THE CIVIL WAR
IN SOUTH CAROLINA

THE CIVIL WAR IN SOUTH CAROLINA

SELECTIONS FROM THE
SOUTH CAROLINA HISTORICAL MAGAZINE

Edited by
Lawrence S. Rowland and Stephen G. Hoffius

HOME
HOUSE
PRESS

CHARLESTON, SOUTH CAROLINA

The Civil War in South Carolina:
Selections from the *South Carolina Historical Magazine*
Edited by Lawrence S. Rowland and Stephen G. Hoffius

Published by
Home House Press
109 Broad Street
Charleston, South Carolina 29401
www.Homehousepress.org

Articles from the *South Carolina Historical Magazine* Copyright © 2011 South
Carolina Historical Society
Frontmatter and backmatter Copyright © 2011 Home House Press

Graphic design: Paul F. Rossmann

For information on the *South Carolina Historical Magazine* or the South
Carolina Historical Society:
South Carolina Historical Society
100 Meeting Street
Charleston, SC 29401
(843) 723-3225
www.southcarolinahistoricalsociety.org

First printing 2011
Printed by McNaughton & Gunn, Saline, Mich.
ISBN: 978-0-9845580-2-5

TABLE OF CONTENTS

INTRODUCTION .... *ix*

THE SECESSION CONVENTION:
"A NIGHT OF BONFIRES AND MUSIC"

"Extracts from the Schirmer Diary, 1860" 3
"Membership of The South Carolina Secession Convention,"
    by Ralph Wooster 4

ATTACK ON FORT SUMTER:
"ROCKETS' RED GLARE"

"Extracts from the Schirmer Diary, 1861" (Part I) 19
"Extracts from the Schirmer Diary, 1861" (Part II) 20
"The Evacuation of Fort Moultrie, 1860," by Frank E. White Jr. 22
"Robert N. Gourdin to Robert Anderson, 1861,"
    contributed by Samuel G. Stoney.. 27
"The Battle of Fort Sumter as Seen from Morris Island,"
    by F. L. Parker 32
"William Gourdin Young and the Wigfall Mission—
    Fort Sumter, April 13, 1961," by May Spencer Ringold 39
"Eye Witness to Fort Sumter:
    The Letters of Private John Thompson," by Ron Chepesiuk 49
"The First Shot on Fort Sumter," by Robert Lebby, M.D. 57

THE OCCUPATION OF THE SEA ISLANDS:
"THE FIRST BLOW HAS FALLEN IN THE REBEL NURSERY"

"A Michigan Regiment in the Palmetto State,"
    by George M. Blackburn 65
"Generals David Hunter and Rufus Saxton and Black Soldiers,"
    by Howard C. Westwood.. 76
"Lowcountry Rail Line Threatened: The Battles of Pocotaligo and
    Coosawhatchie, October 22, 1862," by W. Eric Emerson.............. 93
"Occupied Beaufort, 1863: A War Correspondent's View,"
    edited by P. J. Staudenraus 104
"Laura M. Towne and the Freed People of South Carolina,
    1862-1901," by Kurt J. Wolf 113

THE SIEGE OF CHARLESTON:
"WATER WAS SCARCER THAN WHISKEY"

"The Confederate Diary of William John Grayson,"
edited by Elmer L. Puryear 141

"'Brother against Brother': Alexander and James Campbell's Civil War,"
by J. Tracy Power 154

"An Affair of Honor at Ft. Sumter," by C. Russell Horres Jr. 165

"Battery Wagner on Morris Island, 1863," by John Harleston 183

"Morris Island: Victory or Blunder?" by John E. Florance Jr. 196

"Roswell Sabin Ripley: 'Charleston's Gallant Defender,'"
by C. A. Bennett, M.D. 206

"'The Bombardment of Fort Moultrie, November 16, 1863'
by Conrad Wise Chapman," by Ben Bassham 223

"'It Will Be Many a Day before Charleston Falls': Letters of a Union
Sergeant on Folly Island, August 1863-April 1864,
edited by Edward G. Longacre 234

SHERMAN'S MARCH:
"TAKING ALL HER JEWELS AND EVERYTHING OF VALUE"

"Sherman Marched—and Proclaimed 'Land for the Landless,'"
by Howard C. Westwood 263

"A Confederate Victory at Grahamville: Fighting at Honey Hill,"
by Leonne M. Hudson 281

"The Fall of Charleston," compiled by Viola Caston Floyd 295

"An Eye Witness Account of the Occupation of Mt. Pleasant,
February 1865" 302

"Sherman's Army Comes to Camden: The Civil War Narrative of
Sarah Dehon Trapier," by Karen D. Stokes 309

"Sherman at Cheraw," by Larry E. Nelson 332

"The Last Officer—April 1865," edited by John Hammond Moore .. 357

WAR WITHOUT END:
"RAVENOUS FOR PLUNDER"

"The Federal Pillage of Anderson, South Carolina: Brown's Raid,"
by Thomas Bland Keys 373

"When the Yankees Sacked Greenville: Stoneman's Raid, May 2, 1865,"
by Nancy Ashmore Cooper 380

"Skirmish on Crescent Ridge: The Last Clash of the War Between the
States in South Carolina," by John B. McLeod 384

BUSINESS: "MIXING PROFIT AND PATRIOTISM"

"A Businessman in Crisis: Col. Daniel Jordan and the Civil War,"
by Henry Carrison 389
"10 Rumford Place: Doing Confederate Business in Liverpool,"
by Wesley Loy, ... 416

TECHNOLOGY: "AT THE EDGE OF MODERN TIMES"

"Captain Langdon Cheves, Jr., and the Confederate Silk Dress Balloon,"
edited by J. H. Easterby 443
"David C. Ebaugh on the Building of 'The David'" 451
"Charleston's Civil War 'Monster Guns,' the Blakely Rifles,"
by C. R. Horres Jr. 456
"The Confederate Gunboat 'Pedee,'" by Leah Townsend 478

THE HOMEFRONT: "HOPING FOR BETTER TIMES"

"Exhumation of the Body of John C. Calhoun" 489
"The Confederate Receipt Book: A Study of Food Substitution in the
American Civil War," by Frances M. Burroughs 491
"Disloyalty in the Upper Districts of South Carolina During the
Civil War," by James T. Otten 511
"Elizabeth Jamison's Tale of the War," edited by David J. Rutledge .. 527
"'Robbing the Owner or Saving the Property from Destruction?'—
Paintings in the Middleton Place House,"
edited by Harriott Cheves Leland and Harlan Greene 553

ERRATA 565

ABOUT THE AUTHORS 567

OTHER CIVIL WAR ARTICLES IN THE
SOUTH CAROLINA HISTORICAL MAGAZINE 571

INDEX 573

INTRODUCTION

In the 1880s, when South Carolina was in its third decade of poverty following the American Civil War, Episcopal priest A. Toomer Porter encountered Christopher Memminger, a generation older and considered one of the wise men of the state. "Mr. Memminger," said Porter. "I am now as old as you were when this city and State went wild; why did not you older men take all of us young enthusiasts and hold us down?" Memminger replied, "Oh! it was a whirlwind, and all we could do was try to guide it." Memminger served as Confederacy's first secretary of the Treasury.

It's almost impossible for twenty-first-century Americans to imagine the fervor for secession and war in South Carolina in 1860. Any rational comparison of resources—population, wealth, industrial base, transportation resources, arms—would have shown that it would not be a fair fight. The Confederacy could have won that struggle only by the most twisted form of logic, such as if the North had refused to fight, or if most foreign countries had refused to trade with the U.S. And yet white Southerners not only agreed to take on the United States in battle, they thrilled at the opportunity. When secession was endorsed by a unanimous vote of South Carolina delegates, one Charleston businessman recorded in his diary, "it was announced by the firing of Guns, and ringing of Bells, and in the night Bonfires and music." Teenaged boys yearned for the chance to fight, men walked away from their farms and businesses, and women cheered them as they marched down the road. It was the honorable and exciting thing to do, and that alone seemed to justify their actions.

America's great Civil War, the most consequential and transformative event in United States history since the founding of the Republic, began in Charleston Harbor in 1860 and 1861. The political movement that led to the secession of the southern states had its birth in the South Carolina Lowcountry. It is difficult to overstate the importance of that conflict. The Civil War began as the second American war for independence and ended as the second American revolution. The Confederate states failed to achieve their independence but the "Reconstruction" of the Old South that followed was the most profound social, political, and economic revolution the nation has ever experienced. Eventually some of the Reconstruction changes were reversed, but the bulk of them remain the basis of American society to this day, enshrined in the 13th, 14th, and 15th Amendments to the Constitution.

The accumulated triumphs and tragedies of the Civil War have transfixed the American historical memory like no other event. The principal triumphs of the war were the preservation of the Union and the emancipation of 3,500,000 Americans. The accumulated tragedies were the deaths of 600,000 young Americans and the impoverishment of the American South for five generations. Five generations! Imagine your state impoverished from the time of your grandparents until your grandchildren became adults. In South Carolina, between 31 percent and 35 percent of the white men of military age died as a consequence of the Civil War, an irreparable loss to a small state. Citizens, students, and tourists today flock to Charleston Harbor to tread the hallowed ground and to learn how these momentous events began.

South Carolinians have always honored our historical distinction and have worked to preserve the memories and artifacts of our celebrated past. One of the great repositories of South Carolina's historical memory is the South Carolina Historical Society, founded in 1855 and now headquartered in the Fireproof Building on Meeting Street in Charleston. One of the most enduring contributions of that private society is the publication, for 112 years, of the *South Carolina Historical Magazine*, the quarterly publication of the state's history. (From its origin in 1900 until 1952 it was known as the *South Carolina Historical and Genealogical Magazine*.) Within its pages have appeared scholarly treatises on five hundred years of Carolina history, including nearly a hundred articles on various aspects of the Civil War. In honor of the sesquicentennial of the Civil War, the editors of this volume have selected the most informative of those articles for re-publication. (And we've fudged a bit by also publishing three articles that appeared in *Carologue*, the Historical Society's popular general-interest magazine.) These articles have been divided into six sections representing a rough chronology of the major events of the Civil War in South Carolina. Many of these articles are works of accumulated scholarship and many are edited contemporary letters, diaries, and memoirs of the events of the Civil War.

Despite the long list of articles in the Table of Contents and the heft of this volume, many fine articles were left out. Nothing was included, for instance, of South Carolina soldiers' experiences in battle beyond their own state, though many articles address that subject. Nor were any of the long narratives included, the collections of letters that sometimes filled issue after issue. (All the *SCHM* articles related to the war that are not included in this volume are listed in an appendix, and many are well worth studying.) But this collection shows cities under siege and women and children left behind, the military campaigns, the financial struggles, the technological innovations. Much more could have been included—that's one of the reasons the war is still such a hot topic of discussion and academic inquiry—but this volume includes a good summary of what happened to South Carolina, for much of the war the center of the nation's attention, and to South Carolinians.

Who were those men who voted unanimously for South Carolina to secede from the Union, the first state to do so? The section on the Secession Convention contains one scholarly article that identifies all of the 169 delegates to the convention and the signers of the Ordinance of Secession. It was an impressive group. Among them, as Ralph Wooster explains, were four ex-governors, three future governors, prominent educators, leading industrialists and railroad men, some of the great planters of the South, four former United States senators, and five former United States congressmen. Wooster describes the delegates in detail: their ages, places of birth, occupations, and wealth. (Since Wooster's article, other authors, including Charles H. Lesser in *Relic of the Lost Cause: The Story of South Carolina's Ordinance of Secession* and John Amasa May and Joan Reynolds Faunt in *South Carolina Secedes*, have provided further analysis of the convention membership.) Also included here is an eyewitness diary account of Charleston during the excitement of the Secession Convention. "Thus is the commencement," wrote Jacob Schirmer on December 20, 1860, "of the dissolution of the Union that has been the Pride and Glory of the whole world."

The section on the attack on Fort Sumter contains several contemporary eyewitness accounts of the first shot and bombardment of the federal garrison. Included are details rarely reported in histories—like the suspicious-looking rowboat that approached nervous Confederate troops on Morris Island in the dark of night. Confederate assistant surgeon Francis LeJau Parker wrote in his journal that rebel troops opened fire half an hour after midnight on April 13, only to discover that they weren't attacking the enemy but two southern soldiers returning from revelries in Charleston. Eight hours later, Parker noted, "we are lighting cigars when cheer after cheer reaches our ears. Out we run pell mell—Fort Sumter is on fire, hurrah, ... the cheering is deafening." Included in this section are both northern and southern views of the bombardment, surrender, and evacuation of Fort Sumter.

The third section deals with the Union occupation of the sea islands south of Charleston. On November 7, 1861, the largest armada assembled by the U.S. Navy to that time seized Port Royal Sound after a six-hour artillery duel with the outgunned Confederate forts. Hilton Head Island was soon overrun by twelve thousand soldiers and marines from the expeditionary force. Hilton Head was transformed into the headquarters of the U.S. Army's Department of the South, and Port Royal Sound became the home base of the South Atlantic Blockading Squadron whose menacing guns lurked off of Charleston Harbor for the rest of the war. Soon, all the sea islands around the old town of Beaufort were occupied by Union forces. Beaufort and neighboring Bluffton, once the seedbed of the secessionist movement in South Carolina, were abandoned by virtually all the white residents—"the skedaddled Caesars," as a correspondent for a California newspaper described them. That journalist provides a detailed view of Beaufort in June 1863, nineteen months after the northern troops first arrived. "Pianos were broken up and their 'innards' taken out to make bird cages...; portraits of distinguished secesh were bayoneted.... I have seen many a sofa, chair and table of costly make and finish making itself useful in the tents of the honest patriots around this town, and books, pictures, and even furniture and other articles have been sent home by the officers and men of the army of occupation. Private property was not respected, and no limit has ever been fixed here as to how far spoilation should go." The occupied sea island enclave, or, as one Michigan volunteer called it, "the rebel nursery," became the center of the "Port Royal Experiment" by which northern missionaries attempted economic, educational, and social experiments anticipating the emancipation of the thousands of enslaved men, women, and children who lived there. Historian Willie Lee Rose called it the "Rehearsal for Reconstruction" (1964). One of those missionaries was Laura Towne, the subject of an article, who stayed in South Carolina for forty years.

It was from the occupied sea islands that the Siege of Charleston was launched. Throughout the war, Union forces from Beaufort and Hilton Head attempted, unsuccessfully, to break the Charleston and Savannah Railroad, which linked those two large Confederate garrisons. The largest of those attempts, the Pocotaligo Raid of 1862, is thoroughly presented in W. Eric Emerson's article from *Carologue*. The occupied sea islands were also among the first places in America where those who had been enslaved were recruited into the U.S. Army to fight for their own freedom.

The siege was the largest military event of the Civil War in South Carolina. From the sinking of the "Stone Fleet," a Union attempt to block Charleston Harbor in December 1861, until the evacuation of Confederate forces on February 17, 1865, Charleston was almost continuously attacked by Union military and naval forces. It was the longest siege in North American military history and while it continued Charleston became the most heavily fortified city in America. Despite diminishing resources, Confederate forces successfully defended the city for more than three years, evacuating only when General William Tecumseh Sherman's sixty-five thousand Union troops appeared on their flank in February 1865. The high point of the siege was the famous 1863 assault on Confederate Battery Wagner on Morris Island by the African-American volunteers of the 54th Massachusetts Regiment, a deadly battlefield that historian Stephen R. Wise has called the "Gate of Hell" (1994).

During the autumn of 1864, Sherman's western army conducted its famous March to the Sea, rending the heart of the Confederacy and presenting the conquered city of Savannah to President Abraham Lincoln as a Christmas gift. As 1865 opened, his troops set the torch to South Carolina. The articles in this section begin with the preliminary Battle of Honey Hill in November 1864, and end with Sherman's conquest of Cheraw, his last stop in South Carolina before marching his troops into North Carolina. The evacuation and occupation of Charleston and Mount Pleasant are related in eyewitness accounts. The final article in this section presents a first-hand account of Potter's Raid of April 1865. It was the last official campaign of the war in South Carolina and included the last skirmishes of the exhausted Confederate forces.

The final surrender of the Confederate army occurred at Bennett Place, near Durham, North Carolina, on April 26, 1865, but for South Carolina the war was not yet over. On May 1, 1865, the town of Anderson was pillaged by Union cavalry after local residents put up resistance, and on May 2 a detachment of General George Stoneman's cavalry raided Greenville. That same day, a group of Greenville home guards exchanged fire with a troop of Union cavalry at Crescent Ridge south of town. The Union cavalry spared their captives and refrained from burning Greenville. In the Upcountry, Crescent Ridge is considered the last engagement of the war. These events are well chronicled in two articles from *Carologue.*

That's the story of the military in South Carolina. But much more was going on in the Palmetto State. People still had to make a living, and the story of Daniel Jordan's efforts to earn a living in Georgetown County tells us much about the chaos of war. Jordan, who bought Laurel Hill plantation in December 1859, tried his hand at rice and turpentine and shipping, owning plantations and leasing others, but the economics of the war doomed all his efforts. Meanwhile, in England, southern businessmen who were far more successful than Jordan tried their best to funnel their wealth to the Confederacy. As Wesley Loy writes, throughout the war "the house of Fraser, Trenholm and Company rendered yeoman service to the Confederacy, though the firm tried not to sell out profit to patriotism."

One of the plans of the principals of Fraser, Trenholm was to construct for the Confederacy some of the most powerful weapons ever built, two sixteen-foot-long Blakely rifles. According to C. R. Horres Jr., "Some felt the fate of the Confederacy rested on their success." The ardor of war inevitably produces advances in technology, and the Civil War was no exception, though some of the results—clearly not the Blakelys—seem somewhat innocent today. South Carolinians, for instance, bought up all the silk that would have been routed to women's dresses to fashion a reconnaissance balloon. Surprisingly, one subject that almost never came up in the pages of the *South Carolina Historical Magazine* was the *H. L. Hunley*, the first submarine to destroy an enemy ship in battle. Sunk (for the third time) in February 1864, the *Hunley* is a major subject of interest today, but until its recovery from Charleston Harbor waters in August 2000 it seems to have been more of a footnote than a major story. (In one of the few references in the *SCHM*, Harriott Middleton wrote to her cousin Susan Middleton on October 18, 1863, "You see eight more men have been drowned in the diving-boat. They were experimenting with her. Went down safely and rose under a vessel in the harbour—tapped on her bottom to show they were there—but the next time they dive[d], something went wrong, and she filled...." Isabella Middleton Leland, ed., "Middleton Correspondence, 1861-1865, *SCHM* 64 [October 1963], 214.)

Finally, we offer a few fascinating glimpses of the Homefront, the people who were left behind. All five pieces are intriguing: A first-person account of how a small group in Charleston disinterred the coffin holding the body of John C. Calhoun, and moved the remains of the great man elsewhere, for fear that the Yankees, expected to reach Charleston soon, would snatch it; a homemade recipe book on how to substitute for those ingredients that were then unavailable, producing, for example, coffee made of sweet potatoes (written on the back of a Confederate bond); a study of the widespread Unionism in the South Carolina backcountry;   the wrenching memoir of Elizabeth Jamison, whose husband presided over the Secession Convention, and whose story, as her editor explains, "began with privilege and ended in poverty"; and, finally, an account of the struggle by Williams Middleton to reclaim paintings and other artifacts that had been removed from Middleton Place Plantation at the end of the war—were the Yankees "Robbing the Owner or Saving the Property from Destruction?"

This collection is as good as, and as weak as, the quality of scholarship in the state's leading historical journal. One of the interesting discoveries in reading through the entire 112-year history of the *Historical Magazine* is to realize how few articles on the Civil War were published in the first decades. A contemporary account clarifying who fired "The First Shot on Fort Sumter," was published in 1912 (and is included here). No other article on the war appeared in the first thirty-eight years of the publication. This journal, primarily under the leadership of Joseph W. Barnwell, concentrated almost exclusively on South Carolina's colonial and revolutionary-era history. Certainly South Carolinians discussed (and re-fought) the war extensively in the years 1900-1940, but scholars turned their eyes to earlier battles. Two articles on the war appeared in the 1940s, and then the dam began to break in the 1950s and 1960s, as the centennial of the war approached and was recognized.

The first articles include a great number of personal accounts. One imagines South Carolinians uncovering Great Grandfather's diary or memoir and realizing that others would also be interested. These accounts are for the most part presented with minimal commentary. Today's scholars would surround a two-page remembrance with twenty pages of explanation, putting the manuscript into historical context and citing everything ever published on the subject. There's something refreshing about those early, short, powerful articles.

Another interesting aspect of this collection is what is missing: some of the most important events. In addition to almost no commentary on the *Hunley*, there are no articles in the *South Carolina Historical Magazine* or *Carologue* on the burning of Columbia, the single most destructive act of the war in South Carolina.

Many of the articles presented here are the works of stalwarts of South Carolina history in the twentieth century. Sam Stoney, Leah Townsend, J. H. Easterby, John Hammond Moore, Larry Nelson, Harlan Greene, W. Eric Emerson, and J. Tracy Power have all made substantial contributions to the state's historical record. Dr. Power provides an example of how brother fought brother, literally, in the war: Alexander Campbell, color sergeant for a U.S. infantry unit, faced his brother James Campbell, second lieutenant with the First South Carolina Battalion, in the Battle of Secessionville in June 1862. (For more on the Campbell brothers, see Terry A. Johnston's later book *"Him On the One Side and Me On*

The Other.") Seven hundred United States men and boys were killed in that battle, which was located just a few miles from the sands of Folly Beach, today a popular spot for swimming. Almost everywhere we live in South Carolina, and everywhere we travel, the Civil War is still all around us. It is fascinating and awful and sometimes we can't take our eyes away from it, as if we were watching a car wreck. But it's also the most transformative event in our history, and no one can comprehend South Carolina society and politics today without understanding the events of one hundred and fifty years ago.

LAWRENCE S. ROWLAND   STEPHEN G. HOFFIUS
Beaufort   *Charleston*

THE SECESSION CONVENTION:
"A NIGHT OF BONFIRES AND MUSIC"

EXTRACTS FROM THE SCHIRMER DIARY, 1860

April 23. Convention. The great expected democratic Convention commenced its session this morning in Institute Hall, Nothing as large a number here as was anticipated, the Hotel Keepers have been most awfully disappointed in their expectation of Gain.

May 7. This morning's paper gives us the news of an awful accident near Camden when 27 Young Persons were drowned most of them Young Ladies, they went out on a marooning party.

September 8. Yellow fever. The past week there has been some newspaper controversy about its existence. The Bill of Mortality reports 2 deaths. . . .

October 10. Steamer Planter. A trial trip this afternoon. She was built by Jones for Capt. Ferguson for the Pedee river.

November 7. Excitement. Today the excitement has been intense in Broad St in consequence of the supposed certainty of the Election of Lincoln to the Presidency of the U S. The Legislature is now in Session. The money Market is in a most awful State. . . . A Portion of the Federal Officers have resigned. Judge Magrath closed the court and sent up his resignation.

November 9. Excursion. Today the City Council of Savannah pd a visit to our City [to celebrate the opening of the railroad] . . . They were saluted by our Council and taken to the Mills house for a dinner. They were escorted by the Cadets and Washington L[ight] I[nfantry] . . . .

December 6. Convention. Today was the election for delegates for the purpose of the State Seceding, there were a large number of Characters anxious to hand their names down to Posterity as actors in this Southern drama. . . .

December 14. Bells rung most all day in commemoration of the evacuation of the British from Charleston and in the Evg a meeting at Institute Hall to Keep the Secession burning.

December 20. Convention. To day at ¼ past 1 O'C the ordinance of Secession was passed, it was announced by the firing of Guns, and ringing of Bells, and in the night Bonfires and music. Thus is the commencement of the dissolution of the Union that has been the Pride and Glory of the whole world. . . .

MEMBERSHIP OF THE SOUTH CAROLINA SECESSION CONVENTION

By RALPH WOOSTER

On Monday, December 17, 1860, the Convention of the People of South Carolina, called to consider relations with the federal government, convened in the Baptist Church at Columbia. The work of this convention that took South Carolina out of the Union has been the subject of various studies, but little specific attention has been paid to the membership of this illustrious body.[1] Numbering among its members four ex-governors (John Hugh Means, John L. Manning, James H. Adams, and William H. Gist, whose term had just expired) and three future governors (A. G. Magrath, James L. Orr, and John P. Richardson), the convention was truly a gathering of notable persons. Four of the delegates (R. W. Barnwell, T. L. Gourdin, F. H. Wardlaw, and John I. Middleton) had served in the nullification convention of 1832 and the convention of 1852; while three others (R. B. Rhett, Sr., John L. Nowell, and James H. Adams) had served in the 1832 body, but not in the 1852 convention. The convention included prominent educators (R. W. Barnwell, president of South Carolina College, W. P. Finley, president of Charleston College, R. J. Devant, president of the Board of Visitors of the Citadel, and James Furman, president of Furman University); leading industrialists and railroad men (William Gregg, founder of the Graniteville Company, and William W. Harllee of the Wilmington and Manchester Railroad); some of the great planters of the South (Langdon Cheves, John F. Townsend, T. G. Gourdin, John I. Middleton, and John S. Palmer), four former United States senators (R. W. Barnwell, R. B. Rhett, Sr., James Chesnut, Jr., and W. F. DeSaussure) and five former United States congressmen (W. P. Miles, L. M. Keitt, James L. Orr, R. F. Simpson, and J. P. Richardson).[2]

Data from the manuscript returns of the United States Census of 1860 permit various analyses of the characteristics of the members of the convention as a whole.[3] The ages of 158 of the 169 delegates have been ascer-

---

[1] For the work of the convention *see* Charles E. Cauthen, *South Carolina, 1860–1865* (The James Sprunt *Studies in History and Political Science;* Chapel Hill: University of North Carolina Press, 1950).

[2] *Biographical Directory of the American Congress 1774–1949* (Washington: Government Printing Office, 1950).

[3] The writer searched appropriate county manuscript returns of Schedule No. 1, Free Inhabitants, and Schedule No. 2, Slave Population, of United States Census, 1860, for each delegate. Manuscript returns are in the National Archives, Washing-

TABLE 1. AGES

Age of Delegate	No.	Per Cent
20–29	1	0.6
30–39	34	20.1
40–49	49	29.0
50–59	47	27.8
60–69	24	14.2
70–79	3	1.8
Unknown	11	6.5
Total...................	169	100.0%

TABLE 2. PLACES OF BIRTH

Place of Birth of Delegate	No.	Per Cent
South Carolina..................................	144	80.5
North Carolina.................................	5	2.9
Tennessee...	1	0.6
Virginia...	2	1.1
New Jersey.......................................	1	0.6
Massachusetts...................................	1	0.6
Maryland...	1	0.6
England...	1	0.6
Scotland...	1	0.6
Wurttemberg.....................................	1	0.6
Unknown...	11	6.5
Total...	169	100.0%

tained. Table 1 shows that the age group 40–49 comprised 29 per cent of the entire convention; while 27.8 per cent of the convention fell in the age group 50–59 years. Only 35 delegates, or 20.7 per cent of the convention were under 40 years of age. As the median and average age of the delegates was 49.0 years, the convention was therefore comprised primarily of middle-aged men.

One hundred and forty-four delegates, or 80.5 per cent, were born in South Carolina. On the surface this would appear to be a high rate of native-born delegates, but South Carolina was a state that received few immigrants; 96.6 per cent of the entire population in 1860 had been born in South Carolina. Only two other states (North Carolina with five, and

ton 25, D. C. The author used microfilm copies in the Library of the University of Texas, Austin, Texas. A summary of information from these returns may be found in Appendix I to this study. Tables that follow are based upon this Appendix.

TABLE 3. OCCUPATIONS

Occupation of Delegate	No.	Per Cent
Farmer	48	28.4
Lawyer	33	19.5
Planter	33	19.5
Physician	12	7.1
Judge	6	3.6
Minister (Clergyman)	5	2.9
Merchant	4	2.4
Teacher (Educator)	3	1.8
Chancellor	2	1.1
Railroad President	1	0.6
Solicitor	1	0.6
Farmer-Merchant	1	0.6
Broker	1	0.6
Banker	1	0.6
Commission Merchant	1	0.6
Attorney General	1	0.6
President Insurance Co	1	0.6
State Solicitor	1	0.6
Merchant-Planter	1	0.6
Manufacturer	1	0.6
Physician-Planter	1	0.6
Printer	1	0.6
Minister-Farmer	1	0.6
Lawyer-Planter	1	0.6
Unknown	8	4.7
Total	169	100.0%

Virginia with two) were the birthplaces of more than one delegate to the convention. Three delegates at the convention were born outside the United States—one each in England, Scotland, and Wurttemberg. Not a single delegate was born in Ireland, which contributed 1.6 per cent of the total population and ranked third as leading birthplace for South Carolinians, nor in Georgia, which contributed 0.5 per cent of the total population and ranked fifth as leading birthplace.[4]

In regard to occupations represented in the convention, agricultural interests, as might be expected, ranked high. Forty-eight delegates, or 28.4 per cent of the entire convention, were returned as farmers, and thirty-three others, or 19.5 per cent, as planters. As to the distinction between planter and farmer, any person with 20 or more slaves may be considered

[4] See Table 2 for Places of Birth. Figures for state as a whole based on Eighth Census of United States, 1860, vol. (I), *Population* (Washington: Government Printing Office, 1864), 473.

TABLE 4. PROPERTY HOLDING OF DELEGATES

Real Property of Delegate	No.
Below $10,000	30
$10,000 and below $25,000	61
$25,000 and below $35,349 (average)	23
$35,349 and below $100,000	27
$100,000 and above	5
Total	146

Personal Property of Delegate	No.
Below $10,000	11
$10,000 and below $25,000	21
$25,000 and below $68,704 (average)	63
$68,704 and below $100,000	21
$100,000 and below $200,000	24
$200,000 and above	7
Total	147

a planter, but in the Appendix below, terms used in the census are retained. Taken together, planters and farmers (without five delegates who listed their occupation as planter or farmer and something else) comprised 47.9 per cent of the convention. This compares with 46.1 per cent of the entire population of the state listing their occupation as planter or farmer in 1860.

As might have been expected, lawyers were plentiful in the South Carolina convention. Numbering thirty-three members, 19.5 per cent of the entire convention, they far exceeded their percentage in the total population, which was only 0.6 per cent. Physicians, of whom there were twelve; judges, six; ministers, five; merchants, four; and teachers, three, were the other leading occupations represented at the South Carolina convention.[5]

In real property the delegates to the convention for whom figures are available possessed $5,161,765, or an average of $35,349.31; while in personal property they possessed $10,099,766, or an average of $68,704.55. Thus, the average delegate possessed a total wealth of $104,053.86.[6] One hundred and fourteen delegates owned less than the average in real

[5] See Table 3 for occupations of members of the convention. Occupational figures for state are taken from Eighth Census of United States, 1860, vol. (I), *Population*, 454.

[6] Based on data in Appendix I from manuscript census returns. Of the total 169 delegates, real property figures are available for 146, and personal property figures for 147.

TABLE 5. SLAVEHOLDING

No. of Slaves Held By Delegate	No.	Per Cent
No Slaves	16	9.5
1 and under 10	17	10.1
10 and under 20	32	18.9
20 and under 30	11	6.5
30 and under 40	10	5.9
40 and under 50	13	7.7
50 and under 70	29	17.1
70 and under 100	14	8.3
100 and under 200	17	10.1
200 and under 300	9	5.3
300 and under 500	0	0.0
500 and over	1	0.6
Total	169	100.0%

property, while only thirty-two owned more. Similarly, ninety-five delegates owned less than the average in personal property. Thus, the median real property would be $18,875, and the median personal property would be $50,000. The wealthiest delegate at the South Carolina convention was ex-governor John L. Manning of Clarendon, who had $1,256,000 in real property and $890,000 in personal property in 1860.[7]

One hundred and fifty-three members, or 90.5 per cent of the convention, held slaves in 1860. This figure is the more significant if one considers that 61.5 per cent of the convention, or 104 members, owned as many as 20 slaves or more and were in the "planter" class. Furthermore, 41.4 per cent, or 70 members, held 50 slaves or more; and 27 delegates, or 16 per cent of the convention, were very large planters, holding 100 slaves or more. The average holding based on total membership in the convention was 58.8 slaves, while the median was 37 slaves. The large slaveholders of the state were present in great force in the secession convention.[8]

From the foregoing analysis, it is evident that the 169-man body which assembled in Columbia in December of 1860 was primarily a wealthy,

[7] See Table 4 for variations in wealth of delegates.

[8] See Table 5 for variations in size of slaveholdings, and Appendix I for slaveholding of each delegate. The mechanics of working through the manuscript returns and the frailties of human memory made it practicable to search systematically only for slaves held by a delegate in his county of residence. Slaves held in counties other than residence have therefore, with one or two exceptions, been missed.

The largest slaveholder at the convention was John L. Manning for whom census enumerators returned 648 slaves in 1860. In connection with the high proportion of slaveholders in the convention, remember that 57.2 per cent of the total population of South Carolina in 1860 was slave, and there were 26,701 slaveholders.

middle-aged, slaveholding, native-born group of planters and lawyers. Several had had experience in national politics, and practically all had been successful in the economic field. The theory that secession was opposed by the wealthy planters because they had too much at stake to take a chance does not hold up in South Carolina. Neither does the theory that the secession conventions of the South were dominated by small planters and provincial lawyers with a reputation to make, find substantiation in the South Carolina convention; the delegates already had established their positions in Southern society.

APPENDIX

DELEGATES TO THE SOUTH CAROLINA SECESSION CONVENTION OF 1860, WITH A SUMMARY OF DATA FROM MANUSCRIPT RETURNS OF SCHEDULES 1 AND 2 OF U. S. CENSUS FOR 1860*

District	Delegate	Age	Birth Place	Occupation	Slaves	Real Property	Personal Property
Abbeville	John A. Calhoun	53	S. C.	Farmer	135	$50,000	$138,000
	Edward Noble	36	S. C.	Lawyer	19	9,000	20,000
	Thomas C. Perrin	54	S. C.	Railroad Pres.	130	37,000	127,254
	Thomas Thomson	46	Scot.	Lawyer	51	22,250	68,000
	David L. Wardlaw	60	S. C.	Judge	92	20,000	88,248
	J. H. Wilson	35	S. C.	Lawyer	23	8,000	28,000
Anderson	Benj. F. Mauldin	46	S. C.	Minister	19	10,000	30,000
	James L. Orr	38	S. C.	Lawyer	19	35,000	31,200
	J. P. Reed	45	S. C.	Solicitor	27	14,000	40,000
	R. F. Simpson	62	S. C.	Farmer	57	18,748	73,600
	J. N. Whitner	60	S. C.	Judge	43	30,000	150,000
Barnwell	Lewis M. Ayer, Jr.	38	S. C.	Farmer	57	20,000	47,000
	J. J. Brabham	42	S. C.	Farmer—Merchant	52	28,000	16,200
	W. Perroneau Finley	50	S. C.	Lawyer		3,000	10,000
	D. F. Jamison	49	S. C.	Farmer	77	12,000	66,000
	Benj. W. Lawton	38	S. C.	Physician	65	30,000	55,680
Beaufort							
Prince Williams	John E. Frampton	49	S. C.	Planter	131	51,800	10,000
	W. F. Hutson	45	S. C.	Lawyer	4	1,500	15,000
St. Helena Parish	R. W. Barnwell	59	S. C.	Planter	158	16,000	27,000
	Joseph D. Pope	38	S. C.	Lawyer	14	5,000	10,000
St. Luke's	R. J. Devant	55	S. C.	Lawyer	36	7,500	40,000
	E. M. Seabrook	37	S. C.	Planter	40	44,000	136,000
St. Peter's	Langdon Cheves[1]			Planter	289		
	George Rhodes	58	S. C.	Planter	63	35,000	60,000
Charleston							
Christ Church	Peter P. Bonneau	45	S. C.	Farmer	48	12,000	48,000
	W. P. Shingler[2]			Broker	41		

APPENDIX—*Continued*

District	Delegate	Age	Birth Place	Occupation	Slaves	Real Property	Personal Property
St. Andrew's	Alex H. Brown	50	S. C.	Lawyer	53	$35,000	$55,000
	Ephriam M. Clark	46	S. C.	Planter	59	15,500	38,700
St. James' Goose Creek	C. P. Brown**						
	John M. Shingler	62	S. C.	Farmer	10	2,500	6,000
St. James' Santee	Daniel DuPre	67	S. C.	Clergyman	51	10,000	25,000
	A. Mazyck**				73		
St. John's Barkley	William Cain	68	S. C.	Planter	167	33,000	130,930
	P. G. Snowden	37	S. C.	Planter	50	12,000	30,000
St. Philip's and St. Michael's Parish (City of Charleston)	A. W. Burnet[3]		S. C.	Planter			
	H. W. Conner[4]	55	S. C.	Banker			
	Richard DeTreville[5]	58	S. C.	Lawyer	16	18,000	40,000
	Robert N. Gourdin[6]	49	S. C.	Comm. Merchant	1		
	Thomas M. Hanckel	35	S. C.	Planter	11	8,000	8,000
	Isaac W. Hayne	50	S. C.	Attorney-Gen.	11	22,000	6,400
	John H. Honour	57	S. C.	Pres. Ins. Co.	4	10,000	25,800
	Edward McCrady	58	S. C.	Farmer		12,000	2,000
	A. G. Magrath	47	S. C.	Lawyer	10		
	Gabriel Manigault	50	S. C.	Planter	3		35,000
	C. G. Memminger	54	Wurttemberg	Lawyer	15	25,000	150,000
	Williams Middleton[7]	38	S. C.	Planter			
	William P. Miles[8]	39	S. C.	Teacher	9	15,000	30,000
	Francis J. Porcher	60	S. C.	Merchant	16	9,000	25,000
	R. Barnwell Rhett	32		Planter			
	F. D. Richardson[9]	79	S. C.	Lawyer	4	20,000	46,000
	B. H. Rutledge	40	S. C.	Lawyer	4	24,000	18,000
	Thomas Y. Simons[10]	14	S. C.	Lawyer	5	20,000	10,000
	John J. P. Smith		S. C.	Planter		10,100	
	L. W. Spratt		S. C.	Lawyer			
	John Townshend	60	S. C.	Planter	272	246,000	320,000
	Theodore D. Wagner	14	S. C.	Merchant	13	20,000	100,000

District	Delegate	Age	Birth Place	Occupation	Slaves	Real Property	Personal Property
St. Stephen's	T. L. Gourdin	70	S. C.	Farmer	229	$20,000	$115,000
	John S. Palmer†	56	S. C.	Farmer	207	30,000	110,000
St. Thomas' and St. Dennis	John S. O'Hear	55	S. C.	Physician		20,000	5,000
	John L. Nowell[11]	62	S. C.	Planter	133		
Chester	A. G. Dunovant	45	S. C.	Farmer	15	66,000	77,875
	John McKee	36	S. C.	Merchant	10	7,000	29,700
	Thomas W. Moore	50	S. C.	Physician	28	14,250	31,020
	Richard Woods	44	S. C.		85	27,600	76,808
Chesterfield	John A. Inglis	46	Md.	Chancellor	13	17,000	45,550
	Stephen Jackson	52	S. C.	Farmer		10,000	23,000
	Henry McIver	33	S. C.	State Solicitor	14	6,000	26,300
Clarendon	John J. Ingram	39	S. C.	Farmer	30	8,000	44,000
	John L. Manning[12]	44	S. C.	Farmer	648	1,256,000	890,000
	John P. Richardson	59	S. C.	Farmer	174	200,000	225,000
Colleton St. Bartholomew's	E. St. P. Bellinger[13]	43	S. C.	Farmer	192	39,000	102,000
	Merrick E. Carn	59	S. C.	Lawyer	35	10,000	64,000
	E. R. Henderson	51	S. C.	Physician	50	15,000	32,000
	Peter Stokes	38	S. C.	Physician	40	13,500	31,210
St. George's Dorchester	David C. Appleby	53	S. C.	Farmer		20,000	44,900
	Daniel Flud	43	S. C.	Physician	15	1,950	10,000
St. John's	John Jenkins	33	S. C.	Planter	37	8,400	23,850
	George Seabrook	51	S. C.	Planter	10	40,000	64,000
St. Paul's	Joseph E. Jenkins	67	S. C.	Planter	99	26,000	72,000
	Elias B. Scott	55	S. C.	Farmer	59	9,000	53,600
Darlington	Edward W. Charles	54	S. C.	Merchant—Plant.	108	75,000	110,140
	Julius A. Dargan	44	S. C.	Lawyer	52	20,000	84,132
	John M. Timmons	59	S. C.	Farmer	42	81,493	36,301
	Isaac D. Wilson	50	S. C.	Planter	18	65,500	167,600

APPENDIX—Continued

District	Delegate	Age	Birth Place	Occupation	Slaves	Real Property	Personal Property
Edgefield	James P. Carroll	51	S. C.	Chancellor	18	$35,000	$100,000
	R. G. M. Dunovant	39	S. C.	Farmer	47	17,000	49,703
	William Gregg	60	Va.	Manufacturer	14	40,000	250,000
	Andrew J. Hammond	46	S. C.	Farmer	31	19,000	66,700
	James C. Smyly	39	S. C.	Farmer	45	16,700	45,130
	James Tompkins	62	N. C.	Farmer	113	25,000	120,000
	Francis H. Wardlaw	59	S. C.	Judge	18	6,000	20,000
Fairfield	John Buchanan	67	S. C.	Lawyer	52	37,000	76,875
	Henry C. Davis	34	S. C.	Planter	60	14,400	74,365
	William S. Lyles	47	S. C.	Planter	71	18,000	80,705
	John H. Means	48	S. C.	Planter	127	27,144	133,082
Georgetown All Saints	John I. Middleton[14]	60	S. C.	Planter	318	15,000	40,000
	Benj. E. Session[15]	45	S. C.	Farmer	6		
Winyaw	S. T. Atkinson	42	S. C.	Lawyer	18	4,000	23,000
	B. F. Dunkin[16]	63	Mass.	Judge	236		
	Alex M. Forster[17]	44	S. C.	Planter	273	50,000	202,000
	Francis S. Parker	45	S. C.	Planter	221	125,000	130,000
Greenville	W. H. Campbell	35	S. C.	Lawyer	8	17,000	7,500
	P. E. Duncan	46	S. C.	Farmer	59	37,000	100,000
	W. K. Easley	33	S. C.	Lawyer	18	10,000	1,700
	James C. Furman	49	S. C.	Educator	41	19,000	21,556
	James Harrison	46	S. C.	Farmer	52	67,000	83,000
Horry	Thos. W. Beaty[18]	35	S. C.	Merchant	11		
	William J. Ellis	56	N. C.	Farmer	2	3,000	6,925
Kershaw	James Chesnut, Jr.[19]	45	S. C.	Lawyer	76		
	T. J. Withers	55	S. C.	Judge	23	7,000	100,000
Lancaster	W. C. Cauthen	34	S. C.	Physician	12	10,000	28,000
	R. L. Crawford	32	S. C.	Planter	75	25,000	70,000
	D. P. Robinson	40	S. C.	Clergyman	8	5,000	12,000

District	Delegate	Age	Birth Place	Occupation	Slaves	Real Property	Personal Property
Laurens	H. W. Garlington	48	S. C.	Farmer	61	$13,750	$68,000
	W. D. Watts	59	S. C.	Farmer	45	20,000	60,500
	Thomas Wier	60	S. C.	Physician	67	27,000	80,500
	John D. Williams	60	N. C.	Farmer	225	143,000	315,000
Lexington	H. C. Young	65	S. C.	Lawyer	39	10,800	49,600
	H. I. Caughman	57	S. C.	Lawyer	1		1,000
	John C. Gieger	58	S. C.	Planter	72	23,000	60,000
	Paul Quattlebaum	48	S. C.	Planter	40	20,000	40,000
Marion	A. W. Bethea	43	S. C.	Farmer	35	8,500	38,000
	Chesley D. Evans	43	S. C.	Lawyer	12	8,000	15,000
	W. W. Harllee	48	S. C.	Lawyer	35	30,000	40,000
	W. B. Rowell	60	S. C.	Farmer	28	12,000	40,000
Marlborough	E. W. Goodwin	37	N. C.	Farmer	22	2,800	31,000
	William D. Johnson**				77		
Newberry	Alex. McLeod	45	N. C.	Physician-Plant.	92	76,250	135,335
	Joseph Caldwell	52	S. C.	Farmer	66	40,000	139,600
	Simeon Fair	58	S. C.	Lawyer	63	42,000	86,000
	John P. Kinard	48	S. C.	Farmer	106	93,000	160,000
	Robert Moorman	45	S. C.	Farmer	53	6,500	53,000
Orangeburgh							
Orange	D. R. Barton	53	S. C.	Farmer	24	14,000	15,000
	T. W. Glover	63	S. C.	Judge	55	26,000	52,000
	L. M. Keitt[20]	36	S. C.	Lawyer			
St. Matthew's	John J. Wannamaker	59	S. C.	Farmer	103	50,000	83,000
Pickens	Wm. S. Grisham	35	S. C.	Farmer	18	26,000	57,000
	Wm. Hunter[21]	51	S. C.	Farmer	10	5,000	10,043
	Andrew F. Lewis	45	S. C.	Farmer	51	15,000	51,868
	John Maxwell	69	S. C.	Farmer	53	26,830	55,299
	R. A. Thompson	31	S. C.	Printer	7	3,700	11,000

APPENDIX—*Concluded*

District	Delegate	Age	Birth Place	Occupation	Slaves	Real Property	Personal Property
Richland	James H. Adams	48	S. C.	Planter	192	$80,000	$155,000
	W. F. DeSaussure	68	S. C.	Lawyer	20	14,000	53,385
	Maxcy Gregg[22]	44	S. C.	Lawyer	4		
	William Hopkins	55	S. C.	Planter	86	40,000	80,000
	John H. Kinsler	30	S. C.	Farmer	37	18,000	30,000
Spartanburg	Simpson Bobo	56	S. C.	Lawyer	23	45,000	90,000
	J. H. Carlisle	35	S. C.	Prof. of Math.		3,500	7,000
	Wm. Curtis	43	Eng.	Clergyman	7	30,500	49,687
	B. B. Foster	42	S. C.	Farmer	43	10,100	46,300
	Benj. F. Kilgore	40	S. C.	Physician	63	32,000	88,000
	John G. Landrum	49	Tenn.	Minister-Farmer	17	12,000	16,800
Sumter	H. D. Green[23]	30	S. C.	Physician	111		7,500
	Matthew P. Mayes	66	Va.	Farmer	46	15,000	28,600
	Thos. R. English, Sr.	53	N. J.	Clergyman	62	18,000	45,000
	A. C. Spain	39	S. C.	Lawyer	23	7,000	25,000
Union	J. S. Sims	58	S. C.	Farmer	94	45,000	80,410
	James Jeffries	56	S. C.	Farmer	73	4,000	65,000
	Wm. H. Gist	52	S. C.	Farmer	188	80,000	200,000
	J. M. Gadberry**						
Williamsburg	Anthony W. Dozier	58	S. C.	Farmer	136	20,000	113,300
	R. C. Logan**						
York	John G. Pressley	27	S. C.	Lawyer	9	3,700	11,300
	W. B. Wilson	33	S. C.	Lawyer-Planter	37	22,000	30,100
	A. Baxter Springs	40	S. C.	Planter	54	25,000	125,000
	Samuel Rainey	71	S. C.	Planter	69	27,000	72,900
	A. T. Darby[24]				19		
	A. S. Barron	52	S. C.	Physician	27	8,000	27,000
	Robert T. Allison	62	S. C.	Physician	10	16,000	30,500

EXPLANATORY

* Information in this table, with exceptions noted below, is from MS enumerators' returns of Schedule No. 1, Free Inhabitants, and Schedule No. 2, Slave Inhabitants, of United States Eighth Census, 1860. Original returns are in National Archives, Washington 25, D. C. The writer used microfilm copies in Library of University of Texas, Austin, Texas.

** The writer was unable to find these men in Schedule No. 1 of the census, and unable to find information about them elsewhere.

1 The census enumeration does not give Cheves's age, birthplace, and property holdings.

2 The writer has not found W. P. Shingler in the manuscript returns; thus occupation shown here is taken from *The Charleston Directory Containing the Names of the Inhabitants* . . . (Charleston: Mears & Turnbull, 1859), 80.

3 Not found in the manuscript returns; occupation from *Charleston City Directory and Stranger's Guide for 1858* (New York: J. F. Trow, Printer, 1856), 25.

4 The census enumeration does not give property holdings for H. W. Conner.

5 The census enumeration does not give Richard DeTreville's occupation; taken from *The Charleston Directory* . . . (1859), 80.

6 The census enumeration does not give property holdings or occupation for Robert N. Gourdin; occupation shown here taken from *loc. cit.*

7 Not found in the manuscript returns; occupation taken from *ibid.*, 142.

8 Not found in the manuscript returns; information from Francis Butler Simpkins, "William Porcher Miles," in *Dictionary of American Biography*, XII, 616–17.

9 Not found in the manuscript returns; occupation taken from *The Charleston Directory* . . . (1859), 176.

10 There was another Thomas Y. Simons living in Charleston—age, thirty; occupation, lawyer; real property $18,000; personal property, $4,000; slaves, five.

† John Saunders Palmer (1804–1881), held the degrees of A.B. from South Carolina College, 1822, and M.D. from New York Medical College, 1825. Documents owned by Mr. Joseph Palmer of Sumter, show that Dr. Palmer's plantations were Ballsdam (2,700 acres), his residence; "Big Plantation" (1,970 acres), Laurel Hill (1,329 acres), Betaw (c. 1,000 acres), Wee Nee, and Pinelands, in all, more than 6,000 acres. *Editor.*

11 The census enumeration does not give property holdings for John L. Nowell.

12 Of the 648 slaves listed here for John L. Manning, 616 were on his sugar plantation in Ascension Parish, Louisiana. Manuscript census returns for Ascension Parish, Schedule No. 2, 34–42.

13 The data given here combine the returns for Eustus Bellinger and "Establishment E. Bellinger." Eustus Bellinger had real property, $9,000; personal property. $22,000; and slaves, 69. "Establishment E. Bellinger" had real property, $30,000; personal property, $80,000; and slaves, 123.

14 The only J. I. Middleton found is the one listed above, living in the 2nd Ward, Charleston. As 318 slaves were owned by Middleton in various divisions in Georgetown district, it is obvious that he was worth more than the $55,000 shown here.

15 The enumerator neglected to make returns of property for any of the inhabitants of All Saints Parish.

16 The enumerator made no return of property for B. F. Dunkin. Representing Winyaw Parish, Georgetown district, Dunkin owned 97 slaves in Prince George Parish, 135 slaves in Lower All Saints, and 4 slaves in Charleston. He lived in the 6th Ward, Charleston.

17 The slaves listed here for A. M. Forester actually belonged to his wife and six children.

18 The enumerator neglected to make returns of property for any of the inhabitants of the village of Conwayboro, where Thomas W. Beaty lived.

19 Not found in the Free Inhabitants schedule of the manuscript returns; information listed here (with the exception of the slaves found in Schedule No. 2) from James H. Easterby, "James Chesnut Jr.," in *Dictionary of American Biography*, IV, 57–8.

20 Not found in the Free Inhabitants schedule; information listed here (other than the number of slaves) from Robert L. Meriwether, "Lawrence Massillon Keitt," in *Dictionary of American Biography*, X, 294.

21 There was another William Hunter in Pickens district—age, forty-four; occupation, farmer; real property, $5,000; personal property, $7,000; birthplace, South Carolina.

22 Maxcy Gregg lived with Cornelia M. Gregg, age sixty-seven, who had $24,000 in property. The enumerator failed to list Gregg's occupation, which was obtained from S. S. McKay, "Maxcy Gregg," in *Dictionary of American Biography*, VII, 598–99.

23 Census does not give real property holdings.

24 Not found in Schedule No. 1; the slaves listed here for A. T. Darby were found in the Williamsburg district.

ATTACK ON FORT SUMTER:
"ROCKETS' RED GLARE"

EXTRACTS FROM THE SCHIRMER DIARY, 1861

January 1. Fire 1 O'C PM proved to be the residence of G. W. Williams in George St. It originated in the Garret, and the roof all burnt off and the splendid furniture very much ruined.

9. *Star of the West* this Steamer with a reinforcement for Fort Sumter appeared off our Bar early this morning. Our troops were ready for her and commenced a fire from Morris Isld and Fort Moultrie. After several shots she turned around and retreated, it is said two Balls struck her one of which went thro' her we have since heard she has returned to New York.

Accident a Mr. Weeks an Edgefield Volunteer fell out of a window at the Arsenal and carried to the Hospital and died from the Injury and another Mr. Gray from the same was accidentally shot in the Thigh. . . .

News Our political excitement continues unabated, great preparations are making round about Fort Sumter having every appearance that ere long we must have a battle, it is estimated that now nearly 3000 Men are now on duty around the city. On the [?] a large Flag Staff and a Colors hoisted in front of the Courier Office—Vessels have been sunk on our Bar. . . .

February 25. Floating Battery this affair built by Marsh was launched this morning at 8 O'Clock—went off handsomely.

March 4. President Lincoln inaugural address reached us this Afternoon. As was expected quite an excitement, its tone and temper by no means as pacific as it was Supposed it would have been.

March 10 . . . We went to Circular Church being 50th Anniversary of the Bible Society, Address was delivered by Mr. Ralph Middleton and Revd. Mr. [Henry J.] Van Dyck of Brooklyn, N. Y.

19. Snow this morning . . . at daylight was a beautiful scene, everything covered thick. . . .

March 30. Excursion Today all the delegates of the convention now in session were invited by Genl. Beauregard to visit all the various Fortifications in the Harbor, and returned in the Evening very much pleased with the improvements.

Remarks . . . Genl Beauregard has taken full command, Fort Sumter is still in status quo. . . . Nearly all the Houses on Sullivan's Island has been taken possession of by the Soldiers, Martial Law now there, and no one can go the Island without a permit from Genl Dunovant. The Floating Battery has been finished and carried to some point of the coast of which we have not heard. . . .

EXTRACTS FROM THE SCHIRMER DIARY, 1861

April 12. Excitement. This has been a day ever to be remembered, War has commenced in earnest, this morning about 5 O'clock our Batteries opened their fire on Fort Sumter and a continued fire was kept up all day until about 8 O'C PM when there appeared to [be] a cessation and it is said to night, that War Steamers are outside. Troops are coming in from every portion of the country, it is said there are now over 3000 men around our harbor.

[April] 13. During the past night the fire continued at intervals and at day light this morning again commenced, Anderson fired but few guns, at about 8¾ O'C it was discovered that a building in the Fort was on fire, at about 9 O'C Anderson fired the last gun. One heavy volume of smoke gushed from the fire and the fire occasionally increased and then subsided and then burst out again and so continued, all the morning, our [men] continually firing but Anderson never returned it, about One O'Clock the Flag Staff was shot away. Soon after another was raised, having no fire from him, about 2 O'Clock Wigfall and another Officer went over with a Flag of truce and found them all nearly suffocated he advised him to surrender, which he soon after did unconditionally. It is said it was red hot shot from Fort Moultrie that set the Fire, and the whole of the Buildings are burnt, not a Single Person injured during the whole Combat. The excitement in the City at the news of the surrender is beyond description. The War Steamers are laying outside the whole time and never attempted to aid Anderson.

April 14 Our War. Today about 2 O'Clock the Steamer Isabel went to the Fort to take off Anderson and his men, a Salute of Guns were fired as he hauled down his flag and took his departure and about 4 O'Clock a detachment of the Palmetto and Sumter Guards took possession of the Fort and a Salute of Guns were again fired at the Hoisting of our Flag. It is said at the Salute this morning, by some Accident two of his men were Killed, It is also said that the Isabel takes Anderson to New York but his men will be put on board of the Fleet of Ships now outside. Rumor is now afloat that the ships outside intend to make an attempt to recapture the forts. Thus far tonight all is quiet.

April 20.News This past week has been one of almost continued excitement every intelligence bears the impression that a decisive War is about to be inaugurated. The Star of the West has been captured on the Coast of Texas and carried into New Orleans. . . . Considerable force at our Forts repairing the Injuries sustained and putting them in complete repair. We understand they are taking down Stevens battery on Morris Is[land]. Several of our town troops are relieved by County troops and returning to the City.

April 25. Fire Telegraph. For the last few days they have been trying this piece of Humbugery and the squandering of Public money. How it will eventually succeed, is yet to be seen.

April 27. News during the past week . . . the Warlike appearances are increasing very much. . . . Federal Power has stopped the mails and taken charge of the Telegraph thereby cutting off all news. Provisions of every kind have been stopped and seized both North and West coming into this side. There is now scarcely any Bacon or Butter to be had, the latter is now selling at 50¢ . . . .

News . . . Business of every kind almost perfectly paralyzed. Provisions of every Kind increasing in price, vegetables are reasonable . . . .

May 31 News. The War Steamers have again appeared for a Blockade and today they stopped a British Sch[ooner] going out and ordered her back, the British Consul has required an explanation. . . . The Telegraph is now under control and we get no news.

June 3. News. . . . Our new mail arrangement has gone into operation and we now pay 5 cents. All the volunteers have moved from the Island. There are still a large number of regulars down there.

June 13. Thanksgiving day by the President of the Confederacy. It was generally kept our church was very crowded and . . . a Collection was taken up for the aid of the fund to help the destitute families of absent Volunteers when $274.59 was collected.

June 22. Fire Telegraph This heavy and unnecessary piece of City expense is said now to be completed and handed over to the City. Time will show what great advantages will be derived from it. *[marginal note:]* destroyed by the Fire of Dec. 1861

June 28. The Day was ushered in by the Peal of Bells and continued at intervals thru the day. The Palmetto and Moultrie Guards paraded and went over to Mt. Pleasant and in the Evening had an Oration in Institute Hall by B. R. Carroll. In the Afternoon the Zuaves paraded and had a Flag presented to them.

June 29. News . . . The crew of the Savannah has been carried to Fortress Monroe. . . . No arrivals whatever in consequence of the continued Blockade. Some little rice has been brought from Santee by the inland route. This month ends the services of a large number of the Custom house Officers who had received their discharge—no work for them to do.

THE EVACUATION OF FORT MOULTRIE, 1860

Edited by FRANK F. WHITE, JR.

A letter[1] from Captain John G. Foster, army engineer in charge of fortifications at Charleston harbor, vividly describes the reaction of a professional soldier to the evacuation of Fort Moultrie and the firing on the steamer *Star of the West*. Written from Fort Sumter to John H.B. Latrobe of Baltimore on the day following the *Star of the West* incident, the letter recaptures the tensions under which the Moultrie garrison lived during the last week of December, 1860, and the first two weeks of January, 1861.

Following the secession of South Carolina, the position of Major Robert Anderson, commander of United States troops at Fort Moultrie, was an uneasy one. Moultrie was an old fort, weak, and full of cracks in its walls. Of the other fortifications at Charleston harbor, Fort Sumter was not as yet completed, while Castle Pinckney was used only as a storage place for powder. Expected to be attacked at any moment, Major Anderson had no instructions as to the course he should follow. Should the Charlestonians attempt to seize Fort Sumter, Anderson was convinced his position at Fort Moultrie would have been untenable. Consequently, he attempted to do all in his power as a soldier to keep the harbor entrance open and to defend the property under his command.[2]

The letter from Captain Foster describes the preparations which had been made to render Fort Moultrie as defensible as possible.[3] With definite knowledge that an attempt would be made to seize Fort Sumter,[4] Foster had repeatedly urged Major Anderson to evacuate Fort Moultrie and move his entire force into Sumter. Previously, the Secretary of War had authorized the preparation of Charleston harbor defenses on the excuse that complications were arising with England and France over Mexico.[5] For this purpose, Captain Foster had under his control some two hundred laborers. Because of the difficulty of obtaining efficient white masons in Charleston, these laborers were for the most part recruited in Baltimore from men who had at one time worked for Foster.[6] Many of them were not good "Unionists," but Foster paid no attention to their politics because he felt that no serious complications would arise at the fort over that issue. Eventually, most of those regarded as disloyal were shipped off.

Anderson took advantage of the Christmas festivities in Charleston and quietly moved his entire force into Sumter on the evening of December 26, 1860.[7] In this

[1] Original among Latrobe Papers, Maryland Historical Society, Baltimore.

[2] Anderson to Secretary of War Floyd, Dec. 27, 1860. *Official Records of the War of the Rebellion* (herein cited as O.R.), Series I, vol. 1, p. 3.

[3] *See* extracts from Foster's annual report, Oct. 1, 1861. *Ibid.*, pp. 4–5.

[4] Foster to Col. R. E. DeRussy, Commanding Corps of Engineers, Dec. 22, 1860. *Ibid.*, pp. 106–107.

[5] Abner Doubleday, *Reminiscences of Forts Sumter and Moultrie in 1860–'61.* (New York: 1876), p. 21.

[6] *Ibid.*, p. 31.

[7] ̄ ster in an interview with Associated Press stated that Anderson acted on his ̣ponsibility. Baltimore *Sun*, Dec. 28, 1860.

Carolina Historical Magazine 53: 1-5

operation, the boats of the Engineer Department were utilized.[8] While the movement was in progress, it was Foster's responsibility to remain behind at Fort Moultrie as the rear guard, with orders to train his guns on any vessel which might attempt to interfere with passage of the garrison.[9] When all was completed, Foster spiked the guns of Fort Moultrie and destroyed the ammunition and engineer supplies he was unable to send over to Sumter.[10] Then, he rejoined the garrison in its new location.

The letter further tells of the reaction in Charleston to the evacuation of Fort Moultrie. It also reflects Foster's indignation over the firing on the steamer *Star of the West*, and contains a plea to Latrobe to use his influence to try to avert the hostilities which Foster felt were approaching. Latrobe was a man of great influence not only in Maryland but also in the middle states. Foster was moved by reasons of friendship to make his request. Latrobe had been a student at West Point from 1818 to 1821. In addition, he was a friend of Colonel Samuel Moale, Foster's Baltimore father-in-law; and of Edward Moale, who was employed as a civilian clerk at Fort Moultrie. It is further possible that since Foster married Mary S. Moale of Baltimore in 1851, and apparently had been stationed in Baltimore, the two had become friends.

Fort Sumter, S. C.
Jany 10. 61.

J. H. B. Latrobe
Baltimore

My dear Sir:

You cannot think how your note[11] gratified us all, coming to us here in the midst of besieging forces, apparently bent on cementing their insane actions by the blood of their fellow countrymen. It was like the far off bugle notes of advancing succor.

God Grant that the efforts of the patriotic men in the middle states may be crowned with success. But these South Carolinians seem determined to "cement the secession in blood." They seem perfectly insane in their efforts. Yesterday morning they fired upon a steamer bearing the "American flag" *because* she carried the American flag, and was supposed to be the Star of the West with reinforcements for us. The battery that fired is situated on Morris' Island, out of view, behind some sand hills, and about 2400 yards from us.

We are surrounded by batteries, but they can do nothing against us.

[8] Foster's annual report, *op. cit.*

[9] The *"Nina,"* a Charleston guard boat, had been reconnoitering about Sumter for several nights prior to the movement. Foster to DeRussy, *O.R.*, I, 1, p. 106. While the movement was in progress, the garrison made a wide circuit to avoid the guard boat. Doubleday, *op. cit.*, p. 65.

[10] Anderson to Col. S. Cooper, Adjutant General, Dec. 26, 1860, *O.R.*, I, 1. p. 2.

[11] Original was not found.

We can hold out 2 months, easily. I am sparing no effort, as an engineer, to make the fort impregnable, even with so small a garrison as 70 men. I have two assistants Lt. Snyder and Lieut. Meade, whom I keep constantly at mounting guns.[12] We are getting up the columbiads now and in four days will have an overpowering armament.

All are in excellent spirits, both officers and men, and determined to defend the fort to the *last eternity.*

With respect to the movement from Fort Moultrie to this fort, I must say that it met my unqualified approval inasmuch as I had always counseled it from the first. Despairing of having this step taken I had striven with the greatest efforts to make Fort Moultrie (essentially a weak fort) as defensible as possible, and in this spirit had expended over $11,000. and made the work so strong as to astonish and alarm the South Carolinians. I knew for some time before our movement was made, that they intended to seize Fort Sumter, and then, of course, our position at Fort Moultrie would be untenable.

In pursuance of their plans they had, for a week before our movement was made, several steamers, one of them the "Nina," armed with two guns and two companies, stationed every night around Fort Sumter to guard it. They must have looked upon us as a mouse to play with and eat up at leisure; but we gave the cat the slip however, and are now safe in our hole, which may safely be called a *stronghold* (no pun of a malicious character intended). I am willing to bear my full share of the responsibility. The Quartermaster having no funds, I, at Major Anderson's request, furnished all the transportation and every facility.

It was my schooners took over the stores and ammunition, and my boats that took over the garrison. I notified the Major at nightfall that "all was ready," when he marched one half his command to my boats drawn up on the beach, and my oarsmen pulled them like lightning almost under the bows of a steamer from town, while I stood by 6 guns, ready loaded, to fire at any steamer that attempted to interfere with him.

The second trip took all his men, except five (2 sergeants and 3 men) who remained with me, to spike the guns, burn the carriages of those guns that pointed towards Fort Sumter, and blow up the flagstaff, so that none but the "Star Spangled Banner" should ever float from it, You may be assured that I saw the thing well done, and all night long, and during the forenoon of the next day, my whole force of 150 workmen were busy in carrying stores and ammunition to the wharf and my schooners in transporting them to Fort Sumter.

Seeing everything in train, I went to the city to get money to pay off

[12] Lt. George W. Snyder, assistant engineer at Charleston, and Lt. Richard K. Meade, engineer in charge of laborers at Castle Pinckney.

my men. There I found the greatest excitement to exist, and although I saw nothing to warrant apprehensions of personal violence, yet I was informed by many friends to leave the city, because it was generally believed that I had come to blow up the arsenal. Before I left I had the satisfaction of seeing two companies in quick march to seize and protect the arsenal from my incendiary presence.

Returning to Fort Moultrie, I resisted the requests of friends to go to Fort Sumter for fear of an attack, until Major Anderson sent orders to evacuate Fort Moultrie, when all of the rear-guard went over. (Mrs. Foster went with me, with such things as we could take in our hands, Mrs. Smith with her child and mine, went to town).[13]

The same evening Castle Pinckney was taken, and also Fort Moultrie.

My family is now in Baltimore. All the officers have sent their wives off; and we have, emphatically, "cleared the ship for action." If we are attacked here, you will hear of a bloody fight, but I can scarcely believe that they are such lunatics to try us. It is too late now to attempt force with the whole South, but I do hope that a strong force of the Army and Navy may come down here, disembark a force, and take the batteries on Morris I[slan]d, ditto Fort Moultrie, circled by our fire, and then lay Charleston in ashes, in order to avenge the wanton outrage upon the American flag perpetrated by order of the Governor yesterday. Then retire and let them be in *peaceable* separation, if necessary.

You would understand our feelings if you had been outraged and insulted as we have. Twice have they been on the point of restraining me as a prisoner, to say nothing of others.

If you can, by speaking, writing, or talking, avert the terrible calamity of civil war, I implore you to do so. Dont fear us, we can fight our way and die if need be, but try and save "a country" from these fanatical spoilers.

Please present me most kindly to Mrs. Latrobe, and Osmand [sic] and Ferdinand, and Miss Virginia.[14]

Yours Most truly,

J. G. Foster

P.S. My Baltimore workmen deserted me most unexpectedly when I most wanted them. I did *not* require them to fight. I only proposed, a month or so ago, to form an "engineer guard" to protect the fort against a mob, of which there was some fear at the time. Their seditious discussions at the time, caused me immediately to abandon the idea and I told them that they

---

[13] Mrs. Foster with her sister Mrs. Smith left Fort Sumter for the north, Jan. 5, 1861. Samuel Wylie Crawford, *The Genesis of the Civil War* (New York: 1887), p. 133.

[14] John H. B. Latrobe married Charlotte Virginia Claiborne in 1832. Osmun, Ferdinand, and Virginia were their children. John E. Semmes, *The Life and Times of John H. B. Latrobe, 1803–1891*. (Baltimore: 1917), 577–578.

should not only not be armed or drilled, but I would not trust them with a pop-gun. They all with a few exceptions left at the first prospect of a real fight, on the second day after the garrison came over.[15]

Yours, etc.

J. G. F.

[15] Because the garrison was greatly understrength, Foster advocated formation of a "civilian guard" to protect government property in Charleston. However, "he did not judge it proper to give them any military instruction or to place arms in their hands." Crawford, *op. cit.*, p. 71.

ROBERT N. GOURDIN TO ROBERT ANDERSON, 1861 [1]

Contributed by SAMUEL G. STONEY

Robert Newman Gourdin, the son of Samuel and Mary Doughty Gourdin, was born at Buck Hall Plantation, Cooper River, March 29, 1812, and died at Charleston, February 16, 1894. A graduate of the South Carolina College, he was admitted to the Bar in 1834. He later became a member of the factorage firm of Gourdin, Matthiessen and Company, of which his brother Henry Gourdin was senior partner. During his term as alderman of Charleston he negotiated the purchase of the property on the river side of South Battery, so that the White Point Gardens might be extended completely across the southern end of the city. This property was afterwards sold by the city.

On November 7, 1860, Robert Gourdin was serving as foreman of the Grand Jury in the United States District Court in Charleston. On that morning the election of Lincoln was declared. Gourdin announced to the court that the jury, taking into consideration the issues involved and considering that the court was the organ and minister of the Federal Government, respectfully declined to proceed with their presentments. His action was followed at once by the resignation of Judge Magrath, James Conner, the United States district attorney, and the clerk.

The home of Henry and Robert Gourdin [2] was at the north-east corner of Meeting Street and the Battery. Here they dispensed so much hospitality that it was said that the guests of the city were the guests of the Gourdins. It was in this fashion that Major Anderson had become a friend of Robert Gourdin. Anderson had requested Gourdin to become his envoy to Washington, but Gourdin had refused the complicating task.

Private

Charleston 2d February 1861

My dear Major:

Your beef, vegetables and sugar was sent you this morning. I now desire to write you a few lines of a personal and private nature. I hope you have read Mr. Hugers letter carefully and repeatedly, and that

[1] This copy of the original letter in the Robert Anderson Papers, Library of Congress, Vol. 10: 2231, was kindly presented Mr. Stoney by W. S. Swanberg, who used brief excerpts from it in his recently published *First Blood: the Story of Fort Sumter*. A review of Mr. Swanberg's book appears in this issue.

[2] The two Gourdins were among the Charlestonians who after Calhoun's death helped to pay off his debts. Before the evacuation of Charleston they arranged that his body be concealed to avoid the possibility of its being outraged. This *Magazine*, LVII (1956), 57.

you have given to it a candid consideration. It presents points strongly and gravely applicable to your case in the present position of the Country.

I will now advert to your letter of the 28th ulto: and you must not be offended if I venture to comment with freedom upon a portion of it. I think you have fallen into a terrible error, and I would not be your friend did I keep silence in reference to it. In this letter you said, "of one thing all may be assured, that if an attack is made, and I am convinced that the work will be carried, God willing, the Fort will fall into the possession of the state in such a condition that no flag can be raised on its walls. I am opposed to this shedding of blood, but if the strife be forced upon me, and we are overcome by numbers, not a soul will, probably, be found alive in the ruins of the work." I read this declaration with profound, unmitigated regret, for I cannot but regard such a determination altogether inconsistent with your convictions of the right and wrong of this unhappy controversy and with your duty as a Christian man and a Christian soldier. It is your opinion that so many states having seceded, all idea of coercion should be abandoned; that coercion in these circumstances is impossible, and wicked; that it will lead to Civil war, and cannot accomplish the purpose intended, that is preserve the Union—Moreover, your conviction is that the South has been outraged, that her happiness, peace and safety will be sacrificed by the accession of the Black Republican party to power, and you have said that you condemn and despise this party.

Now with these facts and convictions deeply fixed, as I know they are, in your mind, can you believe that the honour and safety of the Government you represent are so involved in the defence of Fort Sumter that, if it is to fall, it must be reduced to ruin, even though every human being wthin its walls shall perish? Review this determination, my friend, it is not the legitimate sequence of your convictions of the right and wrong of this quarrel; it does not bear the test of sober reason, it is not justified by any principle of duty; I am quite sure that humanity and religion condemn it, and the civilization of our age cannot and will not sustain it.

Perhaps, you have been irritated by the bitter feeling in South Carolina in reference to this fort. But discriminate for a moment, and you will probably make some allowance for our people. They, with the people of five other states, have been forced by injustice and outrage to retire from this Confederacy. They have been, and they are still endeavouring to negotiate at Washington a peaceable dissolution of their relations with other former confederates, and to this end they propose to compensate the Government for all property owned by it in So: Ca: and to assume their share of the public debt. And yet, unless Col. Hayne is more successful than the Commissioners the Govt. will persist in holding Sumter, a fort which controuls our harbour, our commerce, and the very safety of our homes. It is natural that our people should feel keenly this state of things in our harbour; but their bitterness is not against you and your Command, but against the Govt, which keeps you where you are, and gladly would they see you relieved from your painful position and departing from them in peace. I believe, as I live in the presence of Almighty God, that the authorities and the people of South Carolina would assail you and your small force *only* under the solemn conviction that the time had come when it is absolutely necessary to have fort Sumter. You have friends here who pray night and morning that this strife may be averted. I am not in the Governors Counsels, but it is my belief, and I entertain it with confidence, that, if it be necessary, to insure the peaceful delivery of Sumter to South Carolina, she will avail of the influence of the Southern Confederacy, that hostilities and civil war may be avoided. No, my friend, in no aspect of this issue can I discover any justification for the resolution expressed in the extract taken from your letter, and I entreat you to reconsider and reflect well upon the subject. The people of South Carolina, if compelled by the Govt. at Washington to attack fort Sumter, should not be regarded as ruthless invaders and aggressors; their relations to that post give them a claim to it which should protect them against being so considered. So much for them, and now one word more in reference to yourself. I repeat, I cannot discover the duty or the honour involved in maintaining Sumter, even to destruction of the works and of every life within its walls. What is to be accomplished by this? Nothing, absolutely nothing, excepting deep self-inflicted wrong by those who sanction and perpetrate the act.

You said to me on Thursday (that is, if I am not mistaken) that the course of Kentucky would influence your decision upon the points we then discussed. You have, no doubt, read Govr. Magoffin's Message, which I sent you. He is clear and strong on this Southern question, and the Legislature has passed a resolution, with only some five dissenting votes, denouncing the doctrine of coercion and declaring that Kentucky will make common cause with the South if coercion is attempted with any of her Sister Southern states. I wish you had some of your old and confidential friends at hand, with whom you might confer at this important moment. But you will, I am sure, receive with kindness what

I have written. If there is in this letter one word, or one expression which offends believe me it was never so designed and forgive me.

I am my dear Major, Yours with regard

ROBERT N. GOURDIN

Major Robert Anderson, Fort Sumter

Saturday night

My letter was written this morning, alone in my chamber, I have been reading it before closing it for the mail, and this idea of destroying Sumter and perishing in its ruins, because it may not be defended, seems to me so extraordinary that I am constrained to recur to the subject.

You have said to me repeatedly that the Govt. should withdraw the troops from this harbour. Still, it does not, and you and our people are kept, through its agency, in a false relation to each other—a relation mutually deplored. God grant that the Govt. may see, as you and I do, that a Southern Confederacy is inevitable, and that humanity, justice, and the civilization of the age demand that this resolution shall be bloodless. I hope with you that it will. But suppose we are disappointed in this; and it resolves to hold this fort after every proper effort is made by the South to induce it to retire, and to retrocede it to this state, and a conflict is, ultimately, the consequence. If it should be your fate to be overcome, would you terminate the unhappy struggle by the horrible tragedy indicated in your letter? God of mercy and Justice forbid it, and save you from an error so fatal. It seems to me that having faithfully, bravely, and gallantly defended your post, if defend it you must, duty to yourself, and to those committed to your charge would require you to submit to that which you may not have the power to avert. Who would condemn you—Who would dare even to censure you for having terminated a conflict when its prosecution had become unavailing and hopeless? On the other hand, if in obedience to a false conception of duty or of honour you sacrifice, recklessly and heedlessly, your own life, and the lives of others, what will be your record here, and hereafter?

My dear Major, do not regard me as presuming to [*illegible*] you— As you know, I feel deeply on this subject, and will do every thing that an honourable man may to avert strife and secure peace. But, if strife must come, I will gladly labour to mitigate its horrors, and assuage the sufferings it will entail upon the country. God bless and direct you. I am your friend

ROBERT N. GOURDIN

P. T. O.

I have not written to Mr. Holt, as I said I would, advising the arrangements in reference to your mails and supplies as being now established. I wish you would have this matter well understood in Washington. Should Mr. Holt answer my letter, I will touch on these matters in my next to him.

Yours,

R. N. G.

THE BATTLE OF FORT SUMTER AS SEEN FROM MORRIS ISLAND

By F. L. PARKER

Francis LeJau Parker, a native of Abbeville District, was born September 22, 1836, at Rocky Grove Plantation. In April 1861 he was stationed at Morris Island as Assistant Surgeon, C.S.A., later rising to the rank of Division Surgeon. He died in Charleston December 15, 1913. His eye-witness account of the bombardment of Fort Sumter has been contributed by his daughter, Miss Ellen Parker of Charleston.

11 April.

For days the community had anticipated commencement of hostilities, public suspense was at its height; for weeks troops, munitions of war, stores of all sorts were daily being carried to the different fortifications in the harbor. At last on the 11 inst. it was known that Gen. Beauregard had sent at 2 p.m. to demand the surrender of the formidable fortress, Fort Sumter. Dispatches continued from Major Anderson to Beauregard during the afternoon and during the night—see correspondence published in papers. In the meantime the different commands were ordered to look out for the signal shell from the battery at Fort Johnson. The last boat bringing troops and munitions of war left Morris Island at five o'clock. All eyes were turned towards the signal point. Eight o'clock came, no shell. Nine o'clock came and passed and still no sign of commencing hostilities. We began to think there would be no fight, men wondered why; some said they knew it would be so. At this time the troops at the batteries were dismissed, the sentinels placed at customary posts, men retired to their tents, disappointed and perplexed. The camp was noiseless, everything was hushed in sleep, the sentinels alone wakeful and alert kept guard, with unweary eyes alternately turned to Fort Johnson and to the Bar, looking for the expected fleet. The guard boats, ever watchful, with their friendly lights sailed on the outskirts of the harbor, scanning the horizon for the first sign of Lincoln's men of war. All this time negotiations were going on between Charleston and Sumter, and so night passed on.

12 April.

4 a.m. Action opened by a shell from Fort Johnson on James Island, the sound of mortar awoke all camps. The sentinels gave the alarm and fired their guns. Men were seen emerging in hot haste from their tents

and running quickly to their respective batteries. Surgeons with bandages and lint in hand, with pocket case under their arms, with laudanum and chloroform and splints, all hurried to the posts assigned them. And now shell answers shell and batteries from the various points send back to each other their warlike sounds until the whole circle plays on Sumter, lighting up momentarily her guns' outlines, scarcely visible in the morning light.

There stands the bold defiant fort, as quiet as death. No light is seen, not a sign of life appears, not even a sentinel can be distinguished, but high above her floats her proud banner, the Stars and Stripes, the flag which for 75 years has never quailed before an enemy or fallen in disgrace.

The ball is fairly opened—Morris Island from end to end is alive with men—officers and aides hurrying to and fro, the mortars and batteries fire at regular intervals. The question is asked on all sides, what is Anderson doing? Why doesn't he return fire? Admiration bursts from all sides as the flag still waves defiantly aloft, seemingly careless of damage or of the shot and shell whistling around her. Major Anderson is not asleep. Sumter has opened. Crash goes her balls upon the iron battery [1] and the 42 pound battery; they strike on houses and ricochet far out into the marsh and creek. Shot succeeds shot; now she answers Moultrie and is paying her regards to the floating battery.[2] Our men are being

---

[1] One of four batteries located on Cummings Point, "this first iron-clad armored fortification ever erected" was designed and built by Col. Clement H. Stevens, a cashier in the Planters and Mechanics Bank of Charleston. The battery was constructed of heavy timbers reinforced by railroad T iron laid at an angle of approximately forty degrees.

"Fort Sumter was distant one thousand three hundred and ninety yards. Behind this 'slaughter-pen,' as many called it, the Palmetto Guard, Captain G. B. Cuthbert, fought through the 12th and 13th of April, 1861, pouring a heavy fire into the gorge of Sumter, which replied with a severe but ineffectual fire from her heaviest guns. At the close of the engagement 'Stevens' Battery' was almost intact, only an iron cove of porthole being displaced and one gun dismounted. Not a man of its garrison was hurt. This astounding success established the value of iron armor . . . and this experiment has revolutionized the navies of the world." _Yearbook of the City of Charleston, 1884,_ p. 352.

[2] ". . . the 'floating battery' was protected by a high bulwark and slanting roof of heavy timber, covered with iron plates of one and a half to two inches thickness; its armament was four 42-pounders. It was frequently hit but not seriously damaged by the guns of Fort Sumter. The projector and constructor was Lieutenant J. R. Hamilton of Charleston, an ex-officer of the U. S. Navy and, later, of the Confederate Navy." John Johnson, _The Defense of Charleston Harbor_ (Charleston, 1890), Ap. xxxvi.

The battery was located at this time off the west end of Sullivan's Island.

made acquainted with the sound of balls—they are falling all about us. The action is general.

10 a.m. Firing is perfectly regular, everybody is cool and calm; they neither fire before or after the minute—"no one is hurt", our men are getting used to the machine—a ball from Sumter comes, is buried in the sand or goes whizzing away into the marsh or up the Island; a moment after a hundred heads are seen upon our traverses watching for another ball from Sumter. There it comes; "Look out" is the cry; down go our men, not a head can be seen, the ball has passed; up again we go and so this continues. Now we have got the range. Our shells fall and burst upon the parapet, others fall within and burst. The rifle cannon, the point and iron batteries are telling on Sumter's walls, clouds of brick and mortar rise from her impenetrable walls. Our men watch with great interest every shot and mark its effect. Cries of that's a good one, hurrah for that one—bad—poor—try it again.

10½ a.m. The middle porthole of the iron battery struck by a 10-inch columbiad and the window so badly injured that the gun cannot be used immediately. They will send to town for blacksmith and instruments. Two other guns keep up the firing. The point battery is doing great execution.

1 p.m. Sumter's casemate guns dismounted or so injured that he has left the Morris Island side of the fort; he is combatting furiously with Moultrie and the floating battery, and occasionally at Fort Johnson. The fleet has arrived, is now off the Bar. It numbers three steamships and one transport vessel—*Pocahontus, Pawnee* and *Baltic*—they are signaling Fort Sumter. All eyes turned on these vessels; we will have hot work tonight, tide high between seven and eight.

7 p.m. Firing and shelling continue. Fort Sumter answers defiantly. Night black and stormy, rain is falling with lightning and thunder. Batteries are manned, everyone at his post, fleet expected every moment, hot work anticipated.

10 p.m. Tide going down, no signs of fleet, miserable cowards. Anderson has just signaled them. They answer but remain inactive, calmly gazing at the battle; the execrations of our men are loud against them and yet our navy officers say their commander [3] is brave. Can it be so! We doubt it.

Rain is falling, night darker, if possible, than at seven o'clock. Our men disheartened at the cowardice of fleet, disappointed that the causal

---

[3] Capt. Gustavus Vasa Fox.

batteries (built for a cause) are not to be engaged in the fight, drenched to the skin, are dismissed from the guns; shot from Fort Sumter has not raked the Island since one o'clock, but it is thought best to seek the Rat Holes. Numbers are crowded into these little cramped uncomfortable places. Tired with the fatigues of two days and nights of watching and work, we fall into a nervous, unsettled sleep. We may be aroused in the next hours to meet the evening's boats on the Beach. Again the sentinels, wrapped in cloaks, walk their lonely posts in the drenching wet. Occasionally the lightning flashes over the sea, their eyes are turned towards the menacing ships of war, but no boats appear, they still look calmly and basely upon the progress of the bombardment. Will they gaze inactively forever?

[13 April]

12½ a.m. at night. Secure in our ratholes we are now sound asleep. Just about us we hear the startling cry of sentinels, corporal of guard, bam! bam! boat in the traverses opposite Lamar's Battery; muskets are fired in quick succession; bam! goes a 24-pounder from Nordhen's Battery. The flash lights up the beach, one boat is seen, some of our men are on the water's edge—they seize the head of the boat, waist deep in water when the cry of "Clear the beach, we fire" rises above the din of musketry and shouts of men—the boat is free again—a clearance of our men is made—Leizeman's 24-pound howitzer belches forth, the grape-shot whistles over the heads of our men and splashes around the boat. It is now ascertained that there are but two occupants on board. These have thrown themselves flat in the bottom and vociferously cry "Friends, Southern Confederacy, don't shoot for God's sake!" Again the boat left to itself is carried down by the waves along the beach; now it is opposite to Leizeman's battery. His men with muskets in hand run to the beach, they join Lamar's men; now the musketting recommences, the frightened sailors cry lustily "Don't shoot, we are friends". The boat drifts unguided by the current, it approaches a second time the shore. Our men rush in and seize the two men, the causes of alarm. They prove to be two drunken fishermen who had brought two members of the Palmetto Guard to the Point in the afternoon. They had missed their way and had attempted to land until discovered, when fear deprived them of their senses. They are taken to Lamar's Battery where they fall asleep while reciting their adventures, more frightened than hurt. By this time the whole island with bags, nets and men, and two companies of Infantry are marched down to this part of the Island near the Point, in case of another surprise. The alarm subsiding and the rain still falling, our men seek shelter in "ratholes" talk about the little skirmish and gradually fall asleep.

7 a.m. Saturday morning. No other alarm during the night; mortar and guns playing unceasingly on Sumter. The firing has continued all night through, less energetically than during the first day. Sumter replies briskly to Moultrie and floating battery. She seems to have forgotten Cummings Point and Morris Island batteries entirely. Her ceasements and parapets towards this side are badly battered, the walls seem completely honeycombed. The sun has risen, the lingering clouds are flying across the heavens, everything looks bright and cheerful, our men are in fine spirits and the firing is steady, continuous and determined. Sumter shows no signs of yielding.

8½ a.m. Most of our troops at breakfast, my mess are seated at table for first time in 40 hours. We are discussing the result of yesterday's shots. The little skirmish of last night is told and the laugh is at the expense of the two poor devils who caused the alarm, and who cried so lustily "don't shoot, we are friends". One remarks how quickly we are accustomed to Sumter's shots. Would our friends think we could so casually take our meal while amidst the cannon balls!! Our meal is over, we are lighting cigars when cheer after cheer reaches our ears. Out we run pell mell—Fort Sumter is on fire, hurrah, thousands stand on sand hills, embankments and traverses, the cheering is deafening. It goes on from hill to hill till it reaches the farthest end of the Island. Now we have him—but no, there wave the Stars and Stripes towering above the flames and smoke, cries of what a gallant fellow Anderson is, he is all pluck, pluck to the backbone. And now the shot and shell fall like hail on Sumter. Every battery redoubles its fire. Shells burst amongst the flames and shot after shot in quick succession, pound the front walls; brick and mortar fly. The eastern part of the building is the part on fire.

10½ a.m. Sumter still fires on Moultrie. Occasionally she pays her regards to the Floating Battery—flames are subsiding. Our efforts are directed towards the southern part of the building. The wind is favorable, if that part catches Sumter is ours.

12 M. Whole fort is on fire. Shells, hand grenades and cartridges burst momentarily on the parapets and ramparts—great cheering on our side. The Stars and Stripes still wave defiantly amongst the smoke and flames. We admire Anderson for his pluck but let fly our shot and shell with a will.

¼ to 1 p.m. Sumter's flag shot down by a ball from Moultrie or the Floating Battery, immense cheering, the hills swarm with men, slight cessation of firing on our side. It is thought that the gallant Major will take the opportunity of surrendering.

A consultation of the general's staff is held, it is determined to send a messenger to Sumter. Senator Wigfall of Texas, aide to General Beauregard, volunteered to go, a small boat is manned by two negroes. Gourdin Young of Palmetto Guard accompanies Wigfall—off they go, a dangerous experiment. All the points except Morris Island are pouring the missiles of destruction in and about Sumter. Every eye is turned to the little boat on her errand of danger and mercy. Shot and shell fall all around her, on she goes, will she reach the Fort?

Anderson raises the Stars and Stripes on southern ramparts—cheers for the gallant Major—he fights like a perfect devil—we call to the boat, flag up, come back, but no—they are too far to hear, on goes the fearless little boat. Moultrie, floating battery and mortar redouble their fire. Sumter enveloped in flames and smoke answers—she fights to the last moment—Islands silent.

¼ past 1. Boat reaches wharf, Wigfall crawls through a porthole pushing white flag before him, intense excitement.

½ past 1. White flag on battlements, hurrah! cries of white flag, great cheering, she surrenders, wildest scene on Morris Beach, immense cheering, Hurrah for South Carolina!

10 min. to 2 o'clock. Boat returning. Wigfall waving his hat—cheers—she nears the shore, he stands erect and shouts "Sumter is ours" —Hurrah, hurrah, hurrah, three cheers boys,—boat in surf, men rush in and seize Wigfall and Young—they raise them on their shoulders, great cheering—Wigfall shouting, men scrambling, hats waving, hurrah for South Carolina. Now he communicates with General [James] Simons —hush, quiet a moment, interest intense.

Major Whiting, aide to Gen Simons, says for him Fort Sumter is unconditionally surrendered to Brig. Gen. Beauregard Confederate State Forces. Gen. Simons requests that the soldiers will now return to their posts, await the fleet, which we will treat as we did Fort Sumter—Three Cheers for Beauregard—such cheers as they were!! Three for South Carolina and a thousand mouths expand, a thousand throats belch out hurrah, hurrah, hurrah, it was a good sight and a devilish cheer. Three cheers for Palmetto Guard—they are given with a will—everybody cheers for himself and for everybody else, and now such shaking of hands, such tossing of hats, such screams, such hugging. Damn it old fellow, give us your hand, hand we give then held. Everybody goes and looks a drunk—everywhere you hear a little independent hurrah, let's take another drink.

¼ to 5 p.m. The excitement consequent upon the surrender of Sumter still continues unabated. Many hundreds of soldiers belonging to the Infantry from the upper part of the Island continue to come to the Point to get particulars and to receive the congratulations of their friends.

5 p.m. Fresh excitement is caused by the appearance of a boat from the fleet sailing for Moultrie. The sandhills and traverses are crowded by anxious spectators; one shot from G[regg] Battery across her bows—she keeps on, another shot splashes water all over her—hurrah shouts the crowd—in a moment her sails fall, she changes her course and rowing approaches Morris Island Shore, as she approaches sentinels are placed to keep off the crowd—officers communicate with her. Her commanding officer requests permission to visit Sumter—refused; Sumter's Commander is officially announced. Commander asks permission to come and take Anderson and men out, refused; boat is told to come again at 9 a.m. tomorrow for an answer on condition that no attempt is made on part of fleet to reinforce the fort.

9 p.m. Our Mess is once more together discussing events of the day and eating supper. It is the first time that we have all met together for forty hours.

WILLIAM GOURDIN YOUNG AND THE WIGFALL MISSION— FORT SUMTER, APRIL 13, 1861

MAY SPENCER RINGOLD [*]

Accounts of the fall of Fort Sumter on April 13, 1861, have given due attention to the role of Louis T. Wigfall, aide-de-camp to General P. G. T. Beauregard, in his unauthorized effort to obtain a cease-fire order from Major Robert Anderson, Federal commander of Fort Sumter. On the afternoon of the surrender, commandeering a small boat and the services of Private William Gourdin Young of the Palmetto Guards and three Negro oarsmen, Wigfall had set out from Cummings Point and, under fire of Confederate guns from Fort Moultrie, had made his way with difficulty to Fort Sumter and into the presence of Major Anderson. In Wigfall's words, "There has been enough bloodshed already".[1] By the time of the arrival of an official party dispatched some hours later by Beauregard to offer assistance to Anderson in the burning fort, Sumter's guns were silenced and a white flag was mounted on its ramparts.

Wigfall's report to General Beauregard praised the efforts of Private Young in assisting in the Colonel's self-imposed mission.[2] And historians of the battle for Fort Sumter have made reference to Private Young's part in the venture.[3]

The young private who found himself a some-what reluctant participant in the dramatic incident was one of three sons of Anna Rebecca Gourdin Young and Thomas John Young. The father was Assistant Rector of Saint Michael's Church in Charleston at the time of his death in 1852. The widowed mother with the children made her home with her brothers, Robert Newman and Henry Gourdin of Charleston, where

---

[*] May Spencer Ringold was a member of the Department of History and Government at Texas Woman's University, Denton, Texas, and now lives in Winona, Miss.

[1] James Chester, "Inside Sumter in '61," in *Battles and Leaders of the Civil War* . . ., edited by Robert Underwood Johnson and Clarence Clough Buel (4 vols., New York, 1956), I, 73.

[2] Louis Wigfall Wright, "Memories of the Beginning and End of The Southern Confederacy," *McClure's Magazine* XXIII (September, 1904), 453-54, for report of Wigfall to Beauregard. This article carries a photograph of William Gourdin Young on page 458.

[3] Charles Edward Cauthen, *South Carolina Goes to War, 1860-1865* (Chapel Hill, 1950), p. 132; W. A. Swanberg, *First Blood, The Story of Fort Sumter* (New York, 1957) pp. 318-20.

The South Carolina Historical Magazine 73: 27-36

the family remained together until each of the boys married and set up a separate establishment.

In 1904, under pressure from friends, William Gourdin Young sketched the following reminiscent account of his experiences with Wigfall on the historic day. The original manuscript has recently been acquired by the South Carolina Historical Society, Charleston, South Carolina, as part of a collection formerly belonging to Miss Isabel De-Saussure, now deceased. A duplicate in typescript has lain in the Robert Newman Gourdin Papers at Emory University, Atlanta, Georgia, for many years.[4]

*   *   *   *

The writer, reared from his earliest recollection in the doctrine of state's rights, completed his collegiate education in the year 1850. Though blessed with little ambition beyond the desire for a happy and prosperous domestic life, certainly with no taste for military glory, he found himself a member of the Palmetto Guard, a company organized to sustain the action of South Carolina should she have found it expedient to withdraw from the Union when the question was being agitated at that time. The majority in the State having pronounced against action without co-operation, the writer spent the next four years in Europe, and on his return did not renew his connection with the company until the ordinance of secession was passed in 1860. He then being a young man of thirty found himself one of the old men of the command.

The Palmetto Guard was at that time a rifle corps connected with the 17th Regiment, South Carolina Militia, composed of an educated, energetic, well-to-do class of young men who at once took a prominent part in what was to be done. Their first military duty was to guard the U. S. Arsenal after its capture by the Washington Light Infantry. They were then ordered for duty at the Lighthouse on Morris Island, where they enjoyed a pleasant picnic; a life rather irksome to myself, from which, however, I was soon relieved, being detailed to assist in the engineer department then very actively engaged in preparing for the attack on Sumter, and the defense of the harbour.

The next position assigned the company was to act as artillery and take charge of various batteries at Cummings Point: the Stevens Iron battery with its three 8in Columbiads; the 42 pounder battery; three guns; the North battery, three pieces; and the rifle cannon, presented

---

[4] There are three major collections of letters and papers of the Gourdin-Young families: The Robert Newman Gourdin Papers, Emory University; the Robert Newman Gourdin Papers, Duke University; and the Gourdin-Young Papers, Georgia Historical Society, Savannah, Georgia. Smaller collections appear at the University of Georgia Library, Athens, Georgia, and at the Library of Congress.

to the State by Mr. [Charles K.] Prioleau. I returned to the command when the attack on the fort was determined. At the same time the venerable Edmund Ruffin of Virginia joined us, and I lost my place as the old man of the company. Mr. Ruffin insisted that he should be an active member and take his share in every duty; it was arranged that he should do just enough to satisfy him that he was not neglected. The old man managed to keep up with the boys, had a good time, fared sumptuously every day, and set an example of moderation in partaking of the good things furnished by our families & friends; an example not always followed, but we were not a very bad lot.

On the afternoon of the 11th April, 1861, the order was given to march to the batteries and take our positions at the guns to commence the fight, which order was promptly obeyed. I confess to a rather solemn feeling when I took my place in the ranks. I was not quite as buoyant as the boys who had no wives at home, and was not sorry when the order came to return to camp.[5] I was not spoiling for a fight and hoped that Major Anderson being of the same mind would conclude to accept the inevitable and evacuate peaceably. On reaching camp we were dismissed with instructions to be ready to double quick to our posts at the signal gun from Fort Johnson, which signal would likely be heard before daylight the next morning.

At 4:30 A. M. on the 12th Capt. [George S.] James[6] fired a mortar from Fort Johnson and we were in our places ready to take up the firing when our turn came in the regular routine arranged for the fight. The command was divided into two sections. I was assigned to the second and with my comrades of that division instructed to remain in the bomb-proof until ordered for duty. I have read and heard much about the bomb-proof members of the army, but from my experience on this occasion was not favorably impressed with the desireableness of the situation. The atmosphere was intolerable, and one by one we deserted our post and took position behind the embankments and viewed the fight. Sumter opened fire on us about 7:30 o'clock, when one of our officers discovering our position ordered us back to our shelter. But the place was intolerable, and we were soon out again. Perhaps if the enemy had been provided with shell, we would have found the place more endurable. At mid-day I was ordered to take my place in the fight in the mortar battery, and no doubt did so with more confi-

[5] William Gourdin Young was married before the war to Theodora, daughter of Mrs. A. T. Gaillard.

[6] Captain James was commander of the mortar battery at Fort Johnson on James Island, the island being under the command of Major N. G. Evans.

dence than if I had been in the first division, as up to that time no one had been hurt, and it was found that the enemy had no shell. The works were a great protection to us against solid shot, most of them passing over us into the marsh beyond. A few spent balls rolled into our battery but did no harm. I remained on duty until night, at which time a rain coming up with thunder and lightening, I took protection under the Stevens battery, avoiding the bomb-proof. At this time it was quite dark and a shout being heard from the harbour it was feared that the fleet had sent in boats and were reinforcing the fort. I mounted to the top of the Iron battery, the guns of the fort were paying us no attention at the time, and when the lightning flashed, could see the fort and reported to Capt. [G. B.] Cuthbert[7] that there was no landing being made at the wharf. The shouts continuing, it was feared that perhaps a landing on the beach to capture our batteries might be attempted. The Capt. called for six volunteers from those off duty to accompany him to the beach and investigate the matter. Being disengaged I took a rifle and was one of the squad. The night was very rainy and dark and we could see nothing except when the lightning flashed. Hearing nothing more the Capt. left us with instructions to fire a gun should he be required. We took position at intervals and marched up and down the beach. In a short time the shouts were again heard and a boat came in view, evidently the occupants having no control of it, and it was being driven on the beach. I advised that one of the squad should fire his piece over the boat to summon the Capt. selfishly wishing to reserve my shot for actual work should it be found necessary. Three of the men became excited and fired into the boat. The crew at once surrendered. The boat being near the shore, they escaped to the beach, giving themselves up just as the Capt. reached us. They proved to be some of our own men who had too much to drink and had attempted an excursion towards the city, lost their way, and were unable to manage their boat. They were placed under guard, but the happy result of the fight next day enabled them to escape with the short confinement for the night. The boat was washed ashore the next morning when the marks of the three shots were apparent. The crew had a narrow escape. I remained on the beach all night, and in the morning again took my place in the mortar battery, being relieved from duty at mid-day. At this time the fort was in flames and had discontinued to fire on us, only sending a few shots at long intervals towards Moultrie, our men cheering every shot they made. All attempts to keep the men in the bomb-proof had been abandoned, and when off duty we wandered

[7] Captain Cuthbert was in command of the Palmetto Guards.

from under the protection of the fortifications. Seeing a boat land in the creek bank of the Island, I went to meet it, hoping to get some news from the other forts engaged in the fight. The boat proved to be from Charleston bringing some of our men who had been sent the night before to repair the damage done to one of the shutters of the Iron battery. Returning I was hailed by two officers and instructed to stop the boat which was about leaving for the city. The officers proved to be Col. [Louis T.] Wigfall and Capt. [A. R.] Chisolm.[8] On reaching the boat, Col. Wigfall proposed to embark at once for the fort. At the time, the harbour was quite rough, and the boat being small, leaking, and without a rudder, Capt. Chisolm pronounced it unsafe, stating at the same time that his boat was in the creek a short distance off and that he would have it brought. Col. Wigfall demurred at the delay, saying that the fort was on fire, the flag down, and in all probability the garrison was in great danger and unable to make their wants known. Capt. Chisolm, however, insisting on going for his boat; Col. Wigfall, under great excitement, exclaimed: "A brave garrison is in great danger, likely to perish for want of help" and that if he could find any one to go with him, he would venture in the small boat at once. He turned to me and asked if I would go with him. I was aware then who he was and replied that I was a private engaged in a fight and did not know if I could leave my post without proper authority. He then gave his name, saying that as aide to Gen. Beauregard, he was authorised to give the order and would do so if I was willing to risk it with him. I at once assented; we embarked and started for the fort with three Negro oarsmen. When we had left the shore, I asked him what was his object in going to the fort. He said he was sent by Gen. [James] Simons [9] under a flag of truce to know if the flag being down and not replaced, it was Maj. [Robert] Anderson's intention to surrender and to offer aid if it were required. I asked how he expected to be received when he carried no flag; he replied he had forgotten all about it and had no flag. He then drew out his white handkerchief and passed his sword through two corners of it. I caught it just as the wind was taking it away. I then cut two strings from my shirt sleeve and, while he held the sword, fastened the handkerchief to it. Against my advice he stood up in the boat, so that the small flag could be seen. The attempt nearly upset us, and he had to resume his seat. We had not proceeded far when a shot from Moultrie came across our bow. I remarked that it was no doubt intended to prevent our proceeding fur-

---

[8] Both officers were serving as aides-de-camp to General Beauregard.

[9] General Simons was in command on Morris Island.

ther as Sumter had resumed firing. The Col. said he would not abandon his mission at the command of Moultrie. In a few moments we had another shot so near it looked as if it was intended to hit us. The Negroes then became frightened and stopped rowing and got into the trough of a rough sea that bid fair to swamp us. With some persuasion we got the Negroes to work again, two of them at the oars, the third bailing the boat which was more than half full of water. A third shot then splashed water over us which satisfied us that Moultrie intended to sink us. Gen. [Roswell] Ripley [10] informed me afterwards that he had ordered the boat sunk when we would not obey his first signal; he said "Some d...... politician was meddling with what he had no business and he intended to sink him." It was with great difficulty that the Negroes could be kept to their work and the boat saved from swamping. I urged on them the importance of getting under the shelter of the fort. On reaching it, however, we found our condition not improved, for the shot and shell from our batteries on the other side of the harbour rendered our position a very dangerous one. Every shot that hit the parapet of the fort sent a shower of brick bats around us, and the shot itself fell too near us for our comfort. Fortunately most of the mortar shell was well aimed and fell within the fort. We were not able to take our boat to the landing as all around it was full of debris shot away from the walls. The situation was a most desolate looking one; the large door at the entrance into the fort from the wharf had been shot away and burnt; the gun mounted at the back of it to sweep the wharf in case of an assault dismounted and the carriage smouldering, as also [were] portions of the doors hanging to the hinges. There was no one who saw our approach, and we had to call in hopes of attracting attention. Not succeeding in doing so, Col. Wigfall directed me to land and make the effort near the gateway. I had to wade up to my waist to reach the landing and succeeded no better. Col. Wigfall then landed and joined me, saying he feared we had come to the habitation of the dead. We then determined to make our way towards the side of the fort facing the city; we considered the gateway too hot to venture on an entrance. At that point we had gone but a short distance when we perceived that our crew were about leaving us. I returned to take charge of the boat and Col. Wigfall proceeded in his efforts to enter the fort. Before I could reach the boat, the crew had pushed off and I had to threaten them with my drawn pistol to bring them back. I then made them disembark and ranged them close under

[10] At this time Ripley was a lieutenant-colonel in command of the artillery on Sullivan's Island.

the wharf, two of them holding the boat to prevent its being dashed to pieces, and the third to bail it. Just as this arrangement had been completed, Major Anderson with an attendant emerged from the gateway and demanded what we were doing at the fort. I replied that we had come with a flag of truce, but not being able to attract the attention of the garrison, the officer had gone around to the other side of the fort in hopes of making an entrance. The Major then reentered the fort, but returned in a few moments, saying he could find no officer and demanded that I should come to him. I said if I left my boat, the crew would desert with it. He insisted that I should come, but I refused unless he would send someone to take charge of my boat. The Negroes asked the Major for God's sake to send and find them a safe place, to which he replied that they were in as safe a place as was to be found in the neighborhood. While this discussion was taking place, an officer called to Major Anderson saying that Col. Wigfall was in the fort waiting to see him. In a short time after this the firing ceased, but the Negroes were very uneasy at the long delay and urged that we should go, saying they must have killed the other gentleman, and I would share the same fate if I remained. In about a half hour, Col. Wigfall reappeared, saying that the fort had surrendered and the white flag raised.

On our way back to the Island it was amusing to listen to the remarks of the Negroes. One of them said, "I hope if I ever bring another buckra man to a fight, the Lord will kill me." The second said, "'Now that it is all over and I am alive, I am glad I came. It will be a good thing to tell my wife." The third said, "That may be so, but I would not like to try it again." I was somewhat of his opinion but did not care then to express it.

Thinking that I was entitled to some consideration after the danger I had encountered, I said to Col. Wigfall [that] as I had accommodated him in going to the fort, he should arrange to take me to Charleston should he be ordered to announce the surrender to Gen. Beauregard; that while on duty the night before, camp had been moved and all my clothing lost and I would have a very unpleasant night if I could not get home and get dry raiment. To this he assented.

The beach was crowded with officers and men to meet us and [they] were wild with enthusiasm. When it was announced that the fort had surrendered, we were taken from the boat and carried on the shoulders of the men. Gen. Simons, who commanded on the Island, was among those who met us and informed Col. Wigfall that he was to proceed at once to the city and carry the tidings to Gen. Beauregard. The Col. remembered his promise to me and a ready assent was granted his request. Capt. Chisolm had his boat ready and the party embarked for the city; it consisted of Ex-Gov. [Richard] Manning, Cols. Wigfall and [James] Chesnut, and Capt. Chisolm. We were about starting when someone said we should not go without a flag, and one of the officers of the Palmetto Guard offered that of our company, which was accepted and entrusted to my care; the other flags were brought at the last moment and we started with all flags flying. Our way was across the back of Sumter and when we approached it, we saw that a number of the garrison were seated on the outside, no doubt to escape the heat and smoke of the burning fort. The gallant Wigfall remarked that it was ungenerous to flaunt our flags in the face of a fallen foe, and it was arranged that we should dip them when passing.

A steamer from the city met and took us aboard. Not having rested the night before I was soon asleep on the soft side of a bench; but my nap was a short one, for I was aroused by a shake from Col. Wigfall who informed me that we were approaching the city, and that I must prepare to take my flag and go with the party to Gen. Beauregard's headquarters at the Institute Hall. I asked to be excused, as my object in requesting to come to the city was to get home, relieve the anxiety of my family, and get dry raiment. He insisted that I should not be excused, saying that I had acknowledged his authority when I went with him to the fort and that it was a duty I owed to my company to present its flag at headquarters when the opportunity was given me.

As the steamer neared the city, the wharf to which it was making was thronged with citizens of all classes, and the Capt. of the boat was requested to make for another wharf so as to avoid the crowd. But it was of no avail; when the boat reached the shore, the crowd was upon us. Immediately on landing Col. Wigfall was taken possession of and borne away on the shoulders of the crowd, the rest of us escaped like fate with a hard struggle. To avoid attracting the crowd on our way to the Hall our flags were furled, but that of the Palmetto Guard being on a long staff could not be concealed, so we were in a press during our entire progress. I was a sorry looking object without jacket; trousers shrunk six inches too short; shirt torn; it and my face black with smoke. As I walked with Gov. Manning and Col. Chesnut in their bright blue uniforms, I was taken for a soldier in charge of the two captured officers of the fort. I was asked, in an undertone, which was Major Anderson, and if the other was Capt. Doubleday. On reaching the Hall we were admitted and the doors quickly closed to keep out the crowd that were clamoring for the news. We found that Col. Wigfall had arrived before us, and he introduced me to the General who made a few complimentary remarks as to the conduct of my company during the action and retired with his officers into his private office. I thought the time was come to make my escape, but the door was locked and the guard said he was instructed not to open it without orders from an officer. I was, however, soon released, for the throng outside beat against the doors, demanding that some one should come out and give them the news. The Gen. came out of his office, saying that it was impossible to transact any business, and seeing me asked if I would take the flag out and try and satisfy the people. The door was unlocked and I escaped, but was made to mount the stepping stone in front of the Hall, unfurl the flag, and give the news. This proved an endless work, for as fast as one set moved off, another closed in and the story had to be repeated again and again. At last my earnest request to be allowed to go home and rest was granted; and I took my way thither accompanied by the crowd, who then dispersed, saying that they would return when I had rested and have a speech, an ordeal about as unsuited to my taste as a fight. I escaped it, however, saying that I was due at my post on the Island. It, however, took the night in the city to rest.

On arriving at home I found the family had just returned thanks for my safety. The news of my being in the city had reached them before. A Negro boy servant in the family had been in the crowd and seeing me rushed home with the news that I was "crooking arms with Gen. Anderson."

From the top of my residence a good view could be had of the harbour and fight and all the family had assembled there (four generations).[11] They had viewed the picture of the boat's visit to the fort, saw the shot nearly strike it; and not knowing that one in whom they were so nearly interested was an occupant of it, pronounced it a foolish risk, and said if sunk the fate was deserved.

I returned to the Island next morning and found that the Palmettoes were selected from the troops on Morris Island to be one of the companies present at the evacuation and to garrison the fort for the night. I was one of the sentinels on guard outside the fort during the evacuation. The fort was surrounded by boats of all kinds to view the pageant and my duty was to prevent their too near approach and if necessary to suppress all unkind remarks. This latter instruction was useless, for the kindest feeling prevailed, and Major Anderson was as

---

[11] According to the Charleston *Directory* of 1860, William Gourdin Young and his family resided at 4 Church Street, Charleston.

popular with our people as Gen. Beauregard himself. Even Capt. [Abner] Doubleday escaped the rebuke his malignity towards our people deserved;[12] his misfortune protected him.

Mr. Ruffin bore our company flag when we entered the fort, and as one of the color guard I was to take care of him, a duty in which I failed as I allowed him to fall into an old well. Fortunately, he was not hurt.

It may be supposed Sumter was not a very desirable place to spend the night; the fire had not yet been extinguished; and we had to assist in working the hand fire engines to keep it under. Later on in war our soldiers held this fort when in a much more delapidated condition and against the powerful iron-clad fleet.

We were relieved from duty at the fort next day and returned to our homes for a short time.

The above reminiscences were written by me for Mrs. W. G. De-Saussure at her request.

W. GOURDIN YOUNG,
Charleston, Sept. 15th, 1904

[12] Abner Doubleday in *Reminiscences of Forts Sumter and Moultrie in 1860-'61* (New York, 1876), revealed a somewhat uncompromising attitude toward Southerners, slave-owners, and secessionists in general.

EYE WITNESS TO FORT SUMTER: THE LETTERS OF PRIVATE JOHN THOMPSON

Ron Chepesiuk*

With the passage of the Ordinance of Secession on December 20, 1860, South Carolina presented demands to President James Buchanan calling for the removal of all Union troops from Charleston Harbor and the forfeiture of all Federal property within the state. Six days later, Major Robert Anderson, the commander of the Union forces at Charleston, secretly removed his troops from Fort Moultrie on Sullivan's Island to what he believed would be a more defensible position at Fort Sumter. When Buchanan refused to agree to the demands of the South Carolina commissioners, Confederate troops seized the United States Arsenal at Charleston.

Buchanan then attempted to relieve Anderson's garrison by sending the *Star of the West*, an unarmed warship loaded with provisions and reinforcements. Heavy fire from shore batteries repulsed the ship, and it was forced to return to New York.

On April 6, the new president, Abraham Lincoln, notified South Carolina authorities that a ship was on its way to Charleston, carrying no troops but only provisions for Fort Sumter. But on April 11, suspicious of the movement and fearful of a prolonged Federal occupation, Gen. Pierre G. T. Beauregard, the local Confederate commander, demanded that Anderson surrender immediately. Anderson's offer to surrender in a few days when his supplies would have been exhausted was refused by Confederate authorities. At 4:30 in the morning of April 12, the Confederate shore batteries opened fire on Fort Sumter. The next day, after a bombardment of thirty-four hours, Anderson surrendered. The Civil War had begun.

Two of the most unique and significant reports concerning these momentous events are to be found, not in an American archival institution, but in Belfast at the Public Records Office of Northern Ireland. They are the letters of John Thompson, a private who was part of the Federal force at Fort Sumter, serving in Company E, 1st United States Artillery.

Not much is known about the life of Private Thompson. According to his military records preserved in the National Archives in Washington, he was born in Anticlave, County Londonderry, Ireland. On

*Associate Professor and Head of Special Collections, Winthrop College, Rock Hill. The author acknowledges the support of the Winthrop Research Council in the preparation of this article.

The South Carolina Historical Magazine 85: 271-279

September 25, 1856, at the age of twenty-two, he enlisted at Philadelphia. With blue eyes, fair complexion and dark hair, he stood five feet and five inches tall. Given the style and content of the letters, it is curious that Thompson gave his occupation as laborer. His wife Mary Charlotte was with him at Sullivan's Island at least in September 1860 for she is listed as a sponsor at the baptism of a child of another Irish garrison member. Thompson's term of service expired on September 28, 1861, and he was discharged.

The first of the two letters, both written to his father, Robert Thompson of Anticlave, gives a graphic account of the tensions and events in the "cold war" period preceeding the bombardment. The second letter, written a few days after the evacuation of the Federal troops from Fort Sumter, describes the atmosphere existing in the garrison while it was under heavy fire.[1]

Fort Sumter So. Carolina
February 14th 1861

My Dear Father

Your letter dated January 11th has been duly received, and I am exceedingly glad to hear of your welfare. You are anxious you say in your letter to know all the war, or properly speaking the rebellion of South Carolina. I shall endeavor to describe what has come under my notice. Ever since the election of President in November last great disatisfaction has prevailed in the Slave States, and during December this State formally sexcede from the Union, and openly threatened to take forcible possession of the Forts, Arsenals and other public property in this harbor. This they were certain could be easily accomplished, as two of the three Forts in this harbor were without any Garrison, and the third, Fort Moultrie being garrisoned by only

[1] Public Records Office of Northern Ireland, Belfast; National Archives, Washington; Register of St. John's (now Stella Maris) Catholic Church, Sullivan's Island. The author appreciates the assistance of Dale Phillips, Park Ranger with the Fort Sumter National Monument, who supplied the baptismal record.

John Thompson Letters (T1585), Public Records Office of Northern Ireland. The author acknowledges the kind permission of the Office to publish these letters. They form part of a modest collection of papers relating to S. C. history. Subjects include emigration, British siege operations at Charleston in 1780, trade between Ireland and S. C., and life in America.

Bernard Crick, *A Guide to Manuscripts Relating to America in Great Britain and Ireland* (Westport, 1979); John W. Raimo, *A Guide to Manuscripts Relating to America in Great Britain and Ireland,* rev. ed. (Westport, 1982).

seventy five United States Artillerymen.[2] Certain of success they vigorously set about warlike preparations, all the time keeping a very strict watch on the helpless little Garrison of which I formed a member. Steamboats were nightly set to watch us to prevent our moving to Sumter, a far more formidable, may I say almost impregnable work situated directly opposite us, and distant about a mile. Our Commander set about fortifying himself in Moultrie, with such unparalleled vigor that our opponents soon became thoroughly convinced that he intended to make a desperate stand in the position he then held, and the duty of watching us was performed with a laxity corresponding to the strength of their conviction. So completely did our Commander keep his own counsel, that none in the garrison officer or soldier ever dreamed that he contemplated a move, until the movement had actually been made. On the night of the 26th Dec. shortly after sun down, we were formed in heavy marching order, and quietly marched out of Moultrie leaving only a few men behind on Guard, and embarking on board a number of small boats that in readiness were safely landed in Sumter. The consternation of the Carolinians may be imagined next morning when they observed Fort Moultrie enveloped in flames and smoke and at noon saw the Stars and Stripes proudly waving from the battlements of Fort Sumter. What they feared, and endeavored to prevent, had taken place, and they had that pleasure of witnessing Uncle Sam's troops in a position scarcely assailable in any other way than by the slow process of starvation. During the night of the 26th the men left behind spiked all the guns, and then set fire to the gun-carriages etc. at the abandoned Fort and then left it to quietly be taken possession of by the troops of South Carolina. This they were not long in doing, they can scale the walls of an *unoccupied*[3] Fort with a gallantry highly commendable. In fact their martial ardor seemed to have taken a turn in this direction for the same day they assaulted the remaining *empty* Fort in the harbor and amid shouts, exultantly raised their Palmetto flag, to announce their bloodless victory. Of course they were boiling over to attack Sumter, and tear down the cursed Stars and Stripes, but of course they haven't done it yet, and if they do and live it will only be to repent their rash folly and mourn

[2] Published accounts vary as to the number of men under the command of Major Robert Anderson. One source, John G. Nicolay, *The Outbreak of Rebellion* (New York, 1881), p. 63, gives eight officers and 60 enlisted men. Another source, George Fort Milton, *Conflict: The American Civil War* (New York, 1941), p. 26, gives nine officers and 74 enlisted men.

[3] All words underlined in the letters have been italicized.

their loss. Fort Sumter which we now occupy is a five sided brick work, walls from 12 to 5 1/2 feet thick mounting three tier of guns of the heaviest calibre, and completely surrounded by water. It is situated on the very edge of the ship channel, so that every vessel passing in or out of the harbor passes directly under our guns. In fact, it is the key of the harbor and completely commands all the other fortifications. Sumter was far from being in a defensible condition, very few guns were mounted and everything was in admirable confusion. However we went to work assisted by 50 or 60 laborers, and now we can say *We are ready.* The Carolinians have been by no means idle all this time however. At the nearest point of land on Morris Island about 1400 yds. distant they have constructed very formidable batteries, and are now I may say just as ready as we are. We are in daily expectation of a commencement, which must come from them as our orders are to act strictly on the defensive. That they intend to bombard us is evident, and that they will attempt to breach this work at its weakest point is equally sure, but we are sure their attempt will prove a failure. They may starve us out and harass us meantime by shelling our position, but we all feel confident that assault if attempted will prove a signal failure. Inside here we are all, thank God, in excellent health and spirits, in fact a more contented lot of men would be hard to scare up. We are only seventy five in number and have now only about twenty laborers,[4] the rest having taken their leave of us, no doubt *thinking* discretion was the better part of valor, and we are opposed to at least ten or twelve thousand Carolinians,[5] our Commissariat scarcely in a condition to stand a long siege, cut off by the batteries of the enemy from reinforcement and supplies, depending on them for mail facilities etc.; and yet we are confident and contented because we all see the strength of our position and know that the *chivalry* of South Carolina are effectually scared to attack the frowning fortress the possession of which they so much desire. So matters stand at present, but how long they may continue so is a mystery.

You need not be in any unnecessary anxiety on my account, for to tell the truth in spite of all their bluster I am almost sure they never will fire a shot at us, indeed I think they are only too glad to be let alone. I am in excellent health, and hope you all are enjoying that same blessing. At the expiration of my time I shall doubtless return to

[4]One source states that, in addition to Anderson, his officers and soldiers, there were eight musicians and 43 non-combatant workmen. Nicolay, *Outbreak of Rebellion,* p. 63.

[5]The Confederate force was estimated to total approximately 7,000 men, with 47 mortars and guns. Milton, *Conflict: The American Civil War,* p. 26.

see you all and give you an account of America verbatim. Keep up this correspondence. A letter from home is very refreshing in a place like this. I will endeavor to keep you posted when oportunity offers regarding events on this side Jordan. Give my respects to all my friends and acquaintances, and believe me

Your affectionate son
John Thompson

Fort Hamilton[6] New York
April 28th 1861

My Dear Father,

I have just received your welcome letter and am exceedingly glad to hear of your welfare. Since I last wrote I have passed through not a few exciting scenes. In my last letter I brought the history of our present difficulties down to our safe arrival in Fort Sumter. Well as time wore on the clouds of disunion thickened around us and we were being gradually hemmed in by formidable batteries erected under our very noses. Our Government suffered matters to go so far that the re-enforcement or relief of Sumter was declared an impossibility to any force under twenty thousand men. Thus we were left at the mercy of the rebels, dependant on them for supplies and completely surrounded by their hostile batteries. They no doubt expected that we would surrender without a blow, but they were never more mistaken in their lives. Our supply of breadstuffs was fast giving out and the Carolinians knew it. They had cut off all communication with the shore, and starvation was staring us in the face. We had been on 3/4 rations for a long time and on the 8th of April a reduction to half rations was made and cheerfully submitted to, the hope of being re-enforced or with-drawn having not yet entirely left us. On the eleventh one biscuit was our allowance, and matters seemed rapidly coming to a crisis. The rebels had doubled their watchfulness and we were certain that something was in the wind. On the afternoon of the 11th about 4 o'clock, three officers from the rebel army made their appearance under a flag of truce, and formally summoned our gallant Major to surrender. This of course he refused to do. About one o'clock on the morning of the 12th another messenger notified us that Genl. Beaure-gard, the rebel commander would open fire on us immediately. This

[6]Fort Hamilton was built in 1831 on the narrows opposite Fort Wordsworthy, Staten Island. Today it is a residential section of the Brooklyn borough of New York. Leon F. Seltzer, ed., *The Columbia Lippincott Gazateer of the World* (New York, 1966), p. 629.

message found our little garrison, only 71, enjoying their usual repose, but they had taken the precaution of moving their blankets under the bombproofs in anticipation of a bloody melee before morning. The word was quietly circulated through the men that it was time to be up and get ready. At 3 o'clock we hoisted our colors the glorious "Star Spangled Banner" and quietly awaited the enemies fire. Long before daylight, at 4 1/2 a.m., the first shell came hissing through the air and burst right over our heads. The thrill that ran through our veins at this time was indescribable, none were afraid, the stern defiant look on each man's countenance plainly told that fear was no part of his constitution, but something like an expression of awe crept over the features of everyone, as battery after battery opened fire and the hissing shot came plowing along leaving wreck and ruin in their path. The rebels for some time had all the play to themselves as our batteries were not opened until six and a half in the morning.[7] It would be useless for me to attempt to describe the scene for the next four hours. If viewed from a distance it must have been grand. The men were eager for the work, and soon had become perfectly familiarized to the bursting of bombshell, not that they had forgotten the destructiveness of these customers. The nimbleness with which they dodged into the safest corner on the approach of one of these messengers put that question beyond doubt. The battle raged on both sides for about two hours, when the fire from Fort Moultrie began to slacken. This, added to the fact that we had nobody hurt on our sides raised a cheer from our begrimed cannoneers, and the bombardment continued. We had been playing on the magazine of Moultrie with considerable effect, for the Carolinians admitted that they left the Fort entirely for some time thinking we were using red hot shot. The batteries doing us most damage were on Morris Island, distant about 1400 yards mounting heavy 8-inch Columbiad guns, and what was worse for us a 24 pounder Rifled Cannon throwing shaft and shell similar to those used with the Armstrong gun. This shot with astonishing precision. Almost every second shot would come in through the embrasure, and those who failed to come in had struck all round the embrasure knocking it completely out of shape and endangering the men's lives inside from the shower of broken brick knocked loose at every shot. Here we had three men slightly wounded in the face not so severely as to require the services of a surgeon. Towards mid-day we could distinctly see a fleet of three war vessels off the bay, and we were certain they were an expedition fitted out to relieve us, and the hopes of speedily getting

[7]The first answering round was actually fired at about 7:30 a.m. Mark Mayo Boatner, III, *The Civil War Dictionary* (New York, 1959), p. 300.

assistance compensated for the lack of anything in the shape of dinner. The action continued without any unusual occurrence until dark when the word was given cease firing for the night. After loading our guns with grape and cannister and posting a sufficient guard we went to sleep by our guns in the safest places we could get. So ended the first days bombardment, with none injured on our side, it was something miraculous, and as our Commander said, certainly, "Providence was on our side." The damage done to our Fort however was considerable. Our quarters, especially the officers, were knocked into a cocked hat and had been three times on fire from the bursting of shell. The enemy kept up a slow but steady fire on us during the entire night, to prevent our getting any rest, but they failed in their object, for I for one slept all night as sound as ever I did in my life. We confidently expected the fleet to make some attempt to land supplies and re-enforcements during the night, it being as dark as pitch and raining, but we were disappointed. Morning dawned and with appetites unappeased and haggard look, although determined and confident, all took their positions for the days work. The second day opened on us with a fair prospect for us, we could distinctly see the destruction our first days fire had worked, and our guns were all just as we wanted them, so we anticipated a good days work. But alas, shortly after we had got everything in full blast, the quarters were again observed to be on fire. The enemy seeing this cheered and doubled their fire with red hot shot, and it very soon became apparent that the quarters must be allowed to burn. Our magazine was becoming enveloped in flames, and our own shell were constantly bursting around us and the increased fire of the enemy made our position at this moment not to be envied. Forty barrels of powder taken from the magazine for conven-ience had to be thrown into the sea to prevent an explosion,[8] and the fire from our guns for the time being ceased, we only returning a shot every two or three minutes to let them know we were not giving up yet. The heat and smoke inside was awful. The only way to breathe was to lay flat on the ground and keep your face covered with a wet handkerchief. About this time we had our first man seriously but not fatally wounded. A large piece of shell tearing some frightful flesh wounds in his legs. He is now doing well. As the smoke began to clear away a little and our batteries about to be opened more generally, some excitement caused our cannoneers to congregate on the left

[8]One account states that heat from the fire was so great that more than ninety barrels of powder were emptied into the sea. Only four were saved, and they were all eventually used. Walter Gaston Shotwell, *The Civil War in America* (New York, 1923), p. 85.

where I was stationed. All were armed with their muskets. It turned out to be Col. Wigfall[9] with a white flag. Myself and another country-man were at the embrasure when the individual above mentioned made his appearance, and we stubbornly refused him admittance for a while, but he begged so hard, exhibited the flag he carried and even surrendered his sword, that at last we helped him in. He begged us to stop firing. An officer answered "We obey no orders here but those of Major Anderson." He then desired to be shown to the Major who at this moment made his appearance. He begged the Major "For God's sake to stop firing and they would grant any terms." This the Major after a little deliberation deemed satisfactory and the word was passed "cease firing." Previous to this however Wigfall had been waving his handkerchief from an embrasure, but the smoke was so thick that it could not be seen, and the batteries who were not aware of Wigfalls presence still kept firing. At the rebel gentleman's request the white flag was shown from our ramparts, and the firing ceased. As soon as all was quiet the flag of truce was hauled down, and our Commander submitted or rather dictated his terms; which were that we should leave with the honors of War, salute our flag, and be furnished with transportation anywhere North we desired. Thus ended the fight and here I am without a scratch, no one being wounded in the fight but the man above aluded to.[10] I forgot to mention that during the fire on the second day our flag was shot down, but it only remained down a few moments when it again floated from our ramparts nailed with ten-penny nails to a new stick.

Your affectionate son
John Thompson

[9]Louis Trezevant Wigfall was born to a planter family on April 21, 1816 in Edgefield District. As a young man, Wigfall fought political duels with Thomas Bird and Preston Brooks, and as a result, he moved to Marshall, Texas, in 1848. Here he served as a Democrat in the state senate and the U.S. Senate. An ardent champion of secession, he was one of the authors of the Southern Address which was signed on Dec. 14, 1860, and urged secession and the organization of the Confederacy. He arrived in Charleston for the bombardment and to push for the surrender of Fort Sumter. He went to Fort Sumter without the approval of the Confederate authorities. On Oct. 21, 1861, he was commissioned a brigadier general in the Confederate army but resigned on Feb. 18, 1862, to gain a seat in the Confederate States Senate. Jon Wakelyn, *Biographical Dictionary of the Confederacy* (Westport, 1977) pp. 437-438.

[10]When the fiftieth round of a planned 100 round salute was fired, an accidental explosion of powder occured. A private named Hough became the first Federal soldier to be killed in the Civil War. Boatner, *The Civil War Dictionary*, p. 300.

THE FIRST SHOT ON FORT SUMTER.

By Robert Lebby (1833-1910), M. D.

The following paper was prepared about 1893, by the late Dr. Robert Lebby, for many years quarantine officer of the State of South Carolina at the port of Charleston, and by him given in 1906 to Mr. A. S. Salley, Jr., Secretary of the Historical Commission of South Carolina, for permanent preservation by the publication thereof. Mr. Salley permitted *The News and Courier* to print it in its issue of Monday, September 3, 1906, and presents it here for the twofold purpose of preserving a most conclusive presentation of evidence regarding the firing of the first hostile shot on Fort Sumter and of carrying out his promise to Dr. Lebby to have the paper published in permanent form.

April 12, 1893, will be the thirty-second anniversary of the first shell fired at Fort Sumter, and is generally considered as the opening of the terrible struggle between the Northern and Southern sections of this great country—the one ostensibly for the preservation of the Union of these United States; the other for the maintenance of their rights under the Constitution of that Union, which they felt were being wrested from them by a fanatical element at the North.

Much has been written to prove the particular individual who fired the first shell at Fort Sumter, and thereby establish 'the fact of a questionable honor of having inaugurated the most momentous struggle in the history of the world, both as to its duration and the numbers engaged in it, and the tenacity with which those of the weaker section maintained themselves against those of the stronger, with the whole of Europe to recruit their armies from and all the resources which their open ports afforded.

I purpose, as a witness to this opening episode in the great drama, beginning April 12, 1861, to give my recollection of it, along with that of others who were on the historic spot of Fort Johnson at that time, as there are but a few now left who were there and witnessed what took place thirty-two years ago, in order that when the history of this gigantic struggle may be written in after years, some items may be obtained that will assist in its compilation.

In order that one not present on the spot may understand the situation of affairs at Fort Johnson at that time, I will state that there were two mortar batteries erected at Fort Johnson for the reduction of Fort Sumter. One situated on the front beach, midway between old Fort Johnson and the Lazaretto point, and directly west of Fort Sumter, and known as the beach, or east, battery (This was the most vulnerable and the weakest line of Fort Sumter), and the other was located due northwest of the former on a hill near some houses and contiguous to the present quarantine residence. The remains of this battery are still plainly visible. It was known as the hill, or west, battery. The east, or beach, battery has been washed away by the sea, but I have saved the timber that was used in the construction of the magazine. This comprises the topography of the offensive works at Fort Johnson for the reduction of Sumter on April 12, 1861.

The post of Fort Johnson consisted, at that date, of these two batteries of mortars and a company of infantry as reserves, all under command of Captain George S. James, South Carolina State troops.

The battery on the beach, or east, was under the immediate command of Captain James, with Lieutenant Henry S. Farley as lieutenant, and the battery on the hill, or west, was under the immediate command of Lieutenant Wade Hampton Gibbes, I think with Lieutenant J. McPherson Washington as next, and the company of infantry, as reserves, was commanded by Lieutenant Theodore B. Hayne, and was stationed near the old Martello Tower, about 400 yards in the woods, to the northwest of the hill, or Gibbes, battery.

I have been thus particular in the location of the battery and its officers for reasons that will be apparent hereafter, and they are facts that cannot be contradicted.

The first point to be established is from what battery was the first mortar shell fired?

General Beauregard, *Military Operations,* page 42, chapter 4, last paragraph, says:

From Fort Johnson's mortar battery at 4.30, A. M., issued the first shell of the war. It was fired not by Mr. Ruffin, of Virginia, as has been erroneously supposed[1], but by Capt. George S. James, of South Carolina, to whom Lieut. Stephen D. Lee issued the order.

Captain Stephen D. Lee, an aide of General Beauregard's, and who, with Gen. Chesnut, informed Major Anderson that fire would be opened on Fort Sumter, says:

The first fire was from James's battery.[2]

Mr. Edward H. Barnwell, of Charleston, who was present at Gibbes's battery at the opening, says:

The first shell fired at Sumter was from James's east battery (or the beach battery); the second was from the west (or hill battery). I was at this battery among some houses, one of which our forces tried to blow up, being too near the battery (Greer's house). This was the battery under command of Lieut. W. H. Gibbes.

Dr. W. H. Prioleau, surgeon of the post, who was at the east, or beach, battery when the first shell was fired, states:

On the morning of April 12, 1861, as soon as orders were received to open fire on Fort Sumter, we repaired to our posts, and twenty-five or thirty minutes after 4, A. M., by my watch, which I held open in my hand at the time, the first gun was fired, this being the right-hand mortar in the battery on the beach. I cannot recollect who pulled the lanyard, but this gun was directly in charge of Lieutenant Henry S. Farley, who, as well as I can recollect, sighted the gun. Captain James giving the order to fire.[3]

---

[1]"The venerable EDMUND RUFFIN, who, as soon as it was known a battle was inevitable, hastened over to Morris' Island and was elected a member of the Palmetto Guard, fired the first gun from STEVENS' Iron Battery. All honor to the chivalric Virginian! May he live many years to wear the fadeless wreath that honor placed upon his brow on our glorious Friday."—*The Charleston Daily Courier,* Saturday, April 13, 1861. (Note by A. S. S., Jr.)

[2]Vide Southern Historical Society Papers, November 1883, and other papers of Gen. Lee.

[3]Note this evidence.

Colonel Henry S. Farley, now of Mount Pleasant Military Academy, Sing Sing, New York, who was a lieutenant with James in the beach battery, states in a letter to me:

The circumstances attending the firing of the first gun at Sumter are quite fresh in my memory. Captain James stood on my right, with watch in hand, and at the designated moment gave me the order to fire. I pulled the lanyard, having already carefully inserted a friction tube, and discharged a thirteen-inch mortar shell, which was the right of battery. In one of the issues of a Charleston evening paper, which appeared shortly after the reduction of Fort Sumter, you will find it stated that Lieutenant Farley fired the first gun, and Lieutenant Gibbes the second.[4]

I will now give my personal recollections of the affair. I am a native, and was a resident and practicing physician of James' Island at the time the first gun was fired, and consequently was perfectly conversant with the topography of the location, and having been a college acquaintance of Captain James, was invited by him the previous day, April 11, to be on hand if anything transpired to require my services. I accepted his invitation and remained to witness the first, and last, gun fired at Sumter at that time.

My recollection of the matter is that on the morning of April 12, 1861, about ten minutes before 4, A. M., Captain S. D. Lee, with two other gentlemen, having just returned from Sumter, passed a group of four gentlemen, I among the number, and inquired for Captain James's quarters, and when directed to the house occupied by Captain James, remarked on passing, that the ball would soon be opened.

A short time elapsed, when Captain James and others passed to the beach, or east, battery, and Captain Lee and his party went on down to the wharf. I was midway between the houses on a bridge that connected the beach and the hill, where I could see the fire of either battery, and at

---

[4]"At thirty minutes past four o'clock the conflict was opened by the discharge of a shell from the Howitzer Battery on James' Island, under the command of Captain GEO. S. JAMES, who followed the riddled Palmetto banner on the bloody battle fields of Mexico.

"The sending of this harmful messenger to Major ANDERSON was followed by a deafening explosion, which was caused by the blowing up of a building that stood in front of the battery.

"While the white smoke was melting away into the air another shell, which Lieut. W. HAMPTON GIBBES has the honor of having fired, pursued its noiseless way toward the hostile fortification."—*The Charleston Daily Courier,* Saturday, April 13, 1861. (Note by A. S. S., Jr.)

4:30, A. M., a shell was fired from the beach, or east, battery, commanded by Captain James.

The second report heard was the blowing up of Greer's house, contiguous to the hill battery, commanded by Lieutenant W. H. Gibbes, and the second shell was fired from this battery under Lieutenant Gibbes. The firing then became general around the harbor batteries bearing on Sumter.

We have, therefore, the concurrent testimony of General Beauregard, who ordered the fire to commence; of Captain Stephen D. Lee, the officer extending the order; of Lieutenant Farley, who was in the battery when the gun was fired, and of the medical officer, Dr. W. H. Prioleau, who was on duty in the battery; also of Lieutenant Edward H. Barnwell, who was present at the hill, or Gibbes, battery, and of myself, who all bear witness to the fact that the first shell was fired from Captain James's battery on the beach. How, then, can anyone claim that the shell was fired from any other point with this weight of evidence against it?

As to the question of who pulled the lanyard of the mortar from which issued the first shell, there are only two living witnesses that I am cognizant of who were in the battery at the time of the fire, viz: Colonel Henry S. Farley and Dr. W. H. Prioleau. Colonel Henry S. Farley asserts in a letter to me that he pulled the lanyard by Captain James's order, and Dr. Prioleau asserts that Lieutenant Farley had charge of the right gun of the battery, and that the first fire was from that gun, Captain James giving the order to fire, and it is reasonable to conclude, therefore, that Farley pulled the lanyard. Certain it is that either James or Farley fired it, but, as Captain James gave the order to fire, it must have been Farley, as James would never have given himself the order to fire. The order, therefore, must have been given to Farley. I, therefore, conclude that Lieutenant Henry S. Farley fired the first gun at Sumter by Captain James's order.

The Occupation of the Sea Islands: "The First Blow Has Fallen in the Rebel Nursery"

A MICHIGAN REGIMENT IN THE PALMETTO STATE

By George M. Blackburn *

As the great fleet of Union ships approached the coast of South Carolina in November 1861, soldiers aboard the transports strained their eyes for their first glimpse of that fabled rebel state. One unit of that expedition, the Eighth Michigan Volunteer Infantry Regiment, was especially eager to strike a decisive blow against the "arch-traitors of the Union." Composed largely of men from the northern, frontier settlements of Michigan, these men were staunchly pro-Union, and many were staunchly anti-slavery. Certainly they sensed the obvious contrasts between their home and coastal South Carolina, a semi-tropical region, inhabited by wealthy plantation owners who were secessionists and slaveholders. It is no wonder that the Michigan frontiersmen were struck by the contrasts, recorded their impressions, and remembered their stay in South Carolina for the rest of their lives.[1]

These men enlisted in the Eighth Michigan during the summer of 1861. They were sworn into Federal service at Fort Wayne, Detroit, in September, transferred to Washington, D. C., in October, and then moved to Annapolis, Maryland, in November. There the Michigan regiment heard "with boyish glee" that they were assigned to General Thomas W. Sherman's expedition.[2] (By the end of the war this commander had acquired the dubious distinction of being known as the "other" General Sherman.[3])

Already General Ambrose Burnside had made a successful attack upon the North Carolina coast, and President Abraham Lincoln had

* Dr. Blackburn is associate professor of history at Central Michigan University, Mount Pleasant, Michigan.

[1] "Some of our men a healthy & strong type of farmer lads were not over clean about their persons." In the voyage from Annapolis to Port Royal the Eighth Michigan was billeted with the 79th New York, who came "mostly from the Bowry . . ., natty in dress and toilet, which caused our Regt to be branded as the dirty Michiganders . . . violent scrapes and a free for all were of daily occurence." Hatred between the two regiments was ended after heroic fighting at James Island, and the ties between the diverse units became "stronger than those of a bloody brotherhood." Arand Vanderveen, October 7, 1915, in records of the Michigan Loyal Legion, Historical Collections, the University of Michigan, pp. 7-8.

[2] Reminiscences of Oren Bumps, in records of the Michigan Loyal Legion, Historical Collections, the University of Michigan, p. 1. Hereafter cited as Bumps' Reminiscences.

[3] Bruce Catton, *This Hallowed Ground*, Garden City, New York, 1956, p. 85.

approved a second descent. The purpose was to secure a naval base for blockade operations and also a base for attacking the interior of the Confederacy.

The Sherman expedition left Annapolis in September 1861, paused at Norfolk several days, weathered a terrible storm,[4] and then continued to the coast of South Carolina. The expedition was certainly no secret; both Northern and Southern newspapers speculated about its destination, though the point of attack was finally decided by Sherman and the naval commander, Flag Officer Samuel DuPont, only after the fleet was on the high seas.

Sherman and DuPont determined to seize Port Royal, South Carolina, an excellent natural harbor, which was to serve the Union fleet as its principal base of operations for the Southeastern Atlantic area.[5] Frantic efforts to prepare a successful defense were hopeless from the start. The two forts guarding Port Royal Sound, Fort Beauregard and Fort Walker, were inadequately gunned and manned; "defended with the valor of the brave,"[6] the forts surrendered to the overwhelming power of the Union fleet. Dismayed at the Union success, white inhabitants of the area fled inland.[7]

Understandably, the exuberant Northern invaders reacted to the capture of the forts in a different manner. Michigan troops regarded their fall as an event which would go down in history. When the Stars and Stripes were raised over the former Confederate positions, "there arose such a shout from our fleet, as it has been the fortune of few to hear, in the course of an exceeding long life."[8] A Michigan soldier rejoiced in the irony that South Carolina, the first state to secede, should suffer one of the first blows in the war. "How good . . . that this first blow has fallen in the rebel nursery. South Carolina ought to suffer, for it is from her teachings—the heresy of states rights—that all our troubles proceed."[9]

Gleeful at the fall of the forts, members of the Wolverine regiment relished reports of Southern panic and drew conclusions, later proved

[4] When the rumor spread that the ship was foundering, "the excitement was appalling, but with swearing of the Highlanders [79th New York] and the praying of the Michiganders she weathered the storm . . . ." Bumps' Reminiscences, p. 2.

[5] Daniel Amen, "DuPont and the Port Royal Expedition," in Battles and Leaders, New York, 1887, I, 671-691.

[6] Bumps' Reminiscences, p. 3.

[7] Detroit Free Press, January 12, 1862.

[8] (Flint, Michigan) Wolverine Citizen, November 23, 1861.

[9] Lansing Republican, November 27, 1861.

false, about Southern bravery. One Michigan newspaper quoted an alleged statement by Governor Francis Pickens that South Carolinians were "born insensible to fear, [yet they] behaved precisely as we all expected them to. They ran away!" [10] One Northern colonel was convinced that his single regiment could capture Charleston, so great was the Southern "panic." [11] In a cocky manner, one soldier drew an historical parallel: history had shown many Knights, such as Knights of the Red Cross, and Knights Templars, but it took this war to "produce an Order of . . . . Knights of the nimble feet." [12]

Whatever the views of the Michigan soldiers, the Federal commander, General Sherman, was unwilling to operate on the assumption of Southern panic. Procrastinating and dawdling, he kept his troops huddled under the protective guns of Union warships along the coast. As a matter of fact, the Michigan troops later drastically revised their impressions of Southern fighting ability and honor. After a disastrous Federal assault on James Island in June 1862, a Michigan officer pronounced the enemy "An honorable foe, . . . in everything honorable, and I esteem these men no mean foe physically." [13] Noting that many of his comrades had been taken prisoner, he felt confident that they would be well treated.

> There are many stories in circulation with regard to barbarities perpetrated by the enemy upon our wounded in other localities but here in our intercourse with these men wherever [we] expect to find them most bitter they have proved themselves a fair foe. We came here upon their soil & have advanced our Pickets continually upon them, & though at first this was always attended with skirmishing & our stations often placed very near theirs, yet in no case have their Pickets fired upon ours after they have been posted. The second day after the Battle [on James Island] we offered a flag of Truce, were received by them fairly, furnished such information with regard to our wounded & missing as they could then give & the next day furnished with a list of the wounded who had been conveyed to Charleston for medical treatment so far as their names were ascertained & the day after with a corrected list. They also received clothes & other necessaries from us for our wounded. I have never cherished a bitter feeling toward these men which would prompt to the

<hr>

[10] *Ibid.*, December 4, 1861.

[11] (Jackson, Michigan) *The Weekly True Citizen,* January 15, 1862.

[12] John C. Buchanan to his wife, Sophia, Beaufort, May 11, 1862, in Bingham Papers, Clarke Historical Library, Central Michigan University. All letters written by Buchanan and his wife are from this collection unless otherwise noted.

[13] John C. Buchanan to Sophia, Hilton Head, July 7, 1862, in Buchanan Papers, Historical Collections, University of Michigan.

exercise of any cruelty, but have regarded them as foes to my country who must be subdued in *war Enemies* & freely acknowledge that I have been surprised at the honorable course pursued in this case by them.[14]

But the Michigan men learned this later. In the meantime the South Carolina coast around Port Royal was open to easy Yankee occupation. Michigan troops curiously observed the countryside, so different from their own home. The South Atlantic coast was penetrated by innumerable waterways; fish, deer, turkey and other wild game abounded. More to the point and of immediate concern to troops who had been on a lengthy sea voyage, the arable land was extremely fertile, producing a veritable cornucopia of good things to eat.

While on shipboard, the troops had been "alternately starved and stuffed with 'sea pie' " (a dish supposedly made from the litter and washings of the deck), so that the troops praised "the day our feet were permitted to press the inviting soil of the Palmetto State." [15]

> What a rejoicing and what a confusion! A more hungry, empty, knock kneed, independent lot of gormandizers never were assembled together before. In less than an hour nearly every man was in search of something to eat. . . . Some of my men . . . were not long gone before beef, mutton, turkeys, chickens, sweet potatoes, oranges, pea nuts, honey, oysters, fresh fish . . . came pouring into camp. Men now live luxuriantly but not prudently. The consequences are that they are soon sick.[16]

Lieutenant John Buchanan reported that coastal South Carolina was "a Beautiful Place" abounding in "Cotton, Oranges, Sweet Potatoes, figgs, etc. The foliage Green as midsummer & beautiful in its very luxurience. There are a great variety of trees & shrubbery & entirely different from ours in our Mich. Home. The cotton shrub was quite a curiosity to me, as was the Orange. The fruit is delicious." [17]

Writing many years later, a veteran recalled Hilton Head Island as "a paradise with its shell road ten miles across on either side lined with moss covered live oak and here and there a magnolia giving forth its fragrance, and charming in its beauty." During the winter of 1861 the Michigan troops lived "like princes on the abundance of the land and sea. Lucious blackberries which grew in profusion on low vines, covered the fields, pea-nuts and sweet potatoes in abundance for the dig-

14 John C. Buchanan to Sophia, James Island, June 22, 1862.
15 *Wolverine Citizen,* December 7, 1861.
16 *The Weekly True Citizen,* January 22, 1862.
17 John C. Buchanan to Sophia, Port Royal, November 12, 1861.

ging, oysters gathered at low tide by the darkies, were plenty and cheap and the hoe cakes prepared by the good old colored aunties who had catered and cooked for the aristocrats of the land were good substitutes for the ordinary soldiers diet." [18]

The climate was equally welcome. The surgeon for the Michigan unit regarded the area "as one of the finest countries to live in on the continent." Since taking possession of Hilton Head Island, there had been only two or three days that he felt like wearing an overcoat and there had been but two light frosts, so that the vegetation remained as green as it was in September. "Today you can pick a boquet of beautiful flowers, even the roses are budding and blossoming. . . . It is now 9 o'clock in the evening, and yet I set in my tent sweating just as I used to do in my office last August." [19]

Needless to say, all remarks on South Carolina were not quite so favorable. One correspondent reported that fleas were a "great annoyance," whose "appetite seems never satisfied, and whose operations are very irritating both to the spirit and flesh." They bred with "remarkable fecundity" in the hot, dry sand. One Northerner filled a half-ounce vial two-thirds full of fleas from his blankets over a two-week period. Every soldier from the Major General down can "boast at least a square foot of blotches on his person. The bird known as the mosquito also attains a good degree of size and ferocity." [20] Some soldiers complained that the water was brackish, that the mid-day sun heated the sand so that it was "almost unendurable to pedestrian," and the glare of reflected light on the ocean was "trying to the eyes of all. . . ." The intense heat caused rapid cooling at night, which produced "dews almost like rain, which soak through tents, blankets, clothing, etc., etc., and is a strong element in the production of disease among the men." [21] James Island was a "low, marshy unhealthy place unfit for the habitation of man. It looks as though it might have been the last place made in finishing up creation when there was a scarcity of materials for making dry land. . . . The undergrowth is so thick that *Fancy* Snakes run through upon the *Bushes* which in any decent country is contrary to *nature*." [22]

But such complaints were not typical. The commander of the Michigan regiment noted in January that "the windows of my room are open,

---

[18] Bumps' Reminiscences, pp. 4, 5-6.

[19] *Lansing Republican*, December 18, 1861.

[20] *Detroit Free Press*, May 24, 1862.

[21] *Wolverine Citizen*, May 3, 1862.

[22] John C. Buchanan to Sophia, Hilton Head, July 7, 1862, Buchanan Papers, Historical Collections, University of Michigan.

balmy breezes waft the song of birds to the ear, and fresh flowers and green leaves gladden the eye." [23] After returning from a visit to his Grand Rapids home, Lt. Buchanan wrote to his wife: "here at last in this pleasant land. So different from our own loved home, a fairy spot, beautiful with flowers, laden with perfume. The contrast is indeed very great. I thought the place lovely in its winter garb, now it is enchanting. The same Majestic Oaks . . . their leafy boughs . . . furnish us a welcome shade, a real luxury, strange as it may seem to you when vegetation is just starting. . . ." [24] The same soldier had previously noted that the "soil is fruitful, the Climate far ahead of our northern States for many kinds of produce." Buchanan made this remark in commenting on the theory that the North might starve out the Confederates. This theory "seems foolish to me," if South Carolina be taken as an example of the South, since there is an "abundance to eat & the probability is they can raise more." [25]

The Michigan troops noted other impressive features. Beaufort was "one of the most splendid places that I have seen in a long time. The houses are furnished with the heaviest kind of mahogany furniture," and (seemingly the ultimate praise) "about every house contains a fine piano." [26] Another soldier noted that houses in the area were "furnished with the most costly furniture, principally of foreign manufacture, such as sofas, chairs, pianos, and one room with some of Phelan's *best* billiard tables." [27]

The Michigan soldiers spoke from first-hand observation in describing the contents of houses. One told of a raid in which troops marched to a planter's house, stacked arms, appointed guards, broke ranks, and marched to the house. "The first pitch we made was for the house, not so much after plunder, perhaps, as through curiosity to see what we could find, and it may be to get something soft to go with our hard bread for dinner. . . ." After helping themselves to cream, milk, butter, preserves, and jam, among other items, the soldiers

> visited, in great haste, each one trying to be first, all the different rooms, but especially the little drawers of the different Bureaus in each room. We also paid some attention to the stands, trunks, boxes, library, &c., and we found abundant evidence everywhere (but especially upstairs in the young ladies room) of cultivation, education and refinement. Of

[23] *Wolverine Citizen*, March 8, 1862.
[24] John C. Buchanan to Sophia, Beaufort, May 4, 1862.
[25] John C. Buchanan to Hannah Bingham, Beaufort, January 19, 1862
[26] *Wolverine Citizen*, January 4, 1862.
[27] *The Weekly True Citizen*, January 22, 1862.

course I cannot enter into a detailed account of these things, but I will simply say that each one appropriated to himself those things that seemed most pleasing in his own eye. However I found myself in a predicament a good deal like the Irishman, who on coming from his own country to this land of plenty, and seeing a dollar in the road thought it beneath his dignity to stop to pick that up, but would wait his chance for a five. I presume he is waiting yet, and so with me. . . .[28]

Not all the soldiers, however, waited for a five. Abundant evidence proves conclusively that widespread looting occurred, even though it was expressly forbidden.[29] Still, the soldiers should not bear the only blame for looting; in fact, Negroes were charged with doing most of the damage.[30]

One soldier recalled finding a locked trunk in a house which he did not have the courage to open, but a colored woman took it and ran away with it. Soldiers also found a cask of the best crockery and glass buried in the yard; while the soldiers did not want it, the colored "brethern" took it.[31] The houses of Beaufort were beautiful on the out-side and gardens uninjured, but the "interiors were in a awful state, little better than a chaos of broken furniture, torn books and engravings, old letters, &c." Negroes said the damage was done by "country people," meaning the field hands.[32]

Clearly the Michigan soldiers were impressed by certain material features of coastal South Carolina. They also had some distinct impressions of the wealthy plantation owners who inhabited the area. Most descriptions involved self-conscious references to the high social class of the residents of such places as Beaufort as contrasted with the more plebeian Michiganians, "mud sills," or "Hessians as they call us. . . ."[33]

Buchanan wrote that in May the first families of South Carolina "were wont to take residence in Beaufort. They are not expected this season & it is thought by some, that some other place would be more pleasant for them, especially as the *mud sills* are here & of course could not be expected to appreciate the intelligence, refinement & chivalry of the higher born."[34]

[28] *Grand Rapids Enquirer Weekly,* January 29, 1862.

[29] *Wolverine Citizen,* December 28, 1861.

[30] *Grand Rapids Weekly Enquirer,* November 27, 1861; *The Weekly True Citizen,* January 22, 1862.

[31] *Grand Rapids Weekly Enquirer,* January 29, 1862.

[32] *Ibid.,* November 27, 1861.

[33] John C. Buchanan to Sophia, Port Royal, November 12, 1861.

[34] *Ibid.,* Beaufort, May 11, 1862.

The theme of "mud sill" versus chivalry was fairly common in letters written home. The colonel of the Eighth Michigan sent home two letters "written by the *chivalry* of that section, which bear the mark of the 'first families' by the poor spelling and ungrammatical sentences." [35]

Although Michigan soldiers acknowledged that the Port Royal residents were upper class, and displayed obvious signs of wealth, Buchanan claimed he saw little evidence of thrift or energy in the South. "The soil is fruitful, the Climate far ahead of our northern States for many kinds of produce. Could our northern Energy be transplanted to this Clime, the change would be startling. This might be made an Eden, but never while a portion of the human family are held in such a Bongage." Buchanan also charged the chivalry with arrogance: "The heaven gifted people born with a whip in their right hand, a spur on their right heel, no doubt to designate them as those foreordained to whip & ride the rest of the world generally." [36]

The invading forces had to draw conclusions about white South Carolinians from inference. On the other hand, their observations of Negro inhabitants were direct. In fact it was impossible to avoid contact with the colored folk who flocked to Northern lines as soon as the landing occurred. Federal troops frequently conversed with the Negroes and prized some of their remarks. The servant of General Thomas Drayton, Confederate commander at Port Royal, quoted the General as claiming during the bombardment of the forts of Port Royal that "the devil nor G--d A--y can't take that fort." Upon realizing that surrender was inevitable, the General called for his horse, and "as the darkey helped him into his saddle he said, '*Massa Drayton, God Almighty come, but de Yankees come wid him.'*" [37] Another old Negro was heard praying vigorously that "de Lord would bless *dese* d--d Yankees." [38]

Not all the Federal troops were amused, however. In a letter to a Michigan friend, one officer snorted that "I wouldn't give the Servant I brot from New York for all the Contrabands I have seen about our Camps. Most of them are very stupid fellows, and very lazy. . . ." [39]

A veteran recalled many years later the "many handsome molatto girls, formerly house servants, who made a dashy appearance arrayed

[35] *The Weekly True Citizen*, January 2, 1862.

[36] John C. Buchanan to Sophia, Beaufort, December 22, 1861, May 11, 1862; Buchanan to Hannah Bingham, Beaufort, January 19, 1862.

[37] *The Weekly True Citizen*, January 22, 1862.

[38] *Lansing Republican*, February 12, 1862.

[39] James Green to Angie Bingham, Birds Island, Georgia, March 12, 1862, Bingham Papers, Clarke Historical Library, Central Michigan University.

in the gowns of their former mistresses." He also noted that at first the Negroes "regarded us as their saviours and were excessively polite, getting entirely off the sidewalk, doffing their hat with a 'Good mawnin Massa' but with familiarity and the joking of the boys they soon wanted the entire sidewalk to themselves." [40]

These observers believed it impossible to escape involvement in the slavery question. It might have been easy to say that "it is an awful thing to let the negro mix up" in the war, "but when you get down here among *the thing* itself, and hear and learn, and see, . . . you become enlisted in sympathy from daily sight." [41] Lt. Buchanan was certainly sympathetic.

> Here . . . you see slavery as it is, poor Helpless Beings occupying the Plantations, deserted by every white Inhabitant, really incapable of doing anything without a Master. . . . These beings live in Houses white washed without, squalidly wretched within, the little Darkeys looking & acting as amusing as any of our northern Babys, perhaps using their Hands a trifle more for *scratching* purposes. I saw one mother catching vermin from the Wool of a nursing Child at Gen Draytons Plantation, which I visited when on Picket Duty. I said Aunty what are you doing there. Her only [reply] was a hearty laugh participated in by all the negroes. They seem to enjoy themselves in their Condition. Of course their wants are few. One of the Head negroes of this Plantation told me that for some time past, the times had been very hard & many of them had only a little corn to eat. [42]

The Michigan soldiers also agreed that "These Negroes have a truly wonderful Talent for music. I have never seen better time than in their singing & Dancing. All sing, & all Dance, from Childhood to old age." [43] Others were fascinated with the religious services of the Negroes, in particular the Negro "Shout." [44]

Sympathy for the slaves, however, did not necessarily extend to acceptance of abolition. A change of policy and commanders showed that. General Thomas Sherman, "an old fogy, dispectic . . . afraid of offending the enemy by destroying their property," [45] was replaced by

---

[40] Bumps' Reminiscences, pp. 4, 6.

[41] *Lansing Republican*, January 29, 1862.

[42] John C. Buchanan to Sophia, Port Royal, November 12, 1861.

[43] *Ibid.*, December 29, 1861.

[44] For references to Negro music and religious services see author's edition of *The Diary of Captain Ralph Ely of the Eighth Michigan Infantry*, Mt. Pleasant, Michigan, 1965, pp. 24, 25, 26.

[45] W. Ely Lewis to O. L. Spaulding, Beaufort, January 14, 1862, Spaulding Papers, Historical Collections, University of Michigan.

General David Hunter. The latter barely arrived in South Carolina before issuing his famous order freeing slaves in the Southern Department. "This caused wild excitement. . . ." [46] The commander of the Eighth Michigan reportedly urged his officers to resign and go home rather than obey the order. It was even said that he would surrender to the Confederates rather than serve under Hunter, because he had enlisted to preserve the Union rather than abolish slavery. [47] No doubt the officer was relieved when President Abraham Lincoln revoked Hunter's order.

Hunter later enlisted Negroes as soldiers, which one German speaking soldier regarded as "a shame for the entire American people and especially a disgrace for the military. . . ." When Hunter sought to secure white officers to command the colored troops, the correspondent of the *Detroit Free Press* exploded: "to the everlasting honor of the [Eighth Michigan] regiment, there was but one man found sunk so low as to allow himself to be used for any such purposes." He continued:

> Tell the friends of the constitution in Michigan, if this war is to be turned into a crusade against any part of our country, and if we are asked or expected to stand shoulder to shoulder on an equality with a negro, as a soldier, the regiment here may be reckoned out, for every officer, from the highest to the lowest will throw up their commissions, and retire from service. There is such a storm brewing here that I think the whole thing will be abandoned, and the negro be again used as he has been—to do the drudgery in the army, unloading vessels, making breastworks, in short, using him anywhere to save a white man's muscle, except with a gun. Thirty thousand of them would be whipped by five hundred white men. [48]

Undoubtedly this reporter reflected anti-Negro sentiment by no means absent in Michigan at the time, as the files of the *Detroit Free Press* amply demonstrate.

But it was not only the "copperhead" Detroit newspaper which seriously questioned the use of Negroes as soldiers. Lt. Buchanan, a strong anti-slavery man, was convinced slavery caused the war, and that slavery must be wiped out. Yet he doubted the wisdom of an even earlier proposal by Simon Cameron, secretary of war in Abraham Lincoln's cabinet, that the former slaves be armed. Such a measure would "en-

[46] John M. Bessmer to John Weissert, Beaufort, May 18, 1862, Historical Collections, University of Michigan. The letter was written in German; this reference is to a typescript in English.

[47] *Lansing State Republican,* October 5, 1864.

[48] John M. Bessmer to John Weissert, May 18, 1862, Historical Collections, University of Michigan; *Detroit Free Press,* May 24, 1862.

gender strife & divide the Councils of the nation, & may embitter the minds of many who are really Union Men. I have seen none of these *Colored Gemmen* as yet who would be capable of fighting, & will venture the assertion, such is their servility that fifty of their Masters would put to flight a Reg—of them. Poor helpless creatures. . . . It would be equal folly to employ them on either side." Curiously enough, some nineteen months later, Buchanan changed his mind, praised Negro troops highly and confessed "I would as soon they would shoot *Mr. Reb* as to do it myself." [49]

But a New England abolitionist, a missionary to the South Carolina Negroes, concluded that "one might as well think of a combination among the Boston kittens to scratch the eyes out of all the Boston dogs as to look for an insurrection in this State, if the negroes on these islands are a fair sample of those on the main. . . ." [50]

The Michigan men soon learned that debate over the military capabilities of Negroes would be replaced by action—a movement toward the Confederate stronghold of Charleston. Federal forces landed on James Island and were repulsed with heavy loss in an assault on Southern fortifications. The Eighth Michigan was particularly hard hit. Within a few weeks the Michigan unit was ordered to the Washington area. Their South Carolina tour of duty had ended.

For the "Wandering Eighth" there were many campaigns and battles in the future, but, one wrote home, "the records of our South Carolina campaign are dear to our memories." [51] The men "sigh[ed] for Beaufort often" when they were enduring the miseries of campaigning before the battle of Fredericksburg.[52] Maybe it was because she had enjoyed reading her husband's description of South Carolina, that Buchanan's wife requested him to "give me a little idea of the surrounding country. Whether you like it as well as Beaufort. I have always imagined the latter, place, as a little fairy land." [53] Reminiscing before a veterans' group many years later, one veteran told his comrades that "the dream of that winter is the sunshine of my soldier life." [54]

[49] For discussion of Buchanan's ideas on this topic see my "The Negro as Viewed by a Michigan Civil War Soldier: Letters of John C. Buchanan," *Michigan History*, XLVII (March 1963), 75-84.

[50] Edward S. Philbrick, September 27, 1862, quoted in *Letters from Port Royal Written at the Time of the Civil War*, ed. Elizabeth W. Pearson, Boston, 1906, p. 89.

[51] *Wolverine Citizen*, March 28, 1863.

[52] John C. Buchanan to Sophia, Falmouth, Virginia, November 20, 1862.

[53] Sophia to John C. Buchanan, Grand Rapids, August 5, 1862.

[54] Bumps' Reminiscences, p. 4.

GENERALS DAVID HUNTER AND
RUFUS SAXTON AND BLACK SOLDIERS

HOWARD C. WESTWOOD*

"Hunter was not suited to the work and . . . Rufus Saxton was."

That, says Dudley Cornish in his superb *Sable Arm*, probably was
the "conviction" of Secretary of War Edwin M. Stanton that caused him
to refuse to recognize a regiment of blacks recruited by Major General
David Hunter on South Carolina's coastal islands in the summer of 1862,
but at the same time to authorize Brigadier General Rufus Saxton to
enlist blacks of that region into the army. Cornish finds Stanton's action
"hard to understand."[1] Understanding is enlightened by a close look at
what was happening on the Sea Islands. It was a time when the President
was tiptoeing toward a change in the nation's traditional policy that only
whites would be allowed to be soldiers. Hunter did not smooth the way;
Saxton did.

At the end of March 1862, Hunter had arrived at Hilton Head to take
command of a newly designated Department of the South, defined to
include the States of South Carolina, Georgia, and Florida.[2] The department resulted from a navy-army expedition, commanded by Flag Officer
Samuel F. DuPont and Brigadier General Thomas W. Sherman, that in
early November 1861 had captured Port Royal about mid-way between
Charleston and Savannah. By the time of Hunter's coming, DuPont and
Sherman had occupied the strip of coastal islands from twenty or so
miles short of Charleston to the vicinity of Savannah, and some coastal
points beyond in Georgia and northeast Florida. All along the Union had
held Key West and soon after Hunter's arrival other Union forces took
Apalachicola and then Pensacola on the Florida Panhandle. The troops
in Hunter's department never would number more than about 18,000.
Probably no general's command throughout the war was spread so thin
over an area so wide.[3]

The Union's position seemed to offer opportunity to attack Savannah or Charleston or both, each an important Confederate port. Even

---

* Counselor in the law firm of Covington and Burling, Washington.

[1] Dudley Taylor Cornish, *The Sable Arm*, (New York, 1966), p. 53.

[2] *Official Records of the Union and Confederate Armies*, ser. 1, 6.248, 257, cited as
ORA.

[3] *Report of the Joint Committee on the Conduct of the War*, H. Rep., 37 Cong., 3d Sess.
(Apr. 6, 1863), 3:292-95, 302, 304, 309, 322, cited as *JCCW Report; ORA*, ser. 1, 6:237, 263-64;
14:362; George Linton Hendricks, "Union Army Occupation of the Southern Seaboard"
(Ph.D. Diss., Columbia Univ., 1954, Libr. of Cong. micro.), p. 7; Shelby Foote, *The Civil War*,
3 vols. (New York, 1958-74), 1(1958):353.

The South Carolina Historical Magazine 86: 165-181

before his relief by Hunter, Sherman had forces poised for an assault on Fort Pulaski that guarded Savannah's outlet to the sea. Within days after Hunter took over, that assault was made with complete success. But a greater force would be required for capture of either port. The Union high command's priorities were elsewhere: Virginia, West Tennessee, and an imminent move on New Orleans. The Port Royal expedition had been designed initially only to secure anchorages for the Union's blockading fleet. That purpose had been more than fully achieved.[4]

General Hunter, however, was hungry for further conquest. While *en route* to supersede Sherman, he had written Secretary of War Stanton that if he were reinforced by only one division he could almost guarantee that he would have the Stars and Stripes waving over Fort Sumter by the anniversary of its surrender to the Rebels.[5] One of the first things that impressed him, on his arrival, was the presence within his lines of a reservoir of loyal manpower that would need only arms and training to augment his army were he able to draw upon it. That reservoir was many hundreds of blacks, lately slaves on the Carolina sea island plantations.

When General Sherman's army had landed, nearly all the whites for many miles on either side of Port Royal had fled, but their slaves had stayed. It is said that only one white man had remained in Beaufort, the "metropolis" of the area. The blacks were nearly as many as Sherman's invading troops. The problem of care and governing of a large slave population was then quite without precedent for a Union army, and for some weeks the blacks seemed to Sherman a baffling burden. But he and his quartermaster, Rufus Saxton, then a captain, bent to the task. In time, Sherman made imaginative provision for the blacks' employment on the plantations and their education.[6] Moreover, help came from the Treasury Department which was given responsibility for abandoned properties. In early March a Treasury agent of exceptional vision, Edward Pierce, brought a band of 53 people, including a dozen ladies, supported by private associations in the North, to take on plantation management and the teaching of the blacks, adult and children. They are known to history as Gideon's Band, their program as the Port Royal Experiment.[7]

[4] *JCCW Report*, 294-99, 302-06, 309-10; Port Royal, S. C., *The New South*, Aug. 23, 1862; Horace Greeley, *The American Conflict*, 2 vols. (Hartford, 1866), 2:457-58. Very significantly, Sherman reported on his return to Washington in April that the troops in the Port Royal area were far more than needed merely to hold the Union's position. *JCCW Report*, 295, 309.

[5] *ORA*, ser. 1, 6:254.

[6] *JCCW Report*, 327; *ORA*, ser. 1, 6:203-05, 218, 222-23; Hendricks, "Union Army Occupation," 9-16.

[7] Edward Pierce, "The Freedmen at Port Royal," *The Atlantic Monthly* XII (Sept. 1863): 296-98; Hendricks, "Union Army Occupation," pp. 43-54; Willie Lee Rose, *Rehearsal for Reconstruction* (New York, 1964), pp. 19-31, 43-69; Port Royal, *The New South*, Mar. 15, 1862.

When Hunter arrived he found that program well begun, with busy communities loyal to the Union. It was in their men folk that he saw potential Union soldiers. More than that, he envisioned attracting thousands more blacks, escaping masters beyond the Union lines. On April 3, only the fourth day after his arrival, he wrote Secretary Stanton asking for 50,000 muskets "with authority to arm such loyal men as I can find in the country, whenever, in my opinion, they can be used advantageously against the enemy." To distinguish such men he asked for 50,000 pairs of scarlet pantaloons.[8]

Immediately thereafter, on consultation with a dynamic black preacher, Abram Murchison, Hunter arranged for a meeting of black men on Hilton Head to get names of those willing to "take up arms in defense of the Government and of themselves." The meeting, on April 7, was conducted by Murchison and two whites, one a plantation superintendent. Response, at first, was favorable. Hunter soon had a list of 150 willing blacks not too old for military service. While evidence is fragmentary, it appears that the early response encouraged Hunter to continue such solicitation into early May.[9] Though he had no reply to his April 3 request to Stanton — indeed, there never would be a reply — the *New York Times* reported on May 1, in a dispatch from its correspondent at Port Royal, that the War Department's original instructions to General Sherman had conferred "fullest power" to employ blacks "even in arms" and that it seemed that Hunter would exercise that power.

While the instructions to Sherman did continue to apply to Hunter, the *Times* man overstated them. Issued in October 1861, just before embarkation of the Port Royal expedition, they provided that Sherman could avail himself of the services of anyone willing, "whether fugitives from labor or not," either as "ordinary employees, or, if special circumstances seem to require it, in any other capacity, with such organization (in squads, companies, or otherwise) as you may deem most beneficial to the service; this, however, not being a general arming of them for military service." The phrase after the semi-colon had been inserted by the President himself when the draft was submitted for his approval. Thereafter the War Department had construed the instructions to mean that blacks could be armed "in cases of great emergency" but "not under regular enrollment for military purposes."[10]

Thus it was clear, in the spring of 1862, that the Union high command had allowed no departure from the policy prevailing after the War of 1812 that the black man, free or slave, could not become a United

    [8] *ORA*, ser. 1, 6:263-64; ser. 3, 2:292.
    [9] *New York Times*, May 1, 1862 (dispatch from Port Royal); *ORA*, ser. 3, 2:29-30, 53; Thomas Wentworth Higginson, *Army Life in a Black Regiment* (Boston, 1870), pp. 272-73.
    [10] *ORA*, ser 1, 6:176-77; ser. 3, 1:609-10, 626; 2:30; A. Howard Meneely, *The War Department, 1861* (New York, 1928), pp. 341-43.

States soldier. There always had been black sailors; already during the Civil War even fugitive slaves had been taken into the navy. But the army was a different matter. Hunter, as the army's fourth ranking major general, knew that full well.[11]

Still, Hunter was authorized to arm his blacks "in cases of great emergency" otherwise than "under regular enrollment." There were obvious possibilities of "great emergency." On April 22 Hunter wrote Stanton that the enemy had 65,000 troops at Charleston, Savannah, and Augusta who could be quickly combined against him. Were he not reinforced, he warned, he might have to draw his troops back into very limited enclaves.[12] That, of course, could expose to the Rebels some of the plantations. Then on May 3 came an occurrence that could lead to another kind of "emergency." On that day the barge of the Confederate commander at Charleston was delivered by its slave crewmen to Union blockaders. The crewmen gave information regarding the Charleston defenses that prompted one of Hunter's chief subordinates, Brigadier General Henry W. Benham, to propose a Charleston attack. Benham was told to perfect a plan.[13] Any such move would require concentration of Hunter's forces on approaches to Charleston, drawing from the screen protecting the rest of his domain. That would create an "emergency" indeed.

As Benham began his planning Hunter did some thinking on his own. His campaign to list names of blacks willing to "take up arms" had not gone well after the initial response. Though Treasury agent Pierce was cooperative, most of the blacks were so enjoying their new found freedom as employees instead of slaves that they were averse to the restriction and danger of military life; on one island but a single man had agreed to be listed.[14] Hunter decided — evidently without consulting

---

[11] Cornish, *Sable Arm*, Foreword; Fred A. Shannon, "The Federal Government and the Negro Soldier, 1861-1865," *Journal of Negro History* XI (1926): 564-65; Herbert Aptheker, "The Negro in the Union Navy," *Journal of Negro History* XXXII (1947): 169, 170-74, 179; *Official Records of the Union and Confederate Navies*, ser. 1, 6:252, 409, cited as *ORN;* Elon A. Woodward, *The Negro in the Military Service of the United States, 1639-1886*, 2:838, 888; Records of the Adj. Gen. Off., 1780's-1917, National Archives, RG 94; Ezra J. Warner, *Generals in Blue* (Baton Rouge, 1964), p. 244.

[12] *ORA*, ser. 1, 14:337.

[13] *ORA*, ser. 1, 14:983; John D. Hayes, *Samuel Francis DuPont — A Selection from his Civil War Letters*, 3 vols. (Ithaca, 1969), 2:50.

[14] *ORA*, ser. 3, 2:53; Elizabeth Ware Pearson, *Letters from Port Royal* (Boston, 1906), p. 40; Rupert Sargent Holland, *Letters and Diary of Laura M. Towne* (New York, 1912, reprinted 1969), p. 37; Higginson, *Army Life*, pp. 272-73.

anyone, even his own generals — to intensify this effort and not only to step up his listing campaign but to begin actual organization. As late as May 7 he was still simply having names solicited. But by the next day he had decided "to enlist two regiments to be officered from the most intelligent and energetic of our non-commissioned officers" and had actually named the men from an engineer regiment to be captain and lieutenants of Company A of the first regiment. On the following day, May 9, he issued an order to be transmitted to subordinate commanders in the area "to send immediately to these headquarters, under a guard, all the able-bodied negroes capable of bearing arms."[15]

On the same May 9 Hunter issued another order proclaiming the emancipation of all slaves in South Carolina, Georgia, and Florida, whether or not within Union lines.[16] Back in the summer of 1861 Major General John C. Fremont had proclaimed emancipation of the slaves of all enemies of the Union in his command in Missouri. The President had set aside that decree.[17] Nonetheless, Hunter now went Fremont one better. His decree covered slaves not only of enemies but also of masters who might be loyal. There is no evidence of what Hunter deemed his authority to emancipate; he did not even report his action to the War Department.[18] It was, however, reported in the northern press, and on May 19 the President issued a proclamation announcing that if there had been such a decree it was voided, that whether the Executive's war powers included the power to emancipate and whether it should be exercised "are questions which under my responsibility I reserve to

---

[15] *ORA*, ser. 3, 2:29-31, 52; Woodward, *The Negro in Military Service*, 2:846-49.

[16] *ORA*, ser. 1, 14:341.

[17] Allan Nevins, *The War for the Union*, 4 vols. (New York, 1959-71), 1(1959):331-36.

[18] The instructions to General Sherman (applicable to Hunter) directed that he be guided by the "principles" of instructions to Maj. Gen. Benjamin F. Butler at Fort Monroe in the summer of 1861 and attached copies. As printed in *ORA*, ser. 1, 6:176-77, the Sherman instructions give incorrect citation to the Butler instructions; correct citation is *ORA*, ser. 1, 6:243; ser. 2, 1:754-55, 761-62. The Butler instructions forbade interference with slavery, except that a fugitive was not to be returned to his master involuntarily. Nonetheless on April 13, just after the capture of Fort Pulaski, Hunter proclaimed the freedom of all slaves of "enemies" at Pulaski and on its island, Cockspur. Though that decree was reported in the Northern press it evoked no disapproval from higher authority. *ORA*, ser. 1, 14:333; *New York Times*, April 19, 1862.

Thus if Hunter had been one to bother with justification of his actions he might have argued that no disapproval of his Pulaski emancipation indicated a change in War Department policy. Also he might have argued that the Presidential action respecting the Fremont proclamation was not an applicable precedent since that proclamation had applied to a loyal state, Missouri, whereas his of May 9 applied to three rebel states.

myself." At that time, indeed, heated debates in Congress on a variety of proposals showed that the issue of emancipation, however limited, was explosive, especially among representatives of border slave states.[19]

The coincidence of Hunter's emancipation decree and his order to round up able-bodied blacks suggests that he hoped by the decree to win the confidence of the blacks and so facilitate organization of his proposed regiments. If so, he miscalculated.

Implementing instructions for the round-up reached Treasury agent Pierce and the plantation superintendents late on Sunday, May 11. That night squads of soldiers were deployed to carry out the round-up the first thing the next morning. Pierce was appalled. Hunter's order read as though all able-bodied men were to be conscripted into the military. That would play havoc with work on the plantations. Moreover, southern masters long had spread the rumor that blacks falling into Yankee hands would be sent off to be sold in Cuba. An abrupt round-up by squads of soldiers would create panic. By the morning of May 12 Pierce was at Hunter's headquarters to follow up a strongly protesting letter he had written the night before. Hunter assured him that only willing men would be enlisted and that plantation foremen and plowmen would not be included in the round-up. But he would not accede to Pierce's plea to defer the round-up.

The scenes on the plantations that morning were fully as sad as Pierce feared. The superintendents, though as appalled as Pierce, loyally cooperated with the military and sought to avert panic. But panic there was. In some places the men fled to the woods, with soldiers trying to hunt them down. Women wailed. And men between the ages of 18 and 45 who could be found were marched off under guard. Five or six hundred were brought to Hunter's headquarters. The next day, May 13, Pierce dispatched to Secretary of Treasury Salmon P. Chase a full report, with documentation, angrily protesting. One of the supporting documents was a letter to Pierce from a plantation superintendent saying, "Never, in my judgment, did major-general fall into a sadder blunder and rarely

---

[19] *ORA*, ser. 3, 2:42-43.

Consideration of emancipation questions in the 37th Congress is well reviewed in Leonard P. Curry, *Blueprint for Modern America* (Nashville, 1968), pp. 36-74. Hunter's blindness to the delicacy of the emancipation question is revealed by the assertion in a Port Royal newspaper, operating under military auspices, that since there had been "no official notification" of the President's disavowal Hunter's emancipation was in full force, and by Hunter's own assertion in later years that the President had "rejoiced" in his action since no word of disapproval had been sent to him. Port Royal, *The New South*, Aug. 23, 1862; David Hunter, *Report of the Military Services of David Hunter* (2d ed., New York, 1892), p. 17.

has humanity been outraged by an act of more unfeeling barbarity." On May 21 Chase forwarded to Stanton the Pierce report with its documentation in order to give Stanton "a correct view of the state of things." Hunter himself made no report, so just what he was up to was not clear in Washington.[20]

True to his word to Pierce, Hunter confined his "recruitment" to the men who professed to be willing and soon, of those who had been marched off, some drifted back home. But Hunter was persuasive and many remained; organization of a regiment began. Hunter assigned as its colonel one of his own staff officers, his nephew by marriage. The other officers were designated from non-commissioned ones of his army. Recruiting effort continued after the round-up but response was limited. Hunter's original plan to have two regiments was soon abandoned. The one regiment, even weeks later, seems never to have been more than 1,000 and may not have exceeded 800. The strong arm round-up left a bad impression with the black community that lingered for many months.[21]

Hunter, in any case, had much more than black recruiting to demand attention. At sunrise on May 13, the day after the round-up, the dispatch boat of the Confederate commander at Charleston was delivered to Union blockaders by her slave crewmen, led by a remarkable young black, Robert Smalls. Even more than the crewmen of the Confederate commander's barge who had escaped ten days earlier, Smalls was thoroughly familiar with the Charleston defenses, notably a recent deployment that seemed to leave a wide opening for Union attack. That night Smalls was brought to Port Royal to tell his story to Flag Officer DuPont. His information was passed on to General Benham for use in his planning of a Charleston attack; on May 17 Benham submitted his final plan.[22]

Hunter soon began preparatory moves toward Charleston. The moves, however, took time. Extensive reconnoitering was necessary, and concentration and advance of Hunter's forces were slow because of inadequate transport on shallow coastal waters and marshy land. Also, eventually, troops had to be brought up from Key West for some protection of uncovered plantations. It was a full month from the time Benham

[20] *ORA*, ser. 3, 2:50-60; Pearson, *Letters*, pp. 37-42, 51; Holland, *Towne Letters*, pp. 41-54; *National Intelligencer* (Washington), May 28, 1862, quoting May 14 dispatch to Boston *Journal*.

[21] Pearson, *Letters*, pp. 50-51, 54; Holland, *Towne Letters*, p. 54; *Cong. Globe*, 37 Cong., 2d Sess. (1862), 3123; *National Intelligencer*, May 28, Aug. 13, Aug. 18, 1862; *Washington Evening Star*, Aug. 19, 1862; Hendricks, "Union Army Occupation," p. 67.

[22] *ORN*, ser. 1, 12:807, 820-21; 13:53; *ORA*, ser. 1, 14:983-86; Benjamin Quarles, "The Abduction of the 'Planter,' " *Civil War History* IV (Mar. 1958): 5-10.

submitted his plan before the moves came to climax. Benham, in field command, at length was in sight of Charleston's spires. Hunter ordered that he establish a secure position for a later attack on the city. In an effort to do so Benham, on June 16, assaulted Confederate works in what became the battle of Secessionville. The attack was a dismal failure. That ended the moves, though some advanced positions were maintained.[23]

The black regiment had not been even remotely involved in Benham's venture. Benham had wanted it sent to him.[24] But there is no evidence that Hunter had permitted it to leave Hilton Head, its place of encampment. By June Hunter's nephew had been succeeded as its colonel by the son of Maine's powerful Senator William P. Fessenden. Red pantaloons had come for the blacks' uniforms and they were armed and drilled diligently. But otherwise, apparently, their only employment was on work parties, notably in loading and unloading vessels.[25]

To this point Hunter might have sought to justify his black "soldiers" by stretching somewhat the instructions to General Sherman, now applicable to Hunter, regarding employment of blacks. The instructions allowed organization of blacks "in squads, companies, or otherwise" and, in "special circumstances," their employment not only as "ordinary employees" but otherwise, and, as we have seen, the War Department had construed the instructions to permit arming of the blacks in "great emergency" short of "regular enrollment." It might have been argued that, with all that confronted his white army and with "emergency" threatened, Hunter was authorized to organize and train in the use of arms able black men while employing them in work parties. Whether that indeed was Hunter's rationalization at the time is unknown. He still had not reported his action to Washington. But in late June he was required to report. As we shall see in a moment, that report put him in an untenable position.

It is possible, indeed probable, that Hunter himself never would have had to tender an explanation had not chances of war delayed the implementing of a decision that Secretary of War Stanton made in late April. That was a decision to send back to Port Royal Rufus Saxton, who

[23] *ORA*, ser. 1, 14:41-104, 979-83; Letters Received, Adj. Gen. Office, 1861-70, No. 1063 S, Rufus Saxton to Stanton, June 30, 1862, NA, RG 94; *New York Times*, June 28, 1862; Greeley, *American Conflict*, 2:460-62.

[24] Register of Letters Received, Dept. of South, from Gen. H. W. Benham, June 11, 1862, NA, RG 393.

[25] Register of Letters Received, Dept. of South, from Col. N. W. Brown and enclosure, June 24, 1862, NA, RG 393; Holland, *Towne Letters*, p. 71; *New York Times*, June 17, July 2, July 9, Sept. 15 (Rev. Mansfield French speech in New York), 1862; *National Intelligencer*, June 28, 1862; Higginson, *Army Life*, p. 73. I have found no formal records of the regiment.

had been General Sherman's quartermaster, to take charge of the blacks in Hunter's department.

On Hunter's arrival at the end of March, General Sherman and Captain Saxton had returned to Washington for reassignment. Within days each was called to testify on the Port Royal situation by the Congressional Joint Committee on the Conduct of the War, a committee just then exceedingly active and especially intimate with Stanton.[26] As quartermaster, Saxton had been closely involved with the Port Royal blacks. The Committee was interested in his appraisal of them; he strongly emphasized their effective cooperation in the work there and his confidence in them.[27] The President already had directed that Saxton be vaulted to the rank of brigadier general, and on April 29, shortly after his testimony to the Committee, he had an order from Stanton to return to Port Royal to assume responsibility for the blacks in the department, subject only to Hunter's general authority.[28] Saxton likewise had a conference with Treasury Secretary Chase, whose concerns, of course, also were involved. It seems that there had been discussion of Hunter's April 3 request for 50,000 muskets and scarlet pantaloons and for authority to arm "loyal men" for use "against the enemy," because Chase's diary noted that Saxton told him that Stanton had authorized procurement of "one or two thousand red flannel suits for the blacks, with a view to organization," but no muskets.[29] Thus Hunter's April 3 proposal to add black soldiers to his army had met with no favor in Washington.

Saxton at once busied himself in assembling a staff and preparing to leave. On May 15 he sailed from New York.[30] Word of his mission already had reached Port Royal. When Treasury agent Pierce had his meeting with Hunter on May 12 to protest the round-up, Hunter had recognized that on Saxton's arrival the question of going ahead with the black regiment would be for Saxton to decide.[31] But Saxton did not get there as planned. His ship was wrecked.[32] Then as he prepared to start anew

[26] Howard C. Westwood, "The Joint Committee on the Conduct of the War," *Lincoln Herald* 80 (Spring 1978): 4-5.

[27] *JCCW Report*, 322-30.

[28] Adj. Gen. Office, Register of Letters Received, 1819-1889, 38(1862):913, NA, RG 94, M 711, Roll 35; *ORA*, ser. 3, 2:27.

[29] David Donald, ed., *Inside Lincoln's Cabinet — The Civil War Diaries of Salmon P. Chase* (New York, 1954), p. 71.

[30] Dept. of South — Special Orders, General Orders, Circulars of Gen. Saxton, May 1862-Dec. 1863, special orders at first two unnumbered pages, NA, RG 393; *New York Times*, May 16, 1862.

[31] *ORA*, ser. 3, 2:52, Pearson, *Letters*, p. 48.

[32] *New York Times*, May 22, 1862.

another delay intervened. Stonewall Jackson was threatening Harpers Ferry. Stanton and the President rushed Saxton to command that vital point during its crisis. He met the challenge brilliantly, winning a special commendation from Stanton and in after years a Medal of Honor.[33] Eventually back in Washington, it was not until June 16 that Saxton received a reissue of Stanton's order to proceed to Port Royal. The reissue contained a significant addition giving him police power necessary for the security of the people to be in his charge. This time Saxton did get to Port Royal — but not until the very end of June.[34] By then Hunter long since had organized the black regiment.

Just before Saxton's arrival Hunter, on June 23, had sent to the War Department a report on the regiment. Report finally had been demanded. On June 5 a leading member of the Kentucky delegation in the House of Representatives tendered a resolution directing Stanton to inform the House whether Hunter had been authorized to organize, or had organized, a regiment "of black men (fugitive slaves)." On June 9 the resolution was adopted without objection. On June 14 Stanton responded that Hunter had not been so authorized, that the War Department had "no official information" whether he had done so, and that a copy of the resolution was being sent to him with instructions to report immediately.[35]

Hunter's report could hardly have been better designed to complicate the President's effort to assure the loyalty and support of the Union's border slave States, notably Kentucky. Sarcastic, even arrogant, Hunter said that he had no regiment of "fugitive slaves." He did have "a fine regiment of persons whose late masters are 'fugitive rebels' " and they "are now, one and all, working with remarkable industry to place themselves in a position to go in full and effective pursuit of their fugacious and traitorous proprietors." On July 2 Stanton transmitted the report to the House. On its reading it created merriment among many and its printing was ordered. But Kentuckians saw in it nothing

[33] Dept. of South — Special Orders, General Orders, Circulars of Gen. Saxton, May 1862-Dec. 1863, note at second unnumbered page and general orders at following eight unnumbered pages, May 26 to June 2, 1862, NA, RG 393; Rufus Saxton file, Letters Received by Appointment, Commission and Personal Branch of the Adj. Gen., File No. 1302, ACP 1879 (containing several documents relating to Harpers Ferry episode and Medal of Honor award), NA, RG 94; Hendricks, "Union Army Occupation," p. 46.

[34] *ORA*, ser. 3, 2:152-53; Letters Received by Adj. Gen. Office, 1861-70, No. 1063 S, Saxton to Stanton, June 30, 1862, NA, RG 94.

[35] *Cong. Globe*, 37 Cong., 2d Sess. (1862), 2587, 2620-21, 2762; *ORA*, ser. 3, 2:147-48.

[36] *Cong. Globe*, 37 Cong., 2d Sess. (1862), 3087, 3102, 3109, 3121-27; H. Rep., 37 Cong., 2d Sess. (1862), Ex. Doc. No. 143; *ORA*, ser. 3, 2:196-98.

funny. Nor could it be squared with the original instructions to General Sherman for it seemed unmistakably to say that the regiment was about to be used for offensive action, not simply to meet a "great emergency."[36]

In fact, however, the regiment was in no such condition as Hunter seemed to assert. The men had taken to drill and would make a good impression on parade. But since Hunter was treating them as "soldiers" — not the non-soldiers contemplated by the Sherman instructions — he had no way to pay them; funds simply were not authorized. Their brother blacks were earning wages as officers' servants and army laborers, to say nothing of the workmen busily engaged on the plantations. It is no wonder, then, that there was rising discontent among the "soldiers." Moreover, the discontent was fed by humiliating ridicule they met with from many white troops. Desertions soon had begun and grew, as Saxton was to find. Some of the "soldiers" even tried to flee to slavery's land. Guards from white units had to be thrown around the regiment's camp.[37]

Why Hunter had never requested Washington's approval of his regiment must be left to speculation. In any event on July 11 occasion arose — he thought — to ask again, as he had on April 3, for general authority to enlist black soldiers. Late that day he received an urgent request to send to Virginia all the troops he could spare. (In Virginia there had been the Seven Days Battles.) That night Hunter wrote Stanton that he was sending six regiments, requiring him to evacuate one of the long held islands — he actually was to evacuate two — and that he might have to give up Beaufort. "I most earnestly beg that by return mail you give me full authority to muster into the service of the United States, as infantry, all loyal men to be found in my department, and that I be authorized to appoint all officers. This has now become a military necessity in this department."[38] Dispatch of troops to Virginia was to leave Hunter an army of but 13,000 in his entire department.[39]

It happened that on July 17, about the time Hunter's request reached Washington, Congress adopted a statute authorizing the President to receive blacks into the service of the United States either as

---

[37] Woodward, *The Negro in Military Service*, 2:907-08; Pearson, *Letters*, p. 100; Higginson, *Army Life*, pp. 43, 273; *New York Times*, July 19, Aug. 22, Sept. 15 (Rev. French speech), Sept. 24, 1862; *National Intelligencer*, May 19, Aug. 13, Aug. 16, Aug. 18, Sept. 23, 1862; *Washington Evening Star*, Aug. 19, 1862.

[38] *ORA*, ser. 1, 14:363-64. Hunter actually sent seven regiments. Though the War Department was to point out to him within a few days that it had sought only what Hunter could "spare," Hunter soon was urging that he be reinforced both to re-occupy the two evacuated islands and to establish new strong positions. *ORA*, ser. 1, 14:365-66.

[39] *ORA*, ser. 1, 14:367.

laborers or for "any military or naval service."[40] The President, of course, already had that authority; all along blacks had been in the military service as laborers and, in the navy, not only as laborers but as crewmen, and there had been no law preventing him from also enlisting black soldiers. Hence the statute did not enlarge the President's authority. Moreover, that a Congressional majority approved such authority did not mean that its exercise would be any more welcome in the border States or lessen the prejudice against black troops that prevailed in the army, as shown by the ridicule Hunter's regiment was receiving from his own white troops. But the statute did prompt Stanton to present Hunter's request at a Cabinet meeting on July 21. Discussion continued the next day. Stanton and Chase, supported by Secretary of State William H. Seward, favored granting the request, and no Cabinet member opposed. The President, however, remained "averse to arming negroes." Discussion ended with the President's saying that he would go no further than to allow local commanders "to arm, for purely defensive purposes, slaves coming within their lines."[41] Hunter's request to rebuild his army with black men was not granted.

Of the "soldiers" in Hunter's black regiment only a fraction remained after persistent skedaddling, and he could not bring himself to deal severely with deserters whom he had never paid. Finally he gave up. On August 9, to the wild joy of the "soldiers" still in camp, he disbanded the regiment, notifying Stanton in a letter the next day.[42]

Hunter had become thoroughly disenchanted with a command charged not with conquest but with little more than maintaining anchorages for the navy. Already he had applied for leave of absence. In late August it was granted. In early September he departed; a superseding commander was coming.[43]

[40] 12 *U. S. Statutes*, Sec. 12, p. 599.

[41] Donald, *Inside Lincoln's Cabinet*, pp. 96, 99-100.

[42] *ORA*, ser. 3, 2:346; Holland, *Towne Letters*, p. 84; *National Intelligencer*, Aug. 18, 1862; *Washington Evening Star*, Aug. 19, 1862. Hunter's disbandment of his regiment came abruptly; as late as Aug. 4 he had written Stanton again, this time specifically asking for approval of the regiment, with authority to pay the men, and still insisting that he could organize many more if permitted. *ORA*, ser. 3, 2:292.

[43] The leave granted was for sixty days. *ORA*, ser. 1, 14:376. Search for Hunter's application for leave has disclosed only a notation that he had applied for it on July 30. Register of Letters Received by Hdqrs. of the Army, No. 114, NA, RG 108. So it is unknown whether Hunter also sought a transfer. But on his departure on Sept. 5 it was understood that his return was unlikely, and he was to tell the press that he had sought other assignment because he could not get troops for "offensive service." Holland, *Towne Letters*, p. 90; Port Royal, *The New South*, Sept. 6, 1862; *New York Times*, Sept. 10, 1862. Maj. Gen. Ormsby M. Mitchell was assigned to the department command on Sept. 1; Stanton told him to get to Port Royal promptly. *ORA*, ser. 1, 14:380-85.

General Saxton, in the meantime, had been a very busy man with a mission then unique in the Union's military experience. On his arrival at the end of June he was well received on the plantations because of a favorable impression left by his service under Sherman. Hardly had he begun to get settled when he had to deal with hundreds of refugees from the two islands evacuated by Hunter's army. Also critical was the problem of the vulnerability of the plantations to Rebel raids. Earlier Hunter had agreed to supply the plantations with arms — well within the Sherman instructions — but it had not been done until Saxton came. Saxton had twenty to thirty muskets distributed to each plantation with orders to instruct the people in their use. On at least one of the plantations the people were delighted and every evening drill in their use was conducted, though on another fear of impressment — lingering from memory of Hunter's May round-up — created suspicion of drill. Nor was threat of enemy raids Saxton's only problem; in time Hunter had to assign Saxton three white companies to deal with pilfering from the black settlements by Union troops.[44]

It was not until early August that Saxton was able to get away from Port Royal to survey his domain down the Georgia coast into Florida. He started on August 5 with his first stop at St. Simon's Island, where a special problem had been reported. Then guarded only by the navy and the local blacks with their limited number of muskets, St. Simon's was infested with Rebel intruders. Saxton took there additional muskets and Company A of the black regiment. That was the company for which Hunter himself had picked the officers; it was a well trained, effective unit. On arrival Saxton found that blacks had suffered casualties in fighting the intruders and that Rebels were still in hiding on the island. Company A was needed and Saxton left it there.[45]

Saxton's coastal tour took ten days. On his return he learned of the disbandment of the black regiment but no word of disbandment was sent to Company A. Saxton also found that Hunter had been ordered to ship his only cavalry regiment to Virginia and that this had led Hunter to decide to abandon all the Carolina area beyond the immediate environs of Port Royal, even the town of Beaufort. Gideon's Band was horrified.[46]

---

[44] *ORA*, ser. 1, 14:375-76; Holland, *Towne Letters*, 73-81, 84; Pearson, *Letters*, 89; Woodward, *The Negro in Military Service*, 2:929; *New York Times*, July 2, Aug. 26, 1862.

[45] *ORA*, ser. 1, 14:375; Woodward, *The Negro in Military Service*, 2:929; Susie King Taylor, *Reminiscenses of My Life in Camp* (New York, 1902; reprinted 1968), pp. 12-15; *New York Times*, Aug. 22, 1862.

[46] *ORA*, ser. 1, 14:374; Pearson, *Letters*, p. 84. An officer of the troops from Hunter's command sent to Virginia had reported to Stanton that Hunter's remaining army was adequate and its cavalry not needed. *ORA*, ser. 1, 14:368-69.

Saxton reacted at once. On August 16 he wrote a most important letter to Stanton. He requested authority "to enroll as laborers ... a force not exceeding 5,000 able-bodied men from among the contrabands ... to be uniformed, armed, and officered by men detailed from the Army." He described conditions on the islands, including what he had found on St. Simon's, and urged that the force he requested could assist in the work on the plantations, guard the people, and "in the event of any emergency" immediately provide aid. Saxton's letter was clever. It did not refer to "soldiers" but only to "laborers." And it seemed within the principles of the War Department's long standing interpretation of the instructions to General Sherman.[47]

Either the letter or a copy was taken to Washington by Rev. Mansfield French, one of the leading Gideonites, accompanied by Robert Smalls, who had become a national hero. They brought word that the Saxton proposal had the backing of both Hunter and DuPont. In Washington they saw Stanton and Chase.[48] Stanton acted promptly. On August 25 he wrote Saxton, authorizing him to enroll up to 5,000 black laborers in the Quartermaster's service. But he went further, and beyond Saxton's request. He added:

> In view of the small force under your command and the inability of the Government at the present time to increase it, in order to guard the plantations and settlements occupied by the United States from invasion and protect the inhabitants thereof from captivity and murder by the enemy, you are also authorized to arm, uniform, equip, and receive into the service of the United States such number of volunteers of African descent as you may deem expedient, not exceeding 5,000, and may detail officers to instruct them in military drill, discipline, and duty, and to command them.

In closing, Stanton's letter noted that a recent act of Congress (the July 17 statute) provided that blacks "received into the service of the United States who may have been the slaves of rebel masters" would be "forever free" and so would be "their wives, mothers and children." Stanton

---

[47] *ORA*, ser. 1, 14:374-76. Rose, *Rehearsal for Reconstruction*, p. 190, mistakenly states that Saxton's letter "envisioned expeditions into coastal districts to capture enemy salt works and to destroy property." It was not Saxton's letter but Stanton's reply that, as we shall see, rather vaguely authorized operations of that nature.

[48] Mansfield French to George Whipple, Aug. 23 and Aug. 28, 1862, Amer. Missionary Assn. Archives, Nos. HL 4517 and 15901, Amistad Research Center, Dillard Univ.; 17 Cong. Rec. App. 319-20 (1886; speech of Cong. Robert Smalls); *National Intelligencer*, Aug. 30, 1862; Okon Edet Uya, *From Slavery to Public Service: Robert Smalls 1839-1915* (New York, 1971), pp. 17-19. Smalls' national renown was notable. *New York Times*, Oct. 3, 1862.

directed Saxton "and all in your command" so to "treat and regard them." Stanton insisted that French and Smalls deliver the letter in person.[49]

Thus did the Union, for the first time, authorize black troops.

Saxton's letter and the advocacy of French and Smalls had a further effect. An order was sent to Port Royal to keep the cavalry there and "to hold the islands now occupied." When French and Smalls returned, the cavalry regiment, that had boarded ship, was disembarked. Lifted was the Gideonites' gloom at Hunter's threat to abandon most of the islands.[50]

For Saxton himself Stanton's authorization meant a renewed commitment to his work at Port Royal. While French and Smalls had been on their mission word had come of Hunter's leave of absence, with indications that he was to be superseded. Saxton assumed that Hunter's next in command would be his successor. With that officer Saxton had been in constant, bitter clash. Perhaps impulsively, Saxton at once had written Stanton asking for assignment elsewhere because of that clash. He had prepared to go North with Hunter on plantation business and, very probably, to pursue his request for transfer. French and Smalls returned to deliver Stanton's letter to Saxton just before Hunter's departure. The authorization for Saxton to recruit and organize black troops meant that he would not be at the mercy of Hunter's successor. That quite changed Saxton's attitude. At first Saxton hesitated about leaving with Hunter, but finally decided to go. It is apparent that face-to-face dealings in the North would facilitate handling all that he now had to accomplish in the South.[51]

---

[49] *ORA*, ser. 1, 14:377-78; French to Whipple, Aug. 28, 1862, AMA Archives, No. 15901. Stanton somewhat overstated the statute's emancipation provision for wives and children; their master, too, had to be rebel. 12 *U. S. Statutes*, Sec. 13, p. 599. On an even more important point Stanton was careless. He said that the black soldiers' pay would be the same as that "allowed by law to volunteers in the service." Understandably Saxton was to interpret this to mean that black pay would be the same as white pay. Woodward, *The Negro in Military Service*, 2:983-84. But the statute imposed a substantially lower pay for blacks. Had it not been for the statute, black pay would have been the same as white pay. *Case of Rev. Samuel Harrison*, 11 Ops. Atty. Gen. 37 (1864); *Pay of Colored Soldiers, ibid*, p. 53.

[50] *ORA*, ser. 1, 14:378, Holland, *Towne Letters*, p. 90; Pearson, *Letters*, p. 86.

[51] Holland, *Towne Letters*, pp. 90-91; Pearson, *Letters*, p. 86; Port Royal, *The New South*, Sept. 6, 1862; *New York Times*, Sept. 10, 1862. Hunter's next in command was Brig. Gen. John M. Brannan, who was left in charge on Hunter's departure. *ORA*, ser. 1, 14:380. Saxton's relations with Hunter had been relatively smooth, but it had been quite otherwise with Hunter's subordinates, notably Brannan. Rufus Saxton Letterbook I, 1-39, Saxton Family Papers, Yale Univ. Saxton's request for reassignment is at pp. 39-40 of this Letterbook. He did not yet know that Gen. Mitchel, not Brannan, would succeed Hunter.

Saxton was back by mid-October. One of his first acts was to inform the captain of Company A, who had come up from St. Simon's to remind the command of his existence, that the company would become the core of a new regiment, with pay for its men and recognized commissions for its officers. Ultimately that captain became the lieutenant colonel of the new regiment.[52]

Thus, on the issue of black troops, Hunter had been left dangling but, at almost the same time, Saxton was given even more authority than he had requested. That, I submit, is not "hard to understand." Few issues were more delicate for the Union government in 1862. Hunter, heavy handed, had gone ahead without even reporting his action; then, when required to report, had seemed to say that he was readying blacks for offensive warfare; and finally had persisted in seeking authority to rebuild his depleted army so without limit as to make it possibly even more black than white. Hunter's cause was hopeless; even after the authorization to Saxton, the Executive still was firm in refusal to authorize blacks as all-purpose soldiers.[53] Saxton, on the other hand, with cautious restraint, had sought no more than leave to arm black workmen to help protect the communities from enemy raids. At that not even Kentuckians could cavil. Jefferson Davis himself later was to say to his Congress that "the use of slaves as soldiers in defense of their homes . . . is justifiable."[54]

Thus Saxton gave Stanton the opportunity to push open a bit the door left slightly ajar by the President at the July Cabinet meeting where he agreed that slaves could be armed for defense. Stanton allowed a limited black soldiery to protect their homes. And in his letter he added

---

[52] *ORA*, ser. 3, 2:663; Higginson, *Army Life*, pp. 275-76; Taylor, *Reminiscences*, p. 15.

[53] Senator James Lane of Kansas, as recruiting commissioner in that State, had been taking blacks. *New York Times*, Sept. 13, 1862. But in August and September 1862 Stanton insisted to him that he had no such authority. *ORA*, ser. 3, 2:312-13, 445, 582; Cornish, *Sable Arm*, pp. 69-78.

On Aug. 22, 1862, Gen. Butler, in New Orleans, ordered enlistment of volunteering free blacks who had been in Confederate Louisiana's State militia, "subject to the approval of the President of the United States." His order provided that they were to " 'defend their homes.' " By coincidence that asserted purpose was strikingly similar to the authorization Stanton was about to give Saxton. Butler promptly sought the War Department's approval. But not until late November was a response sent him; then he was told to use his own judgment. In the meantime he had gone ahead, organizing three black regiments without limiting enrollment to pre-war free blacks. *ORA*, ser. 1, 15:162, 555-57, 601; ser. 3, 2:436-38; Cornish, *Sable Arm*, pp. 65-67. Howard C. Westwood, "Benjamin Butler's Enlistment of Black Troops in New Orleans in 1862," *Louisiana History* XXVI (1985): 5-22.

[54] Message to Congress, Nov. 7, 1864, James D. Richardson, *Messages and Papers of the Confederacy*, 2 vols. (Nashville, 1905), 1:495.

a very ambiguous sentence authorizing Saxton also "to withdraw from the enemy their laboring force and ... to weaken, harass, and annoy them." This enabled Saxton, as he carefully pursued a course of training of the men being recruited, in November to send some companies raiding into enemy territory. Pridefully he reported to Stanton on their fighting skill and their capturing "from the enemy an amount of property equal in value to the cost of the regiment for a year."[55]

By that time the politics of the war had moved beyond where it had stood in the summer, and the President had moved with it. The Final Emancipation Proclamation of New Year's Day authorized the freed slaves to "be received into the armed service of the United States" for garrison duty and to man vessels. And within days thereafter the Executive was taking further action allowing the black man, whether freed slave or free born, to become a full scale Union soldier.[56]

Saxton the cautious, French the Gideonite, and Smalls the hero had fashioned the first breach in the President's bar. Even after the breach had widened there persisted gross discrimination against the blacks in pay and otherwise. But the breach was a vital opening to the long path the black man would travel to win recognition as a man.

---

[55] *ORA*, ser. 1, 14:189-93, ser. 3, 4:1027. The training and organization of the regiment are reviewed in Cornish, *Sable Arm*, pp. 81-92.

[56] James D. Richardson, *Messages and Papers of the Presidents*, H. of Rep., 53 Cong., 2d Sess. (1897), Misc. Doc. 210, 6:158; Cornish, *Sable Arm*, pp. 100-01, 104-06.

LOWCOUNTRY RAIL LINE THREATENED:
THE BATTLES OF POCOTALIGO AND COOSAWHATCHIE,
OCTOBER 22, 1862

W. ERIC EMERSON

The fall of 1862 there were few illusions in either the North or South that the end of the Civil War was in sight. The fortunes of the conflict had ebbed and flowed for both sides. September and October had been particularly active months, with three failed Confederate offensives ending at Corinth, Mississippi, Perryville, Kentucky, and Sharpsburg, Maryland. A battle near the latter location had resulted in over 23,000 casualties, making September 17, 1862, the bloodiest day in American history. In the lowcountry of South Carolina, however, the war had moved at a much less destructive pace. October 1862 would witness an acceleration of combat operations along the South Carolina coast, due in large part to the efforts of a new commander of the Union Department of the South. His goals were to aggressively pursue the war throughout his new command, and the first step would be to destroy an important railway linking Charleston and Savannah.

One and a half years earlier, on April 19, 1861, several days after the bombardment of Fort Sumter, President Abraham Lincoln issued a "Proclamation of Blockade Against Southern Ports," which authorized the blockade of South Carolina, Georgia, Florida, Alabama, Mississippi, Louisiana, and Texas. Nearly seven months later, on November 7, 1861, a Union flotilla under the command of Admiral Samuel F. Du Pont captured Port Royal Sound, and with it Hilton Head Island, the surrounding islands, and the following day, Beaufort and its environs. Port Royal Sound was one of the finest deep-water ports on the Atlantic seaboard, and Du Pont's victory gave the Union Navy a strong base of operations to blockade South Carolina, Georgia, and east Florida.

Within a short time after establishing an operating base at Port Royal, Union warships had cordoned off Charleston, Savannah, and all other ports south of Georgetown, S.C., making them difficult to reach except by the most daring blockade-runners. Even with an effective naval blockade in place, the capture of Savannah and Charleston remained a priority for Union commanders. Of the two cities, Charleston was the more valuable. As the birthplace of secession and the site of the war's first shots, Charleston was perhaps the most symbolically important Union objective of the war. Its capture would be a boon for Union morale and a notable laurel for any commander who could seize the city.

Neither the capture of Charleston nor Savannah, however, would be easy tasks. On November 5, 1861, two days before the battle of Port Royal, the Confederacy constituted the coasts of South Carolina, Georgia, and east Florida as a department under the command of Confederate General Robert E. Lee. Upon taking command, Lee devised and implemented an intensive construction project to erect a defensive network along the coastline of his newly formed department. Critical to these defenses, and of some concern to local residents, was Lee's decision to abandon exposed coastal fortifications, which Union amphibious forces could easily captur. Instead, he concentrated his department's efforts on securing the waterways that led inland from the coast. Lee's plan called for the construction of fortifications at critical

Carologue 20, No. 2 (Summer 2004), 6-19

points along rivers and tributaries and the placement of pickets, who could give early warning of any Union movements, along likely avenues of approach.

Critical to Lee's defensive plans for the coast were two inventions that would see their first widespread military use during the Civil War: the telegraph and the railroad. Upon discerning any movement of enemy troops or vessels, Confederate pickets would send a rider to a nearby telegraph operator. The telegraph operator would relay the information to local commanders, who would then pass the information to Confederate commanders in Charleston and Savannah. Using the Charleston and Savannah Railroad, a militarily important transportation link completed in 1860 that connected the two cities, the Confederates could shuttle waiting troops in either or both cities to any point on the line to face a Union threat. This allowed local Confederate commanders to defend the large area between the two cities with relatively few troops.

In the spring of 1862 Union forces based on Hilton Head Island launched probing attacks at sites in Florida, Georgia, and South Carolina to test local Confederate defenses. On May 29, 1862, as part of this effort, Brigadier General Isaac I. Stevens, commanding the Second Brigade of the Northern District, Department of the South, launched a raid north of Beaufort to destroy portions of the Charleston and Savannah Railroad at Pocotaligo Station. During this operation Stevens' troops nearly reached the railroad before Confederate cavalry turned them back. The near success of the movement against Pocotaligo gave Stevens hope that a larger raid could sever the vital rail link. Before he could try again, however, Confederate forces abandoned Cole's Island at the mouth of the Stono River, and Stevens and his brigade were ordered to James Island, where they participated in the Secessionville campaign. Afterwards, he and his brigade were sent to Virginia, where Stevens was killed on September 1, 1862, at the battle of Chantilly.

On September 17, 1862, Union Major General Ormsby M. Mitchel assumed command of the recently constituted Department of the South, which was headquartered at Hilton Head Island. Mitchel had graduated from West Point in 1829 and served as director of the Dudley Observatory at Albany, New York, prior to the war. Since the outbreak of hostilities, he had shown an aptitude for command. Referred to by his men as "Old Stars," Mitchel commanded the Third Division of the Army of the Ohio. He participated in the capture of Nashville, Tennessee, in February 1862, and he and his men captured Huntsville, Alabama, on April 11, 1862, after driving deeper into Confederate territory than any other Union commander to that point in the war. Mitchel also had authorized the famed Andrews Railroad raid, which sought to sever the Western-Atlantic Railroad that connected the eastern and western regions of the Confederacy. For his capture of Huntsville, he was promoted to major general, but he was relieved of command due to his inability to get along with officers of equal or lesser rank. Shortly thereafter he was placed in command of the Tenth Corps and the Department of the South.

Mitchel believed that Major General David Hunter, the department's previous commander, had not been aggressive enough, and he was intent on actively pressuring Confederate defenses in South Carolina by focusing, as he had with the Andrews raid, on destroying a crucial rail line. By late October 1862 he had completed plans for another Union attempt to break the Charleston and Savannah Railroad at Pocotaligo. In official reports Mitchel later claimed that he hoped to make a "complete" reconnaissance of the Broad, Coosawhatchie, Tullifinny, and Pocotaligo Rivers, while testing his department's ability to rapidly move a Union force into enemy-held territory. He also asserted that he sought to gauge the strength of Confederate forces guarding the railroad and have his men destroy as much of it as possible in a single day.

Mitchel's true objectives for the operation remain somewhat of a mystery. One officer later wrote that Mitchel intended to destroy the railroad bridge over the Pocotaligo, sever communications between Savannah and Charleston, and then attempt to capture Savannah before reinforcements could arrive. Admiral Du Pont later wrote that the attempt to destroy the railroad bridges was intended as a feint to draw Confederate attention away from the Ogeechee River and Fort McAllister in Georgia, which were Mitchel's true targets. Whatever the long term goals for the operation, Mitchel's immediate focus was the destruction of the railway.

Having commanded large-scale raids in the past, Mitchel knew success depended on thorough preparations. In the days preceding the operation, he sent scouts and spies to all critical points on the railroad and dispatched a party to cut the telegraph wires between Savannah and Charleston. His scouts examined all tributaries of the Broad River, gauging their depth and searching for viable landing points, and he ordered his engineers to convert two large flat boats into artillery transports with hinged aprons.

Facing this amphibious assault were the Confederate troops of South Carolina's Third Military District, commanded by Col. William S. Walker. Walker was a West Point graduate and professional soldier who had seen service during the Mexican War and in the far West. He had less than 1,000 men under his immediate command, most of which were cavalry serving as pickets on the coast. In any major engagement he would have to gather his outlying troops for battle. Once consolidated to face a Union threat, a sizeable proportion of Walker's force would have to serve as horse holders and would therefore be prohibited from participating in a fight.

Walker's troops had repelled the Union raid on the Charleston and Savannah Railroad on May 29, 1862, and he had learned some valuable lessons. During the earlier operation his cavalrymen were badly outgunned, since most were armed with sabers, pistols, and in some cases, shotguns. Only one company that participated, the Rutledge Mounted Riflemen, was armed with rifles, which they used to good effect during the battle. At a critical moment in the action, the short range of his men's pistols and shotguns forced them to wait until Union forces were within forty yards before firing. A large number of Walker's troopers, armed only with sabers, were forced to serve as horse holders in the rear of the Confederate battle line.

Following the May 29 raid Walker worked diligently to address this inadequacy. A blockade-runner arrived in Charleston with a shipment of short Enfield Rifles, which Walker secured for distribution to some of his cavalry. The decision to arm his men with Enfields was not a popular one. At least one company complained that the rifles detracted from their ability to engage Union cavalry in more traditional close combat with sabers, thus limiting their effectiveness.

Though Walker's small command was better armed than during the first raid on Pocotaligo, a number of factors favored their opponents as the operation began. Mitchel's raiding force included 4,500 men, several times larger than any force that Walker could initially gather to stop him. Mitchel also had naval gunboats that could provide fire support for his men as long as they remained near navigable waters. Under the right conditions, Mitchel also believed that he held the advantage of surprise. He could strike at any point along the rivers and tributaries that comprised

South Carolina's Third District and then force Walker to hurriedly gather his troops at that point to meet the threat.

Walker hoped to counter Union advantages through a variety of measures. Out of necessity he violated the military maxim that dictates a commander concentrate his forces in the presence of a numerically superior enemy. Instead, he spread his small, highly mobile command at picket posts throughout the district to serve as an early-warning system. Walker would hear of Union movements from his pickets and thereafter could concentrate his forces where needed while telegraphing Charleston, Savannah, or both for reinforcements, which would quickly arrive on the Charleston and Savannah Railroad. Walker and his men also had an intimate knowledge of the Third District and the natural obstacles that could impede a Union advance, and Walker planned to use this familiarity to his advantage.

Following his scouts' extensive reconnaissance of the area near Pocotaligo, Mitchel finalized his plan for the raid. At Hilton Head Island, he would load a force of infantry, artillery, and cavalry aboard a naval flotilla that would transport his men up the Broad River and disembark them at Mackay's Point. Mackay's Point is located at the tip of a peninsula formed by the Broad and Pocotaligo Rivers. From there his men would push northward until reaching and destroying the railroad bridge over the Pocotaligo River. East of the bridge was Pocotaligo Station, which was surrounded by a number of buildings, and south of that the village of Pocotaligo, or Old Pocotaligo as it was referred to at the time. A wide country road running the length of the peninsula would provide the Union troops an ideal avenue of approach, while the Broad, Tullifiny, and Pocotaligo Rivers would protect the column from flank attack and allow Union gunboats to provide fire support as the column advanced. Mitchel estimated that the distance from the landing site to the railroad was seven to eight miles, and he was optimistic that his force could easily destroy the railroad and return to their embarkation point within twenty-four hours.

As the date for the expedition's commencement approached, Mitchel became ill. Unable to personally lead his new command, he placed operational control of the mission in the hands of Brigadier General John M. Brannan, the Department's second in command and occasional commander, who also was in charge of the department's First Brigade. Brannan was an 1841 West Point graduate and a professional soldier. He had commanded the Department of Key West for a brief time before being transferred to the Department of the South. He also had proven himself a capable commander during the Union victory at St. John's Bluff in Florida on October 1-3, 1862, so he was a logical choice to lead this expedition.

On the afternoon of October 21, 1862, Brannan began loading his troops onto their transports at Hilton Head Island, while he made last-minute preparations. Brannan's men had been issued five days worth of rations, 100 rounds of ammunition, and small bundles of pine kindling with which to burn railroad bridges. They also received instructions on how to destroy railroad track. To ensure his flotilla's movement to the landing site, Mitchel employed former slaves to pilot his larger vessels and placed signal officers aboard each ship to expedite communications.

Despite these precautions, problems began to mount even before the expedition set sail. As darkness fell on Hilton Head Island, a fog rolled over Port Royal Sound, and smoke from the expedition's steamers helped diminish visibility. Communications quickly broke down. The flotilla, consisting of fifteen vessels, including gunboats, steamboats, and transports (three of which were towing flatboats and landing craft) left Hilton Head at 11:00 P.M. Around midnight the expedition's flagship, the *Paul Jones,* displayed three red lights, which was the signal for all vessels to begin moving up the Broad River. The *Conemaugh,* third vessel in the convoy, did not receive the signal and quickly ran aground. Two other ships in the convoy, the *Marblehead* and the *Water Witch,* ran afoul of each other, fell out of line, and did not get underway again until morning.

As the *Ben Deford,* Brannan's command ship, reached the mouth of the Broad River, he gave orders for the steamtug *Starlight* to tow four launches of soldiers up the Broad and Pocotaligo Rivers to capture Confederate pickets before they could spread word of the coming Union landing. One group, comprised of ninety-five men under the command of Captain Gray of the 7th Connecticut, was to land two miles north of Mackay's Point on the west bank of the Pocotaligo. Once ashore, they were to cut off and capture all Confederate pickets south of their landing site. Another force, comprised of twelve men and commanded by Lt. Samuel M. Smith of the 3rd New Hampshire, was to proceed up the Pocotaligo River and capture the Confederate pickets on the east bank of the river at Bray's Island.

Capt. Gray's guide, a former slave, led the Union launches past the proposed landing site and further upriver. By the time Gray realized his error and returned to the planned landing site, it was daylight and the main Union force was already disembarking at Mackay's Point.

Further to the north, Lt. Smith's group was having much better luck. Smith's men proceeded up the Pocotaligo until they reached Cuthbert's Landing on Bray's Island, where they landed, went inland, and captured seven Confederate pickets. The Union soldiers and their prisoners then proceeded back to the landing site. From there they traveled by launch downriver to Mackay's Point to deliver the prisoners to Gen. Brannan.

As Union ships approached Mackay's Point in the early morning of October 22, the expedition's misfortunes continued. One of the large transports ran aground before it could disembark its troops. This incident delayed the offloading of some troops for hours. Dawn broke over a scene of confusion at 6:08 A.M., yet Brannan hoped that the previous night's missteps had faded with the waning darkness. Shortly after daybreak Brannan met with Colonel William B. Barton of the 48th New York. He dispatched Barton with a force of 300 men from the 48th, fifty men from the 3rd Rhode Island Artillery, and fifty men from the 1st New York Volunteer Engineers to move up the Coosawhatchie River aboard two transports and two gunboats to destroy the railroad line near Coosawhatchie. Brannan hoped this would create a diversion and draw Confederate attention away from the main attack at Pocotaligo. Meanwhile, Union ships continued to straggle into the landing site and began to ferry Brannan's men ashore in small boats. By midmorning the rest of the flotilla arrived off Mackay's Point and began to unload troops.

As Brannan attempted to bring order from the confusion at Mackay's Point, Colonel Walker received valuable information regarding Union troop movements and quickly took action. Brannan's failed efforts to capture Walker's pickets along the Pocotaligo River left the Confederate communication system intact, and at 9:00 A.M. Walker received word of the Union landing at Mackay's Point. He also learned that Union ships were moving up the Coosawhatchie River towards the railroad. Walker quickly telegraphed Brigadier General Hugh W. Mercer in Savannah to rush reinforcements to the town of Coosawhatchie and General P. G. T. Beauregard in

Charleston and Brigadier General Johnson Hagood in the Second Military District to send troops to Pocotaligo. Walker then ordered the Lafayette Artillery, a section of the Beaufort Volunteer Artillery, and portions of the 11th South Carolina, which were stationed at Hardeeville and Coosawhatchie, to concentrate at the latter location to protect the railroad there. He also ordered Col. Charles J. Colcock's 3rd S.C. Cavalry, which consisted of five companies along with three troops of sharpshooters, to move toward Coosawhatchie. Walker then ordered the remainder of his troops to gather north of Mackay's Point near Caston's Plantation.

Just after daylight on October 22 Brannan realized that he had lost the element of surprise, and with it, the initiative. Lt. Smith's Confederate prisoners from Bray's Island claimed that they had known of the expedition for several days. Confederate Captain Manning Kirk and his company of Partisan Rangers had captured two captains and six privates from the 6th Connecticut Regiment on Chisolm's Island on October 19, and these men were thought to have given information regarding Union intentions. True or not, the pickets' knowledge of a pending Union operation must have been disheartening for Brannan. Regardless, at 8:00 A.M. he began to move his First Brigade northward from the landing site, across a long causeway and up Mackay's Point Road. Meanwhile, the Second Brigade, commanded by Brigadier General Alfred H. Terry, was still off loading from their transports. After the First Brigade had moved some distance up the road, Brannan ordered a halt so that the remainder of his troops could disembark and assume their places in the line of march.

By around 10:30 A.M. the men of Terry's Second Brigade were on the road, and Brannan ordered the column forward. Roughly two miles from the landing, soldiers of the 55th Pennsylvania spotted thirty to forty Confederate cavalry pickets, who retired slowly as Brannan's men advanced. The Union troops then marched unimpeded for five miles until they reached a cornfield near George Elliott's Plantation. Of these first few uneventful miles of the trip, one Connecticut soldier noted, "We passed many recently deserted plantations, pushing on over corn and cottonfields, through ditches and swamps."

As they approached Elliott's Plantation around noon, Brannan's force got its first taste of Confederate resistance. Earlier that morning Walker had ordered Captain Stephen Elliott and the Beaufort Volunteer Artillery, two companies of cavalry commanded by Major Joseph Morgan, and two companies of sharpshooters under the command of Captain J. Blythe Allston, to delay the Union advance. After opening fire on the advancing Union troops, the Confederates retreated north along the road to Caston's Plantation (or Hutson's, as it is referred to in some reports). There, Elliott disregarded nearby Confederate fortifications and placed the Beaufort Artillery's guns in tall grass on both sides of the road along the crest of a small rise. From there they overlooked a marsh and a causeway, which they could sweep with their fire as the Union troops advanced.

Just after noon, the lead elements of Brannan's First Brigade appeared on the road marching north in pursuit, and Elliott's guns and the supporting cavalry and sharpshooters again opened fire. Brannan's skirmishers returned fire, while the brigade performed the time-consuming task of forming battle lines. Major Morgan, in command of the two Confederate cavalry companies, was wounded shortly after the action began. After briefly stalling the Union advance at Caston's, the Confederate force withdrew northwards on Mackay's Point Road. Before departing, they removed boards from a bridge crossing the causeway to further slow Brannan's advance.

Elliott's delaying actions bought time for Walker to gather his forces near Frampton's Plantation, which was one and a half miles to the north. There, Walker deployed his men on either side of Mackay's Point Road, behind a marsh that stretched the length of the Confederate front. Again, a narrow causeway with a bridge bisected the Confederate position, and Elliott's men pulled up boards from the bridge after crossing it. Woods skirted the edge of the marsh on both sides of the causeway. As Elliott had done at Caston's Plantation, Walker placed his artillery in an exposed position near the road, where his guns could do the greatest damage to the advancing Union troops as they moved up the causeway.

Among the Confederate troops gathered at Frampton's Plantation were Captain Benjamin H. Rutledge and the Charleston Light Dragoons. Rutledge had attended Yale, was a Charleston attorney, a signer of the Ordinance of Secession, and, like his men, a member of one of South Carolina's oldest and wealthiest families. At Frampton's Plantation, the Dragoons numbered nearly forty men and had just rotated off picket duty near Port Royal Ferry. Earlier that morning, Walker had ordered the unit to Old Pocotaligo, which was seven miles from their encampment. Rutledge led the unit there and then south to Frampton's Plantation. They arrived just as Elliott's force finished disabling the bridge over the creek, and they were greeted by cannon fire from a Union gunboat that had made its way up the Pocotaligo River. The gunboat's fire soared harmlessly through the unit's formation, but that event marked the first time that many unit members had been under fire.

Walker placed the Dragoons in the Confederate center, just to the right of the road. Its members dismounted, and horse holders led the animals to the rear. The company quickly sought concealment in the tall marsh grass, along with the rest of Walker's force. As Brannan's men moved up the road, Elliott's artillery, along with Nelson's Battery, opened up on the Union column, this time with telling effect. Union artillery attempted to respond but quickly ran short of ammunition. Brannan tried to sweep the Confederates from their position by ordering the First Brigade forward with disastrous results. The 47th Pennsylvania formed a line of battle and advanced against the Confederates, but, as Brannan later wrote, his troops "were twice driven out of the woods with great slaughter by the overwhelming fire of the enemy, whose missiles tore through like hale." Unfamiliar with the surrounding terrain, Brannan continued to press the assaults through the marsh, while Confederate fire ripped holes in the Union formations.

Walker knew his position had potentially dangerous weaknesses. There was low ground at either end of the Confederate line, and Walker feared that it would not take long for Union forces to cross this ground and strike at his exposed flanks. Though they were doing great damage to the opposing formations, Elliott's and Nelson's exposed gunners were becoming casualties at an alarming rate. As Union troops began to cross Frampton Creek to strike at his flank, Walker ordered a general withdrawal of his men to the next defensive position. The fight at Frampton's Plantation had stalled the Union advance for forty-five minutes.

With the exception of the gun crews, Confederate losses had been light all day. This quickly changed as Walker's force attempted to withdraw under Union fire. The Beaufort Volunteer Artillery had borne the brunt of the fighting for Walker's command since the first engagement near Elliott's Plantation, and they continued to provide fire support as their comrades pull backed. Of this stage in the action, Captain Elliott later wrote that "some halves of heads and legs bear faithful testimony to the accuracy of our fire." The Charleston Light Dragoons, which to that point had suffered no casualties during the war, had three men wounded as they retreated.

Moving northward from Frampton's Plantation, Mackay's Point Road meets the Coosawhatchie Road and turns east toward Old Pocotaligo. Walker withdrew his force toward that town, which proved to be his strongest defensive position. To reach Old Pocotaligo, the Coosawhatchie Road followed a long causeway through a marsh to a thirty-foot bridge spanning the Pocotaligo River. Walker's command quickly retreated over the bridge, and the last troops to cross it pulled up the boards, leaving only the bridge's ropes intact. They also inadvertently left a number of their comrades on the wrong side of the bridge. Captain J. Blythe Allston and two lieutenants from the 1st Battalion, South Carolina Sharpshooters, were forced to lie motionless in the marsh for the rest of the day feigning to be casualties, while Confederate and Union fire passed overhead.

As at Frampton's Plantation, Walker deployed his men on both sides of the road, this time to the north and south along the riverbanks and behind the village's large trees and old houses. Once again, Walker positioned his dwindling artillery in the center, in an exposed position where it could sweep the approaches to the causeway. He held the Charleston Light Dragoons as a strategic reserve one-half mile to the rear.

Brannan's pursuit of the retreating Confederates was delayed for some time while his engineers repaired the bridge over the creek at Frampton's Plantation. When the job was complete, Brannan's two brigades quickly advanced across the bridge and proceeded to Old Pocotaligo, where they took position in a line of woods that faced the town across marsh and river. At that point, General Terry later reported, ". . . the rebels opened a murderous fire on us . . ." Brannan's engineers attempted to cut down trees with which to bridge the Pocotaligo, but the intense Confederate fire forced them to abandon the effort.

As Walker's guns began to find the range of the Union troops stationed in the woods, Brannan brought his artillery forward. Guns from the 3rd Rhode Island Artillery, the 3rd U.S. Artillery, and a group of naval guns from the Wabash attempted to answer the Confederate fire, but were quickly silenced by heavy casualties among the gun crews and a dearth of ammunition. Union troops once again could find no way to reach the Confederate position. The 7th Connecticut Regiment sent a small group of men forward under fire to conduct a reconnaissance of the Pocotaligo River. The party returned and reported that river was narrow, but too deep to ford.

Brannan's men, however, were far from inactive. The 55th Pennsylvania sent two companies of sharpshooters forward along the road to fire on the Confederate artillerymen, who had done great damage to the Union forces all day. Flank companies of the 7th Connecticut armed with Sharps Rifles also opened fire on the gunners. Within a short time, this concentrated fire had killed or wounded most of the Confederate artillerymen.

Under intense Union small arms fire for the third time that day, Walker's artillery was slowly falling quiet. Only one gun of the Nelson Artillery and two of the Beaufort Volunteer Artillery were still in action. To relieve some of the pressure on his gunners, Walker withdrew one gun from the Beaufort Volunteer Artillery north up the McPhersonville Road, which ran parallel to the Union lines. In its new position it was masked from the Union sharpshooters, but it could fire on the left flank of the Union lines with impunity.

As the battle progressed at Pocotaligo, the Union force tasked with destroying the track at Coosawhatchie was doing its part in diverting Confederate attention from the main Union objective. Colonel Barton had taken his force up the Coosawhatchie River aboard the gunboats *Patroon* and *Vixen*, the armed steamer *Planter*, and the armed transport *George Washington*. The latter took a wrong turn up Little Bee Creek and would not participate in the coming action. The *Patroon* and the *Vixen* soon ran aground, and the *Planter* moved as far north as possible until she ran aground roughly one and a half to two miles south of the village of Coosawhatchie. Barton disembarked his men and one naval howitzer on the west bank of the river around 2:00 P.M. and marched west to a road running northward to the village. Barton later reported that "the road proved to be an excellent one, hard and firm . . . trees lined it on either side, with an occasional open field beyond." Once astride the road, they marched north for two miles and easily drove off Confederate cavalry pickets along the way. After hearing a locomotive whistle to his left, Barton realized that the road heading toward Coosawhatchie paralleled the railroad. The whistle he heard was from a locomotive speeding north toward the village with Confederate reinforcements from the 11th S.C. Regiment arriving from Hardeeville, twenty-one miles to the south. Barton quickly formed his men in lines beside the railroad and brought forward the naval howitzer to ambush the passing train.

The locomotive barreled onward, with its passengers unaware of the impending danger. As the engine passed, Barton's men opened fire on the train, killing the engineer, the fireman, Major J. J. Harrison of the 11th S.C. Regiment, and a number of passengers. Barton later characterized the Union fire as being "very destructive." Confederate troops were jammed inside railroad cars and aboard platform cars, and the intense fire forced those aboard to seek cover. Some men jumped from the platform cars and hid in the woods to escape the fire, and at least one battle flag, belonging to the Whippy Swamp Guards, fell from the passing train. Upon learning that the engineer was dead, the train's conductor took control of the engine and pressed on to Coosawhatchie Station to disembark his passengers.

Barton's men captured a number of Confederates who had jumped from the train, along with the battle flag. Hoping to take advantage of the confusion caused by the ambush, Barton ordered part of the detachment from the 1st New York Engineers to begin pulling up rails and to cut the telegraph wire, while he led the rest of the engineers and his men back to the road and northwards towards Coosawhatchie station. There, he hoped to attack the Confederates while they were disembarking from the train. Upon arriving in the village of Coosawhatchie, which was south of the railroad station and the river of the same name, however, Barton ran into Confederate infantry supporting Lt. Bleux's Lafayette Artillery and a section of Capt. Elliott's Beaufort Volunteer Artillery on the opposite side of the road bridge. These Confederates immediately opened fire on Barton's force, which briefly returned fire. Realizing that he could not seize the railroad bridge and fearing the arrival of more Confederate troops from Hardeeville, Barton ordered his troops to withdraw to the waiting Union ships. Barton's engineers, hearing the heavy fire from the north, also began to move towards their transports.

That morning in Grahamville, Confederate Colonel Charles Jones Colcock, commander of the 3rd S.C. Cavalry, had received word from Walker that a Union force was moving toward Coosawhatchie. Colcock, suffering from a high fever, ordered Lt. Col. T. H. Johnson to proceed with the 3rd from Bee's Hill to Coosawhatchie and organize its defense. Johnson was unable to cross the causeway at Bee's Creek due to nearby Union gunboats, so he took his three companies of cavalry on a long detour to Grahamville and from there to Coosawhatchie. They arrived just as Barton began his retreat, and the Confederate cavalrymen harassed Barton and his men as they retired toward their transports.

To impede the Confederate pursuit, Barton ordered his engineers to destroy all of the bridges leading to the landing site after Union troops had crossed. This task the engineers accomplished with alacrity. In response, Johnson dismounted his cavalry and led them on foot in pursuit of the Union raiders. As the Union troops approached their waiting transports, they received succor in the form of covering fire from the Planter and the gunboats to the south. Even after the Union troops were safely aboard, Confederates continued to fire on the vessels until the tide rose high enough for the Planter to be refloated. Barton's force then proceeded back to Mackay's Point, quite content with their accomplishments.

Back at Pocotaligo, the battle had digressed into a stand-off, with both Confederate and Union troops trading desultory fire from some distance across the marshes and river. Walker's gunners continued to fire shot and canister into the woods protecting the Union line, but the fire from the rest of his line had grown sporadic. Around mid afternoon, Walker ordered the Charleston Light Dragoons, his reserves, forward at the double quick to reinforce the left side of his line. To convince the Union commander that reinforcements were arriving from the railroad, Walker instructed the Dragoons to shout loudly as they advanced. The Dragoons moved forward with a thunderous cheer, and other Confederate troops on Walker's line answered with their own cheers, which had the desired affect across the river, where Brannan believed that Confederate reinforcements were arriving on the scene.

The Dragoons' advance temporarily inspired Walker's command, which briefly increased its rate of fire. In response, Brannan committed more reinforcements to the Union line, and their fire, according Dragoon Frank Middleton, "began to increase in intensity until their bullets came as thick as hail . . . a rat could hardly run from tree to tree without being hit." In response, the Confederate fire slackened and nearly ceased.

At 4:00 P.M. Confederate reinforcements, in the form of a detachment of 200 men from Nelson's (7th) South Carolina Infantry Battalion, arrived on the scene after a quick march from Pocotaligo Station. As with the Dragoons, Nelson's men joined Walker's line while cheering wildly, which drew cheers from Walker's commands. Walker quickly committed this unit to the right side of his line near the masked Confederate battery. Nelson's men opened an intense flanking fire on the Union forces.

Across the river, Brannan was reaching his breaking point. At each of Walker's defensive positions, Brannan had formed his men into battle lines and ordered frontal assaults on the Confederate lines. In each instance his men had attacked with vigor and suffered significant casualties but had been unable to drive their opponents from the field. For hours they had merely exchanged small arms fire with the smaller Confederate force. The Union artillery had faced ammunition shortages all day, and as a result had been unable to silence the Confederate batteries. As night approached Brannan could find no visible means to break the Confederate line. Realizing that he and his men would not reach the railroad, he ordered a withdrawal to the landing craft at 5:00 P.M.

As the Union force retreated, Walker sent elements of Captain Trenholm's Rutledge Mounted Riflemen to pursue the Federals, while keeping the rest of his command at Old Pocotaligo to counter a possible Union attack from Coosawhatchie. Because Barton's men had cut the telegraph line near that village, Walker did not learn until later that his men there had driven the Union raiders away from the railroad, which sustained only minimal damage in the form of two rails being pulled up and several loosened.

Though he was probably unaware of it at the time, Walker had decisively beaten a numerically superior force and saved, for the second time, the critical transportation link between Charleston and Savannah. Brannan's command retreated back to Mackay's Point, where it embarked on its transports over the next day before returning to Hilton Head Island. In their wake the Union troops left a trail of discarded equipment and a number of dead. Walker's cavalrymen followed the withdrawing force, but did not press them.

Relying on accurate and timely intelligence, rapid concentration of forces, and effective use of terrain, the Confederate forces of the Third Military District had won an improbable victory, but at a significant cost. Confederate casualties totaled 163 (21 killed, 124 wounded, and 18 missing), when compared with Union casualties, totaling 340 (43 killed, 294 wounded, and 3 missing). For the Confederates, as in numerous other battles during the war, the total number of casualties comprised a much higher percentage of those engaged.

The battles of Pocotaligo and Coosawhatchie would shape the subsequent careers of participants on both sides. For Colonel William S. Walker, the battle was probably the highlight of his military career. Shortly afterward he was promoted to Brigadier General and was thereafter known as "Live Oak" Walker for his skillful defense of Old Pocotaligo. He was later transferred to Virginia, where he lost a foot and was captured during the battle of Ware Bottom Church. He was eventually paroled and spent the rest of the war serving in an administrative capacity. Brigadier General John M. Brannan briefly commanded the Department of the South before being promoted and placed in command of the Third Division of the Army of the Cumberland. He later commanded all of the artillery of that army. Captain Stephen Elliott went on to serve with distinction in defense of Fort Sumter in Charleston Harbor and attained the rank of Brigadier General. He was wounded at Petersburg and later in North Carolina, and surrendered with Johnston's army. He died shortly after the war due to complications from his wounds. Brigadier General Alfred H. Terry rose in rank to command the Tenth Corps of Benjamin F. Butler's Army of the James. After the war he commanded George Armstrong Custer at the time of the Battle of the Little Big Horn. Major General Ormsby M. Mitchel, the architect of the raid on the Charleston and Savannah Railroad, did not live to launch further attacks along the coast. On October 27, 1862, he died in Beaufort of yellow fever.

Today, relatively few people outside of the South Carolina lowcountry know of the battles for Pocotaligo and Coosawhatchie. These engagements, however, shaped Union strategy in South Carolina for the next year and a half. Faced with the difficulties of seizing the Charleston and Savannah Railroad and using it to strike at the back door of Charleston, subsequent Union commanders decided instead on a more direct strategy for capturing that most prized and symbolic of southern cities. Within months Ormsby Mitchel's successor would launch an assault on Morris Island at the mouth of Charleston Harbor in hopes of forcing a Confederate withdrawal from the city. The fight for Morris Island would be epic, and though Union troops would eventually take control of the island, the goal of capturing Charleston would remain illusory until the war's final months.

OCCUPIED BEAUFORT, 1863: A WAR CORRESPONDENT'S VIEW

EDITED BY P. J. STAUDENRAUS *

University of California, Davis

From 1862 to 1865, Noah Brooks, a young, hard-working newspaper reporter, covered wartime Washington, D. C., and subsequently became famous for his reminiscences, first published in 1896 under the title *Washington in Lincoln's Time*. A native of Castine, Maine, Brooks had worked for newspapers in Massachusetts, Illinois, and California before going to Washington in December, 1862, as special correspondent of the Sacramento *Daily Union*. In all, Brooks wrote more than 250 letters covering the activities of the Thirty-Seventh and Thirty-Eighth Congresses, War Department affairs, party politics, and the social life of the capital. In his spare moments he lounged in President Lincoln's study and chatted with the President. The two men first met in Illinois during the Frémont campaign, and in 1858 Brooks covered a portion of the Lincoln-Douglas campaign debates. The President relied on Brook's observations and information, and shortly before he died invited him to be his private secretary. Though Brook's assignment kept him in the capital for the greater part of the Civil War period, he paid a brief visit to Union troops stationed on the Sea Islands in South Carolina. At Beaufort he wrote a careful but now forgotten description of the occupied city and its forlorn inhabitants. Brook's original letter appeared in the Sacramento *Daily Union* on July 16, 1863.

Beaufort, June 17, 1863

AN ANCIENT SOUTHERN TOWN

The lovely town of Beaufort, embowered in groves of orange and magnolia trees, about twelve miles above Hilton Head, on the Beaufort river . . . . has for a century or more been the seat of a wealthy and aristocratic population, and evidences of their taste and love for the beautiful and the sumptuous are yet perceptible in the town, which, though partially dismantled and greatly come to grief, yet shows in its half-ruined and neglected gardens, costly and generously large houses and arbored streets and squares, what manner of people formerly occupied the place.

There is much of the early English style in the architecture of the houses, upon which have been engrafted the features which a Southern

---

* Dr. Staudenraus edited "Letters from South Carolina, 1821-1822" in this quarterly, 58 (1957), 209-217.

climate renders necessary for comfort, and the broad piazzas and verandahs, Venetian blinds and wide halls which one sees in every Southern town are here characteristics of the respectable mansions of the place. Here was the home of the Rhetts, the Barnwells and the Prestons of South Carolina; and the house of Robert Barnwell Rhett, a semi-palatial edifice, is one of the show places of the town of Beaufort. It is now occupied by the United States Tax Commissioners, before whose summary proceedings the broad acres of the fugacious nabobs are fast being changed into farms owned by enterprising Northerners, who speak through the nose, eat codfish and pay their honest debts.

The town must be noisy now compared with what it was in the peaceful days of yore, but it is still so serene and Sabbath-like in its stillness that a sojourn of a day or two here is a most excellent poultice to heal the blows of sound inflicted in a noisy, busy city. The fences and walls which enclosed the handsome private grounds of former inhabitants have been greatly demolished by the rude hand of the invader, and marks of violence and vandalism are everywhere visible; but the sable servants of the departed still stroll about the streets, or loiter in picturesque groups around the wells with their watery burdens on their heads, just as they did in other days.

Many of these remnants of ancient families live luxuriously in the sumptuous abodes of the skedaddled Caesars of Beaufort, and one cannot but be struck with the sharp changes which time has made, when he sees the windows of some ancient and aristocratic mansion swarming with blacks, a group of old crones gossipping on the doorways or sunning themselves on the piazza. Truly, the days of ancient grandeur are forever gone when field hands and wandering contrabands people the halls of the *ancien noblesse of Beaufort.* But as our military men have an exceeding keen nose for good quarters, the best of the houses are occupied as headquarters of the command, and the accursed Yankees have their Commissary, Provost Marshal and other offices in the fine old mansions, which are reserved to the Government for that purpose. Your correspondent is just now comfortably housed in the hospitable quarters of Ralph Trembly, an old Californian, but now the Port Royal agent for Adam's Express. He occupies a fine old mansion, owned by the only loyal resident of Beaufort, a Mr. Fyler, who, faithful among the faithless, clung to his flag and refused to fly before "the invaders." He has his family in the North now, and his comfortable house is "Liberty Hall" to a jolly crowd of good fellows during these scorching hot days.

A VENERABLE RELIC

There are several fine old churches here, of which some are now occupied by colored congregations, and of a Sunday night we hear them shouting out their peculiar religious Ethiopian hymns, as "Gideon's Band," with all of the zeal and unction of the race. But the aristocratic church of the former inhabitants was an old Episcopal church, built in 1724.[1] Here the patriarchs of a former age worshiped God—proceeding to the sanctuary, doubtless, with all the pomp and circumstance of princes, attended by their trains of sable menials, who were allowed to get nearer Heaven but further from the altar by climbing into the broad oaken gallery.

The interior of the church bears a few mural tablets to the memory of distinguished departed ones; but the most of the forefathers of the hamlet sleep in the embowered churchyard—their ivy-mantled tombs, sonorous with sounding eulogy, being now near neighbors to the humbler graves of undistinguished names, whose only epitaph is that they died for their country. The Cuthberts, Rhetts, Draytons, DeSaussures and Habershams sleep as peacefully as though the Yankee invaders of the sacred soil of Carolina were not beside them. Some of these old epitaphs are dated as far back as 1755, and just outside of the church yard wall is one mossy stone which bears the date of 1690. It is curious to note how the more modern epitaphs breathe that spirit of "State rights" and State pride which has greatly caused this war, and which is not seen in the older epitaphs. One peculiar monument, a marble representation of a palmetto tree, shorn of its leaves, bore the following inscription: "Sacred to the memory of Hugh Toland, son of Melvin M. and Eliza M. Sams. Born December 1, 1840; died June 29, 1860. A youthful son of South Carolina, he sought to serve her even while preparing for her better future service, and entered her State Military Academy while in his seventeenth year, carrying with him the impress of his childhood's training. He exhibited toward his Alma Mater a respectful devotion akin to that which animated him as a son. His courteous bearing, high-toned sentiments and exemplary conduct for nearly four years won for him the high esteem of his professors and the affectionate regard of his fellow cadets, who mourn his loss. This tribute is paid by his commanding officer. 'What I do thou knowest not now.' "

There are many monuments in this churchyard to the memory of officers of the Army and Navy, showing how even this small town had its large share in the service of the United States. One obelisk bore

[1] St. Helena's.

upon its faces the names of three brothers who had died in the United States Army, of whom one was thus noted: "Brevet Captain James Stuart, Regiment Mounted Rifles, United States Army, who fell mortally wounded in battle with the Indians in Oregon, while leading his men gallantly to victory. June 17, 1851. (General Jones' report.) He was a gifted, accomplished and noble-hearted gentlemen."

This fine old church, I regret to say, has not been spared from the ravages of war, but shows the traces of the vandal hand upon it. An old English-made organ, which stood in the choir, has been disemboweled by somebody, and the ivory of its keys has been forced off. Its melody hushed, it is a mute but eloquent witness of the ruthlessness of the soldiery who first landed in this quiet spot, where more than a whole century had shed its hallowing influences over the land.

THE GRAND SKEDADDLE

When Hilton Head was captured by the National forces under Admiral [Samuel Francis] Dupont, in November 1861, the news speedily reached Beaufort, which, only twelve miles up the river by a channel practicable for the largest vessels, was the most probable point for the next attack. Accordingly, there at once ensued a grand exodus of the secesh citizens of the place and of the adjoining plantations. Hastily packing up their most portable valuables and gathering a few of their able-bodied slaves, they abandoned all else to the invader and fled, leaving even their dishes upon the tables, provisions in the larder and cattle in the stall. Everything locomotive was pressed into the service, and the long shell road, which, stretching for twelve miles up the island to Port Royal Ferry, and embowered with trees and fragrant flowering vines, had been the famous sporting avenue of Beaufort, became at once a scene of hurrying confusion, dismay and wild disorder, such as only can be imagined. The dreadful cry of "The Yankees are coming!" urged them on in flocks and droves, and all day long the rude ferry boat was employed in carrying the flying refugees across to the mainland, where eight miles more brought them to the crossing of the Charleston and Savannah Railroad on the Pocotaligo.

The wealth had chiefly consisted in land and slaves, and now both of these had suddenly become almost valueless. Their lands were left behind, and only a few of the fugitives could afford to take their slaves along, and for the most part they were left behind to riot in the halls of the Beaufort Montezumas. . . . The slaves, intoxicated with their sudden freedom, ransacked the houses of their proprietors, plundering and gutting the wardrobes of masters and mistresses, jumping, in very wantonness of unrestraint, with their rough shoes on, into downy, snowy beds, dancing upon the polished pianos or marble tables, feasting upon choice dainties, decking themselves with gorgeous finery, and "closing out, regardless of cost." the stores of the town. Probably such another saturnalia was never witnessed before in this country, and such another mad set were never let loose from serfdom as the emancipated slaves of Beaufort, left to shift for themselves by their skedaddling owners. I wish that I could convey to the reader, with all its spirit and unction, the story of the exodus as given to me by one of the slaves of Heyward, a wealthy citizen . . . .

After the Negroes came the soldiers, and they, in very wantonness of destructive mischief, demolished what the first-comers had spared. Pianos were broken up and their "innards" taken out to make bird cages, and their tops used to manufacture in relic boxes; portraits of distinguished secesh were bayoneted; articles of virtue or value gobbled up; and what could be carried off to camp as spoils from the Egyptians was incontinently made off with. I have seen many a sofa, chair and table of costly make and finish making itself useful in the tents of the honest patriots around this town, and books, pictures, and even furniture and other articles have been sent home by the officers and men of the army of occupation. Private property was not respected, and no limit has ever been fixed here as to how far spoilation should go.

In looking upon this lovely spot, consecrated by so many memories of the past, where generations have passed their lives in peaceful content, one cannot but be saddened to see how the accumulations of years have been scattered and how thoroughly the arts and improvements of peace have been laid waste by the hand of war. The rich and aristocratic owners of these seats of ease, favored by nature, ministered to by an obsequious race of slaves, wealthy and growing wealthy, living in ease and comfort, were not content, but, still lusting for more power, and fancying that they were gods and not men, rebelled against their lawful Government, and lo! their judgment has come and the Philistines are upon them.

THE FIRST SOUTH CAROLINA REGIMENT

Among the relics of the past which are still found in Beaufort is a record of the doings of the City Council, or Selectmen, which body was known as the Wardens of the city, and the Mayor was called the Intendant. At the time of "the invasion" Edmund Rhett was Intendant, and the doings under his administration appear to have been chiefly of a magisterial character, most of the cases being trials for avoidance of patrol duty by the citizens, who were fined two dollars therefor, or violation of the peace by the slaves, who were sentenced to ten, twenty or thirty lashes, according to the degree of the crime. One entry, August 6, 1861, two months before the conquest, sets forth in good round characters the fact that "this was the meeting night of the Council, in regular order, but none was held for the reason that most of the Wardens were at Bay Point engaged in military drill." And the very last entry is in October, 1861, thirty days before the Yankees came, which recorded the appointment of a Committee "to meet the Colonel and other officers of the First Regiment of Carolina Volunteers, who are daily expected here, and conduct them to the place pointed out for their camp on the southern edge of the town."

So it appears that the First South Carolina Regiment did garrison duty here for the rebellious town of Beaufort; but another regiment of that name and title is now encamped on the southern edge of the town, perhaps on the very spot where the chivalrous sons of the Palmetto State were welcomed by the hospitable people whom they came to defend. The Colonel of the new First South Carolina is Thomas W. Higginson, formerly a Massachusetts preacher of some repute, and a writer of just renown, as the pages of the *Atlantic* have frequently attested. His officers are from Ohio, New York and New England, and his rank and file are from the scattered remnants of the tribes of contrabands left behind by the fugacious citizens of Beaufort, reinforced by levies from the neighboring plantations. The Reverend Thomas has taken up the sword of the flesh, and, believing in deeds as well as words, has smitten the rebellion upon the thigh with a dart winged from its own quiver. . . .

[Let us] look at the camp, and watch the men as they form upon dress parade tonight. The camp is on a level grassy plain, and is as neat and clean as camp can be. Some of the companies are drilling apart from each other in the camp streets, and the rest of the regiment are engaged in various avocations, "chaffing" with each other and indulging in all of the fantastic tricks which the African so makes a part of his nature. The order to fall into line was obeyed with alacrity, and the different companies came up and formed on in fine style; then the regiment was reviewed by the Colonel and the long double line of black soldiers, dark with their regulation uniform and darker faces, stood motionless to receive the orders of the day.

I will confess that I was astonished at the perfection of the drill of these colored soldiers—it was absolutely perfect, each arm and each musket moving as that of one man. Their parade was equally good, each soldier and rank and file marking time with entire accuracy. The appearance of the regiment was excellent, owing to the fact that the men are all of a uniform height, and well made and stalwart fellows. They are also all of a color, being as black as night—no streaks of Caucasian or mongrel blood among them, which is not the case with the "Bostons," as the Fifty-fourth (colored) Massachusetts Regiment is called. They are of all shades, and show a plentiful streak of Northern amalgamation; but, in sooth, the whole of the colored population in this region is purely African, and shows no trace of other admixture, though I notice that some of the picaninnies, of the tender age of a year or thereabouts, have a bleached look, as though they were coming by a born right to Northern prejudices; some of these milk-and-molasses colored infants wear *brass buttons.*

Colonel Higginson is enthusiastic in praise of his men, all of whom have been under fire, and have behaved well. He uses the law of kindness in the government of his men; appeals to their sense of duty and right as men; places his appeals upon the ground of justice and right, not might. It is, perhaps, questionable if such a course will be advisable in the case of men who have been taken from under the harsh plantation yoke, and have never before known that they were anything but chattels. It would seem that the condition and antecedents of these poor creatures would demand a more gradual emancipation from the yoke of their servitude, and that military discipline should be more rigid and severe over them than over men less accustomed than they to implicit obedience. [James] Montgomery with his men, the Second South Carolina, is more severe, though not unkind nor harsh. He believes that men who have been drilled to slavish obedience must be made to obey slavishly—cheerfully because they are not yet free, but implicitly because they are under strict military rule. The experiment of the two theories is being tried by Higginson and by Montgomery, and the result will be looked for with interest by those who know the difference in the two commanders. . . .

SOUTHERN PLANTATIONS IN NORTHERN HANDS

Some of the finest plantations in South Carolina, or the South, are those in this immediate vicinty. The famous Sea Island cotton, sought for the world over, grows here, and the rich, quick soil yields abundantly of sweet potatoes, corn and other crops, while oranges, lemons, figs and other fruits are abundant. These valuable plantations have passed out of the hands of their former owners, and have been, for the most part, sold under the Act of Congress authorizing their disposal to the highest bidder, in default of the payment of taxes to the General Government. This law, framed to cover the state of facts which forbids the confiscation of real estate, have been availed of by many speculators, who have bought very largely of the Tax Commissioners. The largest purchase in this vicinity is a Boston man, [Edward S.] Philbrick, who has bought over 6,000 acres, at a rate of a little more than one dollar an acre. These 6,000 acres comprise thirteen fine plantations,[2] all of them under fine cultivation and capable of turning out a big crop of cotton. Some of the plantations were redeemed by their owners; some were bid in at the vendue by their loyal friends, and several have been reserved by the Government for public use.

One of these latter class is the Smith estate, a large plantation on the river, a few miles below the town of Beaufort. A horseback ride out there the other day was a new sensation to your correspondent. Through long avenues of live oaks and sycamores, covered with fragrant vines, the air laden with sweetness, the cool fresh air blowing from the bay, one can hardly imagine a more delightful ride. There I saw, for the first time, the palmetto tree in its native glory; a knubby, gnarled tree, ridgy as to bark, straight as to trunk, and shabby as to its palmy crown, it is not a very noble emblem for any sovereign State, but will do well enough for the knubby, wiry and shabby State of South Carolina. A grove of aged sycamores, gray with long festoons of Spanish moss, surrounds the Smith house, forlorn in its ruinous condition; and a still grayer darkey met my inquiry for the overseer with, "We hab no oberseer now, sar; we has a *Superintendent,* sar." Uncle Samuel has Superintendents for his plantations, but no more overseers for Sambo here. The Superintendent informed me that he has about fifty hands on the plantation, all of whom were left upon the place when the proprietor skedaddled for parts unknown. These people are paid stipulated wages for their field work, and have time and ground for cultivating enough corn, potatoes and other vegetables for their support, and they manage, with these and the pigs, poultry and cows which they raise, to live very comfortably and send some surplusage to market. On the plantations owned by private individuals the hands are provided with rations and paid small wages by the proprietors, the Government being surety for their continuance upon the place for the length of time stipulated.

The Smith estate was formerly kept up in considerable grandeur, having a fine house, with a lawn sloping to the river, embowered with oleanders, magnolias and myrtles, the place being surrounded by a hedge of the plant known as the "Spanish dagger," a species of low palmetto,

[2] These included Coffin's Point, Cherry Hill, Pine Grove, John Fripp's Big House, Mulberry Hill, Corner Farm, Morgan Island, and two plantations on Ladies Island. Guion Griffis Johnson, *A Social History of the Sea Islands* (Chapel Hill, 1930), 186.

with long, sharp leaves, and crowned with an enormous crown of brilliant white flowers. Wright, the Superintendent, says that his hands are happy and contented in their new lot, and are ambitious to earn something for themselves. I asked him how much cotton he expected to get from his one hundred acres; and he replied that he could not say, nor could he predict the market price of cotton, but he had set his heart upon making a net profit to the Government of $3,000. . . .

Upon my way back to town I passed a camp of contrabands who have been brought in by a recent raid upon the Combahee by Montgomery. They were chiefly women and children, the able-bodied men, some one hundred and fifty, having been placed in the colored regiment now forming here. Montgomery brought in about six hundred of the Negroes, and, as they are field hands, it is a loss to the enemy, and they will soon be useful when dispersed upon the plantations around here. Meanwhile they receive rations of "hard tack," soap, salt and molasses from the Government stores. They are a curious looking crowd, rough and uncouth, with a lingo of their own which is as much like California-Chinese as any Christian tongue. The poor creatures have been bundled about from pillar to post, from plantation to camp, until they scarcely know where or to whom they belong. But they flocked to the standard of the United States, when they heard Montgomery's steam-whistle and saw the stars and stripes on his gunboats.

THE MILITARY GOVERNMENT

All of the reclaimed territory of the State of South Carolina is under the Military Government of Brigadier General [Rufus] Saxton, whose headquarters are at Beaufort. His dominions are at present somewhat circumscribed, but will doubtless be enlarged before many months have passed. He was also General commanding the district of Beaufort up to the time that General [Quincy Adams] Gillmore succeeded [David] Hunter in command of the Department of the South, when he resigned, his dignity being offended at being placed under an officer whom he himself ranked in seniority of appointment.

Beaufort and vicinity is under the strictest military surveillance, and no one is allowed to pass through any of the numerous lines of fortifications upon the island without being armed with a panoply of passes. At nine o'clock at night the curfew-bell rings, and any imprudent person, white or black, found in the streets after that time without the countersign is summarily gobbled up and kept in the guard house overnight, and until he can satisfactorily account for himself. Here, as elsewhere, the military rule gets the upper hands of all other authority, and is final and as changeless as the law of the Medes and Persians.

LAURA M. TOWNE AND THE FREED PEOPLE
OF SOUTH CAROLINA, 1862-1901

KURT J. WOLF *

ON APRIL 14, 1865 — FIVE DAYS AFTER GENERAL ROBERT E. LEE'S
surrender and exactly four years and a day after the fall of Fort Sumter had
marked the beginning of the Civil War — several hundred northern dignitaries, teachers, federal officials, and former abolitionists gathered amidst
the ruins of Fort Sumter to witness the re-raising of the American flag. As a
crisp northeasterly wind whipped across their faces, they looked upon the
battered ramparts, its walls "deeply indented by the shots hurled against
it," and its sides surrounded by "exploded shells" and "shattered stones."
Brevet Major General Robert Anderson, who had surrendered the fort on
the eve of the war, addressed the audience first. Then the original flag,
long absent, ascended to its former height, followed by the thunder of cannons from nearby forts and vessels that "pealed forth their detonations"
for nearly a half hour.[1]

The next speaker, Rev. Henry Ward Beecher, spoke at great length
(though, according to one source, "quite without fire"). His words often
seemed to remonstrate "the citizens of Charleston when there were not a
dozen there."[2] After glorifying a cause that had delivered "one government, without slavery," Beecher reflected on the future. With slavery extinct and peace embracing the land, the ardent abolitionist proclaimed that
"reconstruction" itself would be "easy." It would require neither "engineer
or architect." But the experience of the steamship *Planter*, floating just outside Fort Sumter, perhaps better exemplified things to come. Its occupants,
former slaves, for some "unexplained reason, had not been permitted to
land and witness the ceremonies." Possibly even more symbolic, in its ne-
glect the *Planter* had run aground, and "no effort of her own could set her

*Former graduate student, University of New Mexico in Albuquerque, and
currently an independent writer living on the west coast.

[1][Justus Clement French], *The Trip of the Steamer Oceanus to Fort Sumter and
Charleston, S.C., Comprising the Incidents of the Excursion, the Appearance, at that time,
of the City, and the entire Programme of Exercises at the Re-raising of the Flag over the
Ruins of Fort Sumter, April 14th, 1865* (Brooklyn, N.Y.: The Union Steam Printing
House, 1865), pp. 45-46, 50, 53-54.

[2]Laura M. Towne to her sister Sophy, Apr. 23, 1865, Penn School Papers, Southern Historical Collection, University of North Carolina, Chapel Hill (available on
microfilm, and hereafter abbreviated PSP). Original documents are maintained by
Penn Community Services, Inc., St. Helena Island, S.C.

Laura M. Towne was part of the large crowd that took part in the ceremony at Fort Sumter on April 14, 1865, when the United States flag again was raised. Photo from the collections of the South Carolina Historical Society.

afloat."[3] In the spring of 1865, African Americans, neglected by their white friends, were already in trouble.

Native Pennsylvanian Laura M. Towne — an abolitionist, teacher of freedmen, and homeopathic care-giver — watched these proceedings with an observant eye. She had witnessed much since her arrival on the sea islands of South Carolina three years before, and she would see much more in the decades to come. Indeed, Reverend Beecher could not have been more wrong about Reconstruction being "easy." Thus far, Towne's efforts to help the ex-slaves had been fraught with difficulty, and the years ahead would prove no less challenging. Volunteering to assist the freed people with education and medicine had thrust her into the heart of a socio-political revolution, where she would remain the rest of her life. From the first, she had recorded her thoughts and perceptions in voluminous diary en-

[3][French], *The Trip of the Steamer Oceanus*, pp. 54, 58, 82. See also Willie Lee Rose, *Rehearsal for Reconstruction: The Port Royal Experiment* (Indianapolis, Ind.: Bobbs-Merrill, 1964), pp. 341-345.

tries and letters, dating from 1862 to 1901. Although several prominent historians have sampled these writings — often relying on a watered-down version of her diary and letters published in 1912 — few have realized what a rich source her writings provide for historians of the Civil War and Reconstruction eras.[4] Therefore, this paper, in part, attempts to rescue Towne's poignant insights from obscurity; at the same time it illustrates how her story deepens our understanding of the South in the latter half of the nineteenth century.

Unlike many of her fellow missionaries who abandoned Reconstruction ideals in the face of adversity, Laura Towne remained the rest of her life in South Carolina, continuing to work from the abolitionist beliefs that had brought her south originally.[5] She had come to the South knowing

[4]Willie Lee Rose leaned heavily on Towne's manuscript diaries and letters for her award-winning *Rehearsal for Reconstruction*. Modern historians of the Reconstruction era — Eric Foner, Joel Williamson, Howard N. Rabinowitz, and James M. McPherson, for instance — have used Towne's insights to support their works. Unfortunately, most rely on Rupert Sargent Holland's compilation, and none have told Towne's story. See Rupert Sargent Holland, ed., *Letters and Diary of Laura M. Towne: Written from the Sea Islands of South Carolina, 1862-84* (Cambridge, Mass.: Riverside Press, 1912; repr., New York: Negro Universities Press, 1969). Holland's edition of Towne's diaries and letters leaves much to be desired, as he deleted many of her most poignant comments concerning the South and the prejudiced southern whites she encountered, as well as other more personal insights. The only article apparently ever written about Towne, published in 1961, primarily chronicles the war years, focusing on educational philosophy, and discusses only briefly the Penn School's growth. Riddled with inaccuracies — such as proclaiming that Towne actually finished her medical degree — the author relied exclusively on Holland's edition. See Gerald Robbins, "Laura Towne: White Pioneer in Negro Education, 1862–1901," *Journal of Education* 143 (April 1961), pp. 40-54.

[5]For sake of comparison, one can review several other missionaries who served on the sea islands, for instance Mary Ames, Elizabeth Hyde Botume, Arthur Sumner, and William C. Gannett. Ames's sojourn was brief, May 1865 to September 1866, because of a decline in Freedmen's Bureau funds, corresponding with waning northern interest in such missionary schools. Botume, arriving in 1863, stayed until the late 1860s, when the political situation became increasingly discomforting. Sumner's negative experiences with the freedmen soured his enthusiasm, cutting his efforts short. Gannett, among the first arrivals, lasted fairly long, departing in 1877 as the political climate drastically changed. See Mary Ames, *From a New England Woman's Diary in Dixie in 1865* (Springfield, Mass.: Plimpton Press, 1906; repr., New York: Negro Universities Press, 1969); Elizabeth Hyde Botume, *First Days amongst the Contrabands* (Boston: Lee and Shepard Publishers, 1893; repr., New York: Arno Press, 1968); for Sumner, see Papers of Arthur Sumner, PSP, and Theodore Rosengarten, *Tombee: Portrait of a Cotton Planter, with the Journal of Thomas B. Chaplin* (New York: William Morrow, 1986), p. 258; for Gannett, see the William C. Gannett Papers, University of Rochester, Rochester, N.Y. and William H. Pease, "Three Years among the Freedmen: William C. Gannett and the Port Royal Experiment," *Journal of Negro History* 42 (1957), pp. 98-117.

virtually nothing about the freed people. Through her dedicated labor and influential contacts, she became one of their staunchest advocates — a very model of perseverance and tenacity.[6] But on April 14, 1865, as Towne absorbed the ceremony around her, the events of her recent past were foremost on her mind.

As the northern visitors to Fort Sumter celebrated that evening in war-torn Charleston, Beecher's suggestion that there would be no "architect" for Reconstruction inauspiciously came true. That same night, at Ford's Theater in Washington, D.C., an assassin's bullet took the life of President Abraham Lincoln. The nation, much like the *Planter*, had lost its rudder — set adrift to the winds of change. And Laura Towne, much like the rest of the nation, would have to redefine her place in a continually changing world.

ON MAY 3, 1825, LAURA MATILDA TOWNE WAS BORN IN PITTS-burgh, Pennsylvania, the fourth child of John and Sarah Towne. Her father had grown up in Topsfield, Massachusetts, her mother in Coventry, England. Unfortunately, Laura's mother died when she was about seven and the family relocated to John Towne's native Massachusetts where they settled in Boston. Like her siblings, Laura received a Boston education. After several years, the family moved back to Pennsylvania — this time to Philadelphia — where the eldest brother had reestablished himself in business.[7] Having been introduced to abolitionism during her sojourn in Boston, Laura enthusiastically fell under the influence of the minister of the First Unitarian Church of Philadelphia, Rev. William H. Furness. Although not a member of the American Antislavery Society, Reverend Furness emulated the passion of his friend and most renowned abolitionist, William Lloyd Garrison of Boston, and fellow Philadelphians James and Lucretia Mott. The intensity of Furness's antislavery sermons increased throughout

---

[6]For one scholar's comparison of Towne and other "devoted" missionaries with those with more "shallow motives," see Martin Abbott, "The Freedmen's Bureau and Negro Schooling in South Carolina," *South Carolina Historical Magazine* 57 (April 1956), pp. 66-67, 77. For another comparison, see Monica Maria Tetzlaff, "Cultivating a New South: Abbie Holmes Christensen and the Reconstruction of Race and Gender in a Southern Region, 1852-1938" (Ph.D. diss., University of Pennsylvania, 1995). For more on perseverance and adaptation of abolitionist sentiment, see James M. McPherson, *The Struggle for Equality: Abolitionists and the Civil War and Reconstruction* (Princeton, N.J.: Princeton University Press, 1964).

[7]Holland, *Letters and Diary of Laura M. Towne*, p. x. For another family history, see: [nephew or niece of L. Towne], "Extracts from the Letters and Diary of Laura M. Towne," p. 2 [n.d., 1910?], unpublished document in PSP, Vol. 3, Reel 18. See also Willie Lee Rose, "Laura Matilda Towne," in *Notable American Women, 1607–1950*, ed. Edward T. James, Janet W. James, Paul S. Boyer (Cambridge, Mass.: Belknap Press of Harvard University Press, 1971), Vol. 3, pp. 472-474.

the 1840s and into the 1850s, despite friction within his congregation. Initially he urged moral suasion and then finally outright defiance against elements of the southern "slavocracy" such as the Fugitive Slave Act.[8] Under his leadership, both personal and professional, Laura Towne's zest for abolitionism grew to new heights.

Endowed with a love of nature and a compassion for both man and animal, Towne intermittently attended the Female Medical College of Pennsylvania in the late 1850s. There she studied under Dr. Constantine Hering though she never finished her education. Dr. Hering later maintained that Laura easily could have attained a degree in homeopathic medicine, but the war effort distracted her, leading to other ventures. Nonetheless, Towne's knowledge of medicine would aid her tremendously in the future.[9]

When the Civil War broke out, Towne was living in a boarding house in Newport, Rhode Island, run by the mother of her closest friend, Ellen Murray. Towne desperately wanted to aid the war effort. While teaching school, she joined the Women's Aid Society and sewed uniforms for soldiers. She even considered serving in Union hospitals, but knew she had at least two strikes against her: her homeopathic background and her gender. The regular "scientific" medical establishment frowned upon the practice of homeopathy, viewing it as "quackery, deception, avarice, falsehood, blasphemy, witchcraft, and almost every other conceivable wickedness and folly." Homeopathic therapy was based on the notion that a disease could be cured by minute, diluted doses of drugs that in full produced effects similar to the symptoms exhibited. Women themselves had just begun to make headway in the medical profession; Elizabeth Blackwell, graduating from Geneva Medical College in 1849, had been the first American woman physician. With service in medicine unpromising, by 1861 Towne had begun to feel restless and "not a bit contented."[10]

Finally in the spring of 1862 Towne's fortunes took a new turn, provid-

[8]Douglas C. Stange, *Patterns of Antislavery Among American Unitarians, 1831-1860* (Cranbury, N.J.: Associated University Presses, Inc., 1977), pp. 126, 131-132; Elizabeth M. Geffen, "William Henry Furness, Philadelphia Antislavery Preacher," *The Pennsylvania Magazine of History and Biography* 82 (July 1958), pp. 259-291. Furness and his wife visited Towne on St. Helena Island after the Civil War.

[9]Holland, *Letters and Diary of Laura M. Towne*, p. x; [nephew or niece], "Extracts," pp. 1-2. The medical school was renamed the Woman's Medical College of Pennsylvania in 1867. See Gulielma Fell Alsop, *History of the Woman's Medical College, Philadelphia, Pennsylvania: 1850-1950* (Philadelphia, 1950).

[10]L. Towne to the Girls, May 15, 1861, Newport, R.I.; L. Towne to the Girls, May 26, 1861, both at PSP. "Quackery ..." quotation by Simpson in William Henderson, M. D., *Homeopathy Fairly Represented: A Reply to Professor Simpson's "Homeopathy" Misrepresented* (Philadelphia: Lindsay & Blakiston, 1854), p. 30. For more on Towne's early war activities, see Holland, *Laura M. Towne*, p. ix; and [nephew or niece], "Extracts," handwritten notes, p. 1. L. Towne to her sisters, May 15, 1861, Newport, R.I., PSP.

ing an opportunity that would change her life. In early April she received a commission from the Port Royal Relief Committee of Philadelphia (PRRC) to set sail for the South Carolina sea islands. The PRRC had formed to send supplies, provisions, and educators to teach freed slaves the "habits of self-support" and to "elevate their moral and social condition." Laura Towne was among the first chosen from Pennsylvania to participate in the cause.[11] Seizing the opportunity, on April 8 she embarked on the steamer *Oriental*. During the voyage she carefully characterized the antislavery sentiments of her fellow passengers in her journal, recording several thoughts about each; but for herself she used just one, telling word: "Abolitionist."[12]

SHE ARRIVED ON THE ISLANDS, IN BEAUFORT, SOUTH CARO-lina, a few days later. The sea islands, situated just off the coast of South Carolina and Georgia, were separated from the mainland by a maze of meandering tidal rivers, palmetto trees, and oaks draped with Spanish moss. Field after field of long-staple cotton, the southern economy's most important crop, stretched across the landscape. The U.S. naval fleet, needing a friendly harbor in southern waters for its blockade of the South, found Port Royal Sound — midway between Charleston and Savannah — to its liking. And so on November 7, 1861, on a day immortalized by the resident slaves as "the day of the Big Gun Shoot at Bay Point," the U.S. Navy overwhelmed Confederate battlements at Bay Point and Hilton Head. All but one southern white residing on the islands fled to the mainland; they left most of their clothes, furniture, food, and other valuable possessions behind, including close to 10,000 slaves. The U.S. forces would station many troops to hold the port, but the immediate question facing the military concerned the fate of the former slaves.[13]

Abolitionists and assorted philanthropists rose to the call of Edward L. Pierce, an agent appointed by Treasury Secretary Salmon P. Chase. Pierce's published reports claimed that the freed people desperately needed educators and clothing.[14] Therefore, after securing federal passes into the war zone, a "motley-looking set" of teachers, missionaries, and appointed plantation superintendents arrived in Beaufort in March 1862, a month before

[11]Hiram Barney to Laura M. Towne, Apr. 3, 1862, Custom House, New York, PSP; "Circular of the Port Royal Relief Committee [Philadelphia]," Mar. 17, 1863, Papers of Arthur Sumner, Vol. 4, PSP.

[12]"Company of Port Royalists which sailed from New York of the Steamer Oriental, Wed. Apr. 9, 1862," Laura M. Towne manuscript diary.

[13]Holland, ed. *Laura Towne*, pp. xi–xii; Rose, *Rehearsal for Reconstruction*, pp. 11-13.

[14]Pierce quoted in "Circular of the Port Royal Relief Committee."

Towne.[15] Mockingly dubbed "the Gideonites" by soldiers, these forty-one men and twelve women held disparate aims. These included educating the former slaves, providing religious instruction, and proving free labor more profitable than slave labor.[16] Of course military officials, fretting over security, held entirely different ideas. Even among the government-commissioned cotton agents and superintendents, some were concerned with freed people's welfare, while others only wished to ensure a crop profitable for the war effort and for themselves. In early April, Laura Towne arrived amidst this confusion of overlapping goals, noting that "there seems ... to be a great want of system, and most incongruous elements here."[17] Tensions between such divergent forces would not soon abate.

SHORTLY AFTER HER ARRIVAL, TOWNE TRAVELED TO THE former Pope's plantation on St. Helena Island, joining the household of Edward Pierce, Susan Walker, Capt. Edward Hooper, Nelly Winsor, and several black servants who had made the transition from serving southern whites to northern whites. Awaiting her niche, Towne initially "kept house," distributed clothing from Philadelphia's Relief Committee, and clerked for Pierce. Everyone there knew she patiently attended to these duties only until more suitable opportunities arose. Towne confided to her sister Rosie, "if I cannot do what I came for ..., that is influence the negroes directly, I shall go somewhere else, for I find we can choose."[18] All the women in the household were occasionally "borrowed" to go "appease the eager anxi-

[15]As described in Edward S. Philbrick to Mrs. Philbrick, Mar. 2, 1862, published in Elizabeth Ware Pearson, ed., *Letters from Port Royal, 1862-1868* (New York: Arno Press, 1969), p. 2. For a complete list of the initial group see Henry Noble Sherwood, ed., "Journal of Miss Susan Walker, March 3d to June 6th, 1862," *Quarterly Publication of the Historical and Philosophical Society of Ohio* (January-March 1912), pp. 47-48. Pierce described the setup on the islands to Chase, as well as the anticipated arrival of Towne, who was "represented as having the rarest qualifications for the work." See E.L. Pierce to Salmon P. Chase, Apr. 1, 1862, in John Niven, James P. McClure, and Leigh Johnsen, eds., *The Salmon P. Chase Papers: Correspondence, 1858-March 1863*, Vol. 3 (Kent, Ohio: Kent State University Press, 1996), p. 161.

[16]Gideon's Band, in the Bible, consisted of 500 Israelites who, armed merely with lamps and trumpets, faced an army numbering in the thousands. Missionaries and philanthropists to Port Royal eventually took a liking to this term, although it was first used in derision. See Ronald E. Butchart, *Northern Schools, Southern Blacks, and Reconstruction: Freedmen's Education, 1862-1875* (Westport, Conn.: Greenwood Press, 1980), p. 3; John R. Rachal, "Gideonites and Freedmen: Adult Literacy Education at Port Royal, 1862-1865," *The Journal of Negro Education* 55, No. 4 (1986), p. 456; Robert C. Morris, *Reading, 'Riting, and Reconstruction: The Education of Freedmen in the South, 1861-1870* (Chicago: University of Chicago Press, 1976), pp. 2-12.

[17]Towne diary, Apr. 17, 1862.

[18]L. Towne to Rosie, Apr. 21, 1862, PSP; Sherwood, *Journal of Susan Walker*, pp. 34, 38.

ety" of the ex-slaves who had "lived on promises" of eventual pay while working in cotton fields for the federal government. The pay accorded these African Americans was usually small (about a dollar per acre cultivated) and often delayed throughout the harvest. Only the white northern women succeeded in calming the fears of the freed people, a contribution Towne considered "quite a triumph after having been rejected as useless" by those who believed a war zone was no place for women.[19]

While some Union soldiers had no qualms about the presence of white women, others took every opportunity to scare any and all civilians, reminding them that the "Secesh," or Confederates, lurked on the opposite shores, a little more than a stone's throw away. Rumors circulated about possible rebel raids on the islands, frightening both civilians and former slaves. Towne claimed most such "stories of danger" originated among "waggish soldiers."[20] Although some raids did occur, and the omnipresent sound of gunfire from the mainland reminded everyone about the nature of their situation, Towne seemed to fear evacuation more than the arrival of the Confederates. She sympathized with the freed people who adamantly believed any reconquest by southern whites would mean death for all blacks. Therefore, when a northern white, Matilda Thompson, panicked over rumors of a raid and fled to Beaufort, Towne labeled her flight "a foolish act" that served merely to frighten the ex-slaves.[21] Nevertheless, other civilians did worry about their proximity to enemy lines. Doubting her usefulness in such a precarious zone, Susan Walker sought advice from Frederic A. Eustis, a Northerner superintending a plantation on Ladies Island. Eustis, influenced by the "health question" — and its implications for women on the sea islands — as well as the overemphasized issue of security, warned her that "women, instead of doing anything will themselves be a care." Several days after her discussion with Eustis, Susan Walker returned to the North for good.[22]

Laura Towne would not be so easily swayed, and she would labor among only a handful of northern women. Not until after the war did women missionaries outnumber their male counterparts. Towne believed

[19]Towne diary, Apr. 28, 1862.

[20]L. Towne to Rosie, Apr. 21, 1862, PSP. Charlotte Forten, an African-American teacher from the North, also saw through the soldiers' statements, and was "not at all alarmed by any of their representations." See Ray Allen Billington, ed., *The Journal of Charlotte L. Forten: A Free Negro in the Slave Era* (New York: W. W. Norton, 1981), p. 144. For a more complete collection of Forten's diaries, see Brenda Stevenson, ed., *The Journals of Charlotte Forten Grimké* (New York: Oxford University Press, 1988).

[21]Towne diary, Sept. 7, 1862; L. Towne to James Miller McKim, Sept. 9, 1862, James Miller McKim Manuscript Collection, Rare and Manuscript Collections, Cornell University, Ithaca, N.Y.

[22]Sherwood, *Journal of Susan Walker*, p. 45.

those women endeavoring to work in the Port Royal experiment must be of simple tastes, tremendous nerve, and strong antislavery sentiments, not women of "more refinement." For herself, she knew the only way to "make amends ... for all the anxiety" she had caused her friends and relatives in Philadelphia about her welfare in the South was to succeed better than she ever had before. But to be at her best she believed she would need the help of her old friend Ellen Murray. And for the next month and a half, she eagerly anticipated her friend's arrival.[23]

In the meantime, just as Towne had taken note of the antislavery sentiment in others during her voyage, she measured the tenor of abolitionism among her island compatriots. Upon her arrival on the islands, Towne commented, "a rather too cautious spirit prevails — anti-slavery is to be kept in the background for fear of exciting the army" which had grudgingly allowed the Gideonites' presence in the first place. She wished all her fellow teachers, missionaries, and philanthropists would forthrightly admit, "We have come to do anti-slavery work, and we think it a noble work." But such was not the case. Although African Americans technically could travel freely — their masters nowhere to be seen — no proclamation of freedom had been offered by President Lincoln. The slaves were merely "contraband" of war.[24]

The abolition sentiments of her fellow Gideonites concerned her for a considerable time. For example, when Edward Pierce recommended that she write to the War Department in May 1862 about the recruitment abuses of blacks by Maj. Gen. David Hunter's men, Towne decided to withhold judgment until she could determine whether Hunter's motives were fully intended to aid the cause of freedom. Biding time, she confined her complaints to her diary and letters as white soldiers hunted black recruits like animals, interrupting baptisms and school sessions. Finally, after spending an evening with General Hunter and his wife, Towne found him to be "more antislavery than expected."[25] Later, when Gen. Rufus Saxton took over Pierce's role as protector of the freed people, Towne found Saxton even more to her liking than Hunter. She described the new general as "very antislavery" and despaired over the lack of other antislavery men on his staff, excepting Capt. Edward Hooper.[26] Similar abolitionist sentiments allowed Towne to cultivate a friendly relationship with General Saxton, making it easier for her to communicate her concerns in the future.

[23]Towne diary, Apr. 17, 1862, PSP. For the role of women in freedmen's teaching, see Jacqueline Jones, "Women Who Were More Than Men: Sex and Status in Freedmen's Teaching," *History of Education Quarterly* 19 (Spring 1979), pp. 47-59.

[24]Towne diary, Apr. 17, 1862. "Contraband" was a term first coined by Gen. Benjamin F. Butler at Fort Monroe, Va., in 1861.

[25]Towne diary, May 12, 1862; Apr. 26, 1863, May 18, June 24, 1862 ("more antislavery").

[26]Ibid., June 29, Sept. 1, 1862.

Regardless of people's antislavery feelings, work remained to be done, and it took Laura Towne only a few weeks to determine the first of her roles. In a letter to her sisters dated April 25, 1862, she wrote, "I have begun my professional career." Apparently T. Edwin Ruggles, a neighboring superintendent, asked her to aid some ailing former slaves, and so she "doctored the half dozen families" on the plantation under his charge.[27] From then on, she found herself reaching out to the plantation people more and more, stretching herself between the dual tasks of medical excursions and distributing goods from Philadelphia. Neighboring northern whites increasingly came to rely on her services as well.

Journeying from plantation to plantation brought Towne into greater contact with the freed people. After just one month she said of herself and other missionaries: "we have got[ten] to calling them [the blacks] *our* people."[28] But such quick identification was not always the case. When she first arrived, she noticed primarily the ex-slaves' dirtiness and poor health, figuring "them about the same as so many Irish."[29] But like many abolitionists, the fear that slavery had permanently defiled African Americans proved unfounded. As the faces of what she initially referred to as the "darkies" came to be associated with names, Towne's diary and letters make it less clear whether the people referred to are black or white. Even more telling, in December 1864 Towne wrote to her family of a dinner she had just shared with two black teachers: "I suppose it would seem strange to you to sit down with two colored people, but to us it is the most natural thing in the world. I actually forget these people are black."[30]

As Towne's understanding of the former slaves improved, so too did her perception of their beliefs and practices. When she attended her first "shout" in 1862 — an African-American religious gathering where blacks danced around in a circle, stamping and singing a chorus — Towne reacted negatively. She thought the shout resembled "the remains of some old idol worship." She said, "I never saw anything so savage."[31] And Towne was not the only white Northerner who found the shout discomfitting. Even Charlotte Forten, a cultured African American raised in a free-black community in Philadelphia, described the shout as a "barbarous expression of religion ... destined to pass away under the influence of Christian

---

[27]L. Towne to her sisters, Apr. 25, 1862, PSP.
[28]L. Towne to Rosie, May 13, 1862, PSP.
[29]Towne diary, Apr. 17, 1862.
[30]L. Towne to Tadie, Dec. 25, 1864, PSP.
[31]L. Towne to her sisters, Apr. 25, 1862, PSP.

teachings."[32] Nonetheless, Towne grew less critical over the years. Not only did she continue to attend such spiritual gatherings, she also began labeling them in her diary as "not so striking" or simply as "a fine shout."[33] After her first year on St. Helena Island, Towne drew up a list of the "Superstitions and Practices" of the freed people in her diary, all negative. However, Towne's respect for traditional African spirituality grew. In 1864 she wrote excitedly about her chance to get to know "Maum Katie," an African woman over one hundred years old who had a "tremendous influence over her spiritual children." Towne described her as "very bright and talkative ... a great 'spiritual mother,'" using only positive connotations. Words like "superstition" disappeared from her writings.[34]

While some of Towne's views changed over the years, one impression that did not change was her abhorrence of violence among the freed people. Whether she believed that their violent behavior directly resulted from the slavery experience is unclear. Regardless, her frequent notes frowning on unrestrained behavior illuminate her ever-present benevolent sensitivities — sensitivities that could only be assuaged and realized, she believed, through the continued education of the freed people. Towne recorded in her diary several occasions when black men beat their wives and children, and one case where a man "nearly killed" an old woman who "hagged him" too much. In another instance, Towne overheard a woman tell her child to get back at another child by taking a brick and walloping the offender's head. Unrestrained behavior also appeared in cruelty to animals. Towne noted with horror an ex-slave "lashing a poor horse furiously ... for no cause whatever," or, even worse, an oxen "flayed, with great skinless welts, and a piece of skin and flesh ... taken out over the tail." For Towne, then, bringing behavior into line through example and education became an imperative.[35]

While the administration of homeopathic aid brought Laura Towne closer to the needs of the freed people, it also brought their physical condition, as a legacy of slavery, before her keen eyes. All the ex-slaves seemed

[32]For other views of shouts, see Pearson, *Letters from Port Royal*, pp. 36, 293; Sherwood, *Journal of Susan Walker*, p. 16; Col. Thomas Wentworth Higginson, *Army Life in a Black Regiment*, edited and abridged by Genevieve S. Gray (New York: Grosset & Dunlap, 1970), p. 15; Arthur Sumner to Lt. Joseph Clark, July 7, 1862, PSP. See also Rose, *Rehearsal for Reconstruction*, pp. 91-93. Charlotte Forten, "Life on the Sea Islands, Part I," *Atlantic Monthly* XIII (May 1864), p. 594.

[33]Towne diary, Aug. 22, 1863, May 28, 1864.

[34]"Superstitions and Practices" from Towne diary, Dec. 31, 1862; Towne to S., Dec. 18, 1864, PSP.

[35]First quotation in L. Towne to Rosie, Nov. 10, 1867, PSP. See also L. Towne to ?, Feb. 15, 1874, and L. Towne to ?, May 29, 1870, PSP. On incident with brick, see Towne diary, Apr. 28, 1862, Apr. 5, 1864. "Lashing" quotation in Towne diary, May 1, 4, 1862.

to be "decidedly unhealthy," with bad hygiene and poor teeth. She re-marked, "What else could be expected on hominy and pork from genera-tion to generation!" In terms of health, the Pennsylvanian claimed that many sea island mothers knew very little about child care, as most had been forced, during slavery, to work in the fields all day. On her excursions among the freed people she also heard tales of a whip with a ball on the end that left a "square welt showing where it had taken the flesh clean out." Towne doc-tored one woman with "ridges as high and long as [her] little finger" across the back who told how four of her babies had been "killed within her by whipping."[36] The Philadelphian would hear many stories about the old slavery days and she would record these diligently in her diary and letters.

The long-anticipated arrival of her close friend Ellen Murray on June 8, 1862, did not bring an end to Towne's homeopathic chores.[37] Although she had looked forward to teaching school with Murray, many other du-ties still required her attention. Therefore, when Murray began instructing black adults ten days after her arrival, Towne continued distributing goods from Philadelphia, aiding the sick, assisting Murray, and otherwise help-ing out around the plantation. In June 1862 she described her typical day as "doing household trifles, at doctoring, at teaching with Ellen, at writing business letters till midnight." Initially, Towne confided in a letter to her sisters that she might be better suited for medicine than teaching. But long nights with the infirm, coupled with the deaths of patients who had trusted her dearly, steadily took their toll.[38] The hectic pace itself, as on August 16, 1862, when she nursed forty-two different people, proved incredibly ex-hausting. At one stretch during the winter of 1864, she found herself wak-ing "every morning about four o'clock and agoniz[ing] over [her] patients." Year after year, small pox, yellow fever, cholera, typhoid fever, whooping cough, and other epidemics swept through the marsh-covered islands at alarming rates. No doctor, regardless of his or her training, could quell the fire. Towne, herself, slowly began to feel overwhelmed and inadequate. Despite reassuring praise from blacks and whites alike, in 1867 she admit-ted she would be "overjoyed" if she could "escape from this part of [her] work," claiming she performed it "badly and very inefficiently." But her medical activities continued, even as her teaching efforts increased.[39]

Towne and Murray began more formal teaching efforts with children

[36]Towne diary, Apr. 28, 1862, Aug. 24, 1863, and May 23, 1862.

[37]Ibid., June 26, 1862. Ellen Murray was born in New Brunswick, Canada, and spent much of her youth in Germany and England. See [no author], [untitled, hand-written document starting "Miss Ellen Murray was born . . ."], Reel 17, PSP.

[38]L. Towne to the Girls, May 5, 1862, PSP. Her realization that others might trust too much in her abilities was most acute following the death of Miss Ruggles. She began to look at her "doctoring" more wearily after this event. See Towne di-ary, Oct. 1, 1863.

[39]Towne diary, Aug. 16, 1862, Jan. 4, 1864; L. Towne to ?, Mar. 3, 1867, PSP.

The Penn School was first housed at the Brick Church on St. Helena. Photo from the Penn School Papers, Southern Historical Collection, University of North Carolina at Chapel Hill.

in early September 1862 — initially as substitutes for another white woman vacationing in the North. Eleven days later, they began their own school in the Brick Church, a Baptist building built shortly before the war. Christened the "Penn School" after William Penn, the school started with forty-one students on September 22.[40] Three days later that number had jumped to seventy-six. By January 1863 the school's enrollment surpassed 150 pupils. However, having so many children in the one-room building made

[40]There seems to be some discrepancy concerning the founding date of the Penn School, depending on what source one uses. Murray, who began teaching shortly after her arrival, uses June 1862 as the starting date. See [Ellen Murray], "The Penn Normal, Industrial, and Agricultural School, St. Helena, S.C.," *Atlanta Seminary*, No. 4 (January 1903). Local historian Edith M. Dabbs, whom several secondary sources use as a reference, claimed the women began their school at the Oaks plantation in early September before moving to the Brick Church when the number of pupils grew too large. Actually, they were only substituting at the Oaks during another woman's "absence" in the North. The secondary works in error (relying on Dabbs) are: Elizabeth Jacoway, *Yankee Missionaries in the South: The Penn School Experiment* (Baton Rouge: Louisiana State University Press, 1980), p. 30, and Francis Harold Jordan, "Across the Bridge: Penn School and Penn Center" (Ph.D. diss., University of South Carolina, 1991), pp. 23-24. Towne, for her part, writes on Sept. 22: "Ellen and I began our school in the Baptist church with forty-one scholars." In an article written shortly before her death, she says that they "opened the Penn School in September 1862, in the Brick Church." See, Towne diary, Sept. 11, 22, 1862; Laura M. Towne, "Pioneer Work on the Sea Islands," *The Southern Workman* 30 (July 1901), pp. 399-400.

teaching difficult. Charlotte Forten joined the staff in October 1862, and later remarked in an article in the *Atlantic Monthly*, "to make one's self heard, when there were often as many as a hundred and forty reciting at once, it was necessary to tax the lungs very severely."[41] Towne managed to refrain from complaining in her diary and letters about school conditions for several years. But by 1864, just before the Penn School's new building was completed, she could hold back no longer:

> How happy we shall be nobody can tell who has not taught in a school where he or she had to make herself heard over three other classes reciting in concert, and to discover talkers and idlers ... while one hundred and fifty more are shouting lessons, and three other teachers bawling admonitions, instructions and reproofs. Generally two or more of the babies are squalling ... [after] five hours foodless on very small and tippy laps [generally, the youths had to bring their tiniest brothers and sisters to school while their parents worked in the fields].[42]

Not only were three classes taught at once, the teachers also had no blackboards to assist them — a significant shortcoming when instructing children who had never been allowed to attend school before.

Meanwhile, Towne continued to serve the medical needs of the five neighboring plantations. Aside from everyday illnesses, she and Ellen Murray often took turns sitting up all night beside some of the critically ill white Northerners. Sometimes Towne traded shifts with other healthy Gideonites. Her diaries contain several references to assisting with a patient until morning, and then, on her way home, stopping to teach school, perhaps followed by even more medical errands. Charlotte Forten said of Towne, "She is housekeeper, physician, everything, here. The most indispensable person on the place, and the people are devoted to her." Towne's duties lightened only slightly in October 1862 when Pennsylvania's Port Royal Relief Committee finally realized how severely she was taxing herself, and relieved her of what, at that point, was her most onerous duty,

---

[41]Towne diary, Sept. 22, 25, 1862, Jan. 12, 1863; Forten, "Life on the Sea Islands, Part I," p. 592.

[42]L. Towne to Rosie, Dec. 18, 1864, PSP. See also, Towne diary, Mar. 25, 1864. For another description of the school setting, see Towne, "Pioneer Work," p. 400.

distributing goods from Philadelphia.[43]

Although her store duties came to an end, her involvement in the daily business affairs of the school intensified. As head of the Penn School, she kept up a flurry of correspondence, informing the school's benefactors of its accomplishments. When James Miller McKim, the leader and most influential member of the Port Royal Relief Committee, visited, he joked with her that he "wish[ed] he could have five minutes' conversation ... without [her] plunging into business."[44] But for Towne there was so much business to take care of. Fortunately, she had developed a knack for administration. She was seemingly involved in everything. Soldiers at the wharf in Beaufort, after seeing repeated shiploads of molasses, herring, hogsheads of pork, and other large boxes arrive for "L. Towne," initially assumed they were intended for a man. When they found out that Towne was a female, the officers later admitted they had expected "a tall, rawboned woman, sitting on a hogshead of molasses." They must have been surprised to see a brown-haired woman with a "sweet voice" of less than average height.[45]

DESPITE HER DRAINING SCHEDULE, LAURA TOWNE maintained a positive outlook that won her much respect and countless friendships. Charlotte Forten, who referred to her as "my good Miss Towne," said of her, "It always does me good just to see her bright, cheerful face." From the first, Towne befriended Edward Pierce, commissioned by Secretary Chase to observe freedmen's affairs. Although Pierce resided with Towne and the others on the Oaks plantation for only a few months, the two built a friendship that eventually spanned a lifetime of correspondence. In July 1862 Towne made use of her standing with him in a last-ditch effort to convince Pierce against "giving up his good work," but he admitted he could not continue "to do work that did not and never would pay." He could not afford to mirror Towne's ideal of volunteer work with-

---

[43]Towne diary, Sept. 1, 24, 1863; Billington, *Journal of Charlotte Forten*, p. 146; James Miller McKim to L. Towne, October 2, 1862, PSP. Research conducted on this article has revealed some significant new information about the life of Forten. The two previous compilers, Billington and Stevenson, in biographical chapters on Forten, were vague on her activities in the decade after she supposedly left the sea islands. Stevenson notes Forten wanted to return to teaching in the sea islands, but poor health kept her away. However, Towne casually mentions several visits by Forten in 1868, 1869, and 1872, as if her visits were among the usual paid by neighboring missionaries. See L. Towne to ?, April 12, 1868; L. Towne to ?, Apr. 11, 1869; and L. Towne to ?, Apr. 14, 1872, PSP.

[44]Towne diary, June 21, 1862.

[45]A tall, rawboned ..." from Towne diary, Feb. 27, 1863; "sweet voice" and height description from [nephew or niece], "Extracts," p. 1. Charlotte Forten initially mistook Towne to be in her early twenties when she was really thirty-seven. Billington, *Journal of Charlotte Forten*, p. 146.

out compensation; his law practice in Boston had languished in his absence. Over the years, however, he would return many times to visit her. In the meantime, other men would take Pierce's place in the Oaks household, the foremost being Capt. Edward Hooper, a member of General Saxton's staff and formerly the treasurer of Harvard. In their nightly conversations about antislavery, the fate of the freed people, and the war raging around them, Towne developed a close bond with him.[46]

Throughout the war, Towne came into contact with several important Northerners. Because of their shared anti-slavery sentiments, she struck up a friendship with Thomas Wentworth Higginson, a fellow Unitarian and colonel of the First South Carolina Volunteers, Colored.[47] She also got to know Gen. David Hunter, Reuben Tomlinson, Sam Phillips, the controversial Col. James Montgomery, Gen. Oliver Otis Howard, and, briefly, Col. Robert Gould Shaw, commander of the 54th Massachusetts.[48] But above all, she befriended Gen. Rufus Saxton, the military governor, who became one of her most significant acquaintances. She called him "one of our best and truest hearted men." He paid repeated visits to her residence over the years and engaged her in discussions over matters both public and private. Saxton proved to be one of her staunchest supporters when the elders of the Brick Church began to complain about the Penn School using their building for all its functions. Saxton promised that no one would move her while he remained in command. More importantly, when the general despaired over the prospect of land sales set for February 1863 — sales that would favor "greedy speculators" and nullify any hope of preemption by the freed people — Towne recommended that he have General Hunter put a halt to it. She wrote, "Saxton caught at the idea," and the next day, "the sales [were] stopped as a military necessity."[49]

Although Towne cultivated many positive acquaintances, her diary

[46]Billington, *Journal of Charlotte Forten*, p. 176. Forten had even better rapport with the affable Ellen Murray than with Towne. Towne diary, July 2, 1862. On Hopper, see L. Towne to Tadie, Rosie, and Kitty, Aug. 26, 1862, PSP; Towne diary, Oct. 10, 16, 1862, Sept. 8, 1863.

[47]Towne diary, Oct. 24, 1863.

[48]Tomlinson went from his post as general superintendent to inspector general of freedmen's affairs in Beaufort. After the war, he spent time as state attorney general, and in 1872 ran for governor on a reform platform. Phillips was nephew of the well-known Bostonian, Wendell Phillips. Montgomery served as colonel of the black Second South Carolina Volunteers, and was a former lieutenant of John Brown. Howard became commissioner of the Freedmen's Bureau after the war. Under Shaw, the 54th trained on the sea islands before its storied assault on Fort Walker.

[49]L. Towne to Rosie; Feb. 7, 1864, PSP; Gen. Rufus Saxton to L. Towne, Oct. 26, 1863, PSP; Towne diary, Feb. 1, 1863. See also Rose, *Rehearsal for Reconstruction*, pp. 202-203, 207, 211-212. Towne was also instrumental in convincing others to arm black laborers in case of Confederate invasion. See Towne diary, July 4, 1862.

and letters show no evidence of courtship or even minor love affairs. If she had significant feelings for either Captain Hooper or General Saxton, she hardly let it show in her writings. And when both men married, she never displayed a hint of jealousy toward their new wives. On one occasion, when a black woman asked Towne what she should name her child, the Pennsylvanian recommended "Matilda Saxton," in honor of the general's wife.[50] Significantly, Towne referred to love in her diary as a "psychological phenomenon." Indeed, she never seemed to long for the affections of a man; by 1868 she believed the only reason to consider having a member of the opposite sex residing on the premises was to bring in wood for the fire and take care of the horses and corn. A man was seen only as a utility.[51] Towne's school came first. Perhaps she realized that if she gave in to a man's affections, she might also have to give up what had become her life's work. Her labors among the freed people gave her a sense of meaning, direction, and importance that she had never experienced before, allowing her to realize the Unitarian goals of perfecting morality and human goodness. Not even frequent pangs of homesickness for her friends and family in Pennsylvania proved strong enough to draw her away.

Towne's friendship with the Canadian-born Ellen Murray obviously afforded her the most comfort. To have another like-minded woman around whom she could count on made difficult times less trying. Even though Murray was a Baptist, the two friends tended to view most issues from the same perspective. Murray served as a teammate and confidante. She loved and spoke dearly of Murray, much as she did her sisters, in a manner not uncommon in the nineteenth century. Otherwise, Towne spent most of her free time on her own, gardening — in which she took great pleasure — or accompanied by her dogs on walks through the woods or bathing in the tides.[52]

Certainly, although most of Towne's dealings with other people were pleasant, different motivations and contrasting goals brought her to odds with some northern philanthropists. For instance, James Thompson, a superintendent at Fripp's plantation, especially incited Towne's ire when he

[50]L. Towne to ?, Feb. 10, 1867, PSP. To honor her old friend, she also named her new colt "Saxton." Towne wrote that Ellen Murray also received "namesake upon namesake" among black children. If any of the ex-slaves named their children "Laura" she was perhaps too humble to admit it. See L. Towne to ?, Nov. 1, 1868, PSP.

[51]Towne diary, Sept. 8, 1862; L. Towne to ?, Jan. 24, 1868, PSP.

[52]L. Towne to ?, Sept. 30, 1869; L. Towne to S., Mar. 12, 1870; L. Towne to ?, June 7, 1874, PSP. See also Carroll Smith-Rosenberg, "The Female World of Love and Ritual: Relations between Women in Nineteenth-Century America," *Signs* 1 (1975), pp. 1-29; Lillian Faderman, *Surpassing the Love of Men: Romantic Friendship and Love between Women from the Renaissance to the Present* (New York: William Morrow, 1981), pp. 145-189.

"talked so boastingly" of the need to maintain order among the ex-slaves by resorting to the whip. Towne thought "he ought never to have come and ought to go home." Another incident arose after superintendent Josiah Fairfield moved into the Oaks plantation with Towne and the rest after marrying Nelly Winsor. Fairfield's brash, forceful style in dealing with the freed people contrasted greatly with Towne's more sympathetic, idealistic actions. As the relationship with Josiah and Nelly Fairfield soured, Towne and Murray decided to move to a new home in St. Helenaville at the beginning of 1864, even though that meant a longer walk to school.[53]

Towne also had her differences with Edward S. Philbrick, a Bostonian who had come south to prove that free labor was more profitable than slave labor. Although she maintained an amicable relationship with him, she came to doubt the depth of his philanthropy. When the issue of possible land sales had everyone talking, Philbrick's belief that the blacks were not ready to own land disappointed Towne. Although she tried to dissuade him, Philbrick insisted it was in the freed people's best interests if he bought up several of the plantations and sold the land to them later when the time was right. Of Philbrick, Towne remarked, "who can convince people against their pockets." Later, in 1864, when Philbrick continued to hold onto the land he had promised to sell, he claimed, at this point in the free labor experiment, it would "not be well for them [the ex-slaves] ... to make money so fast on their cotton." Towne, in turn, "wonder[ed] whether it [was] good for him to be getting rich so fast?"[54]

As the war years dragged on and Towne continued to teach and care for the freed people, other changes occurred in her midst. Towne, Murray, and the African-American household servants they had befriended made several moves, first from Pope's to the Oaks plantation, then to St. Helenaville, and finally to Frogmore where they would spend the rest of their lives. Early on, her brother, William Towne, also came to St. Helena Island and temporarily worked with both the superintendents and the former slaves. He would return to the sea islands off and on throughout the 1860s and 1870s. Also, early in 1863, Ellen Murray's sister, Harriet, and her mother arrived to reside on a plantation nearby. Harriet Murray quickly joined Ellen and Laura Towne as teachers at the Penn School. The school itself underwent changes as well. When the elders of the Brick Church grew uncomfortable with an independent school on the premises, the Pennsylvania Freedmen's Relief Association purchased a three-room, prefabricated school house and had it shipped in sections to the sea islands. With this

[53]Towne diary, Oct. 7, 1862. Thompson's sister, Matilda, later married General Saxton. Towne diary, Apr. 28, June 21, 1863, Jan. 7, 1864.
[54]Towne diary, Feb. 4, 1863, May 28, 1864.

new building, the days of shouting above 150 students came to an end in early 1865.[55]

THE YEAR 1865 BROUGHT MORE THAN JUST A CHANGE OF school houses. In January U.S. Gen. William Tecumseh Sherman's troops — after taking Savannah, Georgia — passed through Beaufort. In the wake of Sherman's army came more than 1,000 African-American refugees who had fled their plantations and followed Sherman throughout Georgia. Seeking food, clothing, and protection, many of these weary refugees set up camp in St. Helenaville. Laura Towne immediately set to work tending the sick, yet disease and death took a heavy toll. Towne encountered one mother who had tied her twelve children to her in order not to lose them during the 100-mile trek.[56]

In late January Sherman's army marched from Beaufort and on to Columbia. After several more months, in April 1865, Gen. Robert E. Lee reluctantly accepted defeat and surrendered his army. Shortly thereafter, the war came to an end. Jubilant, Towne and several other Northerners traveled from the sea islands to Charleston to view the devastation and attend the re-raising of the flag at Fort Sumter on April 14. When Towne returned to the sea islands a few days later, she was crestfallen to learn of Lincoln's assassination. She was most angry that white Southerners would never "have to submit to the man they vowed they would never surrender to." According to Towne, the neighboring blacks at first reacted in disbelief, then fell into despondency. One black man told her, "I have lost a friend.... They call him Sam, ... Uncle Sam." Another wanted to know whether the "Government was dead." Many of the freed people had long associated Lincoln with biblical analogies. He was their "Moses," "their spiritual father." And like Moses, the president would not accompany them to the promised land. Another ex-slave told Towne, "Lincoln died for we, Christ died for we and me believe him de same mans."[57]

As the country looked toward redefinition, Towne and Murray's school continued to progress. By mid-1865 the Penn School had essentially become a high school. In a letter to her sister, Towne wrote, "The children have read through a history of the United States and an easy physiology and they know all the parts of speech.... Ellen's class is writing composi-

[55]In October 1863 the Port Royal Relief Committee officially became the Pennsylvania Freedmen's Relief Association to broaden its scope. See Benjamin P. Hunt to L. Towne, Nov. 2, 1863, PSP. For the Murrays' arrival, see Towne diary, Nov. 9, 1863. For purchase of the school house, see James Miller McKim to L. Towne, Apr. 29, 1864 , PSP.

[56]Rose, *Rehearsal for Reconstruction*, pp. 319-323; Harriet Ware to ?, Jan. 6, 1865, in Pearson, *Letters from Port Royal*, pp. 293-294; L. Towne to the Girls, Jan. 8, 1865, PSP.

[57]L. Towne to Sophy, Apr. 23, 1865; L. Towne to ?, Apr. 29, 1865, PSP.

tions." Indeed, as the years passed, the Penn School became the most advanced on the islands, with Murray directing the highest grade levels, while Towne taught and conducted business. In the meantime, Fanny Murray, another of Ellen's sisters, came to replace Harriet, who had married and returned north. In addition, former students slowly assumed the role of assistant teachers. Although the cast of teachers kept changing, enrollment grew toward 200 pupils. By the 1870s Towne and Murray were forced to turn away all but the most promising students.[58]

As the war came to a close, Towne watched as a handful of whites returned to the sea islands. Unlike the mainland, most of the island plantations had been broken up and sold to either northern superintendents or black workers because of "unpaid taxes." Soon former planters filed suits to reclaim lost lands. Although only a few whites came back, Towne could sense their greater presence on mainland South Carolina. However, by 1867 the "uppish" whites on the islands, mainly native Southerners, decided to have a church of their own, separate from the blacks. Towne labeled it a "snobbish affair," yet was determined to attend both churches, "wishing to have [her] eyes open as to all that [was] going on."[59]

During the late 1860s the political climate, never favorable toward progressive reforms for the freed people, grew even colder. As a result, many of the northern teachers scattered across the islands began returning home. In 1867 Towne herself started feeling less "encouragement" from the Pennsylvania Freedmen's Relief Association (PFRA) as interest seemed to wane over the fate of former slaves. The Penn School had existed solely on charity, and, as funds fell, attendance and the need for money increased.[60]

In 1871 the PFRA folded, leaving the monetary needs of the Penn School to one of its auxiliaries, the Benezet Association, sponsored by the Society of Friends. Initially, the Benezet only agreed to sponsor the Penn School "for at least one year."[61] But Towne and Murray succeeded in keeping the agreement alive by refusing their yearly salaries when funds grew short — a sacrifice that allowed their relationship with the Benezet to continue well into the 1890s. After Towne's brother Henry died in 1875, money left in his will also helped provide for the school during the years when the Benezet funds were most lean. When Henry's money ran out, and the scarcity of support again threatened to close the school, timely donations by friends

[58]L. Towne to Rosie, June 13, 1865; L. Towne to Francis R. Cope, Apr. 9, 1873, PSP. The Penn School had to turn down about 200 applicants in 1877; see L. Towne to Cope Brothers, Nov. 12, 1877, PSP.

[59]L. Towne to Rosie, Aug. 3, 1865; L. Towne to ?, Mar. 3, 1867; L. Towne to L., Mar. 27 1867, PSP.

[60]L. Towne to ?, Mar. 3, 1867; L. Towne to ?, May 29, 1870; L. Towne to Francis R. Cope, Apr. 9, 1873, PSP.

[61]L. Towne to ?, July 6, 1871, PSP. The Ladies' Branch of the PFRA existed one additional year. See Mary Rose Smith to Francis R. Cope, June 3, 1872, PSP.

and family repeatedly kept it alive. To control costs, Towne spent weeks mending old, nearly worn-out schoolbooks, occasionally using "nearly a hundred patches in one book."[62]

During the 1870s, when funds were most slim, the Pennsylvanian could have turned the school over to South Carolina and received state aid. But Towne dreaded what might become of her school in southern hands; she knew that she and Murray might soon become unwanted. Besides, she was well aware of the conditions of the state schools — she had been appointed superintendent of schools for the sea islands and served from 1865 through most of the 1870s. She had seen how funding had appeared in sporadic, insufficient amounts for black schools, shrinking the academic year, in some cases, to three months. Such schools often had "no books, slates, maps, blackboard, etc." Furthermore, these schools' adherence to "the constant use of great strong switches or a leather strap" appalled her. Therefore, Towne contented herself with independence, thankful that the islanders had agreed to pay a tax to support their schools. In the meantime, as the Pennsylvanian waited for South Carolina to reform its educational standards, in the early 1870s the state inquired as to the possibility of former Penn School students joining the teaching staffs of other regional black schools. Henceforth, the Penn School became a fertile recruiting ground for black teachers.[63]

THE RECONSTRUCTION ERA BROUGHT OTHER CHANGES ASIDE from decreasing school funds. The right for African-American males to vote resulted in all kinds of questions and controversies among both supporters and opponents alike. On the sea islands, Towne witnessed an early black Republican meeting where the question about the presence of women at such gatherings first cropped up. Exhorted by outsiders to recognize the women's sphere, the men decided that "the women should stay at home and cut grass." Viewing this, Towne noted that black women had been held in higher esteem during slavery days — they had worked equally in the fields alongside the men, yet "it was the woman's house, the children were entirely hers, etc., etc." But the right to vote had given the men legal superiority and "inflat[ed] the conceit of the males to an amazing degree." She contended, however, that this change would only be temporary, and

[62]L. Towne to Francis Cope, June 9, 1875; L. Towne to ?, Sept. 18, 1877; L. Towne to ?, Sept. 27, 1874, PSP.

[63]L. Towne to G., Mar. 3, 1865; L. Towne to Francis Cope, Dec. 1, 1872; L. Towne to F. Cope, Nov. 13, 1873; L. Towne to F. Cope, Apr. 11, 1874; L. Towne to F. Cope, Feb. 6, 1875, PSP. Blacks began to demand black teachers because white teachers of black schools were often those not good enough for the white schools. See Howard N. Rabinowitz, "Half a Loaf: The Shift from White to Black Teachers in the Negro Schools of the Urban South, 1865-1890," *Journal of Southern History* 40 (1974), pp. 565-594.

"[w]hen women got the vote too" it would be as difficult for black men to accept as for whites. (Notably, she wrote "when," not "if.")[64] In the meantime, women on the islands learned other modes of association and empowerment. Beginning about 1870, Laura Towne and Ellen Murray started a temperance organization called the "St. Helena Band of Hope," which held "regular meetings every fortnight." Murray served as president and Towne as one of the vice presidents. Before long, the youths at the Penn School began learning temperance songs and temperance skits to promote the cause and to educate them against alcohol.[65]

During the late 1870s the right to vote for black males had become a precarious privilege. White Southerners grew more obstinate, and political oppression more sanctified. In 1876 in Beaufort County, when intimidation and threats proved not enough, South Carolina Democrats printed trick ballots for "Union Republicans" that omitted presidential candidates and substituted Wade Hampton, a Democrat, for the Republican gubernatorial candidate. The result? As Towne said, "so many voted for Wade Hampton without knowing it, and for *no* President, thus giving a negative for [Rutherford B.] Hayes."[66] Hampton won his election, while the presidential race between Hayes and Samuel J. Tilden fell into dispute with fraud evident on both sides. Tilden won both the popular and electoral votes, but received one short of the minimum in the electoral college needed to carry the election. A special congressional commission decided on the Republican, Hayes, for president, on the condition that all northern troops would pull out of the South, essentially bringing an end to Reconstruction.[67] Throughout the dispute, Towne observed how white Southerners clamored ominously to "get rid of the northerner" and make "the negro landless." Pointing to Hampton's anti-black rhetoric, his slander of black and white Republicans alike, and his demand to have every Republican expelled until they could "prove their titles in court," Towne claimed one could hear "Hampton's slave-whip cracking" in South Carolina. Furthermore, given President Hayes's acquiescence to white southern injustices, Towne began to wonder if "another [James] Buchanan [sat] in the President's chair."[68]

[64]L. Towne to Tadie, June 1, 1867, PSP.

[65]L. Towne to ?, Feb. 20, 1870; L. Towne to ?, May 29, 1870; L. Towne to Lu, June 22, 1879, PSP.

[66]L. Towne to ?, Nov. 8, 1876, PSP.

[67]For Hampton's campaign, see Joel Williamson, *After Slavery: The Negro in South Carolina During Reconstruction, 1861–1877* (Chapel Hill: University of North Carolina Press, 1965), pp. 405-412. For the presidential crisis, see Eric Foner, *Reconstruction: America's Unfinished Revolution, 1863–1877* (New York: Harper and Row, 1988), pp. 575-587.

[68]L. Towne to Rosie, May 6, 1877; L. Towne to Tadie, Apr. 19, 1877; L. Towne to Tadie, Apr. 15, 1877, PSP.

In the meantime, Towne learned much about the corruption of state politics from a new acquaintance, the former slave Robert Smalls. Catapulted to fame during the Civil War when he stole the Confederate steamer, *Planter*, and delivered it into Union hands in Charleston harbor, Smalls had served as a black representative in South Carolina's state congress. His tenure had ended in the fraudulent, politically charged election of 1878, and Towne filled her letters home with stories of the oppression he had faced. In turn, Smalls illustrated his respect for Towne when he brought a member of the British Parliament, on a "tour of inspection," to lunch with her in 1878.[69]

The southern Democratic resurgence of 1877 left many northern teachers disenchanted, and soon most moved away from the South for good. Yet Towne was determined to stay put. Moreover, she could not keep silent. She remarked, "I am not in a frame for ... peaceful repose. I want to agitate, even as I am agitated." Therefore, after the new state legislature passed a law forbidding districts to levy school taxes — prohibiting what had been one of her school's few sources of income — Towne drew up several resolutions and had Sam Green, a local senator, present them at the district school meeting. The resolutions exempted St. Helena from the new law because all the citizens were tax payers and because even the parents of the seven white children — among the 1,280 total school-age children — favored levying the tax. The resolution "passed unanimously" and Towne hoped that newspaper coverage would "show not only the injustices done in forbidding people's providing for the public schools, ... but also that the St. Helena folks [were] awake to their rights." Five newspapers, both North and South, published the resolution; all lauded St. Helena's actions, yet they also refused to denounce the law that had inspired it.[70]

Nevertheless, other actions by the new state legislature, as well as by local whites, further sparked her ire. Starting in 1877, failure to pay the poll tax in South Carolina — a law targeting blacks — could henceforth result in imprisonment. And once imprisoned, the convict lease program went into effect, under which an African-American male could be "put into the penitentiary and sold out ... as a slave for the time of his sentence."[71] Just

[69][French], *The Trip of the Steamer Oceanus*, pp. 85-86; L. Towne to ?, Oct. 7, 1877; L. Towne to ?, Nov. 6, 1878; L. Towne to ?, Nov. 17, 1878, PSP. See also Williamson, *After Slavery*, pp. 377, 416. For a recent biography on Smalls, see Edward A. Miller, Jr., *Gullah Statesman: Robert Smalls from Slavery to Congress* (Columbia: University of South Carolina Press, 1995).

[70]L. Towne to Lu, Aug. 19, 1877; L. Towne to Rosie, June 17, 1877; L. Towne to ?, July 15, 1877, PSP.

[71]L. Towne to Lu, Aug. 19, 1877, PSP; Foner, *Reconstruction*, p. 594. For a comparison between the convict leasing programs of North and South Carolina, see Matthew J. Mancini, *One Dies, Get Another: Convict Leasing in the American South 1866–1928* (Columbia: University of South Carolina Press, 1996), pp. 198-212.

as bad to Towne, the *Beaufort Tribune* reported that a local black man —
charged but not convicted of hog-stealing — had been whipped by a group
of whites, "so saving the expense of a trial." Such justifications disgusted
Towne. Furthermore, Republican county commissioners were arrested in
1878 because of alleged poor road and bridge conditions and forced to resign, yielding their positions to Democrats. Henceforth, three Democrats
would control an office, where in the last election, only nine of the 918
votes had been cast by Democrats. With such reversals, black sea islanders
who had owned land for the past fifteen years stood to lose everything, as
new lawsuits were destined to pass through corrupted courts. In all, such
flagrant abuses and negations of freedoms signaled for Towne a return of
"slavery times."[72]

Southern outrages, coupled with northern apathy, enraged the former
Pennsylvanian. She filled her letters home with angry words and remon-
strations. Yet she noted that not one of her family members in the North
made even the slightest comment about her published resolutions. Even
the Benezet had not been shaken by her accounts and still felt "much confidence in Hayes." Yet this lack of support did not stymie Towne's desire to
"agitate." In August 1877 a friend sent one of her fiery letters about anti-
school legislation to *The Nation,* where it was subsequently published.
Towne proudly noted that the *Boston Journal* and the *New York Tribune* made
additional remarks about it. Inspired, Towne dashed off another letter to
the *New York Tribune,* this time about the convict lease program, but she
never heard anything. Later she figured that her editorial was "too 'partisan'" for a paper that was such "an ardent justifier of Hayes."[73]

ALTHOUGH THE WORLD AROUND HER UNDERWENT MANY
shifts, one aspect of Laura Towne did not change. She generally stood her
ground against prejudice directed toward African Americans. While others of abolitionist heritage lost interest, Towne persisted in her support.[74]
Sometimes this meant confrontation. One time in 1868, while returning
from the North, Towne and a group of Northerners had to spend the night
in Florence, South Carolina. But the only hotel there was run by a former
Confederate prison keeper. Therefore, Towne and her companions refused
to pay a cent for room and board, desiring only to recline in the sitting

[72]L. Towne to Lu, Aug. 19, 1877; L. Towne to ?, Nov. 6, 1878; L. Towne to ?, Nov. 10, 1878, PSP.

[73]L. Towne to Lu, Aug. 19, 1877; Hannah B. Evans to L. Towne, Jan. 25, 1878; L. Towne to Rosie, Sept. 9, 1877, PSP; C., "South Carolina Anti-School Legislation," *The Nation* 2 (August 1877), pp. 70-71.

[74]For background on others who tried to transform their abolitionist ideals into reality — some less successful than others — see James M. McPherson, *The Aboli-tionist Legacy: From Reconstruction to the NAACP* (Princeton, N.J.: Princeton University Press, 1975), pp. 143-160.

room. Towne got in a tiff with the clerk and lectured him about what Union soldiers had endured "at the hands of the proprietor." She said the clerk "looked enraged, but like all Southerners, was cowed by a bold word straight at him." And Towne was not afraid to use bold words or take a stand. Once when confronted by two different carriage drivers in Charleston, one white and one black, the white warned her not to listen to the "nigger" with the "dirty old coach." She admitted later she "was mad enough to slap his face, but ... just said, 'I would believe him just as soon as you,'" and defiantly stepped into the carriage of the African American, which brought a roar of laughter from black onlookers. Later in 1884 a train conductor struck up a conversation with her, saying that he thought "the whole race of niggers ought to be swept away." Towne wrote, "I told him my business was with that race and that they would never be swept away, so he was disgusted and went away leaving me to read in peace."[75]

Public confrontations with racism continually tried her determination, yet she continued to administer the school to the end of her days. In 1900, the year before her death, she laid plans to have her school continue beyond her lifetime by inviting a representative of the Hampton Institute of Virginia, Hollis Burke Frissell, to visit the school. The Hampton Institute was a black industrial school striving to attain Booker T. Washington's vision of self-improvement and political standing by avoiding agitation.[76] Frissell liked what he saw at St. Helena — an island community virtually isolated from mainland oppressions — and so, with his recommendation, the Penn School became an auxiliary of the Hampton Institute, an extension of an experiment in black industrial education. With Towne's death in 1901, Ellen Murray assumed the role of principal. Murray spent her remaining years thwarting aspects of the school's new industrial orientation, one that differed markedly from hers and the original vision she shared with Laura Towne. After Murray's death in 1908, the recently christened "Penn Normal and Industrial School" marched to a different drummer down a different path.[77]

ENDURING THE HARDSHIPS OF THE CIVIL WAR, AND, LATER, the trials of the Reconstruction era, Towne labored diligently amongst the freed people of South Carolina's sea islands. Her voluminous diary and

[75]L. Towne to the Girls, Oct. 17, 1868; L. Towne to Homefolks, July 9, 1884, PSP.

[76]For a discussion of the transition to black vocational schools, see McPherson, *The Abolitionist Legacy*, pp. 203-223; Edward L. Ayers, *The Promise of the New South: Life After Reconstruction* (New York: Oxford University Press, 1992), pp. 322-323.

[77]Henry Wilder Foote, *The Penn School on St. Helena Island* (Hampton, Va.: Hampton Institute Press, 1904), pp. 10-11. Both Jacoway and Jordan detail the transition to the Penn Normal School before delving into the twentieth-century program; see, Jordan, "Across the Bridge," pp. 37-48; Jacoway, *Yankee Missionaries in the South*, pp. 32-38, 48-49.

letters contain much about the age through which she lived. Through homeopathic medicine and teaching, she came into direct contact with the
former slaves and learned to empathize with their concerns. But this took
time. At first, the depth of abolitionism in her fellow missionaries occupied her thinking. Yet she managed to transform her sentiments into genuine concern for the plight of African Americans. While her perceptions and
ability to understand the freed people improved over the years, her northern sensibilities kept their education directed toward dual goals of self-
sufficiency and moral living, relying on reading, writing, and arithmetic as
a measure of progress. A fellow teacher claimed, "Miss Towne always said,
'The best teacher is the one who teaches the pupils to love learning and
love goodness, whatever else is omitted.'" And considering the positive
response of her pupils, she may well have been one of those "best teachers." Regardless, her willingness to voice her concerns, coupled with her
deft business skills, allowed her to steer the Penn School through troubled
waters. So doing, she lived out her final days on St. Helena Island. Appropriately, Edward Pierce called her "the best illustration of permanence and
perseverance" he had ever known.[78]

Today, the Penn School Historic District stretches beneath many of the
same oaks, draped with Spanish moss, that graced the landscape more than
a century earlier. Next to the old buildings, a marker stands in memory of
Laura Towne and Ellen Murray. Close to where the old school once stood,
a stone tablet — weathered and shaded with moss — stands in the former
Pennsylvanian's memory. Carved by one of her brothers, it reads:

> IN MEMORY OF LAURA M. TOWNE, 1825-1901
> She devoted thirty-eight years of her life to the
> colored people of St. Helena Island and employed her
> means in their education and care.[79]

Considering all her activities, these words say so little, and yet mean so
much.

[78][Unknown], [Untitled document,] [n.d.], 19, Reel 27, PSP; Edward L. Pierce
to L. Towne, Apr. 19, 1868, PSP.
[79]Holland, *Letters and Diary of Laura M. Towne*, p. v.

THE SIEGE OF CHARLESTON:
"WATER WAS SCARCER THAN WHISKEY"

THE CONFEDERATE DIARY OF WILLIAM JOHN GRAYSON

Edited by

Elmer L. Puryear

College of Charleston

Like many Southerners of his day William John Grayson was something of a paradox. Educated in the classical tradition, he felt that his bachelor of arts degree from the University of South Carolina did not prepare him for "any definite or useful employment." While critical of the clergy, he became an assistant to a Baptist minister who was president of Beaufort College. In 1822 he began the practice of law, but soon found doubts about the ethics of his own profession. "Right, justice, truth," he remarked, "are secondary considerations or rather no considerations at all." He belonged to the Nullification Party, but he was opposed to the extreme measures adopted by the Nullificationists. An ardent defender of slavery, he consistently opposed secession. He had no illusions about the seriouness of a conflict between North and South, and he regarded the leaders of secession as demagogues motivated by selfish ambitions and blind to the consequences of their own actions. His proslavery sentiments made him a strong advocate of the Union, because he was convinced, like James L. Petigru, "that war, anarchy, military despotism, would inevitably follow a dissolution of the Union; that secession would impart to the Abolition Party a power over slavery that nothing else could give them—a power to make war on Southern institutions, to proclaim freedom to the Negro. . . ."

Born in Beaufort, South Carolina, in 1788, the son of an officer in the American Revolution, William J. Grayson had a long career of political service to the state. He served in both houses of the South Carolina legislature and for two terms in the House of Representatives in Washington. In 1841 he was appointed collector of customs in Charleston, occupying this post for almost twelve years. Like many other South Carolinians, he terminated a prosperous career with plantation ownership: in 1855 he bought "Fair Lawn" near Charleston.

While Grayson had an active political career, it was for his literary activity that he was most famous. He began writing verse while he was in college, but it was not until he was about sixty-five that he began seriously to write poetry. He published three volumes of poetry: *The Country, Chicora and Other Poems,* and *The Hireling and the Slave.* This latter volume was written in answer to *Uncle Tom's Cabin* and defended slavery on the grounds that the lot of the slave was better than that of the hired wage earner. During the War he wrote the *Life of James L. Petigru* and an *Autobiography.*

In the last period of his life Grayson kept the following brief "Diary" which in the true sense of the word is not a diary. It is rather a commentary

The South Carolina Historical Magazine 63: 137-149

on the events and personages of the War viewed through the eyes of an elderly Southern gentleman who had old-fashiond tastes and great love for the South. The "Diary" is valuable chiefly because it was written by a Southern moderate, whose vision was not clouded by prejudice. Grayson was a cultivated individual with the ability to view events with a rational mind and to express his opinions strongly but clearly.

The editor would like to thank Dr. Robert D. Bass for a typewritten copy of the "Diary." The original is in possession of the South Caroliniana Library, which has generously given its permission for publication. Since the journal covers such a short period, May through November of 1862, it is likely fragmentary.

May 10th [1862]. The battle of Shiloh is announced today in the papers. It was a brilliant victory on the first day. On the second, the victory faded away into a drawn battle and many of its fruits were lost to the Confederates. The plunder of the Federal camp disorganized the victors for a time and arrested the progress of their arms. The stores of good cheer were abundant; the Confederates were hungry and thirsty. They turned from fighting to plundering and sacrificed their laurels in some measure to the indulgence of their appetites. They drank and fought with equal vigour but with different results. It is not the first time that a Southern army has suffered a victory to be turned into a drawn battle from the same cause. At the battle of Eutaw in 1782 the American army drove the enemy from the field of battle to their camp and beyond their camp. Every tent in the camp was provided with a table on which good liquor and food were set out ready for the refreshment of the British troops. The victorious onset was arrested at the tables. The Americans charged the dishes and bottles with great success but in the meantime their opponents rallied, returned to the fight and compelled Greene to retire from the field and postpone the half won victory to a future occasion. The honours of the first day at the battle of Shiloh are due to Johnston although it devolved on Beauregard to announce the victory. Johnston was killed at the close of the day. At his death from the insubordination of the troops or the prudence of his successors in command the fortunes of the day were checked and changed.

12th May. The price of everything grows apace. I gave ten dollars today for a bushel of salt at Bennell's mill. Bacon sells for 45 cents a pound, butter for 75 or 80, lamb for 37½, tea for six dollars, coffee for 75 cents. Every article of clothing is of double, triple, or quadruple prices. But we still have old clothes to wear and something to eat. We are not yet reduced to rats and horse flesh. Fat mules go about the streets unmolested. We have not approached the privations which others have suffered in defense of their liberties and nobody complains of the small sacrifices they have been obliged to make.

May 13th. Our troops have evacuated Cole's island and Battery island at the mouth of Stono river. This is another example of weakness and vacillation in our military rulers; one erects a fortification at enormous expense and another destroys it. Our waggon has a team hitched to each end and they draw in opposite directions—what will become of the waggon? We held the batteries during winter and Spring and at the beginning of the sickly season the troops are removed to places subject to malaria—to the worst enemy they can encounter. Country fever is more deadly than bullet or bayonet.

May 14th. The negro crew ran away today with the Steamer, Planter, and carried her to the enemy.[1] They went off from under the nose of the General's Headquarters, within sight of the guard. The Capt and other officers had gone to their several homes and were quietly in bed. Nobody was left on board but negroes; no guard was provided although idle soldiers filled the streets and the boat was engaged in transporting military stores and cannon, five or six of which were on board. The blacks put up the private signals and passed all the forts without question. A few hours after this event, as if to go from extreme laxity to extreme rigidity, the authorities declared martial law. It has made no change except to annoy the citizens. From no precaution at all we have rushed into every sort of useless and harassing regulation. Market carts are not allowed to pass the city bounds; market boats are compelled to stop, not at the market wharf, but, at Morland's a mile from the market. Passports are required for all persons leaving the city. Women and children are advised, almost obliged, to quit the city and two hours only in the day are allowed for obtaining tickets to leave. An immense crowd assembled at the Provost's office this morning; not one in ten was able to obtain a passport. Requests from the multitude to prolong the time were made in vain; petitions and complaints were treated with contempt. The provost and his subordinates were as inexorable at the ancient judges of the infernal regions.[2] There was one alleviating consideration for the citizen. The city was threatened with

[1] The *Planter* was a "high pressure" cotton steamer of light draught formerly plying on the Pedee river. She was chartered by the Government from Captain John Ferguson as a transport and guard boat about the harbor of Charleston. Her armament was a 32-pounder and a 24 pound howitzer. Charleston *Mercury,* May 14, 1862.

[2] The Provost Marshal was Col. Johnson Hagood of the First South Carolina Volunteers. Charleston *Mercury,* May 15, 1862.

an attack from Lincoln's soldiery. The domestic tyranny would serve as a preparation for the stranger's oppression. We should get accustomed by times to being skinned. If Providence should afflict us for our sins with the foreign despot we should have gone through a training in our home school. It will afford some relief from the ennui of our captivity if it comes, to compare the two doses, the city brewed and the Northern decoction, of vexatious annoyances.

May 16th. The Provost finds it impossible to enforce the absurd regulations with which he began. It is made possible to get a passport without running the risk of being squeezed to death in a crowd. Ladies and children are even permitted to leave town without a passport and it has been discovered by our sagacious rulers that the fittest place for a market boat to land is at the market wharf. We are thankful for this unexpected advent of common sense to our councils and enjoy our liberties with thankfulness.

May 20th. Norfolk, it is reported, has been evacuated by the Confederate troops and the Merrimack has been destroyed. There ends for the present all hope of a Southern navy. The loss of Norfolk involves that of the Navy yard at Portsmouth with its dry dock and ship building facilities. Yet, I believe, the destruction of the Merrimack produced a deeper mortification in the South than all the other losses that attended it. There had been among the people the most exaggerated expectations excited by the appointment of Com. Tatnall to command her. The only fear was that he would be too rash; that he would assail Washington, attack New York, or bombard Philadelphia. Nothing was thought too adventurous for a commander so noted for daring. But let no man be counted happy until death has closed his account with fortune. The Commodore did nothing but blow up the ship. Whether it was his fault or his misfortune will not materially alter his position with the people. Whatever the reasons may be for destroying the vessel, her end was unfortunate for all concerned in it. Suicide is not a meritorious departure from the world for either men or ships and the actors never escape grave imputations. The old Commodore's laurels have been tarnished by his misfortune, we will think, and not by his fault.[3]

---

[3] After the fall of Norfolk Captain Josiah Tattnall decided to lighten and repair the *Merrimac* (Virginia) and take the vessel up the James to aid in the defense of Richmond. When the work of lightening was completed, her draft was too deep for the passage up the river. The *Merrimac's* waterline was now so high that her exposed hull could be shattered by any shot. Captain Tattnall made the difficult decision to destroy the ship, but to save the crew for future use. The *Merrimac* was run ashore and burned. This action brought distress and indignation, and Tattnall was accused of "culpable negligence and improvident conduct." He demanded a

But the world seldom cares to inquire which cause is the true one. To be associated even innocently with such a calamity to the Country ensures to the party the evil eye of the people.

June 2nd. The first consequence from the abandonment of Cole's island is the entrance into Stono of the Yankee gunboats and their shelling the islands on either side. The inhabitants of James Island and John's Island have fled from their plantations and the cattle are eating up the half grown crops. Our general having created the necessity of getting out of the enemy's reach by opening the inlet to his marauders now commands all negroes to be removed. It is more easily said than done. Ripley after seeing his plans counteracted has been ordered to Virginia. Two regiments go with him. General Mercer from Savannah takes his place in the city. New brooms sweep clean. We shall see how the adage applies to the new general. Ripley had outlived his popularity. There is but one step, in such cases, with the good people, from hosannahs to cries of crucify him. Pemberton, our major general, is regarded as irritable, petulant and rude.[4] He scorns civilians and militia generals and has no great regard even for the clergy. One reverend gentleman called at headquarters to intercede for two young men who had got into trouble in camp. The appeal for mercy was contemptuously rejected. The commander in chief, as the divine expressed it, threw up his nose in the air like a wild ass' colt and refused to listen to any intercession for mercy. The decision may have been sound but the manner was ungracious. If he sends the enemy to the right about with as little ceremony we shall nevertheless be satisfied with him. With such an atonement even the clergy will pardon his brusquerie.

June 3rd. The enemy has landed at Legare's place on the lower end of James Island under cover of his gun boats. A small party of Confederates advanced to meet them and a skirmish ensued in which we lost a few men killed, wounded and missing.

Ryan's company captured twenty of their opponents.[5] There was much firing and a great deal of noise during the day and a greater part of the night succeeding. But nothing decisive was attempted to drive the

ever fully forgave him. See William Chapman White and Ruth White, *Tin Can court martial and won an honorable acquittal, though it is doubtful if the South on a Shingle* (New York, 1957), pp. 130-35.

---

[4] The officers referred to were Brig. Gen. Roswell S. Ripley, Brig. Gen. Hugh W. Mercer, and Maj. Gen. J. C. Pemberton. Charleston *Mercury*, May 14, 27, and 31, 1862.

[5] A company known as the Irish Volunteers was under the command of Captain W. H. Ryan.

foe from the island. It would be unreasonable to expect vigour or activity from raw troops. When the war shall have lasted two or three years and regular armies are formed, we will see soldiers more fitted for service because better disciplined than volunteer corps can be. At present our troops so long accustomed to be political masters are not always submissive to the arbitrary tone of military rule. There is an uneasy feeling in the city. It seems to be doubted whether the commanding general means to defend it and whether, like Norfolk, it may not be abandoned without a contest. But surely some port should be kept open for communication with foreign countries and a supply of arms and ammunition. It is a mistake to suppose, as people generally do, that in the Revolution of 1776 we were cut off from all intercourse with neutral nations and that a similar condition could be borne now as they suppose it was borne then. Some portion of the American coast was always open to European adventure and the arrival of guns, powder and clothing, during the Revolutionary war. This is an absolute necessity in the present as in the former conflict.

June 4th. People are moving in crowds from the city. Carts are passing at all hours filled with furniture. The talk in the streets is when do you go; where are you going. Every one take care of himself and the enemy take the hindmost, seems to be the prevailing maxim. My younger folks are gone; some to Newberry; some to Anderson. My wife and I remain. I am averse to play the vagabond at seventy-four. Besides if Charleston falls what part of the country can be safe from the marauding parties of the enemy.

June 6th. The report today is that Mercer goes back to Savannah and General Smith is to take his place.[6] So the generals are kept moving if the troops do nothing. It is to be hoped that the change of Counsellors like their multitude will bring us wisdom and safety. So far we see very little. The evacuation of Cole's island proves to be the source of infinite evil. We have opened the door to the enemy and invited him to come in. He never attempted to enter Stono while Cole's island was occupied. It would have been very difficult from the intricacy, shallowness and shifting nature of the Channel. Now his gun boats occupy the river as they please. The military authorities have begun to make bomb proofs in Meeting street near the ruins of the circular church and are impressing all negroes. The blacks seem to be considered as contrabands on both sides alike. The Federals seize them and put them to work; the Confederates impress them for the same purpose. The owner's rights are postponed in either case. Throughout the country

6 This was Gen. W. D. Smith of Georgia. Charleston *Mercury,* June 7, 1862.

the paramount law of the land is the law of force. The public journals are silent, adherents of the ruling faction are afraid to speak out. The greediness for office and pay is prevalent everywhere at the South as well as the North. There are disinterested men in our Country but we must go about with a lantern to find them. Certainly our chief men, President, Governors, generals, are not of the number. Washington during the Revolution refused all compensation for his services; what leading man of the present day has imitated the example. They all take whatever they are able to pocket from the scantily furnished public purse.

June 8th. The bomb proofs or rat holes begun two days ago are abandoned. So we go with feeble vacillating councils, a ship tempest tost with irresolute or ignorant pilots in command.

June 10th. A skirmish began today on James Island. General Smith made an attack on the Federal force but with very little effect. We had fifty or sixty men killed or wounded and made no impression on the enemy. Doubts are entertained whether the government intends to defend the city. Their stores are ordered away. The banks are moving by the general's advice. I hope he will not bestow all his roughness on his civilian friends but expend it freely on his military foes.

June 12th. The bells, today, were taken down from the steeple of St. Michael's Church to be sent to Columbia. One that I saw in the Portico bears date 1765. They have crossed the Atlantic three times. Sent to this country originally from England, they were carried back at the close of the Revolution by the British troops. Restored to the Church by the exertions of private [citizens], they are now hurried away from apprehension of another enemy less scrupulous than the former plunderer. I don't know whether the Federals have stolen Church bells but they have given abundant evidence of their entertaining loose notions on the rights of private property and have turned churches into stables for the convenience of their cavalry. We could hardly expect much respect from them for church bells whether as private or sacred property.

June 16th. The enemy attacked our battery at Secessionville today, at day light, and were repulsed with terrible slaughter. The battery was held by a handful of men under the command of Major Lucas.[7] The attack was almost a surprise but the defense was heroic and thoroughly successful. The enemy were led into action by three generals. Their

---

[7] The newspaper accounts of this attack make no mention of Lucas. Grayson apparently was referring to Major J. J. Lucas in command of Lucas's (South Carolina) Battalion of Artillery. See John Johnson, *Defense of Charleston Harbor* (Charleston, 1890), p. 36.

number was not short of three thousand sustained by their gun boats and batteries. Their discomfiture was total with a loss, it is conjectured, of a thousand men. It cost the Confederates a number of valuable lives. Among these are some of my old and valued acquaintances, Henry King, John Edwards and others.[8] The cause cannot fail which is consecrated by such sacrifices. But alas! for the hearts of mourning mothers, fathers and friends. We are all too apt to enlist Providence on our side in every quarrel but we may at least hope that he will not prosper the arms of men who come a thousand miles to ravage the homes and spill the blood of Southern men under the false pretence of restoring a Union that all the world sees is past restoration.

June 19th. There has been no movement since the fight of the 16th, but there are a thousand rumours. One is that a great Federal fleet is preparing in the Chesapeake to attack Charleston; that the foreign consuls are warned to prepare for the safety of their people; that a French frigate is off the bar to assist in that purpose; that an English frigate is expected with the same view. The great canard has grown from the fact that a French frigate is below with the usual dispatches for the French Consul. It is announced that an English vessel is stranded on Sullivan's island in attempting to run the blockade. She is said to have a thousand barrels of powder much wanted in the City and a large cargo of other articles of value. Anything is acceptable where every thing is wanting. The vessel has reached the city and proves to be the Memphis.

June 20th. It is impossible to get a correct account of events that pass almost in your presence. A hundred accounts are given of the attack on Secessionville, all from eye witnesses, and yet no two of them alike. It is said that Sir Walter Raleigh saw a tumult at the foot of the tower where he was confined as a prisoner and received an account of it from a half dozen bystanders no two agreeing and all differing from his own version of the story. He concluded therefore that little reliance can be placed on historical narratives. I am afraid they are collections of monstrous falsehoods, a grain of truth perhaps in a bushel of chaff. In this case our own stories differ from each other and the Yankee narrative is at variance with them all. No Confederate general, it seems, was on the field at the beginning of the fight, nor at any time, except it be near its close. It could not have been conducted better however if a dozen brigadiers had been present. History will assign all

---

[8] Capt. Henry Campbell King and Lieut. John J. Edwards were serving in the Sumter Guards of the Charleston Battalion. Charleston *Mercury*, June 19, 1862.

the honour nevertheless to the commanding general in the neighborhood.

June 21. The evacuation of Corinth is reported and the sanguine
and knowing represent the movement as a great strategitical success.
The less confident are not so sure that a retreat can be a triumph. If a
retreat be conducted without loss it is creditable to the general commanding but the laurels gathered in such a field are not enviable. Mo-
reau obtained reputation by escaping from a superior enemy through
the Black forest but hardly so great a reputation as Napoleon in his
advance into Italy. Success is the grand test of merit in military affairs, perhaps in all affairs, or as the French say it is only success that
succeeds. It is not unfailing but the only attainable standard of ability
in war or peace. The conquered Cato may have pleased the Gods but
it is the victorious Caesar who is acceptable to men. If the Federal
army had abandoned its lines, we should have hailed the event as a
victory for the Confederate cause; I am afraid Beauregard's evacuation of his lines and falling back sixty miles was equivalent to a defeat
whatever the military necessity that induced the move.

June 22nd. A gentleman owning a farm in St. Andrews represents
the conduct of our own troops as infamous. They pay no regard to the
rights of property and plunder him openly in his presence, careless of
threat or remonstrance. These are the characteristics of a democratic
soldiery who elect their own officers, among whom private and captain
or Colonel are on terms of familiar fellowship, crack jokes together and
slap each other on the back in a hearty way. War with these people
is a season of licence. The camp is a barbecue ground with the additional convenience over ordinary barbecues that the parties assembled
may plunder any neighbour's house, shoot his pigs and help themselves
without scruple to whatever they may fancy in his field or garden. On
John's island, during the winter, every house abandoned by the planter
was gutted by our troops and the furniture that was not carried away
was wantonly destroyed. Pictures served as targets for pistol shots
or objects for bayonet practice; the window sashes were smashed and
the doors, window shutters and out houses converted into fuel. One
gentleman of John's island saw his chairs on the railroad cars. No destruction of Lincoln's men could be more complete or unsparing. We
are realizing the adage that the laws are silent among arms even where
the arms are in the hands of our own people.

June 25th. It is reported today that a negro has come into our
camp from the Federals on James Island. He is a Georgia runaway who
has seen enough of his Northern friends and is desirous of returning

to his master. He had been employed by a Colonel of the enemy to attend to a horse and took the opportunity of riding the horse to water
to ride off to the Confederate camp. With nominal wages and these
paid by Lincoln's government, the negro performs the same duties to
his Northern as to his Southern master. He enjoys the great advantage
too of being called not a "slave" but a "servant". The return of the
runaway to his former condition indicates sufficiently the benefits of
the change. He reports that the enemy carried from the field on the
16th six hundred and forty killed and wounded; this number with those
buried by our troops and the prisoners taken will fall little short of a
thousand. In these murderous conflicts both parties aver that they are
doing their duty and both have devout men and pious chaplains who
exhort them to perform it faithfully. It tempts us to believe that the
moral sense is no infallible guide in questions of ethics and that Christianity is not a successful teacher of peace on earth and good will towards men. Here are men who come a thousand miles from home to
cut their neighbours' throats. They do this to honour their flag, to restore amity and the Union, and to obtain a farm of rich cotton land on
Edisto island. There is a levity exhibited in their letters picked up on
the battle field, a malignant mockery of all that is sacred mixed up with
a sour spirit of hatred that savours of European Red Republicanism
and New England rancour combined. Our worthy friends of Massachusetts treats us [as] they did the Indians, witches, quakers, Baptists
and other heretics of earlier times. There are many good men at the
North but they are as silent as the grave. There are many pious christians but not a voice is heard in favour of peace. So far as we can
judge from their acquiescence in Sewardism they have fallen into the
strange delusion that Christian Charity is consistent with rape, rapine,
and murder. They pray and preach not for peace but for the more
earnest prosecution of a bloody war and the enactment of general confiscation acts. If any disapprove these things, they do nothing to oppose
them. They are not of the class to which the brave apostle belonged
who fought with beasts at Ephesus. The beasts at Washington have it
all their own way and the Christian brotherhood at the North not only
quietly look on while the brutes rend and devour but stimulate their
appetites to fresh exertions. These things try the faith of good Christians. An old friend remarked to me yesterday that Christianity is a
failure. It inculcates peace and love but has made no progress in changing our nature; war is still as rife in the world as in the palmy times
of paganism. But this is a sorry conclusion for a Christian to arrive at
and not a just one. The religion of love is not without its fruits even

on the field of battle. The wounded enemy now is not commonly put to the sword. He is received in the hospitals of his foe. His wounds are healed and his wants supplied. He is not made a slave nor are women and children sold sub hasta by the conqueror now as in ancient times. In spite of even Butler's brutality let us hold fast to the faith and confide in its future mitigating influences in the world.

Another large steamer, the Hero, has arrived with a cargo of goods. She grounded on the bar in coming in. The crew took to her boats and made for the shore leaving the officers on board. But the tide rose and lifted the vessel. She steamed in past her fugitive boats and came up to the City with no damage but the loss of a few goods thrown overboard to lighten her.

Evans and Drayton [9] are ordered to Virginia with a number of the troops from between Charleston and Savannah. There has not been much activity among our commanding officers along the coast. Their policy is not aggressive. The rule seems to be never to attack the enemy at our door until he attempts to enter it and not to pursue him farther than the threshold when he retreats. The ardor of subordinate officers, it is said, is checked by their superiors. We who are spectators only at a distance are advocates of greater energy. A distinguished gentleman, previous to the attack on Sumter, urged the Governor vehemently and repeatedly to begin it. The governor harassed by his pertinacity, at last offered him to command, with permission to begin the war at his discretion. The importunate gentleman declined the offer. While criticising our leaders we should certainly receive a similar offer in the same way.

26th June. Preparations are made for obstructing the harbour. The people seem to have little faith in them. It would be better perhaps to multiply forts in and above the city, that if the enemy's gun boats pass the forts below they would still be under fire. It ought not to be understood as it formerly was that if a gun boat approaches the city a surrender must follow. Vicksburg has settled that question. If New Orleans, instead of vain attempts to obstruct the river, had erected strong forts near the city, she would have escaped the brutalities of Butler.

27th June. A gentleman from Richmond tells me a shocking story of the scenes exhibited on the way in the transportation of the dead from the field of battle to their friends at home. The condition of the bodies, the offensive smell, the careless manner in which they are handled on the road and left exposed at the depots, make their passage

---

[9] Brig. Gen. George Nathan Evans and Brig. Gen. Thomas F. Drayton. Douglas Southall Freeman, *Lee's Lieutenants* (New York, 1946), II, 63.

anything but pleasant to all who come near them. There is not one man in a hundred who would not avoid any such disposition of his remains. Major Wheat of the Louisiana troops in the battle of Richmond requested, in his last moments, to be buried in the field of battle. It is what every brave soldier will prefer. Let the fallen be buried where they fell. Let friendship erect its monuments there and the country raise a general memorial to its illustrious defenders. It would add infinite interest to the battle field forever. The tombs and the names of the heroes beneath them would court the eyes of all who should visit the spot that will live in history like the field of Marathon. What cemetery could be so sacred and appropriate. I respect with warm sympathy the affection that would see the remains of the departed and join in the last offices of respect that are due to the dead, but it is better to restrain the wish when to indulge it is so painful to surviving friends, when it removes the deceased from his fitting resting place and when in almost every case it would be in opposition to his dying desires.

27th June. While we revile the Yankees we imitate them. It is one of their peculiarities to be always inventing slang words and phrases which they thrust into the newspapers and wear to tatters. We never fail to adopt them. Some time ago, the term was "high falutin", next, "in our midst" now it is "skedaddle". We meet with it in all quarters, North and South. No troops run away or retreat; they skedaddle. We use their manufactured words as we do their brooms and buckets. Everything proves how provincial we were getting to be. Even war and revolution have not broken the chain of habit.

28th June. The heart of the city is moved with a report that a great conflict is going on near the city of Richmond.[10] Every body is alive with anxiety and expectation. Everybody has a word to say as to the proper mode of proceeding. It is the privilege of a free people to criticize its authorities, civil and political, to know every thing, to be familiar especially with military affairs. A story is told of Hannibal being once invited to hear a Rhetoricean discourse on the art of war. If the Carthaginian leader were a sojourner in our city he would meet an instructor at every corner. It has happened by some oversight of Presi-

---

[10] This reference is to Gen. George B. McClellan's attack on the forces of Generals Lee and Jackson. The opposing armies came to blows in what is known as the "Seven Days" (June 25-July 1, 1862). This was a series of battles, beginning with Mechanicsville and ending with Malvern Hill, in which McClellan hammered almost continuously at the Confederate forces defending Richmond. While winning several engagements, McClellan failed to take Richmond, and the South's anxiety turned to joy.

dent Davis that the great strategists are not in the army. They are left at home to supervise the marches and battles of Lee, Johnson and Beauregard. Some of the gentlemen most prominent in hurrahing the people into the contest have never been able even to get into the ranks. All that they have been able to do is to give their opinions and advice freely on the conduct of affairs and on the characters of those who direct them. Unfortunately for the Country, the strictures of these neglected patriots have no influence at headquarters.

June 30th. The English war steamer Racer entered Charleston harbour today and lies in front of the battery. Everybody has an opinion to express. One asks if she saluted the Confederate flag—of course she did nothing of the kind. It is conjectured by another that her arrival indicates an attack on Charleston and she comes to look after English subjects and interests. In another's judgment it indicates a change in England's policy and foreshadows her recognition of the Southern Confederacy. This notion is a very idle one. England's foreign policy consults her own interests only. She acts when these demand it and never before. She stood aside and saw Poland divided and Hungary crushed. She interposed in South America because she hoped to obtain great advantages from the trade of the Spanish Colonies when independent States. She desires Southern trade but will not risk her interests in the North. She will stand aloof from the South during her struggle and be cordial with her when the battle has been fought and the victory won; while we are struggling in deep water she will look on complacently and do by us afterwards as Johnson says Lord Chesterfield did by him—encumber us with help after we have reached the shore. She will not risk the loss of her Northern debts. There is nothing surprising in this. Whatever may be true of individuals, the conduct of Nations is always selfish. It is so at least with what are called free governments. An autocrat may be swayed by generosity or caprice to take part with the weak against the strong; nothing moves a Republic or limited monarchy but gain or ambition.

"BROTHER AGAINST BROTHER": ALEXANDER AND JAMES CAMPBELL'S CIVIL WAR

J. TRACY POWER*

ON MONDAY NIGHT, JUNE 16, 1862, THE UNION CAMPS ON SOL Legare Island, near Charleston, South Carolina, were full of weary, gloomy, and angry officers and soldiers. Many of them were talking about or writing letters home about the battle they had fought that morning, a battle which had taken place near the planters' summer village by the name of Secessionville, and which soon would be known by that name. The fight, which had taken place near the center of James Island, just across the Ashley River from the city of Charleston, had been a disaster for the Federal troops engaged there. General Isaac I. Stevens's division of three brigades had charged a strong Confederate fortification in an ill-advised assault ordered by Stevens's commander General Henry W. Benham. Stevens's division had approached the enemy by advancing down the neck of a narrow peninsula with thick marsh on either side, and his regiments had been forced to crowd together on the high ground instead of attacking in line. His units had then lost their formations, had entered the action piecemeal, and had been repulsed by a heavy fire of artillery and musketry from the Confederate defenders commanded by Colonel Thomas G. Lamar and Colonel Johnson Hagood. By seven-thirty in the morning, after more than three hours of fighting, Benham had finally admitted defeat and had ordered a withdrawal back to his camps near the Stono River. Federal casualties had numbered nearly 700 officers and men, or about one-fifth of the 3500 troops engaged.[1]

One of the better-known Federal units which fought at Secessionville was the Seventy-ninth New York Infantry, commonly known as "The Seventy-ninth Highlanders." Some of the Highlanders were among the few Union soldiers actually to reach the Confederate fort; the unit suffered 110 casualties out of a total strength of 474. This regiment had been organized in New York City in May 1861 and boasted a sizable element of Scotsmen, many of whom had emigrated to the United States in the 1850s. Its first uniforms were bright blue jackets and colorful tartan kilts for the officers, and the same jackets with tartan trousers for the men. Though the Seventy-ninth wore these impressive uniforms when they left New York for Wash-

*Staff historian of the South Carolina State Historic Preservation Office at the South Carolina Department of Archives and History and adjunct instructor of history, Midlands Technical College

[1]See the author's "'An Affair of Outposts': The Battle of Secessionville, June 16, 1862," *Civil War History* XXXVIII: 2 (June 1992).

ington, they wore the regulation blue uniforms in their first battle, the Union defeat at First Manassas in July.[2]

While many members of the Seventy-ninth New York distinguished themselves at Secessionville, Color Sergeant Alexander Campbell was among the most conspicuous of the Highlanders during the battle, as he planted the regimental colors atop the parapet and kept them there until the Federals were forced to withdraw under a withering fire of musketry and artillery. Campbell, most often called Sandy, was twenty-four years old and was a native of Crieff, in the Central Highlands of Scotland. Campbell and several of his brothers had moved to the United States in the decade before the war, eventually settled in different cities, and worked at different trades. When Sandy arrived in New York he lived with the family of Elizabeth Ralston, whose son James was a stone mason and had encouraged Sandy to emigrate from Scotland. Ralston and Campbell moved to Charleston in 1856, where they worked on the new United States Custom House, and where Sandy also served in the "Scottish Guards," a company in the antebellum South Carolina militia. Campbell's stay in South Carolina was a brief one, however, as he returned to New York City by 1859 and married James Ralston's sister Jane.[3] He enlisted in the Seventy-ninth Highlanders when the regiment was organized and fought in the ranks at First Manassas. Campbell was promoted to be one of the regiment's color bearers, with the rank of sergeant, in September 1861.[4] The Seventy-ninth New York took part in the Union occupation of the South Carolina sea islands that fall as part of the newly created Department of the South and would remain in South Carolina for several months.

---

[2]A valuable regimental history is William Todd, *The Seventy-ninth Highlanders, New York Volunteers in the War of the Rebellion 1861-1865* (Albany, N.Y.: Press of Brandow, Barton & Company, 1886).

[3]For the several antebellum South Carolina militia companies, see Michael E. Stauffer, *South Carolina's Antebellum Militia* (Columbia: South Carolina Department of Archives and History, 1991), p. 19. The following story of Alexander and James Campbell is based primarily on seventy Campbell family letters — sixty-six of them wartime letters — in the Personal Papers collection of the South Carolina Department of Archives and History, Columbia (hereafter Campbell Family Papers, SCDAH). The vast majority of these letters were written by Alexander Campbell to his wife Jane. See also Pension Case File of Alexander Campbell, Record Group 15, National Archives, Washington, D.C. (hereafter Alexander Campbell Pension Case File); this valuable file, with extensive biographical material on Alexander Campbell and his family, was brought to the author's attention through the courtesy of Ms. Katherine Dhalle of New Hartford, N.Y., an authority on several Union regiments that saw extensive service in the South Carolina Lowcountry.

[4]Frederick Phisterer, comp., *New York in the War of the Rebellion 1861 to 1865*, 3rd ed. (Albany, N.Y.: J.H. Lyon Company, State Printers, 1912), Vol. IV, p. 2849; Alexander Campbell Pension Case File.

"We have had a fight," Sandy began a letter to his wife Jane late on the night on June 16th. "I am all right ... it was a verry severe fight and we have Lost a good many ... I cant see how Jammie Matthew & me [Jane's brothers James and Matthew Ralston] got of without a scratch." He observed, "the enemy is strongly fortified on this island" — meaning James Island — and then mentioned, "Brother James was in the fort[.] I asked one of the rebels that was wounded and taken prisoner and he told me so."[5]

Campbell's older brother James was thirty years old, a bachelor, and had worked as a drayman and a clerk in Charleston before the war; he had indeed been one of the defenders of the Confederate earthworks that morning. James, like Sandy, had come to the United States in the 1850s, settled in Charleston, and had served in the antebellum South Carolina militia. He had, in contrast to his younger brother, chosen to stay in Charleston when Sandy moved to New York. His old militia company, the "Union Light Infantry," had its own sizable complement of Scotsmen and was sometimes called the "Scotch Company." It entered Confederate service in March 1862 with five other Charleston companies, forming the First South Carolina Battalion. This battalion, commanded by Lieutenant Colonel Peter C. Gaillard, was also known as the "Charleston Battalion." James enlisted as a first sergeant and was elected second lieutenant by the members of his company in May.[6] Though the battle of Secessionville was his first exposure to combat, Lieutenant Campbell's performance there was a notable one. He jumped to the parapet unarmed, rolled a log down onto a group of charging Federals, captured an enemy rifle, and then continued fighting.[7]

Sandy had known for some time that James was serving in the Confederate army, but had only recently learned any detailed information about his younger brother's whereabouts. On June 3, the day after the Federals landed on James Island, the Highlanders skirmished with the Confederates and captured Adjutant Henry Walker of the Charleston Battalion. Walker, himself a Scotsman, remarked, "Had I known I was to have been taken prisoner, I would have worn my kilts."[8] He had a long conversation with Sandy Campbell, saying that he would have recognized Sandy from his

[5]Alexander Campbell to his wife, June 16, 1862, Campbell Family Papers, SCDAH; Alexander Campbell Pension Case File.

[6]Compiled Service Record of James Campbell, 1st (Charleston Battalion) Infantry (Gaillard's Battalion), Compiled Service Records of Confederate Soldiers Who Served in Organizations from the State of South Carolina, War Department Collection of Confederate Records, Record Group 109, National Archives, Washington, D.C., National Archives Microfilm Publication M267, Roll 149 (hereafter James Campbell Compiled Service Record); Campbell Family Papers, SCDAH; Charleston News, March 4, 1907.

[7]Charleston Courier, June 18, 19, 1862.

[8]Todd, The Seventy-ninth Highlanders, p. 142.

resemblance to James. Walker also reported that James had been elected second lieutenant of his company, and was popular with the officers and men. "So you see we are not farr from each other now," Sandy wrote Jane a few days later, noting that Walker also told him, "James talked often about me ... this is a warr that there never was the like of before Brother against Brother."[9]

In the aftermath of Secessionville, letters and newspaper editorials illustrated the Federals' despondency and the Confederates' jubilation. Sandy Campbell called the battle "an unfortunate affair," commenting, "General Steavens the night after the battle cryed like a child about the Loss of so many brave men."[10] Stevens had become colonel of the Seventy-ninth New York after its first colonel was killed and was still quite popular with the Highlanders after his promotion to general. "Our camp has been thrown into deep gloom in consequence of our heavy loss," wrote another member of the regiment, in a letter published in the New York *Times*. "Two more such attacks would effectually dispose of the poor Seventy-ninth Highlanders ... Gen. Benham says every man of the Seventy-ninth deserves a pair of epaulets."[11]

The Charleston newspapers, in contrast, were full of breathless descriptions of southern heroism. The Charleston *Mercury* crowed, "the foe, it is true, displayed admirable courage; the famous Highland Regiment, the 79th New York, occupied the prominent place in the picture, but their desperate onslaughts were of no avail against the stubborn resolve and lofty valor of our brave boys."[12] An editorial in the Charleston *Courier* even mentioned the Campbell brothers, observing that their story was "another illustration of the deplorable consequences of this fratricidal war." While acknowledging that Sandy Campbell "fought gallantly in the late action" and that he "displayed ... a heroism worthy of [his] regiment and of a better cause," the editors noted that James Campbell "was conspicuous and has been honorably mentioned on our side."[13]

On June 18 the Confederates granted a flag of truce so the Federals could obtain information about their dead and wounded within the Confederate lines. Sandy received a letter from James, who had not previously known that his younger brother was fighting near Charleston. "Dear Brother," James's letter began, "I was astonished to hear from the prisoners that you was colour Bearer of the Regmt that assalted the Battrey at this point the

[9]Alexander Campbell to his wife, June 10, 1862, Campbell Family Papers, SCDAH.

[10]Ibid., June 25, 1862, Campbell Family Papers, SCDAH.

[11]Unknown soldier of the 79th New York Infantry, June 18, 1862, published in *Scottish American Journal*, and quoted in New York *Times*, June 28, 1862.

[12]Charleston *Mercury*, June 17, 1862.

[13]Charleston *Courier*, June 19, 1862.

other day." He continued, "I was in the Brest work during the whole engagement doing my Best to Beat you[.] but I hope you and I will never again meet face to face Bitter enemies in the Battle field[.] but if such should be the case You have but to discharge your deauty to Your caus for I can assure you I will strive to discharge my deauty to my country & My cause."[14]

Sandy sent a copy of James's letter to his family in New York, saying, "its rather to bad to think that we should be fighting him on the one side and me on the other for he says he was in the fort during the whole engagement[.] I hope to god that he and I will get safe through it all and he will have his story to tell about his side and I will have my story to tell about my side."[15] The brothers missed a face-to-face reunion by the slimmest of margins. In the afternoon of July 3 James received permission from his captain to approach the Federal picket lines. He wanted to ask if Sandy was wounded and to try to see him for a few minutes. James asked the Union picket what regiment he belonged to, hoping he would hear "The Seventy-ninth New York Highlanders," and was disappointed when the soldier belonged to another unit. Sandy later wrote that James "wanted to see me bad and asked if they would send for me but the officer was afraid to doe it," and James returned to his camp. When Sandy heard that James had tried to find him it was too late to get permission to approach the Confederate pickets. The Seventy-ninth New York left James Island the next morning.[16]

Sergeant Campbell, along with most of the Union soldiers who had taken part in the expedition, spent a few days at Hilton Head and Beaufort. He wrote James while at Beaufort, but never learned if his younger brother had received his letter. The Federals then left for Virginia, arriving at Newport News in mid-July.[17]

SANDY CAMPBELL'S BITTER EXPERIENCE AT SECESSIONVILLE permanently darkened his opinion of life in the Union army. At first, he had often filled his letters home with such optimistic phrases as "I expect we will soon have the ware all over," or "I think the ware will soon come to an end now," or "I cant see how the South can keep it up much Longer," or "O Jane shurely it cant Last Long now."[18] As the war continued, however, Campbell became more pessimistic. In one typical outburst, he wrote, "our regiment feels verry much disitisfied about not getting a chance to garrison some

---

[14]James Campbell to his brother Alexander, June 18, 1862, Campbell Family Papers, SCDAH.

[15]Alexander Campbell to his wife, June 25, 1862, Campbell Family Papers, SCDAH.

[16]Ibid., July 15, 1862.

[17]Ibid., July 15, 29, and 31, 1862.

[18]See, for example, ibid., September 13, November 13, and December 16, 1861, and June 13, 1862, respectively.

place so that they could get a fourlough to see there families."[19] Sandy wrote
his wife that he expected a lieutenant's commission and threatened, "If I
dont get it ... I will throw there Colors at them and goo back to my
company[.] I wont make a target of myself much Longer[.] its called an
honorable posisition but its a verry dangerous one."[20]

Campbell did not get his coveted commission, however, for a few more
months. In August 1862 Stevens's division, which was now part of the
Ninth Army Corps, was sent to reinforce General John Pope's Army of
Virginia. The Seventy-ninth New York participated in Pope's crushing
defeat at Second Manassas, fighting—and losing—on the same ground for
the second time in little more than a year.[21]

In the aftermath of another lost battle, circumstances brought Sandy
Campbell, the colors of the Seventy-ninth Highlanders, and Isaac Stevens
together in dramatic fashion. Stevens's three brigades were assigned to
serve as Pope's rear guard on the Union retreat to Washington after the
battle, and on Monday afternoon, September 1, 1862, his troops encountered Confederate advance units near a ruined Virginia mansion known as
Chantilly. The Confederates were elements of General A.P. Hill's division,
six brigades strong, in General Stonewall Jackson's corps of the Army of
Northern Virginia. They had been marching all day to find the retreating
Federals.

The battle at Chantilly can best be described as a "meeting engagement," in which the opposing forces stumbled onto each other and fought
without any decisive result. Stevens and Hill quickly deployed their
respective divisions and attacked almost simultaneously, while a fierce
thunderstorm added to the drama. The Seventy-ninth New York, its colors
in the forefront, entered the fight at the head of Stevens's leading brigade.
Under a volley of musketry from Hill's Confederates, the Highlanders
quickly lost many casualties, among them four color bearers shot down in
succession.

When Sandy Campbell became the fifth Highlander color bearer
wounded, with a musket ball through his left calf, the flag fell to the ground
and the regiment faltered briefly. Stevens, sensing a crisis, grabbed the
colors from the next member of the color guard. Campbell, lying at
Stevens's feet, yelled, "For God's sake, General, don't *you* take the colors;
they'll shoot you if you do!" Stevens yelled back, "Give me the colors! If they
don't follow now, they never will!" and ran forward shouting, "We are all
Highlanders; follow, Highlanders; forward, *my* Highlanders!" Stevens was
almost instantly killed by a musket ball through the head. When his body
was recovered after the battle, he was still clutching his old regiment's flag.

[19] Ibid., July 25, 1862.
[20] Ibid., July 29, 1862.
[21] Ibid., August 5, 6, and 10, 1862.

A newspaper correspondent for the New York *Tribune*, recording the incident a few days after the battle, called Sandy Campbell "a grizzled old Scotchman," even though he was only twenty-four. The correspondent also claimed, "the language I have given as Gen. Stevens's was taken down upon the field by a member of his Staff."[22] The colonel of the Seventy-ninth New York sent the colors to Stevens's widow several months later, writing her, "although [they are] but a rag, many a brave man would have sacrificed his life rather than anything dishonorable should happen [to] them."[23] After Stevens's death, fellow division commander General Philip Kearny committed his own troops, but when Kearny was killed near dusk the Federals broke off the battle and withdrew.

Three days after the fight at Chantilly, Sandy wrote Jane from Emory Hospital in Washington. His letter began, "My Dear Wife you will not be surprised to hear that I am wounded after such severe fighting as we were in," but reassured her, "I am only slightly wounded. The ball went through it wont amount to much[.] I got it on monday evening in the fight that general Steavens was killed in."[24] His letter never mentioned the dramatic exchange with Stevens over the regimental colors. While still in the hospital, Campbell wrote bitterly of the Union war effort: "What man ... has heart any longer to fight under such generals as we have [?] The[y] seem to want to get men slaughtered, and all to no purpose whatever."[25]

Campbell, on wounded furlough, was promoted to second lieutenant of Company G in October 1862, a position somewhat less exposed than that of color sergeant. He served as a regimental recruiter back home in New York before rejoining the Highlanders in January 1863 and accompanying them on a Federal expedition to Kentucky that spring. Sandy, who was thoroughly disillusioned with the war by this time, believed that he had done his duty and resented being accused of overstaying his wounded furlough. He repeatedly attempted to resign his commission, citing his wound, illness in his family, and business matters that needed his attention. Campbell's resignation was finally accepted on May 7, 1863, at Columbia, Kentucky, citing his disability.[26] Sandy's last letter before he returned home ended hopefully with the comment, "I expect to be with you soon and not

[22]New York *Tribune*, September 8, 1862.

[23]Col. David Morrison to Mrs. Isaac I. Stevens, September 22, 1864, quoted in Hazard Stevens, *The Life of Isaac Ingalls Stevens* (Boston and New York: Houghton, Mifflin and Co., 1900), Vol. II, p. 500.

[24]Alexander Campbell to his wife, September 4, 1862, Campbell Family Papers, SCDAH.

[25]Ibid., September 9, 1862.

[26]Ibid., January 31, February 11, 19, 28, March 4, 8, 13, 18, 31, April 10 and 13, 1863; Phisterer, *New York in the War of the Rebellion*, Vol. IV, p. 2849; Alexander Campbell Pension Case File.

to goo for a soldier again and I Remain Your Long Absent but soon to be Present Husband." Campbell spent the remainder of the war in New York City with his wife and family.[27] In September 1864 he was examined by a board of officers of the Veteran Reserve Corps — a unit in which men who were disabled or otherwise unable to perform combat duty could still perform garrison duty or other light duty if they wished to do so. The board thought Campbell "deficient" in his knowledge of tactics and did not recommend him for a commission in the corps, but commented that he had "merit and capacity" and urged him to study tactics and reapply for a commission. There is no record that Sandy Campbell, who was undoubtedly weary of the war, did so.[28]

THOUGH SANDY'S ACTIVE ROLE IN THE CIVIL WAR WAS OVER, the war was not yet over for his older brother James. Since June 1862 and the battle of Secessionville, Second Lieutenant Campbell and his battalion had remained in the Charleston area, with the Charleston Battalion sometimes serving on James Island and sometimes forming part of the garrison in the city itself. The battalion was in Charleston in the spring and summer of 1863 when Federal forces launched a second major offensive against the defenses of Charleston Harbor.

Battery Wagner, the Confederate fort near the northeast tip of Morris Island, became a focal point for the Union land approach. General Quincy A. Gillmore, commanding the Department of the South, planned to land his infantry on the southwest end of the island and take the fort by a frontal assault. After a small-scale Federal attack was easily repulsed, both the attackers and the defenders prepared for a second larger attempt on Wagner. General William B. Taliaferro, in command of Confederate forces on Morris Island, replaced the garrison in Battery Wagner with fresh troops which included the Charleston Battalion. Gillmore, meanwhile, assembled his Federals for another assault.

On the evening of Saturday, July 18, 1863, after a fierce ten-hour land and naval bombardment designed to weaken the Confederate defenses at Battery Wagner, the Federal infantry moved forward. At almost eight o'clock, about dusk, the first of General Thomas Seymour's troops ad-

[27]Alexander Campbell to his wife, April 29, 1863, Campbell Family Papers, SCDAH. Of the Campbells' six children, three young sons — John, James, and Alexander — died within a few weeks of each other in November and December 1865. Three others — Jennie, John, and Clementine — were born after the war. Clementine Campbell, born in 1871, later lived in Spartanburg, South Carolina, and helped care for her uncle James in Charleston during his last illness.

[28]Office of the Board of Examination, of Officers of the Veteran Reserve Corps, "Report of the Examination of Alexander Campbell, Late 2nd Lieut. 79th New York Volunteers," September 7, 1864, Alexander Campbell Pension Case File.

vanced up the beach toward the fort in an assault doomed to fail. The first brigade, which included the famous Fifty-fourth Massachusetts commanded by Colonel Robert Gould Shaw, suffered appalling casualties from Confederate musketry and artillery. The only Union success of any note occurred after a North Carolina regiment left its position in Battery Wagner and refused to fight, when elements of a second Federal brigade then reached — and entered — the southeast angle of the fort.

When the Confederate defenders realized that the enemy was actually in Battery Wagner, James Campbell volunteered to go there and report back to Taliaferro. He jumped atop the parapet at the southeast angle, demanded that the troops there identify themselves, and was answered by two Union soldiers who lunged at him with their bayonets. "With great presence of mind," reported the Charleston *Courier*, "[he] pushed them off the parapet, both falling ... on their own bayonets."[29] Campbell ordered the rest of the Federals to surrender, but one of them grabbed him by the leg and pulled him down into the ditch below. Of the five Confederates later listed as captured or missing in the night battle, James Campbell was the only officer.[30] All the Union troops, having suffered heavy casualties, were soon forced to withdraw from their positions both inside and in front of Battery Wagner.

John Johnson, in his 1890 history of the siege of Charleston, wrote that James Campbell "paid dearly for his venture ... [the enemy] passed him under heavy fire to their rear."[31] A newspaper account published a few days later reported, "the oath of allegiance was tendered [Campbell] at Hilton Head, but rejected with the utmost scorn and contempt."[32]

Campbell was soon taken to the prison for Confederate officers at Johnson's Island, on Lake Erie just north of Sandusky, Ohio. He was imprisoned there from October 1863 to February 1864, when he was transferred briefly to Point Lookout, Maryland. Though still a prisoner of war, James was promoted to first lieutenant in his old unit — now redesignated the Twenty-seventh South Carolina Infantry — in January 1864. By June of that year he was imprisoned at Fort Delaware, Delaware,

---

[29]Charleston *Courier*, July 25, 1863.

[30]Ibid.; *The War of the Rebellion: A Compilation of the Official Records of the Union and Confederate Armies*, 4 Series, 128 Volumes (Washington, D.C.: U.S. Government Printing Office; 1880-1901), Series I, Vol. XXVIII, Pt. I, p. 406.

[31]John Johnson, *The Defense of Charleston Harbor, including Fort Sumter and the Adjacent Islands, 1863-1865* (Charleston, S.C.: Walker, Evans, and Cogswell, 1890), App., p. lxxxix.

[32]Charleston *Courier*, July 25, 1863.

where he remained until released after the war's end.[33]

James wrote Sandy several letters from the three prisons, asking for news about their family and usually requesting newspapers, money, and clothing. The two corresponded often, but usually did not write much about the war, preferring to discuss the latest Campbell family news.[34] They did occasionally mention mutual friends still in the army, or give news of their respective units. "By the by," James wrote in the summer of 1864, "I saw in some paper the arrival home and reception of the 79th Regt[.] how many of the original Regt came home with them, from the hard service they have seen, I would not think many of them was left."[35] Sandy wrote his brother that he thought James was better off in a Federal prison than with his old unit, which was then fighting near Petersburg under Lee. James answered, "I can apreciate your meaning [but] if I had my choice, I would take my chance in twenty Battles rather than stay another twelve months in Prison."[36]

On June 12, 1865, two months after Lee's surrender at Appomattox and almost two years after his capture at Battery Wagner, James Campbell took the oath of allegiance to the United States government and was released at Fort Delaware. The Campbell brothers' Civil War was finally over.[37]

JAMES RETURNED TO CHARLESTON AND DIVIDED HIS TIME between the city and various farms in Charleston County. After farming for himself on a modest scale, he managed "Oaklands," the Combahee River plantation owned by Rawlins Lowndes, for many years. He eventually bought land along the Ashepoo River and planted there until his death. Sandy, meanwhile, lived in New York City for a few years, but by 1870 had moved to Middletown, Connecticut, where he established a business as "Manufacturer of Artistic Monuments."[38] The two brothers kept in touch over the years, and the last known letter between them is one from James to

[33]Compiled Service Record of James Campbell, Twenty-seventh (Gaillard's) Regiment, Compiled Service Records of Confederate Soldiers Who Served in Organizations from the State of South Carolina, War Department Collection of Confederate Records, Record Group 109, National Archives, Washington, D.C.; National Archives Microfilm Publication M267, Roll 356 (hereafter James Campbell, Compiled Service Record).

[34]James Campbell to his brother Alexander, November 9, 1863, January 17, February 6, 29, June 18, August 10, 26, 18, September 17, October 5, 18, November 4, 1864, January 9, May 5, 1865, Campbell Family Papers, SCDAH.

[35]Ibid., June 18, 1864, Campbell Family Papers, SCDAH.

[36]Ibid., July 10, 1864, Campbell Family Papers, SCDAH.

[37]James Campbell, Compiled Service Record.

[38]James Campbell to his brother Alexander, November 1, 1865, March 5, 1866, October 20, 1886, and undated letterhead, Campbell Family Papers, SCDAH; Charleston *News*, March 4, 1907.

Middletown, Conn.,_____190

By 1870 Sandy Campbell had moved to Middletown, Connecticut, where he established a business as "Manufacturer of Artistic Monuments. Letterhead courtesy of the South Carolina Department of Archives and History.

Sandy, written in October 1886. After describing the aftermath of the recent Charleston earthquake, James answered Sandy's questions about the prospects for work in Charleston. "You propose coming here this winter," he wrote, explaining, "I would be glad to see you, but if you come expecting stone-cutting, I fear you will be disappointed."[39] James, who never married, was an active member of the St. Andrew's Society, the United Confederate Veterans, and the Union Light Infantry Charitable Association in his later years. He was eulogized as a "sterling Scotchman ... and faithful and fearless Confederate soldier" when he died in 1907 at the age of seventy-four, and was buried in Magnolia Cemetery in Charleston.[40] Sandy Campbell survived his older brother by only two years and died in 1909 at the age of seventy-one.[41]

We do not know if the Campbells ever met face-to-face after 1865, swapping old soldiers' tales, but their remarkable letters survive, in a small collection at the South Carolina Department of Archives and History in Columbia. "Its rather to bad to think that we should be fighting him on the one side and me on the other," Sandy wrote a few days after Secessionville. "I hope to god that he and I will get safe through it all and he will have his story to tell about his side and I will have my story to tell about my side."[42] The Campbells' story reminds us that the familiar phrase "brother against brother" has a deeper and more human meaning than we usually recognize.

[39]James Campbell to his brother Alexander, October 20, 1886, Campbell Family Papers, SCDAH.

[40]Charleston *News*, March 4, 1907.

[41]Alexander Campbell to his wife, June 25, 1862, Campbell Family Papers, SCDAH.

[42]Ibid., June 25, 1862.

AN AFFAIR OF HONOR AT FORT SUMTER

C. RUSSELL HORRES, JR.*

DURING THE CIVIL WAR, FORT SUMTER WITNESSED MANY ACTS of remarkable heroism and unselfish service to the Southern cause. Eyewitness chroniclers of the history of the fort and its defenders gave glowing accounts of these deeds while carefully avoiding reference to the fact that the fort and its defenders were involved in one of the most ignominious episodes of Charleston's Civil War history.[1] Events occurred during the beginning of the war that were to contribute to the garrison's loyalty being challenged by the citizens of Charleston and lead to an affair of honor between its senior officers. The duel and its consequences reverberated through Charleston society, the state government and in the top levels of the Confederate government both in Richmond and abroad. This account illustrates the involvement of Charleston society with the Confederate military establishment and provides considerable insight into the circumstances of the times and the Code of Honor of the Old South.

In January of 1860, the newly seceded state of South Carolina prepared to defend itself against the Union by authorizing the formation of the First South Carolina Artillery Battalion. Key positions in the unit were given to those with past military education or experience. However, the strong allegiance to social position held in the South would also see leadership positions falling to those of high political or social standing. This process brought together two men in their early 30s, William Ransom Calhoun and Alfred Moore Rhett, who would be intimately involved in this scandalous incident.

Ransom Calhoun and Alfred Rhett were from prominent South Carolina families and, by most measures, belonged to the highest levels of society. Ransom Calhoun, born in 1827, was the oldest son of John Ewing Colhoun and Martha Maria Davis. Ransom grew up in a magnificent home at Keowee near Pendleton. His aunt, Floride Bonneau Colhoun, married U.S. vice-president John C. Calhoun. As a boy Ransom was a frequent visitor to their

*Independent Researcher, Mt. Pleasant, S.C. The author wishes to acknowledge the assistance of Dr. Ernest McPherson Lander in locating the Calhoun burial site.

[1]John Johnson, *The Defense of Charleston Harbor, 1863-1865* (Charleston, S.C.: Walker, Evans & Cogswell Co., 1890; repr., Germantown, Tenn.: Guild Bindery Press, 1994); Charles Inglesby, "Historical Sketch of the First Regiment of SC Artillery," Pamphlet Collection, Charleston Library Society (hereinafter CLS), Charleston, S.C.

home, Fort Hill, at Clemson.[2] He was admitted to West Point on July 1, 1846, and maintained a balanced academic record across all subject areas during his tenure at the academy. He graduated 27th in a class of 44 in 1850.[3] Although he had intended to follow a military career, he resigned his commission as a brevet second lieutenant of Dragoons in the U.S. Army on April 26, 1851, after nearly a year's leave of absence.[4] His resignation was said to be because of the first secession crisis in South Carolina, and he took a position as ordnance officer for South Carolina to work on preparing the state for war.[5] When the crisis passed, he obtained a position as Secretary of Legation for the French Mission under John Y. Mason in September 1857. He served in this position until March 4, 1861, except for a period from October 1859 to November 1860 when he was chargé d'affaires of the United States to the Court of Tuileries.[6]

Alfred Rhett was the son of Robert Barnwell Rhett, a U.S. Senator from the state of South Carolina. He was born in Beaufort on October 29, 1829. His father, an outspoken proponent of secession, was a candidate for presidency of the Confederacy. His brother Robert B. Rhett, Jr. was the publisher of the *Charleston Mercury*. Alfred graduated from Harvard in the class of 1850 and was a rice planter before the war.[7]

Alfred Rhett's father knew John C. Calhoun well and was his campaign manager for the U.S. Presidency until there was a falling out between them in 1842.[8] This association raises the possibility that Ransom Calhoun and Alfred Rhett knew each other in the years preceding the war. Their formal relationship began when they were both among the founding officers of the First South Carolina Artillery. Calhoun, because of his previous military experience, was named one of four captains of the newly formed artillery

---

[2]Ernest McPherson Lander, *The Calhoun Family and Thomas Green Clemson: The Decline of a Southern Patriarchy* (Columbia, S.C.: University of South Carolina Press, 1983), 154-155, 479. In the mid 1800s, the spelling of this branch of the family was changed from the Irish form of Colhoun to the more familier Calhoun.

[3] Official Register of the Officers and Cadets of the U.S. Military Academy 1847-1850. West Point, New York.

[4] George W. Cullum, *Biographical Register of the Officers and Graduates of the U.S. Military Academy at West Point From its Establishment, in 1802, to 1890* (Boston, Ma.: Houghton, Mifflin and Company, 1892), II, 427.

[5] *Charleston Daily Courier*, Sept. 13, 1862.

[6] Cullum, *Biographical Register*, 427.

[7] Rhett Family History and Geneaology files (30-4 Rhett), South Carolina Historical Society (hereinafter SCHS), Charleston, S.C.

[8]John S. Coussons, "Thirty Years with Calhoun, Rhett, and the *Charleston Mercury*—A Chapter in South Carolina Politics." Ph.D. Thesis, 1971, Louisiana State University, 158, 164-165.

battalion, while Alfred Rhett was given a lieutenant's appointment.[9] Roswell S. Ripley, also a West Point graduate, was named lt. colonel.[10] The unit's first assignment was to garrison Fort Moultrie in preparation for driving Major Robert Anderson out of Fort Sumter.

Rhett's difficulties with Calhoun began during the opening shots of the Civil War, when their regiment served the guns at Fort Moultrie. In the excitement of battle Calhoun, on orders from Ripley to change the pattern of firing on Fort Sumter, by-passed Rhett and gave direct orders to the artillerists. After the battle, Calhoun also ordered Rhett and some of his men who were celebrating on the parapets to return to their stations. Rhett took great offense at these incidents. Unsuccessful in an appeal of his case before a military advisory board, he took to open criticism of Calhoun before other officers of the regiment.[11]

In the months following the seizure of Fort Sumter, many changes occurred in the First South Carolina Artillery Battalion. All of its original captains, except Ransom Calhoun, resigned to accept high positions elsewhere. This opened captain's positions for Alfred Rhett, Thomas Wagner and Joseph Yates. Following the restoration of Fort Sumter, two of the companies were garrisoned at the fort, which became the battalion's headquarters.[12] Under orders from the legislature, early in July Capt. Calhoun outfitted Company A of the unit as a battalion of field artillery and took it to Virginia.[13] In August 1861, Lt. Col. Ripley was promoted to brigadier general in charge of coastal South Carolina defenses.[14] This opening led to Calhoun being given a promotion to lt. colonel of the First South Carolina Artillery.

Calhoun felt that the situation in Virginia demanded that he stay with the battery he commanded in spite of the fact that Joseph Yates had been promoted to captain of that command. Calhoun's friend Capt. Thomas Wagner became incensed that Ransom would not return immediately to Charleston to take command of the First SC Artillery. At this early phase of the war garrison duty in Charleston would have seemed considerably less exciting than the opportunity to engage the enemy in Virginia. It also

---

[9] Inglesby, "Historical Sketch of the First Regiment of SC Artillery," 3-4.

[10] C.A. Bennett, "Roswell Sabin Ripley; Charleston's Gallant Defender," *South Carolina Historical Magazine* (hereafter *SCHM*) 95 (July 1994): 228.

[11] Alfred Rhett, Testimony at Board of Inquiry, Charleston, S.C., Nelson Mitchell Papers, SCHS.

[12] Inglesby, "Historical Sketch of the First Regiment of SC Artillery," 3-4.

[13] *War of the Rebellion: A Compilation of the Official Records of the Union and Confederate Armies* (hereinafter cited as *O.R.*) (Washington, D.C.: Government Printing Office, 1880-1901), Series I, Vol. LXV, 178.

[14] Bennett, "Roswell Sabin Ripley," 229.

appears that Ransom had time to make a number of social calls during his time in Virginia.[15] Thus began a period during which Calhoun and Wagner would not communicate with each other.[16]

In December, Calhoun was still near Centreville, Virginia when the First South Carolina Artillery was authorized to increase to a regiment of ten companies. Calhoun was promoted to colonel of the regiment, Thomas Wagner was promoted to lieutenant colonel and Capt. Alfred Rhett to major as a result of the expansion.[17] Some accused Calhoun of being un-patriotic for staying with the field artillery battalion in Virginia. On December 4, 1861, he bipassed Ripley, and appealed directly to General P. G. T. Beauregard for adjudication of his decision, and sent Ripley a copy of the request. Beauregard, in a lengthy reply, fully supported Calhoun.[18] This action probably contributed later to General Ripley's decision to bring charges against Ransom Calhoun. Civil War diarist Mary Chesnut, who knew Ransom Calhoun through her close friend Sally Buck Preston, recorded on January 6, 1862 that Ripley had arrested Calhoun for writing an insulting letter either to or about General Ripley.[19] When Calhoun finally returned to Charleston, he was disaffected with Rhett, Wagner, and Ripley.[20] Over the next few months, this situation would intensify and discredit the loyalty of the garrison and lead to dire consequences for Calhoun.

The first recorded evidence of discord between the officers of Fort Sumter occurred on April 23, 1862. Colonel Calhoun was at the fort that day and was critical of actions that Major Rhett had taken in his absence. The parties assembled six witnesses in the Adjutant's office and made charges and counter charges concerning their feelings towards each other. Alfred Rhett pressed his witnesses to write letters supporting his view that Calhoun was the aggressor in this incident. Edmund Rhett presented these letters to Calhoun, who declined to comment and promptly returned them.[21]

---

[15] C. Van Woodward and Elisabeth Muhlenfeld, eds., *The Private Mary Chesnut: The Unpublished Civil War Diaries* (New York: Oxford University Press, 1984), 105, 114.

[16] Nelson Mitchell, Board of Inquiry Transcript, Nelson Mitchell Papers, SCHS.

[17] Inglesby, "Historical Sketch of the First Regiment of SC Artillery," CLS, 5.

[18] Nelson Mitchell, Board of Inquiry Transcript, Nelson Mitchell Papers, SCHS, 92-94.

[19] Mary Boykin Chesnut, *Diary from Dixie*, ed. Ben A. Williams (Cambridge, Ma.: Harvard University Press, 1980), 181.

[20] *O.R.*, I, XXVL, 515.

[21] "Papers Touching Interview of April 23, 1862," 4-8, in collection of bound pamphlets with the running title *The Case for Major Rhett* (Charleston: Evans and Cogswell, 1862-1863), The Charleston Museum. These pamphlets belonged to R.B. Rhett, Jr.

Other signs of trouble at Fort Sumter appeared in the spring of 1862, when rumors spread through Charleston concerning the loyalty of Colonel Calhoun's regiment. According to Governor Francis Pickens, "the evil" at Fort Sumter began in the summer of 1861 when Calhoun had been with South Carolina troops at the first battle of Manassas. He was a company commander at the time and had in some way offended Major Thomas Wagner and possibly General Ripley as well. Ripley pressed charges against Calhoun on his return to Charleston, which led to a lengthy court-martial proceeding and wide-spread dissension. During Calhoun's absence for the court-martial, reports claimed that five members of Fort Sumter's garrison deserted and fled to the blockading Union fleet. Pickens asserted that Ripley had left Fort Sumter under the command of only a captain, a "favorite of General Ripley," because he had assigned Major Wagner, second in command, to duties outside the fort.

Thus, Governor Pickens implicated Ripley in the troubles at Charleston for his poor judgment in assigning commanders at Fort Sumter. General Robert E. Lee wrote on May 4, 1862 that he saw no way of correcting matters at Charleston except to relieve Ripley.[22] Charlestonians W. Porcher Miles, W. D. Porter and Mayor A. G. Magrath tried to support Ripley by suggesting to Lee that Ripley be allowed to command Charleston's defense without being under the control of Major General John C. Pemberton, commander of the Department of South Carolina and Georgia. Lee would have no part of such an arrangement.[23] Ripley, who had already displayed his dislike of Pemberton by repeatedly requesting a transfer from the department, was re-assigned to Virginia on May 24, 1862. Lee wrote Governor Pickens on May 29 that the discordance among the officers called to defend Charleston was regrettable. By relieving Ripley, he assured him steps had been taken as far as practical to remedy the "evil."[24]

Further insight into these events is found in Pemberton's reply to former U.S. Senator James R. Chesnut's concerns regarding the loyalty of the Fort Sumter garrison on May 23. Chesnut, Chief of the Department of Military for the state of South Carolina, had information suggesting that disaffection prevailed in a large portion of the fort's garrison, extending to threats of mutiny and refusal to fire on the enemy.[25] According to Pemberton, General Ripley had discovered that the sources that had informed Chesnut of the post's disloyalty were also circulating similar reports in Charleston. Pemberton acknowledged that there might be disaffected individuals among

[22]*O.R.*, I, XXVL, 504, 515-516.
[23]*O.R.*, I, XXVL, 504.
[24]*O.R.*, I, XXVL, 524.
[25]*O.R.*, I, XXVL, 508.

the "rank and file" of Fort Sumter. Indeed, Private John Aiken of Calhoun's command had been placed in confinement and faced a general court-martial for using seditious language in the presence of Mr. James W. Simons, a Charlestonian. Pemberton considered reports that a large portion of the garrison had threatened to mutiny and would refuse to fire on the enemy to be "unfounded rumors," and strongly supported Calhoun.[26] On May 29 General Lee, citing a mutiny at Fort Jackson during the battle for New Orleans, encouraged Pemberton to pay particular attention to the condition of the armaments and feelings of the garrison.[27]

Calhoun did not take the assertions of disloyalty lightly. He had stated to Pemberton that he and the officers of his command "have confidence in the courage, patriotism and discipline of the men."[28] At the end of May, he had each company captain produce an affidavit declaring the loyalty of their commands. These were forwarded to Pemberton's headquarters. From the affidavits, it is clear that the soldiers were much affected by the "very strong sentiment against the troops of this garrison as regards their loyalty."[29] Several thought that the citizens of Charleston had treated them unfairly and that the only resolution was to seek the regiment's transfer. The signature of Major Alfred Rhett, second officer of the First South Carolina Artillery, was notably absent from Calhoun's affidavits. Rhett, who commanded Fort Sumter during Calhoun's absence, should have strongly supported his commander's request for statements of loyalty. Records indicate that Major Rhett was in charge of Fort Sumter on May 13 when Robert Smalls piloted the steamer *Planter* out of Charleston Harbor with a valuable load of artillery.[30] He also was listed as commander of Ft. Sumter in the Confederate army returns of July 1862.[31] General Pemberton noted that he had had personal conversations with Major Rhett during this period, no doubt facilitated by Ripley's removal.[32]

These events occurred during a particularly contentious period for the military leadership at Charleston, a factor that may have contributed to the situation escalating to tragic consequences. In May 1862 General Pemberton, commander of the department following General Lee's departure, generated intense anxiety among the state's leaders with his decision to abandon outlying fortifications near Charleston. His most notable action in this

[26]*O.R.*, I, XXVL, 517.
[27]*O.R.*, I, XXVL, 523; VI, 640-646.
[28]*O.R.*, I, XXVL, 517
[29]*O.R.*, I, XXVL, 565.
[30]*O.R.*, I, XXVL, 15.
[31]*O.R.*, I, XXVL, 591.
[32]*O.R.*, I, XXVL, 590.

regard was his decision to remove armament from Fort Palmetto, which was located on Cole's Island guarding the Stono and Folly River inlets. When word leaked that Pemberton proposed abandoning the harbor forts and defending Charleston from the mainland, even his former ally Governor Pickens deserted him.[33] With Pemberton in trouble with the local citizens, Ripley clashing with Pemberton and Calhoun, and Rhett and Wagner quarelling with Calhoun, little wonder rumors where flying.

By June 25, 1862, despite the stunning defeat of the Union forces at Secessionville by forces under Pemberton's command, General Lee forwarded his recommendation on the Charleston situation to Confederate President Jefferson Davis. Lee, swayed by William Porcher Miles' request for "any other" officer to be put in charge, reported that he saw no way to avoid Pemberton's removal.[34] The pressure to remove Pemberton became so severe that on July 5 Inspector General Samuel Cooper, believing the ailing Maj. Gen. Gustavus W. Smith would assume the command, prematurely ordered Pemberton to report to Richmond for new orders. Pemberton, caught totally off guard, asked Cooper to acknowledge under whose orders was he to report to Richmond. Cooper replied, "the President."[35] Learning that Smith was too ill to accept the appointment, Cooper reversed his orders on July 13.[36] It would be another 60 days before Pemberton would learn his fate, a period in which Charleston would lose both its new commanding general, W. D. Smith, and the senior officers of the First South Carolina Artillery. General Smith would succumb to yellow fever on September 12. Lieutenant Colonel Wagner would die from wounds received on July 17 when cannon at Fort Moultrie burst after being inadvertently double charged. Colonel Calhoun's fate was considerably more infamous. He would be killed in a duel with Major Rhett on September 5.[37]

Leadership of the Department of South Carolina and Georgia fell upon a favorite of Charlestonians, General Pierre Gustave Toutant Beauregard. He was officially appointed to the position on August 29, 1862, but did not learn of the assignment until September 10 due to the orders being sent to his home in Bladen Springs, Alabama. He had only recently reported for duty at Mobile following convalescence from his campaigns in Tennessee.[38]

[33]*O.R.*, I, XXVL, 593-594.

[34]*O.R.*, I, XXVL, 560.

[35]*O.R.*, I, XXVL, 582.

[36]*O.R.*, I, XXVL, 585.

[37]Langdon Cheves to mother, August 2, 1862, Cheves Family Papers, South Caroliniana Library (hereinafter SCL), University of South Carolina, Columbia, S.C.

[38]Alfred Roman, *The Military Operations of General Beauregard* (New York , N.Y.: Da Capo Press Reprint 1994), II, 435.

In view of the contentious nature of the situation, Pemberton was fortunate Richmond honored his request for reassignment rather than leave him as second in command, as had originally been ordered.[39] No doubt troubled by his forced retirement from his 16-month command, Pemberton would not have welcomed receiving the following telegram as he prepared to leave Charleston:

RICHMOND, VA., September 22, 1862

Major-General Pemberton:

Colonel Calhoun's death in a duel being announced in the papers, I desire to call your attention to the 25th and 26th articles of war and to request an immediate execution of them.

G. W. RANDOLPH
Secretary of War[40]

Pemberton, in one of his last official duties at Charleston, responded to Secretary Randolph's request for executing the Articles of War concerning dueling. He convened a court of inquiry the same day he received the telegram. However, with Pemberton reassigned, the business of sorting out the death of Ransom Calhoun would fall upon Beauregard.

In a meeting on September 28, the day before Beauregard assumed command of the department, Governor Pickens described his concerns for the situation at Fort Sumter to Beauregard and felt so strongly that he followed up "specifically in writing."

> The recent difficulties among the field officers (at Sumter) and the death of the two senior officers in command (Calhoun and Smith) and probable suspension of, at least for a time, of the other field officer from actual command (Rhett), make it of the deepest interest to the State and to the country at large to have an artillery officer of high rank immediately appointed to the command of that fortress.[41]

At the suggestion of "prominent Charlestonians," Beauregard responded by requesting the return of Roswell Ripley to the command of Charleston's

[39]*O.R.*, I, XXVL, 601.
[40]*O.R.*, I, XXVL 604-605.
[41]*O.R.*, I, XXVL, 613.

defenses. At the time, Ripley was recovering from a neck wound received at Fredericksburg. On his return, Ripley assured Pickens that a military board had made a thorough examination of the matter of disloyalty and that the garrison appeared to be well disciplined and zealous.[42]

The custom of dueling in America began in colonial days and extended into the 1880s.[43] An extraordinary number of prominent Americans were involved in duels during the early 1800s including dozens of congressmen, several state governors, numerous newspaper editors and a host of prominent planters.[44] Although settled without an actual conflict, an 1842 duel challenge of Abraham Lincoln by James Shields, commander of the Palmetto Regiment in the Mexican War and later a major General in the Union Army, illustrates the degree to which the practice infiltrated 19th century society. Dueling among Army and Navy officers occurred to such an alarming degree in the early 1800s that it led to the inclusion of anti-dueling provisions in the articles of war. During the Civil War, dueling among officers appears to have been almost uniquely a Confederate problem.[45] This in part was due to the practice having become a virtual social institution among the upper class of the South. Military officers of the rank of captain or above were considered to belong to this class.[46] The most notable Civil War duel by rank of the participants was fought on August 6, 1863, near Little Rock, Arkansas between Generals John S. Marmaduke and Lucius M. Walker. Walker, a West Point classmate of Ransom Calhoun and the superior officer, was killed.[47] Brig. Gen. John S. Marmaduke studied at Yale and Harvard Universities before going to West Point. Despite his participation in the duel, Marmaduke received a promotion to major general later in the war.[48]

Dueling in the South was viewed as an incentive to virtue and a shield on personal honor. Although an intangible concept, honor among the southern aristocracy was seen to be no less real and no less valuable than the most expensive and cherished physical possession.[49] The fact that the South

[42]*O.R.*, I, XXVI, 632.

[43]Don Carlos Seitz, *Famous American Duels* (Freeport, N.Y.: Books for Libraries Press, Reprint 1966), 17.

[44]Jack K. Williams, *Dueling in the Old South: Vignettes of Social History* (College Station:Texas A&M University Press, 1980), 12.

[45]Major Ben C. Truman, *From the Field of Honor* (San Diego: Ford, Howard and Hulbert, 1884), 81.

[46]Williams, *Dueling in the Old South*, 12, 27.

[47]Seitz, *Famous American Duels*, 27-28; Official Register of the Officers and Cadets of the U.S. Military Academy 1847-1850, West Point, New York.

[48]Ezra J. Warner, *Generals in Gray* (Baton Rouge: Louisiana State University Press, 1959), 211-212.

[49]Rosser H. Taylor, *Ante-Bellum South Carolina: A Social and Cultural History* (Chapel Hill, N.C.: University of North Carolina Press, 1942), 47, 77.

held on to the practice after it had been largely abandoned in the North is indicative of the South's adherence to the ethics of aristocracy and the psychological chasm between the regions.[50] In the institutionalization of dueling in the South, South Carolina played a significant role. Former governor John Lyde Wilson published one of the few formal declarations of the Code of Honor in 1838. His rationale for such a publication was that establishing a process for cooling off and allowing outside parties (seconds) to attempt peaceful mediation of differences could prevent unnecessary conflict.[51] His publication came 26 years after an act had made dueling illegal in the state.

Legal status had little impact on dueling largely because, when charges were brought, defendants were generally acquitted. South Carolina citizens flaunted the law and newspapers openly advertised dueling schools and courses. In the early 19th century, a dueling society was said to exist in Charleston in which one's position was dependent on the number of persons he had killed or wounded in duels.[52] The exact number of duels fought in the state is not known but is undoubtedly a considerable figure. One South Carolinian reported that he had been a second in 51 duels during the antebellum period.[53]

The practice of dueling in South Carolina was not without its opponents. Charles Cotesworth Pinckney made an early stand against dueling. Alfred Rhett's father Robert Barnwell Rhett, having refused to duel with Jeremiah Clemens when they were both U.S. Senators, was also a noted opponent of the practice.[54] Another notable anti-duelist was Confederate Capt. F.W. Dawson, who came to Charleston following the war as associate editor of the *Mercury*. He left the *Mercury* after a brief period to become part owner and editor of the *Charleston News and Courier* and was challenged to a duel by the manager of the *Mercury*, which he declined on religious grounds. Dawson's strong position against the practice led to his being awarded a Knight of the Order of St. George by the Pope on November 23, 1883. Growing public opposition and a controversial duel between Col. E.B.C. Cash and William Shannon in 1880 resulted in the South Carolina legislature's declaring death in a duel as murder. This law effectively ended the practice.[55]

---

[50]Clyde N. Wilson, *Carolina Cavalier: The Life and Times of James Johnston Pettigrew* (Athens, Ga.: University of Georgia Press, 1990), 86-87.

[51]John Lyde Wilson, *The Code of Honor: or Rules for the Government of Principals and Seconds in Dueling* (Charleston, S.C.: Eccles, 1838).

[52]Truman, *From the Field of Honor*, 79.

[53]Williams, *Dueling in the Old South*, 42.

[54]Truman, *From the Field of Honor*, 78, 442.

[55]Ibid., 88.

At issue for the court of inquiry into Calhoun's death, was the prohibition of dueling among military officers. Calhoun was on leave of absence at the time of the duel, but Rhett was clearly on active duty. Both Calhoun and Rhett had previous experiences with the practice of dueling. While in Paris, Calhoun had his first brush with the Code of Honor when he fought a bloodless duel with a gentleman from New York.[56] Alfred Rhett was also no stranger to dueling; he had been a very controversial second in another famous Charleston duel in 1856 between *Mercury* editor William Taber, Jr. and Edward Magrath, brother of A.G. Magrath, over the paper's publications about his brother. It appears that Rhett had shouted loudly and threatened Edward Magrath. Whatever his intentions, the young editor was killed.[57] Thus by military rank and social standing Calhoun and Rhett fell into the class in which dueling was an accepted means of settling differences, though not legal under state or Confederate Military law.

The court of inquiry into the Calhoun-Rhett affair would last throughout the fall of 1862. A parade of witnesses would testify about the affairs of the duel's participants. The court learned that Alfred Rhett seemed unable or unwilling to let his difficulties with Calhoun drop and, after almost 16 months of consternation, found himself involved in a situation that would escalate into violence. Rhett, along with a number of prominent Charlestonians and military officers, enjoyed the ambiance of the Charleston Club during his time off from his isolated post at Fort Sumter. The Club, a venerable institution still in existence, was located during the Civil War in a fashionable three-story brownstone building on what is now the U.S. Post Office parking lot at the corner of Meeting and Broad Streets.[58] On August 7, 1862, Rhett was in the company of Captain Arnoldus Vanderhorst, Captain Thomas Pinckney, Captain John Mitchel, Mr. George Bryan, Mr. Alfred Huger and others at the club. The group's discussion turned to West Point graduates among the Confederate command to whom Vanderhorst felt much was owed. Rhett, critical of that class of officers, let his feelings be known. Vanderhorst pressed him on the qualifications of Calhoun, his commander and a member of that class of officers. Vanderhorst said that Davis and Beauregard held Colonel Calhoun in high regard. Rhett exclaimed that Calhoun was a "damned puppy." Vanderhorst felt himself insulted and demanded of Rhett that he explain how he intended his comment. Rhett then told Vanderhorst that he could "take it any way he wanted." Vanderhorst left the room, returning in about fifteen minutes as Rhett was about to leave,

---

[56]*Charleston Daily Courier*, Sept. 13, 1862.
[57]Wilson, *Carolina Cavalier*, 94-95.
[58]Charleston *News and Courier*, Dec. 10, 1984.

and told Rhett that he considered his language in front of the assembled gentlemen as insulting and that he would call on him for satisfaction at the earliest hour. Rhett curtly told him that boats left for Fort Sumter at half past 6 o'clock in the morning and 4 o'clock in the afternoon and that any proposition could be carried by either of the boats.[59]

In accordance with the Code of Honor, seconds were appointed to exchange conditions and, more importantly, to attempt a peaceful mediation. Dr. William Huger was the second to Vanderhorst and 22-year old, Irish-born Capt. John C. Mitchel was the second for Rhett.[60] The issue between Rhett and Vanderhorst was quickly pressed and, finding no grounds for compromise, the challenge was scheduled for 6:30 p.m. on August 9 at the farm of Mr. Ben Rhett, located near the present site of the Citadel.[61] Some felt that this haste violated the duty of seconds to attempt a peaceful adjudication.[62] Others believed it was strange that the issue was pressed at all, as Rhett's sister was married to a Vanderhorst.[63] Smoothbore dueling pistols were selected as weapons and the method of firing chosen to be raised shot. This method of firing, by raising the pistol from the side, had been found less deadly than the method of dropping the pistol from a vertical position (dropped shot). Instructions were given not to fire before the word "fire" or after the word "halt." The distance was paced off, the call given and both parties fired without hitting. The seconds again requested an apology, but none was offered. Pistols were reloaded and the duel repeated. On the second round, Vanderhorst fired quickly and missed. Rhett held his fire and, on the order to halt, discharged his pistol into the air. At this point, the issue was declared settled without satisfaction.

In the close social circles of wartime Charleston, Calhoun quickly heard of the insult issued and the duel fought on his behalf. Ransom Calhoun was also known to attend the Charleston Club where Rhett issued the insults.[64] Although there was a growing opposition to dueling, the social order of the Southern elite demanded that a challenge be made if one had been slandered.[65]

[59]Mitchell-Pringle, Board of Inquiry Transcript, 84.

[60]Johnson, *The Defense of Charleston Harbor, 1863-1865,* 208.

[61]W.H. Huger, Affidavit, Arnoldus Vanderhorst Dueling Papers, 1835-1881, SCHS; Charleston *News and Courier,* Jan. 8, 1965.

[62]"A Blunder and its Consequences,"Arnoldus Vanderhorst Dueling Papers, SCHS.

[63]John Marszalek, ed., *The Diary of Miss Emma Holmes 1861-1865* (Baton Rouge, La.: Louisiana State University Press, 1994), 196.

[64]"A Sketch of the Charleston Club," Pamphlet Collection (Vol. 16, No. 2), 10, CLS.

[65]Elizabeth Street Mason, "The Dueling Simons Family," *Carologue* 10 (Winter 1994): 20.

For a military officer, the prospect of being branded a "coward" was unthinkable. On August 13, 1862, Calhoun prepared a written statement foreshadowing the coming events, in which he began, "In view of the probable serious termination of the difficulty between Major Rhett and myself..." In this testament, he claimed to have first heard of Rhett's attacks on him from Captain Joseph Heyward, a personal friend, and in April 1862 had told Rhett in the presence of four witnesses that he was aware of how Rhett had assailed him and that he had not pressed the issue for "patriotic reasons" but that he intended to hold him "to account for it."[66] Col. Calhoun resigned his commission in the Confederate Army for "health reasons" on August 18 and was granted a leave of absence.[67] Through his friend, Colonel Olin Miller Dantzler, Calhoun wrote to Rhett on September 3: "You have on many occasions assailed me with a view to injure my character, and under circumstances which give me a right to demand redress." Rhett obliged him with the satisfaction of a duel. The seconds, Colonel Dantzler for Calhoun and Dr. J. K. Furham for Rhett, were unable to reach a peaceful mediation and a duel was set for 5:00 p.m. on September 5 at the Charleston Oaks Club, then located on the Cooper River just north of Magnolia Cemetary.[68]Attire for the occasion would be uniforms or the dress of a gentleman. In addition to the seconds, Dr. W.T. Wragg, Dr. J. D. Bruns and General James Simons attended. As with Vanderhorst, the raised shot from smoothbore dueling pistols would be the method of dueling. After the seconds tossed a coin for the choice of position, the men paced off a distance of 30 feet. In accordance with the established protocol, the command "Gentlemen prepare to receive the word" was given. This was followed by the question "Are you ready?" On the command "start," Rhett shot Calhoun through the heart; he died quickly.[69]

Before the war, Ransom Calhoun had been a member of St. Paul's Episcopal Church in Pendleton, and he was afforded an Episcopal service in Charleston.[70] The day following his death, a terse bulletin appeared in the Saturday morning edition of the *Daily Courier* announcing that the funeral observance would be that afternoon at 4:00 o'clock at St. Philip's.[71] Following

[66]William R. Calhoun to Mcmillan King, October 16, 1862, Nelson Mitchell Papers, SCHS.

[67]Thomas Jordan, General Order 19, Headquarters Department of S.C., Ga. and Fla., January 30, 1863, SCHS.

[68]Henry A.M. Smith, "Baronies of South Carolina," *SCHM* 13 (April 1912): 77.

[69]Nelson Mitchell, Board of Inquiry Transcript, Nelson Mitchell Papers, SCHS, 6.

[70]Edwin H. Vedder, Records of St. Paul's Episcopal Church, Pendleton, South Carolina, 4.

[71]*Charleston Daily Courier*, Sept. 6, 1862.

a funeral procession through the streets, Ransom Calhoun was buried in the Huger family plot at Magnolia Cemetery.[72] An unidentified female admirer was said to have given the undertaker a splendid bouquet of flowers to place upon his coffin as its was laid in the ground.[73] One such admirer was twenty-year-old Sally Buchanan Preston, who met Calhoun in Paris, where she was in school before the war.[74] His death was part of a series of misfortunes that would befall her admirers. Bishop Howe preached a sermon against dueling at St. Philip's the day after Calhoun's funeral, and an editorial followed in the *Daily Courier* on the evils of the practice.[75]

The events that occurred later would prove almost as contentious as the duel. Charleston society quickly polarized around the issues depending on where sentiment or family loyalties lay.[76] Emma Holmes recorded: "The Rhetts have been hitherto hated enough, now the name is almost execrated—the public are almost unanimous against him."[77]

On September 18 the Charleston Coroner's inquest rendered a unanimous verdict that Major Alfred Rhett, as principal, and all of the parties, as accessories, had feloniously killed Colonel Calhoun. Coroner E. M. Whiting issued warrants for the arrest of all parties involved.[78] News of the death spread and by November had reached England, where Charles Prioleau would write about Ransom Calhoun's life being thrown away, "God knows there are Yankees enough to kill to satisfy any man however blood-thirsty."[79] For nearly two months, the board of inquiry heard testimony concerning the events leading to the duels. They learned of the long-standing disaffection between the two men and of Alfred Rhett's open criticism of his commanding officer. They heard testimony from witnesses who felt that Calhoun had offered Rhett an apology for treating him roughly and that the two men had shaken hands on the matter while standing on the wharf at Fort Moultrie. Rhett's brother testified that Alfred did not consider the occasion an apology.

The most prestigious witness at the hearing was General Ripley, called on behalf of Rhett. On October 30, 1862, Ripley testified that he was aware

[72] Internment Records, Magnolia Cemetery, Charleston, S.C.

[73] Ann Morris Vanderhorst Diary, September 5, 1862, SCHS.

[74] Ann Fripp Hampton, ed., *A Divided Heart: Letters of Sally Baxter Hampton* (Spartanburg, S.C.: Reprint Co., 1980), 102.

[75] Marszalek, ed., *The Diary of Miss Emma Holmes*, 198; *Charleston Daily Courier*, Sept. 13, 1862.

[76] Robert N. Rosen, *Confederate Charleston* (Columbia, S.C.:University of South Carolina Press, 1994), 104.

[77] Marszalek, ed., *The Diary of Miss Emma Holmes*, 196.

[78] *Charleston Daily Courier*, Sept. 20, 1862.

[79] Charles Priloeau to George Trenholm, November 8, 1862 (Copy), SCHS.

of the difficulty between these officers as early as August 1861, when Calhoun wrote Ripley about bringing charges against Rhett. Ripley also testified that he had heard rumors that Colonel Calhoun had made threats against Rhett in a Richmond "house of ill repute." Furthermore, he knew that Rhett had expressed a desire to leave the regiment the previous winter and spring to avoid being under Calhoun's command. Ripley testified that other duels between officers had been fought, and that the articles of war had not been enforced. In cross-examination, Ripley was asked what he would do if a junior officer was insubordinate. Ripley left no doubt that he would quickly bring the officer up on charges.[80]

Alfred Rhett testified on his own behalf that he had been offended by Calhoun, who had waited over a year to give him the opportunity to redress the issue. In the case of the first duel with Vanderhorst, he said he was not the "volunteer," having been pressed by Vanderhorst to comment on Calhoun. Concerning the duel with Calhoun, Rhett felt that Calhoun's challenge was preemptory, leaving him no choice. Rumors spread that Rhett had practiced constantly for the duel before a large mirror in his quarters at Fort Sumter.[81] Testimony established that both parties had practiced. In spite of the arguments presented, the board felt it could not exonerate Major Rhett, finding that he accepted a duel while an officer of the Confederate Army in violation of the 25th Article of War and determined that the matter should be investigated further.

In January 1863 Gen. Beauregard stepped in and closed the proceedings by affirming that it would be unjust to cashier Major Rhett out of the service, when no others had been punished for dueling. Putting the department on notice, he announced that any future duels would be subject to the articles.[82] Even after the pardon, Beauregard continued to receive letters advising him to examine the apprehension of mutiny and treason at Fort Sumter.[83] On January 13, 1863, news broke that Rhett had been placed in charge of Fort Sumter. Calhoun's friends were incensed that Rhett was promoted to the colonelcy vacated by Calhoun's death.[84] Emma Holmes noted in her diary, the appointment was met with "universal indignation."[85]

---

[80]Roswell S. Ripley, Testimony on October 30, 1862, Board of Inquiry Transcript, Nelson Mitchell Papers, SCHS.

[81]Marszalek, ed., *The Diary of Miss Emma Holmes*, 196.

[82]Thomas Jordan, General Order 19, Headquarters Department of S.C., Ga. and Fla., January 30, 1863, Nelson Mitchell Papers, SCHS.

[83]*O.R.*, I, XXVI, 770.

[84]"A Blunder and its Consequences," Arnoldus Vanderhorst Dueling Papers, SCHS; E. Vanderhorst to D.W. Huger, April 6, 1863, Arnoldus Vanderhorst Dueling Papers, SCHS.

[85]Marszalek, ed., *The Diary of Miss Emma Holmes*, 222.

Following Beauregard's pardon, a pamphlet titled "The Case for Maj. Rhett" was circulated among Charlestonians to support Alfred Rhett's position.[86] It was reported that Brigadier General Thomas Jordan, Beauregard's Chief of Staff, thought badly of Rhett and read the pamphlet only at Beauregard's request. Following his reading, he felt the pamphlet cleared Rhett of impropriety in the affair.[87] Any further attempt to discredit Rhett was soon derailed by his outstanding performance as commander of Fort Sumter during the defeat of Rear-Admiral Samuel F. Du Pont's ironclad fleet on April 7, 1863, and the defense of the fort during the subsequent siege.[88]

Colonel Alfred Rhett remained at Fort Sumter until it was substantially demolished by long range Union artillery firing from Morris Island. On September 3, 1863, Maj. Stephen Elliott, Jr. was designated to replace Rhett as commander of Fort Sumter.[89] Rhett was given command of the Fifth Military District consisting of the city of Charleston, Fort Ripley and Castle Pinckney.[90] He remained in this position until Beauregard ordered the evacuation of Charleston on February 17-18, 1865. Attempting to join forces with other Confederate troops to stop Union Major General W.T. Sherman's advance, Charleston's defenders headed toward North Carolina with Colonel Rhett in charge of a brigade.[91] On March 15, elements of Sherman's 14th Corp pressed General Hardee's forces near Averasboro, North Carolina. As the lines fell back, Rhett and an assistant rode out in front of his lines to inspect their pickets and were captured. Rhett, impeccably dressed in a fine uniform trimmed with gold braid and expensive Russian made boots, was taken to General Sherman. To the indignity of his captors, Rhett was invited

[86]*The Case for Maj. Rhett*, Charleston Museum. Section titled *Opinions of General P.G.T. Beauregard and James A. Seddon, Esq.* This section contains telegraphs between General Beauregard and James Seddon, then Confederate Secretary of War, that were not among the official records of the Confederate War Office. The Beauregard telegraph explains that he believed that Major Rhett was entitled to the rank of Lt. Colonel upon the death of Calhoun because Calhoun's logical successor, Thomas Wagner, had been killed in an accident. Seddon concurred with Beauregard on December 29, 1862, that by point of law, Rhett was already the Lt. Colonel. Beauregard ordered Lt. Colonel Rhett to report for duty to Brigadier General Ripley on January 8, 1863.

[87]Susan Middleton to Harriott Middleton, March 20-21, 1863, Cheves-Middleton Papers, SCHS.

[88]Johnson, *The Defense of Charleston Harbor*, 40-61, 146.

[89]*O.R.*, I, XL, 336.

[90]Ibid., 441.

[91]Joseph E. Johnston, *Narrative of Military Operations* (New York: D. Appleton and Co., 1874), 371, 382.

to have supper at headquarters.[92] Rhett, fuming about being captured without a fight, talked with Sherman about mutual Charleston friends that Sherman had made when stationed at Charleston before the war.[93] After being forced to walk to Goldsboro and imprisonment in Delaware, Alfred Rhett's Civil War career ended.

Following the war Rhett returned to Charleston and on August 14, 1866, he married Alicia Middleton Sparks, General Ripley's stepdaughter. After returning to rice planting, he was appointed to the post of Chief of Police for the City of Charleston under Mayors Sale and Courtenay.[94] Controversy continued to follow Rhett in his retirement from the military. General Beauregard published a letter in 1872 implying that Rhett had wanted to abandon Fort Sumter prematurely during the siege of 1863. Rhett's brother challenged Beauregard and numerous correspondants sent letters to Beauregard in support of Rhett. Beauregard suggested to Rhett's brother that he should just let the matter drop.[95] Alfred Rhett died November 12, 1889, and following services at St. Philips he was buried in the Rhett family plot at Magnolia Cemetery, not 50 feet from where Ransom Calhoun was initially interred.[96] No stone exists for Ransom Calhoun in the Huger plot at Magnolia. It is likely that Calhoun's remains were moved to the Calhoun Cemetery overlooking Lake Hartwell near Clemson University, where a headstone bearing his name has been located.[97]

The most perplexing aspect of the affair of honor between Calhoun and Rhett was why Calhoun, with so many opportunities, resisted officially charging Alfred Rhett with insubordination. Rhett's defiance and contempt for his commander was no secret as many witnesses testified. Calhoun's argument was that for "the good of the service" he was prevented from bringing charges, but there may have been other factors that gave him pause. Alfred Rhett was a member of an influential family with access to the press, who could have made a court-martial a public affair.[98] There are other circumstances that reflect on this question. Although Calhoun, while in

[92]Burke Davis, *Sherman's March* (New York: Random House, 1980), 228-229.

[93]William T. Sherman, *Memoirs of General William T. Sherman* (Bloomington, In.: Indiana University Press, 1957), 300-303.

[94]Newspaper Clippings, Rhett Family History and Genealogical Research files (30-4 Rhett), SCHS.

[95]H. Newcomb Morse, "General Beauregard and the Colonel Rhett Controversy," *SCHM* 78 (July 1977): 189-190.

[96]Internment records, Magnolia Cemetery, Charleston, SC.

[97]E.M. Lander and Lewis Patterson, Personal Communication with author, April 6, 1998.

[98]W.A. Swanberg, *First Blood* (New York, N.Y.: Dorset Press, 1990), 8.

Virginia, had written his commander, Colonel Roswell Ripley, regarding Rhett, it appears that Ripley did nothing to settle the dispute. Furthernore, Ripley pressed charges against Calhoun when he returned from Virginia, indicating considerable disaffection between Ripley and Calhoun. On the other hand, it appears that the relationship between Ripley and Rhett was much more than casual. As previously noted, Francis Pickens identified Rhett as "one of Ripley's favorites." Rhett was known to have been a guest at Ripley's dinner parties for visiting dignitaries. Ripley even referred to Rhett's friend and dueling second, Captain John Mitchel, as "his fancy Irishman."[99] Following the war, Rhett's marriage to Ripley's stepdaughter and service as pallbearer at Ripley's funeral are further indications of their close ties. Thus, it appears that Ransom Calhoun could have encountered considerable difficulty in pressing a case against Alfred Rhett with Ripley in place. However, even in the three months after Ripley had been removed, Calhoun did not press charges. Whatever his reasons, Calhoun's failure to act ultimately led to his untimely death, to the loss of an experienced and valued officer, and to a dark chapter in the history of Fort Sumter.

[99]Arthur J.L. Fremantle, *Three Months in the Southern States*, introduction by Gary W. Gallagher (Lincoln, Ne.:University of Nebraska Press, Reprint 1991), 185, 200.

BATTERY WAGNER ON MORRIS ISLAND [1] 1863

By JOHN HARLESTON

John Harleston (October 25, 1831-February 7, 1919), son of Edward
and Anna Isabella (Huger) Harleston, was born in Anderson District, where
the Harleston family spent the summers. He attended Pendleton Academy
until fourteen years of age, and when the Mexican War began, he was anxious
to go to the front. His father, however, took him from Pendleton Academy
and brought him to a school in Charleston taught by Samuel A. Burns, on
Meeting Street near the corner of George. For three years he remained at
this school, and then studied Latin and Greek under Professor Springs, a well-
known teacher of the day, who taught in what was known as the old Pickett
Guard House on Marion Square.

As John Harleston found plantation life on the Cooper River too tame,
he resolved to go West. Leaving Charleston by rail for New Orleans, he there
took a boat to Galveston, whence he traveled by stage to Goliad, and thence
on horseback to San Antonio.

Upon learning that South Carolina had seceded, John Harleston immediately returned to Charleston, where he enlisted and was made a first lieutenant in the Vigilant Rifles, under Captain Samuel Y. Tupper. He was stationed
first at Morris Island, where his tour of duty was in marked contrast to the
later duty of which he writes below. He served courageously throughout the
war, being wounded three times and captured twice. His brother, Frances
Huger Harleston, was killed at Fort Sumter.

After the war, John Harleston worked first at steamboating, and later
in the railroad business. Prominent as a Mason, he was elected to every office
in Landmark Lodge.[2] His recollections of Battery Wagner were written in
September 1902, and are printed here unchanged that punctuation has been
somewhat standardized for the sake of readability.

BATTERY WAGNER

Sepbt 1902

I have been often asked, "What was the tightest place you were
in during the Civil War?" I always answered, "Battery Wagner on Morris Island, and I have been in many tight places: as a prisoner on U. S.
vessels, in the Tombs prison in New York, in Fort Lafayette, in Fort

[1] For a general view of the Union campaign against Morris Island, see J. E.
Florance, Jr., "Morris Island: Victory or Blunder?", this *Magazine*, LV (1954), 143.

[2] Information on John Harleston was supplied from family records by Mrs. E.
Roy Daniell of Charleston, his grandniece.

The South Carolina Historical Magazine 63: 1-13

Delaware, and in the Bull Pens of Logan's Corps, in North Carolina, and the Bombardment and defence of Fort Sumter, and in numerous other places, but of *all*, the last six days before Battery Wagner was evacuated, was the worst."

I was then a private in the Charleston Light Dragoons, afterwards Co. H, 4th S. C. Cavelry. This company was ordered to Charleston from the coast, where it had been on duty for a year or more, helping to guard the Charleston and Savannah R.R. at Yemassee, Pocotaligo, Coosawhatchie, and [all] that country, and arrived at that city, marching by Rantowles in August, 1863, and camped on the Washington Race Course. On August 20th, an order was received from Head Quarters, ordering a squad of one Sergeant, and six privates to proceed to Morris Island, and relieve the squad doing Courier duty there, and 2d Sergt B. F. Huger, and six men were detailed, went to Morris Island that night, and relieved Sergt Hyer and squad, from the 5th S. C. Cavelry.

In the *Year Book of [City of Charleston] 1884*, issued by Mayor Courtenay, and written by R.C. Gilchrist, is a piece called the "Confederate Defence of Morris Island," and in giving an account of the Cavalry, doing duty there, and their duty as Couriers, he says it was done by a Detail of a Lieut. and ten men from Cap. Zimmerman Davis' company, The South Carolina Rangers, and who remained until the evacuation. This is certainly an error. I know that Sergt. Huger and squad relieved Lt or Sergt Hyer on Aug 20th, and that the second squad of Dragoons, of which I was one, relieved Sergt Huger and squad, on the evening of Aug. 31st. Cap Gilchrist was not present at the last days of Battery Wagner, hence this error. I can only remember the names of two of Sergt. Huger's squad, they were A. Burgess Gordon, and Josiah Bedon. I have tried to remember the others, but can't, the three above men are all dead. On the morning of the 31 [st.] Aug. another squad was ordered to relieve the one on Morris Island from the Dragoons. This duty being considered especially dangerous, the men were selected by lot, the 2d Squad were Scrgt. E. C. Holland, Privates Charles E. Prioleau, A. R. Elmore, J. B. Moore, W. H. Fairley, A. R. Taylor, and the sixth man's name, I can't remember, though I thought I never could forget them.

J. B. Moore was a married man, with wife and children, (the only married man of the squad), he was much distressed, and I, getting permission from Cap. Colcock, offered to take his place, and did so. This was how I got on the squad. Had I of known, what was ahead,

I don't know if I should have made the offer, but as I got back in safety, I am glad I did.

On the evening of Aug 31st, about 9 o'clock, the Squad under Sergt. Holland, reported on Southern wharf with Blankets and Revolvers, nothing else, were put in a row Boat with provisions etc. for Morris Island, where we arrived shortly after, and landed on the beach along side of Battery Gregg. As I jumped ashore, the first person I met was Burgess Gordon, of Huger's men. He exclaimed, "Good God Harleston are you here?" I said, "Yes I am here," and told him about taking Moore's place, and he said, "Well old fellow our Boat's ready, and I thank God I am getting away from this place. I tell you it is hell, hell." The next moment he was aboard and off.

Now the rest of this, I know and saw, and although after 40 years, I have forgotten much, I think what I write is nearly correct.

After we landed, we went to Couriers' Head Quarters, which was a small low Bombpr[oof] some 100 yards east of Battery Gregg. It faced the City, and was barely large enough to hold our party.

We had scarsely got there, when there was a call for a Courier. One was wanted to carry the dispatches to Wagner, that came from Charleston with us. I don't remember how it happened, but I was detailed to carry them. Now I knew nothing about the rout or way of getting to Wagner, but one of the men garrisoning Gregg, told me to take a Horse from the stable (or pen it was) which was in a corner of the earth works between Courier quarters and Battery Gregg, lead him down to the Beach, Keeping close to the Breast works, until I struck the water, then mount, turn his head up the beach, and let him go. All I had to do was to stick on, and the Horse would do the rest, and advised me to ride a little flea bitten Grey, whose tail had been cut off by a shell, all but six or 8 inches, and was still raw and bloody.

I followed his advice, and when I got to the end of the curtin wall, and near the beach, I jumped on his back, gave him his head, the little Grey was off like the wind. Straight up the Beach we went, until I could see Battery Wagner looming up in the darkness. The Grey made a swerve to the right, and in a minute stopped short under the walls of Wagner to the right of the Sallyport, before an old Gun carriage that he was accustomed to be hitched to. The stop was so short and unexpected, that I shot forward to his ears and came within an ace of going over, but recovered myself and got back into the saddle, which I was very glad of, for the Sallyport was crowded with soldiers, who would have run me to death if I had been thrown. They yelled and cheered and wanted the news, for they knew I was a new arrival, and were looking out for the first comers. This was my first acquaintance with Battery Wagner.

I remained there the balance of the night and came back to Gregg in early morning. We found five Horses at Gregg, left by the squad from the 5th Cavelry. All, if I remember right, had been hit by minnie balls or shells, and were about half the number originally carried down. Of all these five horses, the little Grey was the best. He was never scared by shot or shell I have seen them bursting all around him until [he was] nearly hidden by the smoke; have seen a 15-inch shell from a Monitor strike the beach, making a hole you could put a cart in, ten or a doz[en] yards in front of him, yet he never slackened his pace, but swerved to the right or left to avoid the pits and ditches made by the shells.

Sergt Huger made a list of his men, including himself, each man, taking his turn to ride as his name came, so all knew when a call came, who was to go. Our Serg[ean]t made out a similar list, but left his own name off, as he had a right to do, being in charge. He never rode, and never saw the inside of Wagner.

Our custom was [that] the man at Wagner remained there day or night, until another came up from Gregg. Then the one who had been there left for Gregg, and the last comer remained at Wagner until relieved in the same way. If dispatches were important, two couriers were sent within ten minutes of each other, so if one got killed, the other might get through. The distance between Battery Gregg and Wagner was three quarters of a mile, and the ride was straight up the beach until you got about 100 yards from Wagner, then you turned to the right and made for the Sallyport. This ride was *always* under fire, very heavy at times, from Monitors and the Ironsides along the beach, and from Land Batteries throwing shells of 100, 200 and 300 pounds, and from the bullets of the Sharpshooters, under whose range you came when a quarter of a mile from the Battery, and the last three or four days before it was evacuated, it was fearful. Three Monitors and the Ironsides anchored off the Beach, close in and spread out along it, never ceased fireing. Day and night, it was kept up in same way.

I have been in Sumter, and other places, but nothing like this was. I don't think any of us expected to get through, and [we] often bid each other good by when we started. I remember going down with Prioleau to the starting point, and watching him ride for Wagner. I did not see how he could get through. It was the day before the Island was abandoned. Three Monitors and the Ironsides were lined along the beach, between Gregg and Wagner, and were hurling shells in every direction. You could see the big 15-inch shells as they left the guns on the Monitors, come swaying along, striking the beach and exploding, throwing up a cloud of sand 20 or 30 feet high, and making a hole where they struck, big enough to put a horse and cart in. Sometimes they went over into the marsh, sending clouds of mud and grass in every way. But we feared the shells from the Ironsides more than all. She would let off a broadside at a time (8 Guns) and her shells you never could tell anything about, until they struck, and if in their range, nothing could save you. The Couriers were in plain view of these vessels when riding in day time, and we used to swear they fired at us. And when you got near Wagner, it was worse, for here you not only run among all the big shells fired at the Fort from the Ships and Land batteries and the little perpendicularly dropping Coehorn Mortor shells, but you had to run the chance from the minies of the sharp shooters, really the worst of all.

Yet through all this, only two men were hurt from Sergt Huger's squad and sent to Hospital, and two from ours (Fairley and Taylor) who were sent to James Island. The wounding of these men left a smaller number to do the work, and it was seldom you were idle, day or night, and for Forty-two consecutive hours this iron hail was falling, and at times the earth trembled like an earthquake. The last days on Morris Island were of simple endurance, and I can't give a better description than by quoting from "The Defense of Morris Island," from *Year Book 1884* [p. 377]: "The burning sun of a Southern summer, its heat intensified by the reflection of the white sand, scorched and blistered your body. An intolerable stench from the half-buried dead, exposed to sight all around, the swarm of flies attracted by the smell and blood, the unventilated Bomb-proofs, crowded with men, many sick, and filled with smoke of Lamps and smell of blood. The din of our own artillery, and the bursting shells of the foe, prevented sleep. The food, however good when it left Charleston, by exposure first on the wharf there, then on the beach at Cummings Point, being often forty-eight hours in transit, was unfit to eat. Water was scarcer than whisky."

The water supply obtained from Barrels sunk in the sand, soon became unfit for use. Dead bodies were all around, and the water smelt and tasted of them, and was half salt anyhow. A limited supply was brought from the city, but this was kept for the wounded. There were some of the wells some distance below Wagner that were

better, but one had to expose himself to reach them. And soon the
Ships found it out by the number of men going there; they soon got
the range, they shelled these places vigorously, and one risked his
life every time he went for water. The way they used to do, was to
get all the canteens they could tie on their bodies and carry, creep on
their hands and knees a half a mile, fill the Canteens, and return in
the same way. The suffering of the garrison, and the patient endurance
in the way they bore it, exceeded anything I ever saw or *heard* of.

Between eight and nine hundred men cooped up in the most foul
Bomb-proof, with barely food and water to sustain life, under a fearful fire day and night so that exposure was death, and for the last
three or four days, not able to exchange a shot with your enemy, just
waiting, and seeing your comrades brought in every hour, mangled or
wounded, was a trial to these brave men. You seldom heard a murmur,
but all must have looked forward to captivity or death. These men, I
call Hero's. Any man will fight when there is an enemy before him,
and he can return blow for blow, or shot for shot, but put him in a
place where he is being constantly shot at, unable to do anything but
sit down and takes what comes without returning a blow, seeing comrades and friends killed all around him, I say if men stand this, there
are no better soldiers or manhood in the world.

I remember one morning at Wagner, a heavy shell from the land
batteries, struck a big square timber over a bombproof off from the
headquarters to the S. E. I think it was used as a hospital. The whole
front fell in, blocking the passage way, and stopping up the entrance,
so those in there (30 or 40 I think) would be suffocated unless relieved.

A detail was put on to dig them out. It was from a Georgia Regiment and was 12 or 15 men. At their head was a Captain, a short,
thickset man, a Captain Benning, brave as a Lion and cool as ice. The
orders he gave were for the men to go into the passage way, one at a
time (for there was room for no more) and dig for five minutes. He
was then relieved by another, and so on. The Captain stood by the
entrance with his watch in his hand to time them. Now that entrance
and passage way was under heavy fire, the shells were bursting every
minute or two, the fragments flying all around, and the smoke often
hiding the man working.

I was standing close by, looking on, when it came to the turn of
a big six-footed man to go in for his turn. I can see him now. He had
on an old blue Yankee Overcoat and just a piece of a shirt under it.

He had a full face, light hair, and blue eyes. His face was white, and as he hesitated and fumbled at his coat, the Captain spoke to him sharply, and he said, "Yes, Captain, soon as I get off this coat." The Captain then looked at him good, and said quickly, "D-d, I believe you are afraid." The man jerked his coat off, threw it on the ground, and made a dash for the passage. I saw his white face when he passed me. I saw him throw out a few spades full of sand, then a shell burst right over him. You could not see for the smoke for a moment, and when I did see, the man was down on his knees, his head in the sand and the end of his back bone sticking out several inches. He had been struck by a fragment across the lines, and nearly cut in two. The body was dragged in, and Cap. Benning picked up the shovel, jumped to the place where the man had been killed, and worked at the sand for more than five minutes. His men expostulated, but he waved them back. This scene made a great impression on me. The men in the bomb-proof were finally dug out.

Another time I was sitting outside of the entrance to head quarters at Wagner, with five or six others. The shelling was heavy. We knew it was not a healthy place, but the air there was a little better and we risked it. After being there about an hour I suppose (for time was nothing), a large shell burst, it seemed to me right among us, (though it was 15 or 20 feet outside). I was knocked over, the bench we were sitting on [was] broken. I saw the fire from the shell, and the place was filled with smoke. Something struck me on the leg just above the ankle, and down I went. I did not know for an instant whether I was alive, or dead. I was partially stunned. The boys grabbed me and the first thing I remember, I was in the operating department, and the surgeon asking me, what was the matter. There was a pile of legs, and arms, and several dead bodies lying around, and the smell, Good Lord! I told him "Nothing, except I was stun'd for a moment." Dr. W. C. Ravenel who was one of the surgeons, came up and asked if I would not like a drink of brandy. I must have looked my astonishment, for he laughed and brought me a tumbler half full. This set me up. I had on a pair of what we called, half English Cavelry Boots, that came half way to the knees. I found that a piece of the brass sabot from the shell had hit me above the ankle, cutting the boot but just breaking the skin. I always thought I got the best of that shell, for without it "no Brandy."

I remember at another time, I was just outside the entrance to the West side. A sentinel was kept there as a lookout to report anything unusual. The mortor shells were coming down pretty thick, and I with others was watching them. The sentinel was hugging the parapet closely, and watching, when a shell dropped very close to him. He made a break for some steps (about 6 or 8) against the wall, and run under them. As he got there the shell exploded, and a fragment took his head, or most of it, off. His cap was pinned to the boards holding the sides, and remained there all that day. After a hurried examination, the body was rolled as close to the wall as possible, and staid there until night, and another man [was] sent to take his place. I don't think the steps were touched. The piece of shell passed between them, and if the man had remained quiet, he probably, would not have been hurt.

The south wall of the Battery facing most of the Yankee Batteries, and the rifle pits of the sharp shooters were near the top of the wall, and [they] had to fire through loopholes made of sand bags. Two Bags were placed at an interval of four to six inches, across these, another bag was placed on them. This formed the loophole, and towards the end, the Yankees had worked so close to Wagner, and had got their shooting down so fine, that all you had to do, was to cover one of these holes three seconds with your cap, and there was a bullet through it. I saw Captain Ogden Hammond one morning (I think he was officer of the day), climb up to the platform, w[h]ere the sharpshooters were, to take an observation. He was very quick about it, but as he turned to leave, a bullet cut his jacket across, from shoulder to shoulder, as if done with a knife. He was not hurt.

I saw one of [our] men push his gun through quickly and fire at a Yankee soldier who had got out of their trenches and was standing up. As he fired, he sang out, "I got him." The next moment, he came rolling down the slope with a bullet through his shoulder. They had got him too. I crawled up once or twice and took a peep at the Yankees working in the trenches, and took a shot for a sharp shooter.

The morning before the evacuation (I think it was), the firing from ships and batteries had been fearful all night, no let up, and daylight brought no relief. I was at Wagner that night for more than half of it, and when daylight came, I walked to the sally port, w[h]ere many men had gathered. When I got there, I met Tom Chapman, a member of the 25th Reg' S. C., a Charleston man, and a well-known character. As I came up, he said, "Harleston, had any breakfast?" and I asked him where he expected any breakfast to come from, when there was not a mouthful in the fort. He pointed to the eastern end of the lines, where a small wooden structure had been built and was used to keep Bacon, and hard-tack in. The heavy firing during the night had cut away the wall under which it was hidden, and as soon as seen, [it] was knocked to pieces. We could see sides of Bacon and Hard-tack scattered around in the sand. Chapman was a dare devil sort of a fellow, reckless and bold. He said to me, "I have been watching and thinking for some time, and I'll tell you what we can do. If you notice, you will find the Yanks are fireing from a battery well up the island, and they are firing in volleys, five or six guns at a time. Now if we wait, until the next volley comes, and then make a dash, one grab a piece of bacon, and the other some biscuit, we can get our breakfast. Will you try it with me?" I considered a moment and replied, "I am your man." "Done," he said, "as soon as the next volly comes, and it will be soon, we will start."

The point we were going to was one hundred yards or more from us. While we were speaking, three men had started to do the very thing we had intended. They crept down the wall towards the beach as far as they could get, keeping out of sight of the Yankees. Then they made a break for the food. They got there, but before they had time to do anything, two of them were dead, lying among the Bacon. The other was hit, but I heard got back. We saw all this. It was over in a minute. Chapman turned in a quizical sort of way and said, "Harleston, I ain't hungry," and I answered quickly, "Neither am I," [and] cursed a bit. No breakfast that morning!

On the afternoon of the 5th, the Yankee signals were read, and it was discovered that Battery Gregg was to be attacked by Boats that night, and preparations were made to receive them. Troops were sent down from Wagner after dark (the 27th Georgia Reg') and others, and the embrasure of one of the Big Guns at Gregg was cut away, so as to allow the Gun to bear on the creek through which the Boats were expected, I got down to Gregg from Wagner about 11 or 12 o'clock that night, and after talking with Charley Prioleau, we concluded to take a hand in the fight, with the Georgians, and went over to where they were [we] found them in line lying down, outside and below Gregg. We tried to get Rifles from them but they had none to spare, but told us they [were] spare Guns at Gregg. Prioleau and myself went there; and after a little talk, they handed us out two muskets with some cartridges and a handful of caps. We went back to where our Georgia friends were, and laid down between them. Prioleau was two or three men to the right of where I was.

As soon as I got there, I bit off the end of a cartridge, and ram'd it in the gun, but it stopped some distance from the bottom, and while I was trying to force it down, and cursing the gun, Prioleau sang out to me, "John, what's the matter?" and I said, "I can't get my cartridge down." He said, "Oh Lord man, the Gun was loaded when you got it." I tried mine with the ramrod, and found it out. The men around had heard us, and were tickled to death. They said, 'Why partner, you ought to be glad. There you have two bullets, and a handful of buckshot in your gun, and we have only one in ours. You ought to be proud. When that load gets among them Yankees, there won't be none left for us!" I told them I did not feel very much elevated by it, and offered to swap guns with any of them, so they could get the honour, and glory. This turned the laugh on them, and an officer nearby came to see what was the matter. They told him and it made him laugh, and he said to me, "Well Courier, what are you going to do about it?" I replied, "Shoot her when the Yanks come, if it is the last gun I shoot in the war." He said, "Good for you, you can fill them old Muskets chock full, you can't hurt them. If I was you, I would put another in." But I declined. The Guns they had given Prioleau and myself were old U. S. flint and steel muskets, altered to percussion, big heavy things, made for work. I was more afraid [of] the kicking than the bursting. I had shot them before on the plantation at Rice Birds.

This was amusement to the fellows, and they passed it up and down the line.

Soon after one o'clock in the morning, we heard two or three shots from the guards down below us, and knew the Yankees were coming. It was not long before the leading boats shot out of the creek, and spread out. Two field pieces on our right opened on them, with Grape and Canister. The Infantry had received positive orders not to fire before the word was given, then to aim straight and shoot low. The next thing the 10-inch Gun from Gregg, that was just behind us and over our heads, let loose. We could see the Boats fairly well then. They were fireing Grape from their Boat Howitzers at us when we got the order to fire. I was all ready. I had the old musket well trained, pressed her hard to my shoulder, and pulled the trigger. I heard her roar above the other guns, and she jumped up and back, clear over my head. I thought my shoulder was knocked out of place at first, but I grabbed for the gun, and she seemed all right. I kept on loading and fireing until orders came to cease. Just then I heard yells for a Courier, and as it was my turn, I gave the gun to Prioleau to return, and in five minutes was carrying the news of the repulse of the Yankee Expedition to Wagner

This account has been spun out, much more than I intended, and an expert writer would have said *all* I have in one-half the space and words. I am not pleased with it, but if I tear it up, I will never write another, and as it is *not* History and may serve to pass the time to some of my family, I let it stand. I would stop now, but for one more explanation, I think absolutely necessary.

Batteries Wagner and Gregg were evacuated beginning the night of the 6th of September 1863, and early morning of the 7th. In Johnson's *Defense of Charleston [Harbor]* (see "Appendix," page 116), Col. L. M. Keitt's report of the evacuation of Morris Island has this in it: "I ordered Cap. Huguenin down, sending word by Private John A. Stewart, Gist Guards, the Cavalry couriers having left without permission" [p. cxix]. Now these couriers were the Charleston Light Dragoons, and the charge is uncalled for. These men were Col. Keitt's equals in *every way*, and four of them afterwards laid down their lives on the bloody fields of Virginia. These are not men to be accused [of] desertion, for leaving without permission is Desertion. I never saw or read Keitt's report until six or seven years ago, and was indignant when I read it, and wrote a *strong* denial, and intended to publish it, but was advised by friends not to. Col Keitt had gone, nearly all the Couriers were gone too, and to start the question would do no good and might make very bad feelings, they said, all that knew the Dragoons would know the accusation unjust.

Now this is what I remember to have happened. The night the Evacuation took place, I was Courier at Wagner. I got up there with dispatches, I should judge, about nine o'clock that night. There was an unusual stir going on when I arrived. Men were hurrying about, orders being issued, and the garrison were assembling. Shortly after, part of the men marched out and took their way down to Gregg, others quickly followed, and in one hour and a half or two hours, the Battery was pretty much deserted. I remained near the Head Quarters. Officers and [men] were passing in and out all the time. I saw Cap. Bryan repeatedly, he passed close to me and saw me, and knew I was a Courier. He appeared to be directing the whole movement of troops, and most successfully did he do it. He was everything then, when the least blunder would have exposed the movement, and the last man there would have been killed or captured. I believe it was *entirely* due to his skill, and coolness that the garrison got away.

I was by those Head quarters when Col Keitt came out with some officers and orderlies, and took his way down to Fort Gregg. I could have put my hand on him. Not a word was said to me by any one. I remained in that Bomb proof, I should guess, from a half to 3/4 of an hour after he left. I can't tell, but the place was deserted. I saw some men with canteens looking around. I went to the Sally port and stood there awhile looking out. I saw some men up on the battery among the Guns. I thought they were spiking them. I was worried, I did not know what to do. I knew the Head Quarters, and garrison had gone, and did not know who was in charge up there at that time, or where to go to find out. There was not a living soul near me. I determined to leave. I started straight out among the sand hills to get some shelter from the heavy fireing, but the sand was so heavy and I was so tired, I struck for the Beach. I did not meet any one on my way down until I reached Gregg.

I passed one dead man soon after I struck the beach, with the surf running in up to his knees. At Gregg, I saw some men, about 30 or 40, getting into the boats that were waiting on the beach; and more men, I took them to be Artillerymen, coming in from the sand hills. I went at once to the Courier Head Quarters. There I found Charles E. Prioleau, and I think Elmore (there was a Courier with him anyhow). Prioleau said, "Why, w[h]ere have you come from? We have been looking out for you for the last two hours, and thought you had been killed, or captured." I explained about my being left at Wagner, and waiting until tired, and I asked what their orders were. They said they had none. I asked where the Sergeant was and was told he had gone out half an hour or more ago, and they had not seen him since. I said, "Let us go and look for him, or somebody in authority, for I have *no idea* of being left here for the Yankees." We went out, down to the boats where men were embarking, then to Gregg. We did not meet the Sergt, or any one who could give us orders or information. One man at Gregg told us the fuse was laid to the Magazine to blow the fort up, just as soon as they got orders, and he wished they would come quickly.

We started back towards the Boats that were comeing and going all the time, and met near them The'o G. Stoney, and upon our report of our fix, and the absence of any officers to report to or get orders from, he advised us to leave in the next batch of boats, then returning. While we were speaking, Mr. Francis J. Porcher came up, and on hearing our position, joined with Mr. Stoney in advising us to leave. They were waiting for the men from Wagner, (Cap. Huguenin, Cap. Pinckney, Lieut. Mazyck and some men,) and there might not be room for us, in their Boat. There were very few men then waiting to get off. They were coming in, in ones and twos, from the sandhills, and when the Boats did come in, Mr. Stoney went with us, and told the officer in charge who we were, and to take us, and we did go, and were put on a River Steamer near Sumter. I believe, Col. Keitt, and all his officers had left Morris Island before I got down there. There was no place for him to hide, and we (the couriers) looked all over the place, from Gregg to the end, and found no officers to give us orders or directions, and I have always thought, and still do think, that the Cavalry Couriers at the evacuation of Morris Island, were deserted (just forgotten), instead of deserting. My finding Prioleau and another at their Post when I came down, shows they had been there all the time, waiting for orders and ready for duty, and if not found when wanted, it was not their fault.

Just before leaving I wanted to shoot the little Grey Horse that had served us so well, but Mr. Stoney would not let me. I took off his bridle, and carried it in the Boat with me to remember him by, and when we got to the Steamer there was a good sea on, and trouble in climbing on board, and I forgot the bridle and left it in the Boat.

We crept in among some No.Cn. troops, and laid on the deck utterly worn out. One old North Carolinian recognized us, and said, "Aint you Couriers?" and when told that we were, said, "Well Boys, I am powerful glad to see you. I never did expect to again. I don't see how you ever did get through. I used to watch you." He then remarked, "I have heard the preachers talk about Hell, a great big hole, full of fire and brimstone, where a bad fellow was dropped in, and I will allow it used to worrie me at times, but Gentlemen Hell can't be worse than Battery Wagner. I have got out of that, and the other place ain't going to worrie me any more!" I went to sleep, and when I woke up, it was day light, and the Steamer at the wharf in Charleston.

No doubt it will be noticed that I speak much of myself in these papers. It is *not* from Egotism. I did *no more* and *not* as much as some of the Couriers. They went through what I did, saw what I did, and run all the risks, and suffered the same privations. I could not see any way but to show what I saw personally. Remember this was written *entirely* from memory, 38 years after they occurred, and I feel memory is very deceptive. I may be wrong in instances, but it is as I now remember.

J. H.

MORRIS ISLAND: VICTORY OR BLUNDER?

BY JOHN E. FLORANCE, JR.*

Charleston is on a peninsula formed by two rivers which also form Charleston harbor, one of the South's finest. In the center of the harbor is Fort Sumter, a well-fortified, closed work of masonry, with five sides and truncated angles. Sumter was the apex of Charleston's defenses. To the north of the harbor lies Sullivan's Island, upon which is Fort Moultrie and various small batteries. South of the eastern tip of Sullivan's Island across the harbor, is Morris Island, a small, narrow strip of land, principally sand. James Island lies to the west of Morris, separated by marshes of two miles width. South of Morris lies Folly Island, cut off from Morris by Lighthouse Inlet, a narrow body of water unnavigable to monitors.

In June 1862, Union forces invaded James Island, but after the Battle of Secessionville, in which they lost 683 men, they retired from the island in good order. Monitors of the federal navy assaulted Fort Sumter unsuccessfully in April the following year, and took such a beating that Admiral Du Pont, in command, advised Washington that renewal of the attack "would have converted a failure into a disaster."[1]

Military leaders in the North agreed that a successful campaign against Charleston should entail the utmost cooperation between land and sea forces. Such had not been the case when the army and the navy had been under the commands of General Hunter and Admiral Du Pont, respectively. It was decided then to replace both of these officers.

A distinguished army engineer, General Q. A. Gillmore, was assigned to take over the land forces.[2] This gentleman had proved his merit at Fort Pulaski in the early stages of the war. The naval counterpart was to be Admiral Foote, but a few days before assuming command, he died of natural causes. Admiral John H. Dahlgren, the gun inventor, was sent to fill the vacancy, and remained throughout the war.

At the time of these changes of command,[3] the North occupied a two-hundred-and-fifty-mile strip of land from Lighthouse Inlet to St. Augustine, Florida, but held no land to the north of Charleston which could aid in capturing the city.

Two of three possible plans of operation had previously proved failures.

* Ensign, U. S. Naval Amphibian Training Command, San Diego, California.
[1] *Official Records of Union and Confederate Navies*, XIV, 3.
[2] Gillmore was appointed chiefly through the efforts of Horace Greeley. S. Jones, The *Siege of Charleston* (New York, 1911), p. 116. Hereafter cited as *Siege*.
[3] 12 June, 1863.

First, for the monitors to attempt to batter or sneak by Fort Sumter was out of the question, for the Union fleet was no more potent than it had been the previous year, and Fort Sumter was still as strong as ever. A second procedure was to cross Lighthouse Inlet, capture Morris Island, and by the use of siege guns, reduce Sumter to a point where the monitors could easily run by it and the harbor obstructions to Charleston's waterfront. Third, Federal troops might attempt once more the occupation of James Island, from whence they would be in a position to put Charleston in immediate peril.

Many persons have disagreed with General Gillmore's rejection of the last mentioned course. James Island undoubtedly held the logical approaches to Charleston, but Gillmore believed the opposition there too strong for his forces to overcome.[4]

Confederate statistics show that General Gillmore's estimate of the relative strength of the opposing armies was grossly in error. General Beauregard, in command of the Charleston area, estimated that during this period he had "but 5861 men of all arms in the First Military District guarding the fortifications around Charleston."[5] Corroborating this is General Ripley's statement in the same volume: "My force in infantry was, in all, 2462 effective—1184 on James Island, 612 on Morris Island, 204 on Sullivan's Island and 462 in Charleston."[6] Why had Gillmore so vastly overrated his enemy?

The invasion of James Island in 1862, in which the Federal troops found a somewhat equal opposing force must have influenced him to some extent. Actually, Confederate troops at Secessionville numbered but half those from the North. Even then General Hunter had attacked the strongest point in a weak line. Had he tried anywhere else along this line, he probably would have succeeded in his campaign.

Just prior to Gillmore's assumption of command, Union forces had commenced strong fortification of Folly Island. These activities had not gone unnoticed in the Confederate camp, however, and Morris Island was reinforced to meet as well as possible any invasion attempt. The day after arriving off Charleston, Gillmore wired to General Halleck in Washington: "The concurrent testimony is that the defenses on Morris Island have

[4] Q. A. Gillmore, *Engineering and Military Operations Against the Defenses of Charleston Harbor in 1863* (New York, 1865), p. 22, footnote.

[5] Alfred Roman, *Military Operations of General Beauregard* (New York, 1884), Vol. II, 109. Hereafter referred to as *Beauregard*.

[6] John Johnson, *Defense of Charleston Harbor* (Charleston, 1890), p. 85. Hereafter cited as *Johnson*.

[7] P. T. G. Beauregard, "Defense of Charleston, South Carolina," *North American Review* CXLIII (July 1886), 44.

undergone a material change within the last three weeks, much to the advantage of the enemy."[8]

In a telegram to the Confederate Secretary of War, May 10, Beauregard reported: "Enemy in force on Folly Island, actively erecting batteries yesterday."[9] Two days later he reported in a similar telegram that General Evans, in command of a brigade on Morris, had reported two enemy brigades on Folly.

At this time, troops were badly needed by southern forces to counteract an expected enemy thrust in the Mississippi River area, and Charleston's defenses were considerably reduced to aid General Pemberton there. Beauregard became greatly concerned over this and reported to his superiors that any further weakening of his command might prove disastrous. Nevertheless, Morris' defenders, along with Negro slaves from the area, busily constructed fortifications in strategic locations, at least to stall an invasion.

Gillmore immediately ordered his gun emplacements on Folly to be augmented. The large sand dunes on "Little Folly," at the northern tip of the island, provided excellent coverage for the workers. Most of the work was done at night to conceal the preparations, and, although the Confederates knew of the activity, they had no concept of its scope. General Ripley, in a report to Beauregard, stated: "On the morning of the 10th [July], the enemy opened a heavy fire on our positions from Little Folly with from twenty to thirty long range guns which he had placed in position during the night."[10] The truth was that these guns, of which there were forty, had been ready for action at least a week.

On July 9th, Federal forces made a diversionary attack on James Island. About 3800 men, embarked upon transports, sailed up the Stono River, disembarked on the island and fought a brief skirmish with the Confederate defenders. They quickly re-embarked and headed home, thinking their mission accomplished. This raid may have diverted attention from Morris, but it diverted no troops, for there were none to be diverted without leaving the island defenseless.[11]

General George C. Strong was chosen to lead the Union assault on Morris. His command consisted of one brigade, enveloping over four regiments of infantry plus detachments of artillerists and engineers. On the night of the ninth, they embarked in small boats and concealed themselves among the tall marshes adjacent to Folly. Early the next morning, the full force of Federal guns opened up on the south end of Morris, and

[8] *Official Records of Union and Confederate Armies*, XXVIII, Part II, 4.
[9] *Beauregard*, p. 107.
[10] *Ibid.*, p. 108.
[11] General Gillmore disagrees; in his report (p. 29) he flatly states that troops were sent from Morris to reinforce James Island.

minutes later, four monitors added their firepower to the barrage. The Confederate batteries, eight guns and three mortars, answered as rapidly as possible. At 7:00 o'clock A.M., the launches commenced their crossing.

The bodies of troops ashore were met by formidable resistance, but the defenders were quickly outflanked and forced to retreat. Union forces virtually chased the Confederate forces up Morris, until they came within range of Battery Wagner's guns. Here they stopped to dig in, fatigued by the hot summer's sun. The southern forces suffered heavily during the day, losing some three hundred men, not to mention the artillery which had defended the lower portion of the island. The monitors moved in to bombard Wagner for the remainder of the day.

Beauregard's account of the affair read: "It was not the erection of the works on Little Folly that caused the abandonment of our position; it was clearly the want on our side of infantry support, and the enemy's superior weight and number of guns, and the heavy supporting brigade of infantry, that swept away our feeble, stinted means of resistance."[12] Nevertheless, some credit must be given to the invaders for their clever concealment of guns on Folly, and for their land-sea coordination.

The Federal forces had captured two-thirds of Morris Island in two days. They now faced the formidable Battery Wagner, known to its enemies as "Fort" Wagner after its stubborn resistance to attack had been proved.[13]

Wagner was indeed a sturdy work, extending across the island at its narrowest part. Its total force was about twelve hundred men, manning guns facing to the south as well as to sea. Its purpose was to prevent the establishment of breeching guns on Morris Island to be used against Fort Sumter.

Before sunup on the morning of the 11th, Union soldiers attacked Wagner, led by four companies of the Seventh Connecticut Regiment. They charged bravely over the sandy approaches to the battery and advanced up to the parapet. One group managed to occupy the south-east parapet. However, the Sixth Pennsylvania Regiment, following the men from Connecticut, was ordered to lie down when the heavy defensive fire commenced, and thereby entered the action too late for adequate support. As a result, the invaders were finally driven back in confusion, and the gallant men who had entered the parapet were forced to surrender.[14]

[12] *Beauregard*, 113.

[13] Battery Wagner was not a work of the most formidable kind, but an ordinary field-work with thick parapets, but with ditches of little depth. General Gillmore contended always that it was 'formidable', on account of its approaches as well as its plan and armament. *Beauregard*, 82.

[14] The Confederates captured 130 prisoners, while suffering 12 casualties; Union losses were reported at 330. *Johnson*, p. 95.

At this point, General Beauregard held a conference with his subordinate commanders to determine whether or not it would be feasible to drive the enemy completely off of Morris. To do this, it would be necessary to conduct the entire operation at night, for with the monitors operating in daylight, the Union forces would hold a decided advantage. Because of this, the idea was abandoned after much deliberation, and plans were adopted to continue a purely defensive attitude.

Meanwhile, the invaders were discussing the ways in which to capture Battery Wagner. A simple charge seemed out of the question, for the battery had been re-inforced, although not nearly to the extent that Gillmore believed. His estimate of the artillery strength of Wagner was fairly accurate: ten to twelve guns, four or five of which covered the land approaches and the rest the main shipping channel to seaward. Actually the defenders manned thirteen guns, most of which were old and dilapidated, and only one, a ten-inch columbiad, which would have any effect on the monitors.

Gillmore feared Wagner so, that he planned for the construction of four batteries of his own to be used against it. These works varied in distance to Wagner from 1330 to 1920 yards and were named Batteries Reynolds, Weed, Hays and O'Rourke. They were to be fortified with a total of thirty-one guns of varying calibre. In spite of a continuous harassing action against their construction, the work progressed with remarkable rapidity, and by the 18th of July, were ready to conduct a maximum effort assault against Wagner.

The defending forces observed the bustling activity in the enemy lines on the morning of the 18th. Troops in large numbers were being sent across Lighthouse Inlet from Folly, taking up positions behind the newly constructed fortifications. Wagner commenced firing at 8:10 A.M. and was joined five minutes later by Battery Gregg, on the tip of Morris Island. By 10:00 A.M., the monitors moved in to a position abreast of Wagner and added their guns to the Federal land fire which had commenced earlier in the morning.

The firing on Wagner that day was something that the soldiers and sailors on both sides would never forget. General Taliaferro, in command of the battery at the time, estimated that "nine hundred shot and shell were thrown in and against the battery during the eleven and a half hours that the bombardment lasted."[15] The total number of guns in action numbered about one hundred, and the smoke from them hung heavy over the island all day. Most of the defending garrison remained under the protection of spacious bomb proofs during the heavy firing, the Charleston

---

[15] *Beauregard*, 118.

Battalion being the exception. These men remained at their posts on the parapets, suffering twenty-eight casualties.

About sundown, the noise suddenly ceased, and the garrison braced itself for an onslaught. At 7:45 P.M., the Confederate forces observed the enemy beginning their advance. Due to the meticulous job of protecting the artillery pieces and powder with sandbags during the day, Wagner was able to fire, along with Gregg and Sumter, on the advancing Federal columns. The leading regiments bravely weathered the fire, except for a group of Negro troops, which fled to the rear in disorder. This served to cause confusion among the supporting forces, and only two regiments were left to stand up against Wagner.

The 31st North Carolina regiment, defending the battery, disgracefully refused to man their position on the south-east parapet, permitting the enemy to rush in unopposed.[16] However, the attack was repulsed with heavy losses to the Union troops, and the small detachment that had taken over the abandoned parapet was forced to surrender to Confederate infantry. The defenders' losses were placed at 174, and, while Federal casualties were never officially given, observers on both sides estimate approximately 3000 killed or wounded.[17] Although both Gillmore and Dahlgren wanted to push the attack the next day, disagreements as to whose forces would play what part led to a stalemate decision, and the idea was dropped.

Immediately after this defeat, the attacking forces commenced digging in to prepare for a siege. Five parallel lines were constructed to repulse any offensive action that might have been undertaken by Confederate forces in Wagner. These lines were carefully planned, and took many days of work to complete. During this time, Confederate sharpshooters took a heavy toll of the laborers, lowering their morale considerably. Indeed, it seems it would have been more humane to charge the garrison until it fell, rather than sit and slowly die from enemy sniper fire.

Pressure at this time was strong in Washington and northern newspapers for action and victory in the Charleston district, but Gillmore still felt he was not yet ready to move against Wagner again. Therefore, he intended to fire over Morris Island with heavy guns, and pound Sumter into submission. To do this, he placed in the first three of the five parallels long range, large calibre guns, aimed to fire high over Wagner.

On the morning of August 17, the guns opened up, aided by Dahlgren's monitors which moved in close to the fort. For seven days the bombard-

[16] This regiment later distinguished itself in action in Virginia. The 51st North Carolina Volunteers retrieved the honor of the state by manning their positions gallantly throughout the battle.

[17] *Siege*, 244.

ment continued. Most of Sumter's artillery had been moved to Gregg and Wagner previously; all but one of those which remained were destroyed by the week's end. But the firing of that one each evening announced to the anxious citizens of Charleston that the fort was still in friendly hands. Sumter's battered walls, however, clearly showed that she could no longer offer any aid in firing against the enemy on Morris Island.

General Gillmore believed that by silencing Sumter he had performed his job, and now expected the navy to move in and demand the surrender of Charleston. Dahlgren, however, feared obstructions at the harbor's entrance, and refused to move his ships until Sumter was actually in Union hands. The lack of army-navy cooperation once more stymied Federal efforts to capture their objective.[18]

The darkest days of the siege were now at hand. Federal forces continued fortifying their parallels, under harassing enemy fire. The number of sick and wounded daily increased, and the morale of the troops and officers was at a low ebb. Public pressure once more bore on Gillmore from Northern newspapers. The point was reached where only two alternatives remained: (1) to abandon the Charleston campaign altogether, or (2) to push forward with increased vigor towards the capture of Morris Island. Gillmore was reluctant to adopt the former course of action, so he decided to try the latter once more.

To divide the attention of Wagner, an amphibious assault against Battery Gregg was planned for the night of September 4. The troops were embarked in barges, and, accompanied by ships carrying howitzers, approached the battery soon after darkness. One boat, however, observed a Confederate vessel leaving Cummings Point, and could not resist firing upon it. Although the boat was captured, the element of surprise was gone, for Gregg had observed the chase and was alerted to the attack. The boats were called off, and the assault postponed until the next night. This time the defenders were well prepared. Holding their fire until the troops were 100 yards off shore, the guns from Gregg sent the enemy reeling back in disorder to their boats, suffering heavy casualties.

The final operations against Wagner commenced on the morning of September 5. The sappers had pushed up to within one hundred yards of the Confederate Battery, and light mortars were brought up to these positions.[19] For forty-two consecutive hours, Wagner was subjected to fire from all the land batteries the Federal forces could muster, plus the highly damaging salvos from the Union flagship, *New Ironsides*. This ship, with her 11 and 8-inch guns, fired richochetting volleys. The shells bounced off the water, and with a low remaining velocity, fell practically vertically

[18] Gillmore, footnote, pp. 63–66.
[19] This was the 5th and final parallel.

into Wagner. This was probably the most damaging fire directed at the battery.[20] At night, calcium lights turned the whole area into brightness.

The Confederate troops huddled in the bombproofs. The many dead who had been buried in and around Wagner lent a horrible stench to the sweltering shelters. The water became polluted and unfit for use, and the garrison came to rely on the precious supply brought over from Charleston. Repairs were impossible under these conditions; the battery soon was unable to fire its last piece of artillery and could not provide even a token answer to the heavy guns of the enemy.

The sappers, meanwhile, pushed up to the parapet of Wagner, outflanking it on the south-east front. The guns from Sullivan's Island to the north and James Island to the west were forced to withhold their fire for fear of hitting friendly troops. There was little danger to the sappers now, and they pushed their work with a new sense of security, even daring to relax during rest periods in full view of the battery.[21]

On the morning of the 6th, General Beauregard received from Colonel Keitt, commanding Battery Wagner, a telegram which admitted that the garrison stood a good chance of being destroyed. A later telegram requested small boats at Cumming's Point that night to evacuate the troops from Morris. Colonel Keitt's final message read:

The enemy's sap has reached the moat, and his bombardment has shattered large parts of the parapet. The retention of the post after tonight involves the sacrifice of the garrison. If the necessities of the service make this advisable, the men will cheerfully make it, and I will cheerfully lead them. I prefer to assault the enemy to awaiting an assault, and I will at four o'clock in the morning assail his works.[22]

Beauregard sent his chief-engineer to Morris to inspect Wagner. He agreed in substance with Keitt's report. Therefore, Beauregard issued the order for the evacuation of Morris Island. Two Confederate monitors guarded the embarkation point, and at nine o'clock the next morning, the movement commenced. By 0115 the next morning the evacuation was completed. The guns in Gregg and Wagner had been spiked, but, owing to a failure of the ignition fuse, did not explode and fell into enemy hands. The loss of men by southern forces was remarkably small considering the vast scope of the operation; 46 men in all were captured by the Union forces.

Thus ended the siege of Battery Wagner and the struggle for Morris

[20] *North American Review*, CXLIII, 52.
[21] Gillmore, p. 72.
[22] *Beauregard*, p. 132.

Island. Gillmore sent to Dahlgren after the capture a message which read: "The whole island is ours, but the enemy has escaped us."[23]

The casualty reports indicate that the Union forces suffered 2318 men killed or wounded on Morris from July 10 to September 7, while Confederate casualties were but 641.[24] It is easily seen that the Federal army suffered a defeat as far as numerical losses were concerned, but the question is, was this loss offset by tactical gains?

First, consider the purposes for the campaign. Gillmore's plan was to capture Charleston, and to this end he thought it necessary to capture the whole of Morris Island. This would permit free access to the harbor by Dahlgren's fleet. Morris was captured, Sumter was demolished, but still the Union forces got no closer to Charleston until its evacuation at the close of the war.

But why did Beauregard hang on to Morris until the bitter end when by his own admission he knew the outcome was inevitable?[25] The answer to this seems twofold: First, he was diverting the enemy from the much more important James Island, from which Federal forces could seriously endanger Charleston. As stated earlier, one of Gillmore's first and primary mistakes was to invade Morris instead of James Island. Once Beauregard realized that his adversary had committed this error, he was determined to bluff his way through, leading Gillmore to believe that the Confederates had pinned all their hopes upon the successful defense of Morris. Secondly, the campaign was drawn out for the reason that it gave Beauregard valuable time to build up his inner defenses for the protection of Charleston.

General Gillmore criticizes the defenses of Morris in three ways. He says in his report[26] that instead of placing Wagner where it was, a much better protection could have been provided by heavily defending the southern tip of Morris, with a smaller fortification to the rear. This, in his opinion, would have prevented the initial landings on the island, and prevented the destruction of Sumter by breaching batteries. The fact remains, however, the South did not have men or materials to attempt such an undertaking and at the same time provide an adequate defense for James Island. Besides, this plan would have permitted an amphibious attack on the northern end of Morris, an idea which appealed greatly to Dahlgren and Gillmore. It is true that Wagner did not perform its primary duty of preventing the breaching batteries from bombarding Sumter, but it did as well as could be expected.

[23] Correspondence: Gillmore, p. 337.
[24] *Johnson*, appendix CXLII, CXLIII.
[25] Comte de Paris, *History of the Civil War in America* (Philadelphia, 1888), p. 361.
[26] Gillmore, pp. 125–126.

Gillmore also condemned the use of mines by the defenders of Morris, stating that this prevented telling sorties at night into Federal positions. His observations are undoubtably correct, but men are lost in sorties, and the Confederates could hardly afford to lose men. The mines (then called torpedoes) served not only as a passive defensive measure, but also gave warnings of enemy movements.

This third Confederate mistake, according to the Northern general, was the lack of mortar fire by the Wagner garrison. True this type of fire was highly injurious to the sappers, but there were only a limited number of mortars available at the battery, and ammunition for these was a scarce item. It must not have dawned on Gillmore until the final stages of the siege that vertical trajectory was such a potent weapon, for the first use of it by Union forces was in the final bombardment.[27]

As a result of the campaign on Morris Island, the Federal forces had gained possession of a small, narrow strip of sand and marshes. They had captured Battery Wagner, and controlled half of the entrance to Charleston harbor. But they were no nearer Charleston than when the campaign begun! Their navy still refused to enter the harbor because of the presence of Fort Sumter—not the firepower of Sumter, but the mere presence, for Sumter had no firepower left. The only claim that could be made by Northern forces was that they had gained Confederate territory, for which they paid with many lives.

The only conclusions that can be made regarding this campaign are self-evident. The North made a disastrous blunder in attempting an invasion of Morris, and achieved an abortive victory. Had the North initially moved on James Island, or had the perseverance and daring to enter the harbor by sea, the story might have been different. The strategy of the the Confederates was not impeccable, but it was not bad. They at least carried out their assigned mission of keeping the enemy from Charleston, and at the same time, had inflicted a telling toll of casualties on an enemy battling for fruitless objectives.

[27] *North American Review*, CXLIII, 51.

ROSWELL SABIN RIPLEY:
"CHARLESTON'S GALLANT DEFENDER"

by C. A. Bennett, M.D.*

ROSWELL SABIN RIPLEY, REFERRED TO BY HIS CONTEMPORAR-
ies as "Charleston's gallant defender,"[1] has fallen into historical obscurity.
This interesting, though highly controversial, Confederate general is little
known in Ohio, his birthplace, or in Ogdensburg, New York, his childhood
home. Even in Charleston, South Carolina, where he lived, fought, and is
buried, he has been largely forgotten. Despite Ripley's previous popularity
in Charleston, the criticisms of his detractors have outlived the praises of his
supporters.

Ripley's birthplace in Worthington, Ohio, is identified only as the
Ripley House. On the sign in front of this house no mention is made of this
1843 graduate of the United States Military Academy, who later became a
Confederate general. Many are unaware of the major role he played in the
April 12, 1861, Confederate bombardment of Fort Sumter in Charleston
harbor. Ripley fought enthusiastically for the Confederacy in the defense
of Charleston and for a short time was a brigade commander with Robert E.
Lee's Army of Northern Virginia. How did this northern-born rebel attain
prominence in the Confederate Army and why was he so controversial?

Current writers have described Ripley negatively, claiming he was
"irascible and at times hot tempered" with "an inability to get along with his
superiors"; he has been called "even more contumacious than D.H. Hill:
where Hill respected some superiors, Ripley was against them all."[2] This
assessment is contradicted by the positive opinions of Ripley's contempo-
raries, such as that of George C. Eggleston, who for a time served in an
independent battery at Charleston:

> He was portly in person, of commanding and almost pompous
> presence, and yet, when one came to know him, was as easy
> and unassuming in manner as if he had not been a brigadier
> general at all....

*Independent researcher, Dublin, Ohio. He is a member of the Sons of
Confederate Veterans and the Military Order of the Stars and Bars.

[1]Charleston *News and Courier*, March 30, 1887.

[2]E. Milby Burton, *The Siege of Charleston 1861-1865* (Columbia: University of
South Carolina Press, 1970), p. 64; Stewart Safakis, *Who Was Who in the Civil War*
(New York: Facts On File Publications, 1988), pp. 545-546; Clifford Dowdey, *The
Seven Days: The Emergence of Robert E. Lee* (Little, Brown and Co., 1964) p. 186.

He was not a good martinet, but he was a brave, earnest man and a fine officer, of a sort of which no army can have too many.[3]

A former staff officer, Colonel E. M. Seabrook, stated, "He always endeavored to bestow upon his subordinates, officers and men, the full measure of praise due them."[4] His former West Point classmate Confederate General Samuel G. French remarked, "He was generous, openhearted, outspoken; harbored no resentments.... His cheerful presence dispelled all unnecessary solemnity.... [H]is generous and unselfish disposition formed friendships among his classmates that lasted through life."[5]

Following his graduation from the U.S. Military Academy in 1843, Ripley served nearly ten years in the artillery service. Breveted twice for "gallant and meritorious conduct" during the Mexican War, Ripley ended his U. S. military career at Fort Moultrie, South Carolina, when he resigned on March 2, 1853.[6] On December 22, 1852, Ripley married Alicia Middleton Sparks, the widow of William A. Sparks and daughter of John and Mary Middleton. Ripley is said to have "gone into business in Charleston as agent for a rifle company."[7]

While the United States drifted toward dissolution and war, Roswell Ripley attempted to help his adopted state of South Carolina prepare for secession. On March 3, 1860, Ripley sent letters to the governors of Alabama, Georgia, and South Carolina. He wrote regarding the "armament of the Militia and volunteers of the Southern States," and advocated the building of an armory.[8]

Ripley's efforts for South Carolina also included at least one trip north to buy arms. From the Continental Hotel in Philadelphia, on November 7, 1860, Ripley wrote to General States Rights Gist in South Carolina encouraging legislation for an armory, but stated, "what you want first is arms." He commented that he was delayed in Philadelphia "partially on business

[3]George C. Eggleston, *A Rebel's Recollections* (New York: Hurd and Houghton, 1875), pp. 164-165, 168.

[4]Col. E. M. Seabrook, *Address Delivered at the Unveiling of the Ripley Monument* (Charleston, S.C.: Daggett Printing Co., 1894), p. 12.

[5]Samuel G. French, *Annual Reunion of the Association of the Graduates of the USMA* (E. Saginaw, Mich.: Evening News Printing and Binding House, 1887), pp. 63-64.

[6]G. W. Cullum, *Biographical Register of the U.S. Military Academy, 1802 to 1890* (Cambridge, Mass.: Riverside Press, 1891), Vol. II, p. 157.

[7]Dumas Malone, ed., *Dictionary of American Biography* (New York: Charles Scribner's Sons, 1935), Vol. VIII, pp. 62526, s.v. "Ripley, Roswell Sabine" [sic] by J. G. deRoulhac Hamilton; W. A. Swanburg, *First Blood: The Story of Fort Sumter* (New York: Charles Scribner's Sons, 1957), p. 307.

[8]R.S. Ripley to W.H. Gist, March 3, 1860, Compiled Service Records of Confederate General and Staff Officers, R.S. Ripley, MC #331 Roll 212, S.C. Department of Archives and History, Columbia, S.C. (hereafter Compiled Service Records).

Roswell Sabin Ripley. According to one contemporary, "He was portly in person, of commanding and almost pompous presence, and yet, when one came to know him, was as easy and unassuming in manner as if he had not been a brigadier general at all." Photo courtesy of the Massachusetts Commandery Military Order of the Loyal Legion and the U.S. Army Military History Institute.

of that nature."[9] Following South Carolina's secession on December 20, 1860, and the evacuation of U. S. forces from Fort Moultrie to Fort Sumter in Charleston harbor, Governor Francis Pickens appointed Ripley major of ordnance at Fort Moultrie. When Major Robert Anderson moved to Fort Sumter he had ordered his men to spike Moultrie's guns and burn the gun carriages. At Fort Moultrie, Ripley's "indomitable energy and his great mental ability were exercised by day and by night, in repairing the guns and hotshot furnaces, and putting the fort in a condition to retain her ancient

[9]R.S. Ripley to S.R. Gist, March 22, 1860, Compiled Service Records.

name."[10] On January 28, at the request of Governor Pickens, the South Carolina Senate confirmed Ripley's nomination for lieutenant colonel of the Battalion of Artillery.[11]

By March 1, 1861, the Confederate States of America had assumed control of the military in Charleston and President Jefferson Davis selected General P. G. T. Beauregard to command the area. On April 11 the Confederates, learning that Fort Sumter would not be abandoned but would be resupplied and reinforced, demanded the fort's evacuation. At 4:30 a.m. the next day, a signal shell fired from Fort Johnson on the opposite side of the harbor opened the attack on Fort Sumter. Ripley's artillery began firing immediately. The artillery duel lasted throughout the day, slackened during the night, then resumed the next morning. As Ripley described the action from Fort Moultrie:

> The shot, both hot and cold, crashed into the quarters of Fort Sumter and along the parapet, rendering the extinction of the flames difficult, and lighting up new places to windward. It became evident soon that the enemy was worsted, but to insure the result orders were passed to each of the batteries to redouble their fire.[12]

Abner Doubleday, then a U. S. captain at Fort Sumter, knew Ripley was in command at Fort Moultrie. According to Doubleday, "I was told ... [Ripley] took pains to denounce me as an Abolitionist, and to recommend that I be hanged by the populace as soon as caught." Doubleday spoke despairingly about Ripley joining the Confederacy, but added, "being a man of talent, and a skillful artillerist he did us a great deal of harm." Doubleday added:

> About 8 A.M. the officers' quarters were ignited by one of Ripley's incendiary shells, or by shot heated in the furnaces at Fort Moultrie.... [T]he hot shot soon followed each other so rapidly that it was impossible for us to contend with them any longer ... the wind drove the smoke in dense masses.... It seemed impossible to escape suffocation.... Some ... posted

[10]Seabrook, *Address, Ripley Monument*, pp. 4, 5.

[11]President of South Carolina Senate to Gov. Pickens, January 28, 1861, E.M. Law Papers, Southern Historical Collection, University of North Carolina, Chapel Hill, N.C.

[12]*War of the Rebellion: A Compilation of the Official Records of the Union and Confederate Armies* (Washington, D.C.: Government Printing Office, 1880-1901), Series I, Vol. I (hereafter cited as *O.R., Series I* unless otherwise noted), pp. 260, 301, 41.

themselves near the embrasures.... I crawled out one of these openings, and sat on the outer edge; but Ripley made it lively for me there with his caseshot, which he spattered all around. Had not a slight change of wind taken place, the result might have been fatal to most of us.[13]

Following the surrender of Fort Sumter, the honor of occupying it was given to Ripley and the South Carolina Palmetto Guard. Under Ripley's command, the reconstruction of the badly damaged fort began immediately. Governor Pickens wrote to President Davis, stating, "Ripley is by far the most efficient and thorough officer here, and has been working night and day to put Sumter in fighting order.... I owe him more than any other single man, and the people of Charleston know it."[14]

SHORTLY THEREAFTER, RIPLEY'S PROBLEMS, DISSATISFACTION, and reputation as troublesome began. Previously, Ripley had been considered reasonable in regard to rank and command. In an early letter to Leroy P. Walker, the Confederate secretary of war, Ripley stated:

I have the honor to apply for the commission of Colonel or of Lieut. Colonel of Artillery in the Army of the Confederate States of America. I mention the second rank as I do not wish an application or claim of mine to interfere with those of an officer who has seen more active service in the artillery arm than myself.[15]

As the months passed following Ripley's efficient performance at Forts Moultrie and Sumter, he became increasingly frustrated by his lack of promotion. Late in July 1861 rumors circulated in Charleston that Ripley intended to resign for that reason. A letter to Ripley from "patriotic and representative citizens" of Charleston, dated July 29, 1861, stated in part: "This whole community would regard such resolution on your part as nothing less than a public calamity, we entreat you to pause, and, if possible, to refrain.... Our conviction is, that our indebtedness to your wisdom is beyond being measured." Ripley yielded to their request and remained in the service. By August 21 he had been promoted to brigadier general and was in command of the Department of South Carolina and its coast defenses.[16]

[13]Abner Doubleday, *Reminiscences of Forts Sumter and Moultrie* (New York: Harper & Brothers, 1876), pp. 154-157.

[14]Burton, *Siege of Charleston*, p. 57; John Johnson, *The Defense of Charleston Harbor, 1863-1865* (Charleston, S.C.: Walker, Evans & Cogswell Co., 1890; repr., Freeport, N.Y.: Books for Libraries Press, 1970), p. 18; *O.R.*, Series IV, Vol. I, p. 318.

[15]Ripley to Walker, undated, Compiled Service Record of R. S. Ripley.

[16]Seabrook, *Address, Ripley Monument*, p. 7; *O.R.*, Vol. 6, p. 267.

In early November 1861 Robert E. Lee assumed command of the coasts of South Carolina, Georgia, and East Florida, Beauregard having been transferred earlier to Virginia. At this time Union naval forces were concentrating off Beaufort and Port Royal, South Carolina. On November 7 they launched an overwhelming attack and captured the Confederate installations at Port Royal Sound. Ten days later, in the reorganization of the coastal defenses, Lee reduced Ripley's command to that of the water and land defenses of Charleston.[17]

In late November differences arose between Lee and Ripley as to the proper defense of Charleston and the coast. Robert E. Lee was not yet the revered figure he would become in Confederate history and until then had participated only in the rather unsuccessful western Virginia campaign. Therefore, it does not seem remarkable that Ripley might disagree with Lee. On November 26 Ripley advised Lee of the capture of two coastal islands, Otter and Fenwick's, by Union forces. This would allow Ashepoo and Paw Paw river access to the Federals. Proceeding inland, they could then threaten the important railway connecting Savannah and Charleston. Lee's assistant adjutant general, T. A. Washington, responded immediately to Ripley. "The commanding general directs me to say that the enemy can land on all the islands he can approach with his armed vessels, but he will hardly find it to his advantage to hold them after they have been pillaged." Lee instructed Ripley to obstruct the Ashepoo and Edisto rivers, but this response indicates significant differences of opinion regarding the importance of controlling coastal islands in the defense of Charleston. Responding to Lee on December 5, Ripley stated, "it seems to me as far forward as we can go with safety from Charleston the better we are for its defense."[18]

On December 10, from his headquarters at Coosawhatchie, Lee divided the coast of South Carolina into five military districts. He placed Ripley in command of the Second District with his headquarters in Charleston. The Fourth District, extending from the Ashepoo to the Port Royal entrance, was under the command of the recently arrived Brigadier General John C. Pemberton. His headquarters were with Lee at Coosawhatchie. On January 14, 1862, soon after arriving in South Carolina, Pemberton was promoted to major general, thus outranking Ripley.[19] While the differences between Ripley and Lee primarily involved Charleston's lines of defense, Pemberton's promotion certainly did not help the situation.

At about that time a dispute developed involving Ripley's junior officers and Governor Pickens. In a letter to Lee on December 31, 1861, Pickens stated:

[17]*O.R.*, Vol. 6, pp. 309, 311-312, 323.
[18]Shelby Foote, *The Civil War* (New York: Random House, 1958), Vol. I, pp. 127-130; *O.R.*, Vol. 6, pp. 329, 336.
[19]*O.R.*, Vol. 6, pp. 344-345; Safakis, *Who Was Who*, p. 497.

> I regret to hear and to know of the unpleasant feeling amongst the officers under General Ripley, particularly of the junior officer in the artillery. Appointments cannot be made to please all, ... besides I thought it would be very agreeable to all to appoint a son of General Beauregard.... Why these appointments should create such excitement among the junior officers in Fort Sumter I am at a loss to understand.[20]

Apparently appointments had been given to Beauregard's son and to others, appointments to which officers under Ripley believed they were entitled. If this "unpleasant feeling" involved Ripley, it exemplifies Seabrook's statement, quoted earlier, regarding Ripley's support for his officers and men. On January 7, 1862, Governor Pickens wrote a somewhat contradictory letter to President Davis:

> ... I fear the feeling of General Ripley towards General Lee may do injury to the public service. His habit is to say extreme things even before junior officers, and this is well calculated to do great injury to General Lee's command. I do not think General Ripley means half what he says in his energetic way, but others construe it differently.[21]

The controversy over the defense of Charleston and the coast of South Carolina began to focus on Cole's Island. On February 19, 1862, Lee wrote to Ripley:

> I am in favor of abandoning all exposed points as far as possible within reach of the enemy's fleet of gunboats and of taking interior positions....
> If they [the batteries on Cole's Island] can be reached in great force by the enemy's gunboats they might be suppressed, and the Stono seized as an avenue of approach. If it is necessary to maintain these batteries, they should be made as strong as possible.[22]

Obviously, Lee was not committed to abandoning Cole's Island.

However, in early March President Davis ordered Lee back to Virginia, and Pemberton assumed command of the Department of South Carolina and Georgia. Two weeks later, apparently discounting the significance of Cole's Island, Pemberton ordered the complete withdrawal of troops and

[20]O.R., Vol. 6, pp. 363-364.
[21]Ibid., p. 366.
[22]Ibid., p. 394.

batteries from that island.[23] Although Ripley had disagreed with Lee over lines of defense, subordination to Pemberton's injudicious orders was very difficult. W. Porcher Miles, the South Carolina congressman who chaired the Confederacy's Committee on Military Affairs, received a long letter on March 10 from William H. Trescott, a Charleston native who had been assistant secretary of state in the Buchanan administration. Trescott stated in part:

> Gen. Lee has been relieved and Gen. Pemberton is now in command. Subordination to Lee is one thing, subordination to Pemberton an entirely different thing....
>
> Whatever Gen. Pemberton's reputation and whatever he has done (unknown here certainly) to be made Major General, it is a great and crying injustice to allow him to [outrank?] Ripley in this military district.[24]

Trescott followed this letter with another on April 3:

> Pemberton has ... interfered most injudiciously not only to Gen. Ripley's great dissatisfaction, but to the universal discontent of the whole country....
>
> Every spot of land, every marsh, every island, every creek has been examined, measured, sounded by Gen. Ripley and those under his command: time, money, labour, energy have been expended in preparing these defenses and now General Pemberton is to ride over this country at a hard gallop, look over a map which he can't understand, and all must be abandoned....
>
> I have seen him [Ripley] constantly and closely and I can bear my honest testimony to his energy and ability. I care not what his faults may be, his work stands there to prove his capacity and his fidelity...
>
> [T]his command should be his fully and entirely.... I did hope that Gen. Lee would take this view, but I have been disappointed.[25]

Within three weeks, Trescott redirected his efforts on Ripley's behalf. On April 22, 1862, he urgently telegraphed Miles, "Ripley is very anxious to be relieved and allowed to go [to] Virginia with the troops taken from him for that neighborhood. I am sure his place here cannot be supplied, but it is only justice to him to give him power equal to his responsibilities or let him take

[23]Ibid., pp. 400, 402, 420.
[24]W. H. Trescott to W. P. Miles, March 10, 1862, E. M. Law Papers.
[25]Ibid., April 3, 1862.

the field."[26]

The Confederate government accepted Ripley's request to be relieved of duty in the Charleston area, and he was given command of the Fifth Brigade of General D. H. Hill's division in Virginia. Ripley's brigade participated in the battles of Mechanicsville, Gaines Mill, and Malvern Hill during the Peninsular Campaign. In September 1862 Ripley's brigade crossed the Potomac into Maryland as part of Robert E. Lee's Army of Northern Virginia and was engaged at the battle of Boonesborough. It became heavily involved early in the battle of Sharpsburg (Antietam) on September 17, 1862; there, Ripley was wounded while reforming his brigade.[27] According to D. H. Hill, "Brigadier-General Ripley received a severe wound in the throat from a Minieball, which would have proven fatal but for passing through his cravat. After his wound was dressed, he heroically returned to the field, and remained to the close of the day with his brigade."[28]

During this time, the situation in Charleston deteriorated for John C. Pemberton. Pressure mounted for his removal and on August 29 Beauregard was sent back to South Carolina to relieve him. Shortly after his arrival, leading men of Charleston urged Beauregard to obtain the services of Roswell Ripley. Following the battle of Antietam, Ripley had expressed interest in returning to Charleston and had written to Beauregard, "I would not like the defense of Charleston to go without being in & as we had such good results formerly I really hope that should we be associated again we should be as fortunate. I shall I trust be fit for duty in a few days." In mid-October Ripley arrived in Charleston. As commander of the First Military District, he was to direct his attention "to the defenses of Charleston Harbor, which must be placed in as complete condition for immediate service as circumstances will permit."[29]

In early November Beauregard and Ripley began to have difficulties with Major F. L. Childs of the Charleston Arsenal. General Beauregard had decided he must quickly "rifle and band" as many heavy artillery pieces as possible. Citing the unacceptably slow work of Childs, Beauregard placed the project under Ripley's control and Childs was later arrested for not complying with Ripley's orders. Beauregard and Ripley were in agreement regarding this matter and worked well together with no evidence of discord.[30] In February 1863 Beauregard wrote the following in support of

[26]Ibid., April 12, 1862.
[27]O.R., Vol. 11, Pt. II, pp. 485, 647; Vol. 19, Pt. I, pp. 1032-1033.
[28]Ibid., p. 1027.
[29]O.R., Vol. 14, p. 601; Alfred Roman, *Military Operations of General Beauregard* (New York: Harper and Brothers, 1884), Vol. II, p. 26; Ripley to Beauregard, September 29, 1862, Compiled Service Record of R. S. Ripley; O.R., Vol. 14, p. 641.
[30]O.R., Vol. 14, pp. 689-692.

Ripley's promotion:

> In his present command, as important if not more so than is now entrusted to any Major General in the service, he is daily giving the Country and myself the benefit of his administrative talent and services, and of his untiring energy and zeal in the discharge of his duties as commander of the 1st Military District of South Carolina embracing all the works for the defense of the City and Harbor of Charleston. In numbers his command is that of a Major General.[31]

Serious problems between Ripley and Beauregard's staff developed in early May when Ripley determined that the construction of defensive works on Morris Island had been lagging. This was a major concern with Union forces now on Little Folly Island, in striking distance of Morris Island. Unfortunately for Ripley, he criticized the engineer department of Beauregard's friend, Major D. B. Harris. Harris previously had been on Beauregard's staff, and had been chosen by Beauregard to head that department. There ensued charges and countercharges regarding the lack of supplies, transportation, and inadequate or ineffective utilization of labor.[32] Ripley expressed his frustration on June 6, 1863, to General Thomas Jordan of Beauregard's staff, citing two to three months of "carelessness and inattention of engineer officers."[33] After the war, Ripley published correspondence on this topic. He noted that after June 21, Beauregard reaffirmed that the defensive works were to be supervised by engineer officers, not by Ripley. "Little was attempted," he wrote, "and little accomplished. The enemy attacked and carried the point about three weeks [later]."[34] Ripley was referring to early July 1863 when Federal forces successfully landed on the southern tip of Morris Island. In August Secretary of War James A. Seddon angrily confronted Beauregard and W. P. Miles regarding a letter from Miles which claimed this Union success resulted from Beauregard's lack of forces to defend the island. Seddon replied, "According to my conception, it was not the want of infantry force ... [but], the want of adequate works of defense at the lower end of the island."[35]

In *The Siege of Charleston*, E. Milby Burton blames Ripley for initiating Seddon's reply, although evidence indicates it followed Miles's letter.

---

[31]P. G. T. Beauregard to S. Cooper, February 7, 1863, Compiled Service Record of R. S. Ripley.

[32]*O.R.*, Vol. 14, pp. 938, 956-957, 642, 957-959.

[33]*O.R.*, Vol. 14, pp. 1024-1025.

[34]R. S. Ripley, *Correspondence Relating to Fortification of Morris Island* (New York: John J. Caulon, Printer, 1878), p. 23.

[35]*O.R.*, Vol. 28, Pt. II, pp. 186, 342-343, 297.

Unfairly criticizing Ripley, Burton states that although Beauregard warned him, Ripley was unprepared for the Morris Island attack. However, it must be remembered that it was Ripley who had continually warned Beauregard of the poor defenses on the island's southern end. Union infantry attacks on the island's last stronghold, Fort Wagner, were repelled, but a continuous bombardment forced the defenders to evacuate the island.[36]

Possibly generated by this Morris Island controversy, there appeared the first concerns about what Lieutenant Colonel Arthur J. L. Fremantle described as Ripley's "occasional rollicking habits." Fremantle, a British officer, spent three months in 1863 touring the Confederacy. He visited Charleston in early June and gave this description of Ripley:

> He is a jovial character, very fond of the good things of this life; but it is said that he never allows this propensity to interfere with his military duties, in the performance of which he displays both zeal and talent. He has the reputation of being an excellent artillery officer, and although by birth a Northerner, he is a redhot and indefatigable Rebel.... Nearly all the credit of the efficiency of the Charleston fortifications is due to him.[37]

During the war "there was a semblance of social life" in Charleston and certain of these affairs may have gotten somewhat out of control. By June 24 Beauregard had been anonymously informed that "a portion of this community are much concerned at the conduct of the brigadier general commanding the First Military District on the occasion recently, as it is represented, of a drinking frolic, either in the city or on a vessel in the harbor."[38] District Judge Alfred Magrath and Robert B. Rhett, Jr. interviewed Ripley and assured Beauregard that he would "not be intoxicated, ... or influenced by liquor so as at any time to interfere with the proper discharge of his duties."[39] Despite these problems, in early October Beauregard again requested a promotion for Ripley which was also denied. "General Ripley," he wrote, "is ... an officer of unquestionable professional ability and attainments — an artillery officer of the largest experience, he has exercised a Divisional command for nearly a year, and I believe his sphere of usefulness would be enhanced by this promotion."[40]

In November 1863 the lack of progress on defensive works being

[36]Ibid, pp. 297-298; Burton, *Siege of Charleston*, p. 209.

[37]Arthur J. L. Fremantle, *Three Months in The Southern States, April -June 1863* (Edinburgh: W. Blackwood and Sons, 1863; repr., Time-Life Books Inc., 1983), p. 179.

[38]Burton, *Siege of Charleston*, p. 263; *O.R.*, Vol. 35, Pt. II, p. 634.

[39]*O.R.*, Vol. 35, Pt. II, p. 634.

[40]P.G.T. Beauregard to S. Cooper, October 2, 1863, Compiled Service Record of R. S. Ripley.

constructed on Sullivan's Island precipitated additional charges by Ripley. Citing months of interference, inactivity, faulty dispositions, and a waste of labor, Ripley again criticized the engineers and D. B. Harris. Harris, he wrote, "pursues a course of action looking much like obstruction. That is, being unable or unwilling to effect the necessary purpose, it is endeavored to prevent others from doing it."[41]   Others charged with the defense of Sullivan's Island, Brigadier General Thomas L. Clingman, Colonels D. H. Hamilton and L. M. Keitt, supported Ripley with their endorsements. On January 6, 1864, refusing to hear Ripley's complaints, Beauregard's chief of staff returned Ripley's paper stating "the subject matter in the main cannot legitimately enter into communication from him [Ripley] to these head-quarters."[42]   Undeterred, on April 9 Ripley again wrote of engineering deficiencies and faulty construction, this time concerning the mortar batteries on Sullivan's Island. Ripley stated, "I remained quiescent under the system adopted, and saw the works progressing slowly.... Returning from a leave of absence ... I found ... that the condition of things had not materially altered during my absence." Ripley's typically thorough report included extensive and meticulously detailed memoranda concerning all the batteries on Sullivan's Island. He concluded, "The low places on Sullivan's Island west of Fort Moultrie have not been filled up or drained to any extent, which is to be regretted, as the summer season will bring sickness if the matter is not attended to."[43]

In another change of command, Major General Samuel Jones replaced Beauregard on April 20, 1864. Jones increased Ripley's command, adding the Fifth Military District to Ripley's First. This followed Ripley's performance in the repulse of the monitor attack on Fort Sumter in May which, according to Ripley, "proved a failure to the enemy and demonstrated the power of our heavy batteries, and the skill of our artillerists, officers and men." Ripley and Jones apparently worked well together and had no significant difficulties as of late August. Jones, in his report of August 22, 1864, described the action of the July 1-10 attack on James Island and Fort Johnson: "General Ripley's lines were not attacked, but they were constantry [sic] exposed to attack, and the reduction of his forces to reenforce General Taliaferro imposed greatly increased vigilance on him and his officers, which was met by them with alacrity."[44]

One month later, a letter from Ripley to Adjutant and Inspector General Samuel Cooper precipitated a series of devastating events for Ripley. He requested a decision from Cooper which he hoped would prevent recurrence of a recent problem involving Major John F. Lay, a former inspector

---

[41]*O.R.*, Vol. 28, Pt. II, pp. 515-519.
[42]Ibid., p. 520.
[43]*O.R.*, Vol. 35, Pt. II, pp. 409-422.
[44]Ibid., pp. 445, 500; Vol. 35, Pt. I, pp. 138, 126.

of cavalry on Beauregard's staff, who at that time was an assistant to General Jones. Ripley also stated, "Major Lay had been reported once in writing and several times orally for taking unauthorized and irregular actions as a staff officer." Ripley questioned orders issued by Lay which Ripley thought to be unauthorized by General Jones. Though he had been absent, Jones supported Lay and a bitter confrontation ensued.[45]

In late September 1864 Beauregard, Colonel D. B. Harris, and Lieutenant Colonel Alfred Roman were ordered to return to Charleston to investigate the dispute. Over a year late, Beauregard had just filed his official report covering the action at Charleston during July-September 1863, which included the loss of Morris Island. Although his relationship with Ripley had been strained, in his report of September 18, 1864, Beauregard still praised Ripley: "I have to express my acknowledgements of the valuable services rendered by Brig. Gen. R. S. Ripley.... He was invariably active, industrious, and intelligent and carried out his important duties to my entire satisfaction."[46]

Beauregard arrived in Charleston and began investigating Ripley. Reopening the old issue, he asked junior officers P. C. Warwick and J. L. Fraser (of Jones's staff) whether they had personal knowledge of Ripley having been intoxicated after June 30, 1863. Both officers stated they believed him to have been so on July 2, 1864, which Fraser determined "from his boisterous manner, excited tone, and general appearance." This despite General Jones's positive endorsement of Ripley for that period, cited above. Warwick confirmed the report filed by General Jones, that on September 17, 1864 (in Jones's absence) Ripley went to Jones's headquarters looking for Lay, "very much excited, and in a violent, rude, and insulting manner and language, accompanied with threats to Major Lay, refused to obey or receive orders from [Jones's] headquarters." Sentiment against Ripley increased as General Cooper and Secretary Seddon sided with Jones. Reporting to President Davis, Beauregard recommended that Ripley be relieved of duty in Charleston, "which offers such great temptations and facilities for indulging in his irregular habits." Beauregard wanted Harris appointed to succeed Ripley, and Ripley sent to Petersburg to command Elliott's brigade. He also stated that Jones knew of the accusations by Fraser and Warwick:

> But from his conversation with them as to the particulars of General R's manner and conduct, his knowledge of the general, and his experience as judge advocate ... he was satisfied that a charge to that effect [intoxication] could not have been sustained

---

[45]Ibid., Vol. 35, Pt. I, p. 549; Vol. 35, Pt. II, pp. 162, 628-629.
[46]Ibid., Vol. 35, Pt. II, p. 630, Vol. 28, Pt. I, p. 91.

before a court, and therefore thought it best not to prefer the charge.[47]

Changes in command occurred before this problem could be resolved, and on October 2, 1864, Beauregard assumed command of the two western departments previously under Generals John B. Hood and Richard Taylor. Lieutenant General W. J. Hardee was appointed to replace Jones who was ill, and the Second South Carolina subdistrict was given to Ripley. The newly arrived Hardee was unable to replace Ripley with Harris, as Harris had died of yellow fever. One wonders if the undrained areas on Sullivan's Island, reported previously by Ripley, played a part in this epidemic.[48]

By this time the Ripley-Jones dispute had reached President Davis, who concluded, "If General Ripley had learned from the staff officer before the order was issued that it did not emanate from General Jones, he was not bound to obey it."[49] In November, news of Beauregard's efforts to relieve Ripley reached the citizens of Charleston. In protest, representatives of the city and adjoining parishes petitioned Secretary of War Seddon and President Davis. Endorsed by Governor M. L. Bonham and presented by Senators Orr and Barnwell, the petition stated, "General Ripley in his services for the defense of Charleston has evinced marked military capacity, knowledge, energy, sagacity, and judgement.... [T]he under signed respectfully say that they would regard his removal as a public calamity." Senator Orr stated Ripley had been placed on furlough.[50]

Conditions were becoming cataclysmic for the Confederacy. In September Union forces captured Atlanta and by Christmas they occupied Savannah, preparing to invade South Carolina.[51] Yet in December 1864, despite the impending demise of the Confederacy and all of Ripley's other problems, he managed to join with some prominent Charleston citizens to form a land-development company. The company was to develop 917 acres of "high land with marshes attached" in St. Luke's Parish, Beaufort District. Ripley purchased one share of the company, which was capitalized at $165,000, with thirty-three shares at $5,000 each. A list of the twenty-two other investors includes members of the Bee, Ravenel, Rhett, Heyward, Eason, Gregory, and Claussen families. There is no recorded fate of the company, but for obvious reasons the company most surely failed.[52]

[47]O.R., Vol. 35, Pt. II, pp. 629-633.

[48]Roman, *Beauregard*, Vol. II, p. 278; O.R., Vol. 35, Pt. II, pp. 643-644, 649-650, 639, 422.

[49]O.R., Vol. 35, Pt. II, p. 630.

[50]Ibid., pp. 646-647.

[51]E. B. Long, *The Civil War Day by Day: An Almanac 1861-1865* (Garden City, N.Y.: Doubleday & Co., 1971), pp. 565, 613-614.

[52]Charles Cummings, "Seven Ohio Confederate Generals: Case Histories in Defection," unpublished dissertation, Ohio State University, 1963, pp. 734-735.

Ripley's problems escalated in 1865. In early January Beauregard, who was now in Montgomery, ordered Ripley to report to General Hood. Ripley, on furlough and departing for Virginia, requested an extension of his leave, and asked not to be assigned to a command under Beauregard due to Beauregard's "personal motives of hostility." The next day Ripley's leave was revoked.[53]

On January 28 Major General D. H. Hill, then in Augusta, received a communication from Beauregard's staff ordering Ripley, if he was there, to report to General Cheatham for assignment to Gist's brigade.[54] Evidently, Beauregard did not know Ripley was on leave in Virginia. Twenty years later, in a New York *World* interview, Ripley related that in December 1864, he had written to Governor Magrath of South Carolina regarding the state's defenses against Sherman's approaching army. Governor Magrath "advised me to go to Richmond," which he did.[55] Early in February 1865 Union forces began their march into South Carolina. Beauregard, then in Columbia, still had not found Ripley and expressed his frustration to Hardee. "Should General Ripley be still in Charleston," he wrote, "inquire for [what] reason he has not joined his brigade in Augusta, and order him there forthwith, via Columbia. Should he disobey, send him in arrest."[56] On February 13 Beauregard finally learned that Ripley was in Virginia. After many favorable reports and twice recommending Ripley for promotion, Beauregard responded vehemently: " Brigadier-General Ripley is active, energetic, intelligent, ambitious, cunning and faultfinding. He complains of every commanding officer he has served under, and has quarreled (or had difficulties) with almost every one of his immediate subordinate commanders."[57] In his anger Beauregard grossly overstated Ripley's problems. While he did differ with Lee over Charleston's defenses, he was not alone in his vigorous objections to Pemberton. With Jones and Beauregard, his "complaining" concerned not them, but their subordinates Lay and Harris. Ripley's staff referred to him positively during and after the war.

Ripley's activities from late February until the end of the war are not well documented. According to Seabrook, "General Ripley ... reported to General Johnston on the evening of the Battle of Bentonville.... [H]e was again ordered to South Carolina for duty. Arriving at Chester, South Carolina he heard of the surrender of the Confederate armies and the fall of the Confederacy."[58]

---

[53]*O.R.*, Vol. 47, Pt. II, p. 1001, 1030-1032.
[54]Ibid., p. 1051.
[55]New York *World*, "A Talk with Gen. Ripley," March 17, 1885.
[56]*O.R.*, Vol. 47, Pt. II, pp. 1158.
[57]Ibid., p. 1031.
[58]Seabrook, *Address, Ripley Monument*, p. 12.

INFORMATION CONCERNING RIPLEY'S ACTIVITIES AFTER THE war also is not abundant. After leaving Chester, it is reported that:

> He joined his family at Society Hill, South Carolina, and after a short time went with them to England, and obtained employment in a manufacturing establishment in London....
> [T]he French Government ... offered him a lucrative contract for a large number of rifles ... [but] the machinery was claimed by the United States Government as property of the Confederacy, and this caused the failure of the contract. General Ripley returned to New York.... Having cast his fortunes with the Confederacy, he bore the consequence of defeat bravely, and manfully, without repining.[59]

In New York City Ripley lived "at the New York Hotel for some years, ... [and] made one of that coterie of men — ex-Federals and ex-Confederates — who distinguished themselves in that struggle and who have since made the New York Hotel their headquarters." At this hotel, on the morning of March 19, 1887, Roswell Ripley suffered a stroke and died later that night.[60]

"The Sad and Sudden End of Charleston's Gallant Defender" was reported on the front page of the *News and Courier*. Upon learning that Ripley had requested burial in Charleston, Mayor W. A. Courtenay responded that the city "would esteem it a high privilege to carry out the last wish of the superb old soldier, who, while he lived, loved Charleston."[61]

On Sunday, April 3, Ripley's funeral and burial service took place in Charleston. With all city and port flags at half-mast, the bells of St. Michael's tolled from 8:00 a.m. until 10:00 a.m., the hour of the funeral service at St. Luke's Church. Johnson Hagood, former Confederate general and postwar governor of South Carolina, attended as did the cadets and staff of The Citadel. Pallbearers included former Ripley staff officers Colonels Alfred Rhett and E.M. Seabrook, Lieutenant Colonel P. C. Gaillard, and Major T. A. Huguenin, and former war-time governor A. G. Magrath. As reported in the *News and Courier*, "The City of Charleston ... paid its debt of gratitude to its heroic defender.... It has been many years indeed, since an event of so much significance has taken place in this old city.[62]

Seven years later, Colonel Seabrook gave the dedication speech at Magnolia Cemetery for the unveiling of the Ripley Monument. The Survivor's Association and other Charleston citizens erected the monument of polished Carolina granite. It reads:

[59]Ibid., p. 12.
[60]New York *World*, March 30, 1887.
[61]Charleston *News and Courier*, March 30, 31, 1887.
[62]Ibid., March 31, 1887.

IN MEMORY OF
BRIG. GEN R. S. RIPLEY, C.S.A.
IN RECOGNITION OF HIS MILITARY SKILL
AND HIS
DEVOTED SERVICES IN THE DEFENSE OF CHARLESTON HARBOR[63]

Henry Timrod, the Charleston-born poet later known as the "Laureate of the Confederacy," had written a poem in honor of Ripley, two stanzas of which are on the monument:

> Rich in red honors that upon him lie
>   As lightly as the Summer dews
> Fall where he won his fame beneath the sky
>   Of tropic Vera Cruz;
>
> Gay Chieftain! on the crimson rolls of Fame
>   Thy deeds are written with the sword
> But there are greater thoughts which with thy name
>   Thy country's page shall hoard.[64]

Most modern writers have been excessively critical of Roswell Ripley. Unsubstantiated claims that Ripley was unable to "get along" with both his superiors and his subordinates have been repeated until they have now assumed mythical proportions. Ripley's years of dedicated, productive Confederate service have been forgotten or ignored. Ripley would not tolerate inefficiency or incompetence. His "complaining" was directed against those who were inept or negligent in their duties. His timely, meticulously detailed official reports are indicative of the perfection for which he strived and are contrary to the charges that his performance was impaired by his "irregular habits." Admittedly Ripley had faults and shortcomings. However, the citizens of Charleston still continued to express their appreciation and unwavering devotion at the time of his death, some twenty years after the fall of the Confederacy. There were many who participated in the defense of Charleston during the War for Southern Independence, but one of the most constant and devoted was Roswell Sabin Ripley.

---

[63]Seabrook, *Address, Ripley Monument,* p. 13.

[64]H. T. Thompson, *Henry Timrod, Laureate of the Confederacy* (Columbia, S.C.: The State Company, 1928); P. H. Hayne, *The Poems of Henry Timrod* (New York: Arno Press, 1972) pp. 99-100; personal visit to Magnolia Cemetery, Charleston, S.C.

"The Bombardment of Fort Moultrie, November 16, 1863" By Conrad Wise Chapman

By Ben Bassham[*]

In 1982, a large battle picture, *The Bombardment of Fort Moultrie, November 16, 1863* (Fig. 1), painted in Rome by a young American artist for a client in England, finally came "home" to Charleston, South Carolina, where it may now be seen in the Gibbes Art Gallery. It is arguably the finest-known work of Conrad Wise Chapman (1842-1910), one of the South's most important painters of the Civil War era.

Unknown to scholars of American art until its sale at auction in New York in 1975, the canvas may now be regarded as the largest and most accomplished work in a group of paintings in which Chapman recorded the complete system of Charleston's harbor defenses. Today, thirty-one small oil paintings of this series form the core of the collection of the Museum of the Confederacy in Richmond, and three more depictions of defensive works and numerous studies for the series in oil, watercolor, and pencil are housed in the nearby Valentine Museum. Finally, one more small panel in the Gibbes Art Gallery and one in a private collection in Charleston complete the series. Taken together, with the *Fort Moultrie* the recently emergent centerpiece, this group of paintings factually records detailed evidence of southern military ingenuity. It celebrates a Confederate moral victory: the long, emotionally charged, and nearly successful resistance to a prolonged siege by the odds-on favorites in the struggle, the combined naval and land forces of the North.

A short but significant chapter in the history of that siege is presented in the *Fort Moultrie* painting. In glowing, brilliant hues of blues, yellows, and reds, and in meticulously rendered detail, the artist has represented the exchange of fire between Moultrie's gunners and a column of Union monitors steaming into the harbor. Viewed from the north wall of the fort, the scene spreads out panoramically under a cerulean dome of sky. The artist has dramatically captured a sense of the dominant horizon line of this South Carolina coastal "low country." Only a structure in the left middle-ground, the old "Moultrie House" summer hotel, a signal and lookout tower, and a flagpole, on which flutters the Confederate "Stainless" banner, penetrate into the sky above the horizon. In the foreground, Chapman depicted with textbook accuracy the application of revolutionary new

---

[*] Associate professor of art history, Kent State University.

The South Carolina Historical Magazine 89: 13-23

Fig. 1. "The Bombardment of Fort Moultrie, November 16, 1863." (Courtesy of the Carolina Art Association)

principles of seacoast fortification, in which massive sloping walls of earth and sand replaced the stone and brick of traditional defensive works (Fig. 2). It is an impressive performance by a young man who brought not only artistic talent but first-hand knowledge to the task, for Chapman served in Charleston in a Confederate uniform for seven months during the siege.

Conrad Wise Chapman grew up in Italy and possessed an artistic background — and accent — more European than American, but he began his work in Charleston with all his southern credentials in order. He was born in Washington, D.C., in 1842, the son of the American artist John Gadsby Chapman and his wife Mary Elizabeth (born Luckett), of Alexandria, Virginia; both parents came from old, upper-middle-class Virginia families. Conrad's paternal great-grandfather, John Gadsby, owned and operated prosperous hotels in Alexandria, Baltimore, and Washington, D.C. In 1850, the elder Chapman — ill, worn-out, and still smarting from the harsh criticism heaped on his painting for the Capitol rotunda, *The Marriage of Pocahontas* — took his family to Rome where he hoped to work in peace and raise his two sons and daughter among the community of expatriate American artists and writers in an environment less hurried and materialistic than that of the United States. Conrad and his brother, John Linton, studied art with their father, and by the late 1850s they were both painting pictures of the city's landmarks and its environs for sale to American tourists.[1]

When the news reached Rome of Lincoln's call for volunteers to march on Virginia, Conrad and his brother asked their father's permission to enlist in the Confederate army. When his father refused, Conrad painted several pictures for quick sale and then ran away from home. Unable to reach Virginia by sea because of the Federal blockade of southern ports, he took a British ship to New York and from there made his way to Kentucky where he enlisted in September 1861 in a regiment of the famous "Orphan Brigade." He served in the West for about a year, but for much of that time he was ill and was shuttled from one dismal hospital to another. He recovered long enough to take part in the battle of Shiloh, where he suffered a severe head wound on the second day's fighting. After more hospitalization and further participation in the declining fortunes of the Confederate army in Mississippi, he sought and was granted a transfer to a regiment in Virginia commanded by Brig. Gen. Henry A. Wise, his father's friend and

---

[1] See Georgia S. Chamberlain, "John Gadsby Chapman: A Reappraisal," *Antiques* (June 1958), pp. 566-569; William P. Campbell, *John Gadsby Chapman* (exhibition catalogue), (Washington, D.C.: National Gallery of Art, 1962); and Edward F. Heite, "Painter of the Old Dominion," *Virginia Cavalcade* (Winter 1968), pp. 11-29.

Fig. 2. Detail of "The Bombardment of Fort Moultrie, November 16, 1863." (Courtesy of the Carolina Art Association)

the former governor of the state, after whom Conrad had in part been named.[2]

During the winter of 1862-1863, Chapman's unit took part in the defense of Richmond and saw some action around Williamsburg. There he continued his practice, begun in the West, of sketching portraits of his friends and recording scenes of camplife in his sketchbook. While dividing his time between fighting and drawing, he gained a reputation for daring in the first pursuit and for great descriptive skill in the other. His commanding officer praised his daring in a skirmish at Whitaker's Mill, saying "that he could not restrain the impetuosity of Cooney [Conrad] Chapman and that the fellow fairly reveled in fighting."[3]

In September 1863, Chapman was given further opportunities to display both talents when his regiment was sent to Charleston to take part in the city's defense.

Few engagements in the Civil War generated more public attention on the two opposing home fronts and none was more prolonged than the siege of Charleston, which began in 1863 and ended when the small force of Confederate defenders left the city in February 1865, their position having been made untenable by the advance northward from Savannah of Sherman's army.

With the defeat and the departure of the defenders of the United States forts in the harbor in the first week of the war, the South laid claim to Fort Sumter, Fort Moultrie, Fort Johnson, and Castle Pinckney. But when Maj. Gen. Pierre Gustave Toutant Beauregard returned to Charleston to assume command in September 1862, he found the harbor's defenses and the preparedness of the forces frighteningly inadequate to resist the anticipated Federal assault. Enlisting the aid of Col. David Bullock Harris, an expert at military engineering who had served with him at Centreville, Virginia, and in the West, he set about strengthening and extending the harbor's defenses with the aim of making them impregnable. Today, it is possible to examine a comprehensive record of Beauregard's preparations because he formed a board in 1864 to compile a history of the siege to be comprised of documents, maps, and drawings.[4] As early as September 10, 1863, however, Brig. Gen. Thomas Jordan, Beauregard's chief of staff, had

[2] Ben Bassham, "Conrad Wise Chapman, Artist Soldier of the Orphan Brigade," *The Southern Quarterly* (Fall 1986), p. 40-56.

[3] John S. Wise to Mrs. Joseph Bryan, June 7, 1906. Chapman File, The Valentine Museum, Richmond.

[4] *The War of the Rebellion: A Compilation of the Official Records of the Union and Confederate Armies*. Series 1, Part 2, Volume 35 (Washington, D.C.: U.S. Government Printing Office, 1880-1901), p. 477. Hereafter *O.R.*; also John Johnson, *The Defense of Charleston Harbor* (Charleston, S.C.: Walker, Evans and Cogswell Co., 1890), p. 3.

requested Gen. Wise to release Chapman to his office to make sketches for the ordnance bureau in Richmond; on October 9, Jordan promoted the artist to ordnance sergeant, perhaps in an effort to boost his prestige among the men as he went about his assignment. Clearly, Chapman was proud of this promotion for he recorded his rank along with the title and date of the painting in the lower right corner of the *Fort Moultrie*. Later in the year, official orders referred to Chapman's assignment as that of executing drawings to make up a "Journal of the Siege of Charleston," a suggestion that Beauregard had conceived the idea for a pictorial and written record of one of his proudest achievements before he appointed an official board to carry it out.[5] Writing long after the war, Beauregard recalled that it had become evident to him while at Charleston "that a well-prepared and authentic history of the operations was due as well to the brave forces of the South engaged as to the claims of military study and experience everywhere."[6] But Beauregard also simply liked and recognized the power of pictures. Drawings of Fort Sumter, for example, were photographed and the prints mounted and inscribed by the general with accompanying testimonials to several of its defenders.[7]

From September 16 to March 5 of the next year, Chapman went about his task of collecting material for the projected series of pictures. It proved to be especially dangerous work that fall, as the Federal land batteries on Morris Island and the heavy guns of the ironclads unleashed an almost continuous bombardment unprecedented in the history of war. A friend later recalled that Chapman often sat "on the ramparts of Fort Sumter and other forts under the heaviest kind of artillery fire. Chapman held cannon balls and shells in great contempt."[8]

During this period, Chapman sketched Fort Moultrie three times, including a view of its walls in the background of *Battery Rutledge* (Museum of the Confederacy, Richmond); his first sketch is dated September 16, 1863, his last November 11, less than a week before the engagement depicted in the Gibbes picture.

The Fort Moultrie that Chapman visited in mid-September was a defensive work in transition; it was, in fact, the third Fort Moultrie on the Sullivan's Island site, rapidly being transformed into its fourth form.

From the earliest moments of the Revolutionary War, Sullivan's Island was thought to be the key to Charleston's uniquely shielded harbor, since a fort placed near its southern beach could command the main

---

[5]"Compiled Service Records of Confederate Soldiers," National Archives, Washington, D.C.

[6]Johnson, p. 187.

[7]Ibid., p. 3.

[8]John S. Wise to Mrs. Joseph Bryan, June 7, 1906. Chapman File, The Valentine Museum, Richmond.

shipping channel into the city. The first Fort Moultrie, named for William Moultrie, its first commander and later governor of South Carolina, was constructed in the summer of 1776. Although only partially completed, this palmetto log and sand fort was strong enough to turn back a large British fleet and keep Charleston free until 1780, when it fell to a brief land siege.[9]

After the second Fort Moultrie, a five-sided earth and timber structure that was completed in 1798, was destroyed by a hurricane in 1804[10], work on the third fort began as America prepared for a second war with Great Britain. Polygonal in plan, its 15-foot-high brick walls are sharply angled into bastions on the northern, or landward, side, and present three broad faces, or curtains, along the sea front. Cannons were placed *en barbette* to fire over a low parapet. Inside the walls, barracks for enlisted men, officers' quarters, a magazine, a hot-shot furnace, and other buildings were constructed.[11]

The third Fort Moultrie underwent only a few changes prior to the outbreak of the Civil War: the walls were repaired, a ditch was dug around the work, and strong traverses—sloping walls to shield batteries from flank or enfilading fire — were put in place.[12] In late December 1860, with hostilities growing imminent, the Union garrison abandoned the fort and transferred to Fort Sumter.

When the Confederates took over the fort, they salvaged most of the guns and, in mid-January 1861, built "high and solid merlons, formed of timber, sand bags, and earth ... between the guns" on the southwest front facing Fort Sumter; on that same side an earthen parapet in front of the scarp wall was finished by the end of the month. During the exchange of fire between Moultrie and Sumter on the first day of the war — April 12, 1861 — shot and shell from the Union gunners across the bay did heavy damage to the barracks and officers' quarters — and they were subsequently demolished and removed by the Confederates — but the batteries suffered no damage at all.[13] Perhaps because Moultrie had come through this action so well, and because the threat of a major Union siege did not become apparent until late 1862, little more was done at the fort during the next two years.

[9]Edward Bearrs, *The First Two Fort Moultries: A Structural History* (Washington, D.C.: U.S. Department of the Interior, 1968), pp. 4-12.

[10] Ibid.

[11] Jim Stokeley, *Fort Moultrie, Constant Defender* (Washington, D.C.: U.S. Department of the Interior, 1985), pp. 34-35.

[12] Ibid., pp. 43-44.

[13] Edward Bearrs, *Fort Moultrie No. 3* (Washington, D.C.: U.S. Department of the Interior, 1968), p. 167.

When Beauregard resumed command in Charleston in September 1862, he ordered Harris to undertake the conversion of Moultrie from an exposed masonry structure into a powerful earthwork by banking more sand against the scarp-wall and by constructing even more traverses.[14] The strengthening of Moultrie was part of Beauregard's plan to prepare for the inevitable reduction of Fort Sumter by heavy Federal siege guns placed at the northern tip of Morris Island across the bay. As soon as Sumter was neutralized, Beauregard assumed, the Union land batteries would turn their attention to Fort Moultrie, the last remaining obstacle of any significance.[15] By September 6, ten days before Chapman made his first sketches of the fort, this strengthening was largely completed.

Chapman's painting, assumed to have been executed in Rome two years after the war[16] and based on those sketches, is a faithful record of the changes wrought at Fort Moultrie during the late summer and fall of 1863. Huge "bombproofs," shelters built of palmetto logs piled high with sand and earth and held in place with sandbags and turf, form the eastern and western flanks of the fortress. Clustered around the old hotshot furnace is a small group of tents — the barracks were long gone by then — and two smartly-dressed ranks of riflemen standing rather incongruously at attention while their comrades scurry about serving the batteries. Two huge polygonal traverses shelter the parade ground and the batteries from shell fire that could, and did, come in from a variety of directions onto this exposed fort. The centrally situated traverse doubled as a powder magazine. Six of the eight heavy guns on Moultrie's harbor-front faces are engaged; they are separated from one another and shielded by thick sand and earth traverses built and repaired in the lulls between bombardments by gangs of slaves borrowed from nearby plantations. This was truly defensive warfare with the pick and shovel, and Chapman painted a

[14] Bearrs, *Fort Moultrie No. 3*, p. 172.

[15] T. Harry Williams, *P.G.T. Beauregard: Napoleon in Gray* (Baton Rouge: Louisiana State University Press, 1955), p. 196.

[16] Although Chapman's painting of Fort Moultrie is dated 1867, recently discovered evidence points to an earlier date. On May 27, 1865, his father, John Gadsby Chapman, wrote from Rome to a family friend in New York: "The pictures which [Conrad] painted while here would astonish you, as they did everyone. One, a Bombardment of Fort Moultrie with 150 figures (now in England) would do credit to anyone...." (John Gadsby Chapman to William Kemble, William Kemble Papers, Bedford Hills, New York.) In March 1864, Conrad Wise Chapman left Charleston to rejoin his ailing mother in Rome; by January 7, 1865, he was on his way back to the South to rejoin his unit (John Gadsby Chapman to William Kemble, January 7, 1865, William Kemble Papers). If the Gibbes picture is the one referred to by the artist's father, its date must now be set at 1864.

prominent symbol of this new era in the "still life" of shovels and wheelbarrow on top of the western bombproof.

Harris's modifications to the then-55-year-old fort were prompted by a revolution in military technology: adequate to protect its garrison and armaments from even large shot from smoothbore cannon, the masonry walls of Moultrie would have been reduced to rubble and brickdust by the gigantic, rifled artillery recently developed and brought to bear by Federal forces. Some of the monitors fired shells from fifteen-inch cannons. Weapons such as these had breached the walls of Fort Pulaski in Savannah in less than two days, and were in the process of wrecking Fort Sumter, a contemporary work which, like Pulaski, had been built as part of this country's "permanent system" of seacoast defenses. The Confederate commander and his engineer recognized that masonry forts were obsolete; they abandoned traditional theory and practice and took the necessary steps in order to survive. Because of a greater experience brought on by necessity, the Confederates surpassed Union engineers in adopting new defensive measures, here at Charleston and elsewhere.

The engagement that took place on November 16, 1863, was yet another demonstration, like the more dramatic repulse of Rear Admiral Samuel F. DuPont's fleet of monitors and ironclads on April 7 of that year, of the superiority of the Confederate defenses and their gunners over the persistent, but tactically limited, gunboats of the North. Chapman did not arrive in Charleston until September and could not have seen that stirring earlier battle, an epic entertainment which was viewed by nearly everyone in the city.[17] He was probably an observer of the November 16 fight; indeed, the dates of his preparatory sketches for the paintings indicate that he spent much of October and November on Sullivan's Island.

Here, briefly, is an account of the events that surrounded the moment Chapman depicted: on the night before, Fort Moultrie opened up a heavy bombardment on the Union positions at the tip of Morris Island across the mouth of the harbor. The Federal commander there asked the navy to send in vessels to prevent an anticipated Confederate boat attack. Accordingly, the monitor Lehigh steamed in to take up station between Fort Sumter and Cummings Point in the early hours of the sixteenth. However the tide was going out that morning, and the *Lehigh* came to rest solidly on a sand bar.

At first light, Moultrie's garrison, the First Carolina Infantry, commanded by Captain J. Valentine, caught sight of the *Lehigh*, dead in the water. They opened up on her at 6:45 a.m. and, joined by other Confederate batteries, kept up a steady fire for about the next four-and-one-half hours. Early in the action, three other monitors, the *Passaic*, the *Nahant*, and the

---

[17] E. Milby Burton, *The Siege of Charleston, 1861-65* (Columbia: University of South Carolina Press, 1970), p. 140.

Montauk, came in to attempt to tow the *Lehigh* off the bar and to answer the fire from Sullivan's Island. These four monitors, with the *Lehigh* presumably located on the right, may be seen in Chapman's painting as virtual specks in the water above one of Moultrie's massive corner traverses. The fort was hit several times: a rifled thirty-two pounder was struck and dismounted and a shell exploded in the north entrance, fatally wounding one man and injuring three others seriously. In Chapman's painting, these men are shown being carried, with a tenderness akin to that seen in depictions of the deposition of Christ, into the safety of the western bombproof.

Actually, Chapman's painting is mistitled, for the men of Fort Moultrie gave much worse than they received. While the Union naval commander later reported to Washington that the ship "sustained no real damage," the *Lehigh*'s captain must have had another opinion.[18] His ship, a tiny dot in the water when viewed from Moultrie 2,300 yards to the north, had been struck twenty-seven times. Her deck plates were buckled and she was leaking badly; although she saw further light action after the sixteenth, by the end of the month the *Lehigh* had to be sent to Port Royal for repairs.[19] Although the events of this day figured as only a minor episode in the history of the siege, the morning's battering of the *Lehigh* was a victory consistent with the southern conviction that a just and noble cause, combined with the courage, skill, and pluck of the Confederate fighting man, would ultimately triumph over the advanced technology and greater material wealth of the northern "invaders." Such a victory was especially sweet coming in the same year that had seen the depressing defeat at Gettysburg and the loss of Vicksburg.

The engagement depicted may well have had a special significance to the patron who commissioned the painting, the businessman Charles K. Prioleau, a member of one of Charleston's oldest and most distinguished families, who continued to have close commercial ties to the city after moving to Liverpool, England. Indeed, Prioleau was heavily involved in blockade running between Liverpool and Charleston and early in the war donated a cannon for the defense of the harbor.[20] Prioleau probably bought the painting because he wanted a memento of Charleston's part in the war; many years later, Chapman suggested that Prioleau would have purchased

[18] *Official Records of the Union and Confederate Navies in the War of the Rebellion,* Series 1, Vol. 15 (Washington, D.C.: Government Printing Office, 1902), pp. 117-127, 145-146; *O.R.,* Series 1, Part 1, Vol. 28, pp. 739-742.

[19] May Spencer Ringold, "William Gourdin Young and the Wigfall Mission — Fort Sumter, April 13, 1861," *South Carolina Historical Magazine* (Vol. 73), p. 29. See also Ethel S. Nepveux, *George Alfred Trenholm and the Company That Went To War, 1861-1865* (Charleston, S.C.: Comprint, 1973).

[20] Burton, *The Siege of Charleston,* p. 40; Nepveux, *George Alfred Trenholm,* p. 23.

several more paintings if his business hadn't failed.[21]

Chapman's painting may have been modeled, perhaps on Prioleau's suggestion, on a highly-praised painting of the war, *The Bombardment of Fort Sumter* of 1865, long believed to be the work of Albert Bierstadt, but recently reattributed to John Ross Key, the grandson of Francis Scott Key.[22] Key's painting is strikingly similar to Chapman's in size — twenty-six by sixty-eight inches to Chapman's twenty-eight by seventy-two inches — and in panoramic format. Key, another of the Confederate artists detailed by Beauregard to compile a pictorial history of the siege, and Chapman knew one another and visited Fort Sumter together from December 7 to December 10 in 1863, only a few days after the last great Federal bombardment of the fort had ended.[23]

Although Chapman and Key were the best qualified to depict the Confederate defenses by virtue of their greater military experience, they were not the only artists in Charleston in those months. Historian Alfred C. Harrison, Jr., has found that Charleston, in addition to continuing a tradition of balls, banquets, and picnics, was also a beehive of artistic activity that season, with virtually all of the painters turning their attention to the stirring symbol of Fort Sumter.[24]

However of the paintings produced during this period, the subject of Chapman's monumental, luminous, and meticulously painted canvas in the Gibbes Art Gallery is unique. This painting alone pays homage to the designers of the "new" Fort Moultrie and to the astonishingly skillful men who manned its guns.

[21]Conrad Wise Chapman to Granville G. Valentine, February 23, 1899. Chapman File, The Valentine Museum, Richmond.

[22] Alfred C. Harrison, Jr., "Bierstadt's *Bombardment of Fort Sumter* Reattributed," *Antiques* (February 1986), pp. 416-422.

[23]Johnson, p. 187.

[24]For example, a Columbia, S.C. artist named A. Grinevald painted three pictures of major episodes in the siege (Charleston *Mercury*, August 7, 1863); William Aiken Walker had on display a depiction of the ruins of Fort Sumter (Charleston *Mercury*, October 20, 1863); Lawrence B. Cohen (Charleston *Courier*, January 15, 1864) and George S. Cook (Charleston *Courier*, Spetember 12, 1863) also made Fort Sumter their subject.

"It Will Be Many a Day Before Charleston Falls": Letters of a Union Sergeant on Folly Island, August 1863-April 1864

Edited by Edward G. Longacre

From the spring of 1863 until February 1865 Charleston underwent one of the longest and most debilitating sieges in the history of warfare. The city's harshest period of trial began in mid-August 1863, when Union Major General Quincy A. Gillmore decided to shell the Charleston defenses, including Forts Sumter and Moultrie, with an awesome array of long-range ordnance. From their bases of operations on Morris and Folly Islands, south of the city, Gillmore's cannoneers quickly turned Sumter, the principal defensive work in Charleston harbor, into "a shapeless and harmless mass of ruins." During the first week alone, the besiegers fired over 5,000 rounds (more than half a million pounds of ammunition) into the fortress. Then came several attacks against the city works by members of Gillmore's X Army Corps, aided by a fleet of warships under Rear Admiral John A. Dahlgren. These movements forced the evacuation of Battery Wagner, at the northern tip of Morris Island, on September 7, culminating two months of warfare in that sector.

In August, too, Gillmore began to shell Charleston itself with batteries erected on Morris and Black Islands, firing incendiary shells known as "Greek Fire," as well as more conventional munitions. Within days the lower environs of the city lay in rubble and many inhabitants had been reduced to panic and misery. But, despite Gillmore's expectations, the Charlestonians held out, ensuring that their city would remain in Confererate hands until the closing weeks of the war. With grudging admiration for the inhabitants' tenacity, many of the Federals foresaw a long, protracted campaign that would wreak hardship and suffering on besiegers as well as besieged.

One such realist was twenty-eight-year-old Sergeant Edward King Wightman of the 3rd New York Volunteer Infantry. In letters to his parents, three brothers, and two sisters in Manhattan, he left a graphic and articulate account of the siege—one that (in contrast to most writings by Civil War participants) also abounds in levity and wit. Wightman's facility with the pen stemmed from an unusually extensive education for his day, including postgraduate study at a New York university, and his pre-war profession as a trade journalist. In addition to being a man of letters, the sergeant was a brave and

The South Carolina Historical Magazine 85: 210-224

dedicated soldier—and for that reason he failed to see the close of the campaign to which he had devoted eight months of his life. In January 1865, only a month before Union troops entered Charleston, Wightman was killed while leading a charge across a parapet of Fort Fisher, North Carolina.

The sergeant's correspondence is furnished courtesy of his descendant, Mrs. Edith Wightman Kreitler of Radnor, Pennsylvania. It is published verbatim except for extra paragraphing, punctuation, and a few ellipses.

*   *   *

Folly Island, near Charleston, S. C.
Thursday, August 6, 1863

Dear Parents:—

On reaching the camp of the regiment, at this place, about three hours ago, letters were placed in my hands from you and from Jim and Mary, and it is so long since I have had the opportunity of writing that I have determined to let the [recently obtained clerkship in the] Quartermaster's Department take care of itself for a time while I recount the incidents of the past few days. . . .

In the middle of the night of the 28th of July I was suddenly roused from a sound sleep by the regimental Quartermaster who burst into the tent with eyes wide ajar and informed me that he had orders to prepare to move at daylight with three days rations. I was up in a moment. The Q M Sergt [of the regiment] was called and a consultation held; but the order for removal was written in so general a way that we could not make out whether we were to leave our camp temporarily or for good, taking all our stores and equipage. The Q M was content to go to bed and let things take care of themselves and his sergt very willingly followed his example; but for myself, not wishing to have all the work of starting come in a lump, I visited some of the neighboring Regiments, concluded that we were on a long jaunt, and at once with the assistance of our darkies set about picking up the clothing in boxes, striking and rolling up the tents, etc., so that long before daylight I had everything boxed up.

Shortly afterwards the news leaked out. It was reported that we were bound for Morrison's [Morris] Island, near Charleston, S. C., to assist in the reduction of Fort Wagner. Twenty-two wagons came up to take our luggage. After they were loaded and had started the Quartermaster directed his sergeant to go to the dock at Portsmouth [Virginia], where we were to embark, and superintend the unloading, but the sergeant pleaded inability and I was sent in his place. The wagon train was ahead out of sight, it was raining, and the distance to be traversed was between three and four miles. I growled like a thunder cloud but there was no help for it, and giving my knapsack and haversack in charge to one of the darkies, I set off after them and arrived in Portsmouth in time to have them all safely housed under cover, although in the contest the goods of two other regiments of the brigade were booted out into the storm.

No men had been detailed to unload the wagons and I had to get it done by a squad of contrabands [i. e., freed slaves]. The steamer Adelaide, which was to take us to Charleston, had been delayed and did not come in till midnight. I slept on a bale of hay. At about 2 o'clock A. M. the Quartermaster woke me and said that the troops only would go aboard the Adelaide and that the sergeant and myself were to remain for the present with the luggage. The darkey to whom I had entrusted my personal property has friends in Portsmouth and consequently lingered there until the last moment. Just as the steamer was leaving the dock he came rushing off with the whites of his eyes rolling in a frightful manner, and told me that while asleep on deck both knapsack and haversack had been stolen from him. I tried to get him aboard again so that he might have time to search for them on the passage, but it was too late. Afterwards the knapsack turned up nearly empty. It had been "gone through."

Through the carelessness of the darkey I thus lost my Zouave suit complete, in which I had done all my campaigning [in his former regiment, the 9th New York Volunteers, "Hawkins's Zouaves"]; all my underclothes; my portfolio (Fred's); Abbie's needle book; a host of relics picked up for the girls on half a dozen battlefields; all my papers; my gold pen and pencil case; besides books, my U. S. and rubber blankets, etc. I would rather have given $50 than lost them, but some thing similar has happened once before and when I heard of it I laughed in spite of myself. The haversack (containing a new knife, fork and spoon and three days' grub) has not yet turned up and probably never will. Our company sergeant about an hour ago triumphantly showed me a pencil case and pen he had bought off one of the men on the passage for seventy five cents. It was mine. He knows the fellow who sold it and if I don't haul him over the coals my daddy's not a lawyer. As to Abbie's Testament, containing my photographs of Jim and the girls, a benighted little nigger was found trying to read it on the dock. It was secured and handed to me by a friend. Fred's book of tactics and a couple of other books, together with my overcoat, belt, and belt plate and a pair of white gloves, were also left—quite a little piece of luck for which I congratulate myself. The loss of the underclothes and blanket, as you will probably infer from my last letter, I can readily remedy.

But to return to the dock at Portsmouth. On the second night of our stay at that place occurred a row. Ten men and a sergt had been left with us as a guard over the luggage, and about as many more stragglers were loafing around, perhaps fifteen out of the twenty more or less intoxicated with liquor they had bought or stolen in the city. Among them were a number of Zouaves. Now if there is any one thing the 9th Regiment agree on as a principle, it is that niggers were born to be abused, and "licking a nigger" they count the climax of a drunken spree. As luck would have it our [company] contraband Aaron made himself so forward laughing at their eccentric performances that he attracted their attention, and a couple of them, highly incensed, scaled the boxes on which he was perched and assaulted him with bayonets.

Warned by his yells I rushed to his rescue and fearing that they would murder him (for he is a powerful fellow and struggled terribly against them) I threw myself upon them and grasping the bayonets tried to wrench them from their hands. You would have laughed to see us rolling and tumbling among the boxes, tents, barrels and trunks, legs, arms, heads and feet all mingling and locked together, first one on the top and then another. It was like the mingling of Shakespear's many colored spirits. But finally my hands became so cut and blistered and pricked with the sharp edges and points of the bayonets as they were twisted and wrenched about that I was forced to let go my hold. This untangled the group and Aaron and one of the Zouaves rolled to the ground, while the others remained in my arms.

But unluckily for the poor darkie a dozen Zouaves below were yelling and like hungry sharks waiting to seize him. They jumped on him and kicked him till he was nearly dead and the rascal who held the bayonet struck him a blow across the face which laid open his thick lips with a gash half an inch in breadth, breaking off a couple of teeth besides. A Corporal of the 3rd, who interfered, was knocked down and hit over the bridge of the nose with the bayonet. The assailants then skedaddled, knocking down by the way a herculean contraband belonging to the Lieut. Col. of the 117th N. Y. Vols., and threatening to "lick" the officer [Francis X. Meyer] himself.

I took poor Aaron to the hospital steward and together we managed to sew up his countenance. A big dose of company whiskey was then administered and the patient was put to bed on a box with a tent for his covering. He is now nearly well, but heaving a huge sigh whenever his drubbing is referred to. Quite natural he should. . . .

On Sunday evening (2nd August) the steamer "Escort," somewhat larger than the Harlem [ferry] boats, came up and took our luggage aboard, and on Monday morning, at 8 o'clock, with eight hundred men, including eight companies of the 112th N. Y. and two of the 103rd N. Y., as passengers, we started out upon the Atlantic. With such a boat and such a load a storm would have been fatal to us. I forgot to say that, in addition to our other freight, we had 25 cases of new Springfield rifles, which had just came up for the 3rd in place of the poor [British-made] Enfields we have hitherto used.

Our voyage was a remarkably pleasant one, though the steamer rolled considerably, especially off Cape Hatteras, where a breeze sprang up and sent a few waves aboard. Some of the boys got sea-sick and added to the contents of the ocean. I didn't but slept comfortably on a bed of tents below deck, drawing rations from the haversacks of my friends and living on coffee, hard tack and bacon. We had a new way of making coffee, bye the bye. A cask was filled two thirds full of water, the coffee and sugar dumped in, a pipe reaching to the bottom and connected with the steamer's boiler inserted, steam let in and the whole cooked in four or five minutes. A couple or three casks of coffee sufficed for all on board.

Early on Wednesday morning a cheer awoke me, and springing up I saw before me, about eight miles distant, the solid walls of Sumter and the spires and housetops of Charleston. Close by were a fleet of vessels, prominent among which were the three Monitors, the frigate Wabash and a number of ironclads, while from the sand forts of Morrison's Island an occasional puff of smoke and the booming of heavy guns told that the siege was still in progress. No encampments were to be seen, but after we had got our orders and taken a pilot aboard and neared the shore we gradually traced the outlines of the white tents on the background of white sand which almost appeared to blend with them.

We anchored that night in Stono Inlet [below Folly Island] and this morning, after traversing a straight [strait] as narrow as a canal for two or three miles, brought up at the dock at last and landed on Folly Island. The first thing that attracted my attention was a palmetto tree, reminding me that I am indeed in the heart of the "South."

Our camp is in the midst of the sand hills on the beach of the Atlantic, whose roaring breakers I hear tumbling in upon the shore, as I sit here writing. The boys have already caught a crocodile weighing eleven hundred pounds and one of them has been so unlucky as to have his leg bit off by a shark. The position is a healthy one.

Wells can be dug anywhere and sulphur water is uniformly found at a depth of eight or ten feet. It is altogether preferable to our position at Portsmouth where I was but forty paces from a standing swamp infested with all sorts of vipers. One evening I found a spotted adder more than two feet long in my tent there. I gave the alarm and a dozen of us, deploying as skirmishers outside, arrived with tent pegs, surrounded and dispatched his snakeship as he came out. While there, too, the fatal vapors ensured at least one funeral a day, and sometimes two coffins came by our door in one ambulance, preceded by muffled drums and the comrades of the dead with reversed arms. The order which sent us here was therefore a healthy one. Only the first brigade of our division came. The others remain behind.

I have no time to write more or even to review what has been so hastily scribbled. My health is first rate, weight 157 lbs. Campaigning agrees with me. Fort Wagoner will have to succumb soon. We are close up under it.

The 3rd is engaged in doing picket duty. A rebel shell dropped in the midst of one of our companies, the other day, but only one man was injured. The rest dropped in the sand so suddenly that the danger passed over them.

As ever, I remain
Yr. Aff[ectionate] Son
Ed

*   *   *

Folly Island near Charleston, S. C.
August 24, 1863

Dear Bro[thers]:—

Our mail communication with the North has been interrupted for several weeks in consequence of the operations against Charleston, the government fearing revealation of its plans and strength at this point. I can scarcely write, having a painful felon on one of the fingers of my right hand but as there has been little fighting done here of late I suppose it is necessary in order to assure the folk at home that I am still safe and well.

I left the Quartermasters Dept. a couple of weeks ago in disgust and returned to my company. I was offered a position of Quartermaster Sergeant if I would remain but declined, for the [Chief] Quartermaster is green, often imposed upon, and I have no wish to become implicated by endeavoring to keep his accounts. I was asked to act as Brigade

Quartermaster Clerk but demured and then [was] detailed as clerk to the general court martial sitting in the island but demured again—requesting to act as the company clerk but [the authorities] couldn't see it and [I] requested to be placed in the ranks, where I am at present. While in the Quartermasters I had succeeded in getting two men of the 9th appointed as First Sergeants, [John W.] Knowles of Company C [B] and young [George W.] Rogers of Company H (my old company).

The men of the Third are almost constantly on picket. There are now but about two hundred and twenty men only in the regiment. No drafted men join us and there is the prospect of the organization breaking up. The sooner the better, for a greater collection of stupid rascals, officers and men, I have never met with. I attempted to get transferred to another regiment but unsuccessfully. No position in the Third would be honorable or worth retaining. The Colonel [Samuel M. Alford] and Lieut. Col. [Eldridge G. Floyd] have recently got themselves in hot water by trying to make three year men of two year men. About twenty refused to do duty are now held as prisoners until the matter can be inquired into.

You have probably heard before this of the bombardment of Charleston. The day I joined the company we changed camp further up the island, cutting away an immense quantity of brush and briar wood to make room for our tents. On the 16th inst[ant—i.e., of the present month], in the afternoon, the whole regiment was ordered to Morrison's Island to support the land batteries and the next morning we opened with heavy guns on the rebel works.

The first night we bivouacked on the beach behind sand works, under fire of shells from Fort Johnson [on James Island]. They dropped plentifully around us, but no one was hurt. Next evening we, as we thought we were about to return to camp, were ordered forward and advanced to within 400 yards of Fort Wagner and remained there twenty-four hours with shot and shell of almost every caliber howling and screaming and bursting over our heads. We sat quietly under the "splinter proof" and looked on. Poor Sumpter got an awful peppering by the five hundred pound shots of the monitors and collosal messengers of the big siege guns of the island. We had narrow escapes by the score but only one man was wounded. A night attack had been expected and our pickets were once driven in and we took position at the parapet to meet Johnny Reb but he didn't trouble us further.

On the 18th after dark we started to return to camp. The tide being up we had to wade knee deep in water for a couple of miles. We bivouacked within supporting distance of the works and next day about noon got back to our tents, after an absence of three days and nights without rations, tents or blankets.

The health of the men is not good here. Almost everyone has either a felon or a couple of boils to amuse himself with. The drinking water is bad and the men bathe too much.

Sumpter is breached in several places but I think it will be many a day before Charleston falls. No heavy guns have been fired for three or four days.

In haste,
Ed. K. W.

*   *   *

Folly Island, near Charleston, S. C.
August 30, 1863

Dear Wool [Brother Jim]:—

Your letter of the 18th instant enclosing one from Mary is just received. The postage stamps were very welcome for it is impossible to procure them here.

So it seems you are preparing for jolly times at home. Well, I am glad to hear it. There seems to be no end to my picnic. This changing of spots so often, which you remark upon, according to sound Baptized doctrine an impossible feat for leopards, is yet both pleasant and profitable to that temperament of humanity to which I am assigned. Since I have been out (the first year of my service expired on yesterday) I have visited many cities new to me, such as Phil[adelphia], Baltimore, Washington, Fredericksburg, Norfolk, Portsmouth, Suffolk, etc., besides running like a crazy bedbug, seeking whom I might devour, all over Virginia. I have been over the most terrible battle fields in the country and have seen many of our most formidable forts and earthworks: Newport News, Yorktown, White House, Williamsburg, Fort Monroe and Charleston. I would not have missed [them] on any account—particularly the bombarding of Charleston by our monitors. It is the grandest thing you ever saw. Think of those little cheese boxes, apparently so fragile, hurling their 500 lb. shot with such terrific vim against the crumbling walls of Sumpter and meanwhile riding carelessly at anchor in water seething with foam thrown up by the shots of the rebel guns.

The bombardment has recommenced but it will doubtless yet be many days before we obtain possession of Charleston. James Island [west of Morris and Folly Islands] is covered with hostile batteries and new ones are being erected every day. Both sides exhibit marvelous energy. As for Morrison's Island, we have crept up to Fort Wagner, captured one half of it and are now amusing ourselves throwing hand grenades into the other part. It must soon fall.

Tomorrow we shall move camp further up the island. Good. The water here is worse than miserable—brackish and unhealthy. The felon on my finger has almost kicked the bucket—killed by remedies. Kept me off duty for two weeks.

As for letter[s] from home I am glad and anxious to hear from you all just as often as you can write without inconveniencing yourselves. But I have no right to expect that you should give so much of your time to me. If you may have written weekly many of your letters must have miscarried. It was only a couple of days since I got one from you, Mary, and Abbie, dated July 8. Have any of mine miscarried? Have you had an unbroken narrative from me since I left home? It is rare that we get a mail here and from the letters that I have received to-day it would appear that they are two weeks, at least, on the way. . . .

Perhaps I am just as content for all that. Mary's sketch of herself and the Zou-zou [Zouave] in a previous letter was done in the highest style of art. It tickled me wonderfully.

As ever, Yr. aff. Bro
Ed

*   *   *

Black Island near Charleston, S. C.
September 14, 1863

Dear Bro:—

Oho, you bandy little specimen of the "Harlem Guard." It seems you and the other buddies are rejoicing at having escaped the draft. Well, perhaps the Fates have not decreed that any of you shall lug rifle and knapsack and canteen and cartridges over the sacred soil of Rebeldom. Rest assured of this, though, if you had been sent you would have been roped into a set of secrets which, although the faithful records of your amiable brother may have induced you to think yourselves familiar with, would have racked both mind and body. Nothing but the actual experience could give you an idea of the character of a soldier's life. So, although I should probably return to the field if discharged, I am as glad as you can be that our benevolent Uncle Samuel has seen fit to hold you in reserve. . . .

"But to return to the subject." You will observe that this is headed "Black Island." On the 31st of August the whole regiment was ordered hither on picket duty for ten days. Our wedge tents were left standing in the old camp and we took with us shelter tents and overcoats. Four big whale boats transported us from the norther[n] side of Folly Island (Morris Island) through a meandering swampy inlet to Black Island, between Folly and James, a low marshy strip of ground three quarters of a mile long, covered with tall salt grass except where two low ridges covered with pine trees rise from the sand. Behind these ridges we found a detail of the 117th N. Y. camped and relieved them.

They had already built splinter proofs to retire to in anticipation of being shelled from James Island, which is only about 1400 yards distant and crowded with heavy earth works and batteries. Here splinter proofs are prepared something like a potato house. A long rectangular hole is dug in the ground to the depth of six feet. It is roofed with heavy logs running both length wise and across, the whole sloping toward the front or away from the hostile batteries. The roof rests on stout pillars and is protected on top by layers of sand bags and by loose sand to the height of four or five feet. A narrow appeture is left under the roof in front and a square hole serves as a door to dodge in at. If a shell of any size should strike plump upon such a concern it would of course knock it into a pie. They are chiefly intended as a protection against fragments.

You folks at home laugh at the idea of dodging shot and shell; but it is the nicest thing in the world, as you would be convinced had you see[n] our men when in front of Wagner, bobbing into the holes whenever the sentry shouted "Cover Wagner," "Cover Johnson" or "Cover Gregg" [on the northwest corner of Cumming's Point]. Those lively batteries made us hop around like hot peas on a shovel.

My first picket post was in the top of a pine tree fifty feet from the ground. Sticks had been nailed crossways on the trunk, at convenient distances, to ascend by and a platform constructed for the sentry. From this point a splendid view is obtained of Sumter, Gregg, Wagner, Johnston, Moultrie, of the rebel works on James Island and of our own batteries. I have sat in that cover place by the hour watching the forts as they pumped shot and shell into each other, like a disinterested spectator looking at the war. . . .

James Island looks as though she could blow us out of the water without any effort and we expected she would do it on several occasions. As yet, though, we are undisturbed except by an occasional heavy shell from Johnston and a few light weights from the neighborhood of Secessionville [a battery in the center of James Island].

Our worst picket duty is on the borders of the swamp on the James Island side. There myriads of stout ring-tailed mosquitos "rush" upon the detail the instant it appears and jab their bills in chuck up to the head on the first thrust. Even overcoats are no protection from the torturing rascals, [who] pierce through everything. Sleep is of course impossible with such a ravenous hoard of blood suckers singing and biting and buzzing and picking and screaming and chewing and poisoning, getting up your sleeves and trouser legs, crawling slyly down your neck or dashing into your ears and down your throat wearing a fellow's life out with coughing, slapping, pinching and scratching.

The day following our arrival at Black Island we were set to work to complete the battery of two thirty-two and one one hundred pound rifled guns, with which it was intended to throw "Greek Fire" shells into Charleston. We then threw up an entrenchment six feet high and two hundred yards long, leading from the battery to a bomb proof hospital which was next constructed. The distance from this point to Charleston is between four and five miles, so that the piece had to be given the greatest elevation in firing. The work was done under cover of the woods and when the first shot was fired I was up the pine tree. The shells fell short, and the battery, proving a failure, was removed. We are now building a large stockade fort on the other end of the island and the men of the 3rd dig so well that they have been ordered to stay twenty days instead of ten, as at first proposed.

On the night of the first inst. the roar of the Monitor's guns and the rapid shots of the ironsides roused us from sleep. The ironclads had opened on Sumter. The thundering reports were like the explosions of so many magazines. The earth trembled with the shock of the two broadsides and the concussions were distinctly felt in the air. In the morning poor Sumter looked as if it had been on a bender. No fast man with his hat caved in, cravat awry, waist coat wrong buttoned, coat split in the back, trouser legs half tucked in his boots, ever appeared so hopelessly forlorn. Riddled, battered and mauled, the honey combed walls of this "King of the Harbor" seemed, when the sun shown brightly upon them, dropping black shadows everywhere across the ruins, hardly worth the labor of possessing. Yet it still remains a bone of contention. The rebels hold it but it is harmless for offensive purposes—at least in their hands. The number in the garrison is estimated at from one hundred to six hundred men, who communicate with the city by means of a black steamer. Several small boat expeditions have been fitted out against it but no serious infantry assault has been made. I am ignorant of the cause of delay.

Against Batteries Wagner, Gregg and Cumming's Point, our operations were more successful. Our Monitors and land batteries opened on these Forts on the morning of the 5th with terrible earnestness. Columns of sand and salt spray spurting thirty feet up marked unmistakably the force and accuracy of the solid shot, while the shell, glancing neatly on the parapet, burst like thunderbolts over the center of the enclosures. At times the roar was incessant and the clouds of sand so dense that one could almost swear that Wagner had been loosened from the earth and driven into the air.

The rebels were well casemated or they could not have endured it an instant. Early in the morning of the 7th they endeavored to evacuate but our infantry advanced both on the water and the land side and captured about one hundred. Our loss was but three killed and five wounded. The loss of the rebels must have been severe for the bomb proofs are said to be pelted down. Inside the forts, where our shells burst, holes were found big enough to top a couple of hogsheads into. Many rebel dead had been buried in the works; these the remorseless shells had torn from their resting place and scattered in bloody fragments everywhere. It was like a pest house. In some parts the walls had been almost leveled with the ground. The enemy tried their torpedo [land-mine] tricks and attempted to blow up the magazine, but without success. As soon as we had taken possession Sullivan's, Johnston's and all the neighboring rebels opened but did not deter our men from repairing the works and mounting new guns. All this time the 3rd Reg. was on Black Island.

On the 8th instant the stubborn monitors poked their way out into the harbor and . . . commenced with their usual imperturbability to fire into Sullivan's Island. In about two hours' time there was an explosion and it was reported that the magazine of Moultrie had been blown up. It is now thought to have been something else. About dark the graybacks began to handle their guns with astonishing activity. The whole of Sullivan's Island, to the right of Sumter, was but one sheet of flame. The cannonading soon after ceased. What the result is we do not know.

September 15. I have just received letters from Jim and Mary at home, dated Sept. 8. Mary's account of her trip is very complete and interesting. Ask her to send me the photographs. Remember me to Abbie.

In haste, Yrs. Truly
Ed

P. S. The "Swamp Angel" in the drawing [by Wightman, contained in this letter] originally contained the 200 pounder which fired Charleston. Unluckily it burst. The Rebs don't know it and waste ammunition by the cartload [to try to silence it]. Quite a joke. We laugh a great deal over their plentiful shots, at a deserted underbank. A man occasionally shows himself on the works to keep up the delusion.

E

* * *

Folly Island, S. C.
Tuesday Even. Nov 18 [17], 1863

Dear Bro:—

I have only a few moments before "taps" to tell you of my safe arrival here.

"The Argo" left New York at one and a half o'clock on Wednesday the 4 instant [following furlough]. She was heavily laden with army stores and had also to tow a schooner to Hilton Head, so that our progress was very slow indeed—averaging only about seven miles an hour. The citizens you saw aboard were mechanics in government employ. They became obstreporous shortly after leaving the city, not being satisfied with the soldier's rations provided for them, so that Gen. [Alfred Howe] Terry, who was a passenger, fearing a mutinous outbreak, took military command and organized a guard. Consequently I was up all Wednesday night with bayonet in hand, guarding the engineer's room. But the strategical genius of Wightman soon became so apparent that he was made a corporal on the spot and placed in command of a squad, in which capacity his military bearing was so imposing as to overawe the giddy multitude and squelch all signs of disturbance.

We were five and a half days on the route. Reached Port Royal on Sunday evening at sunset. Stayed over night and at ten next morning embarked on the steamer "Escort" for Folly Island where we landed at sunset on Monday, and an hour afterwards found ourselves once more at home. Part of the voyage was rough and many a Jonah was cast overboard by the unhappy travellers. Luckily, I escaped all symptoms of seasickness. My provisions just lasted the trip out, though I am free to acknowledge that I did "hanker after" the other mince pie which Ell tried to force on me when about leaving the house.

After doubling Hatteras we had real July weather for awhile. Butterflies came aboard and it was too warm to be comfortable except in the shade. On reaching camp, however, a cold snap set in, equal to anything you have yet had at the North. Last night was almost freezing and I lay awake listening to the heavy guns at Cummings Point as they hammered away at Sumter.

An infantry assault is shortly to be made (it is said) by the 7th Conn. Vols. with [Colt's] revolving rifles and scaling ladders in boats especially constructed for the purpose. They are to be supported by another regiment. The assault will probably be made by daylight while there are but few rebs in the fort, our gunboats at the same time engaging the enemy's batteries. The 7th (a splendid batallion) is close to our camp and rehearses its role daily. Success to it.

The island is much more healthy than when I left [in the first week in October]. The cold drives disease away. The number of men on the sick list is comparatively small. The new location of our camp is much better than the last and we have at length found clean water.

I have been all day polishing my rifle and getting it in working order. New furloughs are to be given and a general movement seems as far off as ever. We hear that one Regiment (3rd Infty) is to be separated from the other troops of the division and posted in detachment, in various works, as heavy artillery.

Tell Charley I went to Gen. [George H.] Gordon's Headquarters this morning to see Cooper [a friend from another regiment] but he had gone to St. Augustine, Florida on leave for his health. They think he will resign and not return here.

I have just been weighed and top the beam at 169 lbs. Healthy as a brick. Love to all the phellers.

In haste, yrs.
Ed.

*   *   *

Folly Island, S. C.
November 23, 1863

Dear Bro:—

I wrote to you on arriving here about the 10th instant according to promise. Since that time a change has taken place, both in our position and duties. Just a week ago the 3rd Regiment was broken up into detachments. One company went to Gen [Israel] Vogdes as headquarters guard; six to man the works and guns (they were drilled as heavy artillery at Fort Monroe [Virginia]) at the northern end of Folly Island and there to take charge of four light guns at Pawnee Landing. I am with my company at the latter place. There are two docks here and it is the headquarters of the Post Quartermaster and Commissary. Our picket duty is done. We have only to drill at the guns and to guard them and the camp. During the past week I have been on guard but twice.

The coldness of the weather here when I wrote to you last was due to the prevalence of north winds. The surf lasted but three or four days. Since that time it has been very mild and summer-like—just my kind of weather and agrees with me like a charm. I am in remarkably good condition. The health of the regiment is vastly improved. In place of the eighty on the sick list one month ago there are now but nineteen. . . .

Six officers and twenty five men of the 3rd, it is reported, are to go North to obtain recruits for the Regiment. I think that their chances of success are slim and that after the expiration of sixty days we shall be consolidated. The regiment has no lever to work with. It is but little known and that little is not in its favor. I suppose I might get home with the rest but then doubt the advantages of such a step.

Nothing of moment occurs here and every day promises more positively winter quarters. The bombardment is slowly kept up and there are never wanting rumors of general attacks to be made; yet nothing is done. The 7th Connecticut, who volunteered to assault Sumter, have gone away, it is supposed to their old camp.

As to the 3 year men of the 9th [New York], Col. [Rush] Hawkins' proposition for a transfer has been submitted to them and they have decided to remain where they are. I have communicated the result to Col. Hawkins.

Having nothing more to say I further proceed to say it and subscribe myself

Yrs like thunder, by golly,
Ed K. W.

P. S. Wish I were at home on the 26th [Thanksgiving] to chase folks around the chimney.

Yrs by golly, etc
Ed

* * *

Folly Island, S. C.
December 2, 1863

Dear Bro:—

The first winter months find me "sound and kind, in harness." Folly Island at this session is quite a healthy place. The weather generally is mild and summer like, though for a couple of nights past, following a Northeast storm, ice has formed in the neighborhood. Still the fact that we are pestered with multitudes of flies, almost without cessation, speaks favorably for continued warmth.

There is no military news. We are in status quo. My company acts now as both artillery and infantry. We drill on the guns in the morning, and in the afternoon shoulder our muskets and nearly march our legs off, maneuvering with the division on the beach, fatty Vogdes commanding. Every alternate night I am on picket. Night before [last] I was nearly frozen stiff at it, having been posted where no fires are allowed. Tonight my turn comes again but luckily the weather has moderated. . . .

There are no signs of a general movement. If an infantry attack is to be made we shall first have to be largely reinforced. Perhaps the naval authorities are waiting for the Dictator and other monitors. We have reports of a great victory by Grant in the West [at Chattanooga], but as yet no papers or details. As you may suppose the troops here are jubilant and regard the battle as the most important of the war—one of the finishing blows. On yesterday all of our vessels displayed their colors in honor of the event and the batteries everywhere thundered out their salutes.

> In haste,
> Ed K. W.

* * *

> Folly Island, S. C.
> January 6, 1864

Dear Rod [former classmate Rodney Kimball]:—

Here's a letter to you at last. I should have written long ago had it not happened that the time allowed for such purposes in the Department is limited and I had so many other correspondents to attend to. You'll not be offended when I acknowledge frankly that I rather calculated on your good nature to overlook any seeming negligence while I was hastily forwarding conciliatory messages for more exact correspondents and to testy acquaintences. I don't know what you'll think of me, Rod, when I sheepishly confess that some of them are ladies—a thing to be deplored—an accident—a catastrophe bedoozling to contemplate. Pray for me.

Affairs (in the neighborhood of Charleston) are at a standstill. All our general officers appear to be straddling the fence or sitting in solemn council with straws in their mouths to take a big think, or standing up whistling, with their hands in their pockets; all of which is respectfully intended to convey an idea of "masterly inactivity." To be sure, we throw a shell in the city occasionally, but it isn't expected to hit anybody and we should be very much alarmed if it were discovered that we had accomplished much in this way.

What astonishes us here, is that you folks in the North should continue to imagine that we are going to capture Charleston. We have no such ridiculous aspirations. We are content to live on sand hills, eat salt junk [i. e., salted pork] and drink dirty water. It is true that the [New York] Herald startles us sometimes by showing some trifling advantages we have unwittingly gained; but I solemnly assure you, my dear fellow, that we don't intend to do anything energetic or dashing, and that such little episodes are purely accidental.

The Third Regiment, to which I am at present attached (an Albany regiment by the bye, composed of the most part of sneak thieves and jail birds—delightful associates) has been divided in three detachments and is now serving as light artillery. My Company is posted at Pawnee Landing where there are four guns, two bronze field pieces (six pounders) and two thirty pound Parrots [Parrott rifles]. We guard these and in addition furnish details for half a dozen picket posts. Then we have fatigue work, besides drill and the guns and as an infantry of the line, skirmishes, and so forth.

We live in comparative comfort. We have none of the heavy marching and cold weather of last winter—nothing to compare with our Fredericksburg experiences, though the water freezes here at times. Northern winds always bother us, but when they do not prevail we luxuriate as becomes the inhabitants of "the sunny south." All the troops of this island are provided with wedge tents, which by the order of the surgeons, are raised on logs about two feet from the ground. Many of them have fireplaces and chimneys. Wightman has one and is at this moment toasting his shins at the blazing wood fire. Our bunks are made of crotches of poles and barrel staves combined.

Doubtless you have long since suspected that I have no news to write. You are sharp, sir, sharp. Let me close. I don't know that I am justified in calling this a letter at all. Remember me to Mrs. Kimball and little Kim and believe me as ever

Yours truly,
Ed K. W. Co. H 3rd Infantry, N.Y.V.
Folly Island, S. C.

* * *

Folly Island, S. C.
January 15, 1864

Dear Bro:—

I have to acknowledge the receipt of a vast number of letters from various members of the family since my last. As a consequence I am thoroughly posted in regards to your doings at home during the holiday week previously.

Mary says there is sometimes an interval of three weeks between the arrival of my letters. That cannot always be avoided, for the steamers leave here once a week and very irregularly at that, so that it is no unusual thing for mail to be detained. I intend, however, as nearly as possible, to write regularly on or about the first and fifteenth of each month.

The position of the regiment here is unchanged, though it is rumored that an expedition is about to start soon from Hilton Head to some unknown point. General Gilmore moves his headquarters to that place today. We now suppose that that is where the troops sent from Folly and Morris Island have been concentrated. General Vogdes has gone to New York on a thirty day furlough. He resides in Brooklyn. General Terry (formerly at Suffolk [Virginia]) is left in command. All this looks as if we were not to be disturbed. The prospect of monotonous inactivity is anything but pleasing.

Attempts are being made to re-enlist for three years those men in the Department who have but one year to serve. They are to have $800 to $900 bounty and thirty days furlough. When enough re-enlist to make it an object regiment, regiments are to be sent home en mass. Several have already gone. The proposition is favorably entertained by many of the old members, but there are not enough of them to take the regiment to New York. Furlough, except for re-enlisting men, has been stopped.

The men are still healthy in spite of long continued wet weather and short rations. We are on picket or fatigue duty every day. They alternate. The fatigue is digging—leveling the camp streets (rooting out stumps and so on) and preparing our parade ground. We live on ten hard crackers and two cups of coffee per diem.

Did I tell you I had built a turf fireplace and chimney to my tent? Such is a fact and it makes the house quite cheery and comfortable.

The Herald has nominated General Grant for the presidency. He would be more useful and less dangerous in the field. What are his politics?

Yours truly,
Ed

*   *   *

Folly Island, S. C.
February 14, 1864

Dear Bro:—

My last letter from home was received eight or ten days ago. Mary intimates that a box is about to be forwarded. I am almost sorry to hear it for you know how much trouble there was about the others. We have begun to move here too at last and there is no telling how long the Regiment will remain on the island. Troops are leaving every day, either for home or (it is said) for Florida [for the Olustee campaign].

I have no doubt that you have heard, long before this, more of our movement here than we know ourselves. What the mischief have we been doing? How many of us were killed and wounded in the last fight? did enough get knocked on the head to make a sensation at home? Is there glory enough to cover all the troops or only a hatful or so for General Gilmore and staff? All we know is that Gilmore has taken an expedition to some point farther south, has landed and is now advancing into the interior [of Florida] . . . as though to aid in concert with Grant.

When this expedition left Hilton Head, a second one started from Stono Inlet across the neighboring islands toward the Charleston and Savannah railroads, as a blind. One of the regiments of our brigade, "the 117th of New York," went with the latter. They landed on Cole's Island, passed over Kiavalst [Kiawah] and Seabrook and then crossed to John's Island and proceeded in a northwesterly direction. There were two brigades and two columns. They met the rebs, created a rumpus, burned a bridge and captured a few prisoners. They were then ordered to retire, as our generals were informed that the enemy had detached 8,000 men to meet them. We are told that the movement as a whole was a success.

Infantry and artillery leave the island almost daily to reinforce Gilmore. It is reported that the 3rd will embarck within ten days. Parts of the 89th and 103rd New York Brigade, companions of the old 9th, have re-enlisted and have been sent home to recruit. They have done a great deal of tough marching and fighting and rank among the very best regiments in the service.

On Thursday night last [February 11] at about midnight the rebs opened their guns upon us along the whole line. We were brought out under arms ready to resist and attack and some of our old lady officers were much alarmed. I was detailed to the battery at Pawney Landing where I was assigned a position at the muzzle of a thirty pound Parrot—where I expected to sponge and ram with awful energy. This proved to be no occasion. As present everything is quiet.

The weather is mostly such as you have at home in June but there are cold snaps sometimes, the night is severe and the dews almost as heavy as rain. The health of the men is remarkably good and so forth.

Ed K. W.

P. S. Tell Jim not to direct his letters as hitherto. The address is wrong. Let it simply be Edward K. Wightman, Company H, Third Infantry, N. Y. V., Folly Island, S. C.

Evening—Letters from Mary, Ell, and Jim of February 1st just received.

* * *

Folly Island, S. C.
February 25, 1864

Dear Bro:—

Letters are received from you, Abby, and Mary dated February 6 and 8 and a perfect bedoozler from Ell without date. I am on the quivive for that box—in fact, my eyes have been "peeled" ever since the intelligence reached me. The [steamer] Atlantic left the Head several days ago to return [to New York City] and we expect the Express up every morning.

So you ate my turkey, did you, Booby? I'll have revenge next time I get up to your house. God's blood!! The box would probably have come with the letters had not means of transportation been wanting. All the steamers are busy taking reinforcements to Florida where it is said Gilmore has met with a defeat [at Ocean Pond, February 20]. We hear that his signal books were captured, his plans revealed and his army surprised, and a whole battery captured.

Two small brigades are only left on Folly Island, of which ours is one. We were detailed to man batteries in the works. Johnny Reb has now a good chance to attack us. It is said Beauregard, though, has moved South to give battle to Gilmore. Our General Vogdes, too, has gone and Col. Alford of the 3rd is left in command of Folly and Long Islands. Gilmore has sent to Fort Monroe for reinforcements and the Adjutant General says that when they arrive our Brigade will go South to join the rest—probably within three weeks.

You think the rebs are disorganized and faint hearted. We don't believe the newspaper reports and look for desperate fighting. We are afraid our forces are too much divided.

The women folks speak of my re-enlisting. I shall not re-enlist until my term of service expires and never in the 3rd Regiment.

The health of our men is remarkably good. Mine I believe perfect. Good bye. I'm off on picket.

Ed

*   *   *

Folly Island, S. C.
March 8, 1864

Dear Bro:—

I have just received letters from home up to February 23rd. The box has not yet arrived but is supposed to be at Hilton Head. The expressman tells me that he expects it with the others every day and there is no cause of delay. Probably a deficiency of means of transportation is the trouble. The mail which is due today has not come up and is not looked for for a couple of days.

Our detachment is now employed every day in loading and unloading vessels at the wharf. We have no rest even on Sundays. The citizens who have hitherto done this work have been sent to the Head. Today we have been shipping army wagons. General Vogdes has gone to Florida and Col. Alford of the 3rd is left in command. . . . Vogdes will return, it is said, in a few days.

We have no late news from Florida. No reinforcements have yet arrived from Fort Monroe. There are two brigades on this island and three regiments only on Morris Island. A slow bombardment is kept up on the city of Charleston, but of course no active operations are to be expected in the neighborhood for some time to come. It seems to be the determination of our officers to remain here, if possible, permanently. They may succeed and may not.

I am interrupted here by the cries of a riotous squad of citizens who, it seems, have been ordered up to relieve us, "Z'all right." Bully for us.

I'm in an awful hurry and would not write were it not for mother and the girls, for there is no news. Yes, we have just raised a flagstaff and flag. That's about the sum total.

There is an item for Ell though. You must know that snakes of all kinds abound here. Well, I awoke suddenly three or four nights since and found myself leaning on one elbow and staring through the darkness at the other side of a tent where underneath the bunk several animals seemed to be rolling and tumbling in a fierce conflict. Squeaks, bumps, and hisses alternated with wonderful rapidity. There was an occasional sound, too, like the cooing of a dove. I roused the fellow beside me and suggested it was a snake and rat fight. He agreed. We listened breathlessly, not daring to step out on the floor. Once I reached out my hand toward the matchbox, but a rattling of tins on the shelf suggested adders and lizards and it was jerked back in a very frisky style.

Finally I summoned up pluck to strike a light and discovered— what do you think? Two thundering big tom cats, scrambling around with their ears tucked back, and their tails the size of your office stove pipe. We have never suspected there were any cats on the Island and were wonderfully pleased with our visitors. I sat up half an hour to look at them. In the morning they had escaped.

What's the news? Remember me to the fellas and believe me

Yours truly
Ed K. Wightman

P. S. My offers to exchange the enclosed photograph for another. So may it be. Ask Charlie to send one too if he has any to spare.

Ed

* * *

Folly Island, S. C.
March 21, 1864

Dear Rod,

Something like a month ago I wrote to you but as yet no answer has been received. Perhaps the letter miscarried. How are you getting on at Albany and what is the condition of your health? . . . Drop a line occasionally so that I might keep track of you. I often think of you and picture myself the cozy comforts of your home. Are the Kimball family doing nicely? (The troops remaining in the neighborhood of Charleston are at present quiet and undemonstrative. We have two brigades on this island and three regiments on Morris Island. For defense attacks we depend greatly on strong works immediately between us and the James Island, and upon the gunboats.)

The Third Regiment is falling away and promises soon to give up the ghost as an organization. We have recruiting agents enough in New York and Albany, but the regiment has no reputation to build upon, never having been in an engagement except at that of Big Bethel [in June 1861]. Our men now number at the most about 250 although falsified official reports multiply them, I believe double that. One of the companies has but nine men for duty. Several others have less than twenty. My own company has but fourteen. There is still ten companies, and of course, a super-abundance of commissioned and non-commissioned officers. Such an utterly demoralized, disorganized crowd you [cannot] imagine to be in the army, nor I either, till I saw it. The officers are incapable, the men undisciplined and miserably drilled. Some are too old for the service and some too young. Many complain of having enlisted while intoxicated—others to escape imprisonment of a jail. It is a motley assembly of dissatisfied growlers.

I think you told me while in New York that Kidd, formerly Lieut. in your company, was [New York Governor Horatio] Seymour's military secretary. If you chance to see him I wish you would ask him what is to be done with the 3rd—whether it is to be consolidated and with what regiment and whether it is to be reorganized as a battery. Remember me to everyone and believe me as ever

Yours truly,
Ed. K. W.

* * *

Folly Island, S. C.
March 27, 1864

My Dear Boy,

What's the use of fooling?

I pause for a reply and while pausing will just fill my (your) pipe and light it. Ideas are to be furnished to order if they can't be scratched, or they must be smoked out. Excuse me for a moment. Ow! (Burnt my fingers with a match, upset the tobacco box and woke up my two tent mates, who were sleeping on their bunks.)

Z'all right. Here goes. I received letters from you and Abby dated the 14th and 9th instant respectively, and others from Jim, Charley and Mary. Charley's photograph is very good indeed and the enclosure of postage stamps came in the nick of time. I am glad, too, to have your summary of army news for lately we have been in the dark here as to the military movements in other parts of the country. Since then, however, papers have arrived to enlighten us. We expect to hear of the terrible fighting [in Virginia] within the next three months and perhaps to do a little on our own account.

For sometime back I have feared that the War Department would scatter our forces so much as to tempt the rebels to concentrate successively at different points and overwhelm us in detail. But I conclude from what you hear, that the various expeditions sent out during the winter were merely intended to distract the enemy, to deprive his troops of rest, to retard reorganization and to reconoiter.

It is now time for us to concentrate for the energetic opening of the spring campaign. The promotion of Grant and his appointment to the command of the armies has given great confidence to the soldiers in the Department and they now look to the end as assured. Rumor rides around us busily as ever and every day we are amused with the repeated issue of fresh orders for the movement of the regiment. Only yesterday we were to be assigned as artillerists to Long Island. Today we are to begin to expect a trip to Mobile. Col. Alford is said to have been appointed Brigadier General by the President, but the appointment is not yet confirmed by the Senate. Our Brigade is to be broken up. The 89th and 103rd New York are to report to [General Ambrose E.] Burnside in New York before the middle of next month. [General Benjamin F.] Butler is to send reinforcements to Florida instead of here. [General Robert S.] Foster's Brigade is to return to us. The 117th New York will join Foster and then the 3rd will be left out in the cold. Suppose all this is true. What then? Why, evidently "the cat's run away without the pudding bag's string," which is hardly worth mentioning.

It is pleasant to be able to say that we are more at leisure than heretofore. The crazy commander of the detachment having leveled down all the sand hills in the neighborhood, now rests from his labors. He does nothing now but walk around and round the camp from sunrise 'til midnight with his hands in his pockets, grinning from ear to ear at every remark he can construe as a compliment on the good appearance of the place. It is a mild form of lunacy, and the poor fellow is perfectly harmless. His name is [Captain John] Fay and he grew out of the swamps around Morisania [New York].

I am waiting patiently for the regiment to tumble to pieces. About sixty men will be discharged within the next three months. . . . Those who remain may either be consolidated by special act of Congress or transferred into a Battery.

The weather we have is glorious. "The time of the singing birds has come and the voice of the turtle is heard in the land." The pine trees and palmettoes are putting forth fresh leaves and a new crop of grass is sprouting up. The nights are still cold—sometimes freezing.

On St. Patrick's Day I went on a spree. Luckily our captain [James H. Wicks] is an Irishman. A party of five got a surf boat of a stevador at the dock and rode up the inlets and around the swampy islands. We had previously procured fish lines at the sutler's and provided our-selves with regular genuine Jacob fish hooks. Bullets were used for sinkers. None of your fine brooks. We also laid in a good stock of fisherman's grub, consisting of crackers and cheese. We had the foresight too to make some oyster knives of iron hoops and took with us a liberal supply of pepper and vinegar. I care nothing about line fishing but shell-fishy (joke) thought only of the oysters which grew in great beds along the shore.

The position for fishing was no sooner taken than it was discov-ered that we had neither anchor rope, anchor nor bail. So much for our endeavoring to celebrate an Irishman's birthday. You needn't grin, though, me boy; for you would have given your bandies to be present at the feats which followed. We approached the shore and planted "our gunboats" on an enormous bed of stupendous bivalves. They stood together like a big crowd of fat voters on election day. I grasped my knife, and with that same unerring instinct which guides me in the selection of sweet potatoes and bananas, oysterly raised the fattest of the group and attacked him with a knife. Jerusalem, what a sock-dolager! He looked like Falstaff on the half shell. How hungrily I smiled over that trembling rebel oyster! How I peppered him! How I bathed the poor fellow in vinegar! How I—ah, it takes my breath away to think of it. . . .

Excuse me again, me boy, my pipe's gone out and the "sodger" is warning me from outside that a snake has just run down our chimney. Here goes for the snake. Remember me to the fellas.

Yours truly,
Ed K. W.

P. S. Tell Jim that Lily's letter was received and acknowledged at this time. I should judge from what I hear that about one half of my notes miscarry. Enclosure in the letter.

Your picture of Uncle Sam's review of the candidates for the presidency was stared at by all the gawkies in the company. They thought it the most tremendous hit they had ever seen. It isn't bad. The poor hams, though, were incapable of making those nice discriminations which your gigantic intellect traced out.

* * *

Folly Island, S. C.
April 13, 1864

Dear Bro:—

This is probably the last letter from Folly Island. We are under marching orders to proceed to Fortress Monroe, Virginia, and shall start as soon as relieved by colored troops now on their way. All the white regiments except the 103rd New York (a part of which left for New York last Sunday) will be taken from Folly and Morris Islands. So a report says. We may start tomorrow.

The general opinion seems to be that we are to join the Army of the Potomac but I cannot avoid the impression that we are to advance with the Grand Army up the penninsula. Anyway we are going to help strike at Richmond. The men are in high spirits at the prospect. The leadership of [General George B.] McClellan on the peninsula (where it is suspected he is to take command) is in concert with Grant in northern Virginia [and] will, it is believed, make our Grand Army now concentrating here irresistible, and the fall of Richmond certain.

I cannot tell how glad I am to return again to active service. The avoidance of the second summer in Folly Island is in itself a great point (our camp here is in splendid condition. The parade ground level covered with grass, the streets padded, a staff erected, trees set out with fences and flower beds in front and everything in apple pie order.) Perhaps we take our shelter tents and leave without reluctance.

In great haste,

Ed K. W.

[P. S.] Direct letters to Company H, 3rd N. Y. V., Fort Monroe, Va. until otherwise instructed. Letters of April 5th received. No box.

* * *

As Wightman predicted, his long ordeal outside Charleston was over. Conceding defeat, the War Department recalled his regiment and more than 9,500 other troops from South Carolina and sent them to the Virginia peninsula to take part in a spring offensive against Richmond. In the first week of May these forces, under Gen. Gillmore, were transported to Hampton Roads, where they joined twice as many members of General William Farrar Smith's XVIII Corps, the combined command being designated the Army of the James. Under the overall command of General Benjamin F. Butler, this army waged a long, tedious, bloody—but eventually successful—campaign to capture the Confederate capital.

SHERMAN'S MARCH:
"TAKING ALL HER JEWELS
AND EVERYTHING OF VALUE"

SHERMAN MARCHED – AND PROCLAIMED "LAND FOR THE LANDLESS"

Howard C. Westwood*

When General William Tecumseh Sherman undertook to march from Atlanta to the sea we may be sure that it never occurred to him that he would create a heated controversy over whether black men or white men would own thousands of acres of rich plantation lands along the South Atlantic coast. But that happened.

Not long after Sherman occupied Atlanta in early September 1864, he decided that he ought to strike out for salt water. But not until the second of November did his general-in-chief, Grant, after some hesitation, tell him to "go as you propose."[1] The move seemed risky, for Confederate forces, including considerable cavalry under General Joseph Wheeler, if coordinated and divining Sherman's course could seriously cripple him by persistent harassment far from any base. Nor was it possible to send him help, for it could not be known where he would march; at his outset he himself was not sure whether his destination would turn out to be Savannah or Pensacola or Mobile.[2]

The march began on November 15. While the army was large – about 60,000 infantry, with cavalry of some 5,500 led by General H. Judson Kilpatrick – it was spread wide. There were two wings, each of two corps, each corps in a separate column strung out for miles on different routes, each separated from any of the others by as much as twenty miles. But, though Wheeler's cavalry on occasion kept Kilpatrick busy, deception of the Confederates so succeeded that by December 10, after some three hundred circuitous miles, Sherman had reached the outer defenses of Savannah.[3] Three days later Confederate Fort McAllister, below Savannah guarding a waterway to the sea, fell to his assault and at last he could communicate with the outside world. At once he met with General John G. Foster, heading a small Union army that since November 1861 had been based at Port Royal

* Counselor in the law firm of Covington and Burling, Washington.

He acknowledges the assistance of Dr. Elaine Everly and Mr. W. F. Sherman of the National Archives, and of Mrs. Carol A. Sakosky of the S.C. Department of Archives and History.

[1] *The War of the Rebellion: Official Records (Armies)*, series 1, 39(pt.3):222, 576-77, 594. Citations hereafter to the ORA are to series 1, except where otherwise noted.

[2] *ORA,* 39(pt.3):660-61.

[3] *ORA,* 39(pt.3):713; 44:7-14, 114, 147-48, 212.

occupying portions of the sea islands. Sherman intended to have Foster move a force to the north of Savannah to complete an investment.[4]

Within Savannah Confederate General William J. Hardee commanded some 10,000 troops. Sherman thought there were more. They were well fortified and watery land would allow attack only over five narrow causeways. Sherman took time to get set. To his surprise and chagrin, on the night of December 20 Hardee slipped away to the north before that route could be blocked. Early the next morning Union troops were entering the city unopposed.[5]

When Sherman had confronted Savannah's defenses his army was in superb condition, its morale high.[6] Though at the beginning of his march he did not know what he would propose on reaching the sea, by the time he got there he had so gained confidence in his army that his conclusion was clear: he wanted to drive on northward and, with Grant, quash the rebellion after administering bitter medicine to the South Carolinians who had started it. Indeed, as he had marched through Georgia some Georgians had urged him to give those Carolinians a good taste of the war they had begun.[7] While Grant had held very different ideas, after he and Sherman exchanged messages Grant agreed to Sherman's wish, and Sherman began to ready a northward drive.[8]

The time from December 21, when he entered Savannah, to the end of January was one of the busiest in Sherman's career. Savannah was to be left in Gen. Foster's hands, for whom Sherman had to get reinforcements from Grant. The fortifications around Savannah had to be adjusted to the Unionists' posture. Supplies had to be gathered for a trip that would be longer and much more contested than the journey from Atlanta. Provision had to be made for the 20,000 or so of Savannah's civilians whose money had become worthless overnight and whose link with friends had been severed. And, not least of all, something had to be done about thousands of refugee blacks.[9]

Before Sherman left Atlanta, Grant had suggested that he "move . . . the negroes" from the country he would traverse, adding: "As far as arms can be supplied, either from surplus or by capture, I would put them in the hands of the negro men. Give them such organization as

[4] *ORA*, 44:10-12, 700-02, 855.

[5] *ORA*, 44:10, 12, 727, 728, 771, 786, 959.

[6] *ORA*, 44:8, 13-14, 114, 147-48, 152, 159, 700-02, 726-27.

[7] *ORA*, 44:727-28, 741-43, 797-800.

[8] *ORA*, 38(pt.1):36; 44:636, 726, 728-29, 740-43, 797-800, 820-21.

[9] *ORA*, 44:700-02, 727, 786, 797, 817-18, 841-42; 47(pt.2):18.

you can. They will be of some use."[10] Though Sherman had some blacks among his pioneer corps when he started, and as he marched on welcomed able-bodied black men as laborers in a variety of functions, he did not arm them as soldiers. That is understandable. Combatant blacks in the Union armies were in units separate from the whites. The last thing Sherman needed for the success of his seemingly dangerous march was untrained, undisciplined units.[11] Also, while he doubtless fully understood Grant's point that he "move . . . the negroes" to mean that he should deprive the Confederates of their labor force, he cautioned his commanders that refugee blacks should not "be encouraged to encumber us on the march."[12] That, too, is understandable. Women, children and the infirm would clutter and slow the march and would consume food that might be critically needed by the troops. Unquestionably, early in the march effort was made to minimize the refugees, masses of whom did run to the blue coats, hailing the Day of Jubilee. Unquestionably, too, the effort to minimize met with some success. But as the march proceeded efforts to keep refugees away became lax. There are no reliable figures as to the number who flocked into Savannah with Sherman. There were at least six or seven thousand. But it is quite possible that there were thousands more then or soon thereafter; Sherman once said that one of his wings "reports 17,000 negroes."[13] In any case, the problem of their care cried for Sherman's attention before he moved onward.

Initially, before he entered Savannah, he had assumed that there was a simple solution to the problem – that all he had to do was to order all of the refugee blacks, along with his surplus and broken down horses and mules, sent to General Rufus Saxton who had headquartered at Beaufort, South Carolina, in Foster's department. When the Union landing at Port Royal had occurred in November 1861 the whites had fled the area but their slaves had stayed. In March 1862 the Treasury Department, given responsibility for abandoned property, had launched there what history has called the Port Royal Experiment. Northern businessmen, missionaries, and teachers came to put the blacks to work on the plantations, to teach them, and to introduce them to the way of self-sufficiency as free people. In June

[10] *ORA*, 39(pt.3):222.

[11] *ORA*, 39(pt.3):713-14; 44:59, 159, 166, 212.

It was later implied that Sherman might have armed blacks had he been granted his request for assignment of a Union colonel who was experienced in organizing black soldiers, a request not granted. *New York Tribune*, Dec. 24, 1864, p. 4.

[12] *ORA*, 39(pt.3):701.

[13] *ORA*, 44:13, 75, 159, 166-67, 203-05, 211-12; 47(pt.2):36.

1862 Saxton had been sent there, by special order of Secretary of War Stanton, as the military governor of affairs on the occupied coastal islands. While the Experiment had undergone considerable vicissitude and change during the ensuing two and a half years, by December 1864 there were some 15,000 former slaves busy in their new life, with Saxton the governor and policeman. Sherman thought it quite appropriate that Saxton take on his refugees, and on December 16 ordered that they be sent to Port Royal "where they can be more easily supplied."[14]

But very shortly Sherman had word from Saxton that the problem was not simple. Saxton told him that "every cabin and house" in the area around Port Royal was already "filled to overflowing." Saxton pointed out, however, that St. Simon's Island (below Savannah on the Georgia coast) and Edisto Island (on the Carolina coast between Port Royal and Charleston), once occupied by the Union forces but since vacated, probably were free of Rebels – a sort of no man's land – and had a large number of vacant houses. Saxton thought that those islands could be reoccupied readily by a small force and suggested that the refugees be sent there. It was apparent that Sherman would have to consider the refugee problem more thoroughly.[15]

Then, in early January, Sherman received a personal letter from General Henry W. Halleck, chief of staff in Washington, that certainly made him think twice about black refugees. Halleck wrote that, though Sherman was receiving praise from most people, there were some leading men very critical of his treatment of the blacks, that they thought Sherman rejected the blacks "with contempt." "They say," wrote Halleck, "you might have brought with you to Savannah more than 50,000, thus stripping Georgia of that number of laborers and opening a road by which as many more could have escaped from their masters; but that instead of this you drove them from your ranks, prevented them from following you by cutting the bridges in your rear, and thus caused the massacre of large numbers by Wheeler's cavalry."Halleck knew, of course, that Sherman probably had to discourage refugees because of limited supplies on his march, but, he suggested, perhaps Sherman now could open avenues for the escape of slaves from their masters by arrangement for their subsistence on the

---

[14] *ORA,* 44:701-02, 727, 729-30, 817-18; ser.3, 2:152-53; 4:118-19, 1022-31. A thorough account of the genesis and evolution of the Port Royal Experiment is Willie Lee Rose, *Rehearsal for Reconstruction* (New York, 1964).

[15] *ORA,* 44:787.

coastal plantations. Halleck said that were Sherman thus to foster slaves' escape his critics would be silenced.[16]

If Sherman, on reading Halleck's letter, did not know what was referred to by the charge that he had left refugees to the tender mercy of Wheeler's cavalry, he was quickly to find that the reference was to an incident at Ebenezer Creek about twenty miles from Savannah that had occurred on December 8 and 9 in the march of one of the corps of the left wing. On January 10 Secretary Stanton arrived at Savannah to see what was going on; his visit may have been prompted in part by reports of the Ebenezer Creek incident.[17]

The corps involved had been commanded by General Jefferson C. Davis. Not altogether because of his name, Davis was reputed not to love blacks. Nor had he the reputation of a cool head; in the fall of 1862 he had had a quarrel with his former commanding officer and had killed him.[18] Thus any report of Davis' brutal treatment of blacks would be read by Republican politicians with a believing eye. Even today the Ebenezer Creek incident is recalled as "an inhuman barbarous proceeding." But despite testimony seeming to warrant that label the incident may not have been quite that bad.[19]

Within a week after Sherman's march had started, Davis had warned his corps, "Useless negroes are being accumulated to an extent which would be suicide to a column which must be constantly stripped for battle and prepared for the utmost celerity of movement." Wagons, he said, were too overloaded to allow them to carry also women and children, and he cautioned that "every additional mouth consumes food, which it requires risk to obtain." While, as we have noted, it seems that restraint on numbers of refugees became lax as the march proceeded, this may not have been quite true of Davis' column, especially by December 8 when, being on the extreme left of Sherman's swath, it faced the task of keeping up in the convergence on Savannah. Thus, among the final reports of Davis' units, one regimental report says of refugee negroes: "Large numbers of both sexes and all ages

---

[16] *ORA*, 44:836-37.

[17] Lloyd Lewis, *Sherman – Fighting Prophet* (New York, 1932), pp. 478-79; Earl Schenck Miers, *The General Who Marched to Hell* (New York, 1951), pp. 272-73; Paul M. Angle, ed., *Three Years in the Army of the Cumberland: The Letters and Diary of Major James A. Connolly* (Bloomington, 1959), p. 373; Willard Saxton Diary, v. 26, p. 33, Saxton Family Papers, Yale Univ. Library.

[18] Ezra J. Warner, *Generals in Blue* (Baton Rouge, 1964), pp. 115-16.

[19] Angle, *Three Years in the Army of the Cumberland,* pp. 354-55; Burke Davis, *Sherman's March* (New York, 1980), pp. 91-94.

were prohibited from following the command, in obedience to stringent orders issued on that subject from superior headquarters."[20]

In any event on the night of December 7 the column had reached Ebenezer Creek after a hard march on timber obstructed roads, with Confederate attacks from the rear on Kilpatrick's cavalry and other firing heard in the distance. The creek was wide; the column was entering watery country. Pontoon bridging was required. The bridge was completed at mid-morning of December 8. The corps' crossing was not completed until daylight of December 9, with demonstrations from a Confederate gunboat and troop skirmishing all of the preceding day. After the crossing heavy cannonading was heard from ahead. Sherman's success in deception had fostered an idea that he might be headed for Charleston, accounting, perhaps, for attempted Confederate activity over on the Union left.[21]

In the long crossing of the stream an effort had been made to keep all refugees in the rear, presumably to facilitate the troops' move. When the troops' crossing was completed the bridge was immediately pulled across, leaving a mass of blacks, including many women and children, stranded on the far bank with Wheeler's cavalry soon to come at them. It is said that the refugees panicked, not a few attempting to swim across or to get there clinging to logs, with some assistance from sympathetic soldiers on the other side. Not many made it. Some drowned. Most eventually were picked up by the Confederates. Rumor was to spread that the Confederates shot them down. Of that there is no good evidence and it is most unlikely; much more likely is it that they were simply returned to slave life.[22]

In assessing this incident it must be kept in mind that Davis' position at the creek was ticklish, that in watery country he sometimes was confined to narrow passages that could be blasted by a single opposing cannon, and that he was under great pressure to maintain coordination with the rest of the army on the final approach to Savannah's outer defenses, just then being reached. Indeed over on the Union right wing an officer had managed, on the evening of the day Davis completed his crossing of the stream, to go on ahead of the army and soon got all the way to the coast and reached Foster with word of Sherman's coming.[23] One should be hesitant about condemnation of

[20] *ORA*, 44:186-87, 502.

[21] *ORA*, 44:663, 674; Angle, *Three Years in the Army of the Cumberland*, pp. 349-56.

[22] Angle, *Three Years in the Army of the Cumberland*, pp. 354-55; Davis, *Sherman's March*, pp. 91-94.

[23] *ORA*, 44:699; *New York Tribune*, Dec. 15, 1864, p. 1.

Davis for having the pontoon bridge pulled quickly with Confederates hovering at his rear. Sherman's own judgment, expressed in a January 12 letter to Halleck during Stanton's visit and after Sherman had queried Davis about the creek incident, was that the story of "turning back negroes that Wheeler might kill them is all humbug." At the watercourse, wrote Sherman, Davis did "forbid certain plantation slaves – old men, women, and children – to follow his column; but they would come along and he took up his pontoon bridge, not because he wanted to leave them, but because he wanted his bridge."[24]

Whatever the pro or con concerning the Ebenezer Creek incident, it did make clear that when a Union army was on a swift move black refugees could not be handled adequately by the mere edict that they should not be allowed to "encumber us." Some program was essential for their ultimate disposition that unit commanders could take into account in meeting the exigencies of invasion and that would promise the blacks a haven more secure than the wake of a marching column. Halleck's letter and Stanton's visit made Sherman focus sharply on such a program. On the evening of January 12, at Sherman's headquarters, he and Stanton had a meeting with twenty black churchmen, all but one Savannah residents, including leaders in the black community; the one was a Maryland free black who had been a missionary for the past two years in connection with the Port Royal Experiment. Nine of them had been slaves until Sherman's coming; one of those nine had been a slave of a leading Confederate, Robert Toombs. At the meeting when asked how the blacks could best take care of themselves and assist the Government, their response was that it would be best that they have land to cultivate and so to maintain themselves, with their young men in the meantime enlisting in the army. Then, when asked whether they would rather live in colonies by themselves or be scattered among whites, all but the Marylander said that because of the prejudice in the South they would prefer to live by themselves.[25]

After this meeting, as Sherman explained in a letter to the President a year later, Stanton "was satisfied the Negros could with some little aid from us by means of the abandoned Plantations on the Sea Islands and along the Navigable Waters take care of themselves. He requested me to draw up a plan that would be uniform and practicable. I made the rough draft and we went over it very carefully, Mr. Stanton making many changes."[26] The result was that, on January

[24] *ORA*, 47(pt.2):36-37.

[25] *ORA*, 47(pt.2):37-41.

[26] W. T. Sherman to President Johnson, Feb. 2, 1866, Andrew Johnson Papers, Library of Congress, Series 1, Reel 20.

16 immediately after Stanton's departure, Sherman issued Special Field Orders, No. 15. Foster's command was the Department of the South, embracing South Carolina, Georgia, and into Florida, but the department now had been made subject to Sherman's orders.[27] Thus his Order 15 was the law for that department. It was among the most notable, if not the most notable, of the several military provisions for refugee blacks made during the war.

It provided as follows:

"The islands from Charleston south, the abandoned rice-fields along the rivers for thirty miles back from the sea, and the country bordering the Saint John's River, Fla., are reserved and set apart for the settlement of the negroes now made free by the acts of war and the proclamation of the President of the United States."

The order was to be administered by Gen. Saxton, given the title of Inspector of Settlements and Plantations, with police and general management power over the area.

Whenever "three respectable negroes, heads of families," selected a locality within the specified area for settlement, Saxton was to give them a license, and, under Saxton's supervision, they would subdivide the land in the locality among themselves and others choosing to join them so that each family would have "a plot of not more than forty acres of tillable ground." Saxton was to provide each family head, "subject to the approval of the President of the United States, a possessory title in writing, giving as near as possible the description of boundaries;" such titles would be treated "as possessory." Their possession would be protected by the military "until such time as they can protect themselves or until Congress shall regulate their title."

On the islands and in such settlements "no white person whatever, unless military officers and soldiers detailed for duty, will be permitted to reside; and the sole and exclusive management of affairs will be left to the freed people themselves, subject only to the United States military authority and the acts of Congress." However, the order would not change the existing settlements "on Beaufort Island" or affect "any rights to property heretofore acquired" – referring, presumably, to the whites engaged in the Port Royal Experiment and to property that had been acquired, mainly by Northern whites, under tax sales by the Treasury Department during the war when the old owners were dutiful to the Confederacy instead of to the United States tax collectors.

[27] *ORA*, 47(pt.2):44.

Finally, young black men were encouraged to enlist in the Union army. Saxton was given charge of such recruiting and the organization of black military units.[28]

Sherman's January 12 letter to Halleck had said, "I do and will do the best I can for negroes, and feel sure that the problem is solving itself slowly and naturally. It needs nothing more than our fostering care." Nor, indeed, had Sherman ever been blind to the need to make some provision for the blacks. Even before leaving Atlanta, when he had ordered that refugees should not be encouraged to "encumber us," he had added that "at some future time" he would be able to provide for those "who seek to escape the bondage under which they are now suffering."[29] Surely his Order 15 provided the basis for the fostering care for all the refugees who had followed him to Savannah and who would flock to him when at last he marched on northward through the Carolinas. The fact is that on March 14, after Sherman had emerged at Fayetteville, again to make contact with the outside world via a Union force by then at Wilmington, he ordered that the black refugees "that have clung to us during our march through South Carolina" could be sent to Gen. Saxton back at Beaufort.[30]

If the fighting had gone on for another year or so it is very likely that the kind of self-sufficient black communities envisaged in Sherman's order would have become firmly established and that the social and economic development of the blacks in the South Atlantic coastal region would have been very different. The Port Royal Experiment already had shown considerable success but it was limited to the Port Royal-Beaufort vicinity, and, to Saxton's special distress, allowed for but little land ownership by the blacks. Indeed in Saxton's annual 1864 report to Stanton there was a note of his unhappiness on that score.[31] But now Sherman's order gave Saxton what seemed plenary authority, based on the nearly untrammelled war power of the military, to provide land for the landless over a stretch of hundreds of miles of rich plantation lands. With the imprimatur of Sherman, at that time regarded in much of the North as the nation's greatest hero, Saxton was fired with enthusiasm and hope.

Saxton's hope seemed well grounded. He had visited Sherman at the end of December but apparently had not been encouraged about what might happen to the blacks. However, on Stanton's coming the outlook changed. Saxton had gone at once to Savannah to meet with

[28] *ORA*, 47(pt.2):60-62.
[29] *ORA*, 39(pt.3):701; 47 (pt.2):37.
[30] *ORA*, 47(pt.2):835.
[31] *ORA*, ser. 3, 4:1024-26.

the Secretary, telling of his recent annual report that Stanton had not yet received in which he had objected to the failure to provide for black land ownership; the interview had been "agreeable" and Stanton had promised Saxton "to put him all right," and had sent him back to Beaufort to return with a copy of the report. Saxton had brought it to Stanton just prior to the Secretary's meeting with the black churchmen. Then on January 14 Stanton, on leaving Savannah, came to Beaufort for an overnight stay that proved most congenial, highlighted by disclosing to Saxton an advance copy of Order 15. As though to seal Saxton's authority, there was delivered to him, just after Stanton's departure, his promotion from brigadier general to major general of volunteers.[32]

But the fighting did not last. In only a few weeks it ended. And as it was ending President Lincoln's assassination brought to the presidency a man who did not share Saxton's vision of land for the black man.

During those few weeks Saxton faced a huge task of administration with a limited staff. By early June he was to report an estimate that he had settled 40,000 blacks under Sherman's order. Later he was to reiterate that estimate. But there is no evidence that Saxton was able consistently to follow the method prescribed in the Sherman order – that is, having three black heads of families mark out a settlement and then, under his supervision, subdivide tracts for self-governing communities, with Saxton issuing precisely defined possessory titles to the settlers. That he could have done so in such a short time seems impossible in view of the chaotic conditions in the vast territory, the limited means of transport, the ignorance of the settlers, the shortage of facilities, and the extent and variety of his responsibilities which included, it will be recalled, recruiting of soldiers. The likelihood is that, working under great pressure, Saxton's procedure was makeshift.[33]

As the fighting dwindled — Charleston itself was evacuated in mid-February as Sherman drove northward and isolated it — some of the former white owners began drifting back to the area, seeming to think that somehow they could resume control of the plantations. On

---

[32] Saxton to E. D. Townsend, A. A. G., U. S. Army, Jan. 15, 1865, accepting promotion to major general by brevet, to rank from Jan. 12, 1865, in Rufus Saxton file, Letters Rec'd by Appointment, Commission and Personal Branch of the Adj. Gen., File No. 1302, ACP 1879, RG 94, National Archives; Willard Saxton Diary, v. 26, pp. 25-26, 33-40; William S. McFeely, *Yankee Stepfather* (New Haven, 1968), pp. 47-48.

[33] Saxton to O. O. Howard, June 4 and Sept. 5, 1865, Nos. S-14 and S-83, Letters Rec'd & Registers by the Commr., Bureau of Refugees, Freedmen and Abandoned Lands, RG 105, National Archives, M. 752, Roll 17; Claude F. Oubre, *Forty Acres and a Mule* (Baton Rouge, 1978), pp. 46-47.

April 22 Saxton issued a circular, publishing the key provisions of the Sherman order and giving "unauthorized persons" thirty days' notice to vacate the area; thereafter trespassers would be arrested, to be punished by sentence of a military commission.[34] But hardly had that thirty day period lapsed than two things happened that signaled impending change from what Saxton otherwise might have established, that foreshadowed that the nearly all black enclave from Charleston along the coast into Florida, provided by Sherman's order, would never be realized.

One of these was the implementation of the Freedmen's Bureau Act of March 3, 1865.[35] The Act provided that during the war and for one year thereafter a bureau in the War Department, headed by a Commissioner, would have charge of the affairs of the freed blacks in the Confederate States. It also provided that the Bureau, from land within those states that was abandoned or owned by the United States by confiscation or otherwise, could rent to a male freedman on favorable terms up to forty acres for three years with the freedman's privilege of purchasing "such title thereto as the United States can convey." But the Act did not mention Sherman's order nor did it provide for the exclusion of whites from any area or even hint at the creation of self-governing black communities. On May 12 there took office, as the Bureau's Commissioner, General Oliver O. Howard. He had been Sherman's right wing commander. During the time that Sherman was getting ready for the drive northward from Savannah, Howard had been posted for a considerable time at Beaufort where he had been most favorably impressed with Saxton. On May 22, on the very day that Saxton's April 22 circular had provided that unauthorized whites would be arrested if they had not vacated the area defined in Sherman's order, Howard wrote Saxton of his appointment as the Bureau's Assistant Commissioner in charge of South Carolina and Georgia and, temporarily, Florida. Thus did Saxton lose his autonomy even as the special status of the Sherman lands was clouded.[36]

The second event occurred on May 29, one week after Gen. Howard wrote Saxton of his altered office. The new President Johnson issued a sweeping Amnesty Proclamation for all those who now would take a

[34] Circular No. 4, Apr. 22, 1865, Orders of Asst. Commr. for S. C., Bureau of Refugees, Freedmen and Abandoned Lands, RG 105, National Archives, M. 869, Roll 37.

[35] 13 U. S. Stat.:507.

[36] McFeely, *Yankee Stepfather*, pp. 45-48, 62-64; Howard to Saxton, May 22, 1865, Letters Sent, Endorsements and Circulars by the Commr., Bureau of Refugees, Freedmen and Abandoned Lands, RG 105, National Archives, M. 742, Roll 1.

loyalty oath.[37] While the proclamation excluded various limited classes who had "voluntarily participated" in the rebellion, they were assured that on special application for pardon "clemency will be liberally extended." It was soon to become clear that such assurance was very real. Needless to say, under a Constitution giving the President sweeping power to pardon, amnesty to an old owner seemed to destroy all basis for denying him a return of his abandoned land. The loyalty oath takers were plentiful, and in hardly more time than it takes to tell were clamoring for the lands' return. Nowhere was the clamor to be more persistent than in the area embraced in Sherman's order, and especially in South Carolina where Saxton's work was most concentrated. And it was abandoned lands that were the principal supply for carrying out that order, or, indeed, the land provision of the more general Freedmen's Bureau Act.[38]

On the face of things it would seem that these two events would have ended rather abruptly further administration of the Sherman order. In fact there is no indication that Saxton attempted to carry out the bar against white residents in the Sherman area after expiration of the thirty-day notice in his April circular, and in early June Gen. Howard wrote him that whites should be no more excluded there than in other areas where the Freedmen's Bureau operated.[39] Otherwise, however, Saxton proceeded as though the Sherman order were fully in effect. He had become a crusader for the newly freed blacks. On June 4, in his initial report to Howard as one of the new Assistant Commissioners of the Bureau, he said that his "colonists" under the Sherman order had "many thousands of acres" in cultivation, whence "ample crops will be raised to support the present population, and a large amount of sea island cotton for market will be provided." The crops, he said with pride, "completely astound the former masters who have visited the plantations, while the friends are delighted and encouraged." And in the months following, Saxton continued settling black "colonists" under the Sherman order.[40]

[37] James D. Richardson, *Messages and Papers of the Presidents,* H. Rep. Misc. Doc. 210, Part 6, 53d Cong., 2d Sess. (1897):310-12.

[38] George R. Bentley, *A History of the Freedmen's Bureau* (Philadelphia, 1955), p. 74.

[39] Howard to Saxton, June 8, 1865, Letters Sent, Endorsements and Circulars by the Commr., Bureau of Refugees, Freedmen and Abandoned Lands, RG 105, National Archives, M. 742, Roll 1.

[40] Saxton to Howard, June 4, 1865, No. S-14, Letters Rec'd and Registers by the Commr., Bureau of Refugees, Freedmen and Abandoned Lands, RG 105, National Archives, M. 752, Roll 17; Oubre, *Forty Acres and a Mule,* p. 68.

Meanwhile, the clamor of the amnestied whites for a return of their lands mounted, with a sympathetic ear in the White House. It would seem that the President could have eliminated any claim to the lands by the blacks, and cleared the way for the clamoring whites, by simply disapproving any "titles" that had been issued under the Sherman order. For the order itself, it will be recalled, provided that the "titles" were "subject to the approval of the President." But the President did not resort to that provision. If he focused on it, perhaps he hesitated to resort to it lest that imply that he regarded the Sherman order as still in force. Or perhaps – and this is more likely – the President hesitated lest he alienate some members of Congress whose support he wanted on many other issues when Congress came into session in the following December. Congress had not met since the Presidency had descended on Johnson; at the coming session his whole program for the nation's reunion would be at stake.

In any event, though the President made it clear that he agreed with the clamoring whites that they should have their lands, he stopped just short of peremptorily insisting to Gen. Howard that all the Sherman lands be restored at once. Instead, he told Howard to try to work out, between the white claimants and the black "title" holders, some accommodation – such as agreement by the black to the white ownership in exchange for employment of the black and some tenancy for him and his family.[41] In the meantime Saxton, though by the end of the summer his authority over Georgia and Florida had been transferred to others, leaving him only South Carolina, had been fighting as hard as ever for his "colonists." He urged, to Howard, that when Congress met it would decide that the Sherman order had "all the binding effect of a Statute."[42] While some lands were restored to the whites, many blacks resisted and Howard vacillated, stalled with support from Stanton, and finally, when Congress met, began working with a leading Senator, Lyman Trumbull of Illinois, on proposed legislation that he hoped would be a final solution.[43] At length, in February, Congress did act. It adopted a measure extending indefinitely the life of the Freedmen's Bureau and providing variously for the welfare of the freedmen, including a provision that the holders of

[41] Bentley, *Freedmen's Bureau*, pp. 97-98; Oubre, *Forty Acres and a Mule*, pp. 51-52.

[42] Bentley, *Freedmen's Bureau*, pp. 69, 98-100; McFeely, *Yankee Stepfather*, pp. 126-29; Oubre, *Forty Acres and a Mule*, p. 51; Saxton to Howard, Sept. 5, 1865, No. S-83, Letters Rec'd and Registers by the Commr., Bureau of Refugees, Freedmen and Abandoned Lands, RG 105, National Archives, M. 752, Roll 17.

[43] Bentley, *Freedmen's Bureau*, pp. 99-100; McFeely, *Yankee Stepfather*, pp. 130-48, 195-200.

Sherman "titles" would be confirmed in their possession for three years.[44] While that at least strongly implied that the white man would have the land restored in three years, that doubtless seemed a long time for the old planters to wait before beginning their recovery from the economic chaos left by the war.

During this time the interest of the white planters had been ably represented in Washington by a lobbyist, William Henry Trescot, the "Executive Agent" of the State of South Carolina. Trescot had come to Washington in the fall of 1865 with authority conferred by the South Carolina Convention, and had been busy at the Executive Mansion, on the Hill, and in the War Department. On January 31 as Congress neared its action, Trescot, with associates, met with the President, telling him that Gen. Sherman was in the city and that they understood he would be willing to state what he had meant by his Order 15. The President suggested that they see Sherman. They immediately went to Gen. Grant's headquarters. It happened that Grant was in conference with Sherman and Generals George H. Thomas and George G. Meade. But Grant invited them in, and "they all participated in the discussion of the real meaning of Gen. Sherman's order." The result was that before the end of the day Trescot delivered a note to the President saying that Sherman had said that his order "was meant to be temporary" and that he would "make such a statement . . . upon a reference from you." On the next day the President wrote Sherman asking for a statement of the "purposes" of his order. On the day following, February 2, Sherman replied, "I knew of course we could not convey title to land and merely provided 'possessory' titles, to be good as long as War and our Military Power lasted. I merely aimed to make provision for the Negros who were absolutely dependent on us, leaving the value of their possessions to be determined by after events or legislation."[45] When, a few days later in February, Congress' act

[44] Sen. Ex. Doc. No. 25, 39th Cong., 1st Sess. (1866): 8-10.

The measure also included a section authorizing rental and sale to "freedmen and loyal refugees" of public lands in Florida, Mississippi, Alabama, Louisiana, and Arkansas in plots not exceeding forty acres and another section authorizing the Bureau, if Congress were to provide appropriations therefor, to acquire land "for refugees and freedmen dependent on the government for support" which the Bureau later could sell, presumably to the occupants, at cost. Neither such section made particular provision for Sherman "title" holders, and the latter section was most ambiguous. Ibid., p. 9.

[45] Resolution of Sept. 18, 1865, Committee on Ordinances and Resolutions, Reports and Resolutions, South Carolina Convention (1865), 11-12, S. C. Archives; W. H. Trescot to Gov. Benjamin F. Perry, Oct. 24, 1865, Letters Rec'd and Sent, Sept. 20 – Dec. 21, 1865, Benjamin F. Perry Papers, S. C. Archives; Trescot to Gov. James L. Orr, Feb. 4, 1866, Letters Rec'd, Oct. 11, 1865 – April 3, 1866, James L. Orr Papers, S. C. Archives; W. H. Trescot to President Johnson, Jan. 31, 1866 (two letters), Letters Rec'd by Pres. Johnson Relating to Bureau Affairs, Bureau of Refugees, Freedmen and Abandoned Lands, RG 105, National Archives; Johnson to Sherman, Feb. 1, 1866, Andrew Johnson Papers, Library of Congress, Series 2, v. 3, p. 77, Reel 42; Sherman to Johnson, Feb. 2,

reached the President he vetoed it. Among his many objections to the whole measure he stated that the provision for the Sherman "title" holders violated the white owners' Constitutional rights to their property. The veto came to the Senate where the measure had originated. Thirty Senators voted to override but eighteen voted to sustain, falling short of the two-thirds required to override.[46]

Surely now all the Sherman lands would go back to the white owners with no further controversy. One problem for the whites – that is, the activity of Gen. Saxton, the aggressive crusader for the blacks – had been solved. From about the time when lobbyist Trescot had begun his work in Washington there had been rumor that President Johnson wanted to be rid of Saxton and hoped he would ask to be relieved. But Saxton was stubborn; he refused to quit. Finally, however, in January the axe fell. Saxton was removed. Though offered a Bureau position elsewhere he declined and wound up in Army quartermaster duty far from Carolina.[47] With Saxton out of the way and with the President's veto sustained, Trescot called on Gen. Howard on February 21 and thought he had secured agreement to the issuance of an order for the immediate restoration of the Sherman lands. But Howard worried after their meeting until one o'clock at night; the next day he informed Trescot that he would issue no such order without further instruction from the President. The next day Howard wrote the President that his existing instructions concerning the Sherman lands were that he was to attempt "to make an arrangement mutually satisfactory between the land owners and the resident freedmen." Under those instructions, he noted, many lands had been restored to the whites. But, said he, "In order not to break faith with these freedmen, who had received possessory titles, or who occupied lands under General Sherman's order, I had hoped to render them some equivalent or indemnity; possibly this may yet be afforded them by

1866, ibid., Series 1, Reel 20. Trescot had been prominent in South Carolina affairs for years. R. Nicholas Olsberg, "A Government of Class and Race: William Henry Trescot and the South Carolina Chivalry 1861-1865" (Ph.D. Diss., Univ. of S. C., 1972), Lib. of Cong. microfilm.

[46] Sen. Ex. Doc. No. 25, 39th Cong., 1st Sess. (1866): 1-8; Richardson, *Messages and Papers of the Presidents,* Part 6: 398-405; Cong. Globe, 39th Cong., 1st Sess. (1866): 936-43.

[47] Willard Saxton Diary, v. 26, pp. 218-19, v. 27, pp. 22-23, 51, 59-61, 68-69; purported copy of letter of Dec. 1, 1865, from Trescot to Johnson, Saxton Family Papers, Letterbook 7 (among loose papers); Brief Sketch of the Military Service of Rufus Saxton, p. 3, in Rufus Saxton file, Letters Rec'd by Appointment, Commission and Personal Branch of the Adj. Gen., File No. 1302, ACP, RG 94, National Archives; McFeely, *Yankee Stepfather,* pp. 226-28; Oubre, *Forty Acres and a Mule,* p. 59.

some future action of Congress." He concluded that he still felt "unwilling to make any sweeping restoration of the lands above named to their former owners without more definite instructions than I have yet received either from yourself or the Secretary of War."[48]

Executive Agent Trescot was very much on the job. Gen. Howard wrote his letter in duplicate, one to go through War Department channels and one to be delivered by Trescot himself to the Executive Mansion. Trescot delivered his copy with a covering letter to the President urging that the regular Army authorities in South Carolina (not Howard) should determine whether a white owner was willing to make some fair arrangement with any tenants under the Sherman order, and that Howard should be told to get on at once with all the lands' restoration.[49] While no peremptory order for such restoration was issued, it seems that Trescot's suggestion for having the regular Army authorities handle the matter was – or perhaps already had been – substantially adopted, at least for the area in South Carolina. Howard's view was that there should be restoration only if the white owner and the black "title" holder reached a "mutually satisfactory" arrangement. But the regular Army authorities would restore if only the white owner tendered a deal that they deemed "fair" – whether or not the black "title" holder was satisfied – and even that condition would be imposed only if they found that the Sherman "title" held by the tenant was technically quite correct in its specification of the land he occupied. Howard protested this interference with his administration. Indeed when by early March he had received no new instructions from the President he ordered Saxton's successor in South Carolina to maintain the possession of the "title" holders "until some definite action is had by the Government." As he had intimated in his February 22 letter to the President, he was hoping for some further action by Congress to provide "some equivalent or indemnity" to the "title" holders if the lands were to be restored to the whites. It is not clear how the conflict between the regular military and the Bureau stood when the whole matter finally became academic in July 1866.[50]

[48] Trescot to Orr, Feb. 28 and Mar. 4, 1866, Letters Rec'd, Oct. 11, 1865 – Apr. 3, 1866, James L. Orr Papers, S. C. Archives; Howard to Johnson, Feb. 22, 1866, Andrew Johnson Papers, Library of Congress, Series 1, Reel 20.

[49] Trescot to Orr, Mar. 4, 1866, Letters Rec'd, Oct. 11, 1865 – Apr. 3, 1866, James L. Orr Papers, S. C. Archives; Trescott [sic] to Johnson, Feb. 22, 1866, Andrew Johnson Papers, Library of Congress, Series 1, Reel 20.

[50] Bentley, *Freedmen's Bureau*, pp. 123-24; Martin Abbott, *The Freedmen's Bureau in South Carolina* (Chapel Hill, 1967), pp. 60-62; Oubre, *Forty Acres and a Mule*, pp. 61-67; Trescot to Johnson, Mar. 12, 1866, and copies of Howard to R. K. Scott, Ass't. Commr. for S. C., Mar. 8, 1866, and of Scott's General Orders No. 9, Mar. 7, 1866, Letters Rec'd by Pres. Johnson Relating to Bureau Affairs, Bureau of Refugees, Freedmen and Abandoned Lands, RG 105, National Archives.

At that time Congress again acted. Again it adopted an amendment to the Freedmen's Bureau Act, this time to extend the life of the Bureau for a limited period, with various provisions for the freedmen's welfare, and again it addressed the question of the Sherman "title" holders. But this time it gave in to the white owners. It did provide that any Sherman "title" holders still on the lands could not be ousted until they had harvested current crops and had been fairly compensated for any betterments they had made. Otherwise a Sherman "title" holder, whether or not he had yet been dispossessed, was given no relief except the privilege of buying at $1.50 an acre a twenty acre plot to be provided from several thousand acres in the Port Royal area that the United States had acquired from tax sales during the war. Again there was a veto by a President who seemed to take a dim view of even limited Government aid to the blacks. But this time the veto was overridden. So at last the way was cleared for all the abandoned lands to be restored to the white owners, and finally resolved was the long controversy having roots reaching as far back as Ebenezer Creek.[51]

But when at length the dust of controversy had settled there was something pathetic in the outcome. In the haste, tension, and confusion of Saxton's administration of the Sherman order, settlers' "titles" were not always written with required specificity, many settlers never received any "title" papers at all, and others settled elsewhere than on the locations their papers provided for. Still others, through ignorance or discouragement, had simply given up and wandered away. Furthermore, any "title" holder at a point far from the Port Royal area, even if he heard of the opportunity afforded by the July 1866 statute, probably was reluctant to move there to see what might be available to him.[52] The result is that the books of the United States tax authorities, who issued the allotments from the tax lands, show a total of only 1,398 purchases by blacks pursuant to the 1866 statute. Moreover, while the

[51] 14 U. S. Stat.: 173; Richardson, *Messages and Papers,* Part 6: 422-26; Bentley, *Freedmen's Bureau,* pp. 133-34.

In June Congress had adopted the Southern Homestead Act opening for homesteading some public lands in Florida, Mississippi, Alabama, Louisiana, and Arkansas. It was assumed that blacks could acquire land under that act. It made no particular provision for Sherman "title" holders. Such lands were of inferior quality; for that and other reasons the act had little practical consequence. Bentley, *Freedmen's Bureau,* pp. 134, 144-46.

[52] Probably it will never be known precisely how many "titles" were issued, and when, throughout the Sherman order area from Charleston into Florida because of inadequacy of record keeping at the time, loss of records since, and sheer difficulty in finding what records remain. The most specific effort to tell the story is Oubre, *Forty Acres and a Mule,* pp. 46-71. See also Abbott, *Freedmen's Bureau in S. C.,* pp. 7-16, 54-63; Carol K. Rothrock Bleser, *The Promised Land* (Columbia, 1969), pp. 7-12.

statute provided quite definitely that the plots were to be for twenty acres, any for that amount are almost indiscernible; most were for but ten acres, and not a few for smaller plots, as little as two acres.[53]

How far short that was from the great black enclave that Gen. Saxton thought Gen. Sherman had created.

[53] Heads of Families Certificate Books, Direct Tax Comm. S. C., Nos. D-3 through D-6, Records of Internal Rev. Serv., RG 58, National Archives. Books D-1 and D-2 contain copies of certificates of tax land sales to blacks, numbered 1 through 800, from Dec. 10, 1863, through Nov. 24, 1865. There is a gap between Book D-2 and Book D-3. The latter begins with certificate number 836 on Sept. 21, 1866, the first reciting issuance pursuant to the July 1866 statute. Each certificate thereafter, consecutively numbered, so recites. The last such certificate is in Book D-6, number 2234 of Sept. 23, 1871. The 1866 statute provided that the lands to be sold were to be in St. Helena's and St. Luke's Parishes. The certificates recited, for the earlier years, that they were for land in Beaufort District and, for the later years, in Beaufort County. The District was changed to County in 1868; each contained the two Parishes referred to in the 1866 statute. Letter of June 12, 1981, to the author from William L. McDowell, Deputy Director, S. C. Department of Archives and History.

A CONFEDERATE VICTORY AT GRAHAMVILLE: FIGHTING AT HONEY HILL

Leonne M. Hudson*

A NOTICEABLE OMISSION IN THE HISTORIOGRAPHY OF THE American Civil War is the attention to skirmishes or minor engagements. Minor engagements are often discussed by historians in conjunction with major battles and campaigns; therefore, their treatment rarely goes beyond a glance. The battle of Honey Hill is no exception. This essay presents one of the final engagements of the war along the South Carolina coast, examining the preparations for battle and the manner in which commands were executed. Offering a striking example of how the quality of leadership affected the outcome of the battle, it focuses on the significance of the Confederate victory at Grahamville with regards to the saving of the Charleston and Savannah Railroad, which allowed the Savannah garrison successfully to evacuate that Georgia city in the winter of 1864.

The battle of Honey Hill in Grahamville, South Carolina, on November 30, 1864, was a demonstration of dogged persistence on the part of the Confederate army, as the Northerners attempted to penetrate the coastal region. It was the culmination of previous attacks against the Charleston and Savannah Railroad, which occurred in conjunction with General William T. Sherman's epic march to the sea. The depot at Grahamville was thirty-six miles northeast of Savannah and eighty-four miles from Charleston. In actuality, the battle was fought for the salvation of these commercial cities. The Charleston and Savannah Railroad had become the major lifeline for the two ports since the Federal blockade had brought water commerce to a trickle. A small but determined force of Georgians and South Carolinians withstood an all-day attack by numerically superior Federal forces upon a difficult field of battle.

This battle had its origin in a telegraphic note of November 11 from Sherman to General Henry W. Halleck, chief of staff of the United States Armies. Since Sherman had expected to reach the coast by the first of December, he requested that General John G. Foster, commander of the South Atlantic fleet and army at Hilton Head, break the Charleston and Savannah Railroad at Pocotaligo.[1] Shortly after the war had commenced, General Pierre G. T. Beauregard had warned Confederate authorities in

*Assistant professor of history, Kent State University

[1]For a copy of Sherman's letter to Halleck on November 11, 1864, see U.S. War Department, *The War of the Rebellion: A Compilation of the Official Records of the Union and Confederate Armies* (hereafter cited as *Official Records*) (Washington, D.C.: Government Printing Office, 1880-1901), Series 1, Vol. 39, Pt. 3, p. 740.

The South Carolina Historical Magazine 94: 19-33

South Carolina that the enemy would attempt to destroy the railroad between Charleston and Savannah.[2] Cutting the railroad would have penned General William J. Hardee, commander of the Confederate garrison in Savannah, leaving him without an avenue of retreat. Moreover, a successful lodgement on the Charleston and Savannah would have provided General Sherman with a base from which to operate before risking his troops in battle at either of the well-defended port cities.

In compliance with General Halleck's orders, General Foster designated 6,000 soldiers, including several units of United States Colored troops, six gunboats, and ten pieces of artillery for the purpose of securing for Sherman a foothold on the mainland in the Palmetto State.[3] Every precaution was to be used to conceal from the rebels the movement of the transports as the vessels departed from Hilton Head on November 28 for a place called Boyd's Landing on the south shore of Broad River in Beaufort County. West of Boyd's Landing, nine miles inland, was situated the village of Grahamville with the railroad one mile farther.

SHORTLY AFTER THE PROCESSION BEGAN FROM HILTON HEAD, a heavy fog engulfed the river. So unfavorable were the elements of nature on that night, and so untrained for navigation in such a situation were the pilots of the ships, that many of the boats found themselves on the Chechesse instead of the Broad River. After the proper course was ascertained, the first troops did not arrive at Boyd's Landing until shortly before noon on the 29th and by 4:00 p.m. that day the detachment of cavalry and a large portion of General Edward E. Potter's brigade had arrived on the mainland.[4] General Foster, before returning to Hilton Head, placed General John P. Hatch in command of the Coastal Division with orders to cut the railroad at Grahamville.[5] A West Point graduate, Hatch had been brevetted for gallantry in the war with Mexico. In personal appearance, an expression of confidence and strength emanated from his thick neck, powerful shoulders, and broad chest. But Hatch's army consisted largely of inexperienced soldiers.

The Union forces were wrongly directed towards Savannah by a guide who misidentified a road mark. Actually marching southward in the direction of Savannah, they should have turned to the right at Bolan's Church to reach Grahamville. After marching a few miles in the wrong direction, General Hatch realized that the mistake had been made. This was

[2]Beauregard to John A. Calhoun, January 9, 1862, Pierre G. T. Beauregard Papers, South Caroliniana Library, University of South Carolina, Columbia, S.C.

[3]*Sunday News* (Charleston), December 10, 1899.

[4]Luis F. Emilio, *History of the Fifty-Fourth Regiment of Massachusetts Volunteer Infantry, 1863-1865* (Boston: The Boston Book Company, 1894), pp. 236-238.

[5]*Official Records*, Series 1, Vol. 44, p. 420.

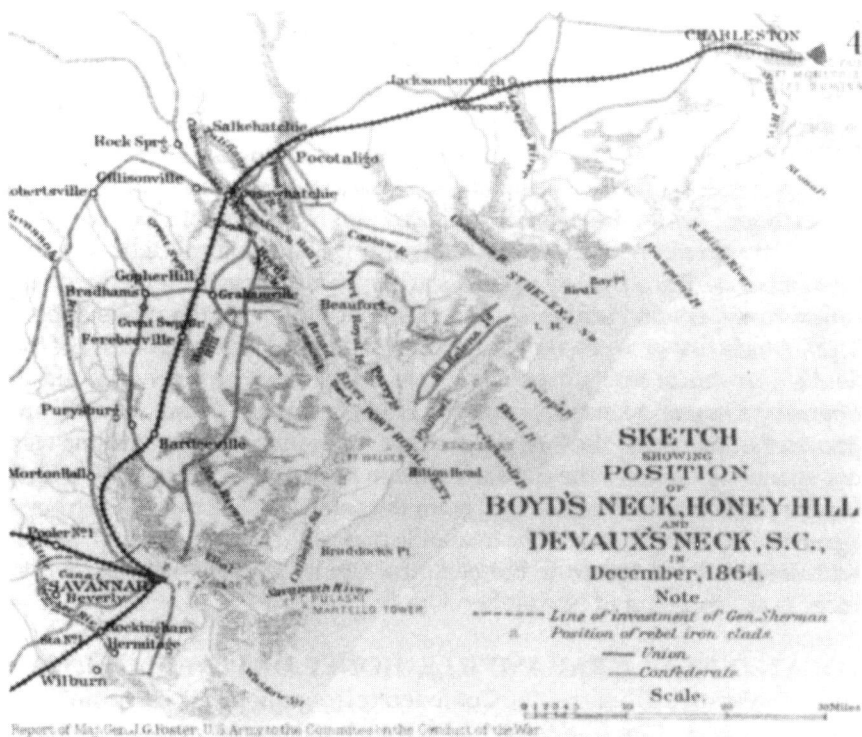

"The Charleston and Savannah Railroad had become the major lifeline for the two ports since the Federal blockade had brought water commerce to a trickle." The Battle of Honey Hill was fought over control of that railroad line. Illustration from _The Official Military Atlas of the Civil War._

a shocking deficiency, considering how close their objective was and the long time available to obtain accurate information about the location of Grahamville. The guide who was employed by General Potter proved to be either untrustworthy or ignorant.[6] Exasperated and frustrated, Hatch retraced his steps and bivouacked at Bolan's Church at 2:00 in the morning of November 30. These events, leading to the failure of the Union forces to seize the Charleston and Savannah Railroad on the 29th or early on the morning of the 30th, helped the Confederates achieve success.

As the Northerners made preparations to cut the railroad, the Confederates were in the process of taking prompt and efficient defensive measures. General Hardee had already instructed General Gustavus W. Smith and the Georgia militia to move eastward in hopes of stopping Sherman's advance. General Smith of Kentucky had graduated near the top of his West

[6]*New York Times*, December 9, 1864.

Point class in 1842. He had established a fine record in the Mexican War and had gained a reputation as a first-rate civil and construction engineer. Smith, as brave as he was obstreperous, had resigned his commission in the Confederate army in the winter of 1863 because Jefferson Davis had passed him over for promotion to the rank of lieutenant general. He relocated to Georgia, where Governor Joseph E. Brown appointed him to command the state troops.[7] Smith departed from Macon on November 25, but progress was slow; therefore, he did not arrive in Savannah until 2:00 a.m. on November 30. Immediately upon his arrival, Smith was presented with an order from General Hardee to proceed at once to the Grahamville depot.[8] The Georgia troops were very much opposed to this request because of the South Carolina militia's previous disregard for Georgia's need for aid in opposing General Sherman's march. However, when General Smith announced to them that their actual purpose for going to South Carolina was not so much to defend the state as it was to keep open a railroad by which reinforcements would be brought in for the defense of Savannah, the troops agreed to leave their state. The available part of the Georgia militia, heavy with fatigue, departed from the beautiful city by the sea for Grahamville early in the morning of November 30th.[9]

LOCATED NEAR GRAHAMVILLE, HONEY HILL WAS AN IDEAL place for the style of defense the Confederate troops hoped to carry out. The geography of the Carolina coast, which was characterized by small streams, miry soil, and impervious thickets, especially lent itself to the defense of that region by small Confederate forces arrayed against superior numbers.[10] Honey Hill was one of the salient positions General Robert E. Lee had fortified along the railroad in 1862. The fortification was positioned on the north bank of a small stream two feet deep and twenty yards wide.[11] The ground between the earthworks and the stream had been cleared of trees but was covered with thick grass, vines, and underbrush. A parapet for light guns had been constructed previously and short trenches for infantry had been prepared. The crescent-shaped fortress terminated suddenly in the swamp. Honey Hill was about ten feet above water level.[12]

[7]Leonne M. Hudson, "The Life and Career of Gustavus Woodson Smith" (Ph.D. dissertation, Kent State University, 1990), p. 312.

[8]*Official Records*, Series 1, Vol. 44, p. 906.

[9]Ibid., p. 415.

[10]George C. Eggleston, *The History of the Confederate War* (New York: Sturgis and Walton Co., 1910), Vol. 1, p. 264.

[11]*Sunday News*, December 10, 1899.

[12]Gustavus W. Smith, "The Georgia Militia During Sherman's March to the Sea," *Battles and Leaders of the Civil War*, Robert Underwood and Clarence Clough Buel, eds. (New York: The Century Co., 1884; Repr., New York: Thomas Yoseloff, Inc., 1956), Vol. 4, p. 668.

The Confederate officer in command of the third military district of South Carolina was Colonel Charles J. Colcock, who was headquartered at Grahamville. A planter before the war, he had done extensive cotton business in several southeastern states. Colcock had also been a railroad entrepreneur and had taken the lead in having constructed the Charleston and Savannah line which he was now defending. A devout Christian, Colcock was a brave South Carolinian who was admired and respected throughout the Lowcountry. The colonel had scheduled his third marriage for November 30, but the exigency of the battle forced him to postpone his wedding for a few days.[13] The outcome at Grahamville might have been different had duty not prevailed over romance. At 7:00 a.m. Colcock was informed by the telegraph operator that General Smith was momentarily expected at the Grahamville station. The Georgia state troops pulled up to the depot at 8:00 a.m.[14]

At 9:00 a.m. approximately one-and-a-half miles in front of the Honey Hill earthworks, the Union troops encountered the first Confederate resistance. This Spartan band was comprised of two small detachments from Companies B and I of the Third South Carolina cavalry. These companies, commanded by Captains John L. Seabrook and Archibald Campbell respectively, aggregated fifty-seven soldiers.[15] The overwhelming numbers of the Federal soldiers slowly forced the Confederate skirmishers backward. So slight was the fighting at this juncture as the Union army approached the fort that, according to one source, the soldiers seemed cheerful and enthusiastic.[16] Continuation of the rapid Federal advance would have guaranteed defeat of the rebels and the loss of the Charleston and Savannah Railroad. The Confederates had to delay General Hatch's force because the Georgia militia had not yet arrived at the Honey Hill fortifications. The only rebel troops on hand to check the Federal advance were the Third South Carolina cavalry. At this critical moment, as the Confederates were being driven back, Colonel Colcock rode to the skirmish line to survey the fighting. He then ordered his men to set fire to the grass; in a few minutes, the grass burst into a blaze and covered the field. A strong wind blowing in the direction of the enemy carried the blaze down on them and they were forced to retreat.[17] Colonel Colcock returned to the breastworks and made the

[13]A. S. Salley, Jr., "Captain John Colcock and Some of His Descendants," *South Carolina Historical and Genealogical Magazine* 3 (October 1902), pp. 230-231. See also William H. Courtenay, "Tribute to Charles Jones Colcock," 1898, Colcock Family Miscellaneous Papers, South Carolina Historical Society, Charleston, S.C.

[14]*Official Records*, Series 1, Vol. 44, p. 415.

[15]*Sunday News*, December 10, 1899.

[16]William W. Brown, *The Negro in the American Rebellion* (Boston: A. G. Brown and Co., 1880; Repr., Miami: Mnemosyne Publishing Inc., 1969), p. 256.

[17]Charles C. Jones, Jr., *The Battle of Honey Hill* (Augusta, Ga.: Chronicle Printing Establishment, 1885), p. 11.

dispositions for the coming battle.

Following the completion of this task, Colcock tendered his resignation from further direction of the battle to Smith, the only general officer present at Honey Hill. In refusing to accept the management of affairs, Smith said, "No, Colonel, you have prepared so fine an entertainment that you must receive your guests; retain charge, and if you wish at any time to consult with me you will find me a little to the rear."[18] For Smith to have waived command of the small army to his subordinate proved that he was indeed a man of impeccable character. However, from a technical point Smith may have questioned his right to command at the battle because some of the troops involved were from the state of South Carolina. Smith was not then a "Confederate" officer but rather a "Georgia" general.[19] The rebel army at Honey Hill numbered about 1,500 effectives.

At 11:00 a.m. the advancing Union troops came unexpectedly upon the main body of the Confederates. The Northerners fired a volley at the rebels and Captain Hal Stuart ordered his artillerists to reply, but "only when they could make a shot tell."[20] The moss-covered trees exploded with canister and musketry fire; thus the battles had begun. Perceiving that the enemy had a strong position, General Hatch directed General Potter to put his troops into the line of battles parallel to that of the enemy. Potter ordered the 127th New York to the extreme left of the causeway and to the right of the road he sent the 144th New York and the Twenty-fifth Ohio. Potter instructed Lieutenant George H. Crocker to occupy the location at the turn in the road with a section of Battery B of the Third New York Volunteers.[21]

As soon as these dispositions were completed, General Potter ordered the Twenty-fifth Ohio, under the command of Colonel Nathaniel Haughton, to drive the enemy from its position with a flank movement, a viable proposition if the Confederates had not been so well intrenched. The Twenty-fifth Ohio moved up the hill through what appeared to be an impervious thicket. Colonel Haughton formed his regiment within a few hundred yards of the rebels' earthworks with the intention of charging their position, which at that time appeared rather weak. A chance of victory escaped the Union forces, though, when the 144th fell back under fire, leaving the Twenty-fifth without support.[22] The aftermath of the retreat on the part of the 144th was that the rebels were immediately able to reinforce their left and pour a murderous fire upon the Twenty-fifth. Despite this fire, the Twenty-fifth was still able to sustain its position until the Thirty-second

[18]*Sunday News*, December 10, 1899.

[19]Hudson, "The Life and Career of Gustavus Woodson Smith," p. 334.

[20]*Sunday News*, December 10, 1899.

[21]Ibid.

[22]Edward C. Culp, *The 25th Ohio Volunteer Infantry* (Topeka, Kan.: George W. Crane and Co., 1885), p. 105.

United States Colored troops came up on its right a few minutes later. The Twenty-fifth did not advance beyond the shallow stream.[23]

The Thirty-second Colored troops were ordered by Potter to carry the Confederates' earthworks. But at the point of their attack, they found the marsh and bushes impassable. A deadly attack of grape, canister, and musketry was opened on the Thirty-second and they were forced to retreat.[24] As the Twenty-fifth and Thirty-second regiments were being repulsed, the Thirty-fifth Colored troops were being gallantly led to the attack by Colonel James C. Beecher, the abolitionist brother of Harriet Beecher Stowe. General Potter ordered Beecher to charge up the Honey Hill road and assay an assault. Dauntless though they were, the swamp combined with the enemy fire to impede their progress and they never reached an effective assaulting position. Having been subjected to a heavy fire resulting in a severe loss of lives, the regiment was forced to retire to the rear of the Third New York Artillery. Colonel Beecher was seriously wounded in this charge, yet he refused to leave the field.[25]

Colonel Alfred Hartwell, commander of the Second Brigade, with eight companies of the Fifty-fifth Massachusetts Volunteers under Colonel Charles B. Fox, moved rapidly to the front. Twice Colonel Hartwell ordered a charge in double column, and twice they were forced to fall back into the line. The road was now "rendered impassable by piles of [the] dead and dying."[26] The Confederates clearly had the advantage due to their tactical position. Within a short distance of the earthworks, Hartwell was pinned beneath his horse in the mud. He was hit three times while he was being carried from the field.[27]

Next, the Union forces attempted a flank movement on the Confederate right where the rebels faced the only situation of extreme danger during the entire fight. Just as the Southerners were being flanked, the Forty-seventh Georgia, having arrived from Charleston, reported to Colcock and were ordered immediately to the right. The Federals attacked with a desperate earnestness. The 127th New York succeeded in crossing the sluggish stream, advancing to within seventy yards of the fort. The regiment held this position for several minutes before being forced to retreat under a thunderous Confederate fire.[28] During the height of the battle, a Confederate officer later wrote, "The noise of the battle at this time was terrific, the artillery crashing away in the center, while volley after volley of musketry

[23]*Official Records*, Series 1, Vol. 44, p. 415.
[24]Brown, *The Negro in the American Rebellion*, p. 256.
[25]*Official Records*, Series 1, Vol. 44, p. 426.
[26]*Sunday News*, December 10, 1899.
[27]*Official Records*, Series 1, Vol. 44, p. 432.
[28]Ibid., pp. 428-429.

ran down both lines and were reverberated from the surrounding forests."[29]

From the right, the Twenty-fifth Ohio and the Thirty-second Colored troops moved from the wood-road to flank the enemy's left position. Reinforcements continued to come, this time in the form of a battalion of marines from the Naval Brigade, organizing on the left of the Thirty-second. Simultaneously, three companies of the Fifty-fifth Massachusetts, commanded by William Nutt, formed to the left of the Twenty-fifth, while the 144th New York remained in a supportive position. This tactical deployment of troops was one of the few times that Hatch displayed generalship worthy of praise. Confederate Colonel Colcock, realizing that the Union troops were about to attempt a flank movement on his left and having no troops to spare from the center or right, ordered Captain Archibald Campbell to extend the intervals of his men. Captain Campbell immediately ordered his soldiers to space themselves thirty feet apart.[30] With the rebels sparsely placed, it seemed doubtful they could have maintained an effective fire along the whole line. At this point, a united frontal assault might have succeeded.

Several incidents in the Honey Hill engagement illustrate the ferocity of the battle and the courage of the men. One Union soldier who was lying down rose up to light his pipe. With pipe in his mouth, a match in his right hand, and the matchbox in the left, a bullet pierced his forehead and killed him instantly. The pipe never left his mouth nor the matchbox his fingers.[31] As a young Confederate trooper discharged his cannon, blood gushed from his mouth, ears, and nose, but he refused to retire.[32]

The artillery of the Union army was not a significant factor in the battle. The unfavorable nature of the ground admitted the employment of only one section of the Union's artillery at a time, thereby leveling out the previous disadvantage held by the southern troops in terms of artillery. Because of the adjacent swamps, the Union artillery could only find a firm firing platform on the road. Furthermore, the Union gunners were at a distinct disadvantage because they had to fire upward; as one Confederate private wrote after the battle, "The Yanks shot [too] high."[33] During the successive charges, the artillery and infantry in the rear could not fire for fear of hitting their own troops. By 2:00 p.m. Battery B of the Third New York Artillery was exhausted, having been engaged since the skirmish on the Honey Hill road earlier that morning. One of the guns had recoiled into a ditch and the artillerists had not the strength to rescue it. The other three guns had

[29]*The Savannah Republican*, December 3, 1864.
[30]*Sunday News*, December 10, 1899.
[31]*New York Herald*, December 12, 1864.
[32]*Sunday News*, December 10 1899.
[33]W. H. Ponder to Rutledge Morgan, July 29, 1899, Caroliniana Library.

overheated and the ammunition was almost completely expended. The Union artillerists were further handicapped when one of the rebel sharpshooters exploded two chests of ammunition.[34] Units of the numerically superior Federal force continued in piecemeal fashion to reach the battlefield.

It was at this point that the Fifty-fourth Regiment Massachusetts Volunteers (Colored) made its entrance onto the battlefield. The most famous black regiment of the Civil War, the Fifty-fourth soldiers were well-prepared for this battle, having had previous experience at James Island, Fort Wagner, and Olustee. The Fifty-fourth was under the command of Colonel Henry Hooper. Upon reaching the battlefield, Hooper was met by Colonel William T. Bennet, the chief of General Hatch's staff to whom Hatch had given orders. Bennet's greeting proved to be little more than a gesture in the direction of the battle accompanied by the order to charge. Hooper naturally asked, "Where?" but received no other reply than "Charge!"[35] Realizing the serious potential damage inherent in carrying out such an order, Hooper moved his men to the left of the road and attempted to carry the Confederate position from there. The natural defenses of the hill, such as its dense underbrush and vines, offered enough of an obstruction to give an extra measure of security to the rebel soldiers.[36] Yet Hooper's failure to charge along the road represented an act of disobedience.

LATE IN THE AFTERNOON, GENERAL HARDEE IN SAVANNAH received a welcome dispatch from Smith.[37] With determination and courage the Union soldiers had been repulsed at Honey Hill. The small entrenched rebel army had decisively defeated the United States troops and had saved the valuable railroad from capture.

General Hatch had simply ordered a series of uncoordinated small units to charge successively by a narrow causeway upon a strongly fortified position defended by artillery and infantry. Moreover, he had failed to take advantage of a promising opportunity at his left. Near the end of the battle, Colonel Hooper made a personal survey of the ground in front of Honey Hill and informed Hatch that the enemy's right could be flanked with just two regiments. Hatch did not take the suggestion seriously, and therefore did not act upon Hooper's advice.[38] Although Hatch rejected Hooper's recommendation, he still did not order his troops to wade the stream. The sluggish stream that flowed in front of the fort offered an obstacle but was

[34]*The Philadelphia Weekly*, May 17, 1884.
[35]Emilio, *History of the Fifty-Fourth*, p. 245.
[36]*Sunday News*, December 10, 1899.
[37]Nathaniel Cheairs Hughes, *General William J. Hardee: Old Reliable* (Baton Rouge: Louisiana State University Press, 1965), p. 256.
[38]Emilio, *History of the Fifty-Fourth*, p. 250.

definitely fordable. This was yet another example of Hatch's failure to command judiciously and utilize his superior force at Honey Hill.

At approximately 4:30 p.m. Confederate General Beverly H. Robertson arrived from Charleston with a portion of the Thirty-second Georgia regiment, a battery of artillery, and a company of cavalry. These constituted an effective reserve, but came up too late to be used in the battle. General Hatch, believing that he could not carry the Confederate works, ordered General Potter to prepare to retire. Potter began making preparations for the retreat and, as darkness approached, the soldiers started clearing the field in successive lines. In hauling back the guns, the 102nd Colored unit lost several men to the punishing fire of Colcock's troops. The rebels made no attempt to advance on their enemy.[39]

FOR THE UNION ARMY, THE BATTLE OF HONEY HILL WAS fought without a plan, without commanding officers near enough to give intelligent orders, without regimental leaders possessing the wherewithal to use good judgment in the heat of conflict. The piecemeal commitment of units threw away the Union's numerical advantage. The Herculean effort by the soldiers at the engagement was wasted because of inferior generalship. In reporting on the conduct of his troops, Potter said, "Nothing but the formidable character of the obstacles they encountered prevented them from achieving success."[40] But the Union general, Jacob D. Cox, was particularly critical of the performance of the northern commanders. "It was a fresh instance of the manner in which irresolute leadership in war," he said, "wastes the lives of men by alternating between an ill-timed caution and an equally ill-timed rashness."[41]

The Confederate leadership proved excellent from beginning to end. As a result of good management, seasoned with good luck, the Confederates brought a force from western Georgia to the coast of South Carolina so opportunely that it moved into position only a few minutes before the start of the battle. In a report of the battle to General Hardee, Smith stated, "I have never seen or known a battlefield upon which there was so little confusion ... and where a small number of men, for so long a time successfully resisted the determination and oft-repeated efforts of largely superior attacking forces."[42] General Smith paid a handsome tribute to Colonel Colcock, remembering him as the gallant South Carolinian who was "entitled to the

---

[39]*Sunday News*, December 10, 1899.

[40]*Official Records*, Series 1, Vol. 44, p. 427.

[41]Jacob D. Cox, *The March to the Sea* (New York: Charles Scribner's Sons, 1906), p. 49.

[42]Smith to Hardee, December [6], 1864, Gustavus W. Smith Collection, William R. Perkins Library, Duke University, Durham, N.C.

honors" of victory.[43] Most of the able officers on both sides were trained at West Point, and many had fought in the Mexican War. Yet, especially on the Union side, these trained and experienced officers were seemingly ineffective.

If casualties are used as a yardstick for determining a winner at the Honey Hill fight, the southern army overwhelmingly would be declared victorious. Smith reported a Confederate loss of eight killed and forty-two wounded. Having been on the attack against entrenchments, the United States bore the brunt of the casualties. Foster reported eighty-eight killed, 623 wounded, and forty-three missing.[44] In describing the battleground, Confederate General James Chesnut said, "It was the bloodiest of fights — a carnage. Before the dead were buried next day, the battlefield was awful to see."[45] According to a Savannah newspaper, "some sixty or seventy bodies were counted in a space of an acre many of which were horribly mutilated by shells, some with half their heads torn off."[46] Captain John J. Ambercrombie of the Union army recalled seeing wounded soldiers creeping "aimlessly about on their hands and knees; some crawled on their bellies, dragging useless limbs behind them."[47] Furthermore, the Honey Hill victory took on added significance for the Confederates because it came late in the war, thereby providing them with the then rare opportunity of scavenging the personal baggage and haversacks of the dead Union soldiers.[48]

The sounds of creaking wagons, the shouts of drivers urging on their mules, and the cries of the wounded pervaded the cold night. Bolan's Church underwent a metamorphosis, from Union headquarters to a hospital. Inside the little white church situated among the moss-hung trees, surgeons had established their operating tables, and the traces of amputations were scattered about.[49] General Hatch's army passed the night at Bolan's Church, gathered around small campfires that illuminated the dark southern sky.

The Confederates who were uncertain of whether the Federals would launch another attack remained in position at the fort throughout the night. The scene at the Grahamville headquarters the next day was one of excite-

[43]Courtenay, "Tribute to Charles Jones Colcock."

[44]*Official Records*, Series 1, Vol. 44, p. 420.

[45]C. Vann Woodward, ed., *Mary Chesnut's Civil War* (New Haven and London: Yale University Press, 1981), p. 684.

[46]*The Savannah Republican*, December 3, 1864.

[47]John J. Abercrombie, "The Battle of Honey Hill," *Confederate Veteran* 22 (October 1914), p. 453.

[48]William Harris Bragg, *Joe Brown's Army: The Georgia State Line, 1862-1865* (Macon, Ga.: Mercer University Press, 1987), p. 104.

[49]*The Philadelphia Weekly*, May 17, 1884.

ment as the Southerners reveled in their victory and gladly welcomed the arrival of additional soldiers. Overall, the Confederate reinforcements were short on quality but long on spirit and enthusiasm. It seemed doubtful that such an exhausted and broken-down force could have sustained a prolonged struggle against the Federals, but Hatch did not order an attack on December 1. That morning General Hardee came to survey the site of the Confederate victory at Grahamville. General Smith, feeling that the necessity to detain the Georgia militia in South Carolina no longer existed, obtained permission from Hardee to return his weary but victorious troops to their own state.[50]

As the Union and Confederate soldiers continued their onslaughts along the South Carolina coast, General Sherman was drawing closer to the beautiful city of Savannah. Once near Savannah, he easily could open communications with the naval and land forces based at Hilton Head. Fort McAllister was the only obstruction preventing Sherman from reaching the sea. It was a bastion situated on an island southeast of Savannah.[51] The capture of Fort McAllister by Sherman's army on December 13, 1864, signaled the end of a 400-mile march and the beginning of the siege of Savannah.

With Savannah about to fall and the continuing attacks of Hatch's forces against the railroad, the prospect of Hardee holding the city was hopeless. General Hardee, disturbed over the deterioration of the situation in Savannah, telegraphed President Jefferson Davis in Richmond: "Unless assured that a force sufficient to keep open my communications can be sent me, I shall be compelled to evacuate Savannah."[52] However, Davis could not honor his request because of the critical state of affairs in Virginia. On December 20, 1864, Hardee ordered the evacuation of Savannah. The procession of troops pouring over the pontoon bridges was a solemn moment, as many of the Savannah soldiers were leaving not only their long-held military post, but their homes as well.[53] Upon crossing the Savannah River they formed a junction with General Samuel C. Jones at Pocotaligo. Without the Confederate victory at Honey Hill, neither the earlier resistance at Savannah nor the evacuation along the railroad would have been possible. General Hardee considered the successful evacuation of Savannah as the crowning achievement of his military career.[54]

The outnumbered rebel soldiers were incapable of preventing the Union army from penetrating the first state to secede. With Sherman

---

[50]*Official Records*, Series 1, Vol. 44, p. 417.

[51]*Richmond Examiner*, December 16, 1864.

[52]*Official Records*, Series 1, Vol. 44, p. 960.

[53]Hughes, *General William J. Hardee*, p. 268.

[54]William Harris Bragg, "An Incident of the Savannah Campaign: The Fight at Honey Hill," *Civil War Times Illustrated* 22 (January 1984), p. 19.

marching across South Carolina, the fortified positions along the vital railroad which had proved to be the military backbone of the coast defense were abandoned by the "faithful guardians" of the Confederacy.[55] The dark clouds of smoke that rose over the Charleston and Savannah Railroad and faded into the heavens were symbolic of the state of the Confederacy by this time. The smoke indicated that the railroad was finally destroyed and the path to the city of Charleston was now open to the Coastal Division under General Hatch. On February 14, 1865, Hardee received instructions from General Beauregard to make preparations silently and cautiously for the evacuation of Charleston.[56] Three days later, the Confederate troops began retreating from the port city in a northward direction, eventually moving toward North Carolina to offer resistance to Sherman.[57] Within a span of two months, Hardee had been forced to evacuate two of the most important commercial cities in the South. Among the Union troops who quickly occupied Charleston were those who had fought at Honey Hill. The vanquished had become the victors. The war's outcome had been delayed but not altered by the battle of Honey Hill.

In retrospect, there was a serious lack of foresight in the preparation for the battle of Honey Hill. It was strange that the pilots of the vessels were not familiar with Broad River, having been in full possession of Hilton Head for three years. A few reconnoitering expeditions up the river would have familiarized the navy with the area and they would have been less likely to have gone astray. Perhaps even more striking was the fact that competent guides could not be found among the South Carolina Negro regiments or the blacks who had migrated from the interior of the state to Hilton Head. The guide who had misdirected the United States Army gave the Confederates the time they so desperately needed to assemble their forces. Even so, a reconnaissance by the first troops who had landed on November 29 would have remedied the mistake of the guide.

During the battle itself, there was a certain amount of poor judgment on the part of the Union generals. If the Federal army had moved from bivouac earlier on the morning of November 30, they could have captured the vital railroad with very little opposition. Furthermore, it was startling that a few rebels could delay the progress of such a large force for so long a time on the Honey Hill road. The strategic and tactical errors of the battle must rest upon the shoulders of the superior officer, General Hatch, who was at the front and directed the operations during the day. Hatch obviously lacked the quality needed to direct large bodies of soldiers in an offensive attack. The battle of Honey Hill served as a testimony to the Confederate troops "of

[55]*Sunday News*, December 10, 1899.
[56]Hughes, *General William J. Hardee*, p. 268
[57]E. Milby Burton, *The Siege of Charleston, 1861-1865* (Columbia: University of South Carolina Press, 1970), p. 316.

what determination and resourcefulness — aided by good fortune — could accomplish against formidable odds."[58]

The victory at Grahamville came at a time in the war when the Confederates virtually had been defeated. It was a splendid triumph for Southerners. Its glorification gave their morale as well as their pride a boost, even though defeat lurked within. The rebel victory at Honey Hill released Savannah from imminent danger and allowed the Charleston and Savannah Railroad to remain a Confederate artery just a few weeks longer. Had the United States Army disrupted the railroad or perhaps achieved a permanent lodgement on the line, it would have been extremely difficult for the Savannah garrison to have retreated in that direction a few days later. Hence, the Confederate victory at Honey Hill may have saved all or part of the force of several thousand soldiers who were to be part of the subsequent resistance to General Sherman in the Carolinas.

"THE FALL OF CHARLESTON"

Compiled by VIOLA CASTON FLOYD*

One hundred years ago this February, Charleston was evacuated by the Confederate troops; the Federal troops entered thereafter. Charleston was evacuated during the evening of February 17, and the early morning of February 18, 1865. With the Federal Army came a New York *Tribune* correspondent who signed himself as "Berwick". His communication written from Charleston in the first few days of the occupation was published on March 4, 1865, in the New York *Tribune*. The article, six columns long, contains approximately 8,500 words. Omitting the greater portion of the reporter's prejudiced observations the factual material is as follows:

THE FALL OF CHARLESTON

Full Account by Our Special Correspondent

Charleston, S. C., Feb. 20, 21, 22, 1865

Here beginneth the reopening of the Tribune's special correspondence from Charleston which has been suspended since the early period of the great Rebellion against . . . the Constitution and Government of the United States.

·   ·   ·   ·

IN THE BAY

We lay off the harbor for several hours before daybreak when the trip to the city was resumed. . . . To the left lay Morris Island, with Fort Wagner and Cumming's Point batteries; further off on the shore, large mounds of sand—the Rebel "Battery B", a little further up with our flag flying over it, Fort Gregg; to the right, on the low sandy shore, with one or two little groves of palmettos near by the earthworks of Fort Moultrie; between them, apparently a mass of ruins, in the middle of the stream, but really one of the most formidable fortifications in the world, was the renowned Fort Sumter; and behind it lay Castle Pinckney, with its cannon pointed at us, and the captured city, where Rebellion was begotten and born and began its career of carnage and desolation.

·   ·   ·   ·

* Mrs. Floyd is the author of *Lancaster County Tours* published by the Lancaster County Historical Commission in 1956. The excerpts printed above were copied from an issue of the New York *Tribune*, dated March 4, 1865, now in the possession of Ned Bailey, Funderburk Street, Lancaster, South Carolina.

The South Carolina Historical Magazine 66: 1-7

First Appearances

The wharves looked as if they had been deserted for half a century—broken down, delapidated, grass and moss peeping up between the pavement, where once the busy feet of commerce trod incessantly. The warehouses near the river; the streets as we enter them; the houses and the stores and the public buildings—we look at them and hold our breaths in utter amazement. Every step we take increases our astonishment. No pen, no pencil, no tongue can do justice to the scene. . . . And, all around this area of desolation are the ruined houses that still stand,—"Gillmore's Town" as the negroes call it.

· · · ·

But however great our astonishment and however awestricken our thoughts were, we remembered that our first duty was to learn for our Northern readers, not what ruin had been brought here but how the city was captured.

So we hurried to the newspaper offices uptown—for their old places of business had been rendered uninhabitable by the shells which sought them out—and found them too.

A Negro Image Breaker

We found The Mercury office deserted—a negro family already quartered in the room which had been the editorial sanctum! In the front room there were four busts of eminent Americans—one of them Calhoun. . . . I said to the negress who showed us into the room:

"That man was your great enemy—he did all he could to keep you slaves—you ought to break his bust."

She said nothing, and as I was occupied in examining manuscripts I did not notice that she left the room. After awhile, having finished my search, I thought that the bust of Calhoun would be a great trophy for the Tribune office, and made up my mind to "spoil the Egyptians" to that extent.

The negro woman was there and I saw that the bust had disappeared. I asked her where it was.

She had "gone done and broke it".

The Evacuation

The recent movements, planned by Gen. Gillmore, along the line of Charleston and Savannah Railroad (under Brig.-Gen. Hatch) and up Bull's Bay (a naval and military expedition under Gen. Potter) alarmed the Rebel military authorities and hastened the evacuation of the city. It was known from Rebel sources that Hardee designed to evacuate the city but it was thought that it would take place on Wednesday, Feb. 22 or later in the week. But Potter's demonstration deceived them (for they believed that they had a very large force while in fact he had but 1,200 men) and they began to leave the city on Friday. Hardee himself left Charleston on Friday night, and the last of the Rebels took their leave on Saturday.

DESTRUCTION OF COTTON AND PUBLIC STORES

Before leaving, details of soldiers were sent to fire every building without exception in which cotton was stored. It is estimated that 2,000 bales were consumed. The western portion of Charleston suffered severely by these fires. The cotton thus destroyed belonged chiefly to the Rebel Government; but hundreds of bales, the property of citizens, shared the same fate. Thirty thousand bushels of rice, government property, and a large warehouse filled with commissary stores were also destroyed. The fire engines were brought out, but were powerless to extinguish the flames. They succeeded only in preventing it from spreading.

HORRIBLE CALAMITY

. . . Some boys discovered where a large supply of gunpowder was stored, and amused themselves with tossing large handfuls of it into the large piles of burning cotton. Suddenly the fire communicated to the magazine, and a fearful explosion took place. The scene is described as being extremely horrible. It is estimated by the citizens that upward of 150 men, women and children perished in the flames and that nearly 200 were injured, burned and wounded. Possibly this may be an exaggerated estimate. . . . This frightful calamity occurred at the North-Eastern Railroad depot, which was totally destroyed. The miserable victims were seen tumbling about in agony, literally roasting alive; their wild shrieks were appalling—and all help was impossible.

DESTRUCTION OF PRIVATE PROPERTY

The flames rapidly communicated to the adjacent buildings and four large blocks were entirely burned down. The fire ravaged Chapel, Calhoun, East Bay and Laurens sts. in the vicinity of the N. E. railroad depot. Two large brick buildings on the corner of East Bay and Laurens sts. and Minonty [Minority?] sts. were also destroyed. An hour later five buildings near the Court-House on Meeting st. were added to the list of losses by fire. The new bridge from the city to James Island [?] was similarly destroyed.

DESTRUCTION OF THE GUNBOATS

While these scenes of horror were going on, the Rebel ironclads were burning. The vessels were named the Palmetto State, the Chicora, and the Charleston. The Palmetto State exploded with a fearful noise about 9 o'clock and the Chicora followed suit shortly thereafter. The Charleston held out till 11 o'clock and then burst asunder. One of these ironclads had 20 tons of gunpowder on board and the effect of its ignition was terrific. Red hot plates were thrown as far as the wharf, and soon set them on fire. But the wharves were saved from destruction by the Fire Department. The gas works were in danger, but were successfully protected. We still have gas, therefore, such as it is—but as it is made wholly of Southern pine, it is far from being a brilliant light. The Charleston Courier of Monday (No. 20,001) mentions a curious phenomenon connected with or caused by these explosions. "The explosions," it says, "were terrific. Tremendous clouds of smoke went up forming beautiful wreaths. A full Palmetto tree, with its leaves and stems was noticed by many observers. As the last wreath of smoke disappeared the full form of the rattlesnake in the center was remarked by many as it gradually faded away."   .   .   .   .

OUR FORCES LAND

Lieut. Col. A. G. Bennett of the Twenty-first United States Colored Troops, Major John A. Hennessy and Lieut. Burr of the Fifty-second Pennsylvania Vols. and Lieut. James F. Haviland, 127th N. Y. Volunteers arrived in a boat at the front of the South Atlantic Wharf at 10 o'clock on Saturday. Col. Bennett sent the following note to the Mayor of Charleston:

> A Surrender Demand
> Headquarters United States Forces
> Charleston, S. C., Feb. 18, 1865

Mayor Charles Macbeth, Charleston

Mayor: In the name of the United States Government I demand the surrender of the city of which you are the Executive officer.

Until further orders all citizens will remain within their houses.

I have the honor to be, Mayor,

> Your obedient servant,

> A. G. Bennett
> Lieut. Col. Commanding U. S. Forces,
> Charleston.

Before receiving this note the Mayor had sent a committee of two Aldermen to Morris Island with a formal surrender of the city. . . .

OFFICERS IN COMMAND

Gen. Schimmelpfennig commanded the Northern District of the Department of the South which extends from Charleston to Hilton Head.

Lieut. Col. Bennett is Provost Marshal and Mayor [Major?] Willoughby, Assistant-Provost-Marshal.

. . . .

VISIT TO FORT SUMTER

On Tuesday we accompanied Gens. Gillmore and Webster to Fort Sumter. Gen. Gillmore generously extended the coveted opportunity to visit the now classical ruin, to a large number of loyal ladies and gentlemen. We went out in the W. W. Coit which soon lay off the fort on the side nearest the city. A steamer had sunk near the Fort. We landed in small boats as the water was quite shallow there. The General and staff and some ladies landed in the first boat. The wall to the fort, looking toward it with back to the city, is about forty feet high, one corner being strengthened with heavy timber work outside. In the center it is perhaps about twenty-five feet high on the average. This side of course has been less damaged than those which were exposed to the fire of the batteries on Morris Island and to the fierce bombardment of the ironclads.

You enter through a very low passage way, a hundred feet or so in length, and emerge into an area of about an acre. Viewed from the inside the walls, or rather defenses, look high and are really formidable.

The fort originally was a pentagon, built of brick, stately and high. Everyone is familiar with its external appearance before the insurrection. Its siege has revolutionized the art of military engineering. It is now shown that the old style of brick or stonewall defenses are far less efficient than earthworks or lines of gabions. Gabions are large deep wicker baskets filled with earth or sea or quartz sand. The brick walls of Sumter that faced Morris Island are almost entirely demolished; but behind where they stood are layers after layers of gabions, with terraces and bomb-proofs both for soldiers on duty at the guns on the parapets and as quarters for officers and men. The defenses average, I should think, about a hundred feet in thickness. Every shell that demolished a portion of the exterior brick wall, therefore only strengthened the defenses, as it tossed the brick from positions where it was of little use to make the interior lines heavier. . . .

The bomb-proofs of the sentinels and soldiers on duty are little steep holes, down which they ran and hid themselves as soon as they saw the smoke of the guns on Morris Island, remaining there until the shell exploded. The heavy siege guns are concealed and protected beneath these impregnable defenses, and are worked in underground galleries. The quarters of officers and men are also bomb-proofs—underground or rather underground rooms; commodious and safe if neither commanding a good view nor extremely luxurious. The area is entirely unoccupied, with the exception of a railway which runs from the entrance toward the officers quarters on the further side. To guard the fort against attack on the sides that have been battered down, there are wires stretched along the parapets, and lines of chiveaux-de-frieze at the bottom to trip up and arrest the charge of an assaulting party. The fort, which looks like a ruin, is thus stronger in its delapitude than it was in its original state. On the left side, looking from the city, heavy timber works protect the old brick walls which are there quite high, but were badly damaged by the bombardment of the monitors under Admiral Dupont.

• • • •

Our flag was hoisted at Fort Sumter on Saturday last by Capt. Bragg, a young officer of Gen. Gillmore's staff. Long may it wave there!

• • • •

Speaking of raising the flag in Charleston reminds me that Maj.-Gen. Anderson has been invited to come down and hoist the original flag over Sumter. The Rebel flag was discovered among the rubbish there. It is as torn and as rent as the Confederacy it represents.

TORPEDOES AND TORPEDO BOATS

It has been ascertained that the Rebels have a number of torpedo boats hidden in some of the creeks twenty-six miles from Charleston. . . .

The river and harbor is being dragged for torpedoes; none have been found yet. On the wharf I saw long bars of iron, about twice the thickness of railroad bars, twenty feet or more in length, with links which connected them and also held the torpedoes in position. Negroes who had worked on them said that these bars had been stretched between Fort Sumter and Sullivan's Island, but that the current was so strong that it had bent the iron and thereby displaced the torpedoes. The Rebels took them up about eleven months ago. There is no doubt whatever that the arrangements of the insurgents for a desperate defense were admirably devised, and that they meant to hold the city to the death had an attack been made from the sea. There is a masked battery at the landing, and strong forts at two or three other commanding positions.

CARTHAGE EST DELENDA[1]

I write this last paragraph in the editorial rooms downtown of the Charleston Mercury. The window glass and sashes are shattered by shot. Over the mantlepiece in pencil marks are written these lines . . . :

For President in 1868
Wendell Phillips of Massachusetts
For Vice-President
Frederick Douglass of New York

Shades of Calhoun—how are the mighty fallen! Surely the great nullifier's bones must rattle in impotent rage at the overthrow of his heathen philosophy.

—Berwick.

[1] The correct Latin inscription is *Carthago delenda est*.

AN EYE WITNESS ACCOUNT OF THE OCCUPATION
OF MT. PLEASANT

February 1865

Henry Slade Tew, 1805-1884, the writer of the following letter, was a storekeeper and the Intendant (Mayor) of Mount Pleasant at the close of the War Between the States. The letter was addressed to his daughter, Emily Jenkins Tew.* He was the father of Colonel Charles Courtenay Tew, the first honor graduate of The Citadel, who was killed in action at Sharpsburg. Several years after the War H. S. Tew went to Dry Tortugas seeking his son whom he had heard was a prisoner there. He did meet Dr. Mudd while there and exchanged gifts with him.

Mount Pleasant
Feby. 26th, 1865

Dear Daughter,

Your absence from home at the time of the evacuation by our troops and the taking possession of those of the U. S. was a great relief to our minds, as our apprehension of insults and violence had been excited by the reports of such conduct elsewhere, and I have prepared this narrative or sort of diary to put you in possession of such facts as transpired and in some of which I was an actor, as may prove of interest to you at some future time may be referred to as part of the history of these eventful times.

You will recollect that for some time before you left, the City and surrounding country was in great excitement at the reports that an evacuation was intended, and these rumors and denials did not cease, up to the moment of the accomplishment of the intention.

On Thursday, the 16th Feby. about three o'clock the military began to impress all the Carts, Wagons, Horses, and Mules in the Town, and then at length all were convinced that the time was come. About 10 o'clock that night Mr. Porcher came to my house, having ridden near 40 miles, to request me to dispose of the Corn on his plantation (about 300 bushels) to the people in such quantities as they needed and to give to such as had no means of purchasing. And, on Friday morning, Dr. Bonneau, who was about removing his family, made the same request

* The manuscript letter is in the possession of Mrs. Courtenay Tew Lindsay of Deland, Florida. The following note is found on the end cover: "A narrative of events attending the evacuation of Sullivans Island as witnessed at Mount Pleasant prepared for the information of my children."

as to Rough Rice (about 400 bushels), but the absence of all the Carts prevented me from carrying out their requests. Directly after breakfast I heard that the Commissary was going to sell at the mill all the stores he could not remove. I went up and suceeded in purchasing some flour and meal for myself, and also in getting a few sacks of each for the poor, which I paid for myself. I had previously collected some Rough Rice and corn for the Poor which I had at the mill and in my store, and had made distribution of about 80 bushels to some of the families— that day Friday was one of anxiety to us all. About dark all the batteries on Morris Island and some of the vessels commenced the most terrible fire I think I ever witnessed in the war, directed at Sullivan's Island principally, though Sumter came in for a share, with the view to cut the bridge and prevent the evacuation of the Island. The fire was incessant and seemed to extend up to our bridge. It was a grand but awful scene. Mrs. Caldwell sent to ask me if I thought she was in danger, and we advised her to come to our house, which she did with her family. The awfulness of that night must dwell in the minds of those who witnessed it as long as memory lasts. In the midst of it, I received a message from Major Vardell to come to his quarters, and went immediately. I found him and his clerks, Tomlinson and Hall, ready to move, and he told me that he had left a quantity of corn in the store at the mill which he wished me to dispose of to the people as early as possible next day at Government price of $5.00 per bushel. He wished the distribution as general as possible, at the same time I heard that orders had been given to burn the mill and contents, about 1,200 bushels Rough Rice of which near 200 was my own, and I had also the stores for the poor in it.

I regarded this as a wanton act of cruelty, as ours was an isolated community having no local source of supply, and all that was in the mill would not have afforded more than would suffice to feed them a month or two, and the destruction of the mill itself would deprive the people of a means of having any rice beat or corn ground, and must cause great suffering. I therefore determined to be there before daylight and endeavor to prevent its destruction. Accordingly I rose before day and went there. Just as the sun was rising a Squad from Bolton's Cavalry rode up with torches. I remonstrated with the officer representing the importance of the mill to the people, but in vain, the order was imperative and at the moment Capt. Bolton himself came up, and to him I also appealed: he admitted the cruelty of the act, knew from his long service at this post that the mill was the only source for the inhabitants to prepare their grain for food, but his orders compelled him to destroy it, and fire was accordingly applied, and the devilish act, I must call it, accomplished.

Before the destruction was completed, I suceeded in getting the mill opened and as my own rice was in sacks, I had it thrown out and distributed to the crowd without distinction of person or color. I then disposed of the corn in the same manner to white and colored trying to make the distribution as nearly equal as I could. Many of them paid but some too needy I gave it to and much no doubt was stolen, as we have had a lawless population for some time in our town.

While these scenes were transpiring over here, those of Charleston must have beggared description,—to us was visible only the awful magnificence of the scene, while the terror, confusion, suffering and crime must have been appalling to the dwellers in the doomed city. The burning buildings public and private the repeated explosions, the gun boats and other vessels burning in the harbor all presented such a scene as but few ever witness in a lifetime, and surely one which none would ever desire to see repeated. Oh God! what a night of horror that memorable 17th of February was.

That which I witnessed on the morning of Saturday while I was on my way to the mill I never can forget during life—it was one of grandeur and awful beauty—the Iron Clads were lying in Cooper River their metal covering a glowing mass of Fire showing with the upmost distinctness every line of their shape contrasted with the dark mass of cloud and smoke in the background, and when the magazine exploded, the Vast mass of livid fire was raised in the air to the height it seemed to me of hundreds of feet and then fell in graceful showers of crimson and their hissing as the waters closed over them I could distinctly hear. As one of the officers of the U. S. fleet told me on Sunday he was watching it and he thought it the most perfect representation of a palmetto tree he could conceive of, and it was so. It rose in an apparently solid mass which might be considered the *trunk* of the tree, and after it attained its altitude, and not till then its cohesion was lost and the fragments began to fall separately—type I fear of the Confederacy to be extinguished in Blood and flame.

About 12 o'clock Saturday three barges landed from the fleet and as I had been elected Intendant by the people on Friday, in that official capacity attended by some of the citizens I surrendered the town submitting to the military authority of the U. S. and was promised protection to persons and private property. The boats were commanded by Lieut. Gifford from the Flagship—they brought a small U. S. Flag ashore and hoisted it for a while on the Light house. The officers were courteous and the men quite peaceful. Many from the fleet were ashore on Saturday and Sunday but we had not yet seen any from the Army from whom we feared violence and insult. All our own blacks boisterous in their reception of the visitors but none that I am aware of had yet left their work or homes. Monday 20th we heard that the troops that had landed at Bull's Bay were marching down and about 11 o'clock the shouts of the negroes apprised us of their arrival. There were three regiments of U. S. colored troops all under the command of Col. A. S. Hartwell, who took his quarters temporarily at the light house. I called on him, told him my name and position and asked protection for the persons and property of the citizens who were mostly women and children and were greatly apprehensive at the presence of the coloured troops. He received me very courteously, and assured me that the fears of the people would prove unfounded as the coloured troops were under better restraint than we imagined and directly placed them in camp and gave stringent orders against straggling from camp and forbidding them to enter houses or otherwise molest citizens. Colonel Hartwell then entered into conversation with me, asked me if I was connected with the Tews of Rhode Island, and if I was favorable to secession, as he had received so many assurances from people that they were not, that he was at a loss what to think and could only judge by the manner and not the language. I told him I would reply with the upmost frankness, that if more than one man in South Carolina out of Fifty told him he had opposed secession they lied, and that for myself, tho a Union man in 1832 and in 1850, yet on the election of Mr. Lincoln I thought all hope of justice to the South in the Union was lost, and I went for secession with vote and voice. He thanked me for the frankness of my reply and said it would be better if all would be equally so. Soon after I left he called on me at home, and I put him in Mr. Whilden's house as "headquarters", by which means Mr. W's furniture has been saved to him as some of the Rogues had broken into the house on Saturday night and stolen. I named the suspected party and on intimation from the Col. the fellow brought it all back the same day. The excitement throughout the day was intense. Many of the negroes from the Plantations came down in the Army train, and together with those of the village made quite a multitude of shouting wild creatures whom the thought of freedom had changed from quiet to transports of uproarious joy. I must tell you what I did for my own. A few days before I gave them $50.00 told them the money would soon be worth nothing and advised them to buy whatever they could then. I also told them that when the troops came they knew they were free to go or stay as they pleased— if they stayed, as long as I had anything to eat they should share as they always had done—Not one answered a word, and I knew of course they would go—they stayed however until Wednesday and then went off without a word of leave taking—Sary setting the example—Louis is gone also, Margaret and Zoe are still here as Elisa is with William and forbids their leaving, but I suppose they will not stay long—this by way of episode—let me resume the narrative, two or three squads of soldiers started into the premises on Monday before guards were placed seeking for tobacco, and stole from me a spy glass (not your brother's) and some trifling articles—the night of Monday passed quietly and we began to hope that under the firm hand and rule of Major Nott the Prov. Mar. things would soon be bearable. When orders came for the Brig. to move to the City and they left us with only six men as a guard and our negroes noisy, stealing all they could lay hands on and moving into the houses that were vacant. It was a sleepless night to us. We all sat up till 4 o'clock. Wednesday was a quiet day. Wednesday night we went to bed very early, no troops yet came over, and we left a light burning. About midnight a ring at the bell and the order to open the house. I put on some clothes, and admitted two soldiers, *white*, who said they came from Sul. Isd. and seeing a light in only my house desired to examine. They asked a number of questions, seemed satisfied with the replies and left. Not long after I heard a clash of arms and soon a knock and request for some Fire. I handed them some matches and all was quiet the rest of the night. Since that night order is fast being restored, the negroes are informed that they are expected to work for their support, and are not allowed to enter houses or committ depredations, and I must say that every officer with whom I have had any intercourse has exibited a degree of courtesy and I must say, a kindness of manner to me most unexpected from all that we have heard of the conduct elsewhere and the threats against So. Ca. particularly. I have had intercourse with Gen. Potter, Col. Hartwell, Lt. Col. Fox, Major Nott, Capts. Taylor Sharp and Abeels, and Lieuts. Pollock & Anderson, besides meeting many Naval and Military on the streets, and I have never either by word or look have been made to feel that I had encountered a foe. I have had no conversation with anyone but Col. Hartwell as before related. Capt. Abeels is our Prov. Mar. but he told me to-day Feby. 28 that this Regt. was about to be withdrawn and the 53rd Pennsylvania to come. So I close the last day of Feby. my dear Daughter, but should any matter of interest occur I will continue my diary for your information.

Our ladies have borne up bravely and have behaved with much prudence.

March 1

The 52nd Regt. Major Hennessy Com'g now garrison Mount Pleasant. Headquarters are now established at Mr. Whilden's house and the proximity to our own dwelling is the best guaranty we can have of quiet and order. The commander seems to be determined to enforce order and maintains stricter military discipline than we have ever had over here before from the troops of *either* army. He does not appear to have much sympathy or regard for the blacks, at least he does not place them above the whites and make all claims and interest subservient to theirs. He called on me and was social and pleasant—his Q. M., Lt. Gilchrist, has been very courteous and accommodating. On the 7th they took possession of my store and placed their Sutler in it, but by arrangement with him, I am to be paid rent. The Sut., Dr. Lowie, (?) is a Scotchman, and seems desirous to settle in business here, and I may possibly find employment from him, at any rate the rent of the store will give me the means of meeting the taxes that will probably be imposed and relieve my mind of much apprehension on that score. 13th. Change again. The 52 is ordered away and their place supplied by the 56th N. Y. 25th Ohio and 35th Penn, the last coloured. The Brigade commanded by Col. Van Wyck to whom I paid my respects. He promised me to supply the wants of the people and has twice had rough rice and corn distributed but the supply is rapidly being exhausted, and then fearful want and suffering must be felt by the inhabitants, none of whom seem to have exercised any forethought in supplying themselves with provisions even those of large means being as destitute as the poorest. Personally I have no reason to complain, but many of the citizens have had their premises depredated on to furnish material for building huts for the troops. The town hall and Market Hall are both torn down, and now the salt works on the coast are being brought in and I hope will supply all they need and stop the destruction in the town.

On Sunday 19th went to Church and in the pew before us was a mulatto girl with a white soldier—we heard he married her Saturday 25th. Attended the funeral of Sally Venning and on Sunday 26th that of little Eddy Royall who died of measles. The whole five of Mr. Royall's children having been taken at one time. On that Sunday the Episcopal Church was taken possession of by negro troops. Their regiment is commanded by Col. Beecher the brother of H. Ward Beecher and Mrs. H. B. Stowe, and we hear that his wife who is with him declines all acquaintance with the whites, but has called upon the colored ladies and invited them to her quarters—from this time forth until matters are settled I suppose that the Church is to be abandoned by the whites, as no one will care to subject themselves to the annoyance of having a colored gentleman or lady perhaps both walking into your pew and overpowering you with their odor or filling you with vermin.

I have planted my Garden and have the promise of an abundant supply of Fruit if I am not robbed, but the Com'g Officer has promised me protection for my fences and thus far, not a twig or board has been disturbed—may it continue and the apprehension of want will be continually diminishing as the products of the Garden and orchard and my cow will materially aid me in feeding the family.

On the 22nd William Lindsay same from the city and he has been staying with Mr. Bennett since the evacuation and has just been able to get over here. I have urged him to stay until he can get something to do. I have taken Wm. Johnson home again, as he was destitute and pauperlike eating and sleeping promiscuously about the Town. On Thursday Mrs. Whitby (Whiley) offered him a situation as clerk, food and washing and six dollars per month. I advised him to accept he is now there and has the chance of supporting himself if he chooses to be attentive.

SHERMAN'S ARMY COMES TO CAMDEN: THE CIVIL WAR NARRATIVE OF SARAH DEHON TRAPIER

Edited by Karen D. Stokes*

SARAH DEHON TRAPIER, THE WIFE OF AN EPISCOPAL CLERGYMAN, spent most of her life in Charleston, South Carolina, where she was born in 1814. Just before the start of the Civil War, the Trapier family moved to Camden, an early market town in the South Carolina backcountry that had prospered during the nineteenth century as a trading center for the cotton plantations of Kershaw District. Despite scarcities and anxieties, the Trapiers remained relatively safe at Camden until the war's final months, when the enemy arrived at their door. In February 1865, the army of General William T. Sherman invaded the town, and Union soldiers occupied and pillaged the Trapier home. The Trapiers, like many others on the Confederate home front, had their lives changed forever by the harrowing encounter. Sarah Trapier's account of what happened was penned within a few months of the events, while her emotions were still raw and the memories fresh in her mind. It was addressed to an unnamed friend or relation, possibly a northerner, to give "some idea of the situation of thousands of others, like our own."[1]

The Trapier Family's Path to Camden

In his autobiography, the Reverend Paul Trapier described his wife, Sarah Dehon Trapier, as "my chief earthly treasure." She was an individual, he wrote, "of rare judgment, of truest affection, and of as brave a spirit as ever was in woman."[2] Sarah was the daughter of Rev. Theodore Dehon (1776–1817), bishop of the Episcopal Diocese of South Carolina.[3] Her mother was Sarah Russell (1792–1857), the daughter of Nathaniel

* Karen D. Stokes is processing archivist at the South Carolina Historical Society. She wishes to thank Joan Inabinet and Charles Baxley for their valuable assistance, as well as the anonymous readers of the South Carolina Historical Magazine, whose suggestions were helpful.

[1] Quoted from Sarah Dehon Trapier's account. See p. 105 of this article.

[2] Paul Trapier, Incidents in My Life: The Autobiography of the Rev. Paul Trapier, ed. George W. Williams (Charleston, S.C.: Dalcho Historical Society, 1954), 19, 35. The original manuscript is part of the Gadsden Allied Family Papers at the South Carolina Historical Society, Charleston (hereinafter cited as SCHS). Unless otherwise noted, all quotations of Paul Trapier are from his autobiography.

[3] Frederick Dalcho, An Historical Account of the Protestant Episcopal Church in South-Carolina (1820; reprint, New York: Arno Press, 1972), 223-232.

The South Carolina Historical Magazine 109: 95-120

Russell (1738–1820), a prominent Charleston merchant.[4] Twenty-year-old Paul Trapier met his future wife in 1826.[5] She was only twelve years old at the time, but as he later wrote, "I think there sprang up then an incipient attachment, which, unconscious probably to both of us, took deeper root than would seem likely from our difference of ages."

Paul Trapier was born in 1806 at his grandfather's country estate, Belvedere, on Charleston Neck. He attended several schools in Charleston, graduated from Harvard in 1825, and subsequently studied for the ministry in New York. In 1830 he was ordained as a priest in the Episcopal church. As a regular delegate to its yearly General Convention, Trapier took an active and significant part in the affairs of the national church. When the South Carolina diocese withdrew to become part of a new church of the Confederate States, he also figured prominently in its councils.[6]

After their initial meeting, Paul Trapier and Sarah Dehon crossed paths again five years later in 1831, when Sarah, along with Paul's sister Alicia, began taking lessons with a tutor at the Trapier home. Paul, by then a member of the clergy, was "charmed" with Sarah's "appearance and manners at the age of 17." The two became engaged the following year and were married on April 27, 1833.[7] Decades later he said of that day, "I secured a blessing second only to that of acceptance with my Saviour, whom I thank unceasingly for giving me such a wife."

George W. Williams noted in his introduction to the Paul Trapier autobiography that the minister's life "began in affluence and ended in poverty, began in happiness and ended in misery." This also was true, of course, of the woman who shared his life for nearly forty years. The young couple spent time during the early years of their marriage at the rectory of St. Andrew's Parish Church, Rev. Paul Trapier's first parochial charge, located on the Ashley River, northwest of Charleston.[8] The St. Andrew's parsonage, Trapier wrote, "was embowered in one of the most beautiful gardens which nature and art can create—more than two hundred varieties of camellia, combined with stately avenues of magnolia, to delight the eye even of European visitors."[9] Of that time, he recalled, "We enjoyed the seclusion very much, as it enabled us to see so much more of each other, and many were the happy days we passed in our diminutive parlor, or in

    [4] N. Louise Bailey, ed., Biographical Directory of the South Carolina House of Representatives (Columbia: University of South Carolina Press, 1981), 3: 625.

    [5] Trapier, Incidents in My Life, 19.

    [6] Ibid., viii, 1, 17.

    [7] Ibid., 19.

    [8] Ibid.

    [9] [C. C. Pinckney, Peter J. Shand, and Paul Trapier], Report of the Committee on the Destruction of Churches in the Diocese of South Carolina during the Late War: Presented to the Protestant Episcopal Convention, May 1868 (Charleston, S.C.: J. Walker, Printer, 1868), 8.

walking about under the trees around the house, with our then only child, the very perfection in our eyes of infant loveliness." Finding that this "lodge in the wilderness" would not do for a permanent home, the couple moved back to Charleston to live with "Mother Dehon" at her elegant home on Meeting Street (today known as the Nathaniel Russell House). Their twelve children were all born at this place, where the family resided for the next twenty-five years.[10]

In 1840 Paul Trapier became the rector of St. Michael's Church in Charleston.[11] He described its congregation as "made up in large part of old families, priding themselves upon ancestry and attached to the church rather because their fathers had been there than from enlightened acquaintance with its principles." Devout, serious, and uncompromising in matters of the faith, the rector attempted changes at St. Michael's that proved controversial, and "after a long struggle of six years," he resigned, though he was consoled by his certainty that he had left behind there "a small but devotedly pious band of Christians, the leaven to leaven the lump of worldliness, and to bring a blessing upon the Church in that Congregation."

Soon after leaving St. Michael's, Rev. Paul Trapier played a principal role in the establishment of Calvary Church in Charleston, a "project for good to the souls of slaves," as he called it. He was appointed minister there in April 1847. Earlier that year, a layman, Henry D. Lesesne, had put forward resolutions at the fifty-eighth diocesan convention "deploring the lack of adequate Church provision for the colored people of the city" and calling for the "establishing and maintaining of a congregation of colored people in Charleston." Trapier stated in his first annual report that the Calvary congregation included "both white and colored," who attended the services and the Sunday School. By late 1849, the growing congregation was worshipping in a new church building on Beaufain Street. Trapier ministered at Calvary until 1856, at which time he resigned due to ill health.[12] In 1855 he published a catechism specifically designed for black communicants.[13]

---

[10] Paul Trapier, The Private Register of the Rev. Paul Trapier (Charleston, S.C.: Dalcho Historical Society, 1958), passim. Their children were: Sarah Alicia (1834-1878), Paul (1836-1855), Frances Dehon (called "Fanny," 1838-1848), Mary (b. 1840), Theodore Dehon (1841-1905), Zoe (b. 1843), Pierre DuGue (b. 1846), Alice Pauline (b. 1849), Elizabeth Shubrick (called "Lillie," 1850-1864), Anne Dehon (b. 1851), Edith Russell (b. 1853), and Richard Shubrick (b. 1856). In his autobiography, Paul Trapier noted that his daughter Mary married Thomas Fisher Gadsden (1839-1891), son of Christopher Gadsden, an Episcopal bishop of South Carolina, in 1866.

[11] Trapier, Incidents in My Life, 20.

[12] Albert Sidney Thomas, A Historical Account of the Protestant Episcopal Church in South Carolina, 1820-1957 (Columbia, S.C.: R. L. Bryan Co., 1957), 202.

[13] See Paul Trapier, The Church Catechism Made Plain, for the Use of Those Who Cannot Read: On the Creed (New York: General Protestant Episcopal Sunday School Union, 1855).

About two-and-a-half years before the war, Paul Trapier was elected to a professorship at the newly established diocesan theological seminary in Camden.[14] He purchased a large house just outside of town called Kamschatka (formerly owned by James Chesnut and his wife, Mary Boykin Chesnut, the famous diarist).[15] Here, Trapier wrote, "I looked forward to passing the remainder of my days most delightfully . . . The students of the Seminary were pious and studious, several of them of rare intelligence." One of these gifted students was William Porcher DuBose (1836–1918), later a Confederate chaplain and renowned Episcopal theologian. When the war began, DuBose, like all of the other seminarians, soon enlisted in military service, and after about a year, the school shut down.[16]

"Dark Clouds Now Gathered Round Us"

Sarah Trapier's manuscript, which is part of the Gadsden Allied Family Papers at the South Carolina Historical Society, was written in 1865. Her narrative commences as her family is well into the third year of their residence in Camden. Full of pathos as well as religious and patriotic fervor, it opens with a description of the vicissitudes and hardships of their lives during wartime, but mainly concerns two fateful months that the Trapiers endured toward the close of the war, in a town that lay in the path of General Sherman's destructive march through the state.

Sherman's campaign across South Carolina began on the first day of February 1865. His army of over sixty thousand men was divided into two wings. The right wing, under the command of General O. O. Howard, included General John A. Logan's 15th Corps. After leaving much of the

[14] Thomas, A Historical Account of the Protestant Episcopal Church in South Carolina, 687-689. The seminary opened in January 1859 and closed in June 1862.

[15] Elisabeth Muhlenfield, Mary Boykin Chesnut: A Biography (Baton Rouge: Louisiana State University Press, 1981), 62. James Chesnut had the house built for his wife, Mary. Kamchatka (also known by this spelling) was named for a Siberian peninsula. The house is extant and is a contributing property to the city of Camden Historic District, which is listed in the National Register of Historic Places. In the 1905 edition of Mary Chesnut's diary, she mentions a trip that she took to her old home in Camden on June 1, 1865: "The Trapiers live there now. In those drawing-rooms where the children played Puss in Boots, where we have so often danced and sung, but never prayed before, Mr. Trapier held his prayer-meeting. I do not think I ever did as much weeping or as bitter in the same space of time . . . He prayed that we might have strength to stand up and bear our bitter disappointment, to look on our ruined homes and desolated country and be strong. And he prayed for the man [Confederate president Jefferson Davis] 'we elected to be our ruler and guide.' We knew that they had put him in a dungeon and in chains." Mary Boykin Chesnut, A Diary from Dixie, ed. Isabella D. Martin and Myrta Lockett Avary (New York: D. Appleton and Company, 1905), 397.

[16] Theodore DuBose Bratton, An Apostle of Reality: The Life and Thought of the Reverend William Porcher DuBose (New York: Longmans, Green and Co., 1936), 45-49.

capital city of Columbia in ashes, Sherman moved his armies northward. At Liberty Hill, in northwestern Kershaw District, General Logan divided his command into two columns and sent a detachment from one, under the command of Colonel R. N. Adams, to raid Camden to the south.[17]

David P. Conyngham, a newspaper correspondent traveling with Sherman's army, described Camden as "a beautiful town" and mentioned its historical significance, noting that two battles had been fought there during the American Revolution. He also related how the mayor and city council had prepared "a very pretty speech and address" for General Sherman on surrendering the town, and that it was "rather mortifying to them to have it unceremoniously occupied by some foragers." Conyngham stated that the first Union forces to arrive at Camden on February 23 were a small group of "foragers," who "skirmished with some cavalry, driving them into the town, and, following them, soon took possession of it."[18]

This "cavalry" defending Camden was a small group of militia composed of elderly men and boys under the command of Col. Burwell Jones.[19] Conyngham reported that on the next morning, Generals Howard and Logan sent in larger detachments, who "destroyed all government property, public stores, the depot, and some public buildings." The federals additionally destroyed "about fifty thousand rations of corn meal, and four thousand bales of cotton" in Camden.[20]

"The storm has at length burst upon us; the anticipated blow has fallen, and Camden has been made to undergo, in her turn, all the horrors of invasion," lamented a local newspaper on March 10, 1865. The same edition gave further details of the sacking:

> The advance body . . . first fired the freight and passenger depots; then the Cornwallis house, also the Commissary store house on the southeast corner of Broad and DeKalb Streets. From this latter building the fire spread south and consumed all the structures on that square fronting Broad Street, down to Rutledge. They also burnt Mr. Geo. Douglas' store, cotton sheds in rear of Gerald's and Bell's stores, and the Bridge over the Wateree River, the Masonic Hall and adjacent buildings. They broke and pillaged all stores, took what goods they wanted and threw the rest into the streets . . . After the cotton and stores had been burned the majority of the Yankees dispersed over the town in small squads to rob on private account . . . The detachment first entering Camden was followed by others, and large forces were camped in the suburbs. In fact the whole

---

[17] John Gilchrist Barrett, Sherman's March through the Carolinas (Chapel Hill: University of North Carolina Press, 1956), 35, 101.

[18] David P. Conyngham, Sherman's March through the South: With Sketches and Incidents of the Campaign (New York: Sheldon and Co., 1865), 343-344.

[19] Thomas J. Kirkland and Robert M. Kennedy, Historic Camden, Part Two: Nineteenth Century (Columbia, S.C.: The State Company, 1926), 163.

[20] Conyngham, Sherman's March through the South, 343.

of Sherman's army was within twenty miles of us. They left the town Saturday night."[21]

Sarah Trapier's account echoes a number of the particulars reported in this article published in the Camden Journal and Confederate, which described Sherman's soldiers as having "run through the gamut, from impertinence to outrage, from pilfering to wholesale spoliation. Many families have been stripped of everything they had in the world. In one neighborhood, where they unearthed buried liquor, they were especially riotous and fired houses with wanton cruelty."[22]

When it was all over, the Trapiers were left with little else on earth except the house that they lived in and each other. "I take refuge in my family," Paul Trapier recorded a few months later, "without which I see not how I could struggle on."

Less than two months after Sherman's armies left, Camden was subjected to another invasion during Potter's Raid, an expedition led by Union general E. E. Potter. His forces left the seaport of Georgetown, South Carolina, on April 5, 1865, headed west, their principal purpose being the destruction of railroads between Florence and Sumter. The general's orders also included a directive that "the food supplies in that section should be exhausted." The infantry troops led by Potter included the 25th and 157th Ohio Volunteers, the 157th New York Volunteers, the 54th Massachusetts Regiment, and five companies of the 102nd U.S. Colored Troops.[23] Eventually, General Potter's force of about twenty-five hundred men reached the vicinity of Camden, where they overcame the resistance offered by a small group of home guard (old men, boys, and furloughed veterans) and entered the town on April 17.[24]

Emma Holmes, a refugee from Charleston living in Camden during this time, recorded a few paragraphs in her diary about Potter's Raid, stating that his troops "committed some gross outrages—violating a young lady at Mrs. Baxley's." She also noted acts of pillaging and related reports of many dead black women and children left along the roadside in the wake of the departing army.[25] Sarah Trapier's account only briefly mentions Potter's Raid in Camden, but she did record that after Potter's army left the town on the April 18, "Numbers of families awoke to find

[21] Journal and Confederate (Camden, S.C.), March 10, 1865, quoted in Kirkland and Kennedy, Historic Camden, 163-164.

[22] Ibid.

[23] Allan D. Thigpen, The Illustrated Recollections of Potter's Raid, April 5-21, 1865 (Sumter, S.C.: Gamecock City Printing, Inc., 1998), ii, 618.

[24] Kirkland and Kennedy, Historic Camden, 174.

[25] Emma Holmes, The Diary of Miss Emma Holmes, 1861-1866, ed. John F. Marszalek (Baton Rouge: Louisiana State University Press, 1979), 434-435.

themselves without a single servant." She added, though, that "none of our servants left us."[26] This was true at the time, but in his autobiography (most of which was written in 1865), Paul Trapier related that all of their slaves had left the family by the end of July.[27] In his official report on the expedition, General Potter noted that "five thousand negroes joined the column and were brought within our lines."[28]

Several accounts written by individuals residing in Camden during the winter and spring of 1865 exist, but few are as lengthy or as detailed as that of Sarah Trapier. The collections published by the United Daughters of the Confederacy contain only a few reminiscences by Camden residents about the time, one of which, by Esther S. Davis, is quoted extensively in volume 2 of the most comprehensive history of the town to date, Historic Camden (1926), by Thomas K. Kirkland and Robert M. Kennedy. The Davis memoir, from 1911, and the recollections of Harriet DuBose Kershaw Lang, published in the South Carolina Historical Magazine in 1958, are among the best known women's narratives concerning this period in Camden's history, but both were written long after the fact.[29] Sarah Trapier's account is rare, then, and all the more significant, because it was recorded (at most) only a few months after the time of the actual events.

An ardent believer in states' rights, Rev. Paul Trapier had rejoiced at the prospect of establishing an independent southern confederacy. The single letter to him from Sarah that has been preserved reveals that she, even as a teenage girl, shared his strong political convictions.[30] But both husband and wife witnessed their hopes crushed. For Paul Trapier, the defeat of the South not only meant the end of the Confederacy, but the end of the American republic. Writing in late 1865, impoverished and embittered, he expressed despair for his country, "all of which," he emphasized, he once used to love as his own.

> I have no heart to derive satisfaction from the glories departed of the first successful Revolution, nor can I do aught else than mourn over those not less magnificent of our late unsuccessful, but heroic, attempt . . . I try in vain to lay hold of something to rest on for a ground-work of hope for the future of my country. The U.S. Constitution has long since been a piece of waste paper . . . [The] right of Secession, for which 13 States have been pouring out the lifeblood of their dearest and their best, is now overpowered by the might of a brutal majority, and the people of those

[26] Quoted from Sarah Trapier's account. See p. 119 of this article.
[27] Trapier, Incidents in My Life, 32.
[28] Thigpen, Illustrated Recollections of Potter's Raid, 612.
[29] See Rives Land Beaty, ed., "Recollections of Harriet DuBose Kershaw Long," South Carolina Historical Magazine 59 (July, October 1958): 159-170, 195-205.
[30] This letter was written during the nullification crisis of the 1830s and is found in the Gadsden Allied Family Papers, SCHS.

13 States after having been over-run and desolated by hordes of cruel soldiers, are drawn in worse than chains of iron back into a Union, which for 40 years has been but an instrument of torture to them. The choicest families of the land are reduced to menial service, and degraded by petty military satraps below their own slaves—and those whom our entire people have been delighting for 4 years to honour are caged and fettered like felons, to glut the vile thirst of a vulgar race for a base triumph over greatness, before which, when it was in power, they trembled, and over which, now that it is fallen, they exult with demoniac malice.

For the next five years, struggling to support his large family, Trapier ministered at several different churches in South Carolina, including the Church of the Nativity in Union, and taught again when, for a short while, the diocesan seminary was reestablished in Spartanburg. In 1870 financial need forced him to accept a position as the rector of a parish in Maryland. His health began to fail the following year, and in 1872, he died.[31] Sarah Dehon survived her husband for another seventeen years, passing away on September 27, 1889, at the age of seventy-four. Both are buried at St. Michael's Church cemetery in Charleston.[32]

EDITORIAL NOTE

In the transcription of Sarah Dehon Trapier's narrative, a few changes were made to punctuation and spelling, principally in the omission of some dashes between words or sentences and in writing out ampersands. All scriptural quotations are taken from the King James Version.

AN ACCOUNT OF THE EXPERIENCES OF THE FAMILY OF THE REVEREND AND MRS. PAUL TRAPIER DURING THE CIVIL WAR

You ask me to give you some account of our family during and since the war; and I will do so, as it will give you some idea of the situation of thousands of others, like our own.

At the commencement of the war, we numbered twelve (my husband and myself and ten children)—of these all were girls, except three, and one of these is a little boy of nine years of age. Our eldest son, our comfort and stay, always delicate from childhood, but brave of spirit and strong in faith, entered the army at the age of 18.[33] Our hearts sank within us

[31] Trapier, Incidents in My Life, 36-38.
[32] Clare Jervey, Inscriptions on the Tablets and Gravestones in St. Michael's Church and Churchyard, Charleston, S.C. (Columbia, S.C.: The State Company, 1906), 270, 315.

as we thought of the sufferings and trials thenceforth to the lot of one so delicately nurtured, so fondly cherished. Little did we know how fearfully were these forebodings to be realized. The first year of the war we never saw him, but he bore up wonderfully under the hardships, fatigues, and want of food, which he constantly endured; and our hearts were cheered by letters full of ardent patriotism, constant hope, and patient endurance; winning by his gentlemanly deportment and faithful discharge of his duties the unqualified approval of his commander and the affectionate esteem of his fellow soldiers. At the end of that time, constant exposure brought on the fever of the climate, and he returned home feeble and emaciated. But we nursed him with the tenderest care, and home joys and home sympathies acted like a charm, and he returned to camp brave and hopeful as ever.

In the meantime our second son pursued his studies at home, and aided his father in every possible way, until the third year of the war, when, at the age of 17, he too entered the army.[34]

My husband, as you know, is a clergyman. He came to our present home advanced in years and broken down in constitution by 25 years of laborious ministerial duties. As Professor in the Theological Seminary of our Church in this Diocese he received a salary of $1500. We owned the house we lived in,[35] and the income from our other property amounted to about $2000; so that at the commencement of the war our large family were able with economy to live comfortably. We knew that this could not last. But we knew the cause to be a righteous one, and we gave ourselves to it, expecting and prepared to suffer.

My children seemed <u>born</u> patriots. Descended on the father's side from those who had distinguished themselves in the first Revolution, and on the mother's side from those who, driven out of France during the Reign of Terror, had become broken-hearted by oppression and suffering, the love of liberty and independence seemed a part of their nature.[36] You

[33] Theodore D. Trapier served in the Marion Light Artillery (also known as Parker's Company).

[34] Pierre D. Trapier served as a private in the Second Regiment, Company F, Confederate States Engineer Corps (the Engineer Corps did not have state designations).

[35] James Chesnut sold the house, Kamschatka, to Paul Trapier in December 1858 for eight thousand dollars. It was sold to Mary M. Kirkland in 1871 for less than half that amount. Kamschatka File, Camden Archives, Camden, S.C.

[36] Rev. Paul Trapier was the grandson of Paul Trapier (1749-1778), a Georgetown planter and delegate to the Continental Congress. Sarah Trapier's grandfather was a French Protestant emigrant who settled in Boston, Massachusetts. Paul Trapier left a history of his family entitled "Notices of Ancestors and Relatives, Paternal and Maternal." It is the first part of his manuscript memoir at the SCHS (which includes his autobiography). An edited and annotated version of the family history was published in the Transactions of the Huguenot Society of South Carolina 58 (1953): 29-54.

will not wonder that they gave themselves heart and soul to the work. The chamber of my grown daughters was soon stripped of the carpet from the floor and the curtains from the bed, and even a part of their warm winter-covering went to minister to the comfort of the poor, suffering soldiers. They knit at even their meals to supply stockings for our armies. I had then four sweet little girls. They called themselves "Us Four," and everyone knew them by that name.[37] Well do I remember the delight with which they packed their first box for the hospital. They earned money by making little fancy articles, and with this they purchased comforts for the hospitals, then crowded with the sick and dying.

During the first year of the war these children earned in this way 50 and 60 dollars. The second year of the war our income from the Theological Seminary was withdrawn for a time, as its exercises were discontinued, because of the enlisting of all the students in the army, and everything advanced in price. But success then waited on our banners and we began cheerfully to deny ourselves many of the comforts we had been accustomed to from childhood. We were at no expense for education, my eldest daughter instructing the younger sisters and their little brother. My husband worked daily in the garden and thus supplied us with many little comforts. He tried at one time to teach a boys' school. But his strength failed and after three months he was obliged to give it up. Providentially at the next meeting of our Diocesan Convention it was generously resolved to continue the salaries of the Professors, and our income became again more nearly adequate to our expenses.

The third year of the war the taxes became enormous, eating up our entire income, and obliging us to live on our capital. Our younger brother, then Rector of St. Philip's Church died this year, worn out by incessant labours for his flock and for the sick, the wounded and the dying at the hospitals.[38] His family (a wife and two children) came to us and are with us now.[39] Our capital was invested largely in Confederate securities, and as the only currency was in Confederate notes, which were at a great discount, we were sinking more and more of our means. Still we never dreamed of the failure of our glorious Cause, and we therefore willingly

---

[37] The Trapier daughters known as "Us Four" were the youngest: Alice Pauline (b. 1849); Elizabeth Shubrick, called "Lillie" (1850-1864); Anne Dehon (b. 1851); and Edith Russell (b. 1853).

[38] Rev. William Dehon (1817-1862). He died late in the second year of the war.

[39] William Dehon's wife was Anne Manigault Middleton Dehon (1820-1876), daughter of Arthur Middleton and Alicia Russell Middleton. She was Sarah Trapier's cousin as well as her sister-in-law. According to the 1860 census, Rev. William Dehon had two children living in that year: William Russell Dehon, age eleven, and Mary B. Dehon, age thirteen.

and cheerfully submitted to increased privations. Tea, sugar, and butter were luxuries reserved for sickness.

Often have we been for months without fresh meat, dessert, or sweet things of any kind. I have seen the little children sit down with all of us to a dinner of a shred of bacon, hominy, and rice, with some preparation of corn, and get up hungry but without a murmur, yea, with smiling faces, assuring us that they would be only the more healthy for going without sweet things for their country's sake, and sometimes they would amuse themselves with descriptions of the wonderful things they would enjoy when peace and independence were attained. Alas this year a great sorrow came upon them. The little band of "Us Four" was broken. Our Lillie, the darling of our hearts, sickened and died. Weeks of suffering and anguish, nights of burning fever, were appointed her. God bless the warm Southern hearts that helped us in this dark hour out their own scanty store! So generously! So unweariedly! Little cups of sugar, papers of tea, a few spoonfuls of arrowroot, little supplies of milk, pats of butter garnished with sweet flowers, would bring a faint smile to her wan face. Especially would we cherish with ever-fresh gratitude the readiness with which a gentleman, twelve miles from us, an entire stranger, offered us the free use of his private ice-house, into which he had collected at great trouble for the use of his own family and of sick and wounded soldiers, that most refreshing and rarest of comforts in the then condition of our Confederacy. Nor can we forget the kindness of our neighbours, who, knowing that we had no means of sending for it, placed their own servants and horses at our disposal, thereby affording to our dear child the very relief she had been longing for most, and relished most highly.

How hard it was to give her up! She had been with us in all our struggles; how sorely we should miss her when her hour of triumph came! Short-sighted affection! Her Heavenly Father knew better. Gradually He reconciled her to the parting. At first it was "Pray for me, Mamma, that I may be better. How can I give you all up! How can I go to the far distant land!" But towards the last a great change came over her. "I want to die." "Pray for me that I may continue His forever and daily increase in His Holy Spirit, more and more, until I come to His heavenly Kingdom." To that "better country"[40] she has gone, and now that we have no other country, and labour awaits those who remain, we know that "He doeth all things well."[41]

[40] Hebrews 11:16: "But now they desire a better country, that is, an heavenly."

[41] From a ballad entitled "He Doeth All Things Well, or My Sister" (1847), lyrics by "F. M. E." and music by I. B. Woodbury; based on Mark 7:37 ("He hath done all things well").

I now pass to the last year of the war. Our pecuniary embarrassments were greatly increased. No clothing could be procured but at an enormous expense. Early in the war we received from Europe through the kindness of a friend, a box containing cloth and the materials for making it up, which proved the greatest possible help to our large family. But this was now nearly exhausted, and the servants were greatly in need. I made coats of carpet for the women and managed to get a suit apiece for the men.

Dark clouds now gathered round us. Instead of hearing of victories, the tidings were often of defeat. From the moment of Gen. Joseph E. Johnston's removal from the command of the army of the West, our doom seemed sealed.[42] As soon as Sherman got into the interior, the difficulty of procuring food for our armies became more and more serious. Our men, however, had learned endurance. They could have borne personal privations. But now a merciless horde were let loose upon the defenseless wives and children of our soldiers. Daily accounts were reaching them of these fearful raids, which left behind nothing but starvation, desolation and dishonour! Ah, little do you know the love, the veneration, the chivalrous devotion the Southern soldier feels for women! Throughout this war she has been his guardian angel, his tender nurse, her prayers strengthening him in his weakness, her sympathy soothing him in his sorrows, her patient example nerving him to self-denial and endurance, her voice encouraging him to deeds of noble daring. Now these loved ones were to be exposed, alone and helpless, to the insults of lawless ruffians, to the lusts of brutal negroes. Can it be wondered that his heart failed him, that his spirit was crushed? Outnumbered by many thousands, food failing, should he persevere in a struggle which must end in defeat, or should he flee to the protection of all he had now to live for?

Up to this time our family had not been visited by any of these fearful raiders. But about the month of January rumours came of their approach. About the same time we learned that our eldest son was ill in Columbia. After an examination by the Board of Surgeons there, he was sent home on a furlough of sixty days. He had been sick a long time, but had endured it patiently till a violent cold brought on a fever with derangement of the liver, spleen and stomach. We were shocked by his emaciation. But we nursed him tenderly, and he recovered slowly, not as on previous occasions of illness, for now the buoyancy of hope was gone.

About the 18th of February we heard of the evacuation of Charleston,

---

[42] General Joseph E. Johnston (1807-1891) was the commander of the Army of Tennessee. Confederate president Jefferson Davis was unhappy with Johnston's strategy of withdrawal before the army of General William T. Sherman and replaced him with General John B. Hood, just before the fall of Atlanta in July 1864. Ezra J. Warner, Generals in Gray: Lives of the Confederate Commanders (Baton Rouge: Louisiana State University Press, 1987), 161-162.

then of the advance of the enemy upon Columbia. All day on the 20th we could hear the booming of the cannon, and the night of the 21st the sky was lighted up by the blaze from the conflagration of that beautiful but ill fated city, the smoke from which obscured the declining sun of the following day. With sad hearts we began to prepare for our turn, our suffering from the same ruthless savages, who had thus sacked and destroyed our capital.

Hastily we gathered together what we valued most, and set ourselves to conceal these in the dead of night; and night after night, when all others were asleep, did my husband and son and nephew, steal out, as if on dark deed intent to secure what of right was theirs, or entrusted to them, and groping their way, with scarcely light enough to see where they were, endeavoured to hide in the ground the silver and jewelry which they knew would be tempting to the cupidity of the marauders, who were soon to be among us. Especially they had to be cautious, as the negroes, it was known, were on the lookout to appropriate to themselves, or discover to the enemy, what would else have escaped the closest search of the latter. We live on the outskirts of the town of Camden, and unfortunately next to a family of Jews of very bad character. They kept a grocery store in the town, where they had large quantities of liquor. This they had been wagoning in open day to their yard, and burying in a large pit within sight of, and with the help of, their negroes. Thus was a new and horrible danger added to our fearful anticipations.

The question pressing most heavily upon us was as to what was to be done with our son. He was feeble. If he stayed he might be carried off as a prisoner, or shot. There was no hospital here for him to go to, and as it was expected that the enemy would approach in one direction, and perhaps not in very large force; it was determined, on the advice of military men, that he should go out on horseback, and conceal himself in the woods, until the advancing army should have passed by. One of our slaves, a boy who had been brought up with him, and who, he trusted, would prove faithful, was to accompany him and take charge of the provisions for themselves and horses. But what a change! From the tender nursing of mother and sisters to cold and rain, privation and fatigue, and harrowing anxiety about us all! Poor boy! I remember well how worn and sad he looked when, on the afternoon of that very day of his leaving us, he threw himself on the bed beside me and exclaimed, "How I should like to rest here for a year!" Alas, he had not rested an hour when the servants came rushing in, crying out, "The Yankees are in the town!" He jumped up, and we all ran downstairs with him. His father was out on one of the horses trying to find out in what direction they were coming. But the other horse was soon saddled. The haversack and blankets were placed on it, and with one hurried kiss and a "God bless you" he went towards the stable. His faithful nurse followed him, and on his return she said, "Poor fellow! He was so weak he had to be helped on the horse." He left word for his father that he would wait in an adjoining wood for the boy with the provisions. In about half an hour his father returned and reported that the Yankees were in Camden. Hurrying the boy off, he joined him in the wood. Here, after making such arrangements as he could for our son's comfort, his father with a heavy heart parted from him commending him to his God and to the care of the servant who seemed to be greatly alarmed.

What a sad circle gathered round the fire that evening! Before we retired to bed, however, we were somewhat relieved by hearing that the report of the enemy's being in the town was false; they were still a few miles distant. The next morning everything seemed tranquil. My little Edith, however, was quite sick, and several of us were in the chamber with her, when about 2 o'clock one of the little girls, going to the window, exclaimed, "Why here is Teedy (Theodore) coming back!" "No," said another, "that man has a blue coat."

"The Yankees! The Yankees!" we all cried out. The children rushed downstairs to their Papa, while I stayed a few minutes to soothe the sick child, who became very much agitated.

When I reached the parlour, I found my sister (Mrs. Dehon), my four grown daughters, my niece and the younger children assembled. Not the slightest symptom of fear or agitation appeared. Several armed men were in the room demanding weapons. "By what authority do you demand arms of women and children?" said my eldest daughter. "By authority, Madam, of the United States," said the officer, apparently a sergeant in command. "I have seen," he added, "many Confederate women, who would as soon shoot a Yankee as eat a dinner." Just then, my husband came in. He had been taken at the gate, to which he had gone to meet the first of this troop, and they had at first spoken of taking him to the general. But, after whispering together for a while, they had told him he must come with them into the house and give up whatever arms were there. He had told them that he had no arms about him, meaning on his person, and they now accused him of lying, when they found there were arms in the house. He repelled the accusation indignantly, but they persisted in it more and more rudely.

When all the weapons of every sort that we had were produced, they took them to the front of the house, and broke the barrels of the guns by striking them on the post of the piazza excepting a very superior double-barreled fowling piece of my nephew's, which the sergeant took a fancy to and carried off. "This is the way," they said, "we do with the arms of rebels."

We were now all assembled in the piazza, ten helpless women and children, my husband standing bare-headed on the steps, his grey hairs, and noble, dignified and fearless mien our only earthly protection. Crowds of soldiers, mostly on horseback, without any order, and apparently under no control came pouring in. One man as he looked up and saw so many girls, said in a tone of peculiarly impertinent inquiry, "Seminary?" "No," said I, "a private house." "Very nice place," said the fellow, "should like to live here myself." "Yes," added another, "very good looking girls too."

An officer, as he rode by, inquired of my husband how many men there were in Camden? "You do not expect me to answer that question, do you?" said my husband. "No," said the officer, "and if you were I should not believe you." "You seem to take me for a Secessionist," said my husband, "and I am neither ashamed nor afraid to say that so I have been and I am. But I am a clergyman, with ten helpless females under my care. I ask a guard for their protection." "You should have thought of <u>that</u>," was the reply, "four years ago," and bidding his men to follow him he rode off, leaving us to the tender mercies of any who might come after him.

As he rode off with most of his squad, one of them lingering a little behind, came up to my husband and presenting his musket, demanded Mr. T's watch. "If you take it," said my husband, "you will be stealing, for I heard your captain just now bid you to go with him." "Say that again," exclaimed the fellow, "and I'll blow your brains out." Whereupon he seized the watch and went off.

Men were now surrounding the house, coming in at the back of it and in front, calling aloud for wine and whiskey. My husband assured them we had no whiskey, as we had not been able to procure any for some time, even as medicine, and that the only wine in the house was for the Holy Communion. One of the officers insisting on our bringing this, we broke and poured out of the window, one of the only two bottles we had, and gave him the other, which he drank the most of and gave the rest to his men. They demanded the key of the cellar saying they didn't believe we had so little and that they would search for themselves. They crowded accordingly into the basement of the house, where we had a pit, in which we used to put ice. They evidently suspected that we had silver there, for they thrust their bayonets down as deep as they could into the sand at the bottom of it, and did in fact come within a few inches of a box containing the chief part of our silver, which as we have learned from our son, he had buried there, under the side of the same pit.

At the same time others in the yard were chasing the pigs, wringing off the necks of the fowls and turning out the cow (which in consequence we lost as also most of our poultry) and doing in short every sort of mischief. It was now near dinner-time. All the morning I had been alternately with the family, witnessing these scenes, or with the sick child, soothing her, and availing myself of the solitude of the chamber to commit them all to the care of Him without whom not a sparrow falleth to the ground. About this time the information of the abundance of liquor next door, began to spread. The inferior officers let the men know that they could get an abundance of it, and with buckets and cans and jugs and tubs they crowded over to the Jews. This gave us a brief respite, and we availed ourselves of it to eat a few mouthfuls of dinner, knowing that we should need all the strength we could get.

We had hardly finished before the current set in again for our house, now more violently than ever. They now clamoured for provisions, coming in at the basement, they dashed right through the windows, shivering not only the panes of glass, but kicking to pieces the sashes, and even the venetian blinds. They evidently were expecting to find in so large a house, an abundant supply, and when on entering the store-room they saw only 4 hams, a ½ barrel of rice, and a couple of barrels of corn, they suspected us of concealing the bulk of our food. Our seampstress remonstrated with them about taking from a clergyman with a large family the little that remained to him. I too reminded them <u>who</u> had said, "If thine enemy hunger, feed him."[43] Some of them seemed abashed, and a young lad said he couldn't bear it as his mother had taught him differently. They took nothing from the store-room, but seeing a barrel of wheat flour in another room, "We'll send the commissary's wagon for this tomorrow," said one of them. We congratulated ourselves that our chief supply of corn (about 75 bushels), which we had put into bins in a room adjoining the stable, was thus far undetected.

A systematic search was now commenced by them for silver and jewelry. Beginning in the lower rooms they now ransacked every sideboard, press, bureau, trunk and drawer. The silver forks and spoons used at dinner, and taken into the pantry to be washed, were soon pocketed. We had asked some of the men for a guard, and we have every reason to believe that the set, who at this time were rifling us, had orders to keep out others, in order that they might carry on their depredations the more methodically and thoroughly, for while they were about this, one or two stationed at the doors, warned off others, and another calling himself a lieutenant, conducted the movements of the rest. They threatened to break open the locks, if the keys were not instantly forthcoming, and one of them, betraying with what practices he was familiar, said, "If I only had a piece of wire, I could open every lock in your house." "I don't doubt it," said my husband, and the man smiled with satisfaction at his recognition of his accomplishment in roguery.

Wherever they went, they were accompanied by my husband and daughters and niece, and sometimes, methought they quailed beneath the steady gaze, the flashing eye, and curling lip of these brave, because innocent and patriotic Southern girls. Thus they saw on the center table

---

[43] Romans 12:20: "If thine enemy hunger, feed him; if he thirst, give him to drink."

in our drawing room two very handsome Bibles in morocco cases richly gilt. These they took up, but laid down again, while the eyes of those in the room were upon them, but when the light was carried out, (it was now night) they whisked off the Bibles, and when we next looked, both books were gone.

As they were going into one of the rooms, "this," said my husband, "is the chamber of one of my daughters." "What of that?" said one of them, "do you think a woman's room is better than any other?" And in they rushed, opening every drawer, tumbling up the dresses, etc. which were in it, and making offensive remarks on them as they threw them on the floor. They did the same in all the chambers. In my sister's room, they insisted upon her opening her desk, from which they took all the Confederate money they found there and some pictures of value. They made my niece open her dressing-case and carried off from it all it contained. "We're only taking this to the quartermaster's," said one of them, as he gathered his spoils into his handkerchief. "You'll have it all back again tomorrow." "You must think us very simple," said my husband. The man smiled, and now Gen. Sherman, we see by the papers, avows that such were his orders.

At length they had gone through all the rooms excepting the one where my sick child was in bed already exceedingly nervous with agitation at what she knew was going on. As the men drew near to the door of that room, my husband remonstrated. But they persisted in their purpose and <u>would</u> go in. As they were about to take up the bed-clothes, he renewed his endeavor to dissuade them. But one of them said, "You can take her up," and the men actually were lifting the covering, when the poor child became violently agitated, and on my husbands exclaiming, "Don't you see how the child is troubled?" as she burst into tears, one of them relented, and said to the others, "Well, let her alone." They went, however, over every other part of that chamber, all round the bed, and peeped under it, and drew out a trunk which was there and opened it. In another trunk they saw a cap of my sons. "Whose is this?" asked one of them. We told him. "Your son's in the artillery," he remarked, "a bullet for him," he added, as he put the cap on his own head.

It was now night: the last room was searched. The ruffians at length were out of the house. The house was quiet; and the sick child slept. I was alone, but as I gazed from my window at the camp-fires so near to us, and knew that hordes of drunken revelers were at that time filling our kitchen and out-houses, my heart sank within me at the thought of the appalling night before us. My young daughters so delicately nurtured, so tenderly cherished! I pleaded with intense earnestness that their Heavenly Father would spread His sheltering wings around them. Descending after a while into the parlour I found them all collected, hovering over a little fire, as we did not dare go out of doors to bring in more fuel, they were talking over the events of the day, when suddenly there was a tramp of footsteps, the doors were thrown open and in rushed several armed men. One who seemed to be in command turning to the others said, "Guards stand at the doors!" They lowered their muskets and obeyed.

My husband was at that moment in another room, soothing the younger children, but he came in on hearing the noise; and all the grown people of our household were thus assembled. The officer inquired if such was the case and on our replying in the affirmative, the fellow threw himself with an insolent air into a chair, saying, "Well, we are Northern vandals, we know you have silver and jewelry. We intend to have it, and if you don't hand it up, we will search your persons and burn your house." Of course, we began immediately to take off our finger-rings, ear-rings and brooches. They insisted that we had other valuables elsewhere, whereupon one of my daughters said, "I have a few coins upstairs." My husband, at my suggestion, remonstrated against her going alone with the soldier, and with difficulty obtained leave to follow her under charge of another of these men. During their absence the remaining one employed himself in lecturing us upon the sin of secession, but was so intoxicated that he had at times to support himself by holding on to the back of a chair.

On the return of those who had gone with my daughter, they demanded who next was ready, and my sister went to her room attended in like manner by one of the banditti, and her valuables left from the previous inspection of her room, were now seized. They then asked my husband if he hadn't any watches. He told them his had been stolen by one of their men a few hours before. "Soldiers don't steal," said the inquirer, "they confiscate. But haven't you any more watches?" On my husband replying that there was an old one, a family watch in his study, the most villainous-looking of the creatures, a young man of peculiarly forbidding countenance and coarse and rude beyond even the others, bade my husband show him the way. He made him open every drawer of his escritoire, from which he took whatever was of the least pecuniary value, among other things a seal. As he took it up, my husband [said], "That was the seal of my grandfather." "Isn't it gold?" was the only inquiry, and on being told that it was, he coolly put it into his pocket. As he was coming out, he said, "You're a clergyman, you tell me. I was once a minister's son, but now I'm a prodigal."

Alas what a history those few words reveal! When this man came back into the room where the rest of us were, they resumed their demands for silver and jewelry. They renewed their threat to search our persons, and as I had on their entrance unclasped a brooch to which I attached peculiar value, I now told them frankly I had it on and would hand it to them as soon as I could find it. They became very impatient and violent, saying we had plenty of jewelry still. The "prodigal" taking the candle from the table said, "Here's the torch," and at the same time taking out his watch and holding it in his hand, he added, "We give you five minutes. Let's have the rest of your jewelry, or we will either search you or burn your house. Now is the day of your salvation."[44]

These last words of blasphemy he uttered with a laugh of scoffing, and a look of fearful audacity, winking to the officer, who professed to be a pious Baptist, and had boasted repeatedly that he was "as good as anybody else." At this crisis we rose in a body, declared that, rather than submit to be searched, we would let the house be burned and with one consent we moved toward the door. They asked "what we were after." "Going for blankets," said my sister, "to protect us from the weather," as it was cold and rainy. This decision seemed to startle them, as they had (according to what we afterwards learned) permission to burn only uninhabited houses. Just then I found the brooch, and as I handed it to one of them, remarked that it was a wedding gift and contained the hair of my father, a Bishop of the Church to which I belonged. He tried to get out the hair, but not succeeding asked, "What are these things?" "Pearls," I said, with which it was set, whereupon he pocketed it.

As we were on our way again towards the door, the "pious Baptist," reeling with liquor, began to assume the part of protector, and said, "They shan't burn your house. They must march over my dead body first," and turning to his associates remarked, "Well they're honest," whereupon he opened one of the doors and they marched out. What a relief to listen to their retreating footsteps! God had indeed proven Himself the "Hearer of Prayer,"[45] and under the shelter of His wings we were protected. They betook themselves to the kitchen where they became so beastly drunk, that profound slumber soon overpowered them all, and thus did the restraining power of God keep us in safety during the long hours of that horrible night! The frightened servant girls ran to us for protection and slept all night in our nursery.

Never shall I forget that night! We separated into two parties, one keeping watch in the parlour, the other in the room of the sick child. The little children, huddled together, wrapt in blankets on the floor, forgot their sorrow in uneasy slumbers. It was raining incessantly, and as our fires burned out and we did not dare to go for more wood, those of us who were in the parlor suffered from cold. The poor children had gone supperless to bed. I would have given anything for a cup of tea or coffee. Of the latter we had a little, but unfortunately the milk curdled, and was not drinkable. Our lights failed, but fortunately we made a discovery of a little flower-trellis. This we broke into small fragments, and the flame we thus kindled gave us a little light and warmth.

---

[44] 2 Corinthians 6:2: "Behold, now is the accepted time; now is the day of salvation."

[45] Psalm 65:2: "O thou that hearest prayer, unto thee shall all flesh come."

Towards morning at my husband's persuasion, while he watched I threw myself on the bed and slept from sheer exhaustion. I awoke at daylight, and hastened to the window. Not a vestige of the enemy was to be seen. But flames rising in different parts of the horizon, shewed how they were employed. Mills, depots and private dwellings were on fire. About breakfast-time kind enquiries from the neighbours with sad, sad accounts of robbery, insult, and drunkenness poured in. How much cause for gratitude! We had been protected from personal violence and injury. Most of our jewelry and silverware had been undiscovered and though our losses were distressing to us, they were nothing compared to those of some others. Our year's supply of corn was as yet untouched. Around our family altar we gathered with thankful hearts, while my husband poured out in fervent prayer our united tribute of praise to Him who had thus far watched over us.

About 9 o'clock, stragglers began to make their appearance in our yard, and as they seemed bent on mischief, asking the servants for that "d——d old rebel" (my husband), we persuaded him to stay in the house. Watching them from my chamber window, we saw them to our dismay break open our corn-room. One of them had a horse, and as he entered the carriage-house and drew out the buggy, we inferred of course, that he intended to carry off the corn. But after trying to put their horse with our harness, we heard them breaking the wheels of the buggy. Leaving it thus rendered useless to us they returned to the corn room and after remaining in it a few moments came out and to our great joy rode off. We advised my husband as soon as they had disappeared to nail up the corn-room that its manifestly unprotected condition might not expose it to robbery. This he did.

And now came our greatest sorrow! I had thrown myself on the bed for a few minutes to rest, when I saw the Irish girl already mentioned enter the room, and looking anxiously at me, whisper something to one of my daughters who started up with an exclamation.[46] I instantly conjectured what had happened. "Theodore has been captured," I said. "Yes," said one of them, "William (the servant who had gone with him) is below and is telling his father all about it."

We all ran downstairs and what a sad sight greeted us. My poor husband! Bravely and nobly had he borne up through all the scenes so torturing to his Southern spirit. But this last was too much. He was weeping bitterly! Bending before him, clasping his knees and sobbing as if his heart would break, sat the poor faithful slave who had just come in.

"Oh, Sir," he said in disjointed words. "I did all I could for Mas Teeah. We wandered about all night in the rain. No one would take us in. About the middle of the night I got Mas Teeah to lie down in an old barn and I

---

[46] Sarah Trapier is referring here to the family's "seampstress." See p. 113.

covered him with both blankets because he was so sick and needed them more than I did. I watched while he slept. The next day we set out again, but lost our way and about 2 o'clock as we were in an empty house, where we had stopped to dry our clothes; just as we were eating a piece of bread, I heard him call out, 'William, the Yankees,' and sure enough five soldiers were coming around the corner. He called to me not to shoot but to give up the arms. Then they took everything from him, blankets, clothes, food, pocket-book, horse, all except the clothes he had on. They did the same to me, taking even to my tooth-brush and comb. I told them how sick Mas Teeah was and begged them to let me go with him, but they wouldn't. An officer took <u>him</u> one way while the men carried me another. And Oh, Sir, they made me drink about a quart of whiskey, and did all they could to make me stay with them. One took me into his buggy, and told me I should do nothing but attend to him, have $10 a month and be free. But I told him I wanted to go home; and so, as soon as I could, I got off, and I've walked 20 miles today, and had to sneak under the house lest they should catch me again."

This was, as well as I can remember it, his sad tale. What a stricken group we were! My husband soon recovered composure sufficient for prayer, and we all knelt down around him, while he poured out our sorrow to Him, whose ears are ever open to unto the prayers of His humble servants, and commended our sick and captive son to His covenant care, entreating Him that he would raise up friends to him and strengthen and sustain him in his feebleness and imprisonment.

We rose comforted, and were just leaving the room when someone ran in crying out, "The stable and corn-room are on fire!" Twas too true! The wretches had concealed in the fodder a slow match, which was doing its work. My husband rushed out followed by all the children. But what could they do! William, still suffering from his intoxication, was the only male, besides my husband on the premises, able to render any aid. Their efforts to extinguish the flames were entirely unsuccessful. The whole pile of buildings was in a few moments one mass of flame. Fences were communicating it to other outbuildings, but with great presence of mind, the female servants under the direction of our daughters, broke these down. Flakes too were falling on the roof of the piazza of our dwelling house. But I stationed a servant girl out of my chamber window with a bucket of water, with which she extinguished the flakes as fast as they fell. The work of destruction was soon over and, ere night closed in, our chief stock of provisions for the rest of the year was a heap of blackened cinders. We remembered the promise of Him who "feedeth the young ravens when they cry."[47] And fully has this promise thus far been fulfilled.

---

[47] Psalm 147:9: "He giveth to the beast his food, and to the young ravens which cry." Sarah Trapier uses the translation given in the Book of Common Prayer, which includes the Psalter, or Psalms of David.

Not a month had elapsed before the sympathy, not of word but of deed, replenished our store-room, if not with abundance, yet with sufficiency. I could fill pages with accounts of the misery which these raiders left in their track. Their treatment of the slaves for whose sake the war was professedly entered into, was atrocious. A gentleman in our neighbourhood assured us that not a female slave on his plantation (with a single exception) was allowed to retain <u>that</u> which should have been dearer to her than her life. This exception, a brave married woman, stood at the door of her house with a log of wood in her hand, and said she would dash out the brains of any man who came near her.

The raiders left Camden on Sunday Feb. 26th, and most devoutly did we pray that we might never see another such set of ruffians. But not two months had passed before another under Gen. Potter (son of the Bishop of Pennsylvania!) was upon us. He brought a large body of negro troops and his special object was to entice away, or carry off by force, our servants. Fortunately a body of our militia were in the town, and another body of our regular army approaching, so that the raiders dared not venture far from their main body nor stay beyond a single night.[48] The next morning, however, numbers of families awoke to find themselves without a single servant, their cooks, chambermaids, washers and men-servants all gone, and many a delicate female, tenderly nurtured and educated in refinement, was obliged to go into the kitchen and betake herself to the wash tub.

But to return to our own family. None of our servants left us. For a month we heard nothing more of Theodore. Our anxiety was intense. At last we learned that he was with Sherman's army, marching rapidly through North Carolina, that the prisoners were on foot and with little to eat. After several more weeks we heard from him from Newberne.[49] What a tale of suffering. Forced marches of from 20 to 30 miles a day, always on foot, the latter part of the journey without shoes or stockings, prisoners' fare, never a word of comfort or sympathy; but if in his feebleness he lagged behind, a threat instead to shorten all his troubles quickly. From day to day and week after week no change of clothing! What wonder that he lived in a kind of stupor until all his sorrows and exposures brought on extreme illness and he was taken to a hospital in Newberne. There they cut off his hair, and plunged him into a cold bath. Then taking away all his clothing, they left him only a blanket to wrap around him, made him walk thus across the yard to a tent where they laid him on a straw mattress, to remain there for four days with no other covering.

---

[48] Potter's troops departed Camden hurriedly after a stay of only one night, due to the threat presented by the home guard in the area, which had been joined by a force of about five hundred Kentucky cavalry troops. Kirkland, Historic Camden, 174.

[49] New Bern, on the North Carolina coast.

There he was found by some benevolent ladies, the spark of life nearly extinct, such treatment having greatly aggravated the disease (dysentery) from which he had long been suffering. The excellent ladies, in the warmth of their true Southern hearts, obtained leave, after great difficulty from the indifference and opposition of those in authority, to take him home and nurse him with the tenderest care. Thus strikingly were our prayers answered! This account we gained little by little at long intervals, as he recovered strength and had opportunities of writing by private conveyances casually occurring; there being at that time no mails even after the surrender of Lee and Johnston's armies, through which Confederates were allowed to communicate with each other. It is not easy to conceive that painfulness of our suspense as months passed by, leaving us still uncertain whether he was dead or alive.

In the meantime public affairs grew darker and darker. Lee's army, it was rumoured, would be obliged to surrender. At first we refused to believe this. But soon accounts reached us of rations being reduced to half a pint of meal a day, and of numbers of men deserting for the protection of their families. Soon after the worst was confirmed. Lee's army surrendered. That of Johnston followed, and we knew that we were a subjugated people. All our sufferings for naught! All our hopes crushed! Everyday by bitter experiences are we made to feel that liberty and independence for us as a people are gone, perhaps forever.

As a family we are nearly ruined. All our business papers were destroyed by Sherman's raiders. Half of our capital, invested in Confederate securities, is gone. The other half, chiefly in Rail Road Bonds, even if recovered, will be almost if not quite valueless, so that the house we live in, with the few acres of land around it, is all we know of that remains to us, except the silver we secreted.[50] But we have one another to love and cling to, willing hands to work, brave hearts to endure, and above all a Heavenly Father to look to, who has promised never to forsake the seed of the righteous. And blessed be God that this is our portion! For truly may I say

> "My boast is not that I deduce my birth
> "From loins enthroned and rulers of the earth
> "But higher far my proud pretensions rise:
> "The child of parents passed into the skies."[51]

---

[50] The family of General James Conner fled to Camden after the evacuation of Charleston, and while there in March 1865, his sister wrote that "Camden has suffered terribly . . . Poor Mr. Trapier and his family were insulted, and lost everything." Mary Conner Moffett, ed., Letters of General James Conner, C.S.A. (Columbia, S.C.: R. L. Bryan Co., 1950), 161-162.

[51] Lines from a poem entitled "On the Receipt of His Mother's Picture Out of Norfolk," by the English poet and hymnodist William Cowper (1731-1800).

SHERMAN AT CHERAW

LARRY E. NELSON*

"THE REGION OF COUNTRY HEREABOUT IS NOT OF MUCH VALUE
to the enemy, either in a military or commercial point of view," wrote
Brigadier General John H. Trapier from his headquarters at Georgetown,
South Carolina, in the fall of 1863.[1] The Confederate commander was
speaking specifically of the port at the mouth of the Great Pee Dee River and
the adjacent seacoast, but his generalization applied to the entire Pee Dee
region of South Carolina. For most of the Civil War, the Pee Dee flowed
unmolested from its origin at the confluence of the Yadkin River and the
Uwharrie River in North Carolina along a southeasterly course through
northeastern South Carolina until reaching the coast at Winyah Bay. The
comparative tranquility of the region came to an abrupt end during the last
few months of the war when the arrival of Sherman's army at Cheraw
dramatically changed strategic imperatives all along the Pee Dee River.

Throughout the Civil War, the principal military developments in the
Pee Dee region and along the nearby seaboard were interrelated. The direct
impact of the war fell first upon Georgetown and the coastal area at the
mouth of the river where the Confederacy undertook defensive measures
and where the routine of the Federal blockade soon began. The military
situation at Georgetown contributed to the decision to locate a Confederate
navy yard at Mars Bluff, about 100 miles upriver, where the C.S.S. *Pedee* was
constructed. The apparent seclusion of the region from military events
encouraged the establishment in 1864 of a prisoner of war camp at Florence,
a few miles upstream from Mars Bluff. The port at Georgetown, the navy
yard at Mars Bluff, and the internment camp at Florence attracted minimal
Federal attention until early 1865 when Sherman's army began moving
toward Cheraw, located on the Pee Dee just below the North Carolina
border 170 miles above the river's mouth.[2] Sherman's advance changed
everything. The Union navy moved against Georgetown; the commandant
of the prison at Florence became anxious to move the prisoners out of
Sherman's path; and the C.S.S. *Pedee* undertook its only combat assignment

---

*Larry E. Nelson is professor of history at Francis Marion University.

[1] J. H. Trapier to T. Jordan, November 23, 1863, *The War of the Rebellion: A
Compilation of the Official Records of the Union and Confederate Armies* (Washington:
U.S. Government Printing Office, 1880-1901), Ser. I, Vol. XXVIII, Pt. II, 521, hereafter
cited as *ORA*.

[2] For mileage along the Pee Dee River, see House Committee on Rivers and
Harbors, *Examination and Survey of Great Pedee River, South Carolina*, 56th Cong., 2nd
Sess., 1900, House Document No. 124, 3, 5.

of the Civil War. The central events of Sherman's march through the Pee Dee region were the clash of Federal and Confederate forces at Cheraw and vicinity, the hurried withdrawal of the Confederates across the Pee Dee River, and the occupation of Cheraw while the Federals bridged and crossed the Pee Dee.

Georgetown, centrally located in the rice growing region of South Carolina, was a minor port with a peacetime population of about 1,500. Although ships of the Federal blockading fleet patrolled the seas off Georgetown and although blockade runners sometimes made daring runs in and out of the port, Georgetown was not well suited to the wartime needs of the Confederacy. The main ship channel at the entrance of Winyah Bay was only eleven and one-half feet deep at normal high tide, significantly restricting the size of vessels that could enter. Transportation above the port was difficult because Georgetown had no direct railroad connection and sharp bends in the lower Pee Dee generally prevented ocean going ships from passing upriver. Cargoes arriving in Georgetown for shipment into the interior usually traveled up the Pee Dee in smaller boats to the Wilmington and Manchester Railroad bridge at Mars Bluff.[3]

For most of the war, Georgetown was poorly defended. In late 1861 engineers established shore batteries on islands near the entrance to Winyah Bay to repel invaders and to protect blockade runners using the port at Georgetown, but requirements for troops and for coastal artillery elsewhere in the Confederacy forced abandonment of these defenses in the spring of 1862. The Union navy soon discovered the lack of defenses in the lower bay and dominated the entrance for the remainder of the war. To command upper Winyah Bay, the Confederates constructed Battery White. Although never quite completed, the battery was well designed, admirably located, and eventually equipped with sufficient artillery to make it formidable, but the size of the garrison was inadequate. General Trapier, who had responsibility for the defense of Georgetown and the adjacent coastline, complained repeatedly that his resources were insufficient and warned that he could not repel a determined assault by even a modest enemy force. Neglecting Georgetown, the Confederacy concentrated scarce resources on the defenses at Wilmington, about 100 miles to the north, and at Charleston, about sixty miles to the south.[4]

[3]Charles Joyner, *Down by the Riverside* (Urbana: University of Illinois Press, 1984), 9-13; George C. Rogers, Jr., *History of Georgetown County, South Carolina* (Columbia: University of South Carolina Press, 1970), 393, 394; J. H. Trapier to T. Jordan, November 23, 1863, ORA, Ser. I, Vol. XXVIII, Pt. II, 521.

[4]Rogers, *Georgetown County*, 394-400; J. H. Trapier to T. Jordan, November 23, 1863, *ORA*, Ser. I, Vol. XXVIII, Pt. II, 521; J. A. Dahlgren to Gideon Welles, February 28, 1865, *Official Records of the Union and Confederate Navies in the War of the Rebellion* (Washington: U. S. Government Printing Office, 1894-1927), Ser. I, Vol. XVI, 273,

When the Department of the Navy at Richmond became interested in building a gunboat on the Pee Dee, the easy access of the Federal navy to Georgetown led to the decision to establish the navy yard upriver at Mars Bluff. The site was well above Georgetown and defended by artillery originally emplaced to protect the railroad bridge. Another advantage of the location was that construction materials could reach the navy yard by rail. Construction of the C.S.S. *Pedee* began in 1863, and after delays in acquiring machinery, the vessel was ready for service by early 1865. A wooden, screw gunboat, the Pedee measured 170 feet in length and twenty-six feet at the beam, drew ten feet of water, and carried a battery of five guns. Somewhat underpowered, the vessel was capable of nine knots under steam. Lieutenant Oscar F. Johnston was the commanding officer with a crew of some ninety sailors.[5] One of the officers, who served in the Confederate navy from the beginning of the war, later said that the *Pedee* was "the best wooden ship built by the Confederacy" he ever saw.[6]

The naval construction on the Pee Dee River attracted the attention of Rear Admiral John A. Dahlgren, commander of the South Atlantic Blockading Squadron. He ordered a reconnaissance of Confederate defenses at the mouth of the Pee Dee, and he obtained intelligence from a Unionist who fled to the protection of the Union navy from the region near Mars Bluff. After careful consideration, Dahlgren suggested to Gideon Welles, United States Secretary of the Navy, an audacious mission involving Union land and naval forces. Dahlgren proposed to seize Battery White, occupy Georgetown, and ascend quickly the Pee Dee River. If successful, the benefits of the operation would include destruction of the gunboat and the nearby railroad bridge. Nothing came of the proposal, but Dahlgren ordered ships blockading the entrance to Winyah Bay to take position in the channel and prevent the gunboat from escaping out to sea.[7]

Another reason for Dahlgren's proposed expedition up the Pee Dee was to reconnoiter the prisoner of war stockade at Florence. Although situated

hereafter cited as *ORN*; J. H. Trapier to T. Jordan, November 23, 1863, *ORA*, Ser. I, Vol. XXVIII, Pt. II, 521-22; J. H. Trapier to G. T. Beauregard, February 17, 1864, ibid., Vol. XXXV, Pt. I, 617-18.

[5]Rogers, *Georgetown County*, 406; William N. Still, "Facilities for the Construction of War Vessels in the Confederacy," *Journal of Southern History*, XXXI (August 1965), 291; S. R. Mallory to W. G. Dozier, December 16, 1862, *ORN*, Ser. I, Vol. XIII, 817-18; J. H. Trapier to T. Jordan, January 26, 1864, *ORA*, Ser. I, Vol. XXXV, Pt. I, 546; S. R. Mallory, Report of Operations, April 30, 1864, *ORN.*, Ser. II, Vol. II, 630, 638; S. R. Mallory, Report of Operations, November 30, 1864, ibid., 532; S. R. Mallory, Report of Operations, November 5, 1864, ibid., 746, 751.

[6]W. F. Clayton, *A Narrative of the Confederate States Navy* (Weldon: Harrell's Printing House, 1910), 106, 114.

[7]J. A. Dahlgren to G. Welles, *ORN*, Ser. I, Vol. XVI, 39-40; J A. Dahlgren to N. B. Harrison, October 29, 1864, ibid., 36.

near the Pee Dee, Florence was not a river town; it was a railroad town. Described by an unfriendly observer as a "railroad eating-house with sleeping-rooms attached," Florence was at the major railroad junction in the Pee Dee region. The Wilmington and Manchester Railroad passed through the town on an east-west axis while the Northeastern Railroad traversed the north-south axis from Charleston to Florence and the Cheraw and Darlington Railroad continued northward to Cheraw. Along the wide main street which fronted on the railroad tracks, the principal building was the two-story Gambel Hotel which catered to the needs of railway passengers. Behind the street in the piney woods were the twenty-five or thirty houses of the residents.[8]

The prison stockade, which was about one and one-half miles east of the town, came into existence during September 1864, shortly after Sherman's army took possession of Atlanta. Fearful that Sherman's troops would reach Union prisoners held at Andersonville, Confederate authorities began moving the prisoners to improvised facilities in Charleston and Savannah. Major General Samuel Jones, the commanding officer in Charleston, was anxious to get the prisoners out of the city and into a more secure location in the interior. He ordered the establishment of a prison camp at Florence and began sending prisoners from Charleston via the Northeastern Railroad even before the prison in Florence was ready. The Florence Stockade, over the several months of its operation, enclosed thousands of captive Union soldiers in remarkable squalor.[9]

Major General William T. Sherman and his army were in Savannah for Christmas 1864, and he moved his forces into South Carolina in January 1865. As Sherman prepared for the march through the Carolinas, he asked the Federal navy to stand ready to offer assistance at the seacoast. He specifically requested that Dahlgren secure the mouth of the Pee Dee River at Georgetown.[10] The march was well underway by late January. The army,

[8]Sidney Andrews, *The South Since the War* (Boston: Ticknor and Fields, 1866), 191-92. A Confederate veteran who passed through Florence on a troop train in 1863 remembered Florence "as a pretty little town in the piney woods." See John Coxe, "Chickamauga," *Confederate Veteran*, XXX (August 1922), 291.

[9]S. Jones to J. A. Seddon, September 12, 1864, *ORA*, Ser. II, Vol. VII, 817; William B. Hesseltine, *Civil War Prisons* (Columbus: Ohio State University Press, 1930), 155, 167-68. For a history of the Florence Stockade, see G. Wayne King, "Death Camp at Florence," *Civil War Times Illustrated*, XII (January 1974), 35-42.

[10]W. T. Sherman to J. G. Foster, January 19, 1865, *ORA*, Ser. I, Vol. XLVII, Pt. II, 97; J. A. Dahlgren, Diary, *ORN*, Ser. I, Vol. XVI, 364-65; L. C. Easton, Report, July 22, 1865, *ORA*, Ser. I, Vol. LIII, 46. The two most important monographs on Sherman's army in the Carolinas are John G. Barrett, *Sherman's March through the Carolinas*, (Chapel Hill: University of North Carolina Press, 1956), and Joseph T. Glatthaar, *March to the Sea and Beyond* (New York: New York University Press, 1985).

making its way through the swamps and across flooded streams enroute to Columbia, encountered no serious opposition from the badly scattered Confederate forces. During the advance, Sherman purposely bypassed Charleston, isolating the city and its garrison of 11,000 men commanded by Lieutenant General William J. Hardee. Under orders from General P. G. T. Beauregard and after consulting directly with President Jefferson Davis, Hardee regretfully and belatedly abandoned Charleston during the night of February 17 and the early morning of February 18.[11] Two days later and about 100 miles to the north, Sherman's triumphant army of 60,000 began its departure from the smoldering ruins of Columbia. Although neither commander knew the precise destination of the other, Hardee and Sherman were, in fact, engaged in a race for the covered wooden bridge over the Pee Dee River at Cheraw.

Situated in a plantation district, Cheraw stood on the right bank of the Pee Dee at the head of navigation. The bridge across the river and the railroad along the right bank enhanced the commercial significance of the town. Cotton and forest products passed through Cheraw down river to the coast and thence to world markets, and goods came upriver from coastal ports for transshipment by wagon into the interior. Along the broad streets of the town were churches, academies, a bank of regional significance, and comfortable homes. The population in the late winter of 1865, variously estimated at 2,000 to 4,000, included refugees from the low country seeking to escape the dangers of military activity along the seaboard.

Cheraw was overflowing with personal property and military supplies. The town was the remotest point in South Carolina accessible by railroad from the coast, and residents of the low country, hoping to store their belongings away from the ravages of war, sent personal valuables and household furnishings to Cheraw. At the same time, considerable quantities of cotton had accumulated in the town because of the blockade at the seacoast. Also arriving in Cheraw were arms, ammunition, and commissary stores of the Confederate government.[12]

Hardee's column traveled a route of 150 miles from Charleston through Moncks Corner, Kingstree, and Florence to Cheraw. Hardee's strategic

[11]Davis to W. J. Hardee, February 14, 1865, *ORA*, Ser. I, Vol. XLVII, Pt. II, 1181; G. T. Beauregard to R. E. Lee, February 16, 1865, ibid., 1202; W. J. Hardee to S. Cooper, February 19, 1865, ibid., Pt. I, 1071; J. E. Johnston to R. E. Lee, February 23, 1865, ibid., Pt. II, 1257.

[12]George W. Nichols, *Story of the Great March* (New York: Harper & Brothers, 1865), 200, 202; J. Fitzpatrick, Report, March 31, 1865, *ORA*, Ser. I, Vol. XLVII, Pt. I, 723; Oscar L. Jackson, *Colonel's Diary* ([Pa.?]: Sharon, n.p., 1922), 190; David P. Conyngham, *Sherman's March through the South* (New York: Sheldon and Co., 1865), 351; Elijah P. Burton, *Diary of E. P. Burton* (Des Moines: The Historical Records Survey, 1939), 67.

objective was to join the Confederate forces which Beauregard was concentrating to oppose Sherman's army. A primary tactical objective for Hardee was to delay the Federal advance by disputing the crossing of the Pee Dee River as long as possible without endangering his own force. Although the railway facilitated the movement, mismanagement by railroaders and the wretched condition of the railroad caused long delays, and the available rolling stock was not adequate to transport the entire force and its equipment.[13] Much of Hardee's column moved slowly over roads turned into quagmires by incessant rains. Flooding on the rivers added to the problems. "Another cause of delay and embarrassment," complained Hardee, "arises from a heavy rise in the Great Pedee and its tributaries, which has carried away some important bridges on the route, thus causing the wagons and artillery to go much out of the way."[14] The head of the column reached Cheraw on February 25 when the rear was still in the low country crossing the Santee River.[15]

Lacking cavalry, Hardee sent scouts, selected from among staff officers and infantrymen at Cheraw, to determine the whereabouts and, if possible, the intentions of the enemy. While pondering fragmentary reports of Federal movements and wondering if Sherman intended to strike the Pee Dee River below Cheraw at Florence, Hardee hastily made preparations to defend Cheraw and the bridge over the Pee Dee River, at least until the remainder of his column arrived. One of the most likely approaches to Cheraw for the Federals was the Chesterfield road which entered Cheraw from the northwest. Chesterfield, a hamlet consisting of a few houses and the district courthouse, was situated about twelve miles from Cheraw.

---

[13]G. T. Beauregard to L. McLaws, February 18, 1865, *ORA*, Ser. I, Vol. XLVII, Pt. II, 1217-18; G. T. Beauregard to W. J. Hardee, February 26, 1865, ibid., 1281; G. T. Beauregard to W. Hampton, March 1, 1865, ibid., 1300-01; Lafayette McLaws, Order Book, 1865, 7-8, Lafayette McLaws Papers, Southern Historical Collection, University of North Carolina, Chapel Hill; Robert W. Sanders, "A Long Hard March," *Confederate Veteran*, XXXIII (July 1925), 255; William W. Henry, *Kid Soldiers of the Sixties* (n.p.: n.p., 1915), 9-10, South Caroliniana Library, University of South Carolina; W. J. Hardee to J. E. Johnston, February 28, 1865, *ORA*, Ser. I, Vol. XLVII, Pt. I, 1072-73. General Joseph E. Johnston relieved Beauregard on February 25, 1865, assuming command of the Army of Tennessee and all troops in the Department of South Carolina, Georgia, and Florida.

[14]W. J. Hardee to G. T. Beauregard, February 26, 1865, *ORA*, Ser. I, Vol. XLVII, Pt. I, 1072. Heavy rains and consequent flooding during February and March are not unusual in the Pee Dee basin. See, House Committee on Rivers and Harbors, *Yadkin-Pee Dee River, N.C. and S.C.*, 73rd Cong., 1st Sess., 1933, House Document No. 68, 31, 91.

[15]McLaws, Order Book, 1865, 8; A. Schimmelfennig to W. L. M. Burger, February 25, 1865, *ORA*, Ser. I, Vol. XLVII, Pt. II, 575.

Another obvious approach was the Camden road which entered Cheraw from the southwest. Both the Camden road and the Chesterfield road crossed Thompson's Creek that originated north of Chesterfield and flowed in a southeasterly direction behind Chesterfield and in front of Cheraw before emptying into the Pee Dee River south of Cheraw.[16]

When configuring the defenses of Cheraw, Hardee took advantage of the natural perimeter provided by Thompson's Creek, a substantial stream that in places was several feet deep and forty yards wide. About ten miles from Cheraw at the bridge on the Chesterfield road, Colonel John C. Fiser's brigade of Georgia infantry with a battery of light artillery entrenched on the left bank of the creek. Some four miles from Cheraw at the bridge on the Camden road, infantrymen constructed an extensive line of strong earthworks at a well chosen site on the right bank of the creek. They also established an advanced position about two miles farther down the road to protect an important cross roads. Only a brigade held the positions on the Camden road at first, but as more troops became available, Hardee increased the size of the defending force.[17] He also made plans for burning the Pee Dee River bridge following the inevitable withdrawal of his corps across the river, but he did not make preparations for positioning troops on the left bank to contest Federal efforts to bridge and cross the stream.

The Federal army began leaving Columbia on February 20, and Sherman's orders were to move on Fayetteville, North Carolina, by way of Cheraw. The important crossing of the Pee Dee at Cheraw was 100 miles northeast of Columbia. With the cavalry on the left and in the front, the Left Wing (Twentieth Corps and Fourteenth Corps) and the Right Wing (Seventeenth Corps and Fifteenth Corps) marched along rain soaked roads

---

[16]W. J. Hardee to G. T. Beauregard, February 26, 1865, ibid., 1282; McLaws, Order Book, 1865, 8-12; W. J. Hardee, "Memoranda of the Operations of my Corps," in Joseph E. Johnston, *Narrative of Military Operations* (N ew York: D. Appleton and Company, 1874), 581; Conyngham, *Sherman's March*, 351; James A. Padgett (ed.), "With Sherman Through Georgia and the Carolinas: Letters of a Federal Soldier," *Georgia Historical Quarterly*, XXXIII (March 1949), 73; U. S. Department of War, *Atlas to Accompany the Official Records of the Union and Confederate Armies* (Washington: Government Printing Office, 1891-1895), Plate LXXX.

[17]J. G. Mitchell, Report, March 30, 1865, *ORA*, Ser. I, Vol. XLVII, Pt. I, 510; F. P. Blair, Report, April 1, 1865, ibid., 381; Matthew C. Butler, "Comrades, Ladies, and Gentlemen," July 27, 1899, *Confederate Veteran*, VIII (January 1900), 32; O. O. Howard to W. T. Sherman, March 3, 1865, *ORA*, Ser. I, Vol. XLVII, Pt. II, 661; M. C. Garber, Report, July 10, 1865, ibid., Vol. LIII, 54; D. H. Poole, Special Orders, February 27, 1865, ibid., Vol. XLVII, Pt. II, 1284; J. C. Rogers, Report, March 28, 1865, ibid., Pt. I, 621; Thomas W. Osborn, *Fiery Trail* (Knoxville: University of Tennessee Press, 1986), 162; McLaws, Order Book, 1865, 13-17; F. P. Blair, Report, April 1, 1865, *ORA*, Ser. I, Vol. XLVII, Pt. I, 381.

and crossed over flooded rivers in the upper Santee River basin. Confederate cavalry skirmished frequently with Union cavalry and infantry while reporting uncertainty about the route and destination of the Federal army. Muddy roads and swollen streams were a far greater impediment to the advancing Federals than was the Confederate cavalry. Delayed at the crossing of the Catawba River due to flooding, the Fourteenth Corps, with the all important pontoon train for the Left Wing, fell several days behind the rest of the army. Sherman learned during the march that a Confederate force was gathering at Cheraw, but reports on the size and leadership of that force were contradictory. In any case, Sherman knew that his army was vastly superior to any which the Confederates could muster at Cheraw.[18]

About the time Sherman's army departed Columbia, a flotilla dispatched by Admiral Dahlgren sailed into Winyah Bay with intentions of subduing Battery White and seizing Georgetown. The port had at last become important to Union purposes. Upon the approach of the Federal ships, the tiny garrison of Battery White spiked the guns and fled. Suspecting that the defenders had abandoned their position, Commander J. Blakeley Creighton of the U.S.S. *Mingoe* approached cautiously, shelled the battery but received no counter fire, and sent ashore a landing party which occupied the fort. Federal forces proceeded past the silent battery and took possession of the town, encountering only brief resistance from a small squad of Confederate horsemen. City officials formally surrendered Georgetown February 25, 1865. The sole reason the Federal navy finally seized the port at the mouth of the Pee Dee River was to open the possibility of communication with Sherman in the event he required it.[19]

Admiral Dahlgren paid a brief visit to Georgetown soon after its capture, and the waters of Winyah Bay held one more terror for him as he departed. Steaming down the bay, his flagship, U.S.S. *Harvest Moon*, struck an undetected Confederate torpedo. The admiral described the sequence of events:

---

[18]W. T. Sherman, Special Field Orders, No. 26, ibid., Pt. II, 445; C. R. Woods to M. Woodhull, February 26, 1865, ibid., 584; A. M. Van Dyke to F. P. Blair, February 27, 1865, ibid., 598; F. P. Blair to A. M. Van Dyke, February 28, 1865, ibid., 611-12; O. O. Howard to W. T. Sherman, February 28, 1865, ibid., 608.

[19]J. A. Dahlgren to Gideon Welles, February 28, 1865, *ORN*, Ser. I, Vol. XVI, 273; J. B. Creighton to J. A. Dahlgren, February 24, 1865, ibid., 276; H. S. Stellwagen to J. A. Dahlgren, February 24, 1865, ibid., 275-76; A. K. Noyes to J. A. Dahlgren, February 25, 1865, ibid., 276-77; R. O. Bush, G. F. B. Leighton, *et al.* to J. A. Dahlgren, February 25, 1865, ibid., 275; J. A. Dahlgren to H. S. Stellwagen, February 28, 1865, ibid., 279.

Admiral Dahlgren's flagship, U.S.S. *Harvest Moon*, struck a mine in Winyah Bay shortly after the capture of Georgetown. This illustration appeared in the *Official Records of the Union and Confederate Navies in the War of the Rebellion.*

> I was waiting breakfast in the cabin, when instantly a loud noise and shock occurred, and the bulkhead separating the cabin from the wardroom was shattered and driven in toward me. A variety of articles lying about me were dispersed in different directions. My first impression was that the boiler had burst. . . . The smell of gunpowder quickly followed and gave the idea that the magazine had exploded.

In a masterpiece of understatement, he added, "There was naturally some little confusion, for it was evident that the vessel was sinking."[20] Within five minutes the ship sank in two and one-half fathoms of water. Dahlgren and all of the officers and crew, save one, managed to escape with their lives.[21]

About 125 miles northwest of Georgetown, Sherman's troops entered the Pee Dee drainage basin toward the end of February, and the first formidable stream they encountered was Lynch's River. Some crossings on this tributary to the Pee Dee River were swollen to three-quarters of a mile, which caused delays. Major General Frank P. Blair managed to get his Seventeenth Corps across Lynch's River well ahead of the rest of the army.

[20]J. A. Dahlgren to G. Welles, March 1, 1865, ibid., 283.
[21]Abstract of Log, U. S. S. *Harvest Moon*, March 1, 1865, ibid.

Moving on the Camden road, he was within thirteen miles of Cheraw by February 28. The Twentieth Corps crossed Lynch's River on March 1 and the next day advanced toward Chesterfield.[22]

Joining Hardee in Cheraw was Major General Matthew C. Butler and his cavalry division that had shadowed the Federal army during the march from Columbia. Under orders from Hardee, Butler posted pickets along Thompson's Creek and went with Major General Pierce M. B. Young's brigade of cavalry to Chesterfield. With the infantry and artillery a mile or two behind Chesterfield on the left bank of Thompson's Creek defending the bridge, Butler moved about two miles in front of Chesterfield where he deployed a strong line of dismounted cavalry behind a breastwork of fence rails.[23]

As both wings of Sherman's army converged in the vicinity of Cheraw, events moved rapidly. On the afternoon of February 28, mounted infantry from the Seventeenth Corps prodded the Confederate defenses on the Camden road. Two days later, skirmishers drove the Southerners from their advanced position, but Blair remained entrenched and waited while the Fifteenth Corps struggled across Lynch's River and moved within supporting distance. During the afternoon of March 2, the lead brigade of the Twentieth Corps, moving on the road from Lynch's River toward Chesterfield, came under sharp fire from the Confederate breastworks outside the town. Two infantry regiments, supported by the rest of the brigade and by artillery, deployed as skirmishers and advanced. A running fight ensued as the Federals drove the Confederates from their breastworks through the town to Thompson's Creek. Partially burning the bridge, the retreating cavalry joined the infantry and artillery already entrenched behind the stream. A brief artillery duel developed, and sharpshooters on both banks continued firing until evening when the Federals posted pickets and fell back about one-quarter mile with intentions of forcing a crossing on the following morning.[24]

[22]O. O. Howard to W. T. Sherman, March 2, 1865, *ORA*, Ser. I, Vol. XLVII, Pt. II, 644; J. A. Logan to A. M. Van Dyke, February 26, 1865, ibid., 583; W. T. Sherman to H. W. Slocum, March 3, 1865, ibid., 667; F. P. Blair, Report, April 1, 1865, ibid., Pt. I, 381; A. M. Van Dyke to F. P. Blair, March 1, 1865, ibid., Pt. II, 632; W. T. Sherman to O. O. Howard, March 1, 1865, ibid., 628.

[23]M. C. Butler to W. J. Hardee, February 27, 1865, ibid., 1288; F. P. Blair to A. M. Van Dyke, February 28, 1865, ibid., 611-12; Butler, "Comrades," 32; N. J. Jackson, Report, March 29, 1865, *ORA*, Ser. I, Vol. XLVII, Pt. I, 599.

[24]F. P. Blair to A. M. Van Dyke, February 28, 1865, ibid., Pt. II, 612; J. E. Johnston to R. E. Lee, March 2, 1865, ibid., Pt. I, 1052; McLaws, Order Book, 1865, 13-15, 17-18; F. P. Blair, Report, April 1, 1865, *ORA*, Ser. I, Vol. XLVII, Pt. I, 381; Butler, "Comrades," 32; Padgett (ed.), "With Sherman," 73; J. L. Selfridge, Report, March 28, 1865, *ORA*, Ser. I, Vol. XLVII, Pt I, 610-11; N. J. Jackson, Report, March 29, 1865, ibid., 599; A. S.

With the Twentieth Corps poised to overrun the Confederate position on the Chesterfield road and with the Seventeenth Corps positioned to assault the defenses on the Camden road, Hardee held a council of war on the evening of March 2 with his ranking subordinates, including Butler who had just returned from Chesterfield. Virtually all of the Confederate column had reached Cheraw from the south, and after discussion, Hardee rightly concluded that the only viable option was withdrawal. He ordered the artillery and supply trains to begin moving as soon as possible to the left bank of the Pee Dee. The troops guarding the Chesterfield road were to withdraw four miles, but the infantry in Cheraw and those on the Camden road were to retire and follow the trains across the Pee Dee. With tar and pitch, readily available from the nearby forest industry, engineer troops prepared the bridge over the Pee Dee for burning. Hardee had no choice but to abandon most of the supplies in Cheraw. Even if his supply trains had been in excellent condition, which they were not, he did not have enough wagons to transport the immense quantity of material which had reached the town by river and rail. He also determined to leave behind several hundred ill and wounded soldiers with their attending surgeons. Through the night of March 2 and the early morning of March 3, thousands of soldiers and their trains moved across the bridge to the left bank of the Pee Dee. As the sun rose, the evacuation was virtually complete.

Butler and his command, assigned as the rear guard, remained on the right bank. The brigade of infantry and the brigade of cavalry were still on the Chesterfield road, and cavalrymen lightly defended the position on the right bank of Thompson's Creek on the Camden road. The orders from Hardee to Butler were to hold the bridge on the Camden road until mid-morning in the expectation that additional cavalry might arrive from Florence. Finally, Butler was to set fire to the Camden road bridge which had been prepared with rosin, torch the abandoned stores in Cheraw, withdraw across the Pee Dee River, and burn the coveted river bridge.[25]

Unaware of the Confederate retreat, Sherman weighed the possibilities from his headquarters at Chesterfield. He was now convinced that the enemy force at Cheraw consisted only of the garrison from Charleston commanded by Hardee. Sherman was eager to attack Cheraw before the Southerners could further strengthen their positions, but he was not

Williams, Report, March 31, 1865, ibid., 584; J. B. Stephens, Report, March 25, 1865, ibid., 854; J. C. Rogers, Report, March 28, 1865, ibid., 621-22; W. Merrell, Report, March 26, 1865, ibid., 629.

    [25]McLaws, Order Book, 1865, 18-19; Butler, "Comrades," 32; Burton, *Diary*, 67; W. J. Hardee to J. E. Johnston, *ORA*, Ser. I, Vol. XLVII, Pt. II, 1320; W. T. Sherman to H. W. Slocum, March 5, 1865, ibid., 691; F. J. Hurlbut, Report, April 7, 1865, ibid., Pt. I, 363; Conyngham, *Sherman's March*, 351.

particularly apprehensive about Southern resistance in the town because he believed Hardee had neither the means nor the intention to mount a substantial defense. Sherman's greater concern was that the Confederates would hold fortified positions on the left bank contesting Federal efforts to cross the Pee Dee which was several hundred feet wide and too deep to ford at Cheraw. "We may," he mused, "have to cross the Pedee with a serious enemy in front."[26] As he recognized, a comparatively small force, well handled, could significantly harass and delay the Federal crossing.[27] "Let us get across the Pedee at all hazards as soon as possible," he concluded.[28] "Once across the Pedee, I don't fear the whole Confederate Army, for if need be we can swing in against the right bank of Cape Fear [River] and work down till we meet our people."[29] Desiring to avoid the need to lay pontoons but recognizing that the retreating enemy might destroy the Pee Dee bridge, Sherman said, "I hardly hope to save the bridge across the Pedee at Cheraw, but it is worth the effort."[30] "I want the Right Wing to move straight on Cheraw," he ordered, "and secure if possible the bridge across the Pedee."[31]

The Federal troops began their assault on the morning of March 3, not knowing that the Confederate retreat was underway. Fording Thompson's Creek well upstream and without opposition, a brigade of the Twentieth Corps flanked the Confederate defenses at the bridge on the Chesterfield road. The flankers moved down the left bank only to discover that the Southerners had quietly abandoned their position during the night. A division of the Twentieth Corps started across the stream and began cautiously moving along the Chesterfield road toward Cheraw. The Confederate infantry, Fiser's brigade of Georgians, had withdrawn first, followed by Young's cavalry brigade. Fiser's brigade was on the Chesterfield road within a few miles of Cheraw at daybreak.[32]

On the Camden road, the Seventeenth Corps began its advance with Major General Joseph A. Mower, a particularly aggressive officer,

---

[26]W. T. Sherman to O. O. Howard, March 1, 1865, *ORA*, Ser. I, Vol. XLVII, Pt. II, 628.

[27]William T. Sherman, *Memoirs* (New York: D. Appleton and Company, 1875), II, 271; William T. Sherman to Pleasant A. Stoval, October 21, 1888, *Confederate Veteran*, XXII (August 1914), 369.

[28]W. T. Sherman to H. W. Slocum, March 3, 1865, *ORA*, Ser. I, Vol. XLVII, Pt. II, 668

[29]W. T. Sherman to O. O. Howard, March 3, 1865, ibid., 661, 662.

[30]W. T. Sherman to F. P. Blair, March 3, 1865, ibid., 666.

[31]W. T. Sherman to F. P. Blair, March 1, 1865, ibid., 631.

[32]J. S. Robinson, Report, March 27, 1865, ibid., Pt. I, 663; N. J. Jackson, Report, March 29, 1865, ibid., 599; J. C. Rogers, Report, March 28, 1865, ibid., 622; A. S. Williams, Report, March 31, 1865, ibid., 584; W. H. Andrews, *Footprints of a Regiment* (Atlanta: Longstreet Press, 1992), 166.

commanding the lead division. In the expectation that the Confederates would burn the existing bridge over Thompson's Creek, the First Regiment Michigan Engineers followed Mower's division to bridge the stream once both banks were under Union control. The skirmish line moved forward anticipating stiff resistance at the earthworks on the right bank of the creek but encountered only light opposition from Butler's withdrawing cavalry. The Southerners set fire to the bridge, but the rapidly moving Federal infantry stamped out the flames and saved the structure. Securing the bridge was a significant turn of events in favor of the advancing Union troops. With the bridge intact, large numbers of infantrymen and supporting artillery moved over Thompson's Creek without delay. Although offering resistance, Butler's cavalry withdrew in haste, and the Federal troops pressed the attack in the new found hope that Hardee's entire corps was in retreat. As the Federal soldiers pushed to the outskirts of Cheraw, the Confederate defenders from Chesterfield arrived in time to join in the rear guard effort. Fiser's Georgians fought a brief but sharp delaying action at the edge of Cheraw while Young's cavalry dashed along the Chesterfield road into Cheraw. Even so, forty-six men were cut off but managed to escape and finally forded the Pee Dee several miles upriver.[33]

Skirmishing heavily, Mower's division entered the town and pushed for the bridge over the Pee Dee. The fighting was house to house in places. A Georgia infantryman recalled: "We had a running fight through the town. The screams of the women and children, the report of the rifles, and the familiar zip of the minie balls made it a scene not to be forgotten soon."[34] To slow Federal progress, Butler deployed his force across the wide streets while withdrawing toward the river. Union artillery opened fire on the hard pressed Confederates who were without cannon.[35] Regarding the effectiveness of the Federal artillery, Edward Wells, one of Butler's cavalrymen, reported: "My horse was killed under me by a cannon ball in one of the streets, the shot passing through him from side to side. I was not at all hurt, my leg only slightly jarred, & splashed with blood from my horse, & my sabre slightly bent by being struck by the ball, as it passed out of the

[33]F. P. Blair, Report, April 1, 1865, ibid., 381; O. O. Howard, Report, April 1, 1865, ibid., 202; Butler, "Comrades," 32; Andrews, *Footrpints*, 166; W. J. Hardee to J. E. Johnston, March 4, 1865, *ORA*, Ser. I, Vol. XLVII, Pt. II, 1320; C. Cadle, Special Orders No. 56, March 2, 1865, ibid., 650; McLaws, Order Book, 1865, 19-21.

[34]Andrews, *Footprints*, 166.

[35]F. P. Blair, Report, April 1, 1865, *ORA*, Ser. I, Vol. XLVII, Pt. I, 381; O. O. Howard, Report, April 1, 1865, ibid., 202; Butler, "Comrades," 32; W. J. Hardee to J. E. Johnston, March 4, 1865, *ORA*, Ser. I, Vol. XLVII, Pt. II, 1320; W. T. Sherman to F. P. Blair, March 3, 1865, ibid., 666; McLaws, Order Book, 1865, 19-21; Osborn, *Trail*, 163.

horse."[36] Sergeant W. H. Andrews of the First Georgia Regulars commented on the consequences of the Federal artillery for the retreating Confederate infantry, "My but it was terrible, as it taken the regiment lengthwise." With grim humor he added, "The rapid fire of the artillery and the shells bursting in our midst made us have a hankering for the opposite bank of the river."[37] In the confusion and haste, the retiring troops had little opportunity to burn the stores abandoned in Cheraw.

The skirmishing at the bridge was desperate. Union troops fought to reach and seize the bridge while the Confederates battled to hold the Northerners in check long enough to escape to the left bank of the Pee Dee and set the bridge ablaze. Sergeant Andrews was among the last Confederates withdrawing across the bridge. "Before we had got more than halfway [over] the bridge," he wrote, "the yankees entered behind us. We had a lively time as we fought through the bridge, some cavalrymen firing the rosin as we fought through.... We left the bridge on fire and full of yankees trying to put it out."[38] An Ohio regiment rushed the bridge while other Federal troops brought artillery and musket fire to bear upon Confederates whom Butler had hastily ordered into position to defend the bridge from the left bank. The Southerners stubbornly held their ground and kept the Federal troops at bay until flames engulfed the structure. Throughout the remainder of the afternoon, Butler's cavalry, joined by infantry and artillery, fired across the river on Federal troops who returned musket and cannon fire with alacrity. Shortly after sundown, the shooting stopped.[39]

Before the fighting at the river ended, Cheraw was under Union control, and Federal commanders moved quickly to consolidate their position on the right bank. Major General O. O. Howard, commanding the Right Wing, sent word to the elements of the Twentieth Corps advancing on the Chesterfield road that Cheraw was in Union hands. Imposing martial law on the inhabitants of the town, he posted a provost guard and ordered a house to house search to gather commissary stores for the army. An inventory of captured supplies and weapons also began. General Blair ordered a regiment from his command to destroy all railroad bridges and trestles within a day's march south of Cheraw, and Major General John A. Logan, who commanded the Fifteenth Corps, organized a mounted force

---

[36]Edward L. Wells to Mrs. Thos. L. Wells, May 1, 1865, in Daniel E. H. Smith, *et al.* (eds.), *Mason Smith Family Letters, 1860-1868* (Columbia: University of South Carolina Press, 1950), 202.

[37]Andrews, *Footprints*, 167.

[38]Ibid.

[39]F. P. Blair to L. M. Dayton, March 3, 1865, *ORA*, Ser. I, Vol. XLVII, Pt. II, 666; Jackson, *Diary*, 189; W. J. Hardee "Memorandum," 581; Butler, "Comrades," 32; McLaws, Order Book, 1865, 21.

for a strike on Florence.[40]

Another concern for the Federals was the C.S.S. *Pedee* that was on the river just below Cheraw. The gunboat was engaged in its only combat mission of the Civil War. As the confrontation between Hardee and Sherman began to develop at Cheraw, Lieutenant Johnston received orders to proceed from Mars Bluff up the Pee Dee River in support of Hardee. Even with the flooding, the crewmen had difficulty finding an adequate channel in which to maneuver their ship. They managed to bring the craft within a few miles of Cheraw and remained until the Federal troops arrived but were unable to assist Hardee's forces. A report that the *Pedee* had exploded about six miles below Cheraw apparently ended Federal apprehensions. In fact, the warship was still afloat and returning to the sanctuary of the navy yard at Mars Bluff.[41]

The principal concern for Sherman immediately after the capture of Cheraw was the situation on the opposite side of the river. Early reports indicated that the Confederates were on the left bank in force.[42] Eager to establish a Federal presence, Sherman ordered, "Make a crossing of and lodgement beyond the Pedee with all possible dispatch, as it is all important we at once hold its left bank."[43] Troops ferried across the river before sunrise on the morning following the capture of Cheraw discovered that the main body of the Confederate army, including the rear guard, had withdrawn, leaving behind pickets who were content simply to monitor Federal progress.[44] Now, only the implacable Pee Dee River barred the Federal advance, but the delay was, as it turned out, just a matter of days.

With a smaller force and with the advantage of the railroad, Hardee had narrowly won the race for the bridge at Cheraw. He held the town long enough to accomplish his strategic objective of bringing his corps from Charleston and moving it across the Pee Dee as part of the broader Confederate effort to concentrate a sizeable force. By holding the town as

[40]Osborn, *Trail*, 163; Second Brigade, First Division, 17th Corps, Itinerary, *ORA*, Ser. I, Vol. XLVII, Pt. I, 96; F. J. Hurlbut, Report, April 7, 1865, ibid., 363; C. Cadle, Jr., Special Order No. 57, March 3, 1865, ibid., Pt. II, 667; C. Cadle to G. A. Smith, March 4, 1865, ibid., 680; A. M. Van Dyke to F. P. Blair, March 4, 1865, ibid., 679; J. A. Logan, Report, March 31, 1865, ibid., Pt. I, 230.

[41]J. A. Mower to C. Cadle, March 4, 1865, ibid., Pt. II, 680; Clayton, *Narrative*, 106; Osborn, *Trail*, 163; Burton, *Diary*, 67; W. T. Sherman to H. W. Slocum, March 4, 1865, *ORA*, Ser. I, Vol. XLVII, Pt. II, 681.

[42]F. P. Blair to L. M. Dayton, March 3, 1865, ibid., 666.

[43]L. M. Dayton to O. O. Howard, March 3, 1865, ibid., 662.

[44]Osborn, *Trail*, 165; C. Cadle to J. A. Mower, March 3, 1865, *ORA*, Ser. I, Vol. XLVII, Pt. II, 667; M. C. Butler to B. Bragg, March 5, 1865, ibid., 1329; G. P. Buell, Report, March 25, 1865, ibid., Pt. I, 467.

long as he did and by destroying the bridge upon his departure, Hardee largely fulfilled his tactical goal of slowing Sherman. Had Hardee exploited the strength of his position on the left bank to dispute the Federal crossing, he could have imposed additional difficulty and delay on the Union army. Instead, he left the river and hastened to join the Confederate force gathering in North Carolina. Later, at Averasborough and at Bentonville, Sherman's Left Wing would feel the impact of Hardee's corps, but in the meantime, the Federal army had unchallenged access to the crossings of the Pee Dee.

George W. Nichols, aide-de-camp to Sherman, recorded his astonishment at the lack of Confederate resistance from across the river. "It is foolish for the Rebels to destroy their valuable bridge when they do not defend the other bank," he wrote. "When they do not prevent our laying pontoons by a more active opposition than we have yet encountered, the delay to us is merely a matter of a few hours. . . . It is incomprehensible to me that the Rebels do not make a more obstinate resistance to our passage of a stream like the Pedee."[45]

Destroying the bridge, the same observer remarked, "is a serious matter to the people."[46] The irony of an officer in Sherman's army expressing sympathy for the misfortune of South Carolinians upon the destruction of a crucial bridge by Confederate troops seems to have escaped Nichols, but of course, the loss of the bridge was a blow to the local economy. In any event, if the retreating Confederates had not burned the bridge, the advancing Federals would have destroyed it after they had passed over the river.

Major General Judson Kilpatrick's cavalry, screening the left flank of the Union army, clashed with Confederate cavalry still on the west side of the Pee Dee in North Carolina. Lieutenant General Wade Hampton's cavalry skirmished with a portion of the Federal cavalry on the evening of March 3, and Major General Joseph Wheeler mounted an attack on Kilpatrick that lasted much of the day on March 4. The Union cavalry began moving down river the next day in the expectation of crossing the Pee Dee on a pontoon bridge. Hampton and Wheeler led their cavalry north in search of a crossing and finally crossed about three days later in the vicinity of Grassy Island Ford, approximately twenty-two miles above Cheraw. Some Confederate horsemen drowned in the perilous crossing.[47]

Sherman ordered his Right Wing to cross the Pee Dee at Cheraw and the Left Wing and Kilpatrick's cavalry to cross about twelve miles upstream in

[45]Nichols, *Great March*, 200.

[46]Ibid.

[47]G. E. Spencer, Report, March 30, 1865, *ORA*, Ser. I, Vol. XLVII, Pt. I, 893-94; J. Wheeler, Report, [April 15, 1865], ibid., 1130; W. Hampton to W. J. Hardee, March 7, 1865, ibid., 1111; William C. Dodson, *Campaigns of Wheeler and his Cavalry, 1862-1865* (Atlanta: Hodgins Publishing Company, 1899), 343; Johnston, *Narrative*, 380.

the vicinity of Sneedsborough, North Carolina. The engineers assigned to each wing were to lay at each location the necessary pontoon bridge: a deck and supporting joists riding on pontoon boats, canvas covered wooden frames, anchored at intervals across the flooding river. The only undertaking more dangerous than crossing on such a bridge was building it. The First Missouri Engineers, pontoniers for the Right Wing, set to work on the morning of March 4 just down stream from the charred ruin of the old bridge. At that point the current was swift and deep, but the high shelving banks restricted the width of the river to about 500 feet. With additional pontoons and bridging materials sent forward by the Fifteenth Corps, the engineers skillfully completed their work by mid-afternoon.[48]

From the outset, problems plagued the bridge near Sneedsborough. Construction was late in starting because the Fifty-eighth Indiana Infantry, serving as engineers for the Left Wing, did not reach the Pee Dee with the pontoon train until noon on March 5. Pegues Ferry, the site selected for the bridge, was three miles below Sneedsborough and posed significant engineering challenges because at that location the current was strong and the river was 920 feet wide. The Fifty-eighth Indiana, not mustered into service as an engineering unit, had acquired its skills through practical experience. While adept at some aspects of combat engineering, the regiment had a record of difficulty with pontooning.[49] The work began in the early afternoon of March 5 and continued for twenty-six hours. "The men worked all night," wrote one of the pontoniers, "but on account of the rapidity of the stream and considerable difficulty in getting anchors to hold we progressed slowly."[50] When the supply of pontoons was exhausted, the engineers took the boxes of army wagons, wrapped the sides and bottom of each with a canvas wagon cover, and anchored these ersatz pontoons in the river. Inadequacies of leadership aggravated the problems, but the barely

[48]Hartwell Osborn, et al., Trials and Triumphs (Chicago: A. C. McClurg, 1904), 194; O. M. Poe, Report, October 8, 1865, ORA, Ser. I, Vol. XLVII, Pt. I, 169; F. P. Blair, Report, April, 1, 1865, ibid., 381; Conyngham, Sherman's March, 354; Osborn, Trail, 168; A. M. Van Dyke to J. A. Logan, March 3, 1865, ORA, Ser. I, Vol. XLVII, Pt. II, 663; J. A. Mower to C. Cadle, March 4, 1865, ibid., 680.

[49]2nd Brigade, 1st Division, 14th Corps, Itinerary, ibid., Pt. I, 109-10; J. C. Davis, Report, March 28, 1865, ibid., 431-32; Clement Eaton (ed.), "Diary of an Officer in Sherman's Army Marching through the Carolinas," Journal of Southern History, IX (May 1943), 247; O. M. Poe, Report, October 8, 1865, ORA, Ser. I, Vol. XLVII, Pt. I, 169, 176; T. Doan, Report, March 28, 1865, ibid., 562; J. C. Davis to R. P. Dechert, February 18, 1865, ibid., Pt. II, 480.

[50]J. C. Moore, Report, March 27, 1865, ibid., Pt. I, 427.

serviceable bridge was finally ready by late afternoon on March 6.[51]

Gathering at the crossing points, well before the bridges were completed, were thousands of troops with their supply wagons, artillery trains, and draft animals as well as the refugees who had followed the army from Columbia with their vehicles and animals. Once begun, the crossing continued through the hours of daylight and darkness for three days at Cheraw and for a day and a half at Pegues Ferry. If the soldiers followed the method used at other crossings, they carried pine torches at night to light their way over the turbulent river. As troops reached the opposite bank, they marched a few miles beyond the stream and encamped to await the arrival of the rest of the army. The crossing was always hazardous and sometimes fatal. A soldier in an Illinois regiment lost his footing near the midpoint of the bridge at Cheraw and fell into the river. He struggled bravely, but the strength of the current and the weight of his knapsack and accoutrements pulled him beneath the surface. He drowned before a rescue boat could reach him.[52]

At both crossings, confusion and congestion were problems, but at Pegues Ferry the condition of the bridge brought additional complications. During the period of the crossing, the churning Pee Dee repeatedly broke the structure, which necessitated tedious delays, sometimes of several hours, while the overworked pontoniers made repairs. Kilpatrick's cavalry and the Fourteenth Corps managed to cross at Pegues Ferry, but the Twentieth Corps marched to Cheraw where the bridge was more reliable.[53]

The movement of troops across the Pee Dee at Cheraw was smoother but not without incident. Between the town and the river was a deep ravine that the columns of troops passed on the way to the pontoon bridge. Thrown into the ravine, to a depth of several feet, were tons of Confederate powder and shells. Soldiers, recklessly setting fire to cakes of powder near the ravine, unintentionally ignited the entire mass. A terrible explosion resulted.[54] Reported one observer: "For fifty rods around the ground was blackened, the trees begrimed and broken, and the hillside torn up, while

[51]Regimental Committee, *Ninety-second Illinois Volunteers* (Freeport, Ill.: Journal Steam Publishing House and Book Bindery, 1875), 223; W. C. Johnson, Journal, 49, Miscellaneous Manuscripts Collection, Manuscripts Division, Library of Congress; H. W. Slocum to W. T. Sherman, March 6, 1865, *ORA*, Ser. I, Vol. XLVII, Pt. II, 704; A. C. McClurg to G. P. Buell, March 6, 1865, ibid., 705.

[52]W. C. Johnson, Journal, 35-38; Jackson, *Diary*, 190.

[53]J. C. Davis, Report, March 28, 1865, *ORA*, Ser. I, Vol. XLVII, Pt. I, 432; W. C. Johnson, Journal, 49-50; A. S. Williams, Report, March 31, 1865, *ORA*, Ser. I, Vol. XLVII, Pt. I, 584.

[54]W. B. Woods to F. H. Wilson, March 6, 1865, ibid., Pt. II, 701.

boxes of ammunition flew into fragments, the shell[s] ascended far in the air bursting at great distances from the scene of explosion."[55] Immediately after the blast, according to another observer, "The men and animals were all stupefied, then the animals stampeded, and it was with great difficulty they were quieted again."[56] Among the large number of soldiers waiting nearby to cross the river, several were wounded and a few were killed.[57]

The explosion damaged and destroyed buildings in the town, causing injuries and generally terrifying civilians. Laura Inglis, member of a prominent family in Cheraw, said of the blast:

> The deafening report and the shock of the explosion, shattering the window panes of about every house in the central part of town, struck terror to the hearts of the people in ignorance of the cause. Together with the fact that a few shells had already been thrown into the town, this gave rise to the report that a general bombardment would follow. This proved to be a false alarm, but in the meantime the streets were soon filled with hurrying groups of townspeople seeking shelter out of range of the shells.[58]

Cheraw remained under Federal occupation while the crossing of the Pee Dee continued. Sherman moved his headquarters to Cheraw the day following its capture and was pleasantly surprised at the extent of the town and with the quantity of seized materials. The original attraction of Cheraw for him was the bridge. He had not known that the town housed a vast quantity of supplies. Included in the captured inventory were twenty-five field pieces, sixteen limbers, sixteen caissons, 3,600 barrels of powder, 5,000 rounds of artillery ammunition, 20,000 rounds of infantry ammunition, 2,000 muskets, 1,000 cavalry sabers, a large amount of material for the manufacture of fixed ammunition, machine tools, one locomotive, twelve or fifteen freight cars, and thousands of bales of cotton. Also captured were commissary stores to fill supply wagons of the Right Wing. Soldiers spiked all of the cannon, except three Blakely guns which they took as trophies, and set fire to railroad facilities, to the warehouses of cotton, and to the military

[55]Nichols, *Great March*, 203.

[56]Osborn, *Trail*, 169.

[57]F. J. Hurlbut, Report, April 7, 1865, *ORA*, Ser. I, Vol. XLVII, Pt. I, 363-64; Burton, *Diary*, 67-68.

[58]Laura Inglis, "A Reminiscence of Sherman's Raid," in *Recollections and Reminiscences* (n.p.: South Carolina Division, United Daughters of the Confederacy, 1990), IV, 305.

The Matheson House served as Sherman's headquarters during the occupation of Cheraw. This is a modern photograph of the structure. Courtesy of Dew James, Director of the Pee Dee Heritage Center.

stores they could not remove. Cheraw ranked with Columbia and Fayetteville as the most important supply depots taken during Sherman's march through the Carolinas.[59]

Cheraw suffered during the four days of Union control. Federal officers gave orders against wanton destruction and pillaging, and the provost guard patrolled the streets. The pious General Howard even issued an order against cursing. Nevertheless, dislocation and destruction prevailed. Soldiers bivouacked in the streets and in virtually every open space while high ranking officers quartered themselves in homes.[60] Virginia Tarrh,

[59]W. T. Sherman to H. W. Slocum, March 4, 1865, *ORA*, Ser. I, Vol. XLVII, Pt. II, 681; W. T. Sherman to F. P. Blair, March 3, 1865, ibid., 666; F. P. Blair, Report, April 1, 1865, ibid., Pt. I, 381; W. T. Sherman to J. Kilpatrick, March 5, 1865, ibid., Pt. II, 693; M. C. Garber, Report, July 10, 1865, ibid., Vol. LIII, 54; Nichols, *Great March*, 199; Fenwick Y. Hedley, *Marching Through Georgia* (Chicago: M. A. Donahue and Company, 1884), 398; C. Cadle to M. F. Force, March 5, 1865, *ORA*, Ser. I, Vol. XLVII, Pt. II, 690; O. M. Poe, Report, October 8, 1865, ibid., Pt. I. 171; Osborn, *Trail*, 168; W. T. Sherman to E. M. Stanton, March 12, 1865, *ORA*, Ser. I, Vol. XLVII, Pt. II, 793.

[60]F. Mott, Special Field Orders, No. 2, March 5, 1865, ibid., 689: F. J. Hurlbut, Report, April 7, 1865, ibid., Pt. I, 363, 364; A. M. Van Dyke, General Field Orders, No. 12, March 5, 1865, ibid., Pt. II, 686; Henrietta Buchannan, "Recollections," in *Recollections and Reminiscences*, IV, 398; Sherman, *Memoirs*, II, 291-92.

whose husband was in the Confederate Army, recorded the abhorrence she felt with Federal troops in and around her home: "The larger portion of our house, during those dreadful days, was occupied by a number of officers and men, and oftentimes the back yard swarmed with the rougher class of privates."[61] To Mrs. C. E. Jarrott, who was just a girl at the time, it seemed that "the whole of Sherman's army" was in Cheraw "with banners flying, bands playing and hundreds of cheering soldiers."[62] Foragers gathered supplies and plunder from homes in the town and the surrounding countryside.

Elizabeth Allston Pringle was a daughter in one of the families visited by foragers, and she later described the experience. The family was having dinner when the soldiers came upon the porch and loudly demanded: "'Whiskey! We want liquor! Don't lie; we know you have it! We want whiskey! We want firearms!'" After entering the house, the men "seemed delighted at the sight of the dinner-table, and for a time were occupied eating and pocketing all that could be pocketed." The intruders went into the storeroom where "they opened box after box." Other solders were upstairs where Elizabeth's "sister was having a trying time. She unlocked her trunk to prevent its being ripped open with a sword, and looked on while they ran through it, taking all her jewels and everything of value, holding up each garment for examination and asking its uses, each one being greeted by shouts of laughter." Not satisfied to search only the house, solders outside were "going all over the yard, running ramrods into the ground to find buried things."[63]

Troops waiting in Cheraw for orders to cross the river found various ways to occupy their time. A Union officer noted in his diary, "I have been wandering through the town today, which is really pretty, with wide streets and avenues bordered with elm-trees, behind which, in the midst of beautiful gardens, are situated tastefully built homes."[64] Other soldiers found less constructive activities. They plundered the valuables sent to Cheraw from the low country, sacked businesses, and started fires. Fires set to destroy supplies and important buildings and fires set for no particular purpose burned the business district of the town. The blaze along the main street threatened to reach the makeshift hospitals housing the sick and injured soldiers left behind when Hardee abandoned the city, but troops of

[61]Virginia C. Tarrh, "Reminiscences," in Mrs. A. T. Smythe, Miss. M. B. Poppenheim, and Mrs. Thomas A. Taylor (eds.), *South Carolina Women in the Confederacy* (Columbia: The State Company, 1903), I, 194.

[62]Mrs. C. E. Jarrott, "Reminiscences," in *Recollections and Reminiscences*, I, 502.

[63]Elizabeth W. Allston Pringle, *Chronicles of Chicora Wood* (New York: Charles Scribner's Sons, 1922), 229, 230, 231, 232.

[64]Nichols, *Great March*, 202.

the provost guard prevented the fire from reaching the hospitals. On March 4, General Mower fired captured Confederate cannon to mark the second inauguration of Abraham Lincoln, and individual soldiers ignited small quantities of powder in what one of them called a "Gunpowder Jollification." The soldiers helped themselves to stores of wine they discovered in the town and celebrated well into the night.[65]

The last significant engagement of Sherman's troops on the right bank of the Pee Dee involved the mounted force sent from Cheraw to Florence. The raid was not a threat to the security of the military prison at Florence because the stockade there was already closed. The advance of Sherman's army from Savannah into South Carolina brought near panic among Confederate officials responsible for military prisons in South Carolina, and Lieutenant Colonel John F. Iverson, commandant of the Florence Stockade, received confusing and conflicting orders for removal of the prisoners from Florence. At first he was to send the prisoners by railroad to southwest Georgia, but Sherman's advance on Columbia cut the railroad well before Iverson could begin the transfer. He subsequently received orders to move the prisoners to Raleigh, but Lieutenant General Theophilus H. Holmes insisted that he did not have enough guards at Raleigh and recommended Greensborough as a suitable destination for the Union captives. The resolution of Iverson's quandary came from an unexpected quarter when in mid-February Lieutenant General U. S. Grant abruptly agreed to a resumption of the exchange of prisoners between North and South. In accordance with the terms of the cartel, the prisoners from Florence were paroled into Federal hands at Wilmington.[66]

From the beginning of the campaign in the Carolinas, Sherman intended to ruin the vital railroad junction at Florence, and destruction of those railroad facilities was the purpose of the mounted strike from Cheraw. Colonel Ruben Williams of the Twelfth Indiana Infantry led two regiments of mounted infantry and a detachment of mounted foragers on the raid.

---

[65]F. J. Hurlbut, Report, April 7, 1865, *ORA*, Ser. I, Vol. XLVII, Pt. I, 363, 364; Burton, *Diary*, 67; Jackson, *Diary*, 190; Osborn, *Trail*, 167, 168; A. M. Van Dyke, Circular, March 4, 1865, *ORA*, Ser. I, Vol. XLVII, Pt. II, 677; J. E. Burton, Report, ibid., Pt. I, 815; Charles W. Wills, *Army Life of an Illinois Soldier* (Washington: Globe Printing Co., 1906), 357; Andrew J. Boies, *Record of the Thirty-third Massachusetts Volunteer Infantry* (Fitchburg: Sentinel, Printing Co., 1880), 113.

[66]H. Forno to Assistant Adjutant-General, March 10, 1865, *ORA*, Ser. II, Vol. VIII, 451-54; J. L. Smith to S. Cooper, March 31, 1865, ibid., 450; J. E. Mulford to R. Ould, February 16, 1865, ibid., 238; S. Cooper to Comdt. of Prisons at Florence, Charlotte, and Salisbury, February 16, 1865, ibid., 238; W. H. Hatch to J. M. Schofield, February 23, 1865, ibid., 296-97; J. M. Schofield to R. F. Hoke, February 23, 1865, ibid., 297; J. M. Schofield to U. S. Grant, February 28, 1865, ibid., 317.

Brigadier General Beverly H. Robertson was in Florence with a brigade of Confederate cavalry reinforced with artillery. Originally part of Hardee's command, Robertson was in the town to interfere with any Union effort to reach Sherman from the seacoast by way of the river or the railroad. The raiders from Cheraw neared Florence on March 5, and skirmishing began on the outskirts of town. The Federals fought their way to the railroad depot but were unable to burn it before being forced to withdraw. Confederate cavalrymen, principally from Tennessee and South Carolina regiments, drove the invaders from the town and at least ten miles beyond. The raiders returned to Cheraw and crossed the Pee Dee on the pontoon bridge.[67]

The successful defense of Florence was one of the few instances in South Carolina when Confederates prevented Sherman's troops from attaining their objective. Robertson saved Florence from the torch, but his victory was otherwise hollow. Williams's troops destroyed the railroad above Florence, and the railroad bridge over the Pee Dee at Mars Bluff was apparently broken by a party of Confederates sent from Fayetteville under orders from General Braxton Bragg to destroy all railroad bridges over streams from the Lumber River south to the Pee Dee. Stranded on the right bank, Robertson's brigade slowly marched upriver, finally crossing at various points well above Cheraw. Robertson was unable to reestablish communications with the main body of the Confederate army in North Carolina until mid-March.[68]

The final day of the Federal crossing over the Pee Dee was March 7. A party of foragers from the Twentieth Corps was the last to cross at Cheraw, and pontoniers raised that bridge by midday. At Pegues Ferry, the crossing of the Fourteenth Corps continued throughout the day and into the night. Engineers of the Fifty-eighth Indiana Infantry worked through the darkness until early morning on March 8 before lifting their bridge. With the recovery of the bridges, the entire Federal army was once again on the march for Fayetteville.[69]

If soldiers guarding the rear of the Right Wing troubled themselves to look back across the river, they saw smoke still rising above Cheraw.[70] The

[67]W. T. Sherman to J. G. Foster, January 19, 1865, ibid., Ser. I, Vol. XLVII, Pt. II, 96; Osborn, *Trail*, 81; J. A. Logan, Report, March 31, 1865, *ORA*, Ser. I, Vol. XLVII, Pt, I, 230; R. Williams, Report, March 6, 1865, ibid., 255; B. H. Robertson to J. E. Johnston, March 17, 1865, ibid., Pt. II, 1421; G. T. Beauregard to W. Hampton, ibid., 1300-01.

[68]R. Williams, Report, March 6, 1865, ibid., Pt. I, 255; A. Anderson to F. L. Childs, February 28, 1865, ibid., Pt. II, 1294-95; O. O. Howard to W. T. Sherman, March 7, 1865, ibid., 713; B. H. Robertson to J. E. Johnston, March 17, 1865, ibid., 1421.

[69]F. J. Hurlbut, Report, April 7, 1865, ibid., Pt. I, 364; J. D. Morgan, to A. C. McClurg, March 7, 1865, ibid., Pt. II, 719; T. Jones, Report, March 29, 1865, ibid., Pt. I. 521; J. Moore, Report, March 27, 1865, ibid., 427.

[70]E. S. Johnson, Report, March 28, 1865, ibid., 368.

town had paid a heavy toll because of its location at an important crossing on the Pee Dee River. The presence of Hardee's troops, the fighting through the streets, and the Federal occupation were remarkably destructive. Fire had consumed much of the town. The wooden bridge across the river was gone. The railroad along the left bank was hopelessly disrupted. And residents had lost much valuable property.

As the Northern juggernaut moved away from the river, Sherman was satisfied. Hardee had escaped, but he had not tarried on the left bank to oppose the Federal crossing. Union troops captured substantial quantities of arms and ammunition and tons of supplies badly needed by the Confederacy. The Federal army moved over the Pee Dee with some difficulty but without major delay. Transportation routes for miles around Cheraw were broken. These accomplishments came with a minimum of casualties among Union soldiers. In retrospect, Sherman considered the capture of Cheraw one of the principal achievements of the campaign in the Carolinas.[71]

All that remained on the river of military significance was the gunboat that had returned to Mars Bluff. Lieutenant Johnston and his officers recognized that an effort to reach open ocean through the now occupied mouth of the Pee Dee River was futile. By the same token, they did not want the vessel simply to fall into enemy hands. They decided to destroy the ship. In mid-March, they sailed into a deep portion of the river just below the navy yard and scuttled their gunboat. The C.S.S. *Pedee*, apparently having never fired a shot at the enemy, settled into the mud at the bottom of the river, and the sailors set out to reach Confederate lines in North Carolina.[72]

Leaving wreckage and desolation behind, the war moved away from the Pee Dee region with Sherman's troops as they advanced into North Carolina. For most of the conflict, the river and adjacent seacoast lacked strategic significance and played only a minor role. The lightly defended seaboard at Georgetown was only occasionally troubled as blockade runners and blockading vessels competed on the nearby sea. The vulnerability of the seacoast at the mouth of the Pee Dee River led to establishment of a navy yard and construction of the gunboat at Mars Bluff. At nearby Florence, Confederate authorities established a prisoner of war stockade where thousands of Federal soldiers languished. The war finally came to the Pee

[71]J. Moore, Report, April 9, 1865, ibid., 188; W. T. Sherman to E. M. Stanton, March 12, 1865, ibid., Pt. II, 793.

[72]Clayton, *Narrative*, 106; W. M. Hunter to S. S. Lee, March 25, 1865, *ORN*, Ser. I, Vol. XVI, 511. When abnormally low water in the Pee Dee River during the fall of 1925 and again in the fall of 1954 revealed the wreck, souvenir hunters and would be salvagers pulled the ship to pieces. See, Florence *Morning News Review*, September 15, 1925; Columbia *Record*, November 1, 1954.

Dee basin with Sherman's army: the Federal navy occupied the seacoast; the river became a significant obstacle for Hardee and for Sherman as they disputed the crossing at Cheraw; Confederate authorities closed the military prison at Florence; and the C.S.S. *Pedee* went to the bottom of the river not far from the yard where it was built. The drama of the Civil War in the Pee Dee region of South Carolina suddenly and swiftly played itself out during February and March of 1865.

THE LAST OFFICER—APRIL 1865

EDITED BY JOHN HAMMOND MOORE[*]

During the final weeks of the Civil War—in fact, at the very moments of the agony of Appomattox—two brigades of colored and white Union soldiers set out from Georgetown, South Carolina, to destroy inland rail communications between Camden and Florence. This trek lasted twenty days, and, even before it ended, word came of a truce in North Carolina between Sherman and Johnston. Only in the vicinity of Sumter and Camden did these Union troops meet any substantial opposition.

The War of the Rebellion contains the official report of this expedition.[1] In all there are ten letters from three generals and several lesser figures. One of the latter, Colonel Edward N. Hallowell, a brigade commander, relates his experiences in terse, military terms. Yet, none of these reports—since they are official—tell us much in the way of interesting detail. However, in the archives of the South Caroliniana Library at Columbia, S. C., there is a brief, but informatitve diary kept by a young lieutenant who accompanied Colonel Hallowell.

Edward L. Stevens of Brighton, Mass., had completed his second year at Harvard when he enlisted as a private in the 44th Regiment, Massachusetts Volunteers, in 1862. Following a six-month hitch he was honorably discharged. Early in 1864, after completing his studies and receiving a Harvard A.B., Stevens—twenty years of age, five feet, ten inches in height with light complexion and blue eyes—was commissioned a second lieutenant in the 54th Infantry Regiment, Massachusetts Volunteers, and in March ordered to report to this unit, an outfit which had pioneered with the use of colored soldiers in 1863. Following a brief sojourn in an army hospital he joined the regiment at Folly Island, S. C. In December 1864 Stevens was promoted to first lieutenant.

His account of this march into the interior of South Carolina, entitled simply "Notes on Potter's Raid," was written in a small, leather-bound notebook. While not complete, it gives us a graphic picture of wartime conditions as viewed by an intelligent, sensitive young man. Lieutenant Stevens describes in detail the condition of plantations and towns, looting by Union men, the stubborn faith of Southern women

---

[*] John Hammond Moore is an associate professor of history at Georgia State College, Atlanta, Ga.

[1] *The War of the Rebellion*, Washington, 1895, series I, XLVII, part I, 1025-1043.

The South Carolina Historical Magazine 67: 1-14

in the Confederate cause, and the condition of liberated blacks. The "Notes" end with the death of First Lieutenant Stevens on April 18, when he died instantly after being struck in the head by an enemy bullet. His body, recovered under fire by two volunteers, was buried at Boykin, but later removed to the national cemetery at Florence, S. C. "Lieutenant Stevens," according to the historian of the 54th Regiment, "was a genial comrade and brave officer. He must have been the last officer, or one of the last officers, killed in action during the Rebellion." [2]

This diary is printed with the permission of the South Caroliniana Library. And, since his words relate closely to those of his commander, Colonel Hallowell's Report is included and printed in italics. [3]

Georgetown, S. C., April 26, 1865

I have the honor to report that on the 5th of April, 1865, my brigade, composed of eight companies Thirty-second U. S. Colored Troops, Col. G. W. Baird commanding, and five companies One hundred and second U. S. Colored Troops, Maj. N. Clark commanding, left Georgetown, S. C., at 8 a. m., on the Sampit or Central road. After marching about three miles in a westerly direction took the road to right toward Black River through heavy pine forests; roads very good. Encamped for night near Johnston's Swamp, about nineteen miles from Georgetown.

April 5th Was on guard last night, and heard that we were to start on a Raid this morning— All sorts of rumors were afloat yesterday, as Gen. [Quincy A.] Gillmore was up to Georgetown[,] remained but a few minutes. A Report is afloat that Lee, since his attack on Fort Steadman[,] is disheartened & wants to come to terms & that Sherman, Grant, Lincoln & Lee are at City Point arranging for terms. Of course we can't trace the report to any reliable source. We think however that Gillmore came here to hurry us off in anticipation of news. We have not the remotest Idea of our destination. We started at Seven & a half this P. M. [4] There are two Brigades of Infantry. The first commanded by Col. P. P. Brown of the 157th N.Y.V. consists of the 54th Mass. Vols., Five co's 102d U. S. C. T.[,] Eight co's 32nd U. S. C. T.[,] thirty or forty cavalry under Maj. [Moses F.] Webster of 4th Mass. Cavalry[,] 2d

[2] Luis F. Emilio, *History of the Fifty-Fourth Regiment of Massachusetts Volunteer Infantry, 1863-1865,* Boston, 1891, pp. 304-305. The picture of Lieutenant Stevens has been taken from this book. It faces page 96.

[3] Capital letters have been added at the beginning of sentences; periods at the end of sentences and to complete abbreviations.

[4] Stevens means "A. M."

Sect. of Artillery under Lt. [E. C.] Clark[,] 3d N. Y. A., the whole force under Brig. Gen. Potter.

I came very near going as Commissary of the Division on Potter's Staff, my name was proposed to him & his Adj. Gen. was about to make the Detail, but Potter did not want to change his commissary as he was to start sooner than he expected. It would have been pleasant duty.

A large train of contrabands came with us for the purpose of getting their families which they had left in Rebbdum. We were marched with great judgement & celerity, especially considering it was the first day out. We halted for rest for ten minutes every hour & had an hour rest at noon. We marched nine miles before dinner and eight after, getting to camp about dark.

I have [George] Broady of Co. H. for Servant. He and [William] Jones make a Team—Uncle Ned Peagram is quite sick, but managed to carry a load to day.

The country we passed through is the most desolate imaginable. We passed but two or three houses all day & those of the meanest Kind. Reminded me of [Edmund] Kirke's "Among the Pines"—I never marched so far or so easily on the first day of a march.

Just after we passed the 16 mile Post we turned to the north on the King[s]tree Road.

On the 6th resumed the march at 6:30 a. m.; country more open and rolling. Marched nineteen miles and camped near Thorntree Swamp.

April 6th Did not sleep much last night[,] two or three shots were fired & we turned out a few minutes. Reveille at five o'clock. Started at 6½, our Brigade in the advance. Marched about eleven miles before dinner, the country much better than that of yesterday. Contrabands joining us and we are collecting horses & mules. I saw a curious sight this morning. About a mile out we came to a house, said to be occupied by a union man. Our boys rushed in & began to slay chickens & take horses so one woman pulled out her handkerchief & waved it as a signal of neutrality, but as it seemed to do no good, she uttered an exclamation & rushed frantically into the house & snatched a table cloth from the Breakfast table & waved it aloft & screamed, "Mr. Officer, see those big men coming in here[!]"

In the afternoon we marched eight miles. We marched to within about Six miles of King[s]tree. The Cavalry to day made some captives, [and] drove a small party of Rebels across the Black River, the latter setting fire to the bridge.

In the evening a great many horses were obtained. Some of them excellent. I carry but little load [—] my canteen, Sword & over coat part of the time, get some forage.

On the 7th started at 6:30 a. m.; general direction northwest; weather good; country still more open. The One hundred and second U. S. Colored Troops were detached from main column to destroy the Kingstree bridge across the Black River. They exchanged a few shots with the enemy, but report no casualties. Two companies of Fifty-fourth Massachusetts Volunteers were sent to destroy the Epps' Bridge. Their casualties were 1 officer (Second Lieut. F. E. Rogers) and 3 enlisted men wounded. We camped at Mill Creek after marching about fifteen miles.

April 7th Notwithstanding the hard march of yesterday, I was in good condition for travelling this morning. We crossed the N. E. R. R. early in the morning—we passed through a fine country to day, a considerable amt. of cotton was found & any amount of Provisions of all Kinds. Parties were out foraging for the Brigade. We burned cotton gins & presses, but no dwelling houses.

We marched quite easily in the morning[,] walking about nine miles. We had an hour & a half for dinner & after marching about a mile halted for some reason or other an hour which I improved by a good nap. We then marched a couple of miles through a fine open cultivated stretch of Land & came to some cross-roads, 8 miles beyond King[s]tree on the road to Manning—Co's H. & A. were sent to the Right to Epp's Ferry across the Black River to burn the Bridge. After going about half a mile we came to a Spot where there had been a Picket fire, from this point there was a Sudden declivity into Black River Swamp. Here was the meanest place I ever saw, black water & black mud. Capt. [Charles E.] Tucker commanded the Party & was mounted. He sent half a dozen men in advance & the rest of us had to wade most of the way above our Knees. We went about two miles & a half & saw a little fire & were in doubt whether it was a Rebel Picket fire, or the bridge burning. The advance waded through a long ford & came within about 50 yards of the bridge, when they were fired on by a party of Rebels concealed across the bridge, which the Rebs had just retreated across & set fire to.

Lieut. Rogers of Co. A. was hit in the Right fore-arm, & Privates J. C. Johnson and J. H. White wounded slightly. We retired, as we had found out that the bridge was burned & we had orders not to have an engagement. We marched back to the cross roads, & found the columns had all marched past, & it was about dark.

We marched rapidly about four miles & found the Regiment encamped for the night. We had a hard march of at least 21 miles[;] found our Servants had not got supper ready. I was well wet through & got to bed late. We have marched 57 miles in three days, pretty good marching.

On the 7th [5] continued the march at 6:30 a. m. in a westerly direction for about five miles, then northwest to the Sumterville road. This course was taken in consequence of a report that the bridges were burned on the main road. We marched through Manning and built the bridges across the Pocotaligo Swamp. . . .

April 8th Off in good season with our Brigade in advance. We got plenty of forage last night from the Party of foragers. I was assigned to the command of Co. A in Roger's place. He rides a horse & comes along with us until we can get to some place to send him to the Coast.

We marched three miles or perhaps a little more, then turned off to the left & went towards the Santee[,] then turned to the right again. Part of the country was very rich. We marched quite rapidly four or five miles without a halt. We made eight or nine miles before dinner, got well rested, then marched rapidly several miles & struck the same road we left early in the morning. I have been unable to ascertain why Potter made this detour, taking us off the road several miles. In the afternoon we went through the finest Kind of agricultural country. Have an intelligent contraband who Keeps us Supplied with Poultry &c.

We crossed considerable many fords & swamps late in the afternoon. I Saw a great sight at dinner— While we were halting the contrabands went by. I would judge 700 or 800 of them of all ages & both Sexes. Little boys & girls of such tender ages, as at home would not be trusted outside the yards, yet these small children Keep up with us marching 20 miles a day. Almost all the little children carry a tub or something on their heads. The women are the greatest sights, some of them are very pert pretty damsels, of all colors. Some attractive old women just alive. Some young women are like brutes almost with bosems as large as a Cow's Bag hanging down. Most of them have a child in arms, a child at the back & a child about to appear. Such a sight for an artist it is to see these poor people just liberated, going on happy, under such burdens as they bear, keeping up with veteran Soldiers in the long wearisome marching. It is Sad & yet encouraging to see the hope in their countenances & their perfect trust in us. What is to become of this Race of uneducated, hopeful, anxious people[?] What a change has the war bro't about!

[5] This is a misprint. It should read the "8th." *The War of the Rebellion,* Washington, 1895, series I, XLVII, part I, 1036.

We entered the town of Manning about dusk after a march of 18 miles at least. The cavalry had gone in before us. All the male population had left in the morning to go to the next town[,] Sumter, where the Rebels are Said to be concentrating all the force they can to defend the town through which the Wilmington & Manchester R. R. runs. Manning is a small town[,] beautiful in appearance. I saw scarcely anything of it. We passed down a fine wide Street. I saw a few buildings[;] we camped in the outskirts of the town. A Cavalryman was killed by a citizen he was talking with, a deliberate murder.

    . . . and at 7 a. m. on the 9th continued the march toward Sumterville. When about three miles from Sumterville we found the enemy intrenched at Dingle's Mill, on Turkey Creek. Their force was estimated at 500 men (mostly militia) and three pieces of artillery. We attempted a flank movement on their left, but owing to the incapacity of the guide were oblidged to return to the main road, when we found that the First Brigade had opened the road and captured the artillery. We camped at Sumterville about sundown.

April 9th   This has been a great Sunday for us. This morning at one o'clock we broke Camp & marched across Black River Swamp where the Black River becomes the Pocotaligo. A detail from the Regiment relaid the planks which the Rebels had thrown off for nearly a mile and a half. We went across to reinforce the Picket line. We walked across Stringers by moon-light. I lay down without blanket at four in the morning & got a nap. Maj. [George] Pope gave Capt. Tucker a mule to day so we have got along easily. Jones got a cart, So we have all our Stuff carried easily— The 1st Brigade has the advance to day. They marched past us about Seven this morning. We are extreme rear to day. We marched through the finest kind of a country to day, full of all sorts of forage & provisions— extensive cotton Plantations. The country showed immense wealth. We must have burned over half a million dollars worth of cotton to day, & I don't believe but what we have more. There were Cotton Gins & Presses, horses[,] wagons & etc. at every house. Not an able-bodied man was seen, all the Whites & blacks have gone to Sumter. The women & children all sit on the Piazzas as we pass. They have a terrible wo[e]begone expression, & no wonder, for it is a terrible thing for an Invading army full of enthusiasm, part of it, before slaves, eager for revenge on their old masters. It is awful for women & children to see the sights they see, but we restrain our men, & altho' I have some difficulty, yet have not heard of any act of wanton conduct on the part of any man in my command.

As I said[,] we destroyed an almost incalculable amount of property to day. To day has been very pleasant for marching, cloudy & comfortable & we have done some of the best marching I have ever saw.

We marched fast & rested little & when we stopped for dinner about one o'clock, we had made fifteen miles. I was some tired as I slept little the night before, not more than three hours. We were very much refreshed by a good long halt for dinner.

Gen. Potter was anxious to take Sumter before dark. We advanced up the road to within about three miles of the place to a cross-road, the plan of attack was for the White Brigade to attack in front while we went to the Reb's left flank. We filed to the right & went considerable distance, & halted & a Skirmish line was pushed out & found a few pickets. We were to advance, when intelligence came which made Col. Hallowell counter-march his Brigade & join the White Brigade. We were greeted by the grateful news that the White Brigade had been very successful[,] had crossed the river & taken two pieces of Artillery & driven the enemy [back]. Part of the 56th N. Y. & 157th were sent to cross below the bridge by a foot path & get on the rebels right flank. This they did in excellent style & with small loss, their advance was so well executed that the Rebels left in hot haste leaving their dead & badly wounded in our hands [&] a few prisoners & two pieces of Artillery. Some of our forces crossed the bridge while it was burning[,] extinguished the fire & the rest crossed on the stringers, the Engineers were on hand & had boards laid on when we got up. Afterwards the cavalry & artillery came across.

As we went across or before it we came to the place where our contrabands were. It is almost incredible that so many could have joined us in so short a time, there were not less than 1000 or 1500 in No. Some of the Prisoners we got were old men, some little boys, the cradle & grave. One of our men said as we went along, there's a Soldier almost old enough to vote, referring to a 75 yr. older. The Rebels scattered & took to the woods & Swamps. We advanced into the town, crossing the W. & M. R. R. Capt. Tucker & Lt. [Stephen A.] Swails were sent to destroy Locomotives & cars & machine Shops, which they did effectually. The Rebels moved their machine Shops from Wilmington to Sumter & had not quite fitted their Shops up, & there were several locomotives here for repairs. There was fine, costly machinery here, which it will be hard for the Rebels to get replaced. We burned lots of cotton. We encamped in a large cultivated field near the centre of the city.— We went through the city singing "Year of Jubilee["] & "John Brown" etc. We came very near capturing the whole Rebel force which numbered about

500. Had our Brigade been sent to the Rebel left earlier so as to have got
on their flank about the time the attack was made in front we would
have bagged them all. They lost several officers—I am alone to night, as
Tucker's stopping at the Depot.

*On the 10th sent the Thirty-second U. S. Colored Troops up the
Manchester and Wilmington road to Maysville to destroy a train of
cars and the railroad bridges. Sent the One hundred and second U. S.
Colored Troops about three miles south on the same road to destroy
bridges. Both detachments were successful and returned to Sumterville
at night.*

April 10th Slept soundly last night, tho' it rained some. Was very
tired last night as we had gone twenty miles before we turned in— To
day we have been resting, tho the Cavalry have been to Manchester[,]
the termination of the road & burned the Depot & a train of Cars—
The 32nd U. S. C. T. went out by another road & burned a long Bridge.
I went along the principal Street of the place to day & saw the cleaning
out the Soldiers had made. The Stores had been entered, Safes broken
open, stores rifled. There was quite a no. of Drug Stores in Sumter, many
more I should judge than the size of the place warranted—they were
nice large Stores, well supplied. There was the greatest conglomeration
of Stuff & all Sorts of Smells. Medical & other Books were all thrown
down together in a confused mass. One of the men got a Sole Leather
valise or trunk from one of these Stores & gave it to me. It was just
what I wanted. I found Several books which I wanted. Many of the
Soldiers entered private houses & took what they wanted, but I could
not hear of any of my men doing so. Sumter is a beautiful place, stylish
people, refined[,] highly educated, Beautiful Libraries & furniture, showing the luxurious style of living the people had. I went down to the
Depot & saw quite a quantity of commissary's Stores abandoned, which
are to be issued to our troops. All our rations were issued to day, two
days & we have to wait for communication with Steamers before we
can get more. Among the Rebel Rations are Pea-nuts! Several Bags
were given to each of our Cos. Captain Tucker had charge of issuing the
Rations.

Some of our officers got things of great value. [Capt. Charles G.]
Chipman found a lot of Shoes, a Sword, fine Dressing-case, &c.— Tucker
got a blue silk Flag, belonging to the Marion men of Combahee. A large
Palmetto tree in the centre & a half moon in one corner—it said "Pocotaligo Oct. 1862" & underneath "Nihil Despondere." This represented
or was given in honor of [Gen. Ormsby M.] Mitchell's defeat on Graham's Neck in '62.

Tucker got some nice China crockery. [Daniel G.] Spear & Rogers got Silver ware, clothing[,] books & the former an artist's Sketch Book— Spear gave me several books of the finest description, of great value to me if I am fortunate enough to get them home. A good many fine Animals were obtained here. It has been splendid to have so nice a rest to day. We needed it, as we had marched at least 95 miles in five days— I am on guard to night. I never saw such a quiet town. Several of the citizens have asked officers to sleep in their homes for protection. [Edward B.] Emerson & Tucker are at houses to night. The men are not half so Secesh as the women—many of them believe that the confederacy is on the eve of establishing Independence. There is a confederate Hospital here, with a no. of Soldiers & Officers sick & wounded. Some of them were well enough to go & fight us then run away & get into bed again when we entered the town— We heard here that Lee had made an unsuccessful attempt on Grant's lines & that Grant had followed up this failure by breaking Lee's lines & taking Petersburg & Richmond, also news came of the taking of Selma[,] Montgomery & Mobile. Potter fired a salute from the captured guns. . . in honor of the victory. Lee & Johns[t]on are Said to have formed a junction & are about to invade the North. May their Invasion prove their ruin. We are extremely anxious to hear reliable news from the North.

On the 11th started at 6:30 a. m. marching southwest through Manchester and camped at the Singleton plantation on the Statesburg road. Sent the Fifty-fourth Massachusetts Volunteers to Wateree Junction, where they destroyed 8 steam-engines and 50 box-cars; they rejoined the command at daylight on the 12th. Their casualties were: wounded, 1 officer (Second Lieut. S. A. Swails) and 2 enlisted men.

April 11th Our regiment & my co. in the advance to day. We proceeded north a short distance, then west & took the road to Manchester, we marched slowly at first, but from nine o'clock we went very rapidly with no more than one or two halts before dinner. We made at least twelve miles before our noon halt. The day was warm & the country had little water so we were hot & tired, but were very much refreshed by a good long halt. The country has been fine to day, but a little more sandy. Plenty of provisions are found, & animals & Poultry— After Dinner, we marched two or three miles & arrived at what was Manchester Depot, where our Cavalry had destroyed the train & depot the day before. The main column halted here, while our regiment was sent to destroy Some Bridges & cars supposed to be on the R. R. Seven miles away. We marched on the sleepers with our tired feet. We had but one Short rest in the whole seven miles. We came to a bend in

the R. R. turning to the west then another to the N. W., then another
North. The W. & M. R. R. ends at Manchester and at a point seven miles
from M. it bends to the north & runs to Camden & to the West & runs
to Columbia. Just before we came to the last bend, we saw that the
Rebels [who] had been recently repairing the road were building a
new turn out & turn table & were getting a double track in one place.
We reached this about dusk & were just turning the bend when we saw
a locomotive, which had got up Steam. Good Shots were sent to the
front & fired, then we all charged & rushed over a tressle Bridge to the
Cars. What Rebels there were left & we had the great satisfaction of
capturing Five Locomotives & thirteen cars. My Co. & F. were sent to
guard the train in the rear while the train was got off. Lt. Swails was
hit by a shot from one of our men, he having got too far ahead. Part
of the regiment was sent to destroy the extensive tressle Bridge over
the Wateree. A Contraband came in & told us there was another train
about a mile farther up the Bridge, so Col. Hooper sent me with my co.
to destroy it, but afterwards thought he wanted the train run down. So
sent Capt. Tucker with me as he understood how to run a train. We
went over this tressle bridge, forty ft. high in some places, stepping
from sleeper to sleeper. It was tiresome to one[']s head & eyes, as we
had to look down so much lest we should make a mis-step which would
be about the ruin of us. We went two miles or more before we came to
the train, which consisted of two Locomotives & 35 Cars, we got up
Steam & ran it down. The fires on the Tressle Bridge were put out &
we ran over the Bridge. It was very dangerous as the train was heavy
& the rails snapped off in some places where they had been burned, but
we kept on. Corp. Nol. [Charles Noe] of my co. fell from a car clear
to the bottom of the tressle bridge hurting himself considerably—

We joined all the trains together making a train of Seven Locomotives & 48 Cars[,] a long train. The train Tucker & I got was loaded
partly with R. R. Iron & Spikes & Glass. The Engines[,] many of
them[,] were in poor repair & we did not get them a[-]going 'till morning, & then we had to run the train down in three parts & set fire to
some of the cars where we were. We attempted too much. We wanted
to run the whole train to Manchester & destroy it there, but the first
train which went down did not get more than half way before a pipe
of the Locomotive burst & the train had to be fired, so all the Cars &
Engines had to be destroyed at that point. One Tressle Bridge was destroyed & part of another.

It was a great mistake not running the whole train back a mile on
the high bridge & setting fire to it, as the cars would have set fire to

the bridge, & the engines effectually destroyed & been dropped into the water. As it was they were destroyed So that they can't be repaired for months & I hope that [by then] Peace will come to us again.

On the 12th the Thirty-second U. S. Colored Troops were sent to Wright's Bluff on the Santee River, distance about twenty-five miles, in charge of contrabands, and with orders to return with rations for the command.

April 12th We arrived back at camp about 8 o'clock, having been walking & working hard more than 24 hours & having but one meal. I don't think I ever did so hard a day's work in my life. We made about 25 miles yesterday— We have marched 120 miles in one week & rested one day in that time so we have marched 120 miles in Six marching days—

We went about five miles this morning & went into Camp. I am almost exhausted with want of sleep & food. We have an almost incalculable no. of contrabands, there are not less than 2500 of them. The 32nd U. S. C. T. has been sent to the Santee with the contrabands[;] they are getting too many for us to guard. The 32nd is to escort the wagon train back. We are out of Rations, & are to live on the country several days until the 32nd gets back[,] probably day after tomorrow. They will have a hard march of 50 miles & the day is hot to day— We are on the Camden road now. I bought a fine Glass (telescope) to day of one of my men. I lay down in the sun & got a short nap & after dinner slept till dusk & turned in after Supper & slept till morning— I was extremely tired & was thankful that we did not have to march. Lt. Spear was sent to forage for the Regiment and brot in considerable provisions.—

April 13th   Has been quiet, one or two regiments have been out & find the Rebels thick around us, 5000 are reported between us & Camden. If so, we had better be getting back to Georgetown. We are very near Columbia, not more than 50 miles & we are halting with our small force in the heart of S. C. Condensed cheek—our confidence carries us farther than our numbers. Have been reading[,] resting & sleeping to day & feel tip top—& ready for more walking any time— A Party of foragers went out to day & got considerable Provisions & Booty —[Lt. Charles O.] Hallett got a Splendid Trunk— We are living splendidly with no expense to us. Poultry, Honey, Potatoes, Corn Bread[,] Molasses, &c— Rogers & Swails went back to Georgetown. Contrabands came in to us by the hundreds to day.

Lieut. [Robert R.] Newell[,] who went to the Santee with the 32 [nd], arrived back last night with dispatches. The train reached the

Santee this noon. The wagon train was loading & is expected here to morrow night—the contrabands were loading— This has been a quiet[,] peaceful day— A mule has been furnished the officers of each co.

The men have got all sorts of musical Instruments, and Keep the Camp lively— There have been acts of vandalism committed by white & black soldiers. People of Sumter tell of the worse than vandalism of Sherman's men at Columbia. I want to be away from such Scenes. Some of the Sumter people have fled from Shells at Charleston only to be robbed by Sherman, & fled from Columbia, because they believed Sumter secure only to lose their last to us. Some of the wealthiest families of Charleston are now at Sumter with barely enough for support.

April 14th Four years ago today the Stars & Stripes were lowered at Fort Sumter & Maj. Anderson marched out as Prisoner of War—as my man Jones says, What has happened to the country & especially to the South since then "Sets a man thinking many a way—" The great[,] great Emancipation of hundreds of thousands of Slaves, the advance of Freedom & liberal Ideas, our Success in arms are very encouraging & lead us to hope for Speedy Peace.

To day we received Some Gen. orders of the War Dept. relative to the raising of the original Flag of Maj. Anderson on Fort Sumter by the Maj. now Brev. Maj. Gen. A Public address by Rev. H. W. Beecher &c. Wish I could be there. We have been waiting for the Rations & 32nd U. S. C. T. to come up from the Santee all day— This morning there was an Inspection to find out what Stuff our men had taken from homes. Instances of vandalism are reported of money & Gold & Silver being demanded of defenceless Women. Some Silver was found. Late this afternoon, twenty or thirty Rebel Cavalry Came down on our Pickets[,] but were driven back after exchanging a number of Shots. The right wing of the Regiment was sent out about two miles, but failed to discern any traces of them. There is a tremendous fire in a N. E. direction, which I can't account for. Just as we came in to night from our Scout, the wagon train came in & Rations are issuing now. There are numerous reports about a heavy Rebel force in the direction of Camden. Col. Chipman is at Nelson's Ferry on the Santee looking for [Gen. Alfred S.] Hartwell who is said to be on an Expedition, but we can learn nothing definite of movements—the 32nd Regt. did not get up with the wagon train which was escorted by the cavalry—

At 2 p. m. on the 15th the Thirty-second U. S. Colored Troops returned and at 3 o'clock the march was resumed. We skirmished with the enemy till dark and then marched in a northeasterly direction till midnight and camped near Jennings' Swamp.

April 15th Fell in early in the morning & waited about without doing any thing until about two o'clock when the 32d arrived from the Santee. The Rebels Showed themselves in large Squads of cavalry to day. So the 25th O[hio] were sent out & Skirmished & had four wounded almost on the first Shot. When the 32d came up the whole column fell in & advanced a little beyond where we went scouting the night before— Here quite a Skirmish took place. We passed the first Brigade & filed to the right to flank the Reb. Skirmish line but it fell back before we could accomplish the object. We had quite a sharp Skirmish which lasted 'till dark. We pushed the Rebs back & turned Sharp off to the E. N. E. & Walked rapidly five miles, then felt our ground slowly till 12 or one when we went into camp being tired & sleepy. Made about 12 miles.

On the 16th started at 7:30 a. m.; country very rolling; passed Brad-ford Springs at noon; skirmished all the afternoon, but it did not retard the march; camped at sundown about twelve miles from Camden.

April 16th Sunday again & tho' it has been a week to day since we entered Sumterville, yet to day we are within seven miles from it. We Started about Seven this morn—our regt. 3d in the Brigade which was in advance. We are making a detour to day to avoid works & swamps on the road to Camden. We have been going in a general N. W. direction to day. The road has been red brick color. The country has been remarkably hilly, the roads however are in splendid condition, made ten miles before dinner. I heard this morning that we took to the Santee 3200 Contrabands & we have hundreds more. Many have come in to day. It is a joyful sight to see families & squads strolling across the fields to join their Liberators. They are welcome & seem to appreciate their freedom. One told me to day that Beauregard went over to the Union side at Kinston[,] N. C.[,] thinking the Confederacy played out.

We advanced only two or three miles this afternoon still keeping on the high table land. Skirmishing commenced soon after dinner. No one was hit on our side. The Rebels left one dead & we took several Prisoners. Encamped at Sunset, having made 12 miles. Conflicting rumors come of the force at Camden. It is estimated from 1 to 5000.

On the 17th started at 6 a. m., and marched to Camden without serious opposition, reaching that point at 6 p. m. On the 18th left Camden at 7 a. m., taking the Statesburg road; found the enemy in force at Boy-kin's Mill. The Fifty-fourth Massachusetts Volunteers and One hundred and second U. S. Colored Troops succeeded in flanking the enemy on our right, and the Thirty-second U. S. Colored Troops, aided by the

First Brigade, were pushed vigorously forward on the center and drove the enemy from their position.

Total casualties in Second Brigade: Killed, 1 officer (First Lieut. E. L. Stevens, Fifty-fourth Massachusetts Volunteers) and 1 enlisted man; wounded, 20 enlisted men. About dark we were joined by Col. H. L. Chipman, with the right wing of the One hundred and second U. S. Colored Troops, he having forced his way through the country from Wright's Bluff with a loss of killed, 1 enlisted man; wounded, 1 officer (Lieutenant Powers) and five enlisted men.

On the 19th resumed the march at 6 a. m.; skirmished all day with loss of—killed, 1 enlisted man; wounded, 4 enlisted men. The enemy made a stand at Rafting Creek, but were soon flanked out of their position by the One hundred and second U. S. Colored Troops and driven in confusion through Statesburg by the whole division. We met with no resistance after leaving Statesburg and camped at Singleton's plantation. The Thirty-second U. S. Colored Troops marched down the Camden Branch Railroad without much resistance. On the 20th the Fifty-fourth Massachusetts Volunteers marched to Middleton Depot and destroyed fifteen steam-engines and a large number of box-cars. On the 21st left Singleton's at 5:30 a. m., taking the Santee road. While near Governor [John Lawrence] Manning's plantation ["Milford"] we were notified of an armistice between General Sherman and the rebel General Johnston. The rest of the march to Georgetown was uninterrupted. We kept to the main road and reached Georgetown at 4 p. m. on the 25th.

During the whole march the troops were in perfectly good spirits, and both officers and enlisted men carried out instructions with energy and cheerfulness.

Enclosed is a nominal list of the casualties during the expedition.

Very respectfully, your obedient servant,

E. N. HALLOWELL,
Colonel Fifty-fourth Massachusetts Volunteers, Commanding Second Brigade, Provisional Division.

WAR WITHOUT END:
"RAVENOUS FOR PLUNDER"

THE FEDERAL PILLAGE OF ANDERSON, SOUTH CAROLINA: BROWN'S RAID

THOMAS BLAND KEYS *

May Day 1865 in Anderson Court House, South Carolina, was balmy spring, and the Civil War, in the southeast, had terminated. Robert E. Lee had surrendered the Army of Northern Virginia to Grant on April 9, and Joseph E. Johnston had capitulated to Sherman April 26. Some of Anderson District's paroled veterans already had returned to their homes and taken up again their civil labors. It was a time of beginning anew. After the despair of the Confederacy's overthrow, affairs could not worsen. With peace there was hope, and all things seemed possible.

On this day Mr. LaFar chaperoned a picnic at Silver Brook for his students, accompanied by a large group of other juveniles of Anderson. There were festivities, and Lillie Hubbard was crowned queen. Miss Harbour's school also was having an outing near Bailey's Bridge on Rocky River, and Janie Pruitt was chosen queen during the revelry.[1] Citizens of the district felt thankful that combat had not reached their lands during the conflict, and the village of Anderson was intact, unlike cities and towns in Sherman's wake.

Unknown to Andersonians, baleful forces had been initiated four days earlier to converge on inoffensive Anderson. At conclusion of Union Major General George Stoneman's incursion from east Tennessee into southwest Virginia and western North Carolina in April 1865, he returned to Knoxville with artillery and prisoners, but left the cavalry division, commanded by Brevet Brigadier General William J. Palmer (colonel of the Fifteenth Pennsylvania Cavalry), in western North Carolina "to obtain forage and to intercept and disperse any bands going south, and to capture trains."[2]

Major General Henry W. Halleck, army chief of staff in Washington, on April 27 sent a telegram to Secretary of War Edwin M. Stanton stating,

* 1721 Flamingo Drive, Orlando, Fla. 32803.

[1] Louise Ayer Vandiver, *Traditions and History of Anderson County* (Atlanta: Ruralist Press, 1928), 114-115.

[2] *The War of the Rebellion: A Compilation of the Official Records of the Union and Confederate Armies,* 128 books and Atlas (Washington: Government Printing Office, 1880-1901), ser. I, XLIX, pt. II: 407 (hereafter cited as *OR*, with all references to ser. I); Robert Underwood Johnson and Clarence Clough Buel, eds., *Battles and Leaders of the Civil War,* 4 vols. (1887-1888; reprint ed., New York: Thomas Yoseloff, 1956), IV: 479, fn.

The South Carolina Historical Magazine 76: 80-86

"have information . . . that Jeff. Davis' specie is moving south from Goldsborough in wagons. . . . I suggest that commanders be telegraphed through General Thomas . . . to take measures to intercept the rebel chiefs and their plunder." [3]

Stanton at once relayed Halleck's counsel to Major General George H. Thomas in Nashville, commanding Department of the Cumberland, and Stanton ordered Thomas to "spare no exertion to stop Davis." [4] Thomas thereupon advised Stoneman, in command of the District of East Tennessee, of the messages, and he directed Stoneman, "If you can . . . get three brigades of cavalry, . . . send them . . . into South Carolina . . . toward Anderson. They may . . . catch Jeff. Davis, or . . . his treasure." [5]

In turn Stoneman sent dispatches to General Palmer and his senior brigade commander, Brevet Brigadier General Simeon B. Brown (colonel of the Eleventh Michigan Cavalry), and ordered Brown to assume command of Colonel John K. Miller's Third Brigade as well as Brown's own Second Brigade, and to move "to Belton or Anderson. From that point scout in the direction of Augusta. . . . The object . . . is to intercept Jeff. Davis. . . . If you can hear of Davis, follow him to the ends of the earth . . . and never give him up." [6] Palmer with the First Brigade was to endeavor to overtake the other two brigades, at which time he would resume command of the division.[7]

Stoneman's orders were received April 29 by Palmer in vicinity of Cowpens Battleground, South Carolina,[8] and by Brown four miles east of Hendersonville, North Carolina, whereupon Brown replied, "the Second and Third Brigades . . . will march this morning for Anderson . . . via Jones' Gap and Pickensville." [9]

Brown's Second Brigade was comprised of three cavalry regiments, Lieutenant Colonel Charles E. Smith's Eleventh Michigan, Major Frederick Slater's Eleventh Kentucky, and Major James B. Harrison's Twelfth Kentucky. Miller's Third Brigade also included three cavalry regiments, Colonel Samuel K. N. Patton's Eighth Tennessee, Colonel Joseph H. Parsons' Ninth Tennessee, and Lieutenant Colonel Brazilliah P. Stacy's Thirteenth Tennessee.[10] Brown's two brigades numbered about 3,600 troopers.

[3] OR, XLIX, pt. I: 546.
[4] Ibid.
[5] Ibid.
[6] Ibid.
[7] Ibid.
[8] Ibid., 547.
[9] Ibid., pt. II: 555. Pickensville was near the site of the present city of Easley.
[10] OR, XLIX, pt. II: 539.

As Brown's flank guards crossed into Anderson District on Monday, May 1, two skirmishes were fought by South Carolina home guards. Near the Thomas Moore home northwest of Piedmont, seventeen miles northeast of Anderson, Colonel Thomas' Greenville Arsenal Cadet Company, joined by Lieutenant W. P. Price and a small band of militia, engaged in a brief fight when attacked by a platoon of blue cavalry, which quickly withdrew, leaving behind one wounded man. Also Captain Jones' Pendleton Home Guard Company of young boys had a brush with the enemy near Pendleton Factory (now La France), ten miles northwest of Anderson.[11]

In late afternoon news reached Anderson that Federals were close by, and parents rushed to the picnic sites and called out that Yankees were nearby and everyone must rush home. Refreshments were abandoned as Miss Harbour and Mr. LaFar hastened their charges homeward.[12]

Historians of the Thirteenth Tennessee Cavalry, a regiment in the Third Brigade, later wrote, "We were now in the Palmetto State, . . . and we did not at that time have many scruples about despoiling the country. We reached Anderson . . . May 1st."[13]

As Brown's vanguard struck the northern limits of the village, "the wild yell of infuriated men, maddened by liquor and ravenous for plunder, was heard."[14] A rising cloud of dust portended their swift approach on Main Street toward the public square. The reckless soldiers fired repeating rifles in all directions. Within five minutes the whirlwind had swept every quarter of Anderson. Screams of women and children added to the din of the storm.[15]

When a squad of Union vedettes arrived, they were encountered by a patrol of Anderson's young men who audaciously attempted to resist the raiders. McKenzie Parker, who had served in the Marion Artillery, aimed his gun at one of the scouts and ordered him to surrender. The Yank told him to put down his weapon, but Parker attempted to fire twice, the gun misfiring each time. The cavalryman at once shot Parker

[11] Vandiver, *History of Anderson County*, 244-245.
[12] Ibid., 115.
[13] Samuel W. Scott and Samuel P. Angel, *History of the Thirteenth Regiment, Tennessee Volunteer Cavalry, U. S. A., Including a Narrative of the Bridge Burning* . . . (Knoxville: P. W. Ziegler, 1903), 241.
[14] James A. Hoyt, ed., "The First Day of May, 1865," Anderson, South Carolina, *Intelligencer*, May 3, 1866, p. 2.
[15] Ibid.

in the chest, felling him. He was borne inside the hotel where he quickly died.[16]

In her home while instructing a pupil in music Caroline R. Ravenel heard shots, and then two children ran in and told her that they had been fired upon. Caroline, looking out a window, saw a bluecoat smite a Negro delivery man with a saber, and then discharge a pistol in a neighbor's yard. The rear of Brown's column closed into Anderson in an hour, and bivouac was made in the square and surrounding streets. The citizenry stayed in their homes, with doors locked and bolted, and blinds drawn.[17]

There was little rest and no security that night. The warriors soon unearthed in a room on the corner of the square a large supply of brandy and wine, which had been stored there by a Charlestonian.[18] Doors were smashed, iron safes were forced open, and contents of houses and store-rooms were stolen or destroyed. The night saw "hideous orgies and rapacious plunderings." [19]

Tuesday at dawn inebriated cavalrymen were sleeping off hangovers, but not for long, as the exhilarating prospect of more loot alerted them to get along with their enterprise. Citizens remained indoors, hoping to protect the residue of their property, but to no avail.[20] At Miss Ravenel's house her uncle, Dr. Henry Winthrop, sixty-two years old, was hanged from the bedstead, with toes just touching floor, beaten on the face with fists and shovel, and his head was rammed against a wall, until, when he believed he was about to be killed, he told his tormentors where he had hidden some gold.[21]

Caroline Ravenel's grandmother and aunt also were menaced with hanging. Day and night successive parties entered and searched all rooms, and rifled trunks, drawers, and wardrobe, and stole money, firearms, corn, watches, jewelry, silver, wine, and a guitar. All in the household were abused by the brutal soldiers, who threatened to kill two or three of them. Even so, the members of this family fared better than some others, and after the nightmare ended, they considered themselves very fortunate.[22]

[16] Caroline R. Ravenel to Isabella Middleton Smith, May 18, 1865, Daniel E. Huger Smith, Alice R. Huger Smith, and Arney R. Childs, eds., *Mason Smith Family Letters, 1860-1868* (Columbia: University of South Carolina Press, 1950), 213.

[17] Ibid., 209; Anderson *Intelligencer*, May 3, 1866.

[18] Mrs. James W. Wilkinson to Mrs. Daniel Elliott Huger, May 11, 1865, *Mason Smith Family Letters*, 208.

[19] Anderson *Intelligencer*, May 3, 1866.

[20] Ibid.

[21] Ravenel to Smith, May 18, 1865, *Mason Smith Family Letters*, 210-212.

[22] Ibid., 209-213.

Blacks, as well as whites, were threatened and harassed, and most of them conducted themselves nobly.[23] Despoiled as Anderson was, the suffering and destruction caused by the Federals were even greater in the surrounding areas.[24]

In February when Sherman had menaced Columbia, part of the Confederate States Treasury Note Bureau there was removed to Anderson and located in the university buildings, and Brown's command thoroughly looted those structures, scattering all the bills they did not keep. After departure of the horse soldiers, scarce sheets of paper, that were intended to have become Confederate currency, blowing along the streets, were salvaged by young ladies for letter writing.[25] Type was strewn upon the floor in the office of the *Intelligencer*, thus preventing publication of accounts of the atrocities at that time.[26]

General Simeon B. Brown, who presided over the sack of Anderson, was 53 years old, a tall and picturesque personage with military manner and a chin beard. In the field he wore a brown hat with brim pinned up. Late in 1862 he had joined the army when the governor of Michigan appointed him major of the Sixth Michigan Cavalry, at which time he was proprietor of City Hotel in St. Clair, Michigan, and was serving as a St. Clair alderman. He was promoted colonel of the Eleventh Michigan Cavalry in December 1863.[27]

On one of Stoneman's earlier forays into Virginia, Brown, commanding a brigade, when surrounded was ordered to cut his way out with two regiments, sacrificing his third regiment. Brown refused to obey, retorting, "Where the Eleventh Michigan and Twelfth Ohio and General Brown go, the rest of the Second Brigade will go; if it be to Kentucky, all right; if it be to Richmond, all right; or to hell, all right." [28] As we have seen, General Brown later kept his word when he visited torment upon the people of Anderson.

23 Ibid., 209, 213.
24 Wilkinson to Huger, May 11, 1865, *Mason Smith Family Letters*, 208.
25 Vandiver, *History of Anderson County*, 235-236.
26 Anderson *Intelligencer*, May 3, 1866.
27 *History of St. Clair County, Michigan* (Chicago: A. T. Andreas & Co., 1883), 670 (photocopy provided by Michigan State Library, Lansing); "A Brave Man—Some Anecdotes of the Late Gen. S. B. Brown," Detroit *Evening News*, March 18, 1893, p. 3, col. 4 (photocopy provided by Michigan State Library, Lansing); "Inns and Inn-Keepers," and "List of Old Time Officials," St. Clair County, Michigan, *Press*, *c.* 1901-1903 (photocopies of clippings from scrapbook provided by St. Clair, Michigan, Public Library); Simeon B. Brown's military service record (Washington: National Archives and Records Service).
28 Detroit *Evening News*, March 18, 1893.

Late Tuesday afternoon, May 2, 1865, Brown ordered the march to recommence southwestward from Anderson, leaving behind his rear guard, "and shortly after dusk the troopers, loaded with ill-gotten gain and stupefied with wine, mounted their fresh steeds obtained in the neighborhood, and followed their doughty leader to other fields of plunder and rapine." [29] By breakfast time on Wednesday, May 3, Brown's rear had departed.[30]

The inhabitants surveyed their community as soon as the foe was out of sight. A year later the editor of the *Intelligencer* wrote, "desolated, . . . Anderson wore a sombre, sad appearance. . . . Her people gathered in knots over the ruins and wreck, and each . . . in saddened tones related an experience of the dread occasion, . . . which will always be denominated 'Brown's Raid.' . . . In the simple annals of our village life . . . [May 1, 1865,] will occupy the most prominent niche of all other days. . . . Its anniversary will ever be recognized." [31]

In Georgia Generals Palmer and Brown rendezvoused and extended the dragnet for Jefferson Davis. On May 6 in Athens, Palmer informed Stoneman,

> I shall send General Bown's and Colonel Miller's Brigades after this duty is over to Greenville, South Carolina, from which place I recommend that they be recalled to Knoxville. . . . The reason that I recommend that [they] . . . be immediately recalled . . . is because their officers for the most part have lost all control over their men. A large number of the men and some of the officers devote themselves exclusively to pillaging and destroying property. General Brown appears to have given them carte blanche in South Carolina, and they are now so entirely destitute of discipline that it cannot be restored in the field and while the command is living on the country.[32]

Near Irwinville, Georgia, Jefferson Davis and party were captured May 10 by Brevet Major General James H. Wilson's cavalry. On May 20 Wilson, in Macon, notified General Thomas that "There is some complaint of Palmer's command by the people, and . . . I would suggest that they be ordered back to East Tennessee, or at least out of the State." [33] The history of the Thirteenth Tennessee Cavalry later divulged, "Some of our men had done some looting at Athens." [34]

[29] Anderson *Intelligencer,* May 3, 1866.
[30] Ibid.
[31] Ibid.
[32] *OR,* XLIX, pt. I: 549-550.
[33] Ibid., pt. II: 850.
[34] Scott and Angel, *History of the Thirteenth Tennessee Cavalry,* 242.

Back in camp near Lenoir, Tennessee, Brown was allowed to resign from the army on June 11, and he went back to his hotel business in St. Clair, and was re-elected alderman.[35]

Later South Carolina Governor James L. Orr, a resident of Anderson District, strove to identify Brown and his command through the War Department, but was apprized that the army register listed no such command.[36]

Brown's City Hotel was destroyed by fire in January 1873; it was valued at $15,000, but was insured for only $10,000. On March 16, 1893, in St. Clair, at the age of 81 years, General Brown "died at home of exhaustion consequent on bleeding piles, obstinate constipation, weak back, and chronic bronchitis." [37]

[35] Brown's military service record; "List of Old Time Officials."

[36] Vandiver, *History of Anderson County,* 241.

[37] Brown's pension application file (Washington: National Archives and Records Service); "This Week Thirty Years Ago," St. Clair County, Michigan, *Press,* January 8, 1903 (photocopy of clipping from scrapbook provided by St. Clair, Michigan, Public Library).

WHEN THE YANKEES SACKED GREENVILLE:
STONEMAN'S RAID, MAY 2, 1865

NANCY ASHMORE COOPER

Although Greenville was far removed from Civil War battlefields, its piedmont location did not totally dismiss it from the sting of military action. Its one-day occupation by Union troops on May 2, 1865, is an event generally overlooked in historical accounts. However, it bears closer examination.

We gain an eyewitness perspective of the day's events largely through family letters and personal reminiscences, which fit together like pieces of a puzzle forming an overview of that one memorable day in May. There were no newspapers or telegraphs and only sporadic rail connections to the "Mountain City," which had remained rather splendidly isolated throughout the war. Therefore, researchers must rely chiefly on individual testimonies of those involved and of lowcountry refugees who wrote their family and friends of their unexpected brush with the military.

In reality the war was over, and yet the Federal scorpion had one final stinging swat left for unsuspecting Greenvillians. On April 9 Gen. Robert E. Lee had surrendered to Gen. Ulysses S. Grant at Appomattox Court House, Va., and on April 26 Gen. Joseph E. Johnston had likewise given over to Gen. William Tecumseh Sherman in North Carolina. On April 14 President Abraham Lincoln was assassinated in Washington, D.C. In the wake of these events, recently deposed Confederate President Jefferson Davis and his cabinet were in retreat from Richmond through the Carolinas and Georgia. Union troops were in hot pursuit of their prey; they left no stone unturned. Thus, upcountry South Carolina fell into their dragnet.

U.S. Army Major-general George Stoneman, commander of the District of East Tennessee, sent out a detachment of cavalry who were led from Asheville into Greenville by Major James Lawson on the morning of Tuesday, May 2. Dubbed thereafter as "Stoneman's men," this brigade—about 200 strong—was neither blood-thirsty nor arson-minded; its motto proved to be Pillage, Pilfer, and Plunder.

They met no local resistance. The earthen embankment just north of town, known as Fort Hatch, had never offered much protection; it was manned occasionally by a combination of Confederate soldiers home on leave and cadets from Columbia's Arsenal Hill Academy. The latter had abandoned it on April 30, just before the raiders arrived.

For the most part, cooperative citizens were treated with courtesy; largely female households were provided a guard, if requested, to ward off stragglers and drunks. Only two deaths are recorded: an inebriated Captain Josiah Choice, who was shot when he threatened to kill anyone who took his horse, and an unidentified

Carologue 10 (Spring 1994), 8-12

black man, believed to have been a former slave of the late Vardry McBee, who was also summarily shot "for impudence." Two may have died later of shock. One house, that of Captain Brooks, was set afire but it did not burn.

Mrs. Caroline Howard Gilman was probably the best known of the Charleston refugees who had waited out the war in Greenville. She did so with her daughters, grandchildren, household staff, and belongings. Mrs. Gilman was a published author and avid letter writer; her extensive correspondence (some of it reprinted in "Letters of a Confederate Mother," *Atlantic Monthly*, April 1926) gives a detailed view of war-time Greenville and especially the May 2 experience.

As soon as the troops neared the Gilman home, Mrs. Gilman's daughter, Caroline Jervey, ran out to the gate and assertively asked to speak to an officer. A polite Lieutenant West came forward and answered her request for a guard. He assigned a "stolid looking" soldier named Shertz to "guard this house strictly, and watch the streets. Let none of our men disturb these ladies."

Albert, one of the Gilman servants, took exception to this new friendship. When asked to "take the gentleman's horse," he replied, "I ain't goin to touch no Yankee horse. Let him hitch him his self."

Seeking philosophical clarity, Mrs. Gilman asked Lieutenant West, "How is it you come to a place like this, where there are only non-combatants, during the Armistice?" He replied, "Oh, madam, the Armistice did not hold after Lincoln's death." Then he rode off, leaving Shertz on guard duty.

The latter soon proved useful when a threatening man appeared on the porch demanding coffee, refusing to believe Mrs. Gilman's contention that she had been without coffee for two months. Shertz pointed his musket at the caffeine-seeker and he soon departed.

Late in the afternoon Lieutenant West returned to the Gilmans' bearing a U.S. flag which he had captured at the Confederate gun foundry. Almost apologetically, he displayed it from the mantel in the parlor. Then he sat down to supper and resumed a political discussion with the family. He asked them why they felt the war had been fought. Louisa Porcher, another Gilman daughter, said it was "to subjugate us and free our slaves." The lieutenant disagreed. "We do not want to subjugate you," he replied, "nor do we want to touch a negro or your institution. The U.S. only wants her own territory, and she will have it."

Meanwhile, another refugee household, that of the Arthur M. Hugers, was experiencing a much higher level of anxiety. Mr. Huger was taken to the depot and held overnight with other prisoners before being released. His wife later wrote to her sister (reprinted in *Mason Family Letters*, edited by Daniel E. Huger Smith et al) that his absence filled her with feelings of "humiliation and constant apprehension." Soon after his departure, she related, a Yankee entered the back door asking for firearms. She immediately gave up the one and only rifle, but he proceeded through the house room by room, searching for others while reassuring her that he had no intention of harming anyone. To her relief he showed no interest in silver flatware, which was clearly visible, jewels, or money. Following this visit, she boldly asked for a guard and received one who remained until dusk, thus calming her nerves somewhat.

Not all households were so fortunate, however. Many were ransacked and stripped of essentially all their valuables. One particularly vulnerable home was Boyce Lawn, a spacious and impressive estate on the edge of town, owned by Dr. James P. Boyce, a Confederate captain and theologian at the local Southern Baptist Seminary. Raiders helped themselves in a frenzied style to his horses, closets, and trunks, "flinging everything about in a wild search for precious things."

It is reported that the intruders held pistols to Dr. Boyce's head, demanding to know where his wife's diamonds and jewelry were. Proving that a soft answer turns away wrath, he coolly explained that when he had heard rumors of their approach on the preceding day, he had packed his family's most valuable possessions in a wagon and had his brother drive it way without revealing his destination. He literally had no idea where his diamonds and silver might be at that moment. Though infuriated, the raiders finally believed him and departed, seizing a number of his personal items, including his easily recognizable watch, cigars, and heavy overcoat.

Main Street suffered greatly. The commissary stores were opened up; empty shops used for storage of lowcountry valuables were cleared out. Storerooms at the Soldier's Rest Hospital were plundered, thus effectively ending the operation of the Ladies' Aid Association that was headquartered there. Caches of salt and other staples were removed from the depot.

The bank, then kept in Beattie's store, was cleverly picked clean. According to one account, the bank-robbing party certainly knew its business. They entered the building and went straight to the cellar, "tapped the wall until the sound changed then tore out the bricks, and appropriated a good many thousand in specie which the careful bank president had very secretly walled in, some months before." The lost funds included $35,000 belonging to the Charleston Bank which had been diverted to Greenville for safekeeping.

"Everything was rifled," Mrs. Gilman wrote in her account. "Books, costly plates, wines, pictures, bed linens thrown in the streets to be picked up by any passerby. All the afternoon we saw white and black laden with goods, passing by the house."

Major Lawson was keenly aware of the advisability of keeping any form of alcohol away from his troops, lest they become excessively rowdy and slip totally out of his control. He supervised the disposition of wine casks stored at David's Warehouse on Pendleton Street; he ordered them emptied into the street, where citizens watched the contents flow along the gutter. A wise move, no doubt. Many families destroyed or buried their liquor holdings as well.

The day was not without some frivolity. Mrs. Gilman reported the story of a pretty fifteen-year-old girl who had no matron to protect her, but she compensated by making fine use of her acting skills. She dressed herself like an old woman and played the role quite convincingly, instructing the servants to feed the raiders who came demanding dinner and bossing her older sister with great authority. When the troops asked her about firearms, she told a servant to bring the poker and shovel!

Unfortunately, one refugee lady, a Mrs. Venning, died about a month later from the shock induced by Stoneman's Raid. The sickly eight-year-old son of a Mrs. Forsyth "fell insensible" when raiders pointed a pistol at him and called him a "Little rebel."

Anyone in Greenville on that May 2 remembered it for years to come. Prince Smith, a black man born on Wadmalaw Island, had been brought to Greenville by his master, along with some seventy other slaves, to escape the coastal war. Interviewed many years later, after he had passed his one-hundredth birthday, Smith clearly recalled: "For almost four years we stayed in Greenville, when suddenly one Tuesday morning bright and early, Sheridan [sic] came into Greenville on horsebacks and order everybody to surrender. Colonels and generals come in the city, without the firing of a gun."

Indeed, the city fathers did not take the raid lightly. They found it particularly galling, occurring, as it did, after the armistice. On May 4 a committee of twelve, which included Benjamin F. Perry and Alexander McBee, signed a petition of redress to the U.S. government (now at the South Caroliniana Library at the University of South Carolina in Columbia) asking the return of "horses, negroes, and other property captured and taken." A list of owners and their losses was appended. Dr. R. D. Long waxed eloquent in his property description: "one fine large bay horse which Maj. Lawson would not allow taken except on condition a good horse be left in his place, but an injured old mare that is now down and unable to get up, was left." There is no evidence that Dr. Long or any other citizens received compensation for their losses.

Despite the extensive plundering of real property there was a remarkable lack of injury or violence during the raid, thanks in large part to Major Lawson's leadership. A retrospective article in the Greenville *Mountaineer* newspaper, which appeared nineteen years later (May 14, 1884), credited the commander as a man of "judgement and rightmindedness." Because of him, the article concluded, "Greenville was spared the fate that befell Columbia and other places in the middle and lower parts of the state."

When the raiders pulled out and went on their way, a great relief was felt in Greenville, but even then all danger was not removed. There was still the threat of an internal enemy—Confederate deserters and draft dodgers who had long been hiding out in the mountainous portions of upper Greenville County, especially in the Dark Corner region. Mrs. Huger wrote her sister in New Orleans that although the Federal raid seemed over, she should "not think of returning to Greenville." As she explained, "The unsettled state of the population in the mountains exposes this place at all times to raids from bushwackers and the anxiety is anything but endurable."

The departing raiders promised that other troops would soon follow, a threat that provoked most women to stay fully dressed and sleep very little for the next several days. However, the threat proved false. The nightmare was over.

Stoneman's Raid may be only a footnote in military history, lasting, as it did, for only one day, but for Greenvillians it was truly a day in May to remember

SKIRMISH ON CRESCENT RIDGE: THE LAST CLASH OF THE WAR BETWEEN THE STATES IN SOUTH CAROLINA

JOHN B. MCLEOD

It has long been thought that the last hostile encounter between Confederates and Federals in South Carolina occurred on May 1, 1865, outside of Williamston. In that skirmish, a group of Arsenal Cadets exchanged fire with some Federal cavalrymen in pursuit of Confederate President Jefferson Davis. Of course, the visit of Stoneman's Raiders to Greenville on May 2, 1865, has been well documented, particularly in the letters of Caroline Gilman. It now appears that a brief but violent skirmish between a group of Greenville home guards and a regiment of Tennessee Unionist cavalrymen took place on present day Crescent Avenue on May 23, 1865. This engagement produced no casualties, but almost resulted in the summary execution of three former Confederates and the sacking of Greenville. Although the Union cavalrymen were justifiably upset after being fired upon, they did not wreak havoc on Greenville. Instead, they simply went on their way back to East Tennessee. This passage of arms is the last documented action of the War Between the States in South Carolina and, with the exception of a few skirmishes in Missouri and in the Indian Territories, was the last such engagement of the entire War.

After General Lee surrendered the Army of Northern Virginia on April 9, 1865, and General Joe Johnston surrendered the Army of Tennessee on April 26, 1865, a number of former Confederates returned to Greenville, most on foot. A Federal garrison had not yet been established in Greenville, although General Van Wyck had been in the area for some time. During the War Between the States, Greenville had been plagued by a number of deserters and draft evaders, commonly called "outliers," who took refuge in the foothills of the mountains in areas such as the "Dark Corner" around Gowensville. During the War, the Greenville District Sheriff, assisted by men organized into a "patrol," attempted to keep the peace.

On May 2, 1865, a group of Union cavalrymen from Stoneman's Cavalry Division paid a visit to Greenville and took almost everything that could be moved. There was little money available since Confederate currency was worthless, and in any event, there was very little to be bought, although a few enterprising Confederates did try to set up stores. The Greenville and Columbia Railroad was not in operation at this time, so Greenville was practically isolated from the outside world.

May 1865 was probably very hot, and life in Greenville was at a fairly low ebb due to the disconsolation caused by the Confederacy's collapse. Former Confederates, arriving home after four years of prolonged conflict, were trying to adjust themselves to normal life. Unfortunately, the War was not quite over.

On May 23, 1865, word reached Greenville that a band of "outliers" was

Carologue 23 (Fall 2002, 22-25

approaching from Anderson District. Sheriff William T. Shumate sent out a call to the former Confederates to form a "home guard" to deal with this threat. A group of distinguished veterans of the late conflict answered the call, including Colonel E.P. Jones, Colonel Charles J. Elford, Colonel B.Burgh Smith, Colonel James McCullough, Captain Leonard Williams, and even an Englishman named Henry Wemyss Feilden, who had fought for the Confederacy. Governor Benjamin F. Perry's son, Hayne, and the Earle brothers also responded to the summons.

This group quickly assembled and went with Sheriff Shumate to the "high ridge" south of the Reedy River, which was known as Crescent Ridge (now Alta Vista and Crescent Avenue). Marching in hot weather was rather thirsty work, and the men refreshed themselves at the mineral springs on Crescent Ridge. Armed with revolvers, muskets, and a few hunting pieces, the group headed east on the ridge in the direction of Lanneau's house (on present-day Belmont Avenue) where they heard the sound of hoofbeats approaching. The group dispersed and took cover in the woods on either side of the track heading toward the Lanneau house. When the first horseman appeared, one of the group opened fire and several volleys ensued. This proved to be a tactical blunder since the approaching horsemen were not "outliers" but rather were troopers of the Thirteenth Tennessee Volunteer Cavalry, U.S.A., on their way home from Georgia after attempting to capture the elusive Jefferson Davis. The cavalrymen, armed with Spencer repeating rifles, returned fire. The home guard, rather nonplussed by this turn of events, chose the better part of valor and took to their heels. Unfortunately, Colonel Jones and two others were rather slow and were bagged by the Union cavalry.

Things did not look good for the former Confederates. The Thirteenth Tennessee Cavalry was the same unit that had pillaged Anderson during the first of May while chasing Jefferson Davis. In fact, the behavior of this regiment had been so bad that their division commander noted that "they are now so entirely destitute of discipline that it cannot be restored in the field and while the command is living on the country." The Federals conferred and decided that summary execution was an appropriate punishment for the captured home guards. The Federals did not even go through the motions of a "drum head" court-martial, but decided that the sentence was to be carried out the next morning.

As time drew nigh for the executions, Colonel Jones (a Freemason) gave his order's sign of distress to a federal officer. This officer, also a Mason, postponed the execution and took the men before the brigade's commander, another Mason, who interrogated Colonel Jones and the others closely and was satisfied with their response that they were not "bushwhackers" and had not fired any shots. Colonel Jones and the others were released and the troopers headed into Greenville.

The citizens of Greenville, obviously fearful of a repetition of the events of May 2, awaited the arrival of the Federal troops with dread. Fortunately for all concerned, the Tennesseans were anxious to return to East Tennessee and were well-behaved. Apparently, there had been some discussion among the cavalrymen about putting Greenville to the torch because of the rude behavior of its home guard. According to a contemporary Union history, it was a near thing:

> The men of Stoneman's division were chagrined by their failure to reap the rewards of the capture of Mr. Davis, particularly after being in close pursuit for over a week. After resting in Georgia for a short period, the three brigades were ordered back to Tennessee.
>
> The return was not without incident. Miller's brigade, while passing near Greeneville [sic], South Carolina, was attacked by a band of guerillas, driving them off in a hail of musketry, capturing two or three. The war being over, mercy was shown and the rebels were spared, as was the village.

Using available resources, the ladies of Greenville prepared a meal for the Union cavalry, and local men provided their horses with forage. After spending the night in Greenville, the Thirteenth Tennessee headed toward Hendersonville and, through Asheville, to East Tennessee. Life in Greenville returned to normal and its citizens awaited the arrival of Federal troops, not as raiders, but as occupiers. Unlike some other communities, Greenville did not suffer greatly during Reconstruction and, in fact, enjoyed a measure of prosperity.

John B. McLeod is an attorney practicing law with Haynsworth Sinkler Boyd, P.A. in Greenville, South Carolina. After graduating from Wofford College and Duke Law School, McLeod served as a law clerk to the late Judge Donald S. Russell and spent four years on active duty with the United States Army. McLeod is presently serving as President of the South Caroliniana Society.

BUSINESS:
"MIXING PROFIT AND PATRIOTISM"

A BUSINESSMAN IN CRISIS :
COL. DANIEL JORDAN AND THE CIVIL WAR

HENRY CARRISON*

IN DECEMBER 1859, WHEN COL. DANIEL W. JORDAN BOUGHT
Laurel Hill, a rice plantation on Waccamaw Neck, he joined the creme de la
creme of South Carolina's well defined antebellum social strata.[1] For
generations, rice plantations had rewarded their owners with fabulous
wealth, political influence, and social exclusivity, and nowhere in the U.S.
was rice production concentrated like it was along the fresh water tidal
stretches of the four rivers emptying into Georgetown's Winyah Bay—a
third of the country's total production.[2]

Plowden C. J. Weston, from whom he bought the plantation, was one of
these "rice princes." Educated at Harrow and Cambridge, Weston owned
three plantations other than Laurel Hill, and when he died in 1864, he left
a library valued at over $15,000 ($149,000 today)[3] and a wine cellar containing
110 dozen bottles of wine.[4] Unlike these established planters, however, Col.
Jordan, 49, who was from North Carolina, had not inherited great wealth,
nor was he dazzled by its brilliance. While the trappings of the rice
plantations—the long avenues of live oaks, the great houses, the elegant
furnishings, the ordered gardens, and the liveried servants—had obvious
appeal for him, Laurel Hill was strictly an investment.

During the eight years he owned Laurel Hill, Col. Jordan was tested as
few men are in business, and his decisions had to be made virtually alone.
Like many of his fellow planters, War, Emancipation, and floods wiped out
his entire investment in rice, a tremendous loss. Yet he survived, invested
again in other businesses, and eventually prospered. Without his propensity
to accept risks, he might have suffered less; on the other hand, without his

---

*Henry Carrison is an independent researcher. Much of the information about
Col. Jordan was taken from the Daniel W. Jordan Collection of over 4,000 letters and
other papers at the Perkins Library of Duke University.

[1] Elected Lt. Col. of the Mississippi state militia in November, 1838. The title,
used by acquaintances, was eventually adopted.

[2] Walter Edgar, *South Carolina: A History* (Columbia: University of South
Carolina Press, 1998), 269.

[3] John J. McClusker, "How Much Is That in Real Money? A Historical Price Index
for Use as a Deflator of Money Values in the Economy of the United States,"
Proceedings of the American Antiquarian Society, 101, pt. 2, (Oct. 1991), 297-373. (1991
figures increased by 15% to adjust to the year, 2000.)

[4] George C. Rogers, Jr., *The History of Georgetown County, South Carolina*
(Columbia: University of South Carolina Press, 1970), 258-259.

**Col. Daniel W. Jordan (1810-1883) in the late 1850s.
Image courtesy of the author.**

personal courage and creativity, he would never have prevailed. Combining intellect, intuition and tough pragmatism, he had both the head and soul of an entrepreneur.

Col. Jordan had prospered in the 1850s as a turpentine producer, although earlier in his career he had known failure as well as success. These experiences had taught him several important lessons that he used to derive a business strategy. He observed that with volume production of commodities such as cotton, turpentine, and rice, unit costs could be reduced significantly. The key was to use labor specialization, task repetition, and incentives to gain efficiencies. Consequently, it was important that he become, and remain, a large slaveowner, and one of the trademarks of his businesses was that they were geared for volume. Another lesson, this one more painful, was that while borrowed money was a convenient source of capital, financial leverage was potentially dangerous because lenders seemed to want their money most at the very time that borrowers were least able to pay. If possible, therefore, a borrower needed access to emergency cash. Finally he had seen that while one's life might be disrupted by events beyond his control, perseverance and flexibility were invaluable tools for survival. In December 1859, as he celebrated the purchase of Laurel Hill with a "Montezuma" cigar and a glass of champagne, he had no inkling that these principles would be so quickly, and so severely, tested.

As a young man in Eastern North Carolina in 1833, having heard stories about the fantastic cotton yields of the newly opened western acreage, he joined the thousands of would-be planters in a mass migration from their worn out Carolina and Virginia farms to Alabama and Mississippi.[5] Unfortunately for him, his timing was bad. After three years of moderately good crops, he had built his Mississippi plantation to about 500 acres and 40 slaves. By 1836, however, he was vulnerable, having borrowed heavily to finance his business—$20,000 to $25,000 (approximately $418,000 today). In mid-1837, burdened with the weight of private speculation combined with the demise of the Second Bank of the U.S., the fragile economy finally collapsed, resulting in the catastrophic "Panic of 1837." Col. Jordan lost his farm, his slaves, and his bride's considerable inheritance, and by the time he returned to North Carolina in 1840, he was literally bankrupt.

It was a discouraging setback, but he was determined to succeed. His timing was considerably more auspicious when he started his turpentine production business in 1843 in Brunswick County, N.C., just south of Wilmington. In the spring of 1845, an industry boom was created when England repealed its import duty on naval stores. The price doubled, then nine months later it increased by half again when a New York dealer tried to corner the market.[6] In 1846, Col. Jordan moved his operation and his family down to Little River, S.C., and by 1859 he owned about 250 slaves and distilled and shipped 10,000 barrels of turpentine spirits and rosin annually to New York, making him for a time possibly the largest single producer in the United States.[7]

[5] During the 1830s and 1840s, South Carolina lost 40 percent of its population, and North Carolina each lost a third, to resettlement in the Southwest. Francis Butler Simkins and Charles Pierce Roland, *A History of the South* (New York: Knopf, 1963), 115.

[6] Percival Perry, "The Naval Stores Industry in the Ante-Bellum South, 1739-1861," Duke University, 1947, doctoral thesis, 247.

[7] There is very little information available on the size of turpentine producers. In his doctoral thesis, "The Naval Stores Industry in the Ante-Bellum South, 1739-1861," approved by Duke University in 1947, Percival J. Perry offers a few facts which serve only as hints. Apparently the number of large full time producers was minimal—perhaps 30 or less—and these operated almost exclusively in North Carolina. James Metts and John A. Avirett, both North Carolinians, owned 65 and 125 slaves respectively. Two of the largest were Daniel W. Russell and James R. Grist, both operating in Brunswick County, N.C. In 1855, Russell owned 25,000 acres of

By 1859 also, circumstances had changed in the thirteen years since Col. Jordan pioneered large scale turpentine production in Little River. Although he owned approximately 15,000 acres, bought for their stands of longleaf pine, competition was moving in, and pine tracts convenient to deep water for transportation were harder to find. In commodity production, cheap, reliable transportation is a critical factor and for him, it was complicated and risky. His production of turpentine spirits and rosin was rafted from his three distilleries on the Waccamaw River down to Bucksport or Bucksville to meet one of the 12-15 New York based schooners he chartered annually to deliver these barrels to his commission merchant in New York. For sailing ships this round trip to Georgetown and back was demanding and dangerous, particularly on the return trip when these "coasters" would be heavily loaded both above and below deck. In the warm months their crews would often be weakened by malaria from the rice field mosquitoes, and during the winter, could find themselves trying to beat against one of the infamous "nor'easters," and at the same time avoiding the shoals and cross currents of "The Graveyard of the Atlantic," Capes Fear, Lookout, and Hatteras, on the lee shore.

However, Col. Jordan had a reason for paying the expensive freight and insurance charges to New York—it gave him access to money. Unlike the Southern banks and Wilmington commission merchants like DeRosset & Brown, the New York merchants would make capital advances, the majority of which he invested in slaves. Resources like this were invaluable to large slave buyers and lessees like Col. Jordan. On the other hand, once a businessman had committed his business to growth, he had to be prepared for the financial pressures of constantly owing large sums of money and for generating sufficient cash flow to service these obligations. In the latter years of the 1850s, the balance of his capital advances from Benjamin Blossom, his New York agent, was $7,000 to $10,000, although there was no note and no scheduled repayment, and his annual cost for leased slaves was about $12,500; combined, it was the equivalent of about $423,000 today.

As the 1850s ended, aside from his normal interest in new ventures, Col. Jordan had good reasons to exit the turpentine business. For two decades, turpentine spirits mixed with alcohol had been marketed as the popular, although volatile, illuminant, camphene. In August 1859 in Pennsylvania, however, a former railway conductor, Edwin L. Drake, discovered an effective means of drilling for oil, and almost immediately kerosene, a brighter burning and safer fuel, was being produced. But the economics of

land and produced $25,000 in sales volume with 150 slaves. By comparison, in 1853, Col. Jordan's sales were approximately $55,000; the number of slaves and acres of timberland he owned at the time are estimates—150 slaves owned and 50 to 75 leased, and 8,000 acres.

turpentine had also deteriorated—materially. Most of the longleaf pine timber along the coast and rivers, especially on those tracts with deepwater access, now bore the familiar "cat face"[8] scars of turpentine production; trees worked for turpentine died after about ten years. Slave prices were determined by cotton; slaves that cost $750 in 1846 had doubled in price to $1,500;[9] the annual rental contracts for slaves had risen to $250/year from $125/year. Charter freight charges in 1860 at 75 cents per barrel were double the 35-cent cost in 1846.[10] Yet along with the diminishing pine forests and the cost squeeze, the base prices for spirits and rosin remained about the same: $.40/gallon for spirits and $1.30/barrel for rosin. As a result, the producers were pressured to increase volume every year just to realize the same income, which required more slaves...and so on.

Having grown cotton and peanuts with varying degrees of success, Col. Jordan did not hesitate to undertake rice planting, although the techniques for planting and growing rice was unfamiliar. In addition to having the Charleston market just 60 miles away, the attractions included a relatively stable plantation life, less travel, predictable prices, a fine rice mill, and a large plantation with no shortage of neighborhood expertise should technical advice be needed. A typical plantation of 600 acres in cultivation might utilize 300 slaves and produce 1,000,000 pounds of rice which, at 3 1/2 cents per pound, would yield an annual income of $35,000 (or $650,000 today),[11] approximately 1 1/2 times what he earned annually from turpentine, and a number of plantations produced twice that amount. However, he did not forget his axiom about needing a fallback for servicing his debt; Col. Jordan readily accepted business risks but was not a gambler. In the event his rice crop failed or was washed out by a freshet, he would retain some turpentine and peanut production, and there was also a salt works on the Laurel Hill property at Magnolia Beach. His next line of defense was to sell Laurel Hill. Finally, and only as an emergency resort, he could sell slaves. With an active market and a slave force heavily weighted to young male field hands, this investment was not only more liquid than most bank notes but the value of slaves had been rising every year since the Panic of 1837 and represented not only the vast majority of his wealth, but also the annual increase in his net worth.

Col. Jordan thought it likely either that the North and South would negotiate a political compromise, or that the North might continue to

[8] So called because of the series of V-shaped scars made on the tree trunk to encourage flow of raw turpentine sap.

[9] Emory Quinter Hawk, *Economic History of the South* (New York, 1934, Reprint Westport, Conn.: Greenwood Press, 1973), 241.

[10] Prices taken from actual contracts in 1846 and 1860.

[11] Charles W. Joyner, *Down by the Riverside: A South Carolina Slave Community* (Urbana and Chicago: University of Illinois Press, 1984), 19-20.

posture and threaten but would not forcibly oppose the South's secession. There seemed to be a reasonable probability that the prosperity of the 1850s would continue into the 1860s. Besides, large rice plantations were occasionally sold but rarely to anyone outside the plantation community— this could be the chance of a lifetime. Therefore, in December 1859, he paid Plowden Weston's asking price of $85,000 with $17,000 cash and a mortgage note for $68,000 and began to reorient his business to planting rice. First, he sold nearly 10,000 acres of timberland to Nicholas Nixon for a $25,000 note.[12] Next he bought about 40 slaves from Effingham Wagner for $44,000, giving Wagner $8,000 cash and notes for the balance.[13] Finally, he liquidated one of the innovative turpentine partnerships he had set up years earlier to give two of his most promising overseers a chance to build their own equity. One of them, Isaiah Williams, had not adapted well to leadership. The other, Eli Parker, had flourished, and while this partnership was reduced in size, Col. Jordan bought a large tract in the lower Santee swamp for Parker to continue producing turpentine. The object was to provide as many slaves as possible for the rice fields. The 1860 census indicates that Col. Jordan owned 305 slaves, making him one of only 84 men in the entire South to own more than 300 slaves.[14]

Committed to learning the nuances of planting rice firsthand, Col. Jordan stayed on Waccamaw Neck all summer instead of taking his family to a retreat as was his practice, and by July his crop looked very promising. The year before, 1859, the plantation produced 672,000 pounds of whole rice, or about $23,000 in revenue, and he expected to produce at least that much income. By October, however, it was evident that his yield would fall short. Actual production in 1860 was 314,000 pounds, which converted to only $11,000—less than half the prior year.[15] The reason for the discrepancy with the crop yield is a mystery, although two factors probably contributed. One was the likelihood that his slaves had not, in one season, made the transition from the piney woods to the rice field. The second resulted from his negotiations with his miller, Thomas Daggett. Plowden Weston's father, Francis Marion Weston, had hired Daggett, an engineer from Massachusetts, to be the miller for the Laurel Hill mill, and when he proved to be not only an excellent miller but a blacksmith and carpenter, either Francis, or more likely, Plowden Weston, made Daggett a part owner in the mill. This arrangement did not suit Col. Jordan, however. To him, ownership of Laurel Hill meant control of the entire operation, including the mill, which

---

[12] Col. Jordan bought his first tract of land in Little River from the brothers, Nicholas and Thomas Nixon, in 1846, and the Nixons had introduced him to peanut farming on a large scale.

[13] Accounting for transaction dated 1/16/60.

[14] Edgar, *South Carolina: A History*, 311.

[15] Laurel Hill rice mill ledger, South Carolina Historical Society.

he later valued at $29,000.[16] Daggett realized this, and by May, 1860, five months after the change in ownership, Daggett decided to leave Laurel Hill, "the situation of my family requiring it." He had just installed a steam powered barrel stave machine and corn-grinding mill at a "cost price" of $6,640.[17] By the fall, the two men had settled on a price. Unfortunately, when Daggett left, Laurel Hill was without an experienced miller, and as a consequence both the quality and quantity of the milled rice suffered.

Further, by the fall of 1860, Col. Jordan was beginning to feel pressure from his lenders. From the professionals, his slave trader in Richmond and his commission merchants in New York and Charleston, he could expect periodic calls for repayment caused by the ebb and flow of money in the economy.[18] However, men from whom he had leased slaves for years on annually renewing notes were requesting full payment, as were those who had sold him land. With an agricultural economy, most families were virtually self-sufficient, had few investment opportunities, and little need for transactional cash, so individual loans was a way to invest. If an individual lender felt that his money was secure, he was usually willing to collect only the going rate of interest, 6 to 8 percent, and to renew his note year after year.[19] But in 1860, with South Carolina's hotspurs threatening to secede if Abraham Lincoln was elected President, the added uncertainty prompted lenders to call in their notes.

With sales of turpentine and peanuts and $7,000 of milled rice that came with the plantation, he managed to satisfy the majority of his small creditors, postponing payment on the total of $23,000 owed to the commission merchants. Col. Jordan had anticipated that the business transition might be

---

[16] Col. Daniel W. Jordan "Diary," January 1, 1868, Jordan Collection, DMC.

[17] Thomas W. Daggett to Col. Daniel W. Jordan, May 8, 1860, Jordan Collection, DMC.

[18] For his sales of turpentine, Col. Jordan was represented in New York by the commission merchant, Benjamin Blossom. For rice, he dealt with the Charleston firm of Mazyck & Howard, and while the relationship with both principals was close, he generally corresponded with Stephen L. Howard. William St. Julian Mazyck was a cousin of Plowden Weston, and since Weston was a creditor, Col. Jordan wanted to avoid a conflict of interest.

[19] In the South capital was a scarce resource and there were many more opportunities to invest than there were available funds. Borrowed money, therefore, was not an option but rather a fact of life, and one requirement for the borrower was that he had to inspire enough credibility to convince suppliers/creditors that he not only could but would perform; i.e., repay them. It was crucial that one's credit reputation be above reproach. No financial statements were ever issued, and usually there was no collateral. On large notes—$500 or more—the creditor required a well known "security" signature, or endorser—usually a large landowner or slaveowner. Col. Jordan might sign hundreds of his own notes in a year's time, and endorse another twenty or thirty. The "securities" on his notes were friends and family; for

tight, but the speed and direction that events were taking made him uncomfortable. It was like being in a small rowboat on a fast moving river—he could hear a dull roar coming from somewhere ahead....and it was growing louder.

However, money and rice yields weren't the only things on Col. Jordan's mind in the fall. of 1860. His oldest daughter, Sarah Victoria, 19, a graduate of St. Mary's in Raleigh and Madame Togno's, a finishing school on Meeting St. in Charleston, and her father's pride and joy, was preparing to marry Ambrose Davie, a recent medical school graduate of the University of North Carolina and a grandson of Gen. William Davie, the Revolutionary War hero, in December 1860. They were married on December 13, a Friday, and a week to the day before South Carolina seceded from the Union.

The immediate reaction of Southern businessmen to the announcement of secession that winter was enthusiasm. With England as a partner, they would be free of the moralistic sermons from the abolitionists, and from their dependence on Northern "capitalists." In contrast, for the Northern merchant who dealt in cotton, rice, sugar, turpentine, and other Southern commodities, secession brought a state of panic. Not only was their source of income threatened but hundreds of thousands of dollars in capital loans owed to them by Southern planters were suddenly in jeopardy. Col. Jordan's New York agent, Benjamin Blossom, was no exception even though he had been unusually clear sighted in the warnings he issued in early December; in fact, the two men represented opposing points of view about the likelihood of war and the consequences of disunion. Col. Jordan, the entrepreneur and optimist, saw the possibilities, whereas Blossom, the conservative, saw the downside. Blossom wrote:

> You seem not to realize what you have to do though with your lauded negro property depreciated 50 percent & all trade & commerce killed for no one knows how long with [—] foes & possible trouble with your negros & the certainty that in less than one year peaceable separation the two sections could drift into war. ..The credit of the South, as of yourself here, is based on the support stable value of Land & Negroes & crops, etc. & the cause lately pursued (because of evils having occurred which will have probably to a great extent [prove] imaginary) has depreciated these millions of dollars & will depreciate them millions and millions more. The peculiar products of the South have declined so that 200 millions of dollars will not cover the loss on Naval Stores, Rice, Sugar, & Cotton

instance, Henry Buck endorsed his $68,000 note to Plowden Weston. In fact, it was not unusual for an endorser, for convenience, to pre-sign a number of printed note forms even though by doing so this endorser would have no idea either of the magnitude or the timing of his potential liability.

Crops, unless things mend & prices recover. The maintenance of the Union alone will cause return of Confidence & recovery of prices.[20]

The financial pressure that began building in 1860 only intensified for the first months after secession, and as a large borrower, Col. Jordan was contending, not only with the large creditors, but with the sudden groundswell towards liquidity. However, nothing—debts, tight money, crop failure, bankruptcy—all his prior disappointments and setbacks combined—nothing could have prepared him for the next letter, which was postmarked "Donaldsonville, Louisiana, and dated February 13th, 1861:

Col. Jordan
Greenville, S.C.

Dear Sir:

"Ere this reaches you, you will no doubt have heard the afflicting news that your poor daughter, M[rs.] Davie and her husband were lost on the steamboat Charmer which was destroyed by fire on Sunday night last opposite the plantation of my son in law M T_____ Gaudet in the parish of St. James about ten miles below this place and some 60 miles above New Orleans.[21]

Given the ambiguity of the address, Col. Jordan may have received the news earlier, but whoever the messenger, the suddenness and finality of the loss of his daughter on her wedding trip must have left him stunned and utterly heartbroken. But he was not allowed time to grieve—the relentless financial pressure did not abate. On February 28, just a week after he learned about Victoria and Ambrose, his Charleston agents, Mazyck & Howard, unaware of the tragedy and under considerable financial stress themselves, wrote: "The statement you make of your affairs seems very satisfactory. We trust you will realize your anticipation. But before these commodities can be converted into money, what is to be done? Your present [debt] to us is about $14,500. Our means are very small & the Banks will do nothing, we already owing them."[22]

[20] Charles W. Blossom to Col. Daniel W. Jordan, December 8, 1860, Jordan Collection, DMC.

[21] ____ Gaudet to Col. Daniel W. Jordan, February 13, 1861, Jordan Collection, DMC.

[22] Mazyck & Howard to Col. Daniel W. Jordan, February 28, 1861, Jordan Collection, DMC.

Another significant pending obligation was his first installment of $6,800 due to Plowden Weston in February 1861. Given the disappointing rice crop from the prior year, and concerned about the mounting financial pressure, Col. Jordan swallowed his pride and approached Weston, hoping that as one of the wealthiest of the rice planters, he would understand the unusual circumstances and postpone the principal payment for six months until the rice crop could be harvested. To his surprise, Weston refused, a decision probably based on the fact that a modification involved his father's estate, which he was not in the mood to change. After protracted negotiations, Mazyck & Howard, who had a large stake in his success, lent Col. Jordan the interest on the Weston note and eventually prevailed upon Weston to postpone the principal payment.

Of course Col. Jordan, no stranger to cash flow related problems, thought he had arranged a reliable fallback. If, in spite of his sanguine expectations, the rice crop failed, he knew he could rely on turpentine and peanuts. His mistake was in assuming that there would continue to be a market. On April 12, when the Confederate artillery opened on Fort Sumter in Charleston harbor some 60 miles south of him, it not only eliminated any further political compromise but also removed Col. Jordan's access to the New York market for the sale of his products. Then to make matters worse, in late June, by order of President Lincoln, Union warships began implementing Winfield Scott's "Anaconda Strategy," a total blockade of the South's key deepwater ports.

Few men could have withstood this financial pressure, combined with the personal tragedy of losing his oldest child and her husband. He was receiving letters about twice a week from a variety of suppliers, large and small, who were concerned about their businesses and who wanted full payment now! Desperate, he was forced to consider desperate measures. A young Georgetown entrepreneur, Sidney S. Fraser, suggested running turpentine through the blockade from Georgetown to England, but his Charleston agent, Stephen Howard, who was his primary source of liquidity, convinced him that the risks were too great.

Because of their relative independence, turpentine slaves had a reputation for being unruly, so when news of the capture of Ft. Sumter filtered through the grapevine, it may have been responsible for three unusual incidents. More likely, with Col. Jordan's finances somewhat in extremis, the slaves may have been irritated about a shortage in provisions. In any case, these incidents were ominous, presaging more trouble to come. On April 18th, four days after Ft. Sumter surrendered, Eli Parker wrote Col. Jordan a note from the Santee tract:

Moses whipped Henderson[23] a day or two ago. I went up there to day & took him—but thought Should have to shoot him but at last he give up - Some one no doubt but our negros broke open a man's House last night & took all the meat he had & even pots plate knives & forks - you had better have those Searched that go to your House. If such goes on there will be no staying here...[24]

Parker wasn't exaggerating. Slavery worked only because Negroes generally accepted their status as slaves, or were compelled to work by judicious use of the threat of punishment—usually whipping. But on the rice plantations in the vicinity of Georgetown, the proportion of black to white was a minimum of 6 to 1 and after 1862, when the planter families began to move away, the proportion increased rapidly. A few weeks later, as a result of a similar incident involving female slaves, Parker received a letter from Susan Moyed asking to be paid for what "Mr Jordan's negros" stole from her. "I am a poor woman and I am not able to lose my things and not get nothing from them..." She asked for $60 for her loss of "1 nice worsted dress, 1 pair of sheets, 2 pretty coats, 1 pair drawers, and some unbleached homespun."[25]

On July 30, 1861, Howard wrote Col. Jordan that several Charleston merchants were planning to run the blockade with a load of naval stores. He commented hopefully, "The general impression in the city is that England & France will soon raise the Blockade, as the slow progress of the Lincoln Army has destroyed the prospect of a short war." The combination of the blockade and tight money had Howard worried. He wrote, "We would not call upon you [for money] at this time if we possibly could get on without it, but our Banks are doing nothing, and as we are not able to sell anything, will require the assistance of our friends to go on..."[26]

In response to Howard's letter of July 30, Col. Jordan sent a load of turpentine spirits to Charleston in August but the vessel was intercepted by the blockade and captured. Adding insult to injury, the yield for the 1861 rice crop at Laurel Hill was even worse than the 1860 crop—it amounted to only 230,000 pounds, or $8,000.

---

[23] Moses may have been a slave driver, or Henderson, an overseer.

[24] E.I. Parker to Col. Daniel W. Jordan, April 18, 1861, Jordan Collection, DMC.

[25] Susan Moyed to E.I. Parker; 1861, Jordan Collection, DMC.

[26] Stephen L. Howard to Col. Daniel W. Jordan, July 30, 1861, Jordan Collection, DMC.

By November 1861 the price for rice had increased to 4 cents/lb. from 2 1/2 cents in September—shortages were beginning to affect prices more than the loss of the export market. Throughout the fall, Howard prodded Col. Jordan to send all the rice he could. In most of these letters, he implores, in effect: "No more money! You need to pay us some of what you owe. We're out of money to lend—there's a blockade here and we have enough trouble finding buyers. You told us you had arranged with a bank to cover your expenses until the crop could be sold. Make them honor their commitments or find another bank to lend you money." Despite the rhetoric however, Howard continued to accept Col. Jordan's drafts—the tradition of service was just too strong.

Frustrated by frequent transportation bottlenecks and soaring freight expenses in the fall of 1861, Col. Jordan bought an interest in a schooner, Laura, to haul his products to Charleston. He was also drafting his own bills of lading, lacking the printed forms. In February, 1862, Captain Chadwick of the Laura sent some disturbing news:

> Col Jordan   Dear Sir   I arived heare Last night from Santee where I left the Laura with parkers son the yankeys have cut off the pasage to charleston they have Sunk 5 of the costers....What do you think best to be done   Come back go up the Santee or fight our way through write me or come down on Thursday if I can get 20 men I can take those barges with (Eds?). I want to go up home to day and will be back Thursday.

> JRChadwick[27]

Now the ships blockading Charleston were not simply watching the ocean entrance; the approaches behind the barrier islands were also being patrolled. Since steam propulsion was needed to transport the rice barrels upriver to the railroad trestles, the owners sold the Laura for $5,000, probably for service as a blockade runner.

As George Rogers explains in his *History of Georgetown County*, the fall of two key Confederate forts on the Tennessee River in early February 1862, Forts Henry and Donelson, created the need to pull replacement troops from the coastal defense and reinforce the western armies. The fortifications ringing Winyah Bay, therefore, were abandoned and a defensive line established further inland.[28] In April and May, 1862, Federal gunboats that had been patrolling the coast, made their first incursions into the rivers, and

---

[27] J.R. Chadwick to Col. Daniel W. Jordan, February 18, 1862, Jordan Collection, DMC

[28] Rogers, *History of Georgetown County*, 396.

were there for the remainder of the war. These gunboats, whose primary mission was to prevent blockade runner traffic, would occasionally harass planters known to be secessionists by burning boats, docks, barns, and mills, and whenever possible offering asylum to the "contrabands," or slaves.

Soon thereafter, as a way to protect their families as well as their slaves, the planters began to leave their plantations for properties they bought up to 150 miles inland. Emily Weston, Plowden's wife, wrote to Benjamin Allston on July 4, 1862, that Plantersville, a community twenty miles inland, was filled to overflowing with planters and that the only families remaining on Waccamaw Neck were the Jordans and the Rosas. David D. Rosa, a New Yorker, was hired by Plowden Weston as a tutor and later he made him the overseer of his plantation, Hagley.[29] Commander Prentiss, officer in charge of the Union gunboats operating in Winyah Bay, reported in May 1862, that, "the rebels are just now very much frightened, and are leaving their plantations in every direction, driving their slaves before them in the pine woods."[30]

With the familiar routes to Charleston cut off by the Federal gunboats, Col. Jordan had two alternative routes to market. His products could to be shipped up the Santee River to intersect the Northeastern Railroad, with Charleston as a destination, or up the Pee Dee River to meet the Wilmington train. The problem, in addition to the basic logistics and the enemy gunboats, was that the wooden rice barrels were heavy (650-720 lbs.) and cumbersome, and there being only rudimentary roads and few bridges, the railroads had a transportation monopoly which they were not bashful about exploiting. For shippers, the service was atrocious. The rice barrels were rolled by hand or lifted with block and tackle, but train cars were open to wind and rain and even with the stout staves and straps, breakage could not be prevented when the barrels shifted or when cars rammed each other (air brakes were a later invention). David Cowan, who managed Col. Jordan's shipments to Wilmington, found the Wilmington and Manchester Railroad particularly frustrating: "the manner in which the R.R. Companies have acted, by breaking Bbls to pieces and carrying them as above stated [ruined by rain water] has worked very much to my injury.... Railroads, like every thing else, are making more money than they know what to do with - and nothing can be done with them."[31]

It is a testament to the courage and fidelity of Mazyck & Howard that they allowed Col. Jordan to continue to draw on their account and thereby

[29] Walton H. Rawls, *A Century of American Sculpture: Treasures from Brookgreen Gardens* (New York: Abbeville Press, 1988), 115.

[30] Rogers, *History of Georgetown County*, 402.

[31] David Cowan to Col Daniel W. Jordan, May 2, 1860, Jordan Collection, DMC.

keep his operation going through 1862. Now that the Confederate harbor defenses had been effectively abandoned, the unopposed Federal gunboats were constantly in Winyah Bay or patrolling the rivers, and slaves were looking for opportunities to escape to one of these vessels. In September, at rice harvest, the gunboat activity on the Waccamaw had increased to a point that Col. Jordan chose not to harvest a majority of his rice crop for fear of losing his slaves. His only large recorded sale in 1862 was a $19,000 sale of turpentine to the Confederate Government in December; $9,000 of these proceeds went to Plowden Weston and $6,000 went to Mazyck & Howard.

That winter, Howard had an intriguing idea—one that had the potential of solving several financial problems simultaneously. The planters had moved inland, leaving Mazyck & Howard with thousands of dollars in unpaid crop advances. As Howard put it: ".....the rice planters are paying us nothing and our balances to them are large and they (are) in no condition to meet them."[32] The plan would involve Col. Jordan buying rice from these absentee planters, including those on the Pee Dee, Sampit, Black, and Santee Rivers in addition to the Waccamaw; Mazyck & Howard would advance Col. Jordan the funds to buy the rice. One of the keys to Howard's plan was getting the products to market, and in that, Col. Jordan had proven to be daring and resourceful. The rice had to be processed, and there was the large rice mill at Laurel Hill. It was dangerous, but the elements were in place to make it possible.

Col. Jordan took most of the risks but if the plan worked, everybody would win. Moreover, the timing was propitious because Howard, who was close to the market, expected a major movement in price to follow the decline in production caused by the planters' leaving. His reasoning went like this: the market price for milled rice was 8 cents, and would soon be 10 cents. It cost 4 to 5 cents/lb. for purchase, milling, and sales commissions, another 4 to 5 cents to get it to the railroad, and 4 to 5 cents rail freight, or about 12 to 15 cents total. Other than possibly transportation, expenses wouldn't change. Now suppose the market price moved to 20 cents and one could buy as much as he wanted. The profit possibilities would be limited only by how much rice could be bought and processed.

The Confederate government was essentially the market because the soldiers had to be fed, and this way, they would get it. For those planters who still had their overseers and remaining slaves planting their fields, they would receive payment immediately and avoid the logistical headaches of milling their rice and smuggling it to Charleston. Col. Jordan would perform that function—he would buy the rice, mill it, and ship it. For

---

[32] Mazyck & Howard to Col. Daniel W. Jordan, February 22, 1863, Jordan Collection, DMC.

Mazyck & Howard, who would underwrite the purchases and sell the rice to the Confederate government, they would earn the 2 1/2 percent commission and perhaps get some prior advances paid. For the government buyers who were having difficulty acquiring rice in quantity, this was a service. For Col. Jordan, frustrated as he was with three unsuccessful efforts to produce a satisfactory rice crop, this not only made sense but played to his strengths—negotiations and logistics. The key was to avoid the gunboats. It proved safer to ship the rice up the Pee Dee by steamer to the Wilmington and Manchester trestle than to ship it seventy three miles up the Santee River and then back down to Charleston on the train.[33]

Their first participant was Henry A. Middleton who owned Weehaw and Kensington on the Black River. George Rogers says of H.A. Middleton that he was the grandson of Henry Middleton, president of the Continental Congress and nephew of Arthur Middleton, signer of the Declaration of Independence. In 1850 he owned 302 slaves and his plantations yielded 900,000 pounds of rice in 1851; he was also "one of the truly rich men in the district."[34] Col. Jordan's only limitation was the amount of money Mazyck & Howard could advance to buy the rough rice. They started cautiously....this scheme was not yet proven and money was scarce.

Howard's intuitions proved to be right. By March 22, 1863, rice was selling for 19 cents to private buyers in Charleston—a phenomenal increase in one of the most important money crops produced in South Carolina. Only a year earlier, which was nine months into the blockade, rice had been selling in Charleston for 3 cents. The Southern economy, however, was fragile since most of the wealth had been invested in slaves, and the chronic shortage of liquid capital, combined with the inability to earn foreign exchange by exporting its commodities, caused the rapid run up in prices.

As the primary buyer, the government had two advantages. One was that they could pay cash for their purchases. Second, they could accept delivery at the trestles where the railroads crossed the river rather than in

---

[33] Wilmington, the South's only large port on the East Coast, was still active and had the added possibility of export whereas traffic in and out of Charleston had, for all intents and purposes, ceased. Until it fell in January, 1865 to a tremendous combined Federal land and naval siege, Fort Fisher, designed on the order of Sevastopol and called the "Gibraltar of America," overlooked the mouth of the Cape Fear River and kept the blockading fleet around Wilmington at arms length. To effectively cut off traffic into and out of Wilmington meant that a blockading fleet had to patrol over fifty miles of the Cape Fear's labyrinth of inlets, shoals, and islands, and the virtual impossibility of doing so made Wilmington the home port for most of the South's blockade runners. It was the Wilmington blockade runners that were largely responsible for maintaining Lee's army in the field and supplied with food and equipment during 1864 and 1865.

[34] Rogers, *History of Georgetown County*, 285.

Charleston or Wilmington where storage was expensive if it could be found. Consequently, the government offered a price substantially less than that offered by the private buyers.

But where was the government getting its cash? This was wartime and Southerners had little money for taxes, yet the government suppliers had to be paid. Consequently, the Confederate Treasury Secretary, C.C. Memminger, chose the only alternative and floated paper currency, or "Confederate money," which was predictably highly inflationary. Like the game of "hot potato," Confederate money was effective so long as the next person would accept it in payment for goods or services—the Confederate government did not compel its acceptance. Patriotism carried it for a few months, but it couldn't last—inflation was inevitable. By March 1863, prices in terms of this currency, were seven times their level two years earlier. However it was the items not produced in the South that were totally out of reach—nails, for example, were selling for $1.50/pound, but only if they could be found.[35]

The planters liked the advantages offered by this venture and the rice kept coming—Alex M. Forster from the Sampit River plantation, Friendfield, sent Col. Jordan a note in April saying that he was loading the Laurel Hill boat and had received $2,000 from Mazyck & Howard for a thousand bushels but that with prices continuing to climb, he wanted to wait before selling any more.[36] J. H. Trapier sent word that he had heard that Col. Jordan was buying rice and asked what price he could get for 5,000 bushels at his plantation on the Black River.[37]

This new venture was very risky in that river steamboats could be intercepted at any time by the Union gunboats and the rice confiscated. Col. Jordan had a several choices—whether to try to ship his rice all the way into Charleston or Wilmington in order to sell to the private buyers at a much higher price, or sell to the government at the river trestle and save the rail freight, and whether to use the Santee or the Pee Dee. The Pee Dee, which went to the North Carolina market, was safer, but initially the prices were lower. Furthermore, the Yankees were not the only ones who threatened to take the rice by force. At first the North Carolina officials, no doubt in response to the need for food for the army but with tight budgets to pay for their purchases, tried intimidation. Cowan wrote to Col. Jordan that the government offered 10 cents for an entire lot and "threatened to Seize (it) unless accepted." Because the "market price" for the few remaining private buyers was considerably higher he refused, but ultimately had to sell. "The

[35] David Cowan to Col. Daniel W Jordan, Sept. 20, 1863, Jordan Collection, DMC.

[36] Alex M. Forster to Col. Daniel W. Jordan, April 1, 1863, Jordan Collection, DMC.

[37] J. H. Trapier to Col. Daniel W. Jordan, July 13, 1863, Jordan Collection, DMC.

next lot of 400 casks I am about to send to other parties @ 13c. Should you Ship after the above, you must make up your mind to abide (the) consequences. I think I can evade them....."[38] This price differential between the government and the private buyers did not last—the government soon realized that if they were going to continue to buy rice in quantity, they would have to accept a price closer to the private rate.

In April, Mazyck & Howard received a large shipment from Col. Jordan that arrived on the 11th "in the most wretched order...."[39] They had asked the government to accept the rice at the river bridge, but because of the condition of the barrels, were refused. This time they couldn't blame rough treatment by the railroad because the barrels themselves were missing hoops and had opened to let in the rain. Three quarters of the barrels were without heads. Mazyck & Howard had a sizable salvage job which they achieved admirably, sold it to the government, and collected $30,932.77. Howard commented that with the threat from the Union fleet, private buyers and speculators were nowhere to be found and the banks had all left town. Out of curiosity, he checked on shipments from other rice planters and found them to be generally undamaged and reported that they were using more and better hoops. Never attentive to this kind of "detail," Col. Jordan assigned supervision to a manager and apparently, since no one expected this arrangement to continue for long, he was more interested in shipping volumes of rice than in slowing the process to emphasize quality.

Shipments of rice were amazingly large and frequent—by late April, Cowan had sold another lot for $27,339.59. "I fear I will not be able to realize 18 cents on the next lot," he worried. "Virginia men don't pay 25c as it will bring no more than that [18 cents] in Richmond."[40] Meanwhile, Parker has been busy in the turpentine business, and sent Col. Jordan an accounting of the filled barrels—over 13,000 barrels of raw turpentine and 2,000 barrels of rosin. Many of the rosin barrels were sunk in black water ponds for security and remained there for the remainder of the war. Even at pre-war prices, the total cache was worth $15,000. Most of this turpentine survived the war and was probably used to pay Benjamin Blossom his accumulated pre-war advances.

Col. Jordan and John LaBruce also operated a salt works on Magnolia Beach and sold salt for $12/bu. Although demand for salt was only occasional, some orders were for as much as 100 bushels, which was

[38] David Cowan to Col. Daniel W. Jordan, March 18, 1863, Jordan Collection, DMC.

[39] Mazyck & Howard to Col. Daniel W. Jordan, April 8, 1863, Jordan Collection, DMC.

[40] David Cowan to Col. Daniel W. Jordan, April 26, 1863, Jordan Collection, DMC.

welcome as a supplement to income.

Early in May 1863, Col. Jordan must have taken some satisfaction in making a $20,400 payment on his note to Plowden Weston. By this time he had paid $46,000 of the $85,000 purchase price. Weston wrote in May, thanking him for his "very prompt and honorable payment of these sums which have proved a great convenience." Confident that he could generate substantial sums from the purchase, milling, and sale of rice, Col. Jordan even asked Weston if he could prepay the bond through the February 1865 installment. Weston replied that he was not anxious to receive the prepayment although he certainly would not refuse it, and would prefer to get it by August when the interest on Confederate securities was reduced. He also mentioned that he was glad that Laurel Hill had not yet suffered from the Yankee raids.[41]

Stephen Howard and David Cowan, Col. Jordan's representatives in Charleston and Wilmington respectively, had their sensitive fingers on the pulse of the market and kept him informed. They were a good team, especially since this was where Col. Jordan's genius lay—in organizing projects, in transportation, in finance, and in logistics. Despite the success of this current venture, it was increasingly apparent that his purchase of Laurel Hill had been a mistake, but when he mentioned his willingness to sell it, Howard reminded him that any arrangement would have to bear the approval of Plowden Weston. To get his approval, the sale could not pay him out early and would have to bring security, or collateral, that would be an improvement on what he currently held. Then there was the question of how the buyer would pay for it. In Confederate money? It was doubtful that Weston would accept it. In fact, the money situation was getting worse daily and Howard was concerned that unless the Confederate government did something soon to restore confidence, this already highly inflated money would be worthless.[42] Cowan described the difficulties in locating private buyers and finding a safe place to store money:

> I can sell any quantity—more at same figure (25 cents); it appears to me to be a good trade—Gov't can move it, individuals cannot. RR Co has no place to store it—Gov't is willing to take it on platform, subject to injury by weather—individuals are unwilling to take the risk...Cape Fear Bank will receive your money on deposit on following conditions—Viz—Charging depositors 1/4 %—

---

[41] Plowden C.J. Weston to Col. Daniel W. Jordan, May 17, 1863, Jordan Collection, DMC.

[42] Mazyck & Howard to Col. Daniel W. Jordan, December 7, 1863, Jordan Collection, DMC.

depositor agrees to take such funds as he deposits—in case the
town is attacked, depositor is to be notified to draw his money—if
he fails to do so, and the money is lost—it is his and not the bank's
loss. I am unwilling to subscribe to any such arrangement, and have
therefore withdrawn my deposits....[43]

This new arrangement had succeeded beyond anyone's expectations;
Col. Jordan's sales for the first six months of providing this service were in
excess of $100,000, and his profit margin, based on his results for February
through June, 1864, was 50 percent—a phenomenal windfall, even in
inflated Confederate money. At the same time, he provided both the
planters and the government a valuable service. Since Col. Jordan was, for
the government buyers, a relatively small supplier, he was paid at the going
rate, a price sufficient to bring not only his rice but quantities from other
sellers, to market. He was paid in Confederate money, but his inventory
turnover was so rapid—a week or two—that the rate of inflation did not
pose a serious handicap. Furthermore, as a net borrower, inflation reduced
the real value of his debt because it allowed him to repay it with cheaper
dollars.

However, though the rice could be easily sold, as the activity of the
Union gunboats accelerated, more rice planters quit planting, being unwilling
to risk losing their slaves to escape or capture. So while he made some rice
sales early in 1864 totaling about $75,000, the daily threat from the gunboats
had its intended effect. Finally, in the late spring of 1864, the Laurel Hill mill
was burned by one of the gunboats and shortly thereafter the Jordans
moved to Camden.

None too soon. By the spring of 1865, with nobody to feed them, and
experiencing for the first time the exuberance of freedom without the
familiar strictly imposed discipline, the former slaves looted, burned, and
stole their way through the rice plantations.[44] There were several reactions
to this military, political, and sociological crisis. One was an unsigned and
undated note that came to Col. Jordan from his Laurel Hill overseer,
probably I. H. Sawyer:

Dear Sir

I write under the most exciting of circumstances—at the fall of
Charleston I tried to move the negros but found that they all wanted
[to] run away. At the same time Columbia fell. I did not know where
I could carry them. I have heard that they passed through your
place & destroyed everything & hoped they could be fed—it would

[43] David Cowan to Col. Daniel W. Jordan, December 8, 1863, Jordan Collection,
DMC.
[44] J.H. Easterby, *The South Carolina Rice Plantation* (Chicago: University of
Chicago Press, 1945), 206.

be impossible to keep them anywhere—the yankees have possession of Georgetown in force & will soon rade through here & destroy everything. The opinion of all influential men is that the negros are a gone question & if so I thought it improper to try & save them. Thought everybody here are taken the oath of allegiance to the yankee Government—thinking of our conversation I went down to town & took the oath. They gave new protection for property only negros—[after?] loose the negros [we] had are better so to save what we can I done it against my will & now regret it.

Ned & Doc have gone to yankees & five of ours all ready—Some will Stay here on the place can't say how many. I will induce all to stay so if we are to have negros after the war we can get at them. Some have lost all. If you think best you could send for them but would take [an] armed force to carry them—then in the condition of the country they would run & go to the yankees. If they all go or nearly so. I wish you had some of the mules if you have need for them.

[At] times like these I am at a loss how to act for the best. I got Mr Ogburn to carry this letter to you & bring an answer to me as it was the only way that I can hear from you. write me everything that you think I may do for the best. Could you not send Joe for some of the mules or Peter if you need them—I may have acted wrong but that was the last resort here to save anything. If [ ] does the yankees at Georgetown they will not rade in less than three or four weeks—if you can send down you would be safe but if I leave all the negros would go at once.

I send your check on Charleston for 2545.40 twenty five hundred forty five and 40/100 Dollars. I can't use it here perhaps you it is what I got for the meat furnished the Government. Col or Mrs J write me conclusions about the matter by [ ]

By April, 1865, the month the war ended, Col. Jordan was in Camden, trying to decide what to do next and corresponding with Eli Parker, his partner in the turpentine business. The first priority was to generate some income, but at least in the turpentine woods, the former slaves were reluctant to work whether or not there was money to pay them. Parker wrote that he had either distilled or saved some spirits which he took to Georgetown to sell but was offered only 60 cents, a premium price before the war but now with the effects of inflation, was unreasonably low. Disappointed, he stored the barrels in a warehouse. The latest market quotation in New York for spirits was $1.85, but people were saying that it could fall to $1.00 because of a new product, kerosene. Parker reported that their turpentine stills were torn up and the copper bottoms were worn out and it would take two or three thousand dollars to restore them to working order. Furthermore, there were no coopers or iron hoops; his suggestion was to use whiskey or beer barrels—they held 25 gallons, cost only 50 cents each, and were the best in the world. The most difficult challenge, however, was to find labor. He continued:

> You were very fortunate that General Potter did not reach your place. You have no idea what influence the Yankees have among the negroes. I saw the provost marshall, [the Col] commanding, and they say that they do not know the disposition that has been made of Laurel Hill or what has become of the mashenary [machinery] you Spoke of—they are under the impression that if you come down and take [possession] that you can retain Laurel Hill. Gilmore is to be military Governor of South Carolina—the yankees say that if every man does not take the oath that the state will be garrisoned by negro troops. The negros here have been very ornery but of late they have been disciplined and punished which has made quite a change—at one time it was dangerous to travel but not now—perfectly safe. I should like to know what our plan will be now to make money....I think you had better come down alone & take the oath & try to save your property.[45]

If there was one thing about business that Col. Jordan understood, chapter and verse, it was the value of labor. Nothing was going to happen anywhere until Negroes could be persuaded to work, whether for food and shelter or for money. On the other hand there was no money to be had. When the slaves were freed, the planters, who represented the wealth in the South, lost 90 percent of the value of their assets, and now that the war was over, Confederate money was worthless. In a letter to Col. Jordan, Charles Alston, in a rather high handed missive, lays much of the blame for the local chaos with the former slaves at Col. Jordan's doorstep.[46] His scarcely

---

[45] Eli Parker to Col. Daniel W. Jordan, May 28, 1865, Jordan Collection, DMC.

[46] Dear Sir - At the request of my neighbors I write to ask you as to your property at Laurel Hill. It is filled up by vagabond negros from all parts of the country who go there when they please—take what they please and are [in] fact destroying what you left of a settlement. They are thus a perfect nuisance to the neighborhood, a harbor for all the thieves and scoundrals who won't work . We know of no person acting as your agent here and I therefore write to know what you intend doing with regard to the property & whether you have abandoned it or whether you have taken steps to recover possession and if so at what day we may expect yourself or agent to occupy and endeavor to keep some order and law on it. As it stands now it is become a positive injury to all of us who are near. It would be some relief even for us to learn that by next January at least these people would be turned off or kept

concealed frustration is understandable. Col. Jordan's response is not available, but in all likelihood he would have explained that he did indeed expect to return but for the moment was attempting to resolve several pressing matters in Camden. The difference in perspective is worth noting. Alston was not interested in Col. Jordan per se; he was interested in restoring and protecting his way of life—the legacy of wealth and privilege that was being threatened. Col. Jordan understood, and was sympathetic, but to him Laurel Hill was an investment, and a marginal one at that. Nevertheless, he did return to Laurel Hill that spring, lived there, and planted rice crops there in 1866 and 1867.

The military rule imposed on the South may have initially been a godsend in insuring law and order. However, within a matter of weeks it was apparent that there would be a leveling bias that could come only at the expense of the relatively wealthy. One of the new rules was that employers were required to get a work contract signed by each worker, all of whom were illiterate. Parker described the reaction:

Dear Sir

    I have at last got all negros here to sign the contract. They go to work munday morning. [I] could not get them to do it before they signed it with grate reluctance and Isaac Reid would not do it and had to take him to Kingstree. he cut up all sorts of shines—Said he would suffer to be Shot down before he would sign it—that he didn't pretend to do anything for any man that he had been under all his life. I go to Georgetown today & will try to get those but fear they will not and as they have been off the place all summer there will be no compelling them. however I will do the best I can. The man has not yet come from Charleston to buy the turp-you had better send Pork at once as I fear they will not do much until they get it. I shall look for coopers & wagon & smith to drive down.

Respect yours
E.I. Parker[47]

under better control. I write you for our situation will be dependable on indeed if all the Planters do not stand by each other in maintaining order. We have already made many things better and if absent Planters return or place agents on their places all might yet go well.

An answer directed to Georgetown at your earliest convenience will oblige
Yours very truly
Charles Alston

[47] Eli Parker to Col. Daniel W. Jordan, September 29, 1865, Jordan Collection, DMC.

It is difficult today, 135 years later, to appreciate the hardships of 1865 and 1866. Of the 60,000 South Carolinians who fought, 21,000 did not return. Sherman and Potter had burned and wrecked businesses, court houses, plantations, railroads, and bridges. The Union military was in charge. There was no money and shortages of everything but tears; slaveowners from South Carolina alone lost nearly $300 million in freed slaves.[48] Negroes were reluctant to work or refused altogether. To survive was hard enough; to operate a business in those conditions was nearly impossible. Yet Col. Jordan was operating four—simultaneously! In 1864 he bought a 2,000 acre cotton plantation in Camden which was being managed by his son. Then there was the turpentine business in the Santee swamp run by Eli Parker, and a cotton buying business in Camden for Theodore Wagner of Charleston.

The fourth business may have been a good idea, but it required persuasion, leadership, money, coordination, nerves, and considerable luck. It involved leasing several of the inactive Georgetown rice plantations. The elements made sense—a number of families had not returned to their plantations, so their land was lying fallow and their former slaves had no work and therefore no source of food. Mazyck & Howard was also interested in generating some revenue. In early 1866, after Col. Jordan had registered his pledge of allegiance to "faithfully support and defend the Constitution ... etc" in the Camden Provost Marshal's Office, he and Dr. John D. McGill leased a Waccamaw plantation, "Prospect Hill," for a year for $2,000 from Benjamin Huger Ward, which they planted as a partnership, along with McGill's Richmond Hill, adjacent to Laurel Hill.[49]

In addition to Laurel Hill, which, of course, he owned, Col. Jordan leased and planted four other plantations:

Rose Hill	Waccamaw River
Longwood	Waccamaw River
Windsor	Black River
Keithfield	Black River

This would mean that Col. Jordan would have hired approximately 500-700 former slaves—the same ones who had been looting and burning— and at least 7 overseers. He bought seed, houses, food, tools, livestock, etc., and as Stephen Howard, who financed this venture, remarked, "you are the largest rice planter in the state and hope you may make enough to let us again be able to quote rice as a staple of the soil."[50] The normal risks of

---

[48] Edgar, *South Carolina: A History*, 374-375.

[49] Col. Daniel W. Jordan, February 9, 1866, Jordan Collection, DMC.

[50] Mazyck & Howard to Col. Daniel W. Jordan, April 30, 1866, Jordan Collection, DMC.

growing rice had not changed other than being multiplied seven times. Money was extremely scarce. But the key factor was still labor and the Negroes were violent and unpredictable. Few people would have dared to invest at all, let alone on a scale that required an up-front rental payment of about $7,500 ($72,000 today), or $1,700 to 2,000 apiece for each of the plantations, before the first seed was planted.

An added complication was that the occupying military had taken over several of the plantations and contracts between the planters and the freedmen had to bear their endorsement. The following agreement may have been typical—clearly this is a cooperative effort between Col. Jordan, the owners, and the Negro workers, and a version would soon come into common practice as "share cropping."

27 March, 66

Dear Sir:

Your note of 22nd inst came to hand this evening.

I will rent the Keithfield plantation for $1750 - being at the rate of $10 per acre, and the mill for $1500.

The rent of the plantation to expire on 1st Jan, 1867; of the mill on 1st April/67.

The party renting to take the seed rice at a valuation to be assessed by three impartial gentlemen—cash payment.

The contract made with the negroes for the present year to continue in force—namely, 1/10 of the whole crop & seed rice at the rate of 2 1/2 bushels per acre to be deducted - the remainder to be divided into two equal portions—one for the planter and the other for the laborers.

The trunks to be kept in good working order.

The mill to be delivered up in good working condition.

The engine to be used if required for threshing out the crop in case the mill is rented separately.

... Yours respectfully
FS. Parker[51]

George Rogers described the dangers of dealing with labor in a litany of examples of violence and contracts broken by the former slaves. Three days after he signed this letter, F.S. Parker, the manager of Keithfield, was

---

[51] F.S. Parker to Col. Daniel W. Jordan, March 27, 1866, Jordan Collection, DMC.

attacked by a mob:

> According to Dennis Hazel, colored agent of Parker at Keithfield, on March 31 freedman Abram quit work and called others from the fields. They armed themselves with axes, hatchets, hoes, and poles and drove Hazel to the boat. "Sampson threw a hatchet after me which struck the water in front of the boat nearly striking me in the head." Parker sent to town for help, and later two Union soldiers and Hazel approached the freedmen. "As soon as we entered the street the people collected with axes, hoes, sticks and bricks and pelted us with bricks and stones and poles, and took the gun away from one of the soldiers." Parker was forced to jump into the river and swim to the other side. Parker swore that no white man could control the Negroes now that they were free.[52]

This was an ambitious endeavor, and though not Col. Jordan's last business venture, in terms of large scale entrepreneurial risk it was to be his last hurrah. Did it succeed? The correspondence for the latter 1860s is sparse, but it appears that it did, although not comparable to the windfall that he experienced with buying, milling, and shipping the rice in 1863 and 1864. However, the acid test of its viability was positive: by the end of that crop year Mazyck & Howard had been repaid all their advances.

In September, Col. Jordan wrote to his wife, Emily, in Camden about his crops and his preliminary arrangements for the 1867 rice season, "Tom Flagg is getting up 50 hands and I have given him where he lives and also the big island. Some of the Weston hands are coming and I really think I shall get 100 to 125 hands on Laurel Hill. I shall interest Dr. Magill in it so he may attend to it. We have rented Bob Nesbit's place near here—Huger [Ward] and myself will work Longwood and also Friendfield, and, I think, Alderly...... Longwood crop is quite good, say 9000 bushels—L. Hill nothing—Rose Hill so so—Fairfield good—Windsor 5000 bushels." He will go to Charleston — there is "broke bone fever" there but no yellow fever.[53]

Apparently Col. Jordan would have three partners for 1867, Flagg, Magill, and Ward.

Unfortunately, their brave efforts to lean against the wind for a second year met with disaster, and Col. Jordan's describes the aftermath in some memoirs that he called his "Diary," written at Laurel Hill:

[52] Rogers, *History of Georgetown County*, 433.

[53] Col. Daniel W. Jordan to Emily Jordan, September 20, 1866, Jordan Collection, DMC.

On this day, January the first, 1868, I have concluded to do what I should have done long years ago; and what I think the duty of the head of every family who wishes to transmit to his descendants the many strange things which are constantly occurring in this uncertain and strange world, viz. a diary of passing events.

This is brought more forcibly to my mind by the wonderful events of the last seven years of war—five of which in actual hostilities, and three made on an unresisting and generous people, by a section of the country, the citizens of which call themselves our brothers— sprung from the same people and speaking the same language. To add to our distress we are threatened by famine. This is brought about chiefly by the meddling of the freedsman's bureau with the labouring population which is composed entirely of negroes who do now, and always did, hate constant labour—indeed will not work without compulsion.

Whilst thinking on this war, made on us for no cause whatever, the changed situation of the people of this our Parish of All Saints is brought forcibly to my mind.. I will name a few only, as all are in about the same situation. The Ward family who owned largely of real estate, and some 1,200 to 1,300 negroes, are now quite poor, having nothing left but the land which is rendered of but little value having no labourers who will work it. The Magills, Alstons, Nesbits are in about the same situation.

The writer of this Journal had, when this war began, settled on Laurel Hill plantation, and engaged in making turpentine in the pine woods, 300 negroes, 100 of whom were able men and also a half interest in 14 men working with E.I.Parker, who he took as an overseer for $200, about AD 1850. The negroes are all gone, and the mill (Rice pounding and Barrel Machines) which cost $29,000 burnt by the Yankees. So I consider my losses about a quarter of a Million of Dollars....

The last year just past has indeed been one of disaster to us. After much struggling to get the negroes to plant a little rice, the freshet of June came and swept off all as low down this river [Waccamaw] as Oakland; and the other rivers did not fare much better. The writer of this has been nearly ruined by this and [the] state of affairs, having been interested in about 800 acres up the river, from which he will not get a single bushel of rice, besides being in debt for supplies.

The state of affairs is indeed gloomy in the rice country; and I doubt if they are much better in the cotton. The planters having generally lost nearly all the rice, and not being able to pay the factors for advances made, leaves the factors unable, if they are willing, to make further advances. Indeed, with the uncertain labour it would seem imprudent for them to do so. What the country will do it is impossible to say.[54]

After the 1867 freshet, Col. Jordan concentrated his efforts on cotton and, like other South Carolinians, struggled through the Reconstruction years before recovering financially. In 1868, with the agreement of the trustees of the Weston estate, he forfeited his $46,000 investment in Laurel Hill, which reverted to his friend and former commission merchant, William Mazyck. Like most of the Georgetown plantations, Laurel Hill changed hands several times before finally being purchased by A.M. Huntington; it was one of four plantations incorporated into Brookgreen Gardens. Perhaps too much had been asked of this and other stately plantations—while they supported the antebellum planter society in grand style, they could not salvage it from the wreckage of the Civil War. Without slave labor these plantations eventually withered and died.

Col. Jordan's approach to business was to assess the circumstances, make a decision, and move on. Sentiment and tradition had their place, but usually not in business. He did not linger over failure, and was open to transactions involving rich and poor, the distinguished and the barely literate. He was a visionary, a risk taker, a survivor of the financial pressure cooker. In some ways an "outsider," he was accepted enough to win election over Charles Alston to the S.C. Legislature in 1850 and was one of only two men, after the founders, ever elected to membership in the Hot & Hot Fish Club, the social inner sanctum for the Waccamaw Neck planters. Unconstrained by their rigid social structure, however, he knew people in every niche of society. The explanation is simple—business was business— to him it was neither a hallowed way of life nor a necessary evil. Indeed, pride, so often misinterpreted as "honor," could often become a handicap, particularly in negotiations. His ability to survive, adapt, and even innovate through these traumatic, wrenching years of transition argues that he was one of the first modern businessmen in 19th century South Carolina.

---

[54] Col. Daniel W. Jordan "Diary," January 1, 1868, Jordan Collection, DMC.

10 RUMFORD PLACE:
DOING CONFEDERATE BUSINESS IN LIVERPOOL

WESLEY LOY*

DURING THE AMERICAN CIVIL WAR, THE CONFEDERACY faced shortages of almost everything, from gunpowder and paper to soap and shoes. Practically every necessity and comfort of life was devoured by the great struggle. Bibles were no exception. The South had always relied on northern and European publishers for its copies of holy scripture, but the war cut off supplies. Bibles were, however, the most prized reading material for Confederate soldiers, and organizations like the Bible Society of the Confederate States and the Virginia Bible Society endeavored to get them from Great Britain. But like most valued commodities, if the Bibles were to pass the U.S. blockade of southern ports, they would do so as contraband. A company in Liverpool, England, was both well-suited and inclined to take on this challenge. In fact, the house of Fraser, Trenholm and Company shipped hundreds of thousands of Bibles, New Testaments, and Psalms across the Atlantic free of charge.[1]

It was not just an abiding devotion to spreading the gospel that prompted this charitable service. The banking and shipping company, operating out of rather plain quarters at 10 Rumford Place, not far from the bustling docks along the River Mersey, actually was working toward a future of immense profit and prestige, a future so grand as to make the gratis shipment of Bibles a trivial matter. It was a future, however, heavily staked on a Confederate victory. Headed by George Alfred Trenholm, a rich South Carolina merchant, planter, and secessionist, the Liverpool company was a close ally of the Confederate government, acting as its European banker and financier. Aside from Bibles, the company hauled aboard its fleet of ships a storehouse of munitions and other supplies vital to the South. It moved thousands of bales of southern capital — cotton — back across the ocean. Although many companies jumped into the risky business of running goods through the blockade, Trenholm's operation stood above the others by its innovation and close partnership with government. As a southern businessman, Trenholm himself was different. He was an uncommonly

*Journalist, Strawberry Plains, Tennessee. The author would like to thank Ethel Trenholm Seabrook Nepveux of Charleston, K.J. Williams of Birkenhead, England, and the staff of the Maritime Archives & Library in Liverpool for their assistance.

[1]E. Merton Coulter, *The Confederate States of America, 1861-1865* (Baton Rouge: Louisiana State University Press, 1950), p. 528; W. Harrison Daniel, "Bible Publication and Procurement in the Confederacy," *Journal of Southern History* 24 (May 1958), pp. 197-199.

strong patriot of the Rebel cause, ultimately serving as secretary of the Confederate Treasury.

Based in a city with deep trade ties to — and strong sympathies for — the breakaway American South, Trenholm's Liverpool business was at the center of efforts abroad to jockey the Confederacy's frail finances, to move vital freight across the sea, and to help Confederate agents outwit their U.S. counterparts in a gritty spy game of the highest stakes. Through all of this, the house of Fraser, Trenholm and Company rendered yeoman service to the Confederacy, though the firm tried not to sell out profit to patriotism. This policy seemed, from a business standpoint, a smart move, though it proved insufficient to spare the company and its principals a harsh fate at war's end.

An important collection of letters to and from Charles Kuhn Prioleau, Trenholm's managing partner in Liverpool, sheds much light on the affairs at 10 Rumford Place and the company's extraordinary partnership with the Confederate government. The collection, held in the Maritime Archives & Library in Liverpool, generally was not known to scholars prior to its purchase from a London bookseller in 1982.[2]

LIVERPOOL:
THE CONFEDERACY'S TRANSATLANTIC CONNECTION

When war between the states broke out in April 1861, Great Britain faced a dilemma. Which side would it support? Some strong voices condemned the irascible South, populated, according to the *London Times*, by a predominantly "poor, proud, lazy, excitable, and violent class, ever ready with knife and revolver, and hating the Negro and his Northern friends with equal hatred." But Britain, and particularly Liverpool, had strong connections to the South. The vital Lancashire textile mills depended on the South for practically all their raw cotton, and the cotton trade naturally was a boon to the gateway port of Liverpool. For decades, "factors" had worked the South, providing planters with advice, credit, supplies, and a way to sell their crops on the big Liverpool and New York cotton markets. Working closely with the factors were firms like Baring Brothers and Alexander Brown and Sons, each of which had thriving Liverpool branches, and which took southern cotton and tobacco crops on consignment from factors in Charleston, Mobile, Savannah, New Orleans,

---

[2]Fraser, Trenholm and Co. Collection held by the Maritime Archives & Library, quartered at the Albert Dock in Liverpool, England. The most important part of the collection is Prioleau's wartime letterbook, produced in Liverpool between 1862 and 1865. Also available are dozens of loose letters sent to Prioleau from George A. Trenholm, prominent Confederate agents, and friends in the war-ravaged South.

and other southern cities.[3] In earlier days, Liverpool and the South had been closely linked in the trade of another valuable commodity: slaves. In short, the South and Liverpool knew one another well, having enjoyed a long and lucrative partnership.

But for Great Britain to throw its support behind the Confederacy — to recognize the independence of the South or to take steps to break the northern blockade — would surely draw the ire of the United States, and perhaps even a declaration of war. With Queen Victoria's Proclamation of Neutrality on May 13, 1861, Britian chose to avoid taking sides. Early on, the South countered with a loose and short-lived cotton embargo, confident that world-powers Britain and France, desperate for cotton to feed their factories and employ their workers, would recognize Confederate independence and help break the U.S. blockade. This "king cotton" policy failed, partly because of unusually large stockpiles of cotton already in Europe in 1861. The glut was aggravated by many profit-minded southern planters who did not agree with the embargo and shipped more cotton. By 1862 the Confederate government itself began to ship out cotton as the only means to pay for vital war matériel from abroad.[4]

A key component of Britain's official neutrality was the Foreign Enlistment Act of 1819, a law that would be the object of fierce legal wrangling throughout the war. Although both sides, the U.S. and the Confederacy, were free to buy guns, ammunition, uniforms, medicine, and other war supplies — and they certainly did — the Foreign Enlistment Act forbade the sale to belligerents of ships armed and equipped for war.[5]

Yet while Great Britain tried to stay neutral, Liverpool — where top-hatted cotton brokers leisurely mingled and traded in the square behind the town hall — hardly followed suit. The city was decidedly pro-South, and many Liverpudlians did much to aid the Confederacy, to circumvent Britain's neutrality laws, and, in addition, to make a profit on the war. All

[3]London Times, Jan. 12, 1861, pp. 6-7; Frank Lawrence Owsley, King Cotton Diplomacy: Foreign Relations of the Confederate States of America (Chicago: University of Chicago Press, 1931), pp. 1-3; Harold D. Woodman, King Cotton and His Retainers: Financing and Marketing the Cotton Crop of the South, 1800-1925 (Lexington: University of Kentucky Press, 1968), pp. 4-18; John R. Killick, "The Cotton Operations of Alexander Brown and Sons in the Deep South, 1820-1860," Journal of Southern History 43 (May 1977), pp. 169-194; Philip Ziegler, The Sixth Great Power: A History of One of the Greatest of All Banking Families, the House of Barings, 1762-1929 (New York: Alfred A. Knopf, 1988), pp. 130-131.

[4]Frank J. Merli, Great Britain and the Confederate Navy, 1861-1865 (Bloomington: Indiana University Press, 1970), pp. 3-23; Owsley, King Cotton, pp. 25-51; Philip Van Doren Stern, The Confederate Navy: A Pictorial History (Garden City, N.Y.: Doubleday, 1962), p. 32; Stanley Lebergott, "Why the South Lost: Commercial Purpose in the Confederacy, 1861-1865," Journal of American History 70 (June 1983), pp. 60-61, 73-74.

[5]Stern, Confederate Navy, p. 33.

this bedeviled Thomas Haines Dudley, the U.S. consul in Liverpool responsible for monitoring the activities of Confederate agents. One observer said Liverpool seemed to fly more Confederate flags than even the southern capital of Richmond. The town organized meetings of the Liverpool Southern Club. Merchants like James Spence lobbied strongly for British recognition of southern independence and invested heavily in Confederate cotton bonds; Spence even signed on as a financial agent for the Confederacy. The local press argued for recognition. And local shipbuilders like W.C. Miller and the Laird yard across the river in Birkenhead — owned by John Laird, who became a member of Parliament at the outset of the war — worked secretly with Confederate naval agent James Dunwoody Bulloch to build ships to attack the North's commercial vessels. Liverpool shipyards also built dozens of fast steamers with names like *Banshee, Phantom,* and *Let Her B* to slip past the blockaders. Liverpool became the hub of efforts to run valuable cargo to the South, awakening in the city "a spirit the like of which had not been known since the palmy days of the slave trade," observed Thomas Taylor, a Liverpool blockade runner. Support for the Confederacy remained strong even as its prospects for victory waned. In October 1864 a lavish five-day bazaar held in Liverpool's classical St. George's Hall — a grand architectural statement of the city's vigor in those days — raised £21,000 to aid southern prisoners of war. Distinguished ladies tended stalls sponsored by all the Confederate states, selling items ranging from portraits of Confederate generals to "a live American rabbit." In sum, "no other city in Britain could with so much cause be accused of unofficially fighting on the side of the South during the Civil War."[6]

Why was Liverpool so inclined to support the South, to ignore the queen's admonition to respect the U.S. blockade? The city's pro-Confederate stance actually ran deeper than the longstanding trade history. On a philosophical level, the U.S. blockade was viewed as an outrageous assault on free trade. Thus, to many Liverpool merchants — residents of a bustling port city in an island nation — breaking a foreign blockade was rather a point of honor. And while many, if not most, British citizens disapproved of the South's embrace of slavery, the blocking of ports was at least as offensive to Liverpool's maritime community as was the peculiar institution

    [6]Merli, *Great Britain,* pp. 61-62; Mary Ellison, *Support for Secession: Lancashire and the American Civil War* (Chicago: University of Chicago Press, 1972), pp. 49, 132; Merli, *Great Britain,* p. 147; Ellison, *Support for Secession,* pp. 51-52; Stern, *Confederate Navy,* p. 36; Arthur C. Wardle, "Mersey-built Blockade-runners of the American Civil War," *Mariner's Mirror* 28 (July 1942), pp. 179-188; Thomas E. Taylor, *Running the Blockade* (London: John Murray, 1896), pp. 9-10, quoted in Ellison, *Support for Secession,* p. 161; Richard A. Warren, ed., "'This Brilliant Affair ...': The Great Confederate Bazaar at Liverpool," *Journal of the Confederate Historical Society* 20 (British) (Spring 1992), pp. 5-12. This article reprints local newspaper accounts of the event. Ellison, *Support for Secession,* p. 167 (final quotation).

In October 1864 a lavish five-day bazaar was held in Liverpool's classical St. George's Hall. It raised £21,000 to aid southern prisoners of war. Photo courtesy of the author.

of slaveholding. In Liverpool "it was rarely held that the North was genuinely concerned to free the Negro from servile labor." The South, in short, had a right to independence, and "whether officially recognized or not, the Confederacy was regarded in Liverpool as a new and separate country." The only caveat was warships. Many Liverpool shippers, though against the blockade and partial to the South, favored the ban on actually equipping ships for war in British ports. They realized that such ships could disrupt their own ventures, such as runs to northern ports, and thereby corrupt the free-trade principle they so prized.[7]

It was in this generally supportive environment that the Liverpool house of Fraser, Trenholm and Company operated on behalf of the Confederacy, and in the service of its own ambition. Agents for the U.S., however, kept a close watch.

FRASER, TRENHOLM AND COMPANY
AND ITS CHIEF EXECUTIVE

Fraser, Trenholm and Company was only one in a network of companies comprising George Alfred Trenholm's transatlantic importing and exporting operation, which owned or controlled about fifty ships. The other companies

[7]John Pelzer, "Liverpool and the American Civil War," *History Today* 40 (British) (March 1990), pp. 51, 49; Ellison, *Support for Secession*, pp. 48 (first quotation), 132 (second quotation); Pelzer, "Liverpool," pp. 51-52.

were John Fraser and Company of Charleston and Trenholm Brothers of New York. Trenholm and his partners also established a strong presence at Nassau, in the Bahamas, and on Bermuda. Close to the southern coast, these island ports served as vital way stations where goods to and from the Confederacy could be stored or broken down into smaller loads for shipment aboard fast, shallow-draft blockade-runners.[8]

It was with the firm of John Fraser and Company that Trenholm, as a teenager, found work as an accountant and clerk. Denied an advanced education by the early death of his merchant father, young Trenholm made the most of his opportunity with the Charleston firm, an old and respected shipper of sea island cotton. By the outbreak of the Civil War, the company's namesake was long dead and George Alfred Trenholm was principal owner and possibly the richest man in the Confederacy, with interests in steamships, railroads, wharves, banks, hotels, cotton presses, plantations, and slaves. He was, by any measure, a pillar of southern and Charlestonian moneyed society, the sort of influential person British journalist William Howard Russell of the *Times* sought out on his highly influential tour of the South in 1861. Tall, white-haired, with a boyishly handsome face and the "manners of a prince," Trenholm was a highly respected businessman who was, according to his own statements, dragged into public service reluctantly, including stints in the South Carolina legislature before, during, and after the war. In Charleston he lived in a showplace of a mansion with great columns and, according to a Confederate midshipman who visited there, a slave doorman "much better dressed than myself, and with the manners of a Chesterfield." Trenholm also had a grand villa called "de Greffin" (his mother's maiden name) in the state capital of Columbia, and he relied on the services of an old, black coachman by the name of "Daddy Peter." He married Anna Helen Holmes in 1828, and they produced thirteen children. Several sons and sons-in-law served in the Confederate army and navy.[9]

[8]Stephen R. Wise, *Lifeline of the Confederacy: Blockade Running During the Civil War* (Columbia: University of South Carolina Press, 1988), pp. 46, 58, 63-65; *Encyclopedia of the Confederacy* (New York: Simon & Schuster, 1993), p. 1618.

[9]Ethel Trenholm Seabrook Nepveux, *George Alfred Trenholm and the Company that Went to War, 1861-1865* (Charleston, S.C.: Self-published, 1973; repr. with epilogue, 1994), p. 6; M. Foster Farley, "'The Manners of a Prince': Confederate Financier George Trenholm," *Civil War Times Illustrated* 21 (December 1982), pp. 18-19; Coulter, *Confederate States*, p. 163; *Dictionary of American Biography* (New York: Charles Scribner's Sons, 1944), Vol. 21, pp. 689-690; William Howard Russell, *My Diary North and South* (Boston: Burnham, 1863), p. 123; Martin Crawford, "William Howard Russell and the Confederacy," *Journal of American Studies* 15 (British) (August 1981), p. 195; James Morris Morgan, *Recollections of a Rebel Reefer* (New York: Houghton Mifflin Company, 1917), pp. 250, 94, 200, 241; Farley, "'Manners of a Prince,'" p. 23; Nepveux, *George Alfred Trenholm*, p. 106. The midshipman, James Morris Morgan, was to become George Alfred Trenholm's son-in-law. The Charleston mansion, Ashley Hall, is now part of a private girls' school of the same name.

George Alfred Trenholm, head of Fraser, Trenholm and Company, put his company solidly behind the Confederacy and provided major financial support himself. In the summer of 1864, Trenholm was pressed into service as the Confederate secretary of the Treasury. Photo courtesy of Ethel Trenholm Seabrook Nepveux.

Although a master of traditional business practices, Trenholm also was a radical. He liked to think big. As a young man, Trenholm wrote fiery newspaper articles under the pen name "Mercator," advocating a railroad link from Charleston to what today are the midwestern states. He was a follower of John C. Calhoun, the South Carolina champion of the right of states to allow slavery and "nullify" federal protective tariffs thought to hurt southern commerce. By 1860 Trenholm, disturbed by the election of Abraham Lincoln as president, was quite prepared to see South Carolina secede to form a new nation. As a member of a commission to ready the state's defense, Trenholm helped build the ironclad gunboat *Chicora* and his partner in Liverpool shipped over a British-built cannon to help bombard Fort Sumter.[10]

Once the shooting started, Trenholm was a committed Confederate patriot, plowing into the struggle not only the resources of his companies but ultimately his leadership. In the summer of 1864, when Trenholm was pressed into service as Treasury secretary, he campaigned hard in the Confederate Congress and in the newspapers for measures like tax increases and even donations of jewelry and silverware to prop up the withering nation's tattered finances. At one point Trenholm donated $2,000 toward a giant New Year's Day appreciation feast for Robert E. Lee's ragged and half-starved Virginia army. But it was late in the war, and "Trenholm wondered throughout the period of his secretaryship why the people could never see and think of the Confederacy as part of themselves — not something far

[10]Farley, "'Manners of a Prince'," pp. 19-20; Nepveux, *George Alfred Trenholm*, pp. 13-15, 17, 23; *Dictionary of American Biography*, Vol. 21, p. 689.

away," writes historian E. Merton Coulter.[11]

Most southern citizens, however, probably did not have the same incentive to win the war as did Trenholm and his partners. The blockade of southern ports, the Confederacy's dire need to assemble a navy, and the problem of getting cash to Europe to buy critical supplies were all major challenges for the new nation. They also represented grand opportunities for Trenholm, who skillfully aligned his companies on both sides of the Atlantic with the Confederate government. With victory, Trenholm's operation would be positioned as the premiere shipper for a new nation, the Cunard of the Confederacy. Indeed, early in the war, Fraser, Trenholm and Company advertised an ambitious new monthly steam packet between Liverpool and Charleston.[12] But as we will see by the letters to and from 10 Rumford Place, even the most patriotic of Confederate businessmen were not thinking "win at all cost." They did not intend to destroy their companies in vain. Nor were they willing to pass up many chances at turning a profit even as the fighting raged on.

MIXING PROFIT AND PATRIOTISM IN LIVERPOOL

In August 1862 Charles Prioleau sent a consoling letter to Theodore D. Wagner, a partner in John Fraser and Company in Charleston. Wagner's brother had died in a military accident, and Prioleau, reckoning that the Yankees were indirectly to blame, wrote Wagner: "I have no heart to allude to business in this letter — all I can say is that the only business that interests me now is how to get you the means of driving these ruffians from your soil and otherwise to injure and annoy them; and I propose taking some heavy risks with this object."[13] Indeed, Prioleau and Fraser, Trenholm and Company did take heavy risks on behalf of the Confederacy — risks that could, with

---

[11]Coulter, *Confederate States*, pp. 171 (quotation), 452-453.

[12]Wise, *Lifeline*, p. 223. The June 1861 advertisement is included in *Official Records of the Union and Confederate Navies in the War of the Rebellion* (Washington, D.C.: Government Printing Office, 1894-1927) (hereafter *Official Records-Navies*), Series 1, Vol. 5, p. 752. The idea of a direct steamship line between Europe and the South was thought to be a vital component of southern independence. However the new line was postponed by Fraser, Trenholm and Co. on the day it was to begin due to uncertainty about entering the blockaded Charleston harbor. By the end of 1861, the idea of starting a steamship line was effectively dead. David Budlong Tyler, *Steam Conquers the Atlantic* (New York: D. Appleton-Century Company, 1939), pp. 298-300.

[13]Prioleau to Wagner, Aug. 28, 1862, contained in Box 8, mcfm. cards 29-32, Fraser, Trenholm and Co. Collection. Wagner's brother, Lt. Col. Thomas M. Wagner, of the First Regiment of South Carolina Artillery, died when a gun at Fort Moultrie burst in July 1862. Battery Wagner, on the tip of Morris Island, was named for him. Robert Rosen, *Confederate Charleston: An Illustrated History of the City and the People During the Civil War* (Columbia: University of South Carolina Press, 1994), p. 106.

victory, position the company for untold prosperity after the war or, with defeat, bring it down.

The financial partnership of George Trenholm's companies and the Confederate government began in earnest three days after the guns began firing on Fort Sumter. Taking Trenholm up on an earlier offer, Confederate Treasury Secretary Christopher Memminger wrote John Fraser and Company for a £5,000 letter of credit for Caleb Huse, an army captain on his way to Liverpool to buy munitions.[14] After nearly a year of haggling, Trenholm's Liverpool firm of Fraser, Trenholm and Company officially became the overseas "depository" for the Confederate government, earning a commission of 0.5 percent, the same rate Barings was believed to be charging the United States for similar services. These negotiations with Memminger — he and his friend Trenholm both were from Charleston — were mere formalities, however. And Fraser, Trenholm and Company was to be much more than a "counting house" for the Confederacy. In the Liverpool firm, the Confederacy had a solid ally in Britain willing to convert its resources — whether Confederate cash, bonds, or raw cotton — into currency good in Europe. The company immediately lent Trenholm's almost unlimited credit abroad to the Confederate cause; it helped negotiate and manage the Confederacy's only major foreign loan, from Emile Erlanger and Company of Paris; and it advised Confederate purchasing and propaganda agents and gave them room to work at 10 Rumford Place. Finally, among the many companies formed to run cargo through the blockade, Trenholm's stood out in the tactics it developed and the chances it took not only to help the government but to enrich company coffers.[15]

Certainly, Caleb Huse and his counterpart from the Confederate navy, James Bulloch, were pleased with the helping hand they received from Prioleau and Fraser, Trenholm and Company. Both these military men were dispatched on harried and seemingly impossible missions to equip a new nation for war. The South needed thousands of guns, big and small, and an entire navy — things that had to come mostly from Europe, as the South was an industrial infant. Early on, Huse and Bulloch had little money to compete with northern agents who also had swarmed to Britain and France to do some serious shopping. Shortly after his arrival in Liverpool in May 1861, a cash-poor Captain Huse tried to close a $195,000 deal for the manufacture of 10,000 Enfield rifles. Prioleau "most generously assumed the responsibility of the entire contract," Huse wrote. "Whenever I have anything to ship I

[14]Raphael P. Thian, comp., *Correspondence of the Treasury Department of the Confederate States of America, 1861-1865* (Washington, D.C.: Published privately, 1879), Appendix 4, p. 62.

[15]Ibid., pp. 250-251, 258-259; Douglas B. Ball, *Financial Failure and Confederate Defeat* (Urbana: University of Illinois Press, 1991), pp. 71-72; Farley, "'Manners of a Prince,'" p. 21.

shall have the able assistance of Messrs. Fraser, Trenholm & Co. Their experience and enthusiasm will enable them to do what no other house in England would undertake. Already their assistance has been invaluable to me. Without them I could have done nothing." Although this gun deal ultimately fell through, the company helped Huse on many other occasions.[16]

Bulloch, in his memoirs, was no less complimentary of Prioleau and Fraser, Trenholm and Company. "Within a month after my arrival, I had not only been able to buy a fair quantity of naval supplies on their credit, but had laid the keel of the first foreign-built Confederate cruiser, and she was partly in frame before the Navy Department had found it possible to place any funds in Europe." That vessel, the *Florida*, would go on to ravage northern commercial shipping.[17]

That Prioleau would be so helpful was not just a matter of doing Trenholm's bidding. As a native of South Carolina, he was, like his superior, both a fervent southern patriot and ambitious capitalist. As president of the Liverpool branch entitled to 5 percent of its profits, he had broad leave to make big decisions — to buy and sell ships or, as we will see, to strike major deals with the Confederate government. From both a business and a personal standpoint, Prioleau's life in Liverpool was good. The youngest son of a Charleston judge, Prioleau became a permanent resident of Liverpool in 1854, and a British citizen in 1863. Still in his thirties when the war ended, Prioleau lived in a "baronial mansion" called Allerton Hall just outside of town. Gleeful Confederate agents, hearing of victory in the first battle of Bull Run, went to the hilltop mansion to raise a Confederate flag. Prioleau took the "acknowledged belle of Liverpool" as his wife, and during the war built her a lavish home in Liverpool's premiere residential district. The townhouse at 19 Abercromby Square, its roof raised two feet above its neighbors by special permission of the Corporation of Liverpool, featured impressive ceiling paintings, including a sabal palmetto — state tree of South Carolina — in the vestibule. Prioleau was, appropriately, treasurer for the great southern bazaar at St. George's Hall, and his wife, Mary Elizabeth, a patron

[16]Captain Huse to Officer of Artillery in Charge of Ordnance Bureau, C.S.A., May 21, 1861, in *The War of the Rebellion: A Compilation of the Official Records of the Union and Confederate Armies* (Washington, D.C.: Government Printing Office, 1880-1901) (hereafter *Official Records-Armies*), Series 4, Vol. 1, pp. 343-346. On the failure of the gun deal, see Maj. Edward C. Anderson and Huse to Secretary of War Leroy P. Walker, Aug. 11, 1861, ibid., pp. 538-542.

[17]James D. Bulloch, *The Secret Service of the Confederate States in Europe or How the Confederate Cruisers Were Equipped* (London: Reichard Bentley, 1883; repr., New York: Thomas Yoseloff, 1959), Vol. 1, pp. 53-54.

of Paris fashion houses, personally tended the South Carolina stall.[18]

Patriot though he was, Prioleau did not allow his enthusiasm for the war effort to cloud his business judgment. In short, Fraser, Trenholm and Company did not exist to win a war, but to turn a profit. And the Confederate government was a major customer. Together, they did startling things. By mid-summer 1861, Confederate purchasing agents in Great Britain had pulled together a storehouse of badly needed supplies — field guns, thousands of Enfield rifles, gunpowder, and ammunition. The problem was how to ship it to the South. The U.S. blockade was on, and British shippers, at least initially, heeded Queen Victoria's order to respect it. Major Edward C. Anderson, in Britain to buy war supplies along with Caleb Huse and James Bulloch, turned to Fraser, Trenholm and Company. Prioleau already had been working on a plan to test the blockade by running a ship laden with a valuable cargo of shoes, blankets, drugs, and other goods into a southern port and then returning with a load of cotton. He told the Confederate agents they could have a share of the cargo space on board the steamer *Bermuda*, but only at a price that Anderson considered "high." Despite considerable efforts at secrecy, U.S. agents in England knew about the ship and were sure she was not bound on "any errand of mercy or peace." Yet they were powerless to stop it. When the *Bermuda* sailed into Savannah, Georgia, on September 18, 1861, and then back out with cotton, it created tremendous excitement. The voyage suggested that the Confederacy's cotton embargo was off, that the U.S. blockade was toothless, and that Prioleau, in the words of the U.S. consul in Liverpool, had "made a fortune by the *Bermuda* venture."[19]

Trenholm's companies defended the high shipping rates — and the

[18]Wise, *Lifeline*, p. 334; "Historical Sketch of the Prioleau Family in Europe and America," *Transactions of the Huguenot Society of South Carolina* 6 (Charleston, 1899), pp. 2-3, 27-30; Morgan, *Recollections*, p. 109; Anderson and Huse to Walker, Aug. 11, 1861, *Official Records-Armies*, Series 4, Vol. 1, p. 541; Adrian R. Allan, *The Building of Abercromby Square* (Liverpool: University of Liverpool, 1986), pp. 12-19, 22-23; Warren, "'This Brilliant Affair ...,'" p. 6. Both of Prioleau's homes are still standing in Liverpool. The townhouse at 19 Abercromby Square is now part of the University of Liverpool. Allerton Hall was heavily damaged by fire in 1994.

[19]Wise, *Lifeline*, pp. 50-52 (first quotation, p. 50; third quotation, p. 52); Peter Barton, "The First Blockade Runner and 'Another *Alabama*': Some Tees and Hartlepool Ships that Worried the Union," *Mariner's Mirror* 81 (February 1995), pp. 45-47; Merli, *Great Britain*, p. 240; Charles Francis Adams, U.S. minister in Great Britain, to Lord John Russell, British foreign secretary, Aug. 15, 1861, *Official Records-Navies*, Series 1, Vol. 6, pp. 176-177 (second quotation, p. 177). Not surprisingly, Trenholm opposed the unofficial cotton embargo, arguing it would result in "a rapid depreciation of the currency of the country." John Fraser and Company to Judah P. Benjamin, acting secretary of war, Sept. 30, 1861, *Official Records-Armies*, Series 4, Vol. 1, p. 633.

This regal townhouse at 19 Abercromby Square in Liverpool was built by Charles Kuhn Prioleau, managing partner of Fraser, Trenholm and Company. A South Carolinian who became a British citizen, Prioleau decorated the house with reminders of his homeland, including a painting of a sabal palmetto on the vestibule ceiling. Photo courtesy of the author.

infuriating prices they charged for the *Bermuda's* goods in Georgia — by pointing out the considerable risk they took in sending the ship. Indeed, the *Bermuda* would be captured on her next try. But in the fall of 1861, when the Confederate agents again had a load of supplies to send, Prioleau's rates were so high that the agents decided on a new tack. They bought a small ship, the *Fingal,* to haul the government's goods. Although the *Fingal* successfully delivered what likely was the South's richest military cargo during the war — and bypassed the high-priced middleman in the bargain — southern leaders ignored the advice of Anderson, Bulloch, and others to form a fleet committed to the government, not profit. Even George Alfred Trenholm and his son, William, had urged the Confederate Cabinet in early 1861 to buy ships, but the idea was rejected for a variety of reasons, including the question of whether it was proper for a government to own a transport company.[20]

Malaise over this question of whether the government needed its own ships inexorably led to dependence on private shippers to bring in the vital war supplies and to carry out increasing quantities of cotton to pay for them. Though good for Trenholm's companies, it was a flawed policy. Not only was the government forced to pay high freight rates, but it became difficult to get space on board ships whose owners were more interested in exporting privately owned cotton to sell for major profits, and importing not war supplies but luxuries that brought top dollar in the suffering South — European silks and satin, spirits and the like. Certainly there was strong

[20]Wise, *Lifeline,* pp. 53-56, 60-61; Coulter, *Confederate States,* p. 290; Ball, *Financial Failure,* pp. 91-93.

demand for such niceties in the South, and rich folks to buy them. "Do have this attended to with care and expedition," a wry Trenholm wrote to Prioleau, in forwarding a southern lady's wish list to Liverpool. "You see the dreadful consequences of this blockade; here is a most charming woman actually destitute of perfume." Gradually, southern leaders tried to rectify the situation with "almost complete state socialism," passing laws to force private shippers to carry government cargo. And eventually the Confederacy at last took steps to assemble its own fleet.[21]

Through every phase, Trenholm's companies were on the leading edge, always finding good opportunities with the Confederate government. A major twist in the evolution of blockade running came at the end of 1861, when the *Gladiator*, a government ship loaded by Huse with war matériel including more than 20,000 rifles, became bottled up in Nassau. Heavily laden, the *Gladiator* had no chance of outrunning U.S. cruisers in the vicinity. George Trenholm "came to the rescue," offering his friend Memminger, the Confederate Treasury secretary, the use of two small, fast steamers, the *Cecile* and the *Kate*, to shuttle the cargo to the obscure Florida port of Mosquito Inlet. This episode launched the intensive practice of using stopover points, especially Nassau and Bermuda, to transfer loads from heavy, oceangoing steamers to stealthy, shallow-draft blockade runners. The government's reliance on private shippers deepened, giving Trenholm the chance to serve both his country and his own companies.[22]

Trenholm's companies again were big winners when the government's policy changed late in the war. In 1864, as part of the Confederacy's struggle to get a better grip on its foreign commerce, Colin J. McRae, the Paris-based agent in charge of all European finances, took steps to assemble a fleet of steamers for the government. McRae's negotiations with one English firm, run by supposed southern supporters Edwin Pinchback Stringer and Edward Pembroke, were unsuccessful.[23] Not surprisingly, McRae found a friend in Charles Prioleau. In a letter to Trenholm, Prioleau explained the deal:

[21]Trenholm to Prioleau, Jan. 10, 1863, Fraser, Trenholm and Co. Collection, Box 1, No. 125; Ball, *Financial Failure*, pp. 96-98; Coulter, *Confederate States*, pp. 289-292, "socialism" quotation, p. 291.

[22]Barton, "First Blockade Runner," pp. 48-49; Royce Shingleton, *High Seas Confederate: The Life and Times of John Newland Maffitt* (Columbia: University of South Carolina Press, 1994), pp. 39-40 (quotation, p. 39); Benjamin to John Fraser and Co., Mar. 22, 1862, *Official Records-Armies*, Series 4, Vol. 1, p. 1017; Wise, *Lifeline*, pp. 58-63.

[23]For a good summary of the muddled state of Confederate financial affairs in Europe, and the appointment of McRae to sort it out, see the letter by Benjamin, now secretary of state, Sept. 15, 1863, *Official Records-Navies*, Series 2, Vol. 2, pp. 496-498. On the negotiations, see Wise, *Lifeline*, pp. 147-148; Ball, *Financial Failure*, p. 98.

I have at the suggestion & request of the Secretaries of the Treasury & Navy entered into a contract with Mr. McRae for supplying 8 Steamers for the use of the Govt and they are all now under way. Two are to be purchased at once, four to be delivered 1st December and two 1st April next. They will cost including outfit & disbursements in round numbers £250,000 and we are to receive a commission on gross cost & expenses of 20%; payment to be made to us out of proceeds of cotton brought out by them and sold by us as usual — one half of each cargo to go towards payment for the boats and the other half towards the general requirements of the Govt.... The boats are *all* to remain our property until *all* are paid for: all risk of loss and capture is assumed by the Govt and should they all be lost they are nevertheless to be paid for on or before the 1st Jany 1866. I think this a very good arrangement for us and it is a very good one for the Govt & I hope you will agree with me.... I am sure we cannot employ our capital better or under a greater service to the Govt than this; they write us that they want Steamers more than anything else and that they have enormous piles of valuable stores actually rotting at Bermuda & Nassau for want of transportation. I think we are doing more in supplying this want than in incurring all the risk ourselves for the purpose of selling them goods in the Confederacy.[24]

Prioleau further steered McRae to the London banking house of John K. Gilliat and Company, where McRae contracted for six additional steamers.[25] Again, Prioleau and Fraser, Trenholm and Company were at the forefront in efforts to supply the Confederacy, while also earning a profit. Not only would Fraser, Trenholm and Company get the generous commission for assembling the ships, it would also earn another commission of 4 percent for selling the government's cotton, according to Prioleau's letter.

DOING CONFEDERATE BUSINESS —
WORTH THE TROUBLE?

Although other southern merchants, such as Gazaway Bugg Lamar of Georgia and his Importing and Exporting Company, took on much government work, there is little doubt that George Trenholm's companies did more for the Confederacy, in the spirit of patriotism, than any other. This

---

[24]Prioleau to Trenholm, June 4, 1864, Fraser, Trenholm and Co. Collection, Box 8, mcfm. cards 313-317.
[25]Wise, *Lifeline*, p. 148.

Fraser, Trenholm and Company built the gunboat, the *Alexandra*, with its own funds as a gift to the Confederacy. Illustration from *Harper's Weekly*, June 6, 1863, courtesy of the author.

surely had to do with Trenholm's strong fraternity with the Confederate leaders, men whose ranks Trenholm joined in July 1864 when he resigned from his companies to take the place of unpopular Christopher Memminger as Treasury secretary. Certainly, Trenholm and his partners strongly courted the government's business, no doubt with an eye on their rosy trade prospects in the event of a Confederate victory. In Liverpool, for instance, Fraser, Trenholm and Company even built a gunboat, the *Alexandra*, with its own funds as a gift to the Confederacy. But enthusiasm for the war effort was limited even in that most patriotic and prosperous "counting house" at 10 Rumford Place, particularly as things began to go sour for the South.[26]

Keeping track of the Confederacy's accounts, paying its bills, working with its myriad purchasing agents — all this apparently wore on Prioleau, a stickler for business protocol. In October 1863 he wrote a long letter to Trenholm, recounting how the company had found a British subject to send, incognito, to Gibraltar to buy an ailing Confederate destroyer, the *Sumter*,

[26]Edwin B. Coddington, "The Activities and Attitudes of a Confederate Business Man: Gazaway B. Lamar," *Journal of Southern History* 9 (February 1943), pp. 3-36; Wise, *Lifeline*, p. 151. On the *Alexandra*, see Philip Van Doren Stern, *When the Guns Roared: World Aspects of the American Civil War* (Garden City, N.Y.: Doubleday, 1965), p. 192.

trapped there by U.S. vessels. Frustrated that Confederate agents had neglected the final details of that transaction and a subsequent agreement to transfer the vessel back to the government, Prioleau told Trenholm the case was "an illustration of ... the impossibility of transacting the business of the Govt with that strict regard to details of method & routine." Without that discipline, Prioleau said, the firm risked "very greatly impairing our own usefulness as active friends & supporters of the cause. As far as the actual payment of money is concerned we are very strict and in consequence have earned the ill-will of certain officers & agents here." Prioleau then offered a surprising recommendation:

> I want you to consider seriously the idea of our giving up the Govt business on this side all together & I would urge it upon you if it were not for the look of the thing while the war lasts. It will not repay us for all the trouble and anxiety and I do not think what we have done has been very much appreciated.

Prioleau the patriot concluded, as he often did, with some encouraging words about family and the war back home, in this case conveying his hopes that Rebel forces could save Charleston "from the foul pollution of a Yankee foot."[27]

Later, Prioleau was forced to get tough with Confederate agents who were flooding Fraser, Trenholm and Company with too many bills and not enough cotton. "I fear I will be compelled to do what I dislike excessively and back out of an offer made," Prioleau said in a terse letter to Caleb Huse, the army purchasing agent, in early 1864. Prioleau had agreed to buy some steamers for Huse, but Huse's Ordnance Department was £70,000 in debt to Fraser, Trenholm and Company. Buying two steamers for Huse would push the debt to £110,000, Prioleau wrote, "far more than I can or ought to advance upon blockade chances." Prioleau went on to vent his frustration over the "recklessness" and possible dishonesty of some Confederate purchasing agents, and he posed a question in defense of his own company's fidelity: "What would Stringer or his tribe charge for advancing the Govt £100,000 in cash & wait his chance to have cotton sent him to pay it?"[28]

A year later, Prioleau wrote again to Huse in London, saying, "the

[27]Prioleau to Trenholm, Oct. 22, 1863, Fraser, Trenholm and Co. Collection, Box 8, mcfm. cards 178-183. Prioleau, for nominal costs, had offered to transfer the *Sumter*, renamed *Gibraltar*, back to the Confederate War Department for use in carrying two immense Blakely rifled cannon to the South. C.R. Horres, Jr., "Charleston's Civil War 'Monster Guns,' the Blakely Rifles," *South Carolina Historical Magazine* 97 (April 1996), p. 119.

[28]Prioleau to Huse, Jan. 12, 1864, Fraser, Trenholm and Co. Collection, Box 8, mcfm. cards 233-237.

Government is now in debt to us for cash advanced £224,125" with another £645,550 in warrants expected — in all, the market value of 30,000 bales of cotton. Even if enough money could be generated to cover the purchasing debt, Prioleau said, what was the point? Tons of supplies were piling up in Nassau and Bermuda with little chance of reaching southern ports, squeezed now by both U.S. ships and approaching armies. "My friend the Confederacy must fight out the remainder of the war under practical isolation from the nations of the East," wrote Prioleau. "... [B]lockade running on the scale it has heretofore been done is at an end."[29]

AGENTS, SPIES, TURNCOATS:
NORTH TRACKS SOUTH ON MERSEYSIDE

An important and fascinating sidelight to the Fraser, Trenholm story is the intense scrutiny the company drew because of its dealings with the Confederacy. During the war, a desperate spy game played out on the wet, windy, sooty streets and docks of nineteenth-century Merseyside as the American consul in Liverpool tried to thwart the efforts of Confederate purchasing agents. Only a short walk separated 10 Rumford Place from the office of U.S. Consul Thomas Haines Dudley, and Dudley and his detectives kept a close watch on the firm. Prioleau, writing to a potential London client seeking the services of Fraser, Trenholm and Company in some secretive matter, waved him off by telegraph: "Consignment to us could not fail to excite suspicion and would be most dangerous and injudicious, an entirely neutral house far better."[30]

The main contestants in this war of espionage were James Dunwoody Bulloch, the Confederate naval agent in Liverpool, and Consul Dudley. Both performed brilliantly for their respective sides. The Georgia-born Bulloch, a former officer in the U.S. Navy and a mail steamer captain before joining the rebellion, landed in Liverpool on June 3, 1861, and went straight to 10 Rumford Place. Though he had been given no funding, Bulloch was under orders to fill an amazing shopping list — everything from ships to pistols to 4,000 pairs of flannel drawers. Unfortunately for Bulloch, the spying had begun even before he arrived on his secret mission. To his "utmost astonishment as well as chagrin," a New York newspaper trailed him to Liverpool with an account of purportedly intercepted telegrams laying out his whole mission. Hence, it was not long before Bulloch noticed "that a private detective named Maguire was taking a deep and abiding

---

[29]Prioleau to Huse, Feb. 21, 1865, Fraser, Trenholm and Co. Collection, Box 8, mcfm. cards 443-447.

[30]K.F. Sirett and K.J. Williams, "Liverpool and the American Civil War: A Confederate Heritage in England," *Journal of Confederate History* 4 (1989), p. 123; Prioleau to A. Hamilton, Dec. 4, 1863, Fraser, Trenholm and Co. Collection, Box 8, mcfm. card 210.

interest in my personal movements." Balding, with great pork-chop sideburns, "magnetic courtly manners" and a good way with the pen, Bulloch managed to cope with spies, the lack of cash, competition from U.S. purchasing agents, poor communications, Britain's thorny Foreign Enlistment Act, and even the petty jealousies of fellow naval officers to accomplish near miracles in Liverpool. With workspace and early financial guarantees from Fraser, Trenholm and Company, he managed to build and spirit out of Liverpool two ships, the *Florida* and the *Alabama*, which captured and burned dozens of northern commercial vessels. He helped send huge quantities of war matériel to the South, and he built fearsome ships equipped with bow rams to breach the blockade.[31]

Intelligence gathered by Dudley was instrumental in the U.S. campaign to pressure the British government into seizing two ironclad rams Bulloch had constructed at the Laird yard in Birkenhead, across the Mersey from Liverpool.[32] Dudley was relentless in his work as consul. Born to Quaker parents and trained as a lawyer in New Jersey, Dudley earned his first legal fee by posing as a slave trader and traveling into the South to retrieve a black mother and three children who were kidnapped for slaves. He was given the Liverpool consul's job — a post once held by Nathaniel Hawthorne — in gratitude for his strong campaigning for candidate Lincoln, to whom he urged no compromise with the South. Dudley's legal training served him well in Liverpool, for the affidavit was his chief weapon. He and the local detective he hired, Matthew Maguire, found more than a few informants, from drunken sailors to dock rats to turncoats, willing to give or sell details about Confederate activities in Liverpool. Tall, dour-faced, his health permanently compromised in a near-fatal steamboat fire in 1856, Dudley was a constant irritant to Confederate agents and Fraser, Trenholm and Company. In fact, he would dog the company for years after the war. In Bulloch's estimation, Dudley "manifested both zeal and ability," though he "often accepted the evidence of talebearers" and — unpardonable in gentleman Bulloch's view — complained to British authorities about Confederate activities with "a reckless disregard of official courtesy." If Dudley's complaints were, in fact, strident, it was because he despised the British policy that placed the burden on the United States, not Britain, to prove violations of the neutrality laws. Indeed, with no subpoena power to

[31]*Dictionary of American Biography*, Vol. 3, pp. 257-258. For Bulloch's initial orders, see Confederate Navy Secretary Stephen R. Mallory to Bulloch, May 9, 1861, *Official Records-Navies*, Series 2, Vol. 2, pp. 64-65. For Bulloch's first report home, see Bulloch to Mallory, Aug. 13, 1861, ibid., pp. 83-87. Private detective quotation in Bulloch, *Secret Service*, Vol. 1, p. 227. For friction between Bulloch and fellow naval officers, see James H. North to Mallory, Mar. 29, 1862, *Official Records-Navies*, Series 2, Vol. 2, pp. 176-177; Bulloch to North, July 10, 1862, ibid., pp. 214-215.

[32]Stern, *When the Guns Roared*, p. 164.

look at contracts, he had a frustrating task. Frequently everyone in town knew the truth, for example, that a particular ship was under construction as an instrument of war for the Confederates. But proving it was another matter.[33]

Dudley worked tirelessly to compile and pass on vital information about suspected warships and blockade runners being built or loaded in England and Scotland. During the first two years of the war, he paid special attention to two handsome vessels being built in yards on either side of the Mersey — one known as the *Oreto*, and the other christened the *Enrica*. Dudley gathered descriptions of the ships, their sailing dates, connections to James Bulloch, and Bulloch's association with the firm at 10 Rumford Place. Dudley's informants even reported that the group of seamen from the *Enrica* was heard playing "Dixies Land" on fife, concertina, and cornopean while crossing on the Mersey ferry. Through guile and good legal advice, Bulloch managed to slip both these unarmed ships out of Liverpool and later equip them for spectacular success on the high seas as the Confederate commerce destroyers *Florida* and *Alabama*.[34]

Dudley was more successful in trying to stop the *Alexandra*, the wooden, screw steamer built by Fraser, Trenholm and Company as a gift to the Confederacy. In a letter to the company, Bulloch wrote that the secretary of the Confederate navy, Stephen R. Mallory, "accepts with pleasure the gunboat you have so generously offered," and thanked the firm for "services in the cause of our common country, very few private individuals of any nation have had either the means or the inclination to render." U.S. officials, of course, did not have benefit of this letter, but they knew the true designs of the *Alexandra*. At the urging of Dudley and his superiors, British customs seized the ship in April 1863 and brought her to trial — a first in the history of the Foreign Enlistment Act. Both North and South eagerly awaited the verdict, which would do much to clarify Britain's shifting policy: Was this a warship for the Confederacy, a violation of Her Majesty's neutrality? Dudley provided the crown with a shocking witness: Clarence Yonge, the disgruntled ex-paymaster of the *Alabama*. Yonge testified that Fraser, Trenholm and Company was "mixed up with" the construction of the *Alexandra*, and that Confederate naval and army agents like James Bulloch had a room to themselves in the company's offices. But the ship was not equipped with guns and the evidence was shaky that she was bound for Confederate military service. The defense alleged that she was built as a yacht. The jury promptly returned a verdict for the defendants, but legal

[33]Brainerd Dyer, "Thomas H. Dudley," *Civil War History* 1 (December 1955), pp. 401-413; Stern, *When the Guns Roared*, pp. 74, 102-104; Bulloch, *Secret Service*, Vol. 2, pp. 314-317; D. P. Crook, *The North, the South, and the Powers, 1861-1865* (New York: John Wiley & Sons, 1974), pp. 293-294.

[34]Stern, *When the Guns Roared*, pp. 141-151.

wrangling and a second seizure of the ship in Nassau effectively held it harmless until after the war.[35]

Early on, the U.S. Consulate in Liverpool was aware of tactics used by Fraser, Trenholm and Company to help bluff their ships past the blockaders. In July 1861 Vice Consul Henry Wilding wrote to Charles Francis Adams, U.S. minister to England, that a ship belonging to George A. Trenholm had been registered at the customs house in the names of two English clerks at Fraser, Trenholm and Company. Wilding said he had "no doubt whatever" that Trenholm's Charleston company remained the real owner and that it was "wrongfully using the British flag." In 1862, in a remarkable letter to U.S. Secretary of State William H. Seward, the tenacious Dudley told of how he personally inspected iron plates being loaded onto a ship that was the subject of a name change and "mock sale" to a Liverpudlian described as "one of the most active and open men in the town in aiding the rebellion" and "one of the tools used by Fraser, Trenholm & Co."[36]

As the war pressed on, Dudley's expenditures for espionage far exceeded the £17 he paid Detective Maguire by the end of 1861. Dudley got a big boost from a man who in many respects was the northern counterpart to George Alfred Trenholm: John Murray Forbes, a wealthy Boston merchant and shipowner. Forbes was sent on a secret mission to England in early 1863, along with fellow shipping magnate William H. Aspinwall, to try to buy ships and thereby keep them out of Confederate hands. Impressed by the level of intrigue at play in Liverpool, Forbes was convinced that a little money spent to stop southern warships like the dreaded Laird rams could save a fortune later, as the United States might go to war with Great Britain if the ships were allowed to sail. Forbes funneled hundreds of pounds to Dudley to expand his intelligence gathering and later convinced officials in Washington to send thousands more.[37]

THE BITTER END

In late 1865 George Alfred Trenholm sent a letter to his young partner in Liverpool with some ideas about how a new venture, the "British and Southern Finance Coy.," could turn a profit off the ruins of the defeated South. South Carolina's piecemeal railroad, Charleston's damaged stores and houses, rich but idle plantations — all needed a shot of new money to bring them to life again. "These ... are the fields of usefulness and profit open to the company," wrote Trenholm. He wrote the letter little more than a

[35]Ibid., p. 199; Bulloch to Fraser, Trenholm and Co., Nov. 24, 1862, *Official Records-Navies,* Series 2, Vol. 2, p. 302; Crook, *The North, the South,* pp. 294-301; Stern, *Confederate Navy,* pp. 166-167; Owsley, *King Cotton,* pp. 429-430.

[36]Wilding to Adams, July 8, 1861, *Official Records-Navies,* Series 1, Vol. 6, p. 47; Dudley to Seward, Sept. 3, 1862, ibid., Vol. 13, pp. 331-332.

[37]Stern, *When the Guns Roared,* pp. 104, 197-206; Crook, *The North, the South,* p. 294; Dyer, "Thomas H. Dudley," pp. 406-407.

month after his release from Fort Pulaski in Savannah, where he and some other members of the Confederate Cabinet suffered the ignominy of imprisonment for their part in the great rebellion.[38]

For Trenholm, the path to prison was rocky. Illness forced him during the Cabinet's flight from the besieged capital of Richmond to hand President Jefferson Davis his resignation on April 27, 1865. Later, Trenholm was ordered to report from his temporary home in Columbia (his beautiful villa de Greffin had burned when the city fell) to U.S. commanders in Charleston. There, a company of black soldiers escorted him down muddy streets to the local jail. Such an occurrence was anticipated, and feared, by Trenholm's partner, Theodore Wagner, who had sent an urgent plea to Prioleau that summer. "The corruption, Black Mail, bribes &c &c are fearful," he wrote. "... I want to be able if the time and moment comes to take advantage of it to save Mr. Trenholm and myself if we can buy ourselves out — this is the reason why I wish the £10,000 sent promptly." Wagner went on to say: "What is doing us a good deal of injury is the report in the papers and about that Mr. Trenholm has secured millions of pounds on the other side. I wish it was so, and I fear they will want to blackmail me badly." Indeed, Wagner, the president of John Fraser and Company in Charleston, did part with a considerable sum when threatened with prosecution for treason, but Trenholm apparently made no attempt at bribery.[39]

Wagner's remark about the alleged post-war fortune held by Fraser, Trenholm and Company in Liverpool points to an issue much discussed through the years. Historians, writing on related topics, have made many sensational but vague statements about how the company fared during the war — that it "fattened prodigiously" or "made tremendous profits, some say as much as four million pounds!"[40] The full and exact truth of the matter is unclear, although some strong clues as to the company's actual wartime fortunes are readily apparent. Not the least of these is the fact that Trenholm

[38]Trenholm to Prioleau, Nov. 24, 1865, Fraser, Trenholm and Co. Collection, Box 1, No. 129; A. J. Hanna, *Flight Into Oblivion* (Richmond, Va.: Johnson Publishing Company, 1938), pp. 238-239.

[39]Trenholm to Davis, Apr. 27, 1865, in Dunbar Rowland, ed., *Jefferson Davis, Constitutionalist: His Letters, Papers and Speeches* (Jackson: Mississippi Department of Archives and History, 1923), Vol. 6, pp. 564-565; Morgan, *Recollections,* pp. 243-246, 250; Wagner to Prioleau, June 9, 1865, Fraser, Trenholm and Co. Collection, Box 1, No. 143.

[40]Edward Boykin, *Sea Devil of the Confederacy: The Story of the* Florida *and Her Captain, John Newland Maffitt* (New York: Funk & Wagnalls, 1959), p. 81 (first quotation); Merli, *Great Britain,* p. 239 (second quotation). Similar assertions have been made, and somewhat debunked, about the supposed fortunes routinely made in running the blockade. See Stanley Lebergott, "Through the Blockade: The Profitability and Extent of Cotton Smuggling, 1861-1865," *Journal of Economic History* 41 (December 1981), pp. 867-888.

and his partners would ultimately see their companies on both sides of the Atlantic crumble underneath the war's heavy fallout.

Unlike other companies heavily involved in blockade running, Trenholm's Charleston and Liverpool houses did not close down at war's end. Both were long-established companies, and certainly the close and steady relationship with the Confederacy, as well as their private ventures, yielded some good returns. But even the cautious Prioleau was bitten by the war's last-gasp mayhem, when Confederate purchasing agents went on a desperate spending spree and sent the bills to the government's banker in Liverpool. The company ended the war still owed £170,000 by the defunct Confederacy. Prioleau intended to sell off Confederate cotton, blockade runners, and other property to erase the debt — to the dismay of British merchants also owed money by the Confederacy — but U.S. authorities soon tied up those assets with a lawsuit. Fraser, Trenholm and Company negotiated a settlement that would have paid it the first £150,000 from the sale of the Confederate property, with the rest going to the United States, but Secretary of State Seward nixed the deal. The company had other problems as well. Not only had it helped sell Confederate bonds in Europe, it had invested in them. And the value of its ships dropped precipitously after the war boom. The company had staked much on a victory.[41]

But the worst was the litigation. Consul Dudley, dogged spymaster during the war, was now seeker and liquidator of Confederate property. James Bulloch, in his memoirs, wrote the outcome:

> Mr. Seward directed the Liverpool Consul to prosecute the suits against Messrs. Fraser, Trenholm and Co., and that unhappy firm was pursued with relentless zeal, and was so persistently involved by their persecutors in Chancery and other proceedings, that it was hardly possible for the partners to give due attention to their private business, and finally their financial credit was affected, and they were reduced to commercial ruin.[42]

Fraser, Trenholm and Company declared bankruptcy in May 1867. A Liverpool paper reported that the firm had liabilities in excess of £1.2 million and assets of about £290,000, including Charles Prioleau's private estate. The respected southern business magazine *De Bow's Review* commented that the failure of the Liverpool firm and the subsequent troubles of John Fraser and Company "is one of the heaviest disasters that could have befallen" Charleston, which had "absolutely depended" on the helping hand of Trenholm's firms after the war. The U.S. government also

[41]Bulloch, *Secret Service*, Vol. 2, p. 418, 423-426; Wise, *Lifeline*, pp. 222-223.
[42]Bulloch, *Secret Service*, Vol. 2, pp. 426-427.

A memorial to Confederate naval officer James Dunwoody Bulloch is located in Toxteth Cemetery, Smithdown Road, Liverpool. The inscription reads in part, "Strong ties of common ancestry existed between the Confederate states and the mother country England. Warm ties of friendship developed between Bulloch and the English people. At the end of the war he chose to remain in Liverpool. American by Birth, Englishman by Choice." The stone was raised by the United Daughters of the Confederacy in 1968. Photo courtesy of the author.

sued the Charleston house, even alleging that it was an arm of the Confederate Treasury. The company was finally liquidated under the claims of the federal government and other creditors.[43]

What conclusions may we draw from the story of George Alfred Trenholm, Charles Prioleau, and the "counting house" at 10 Rumford Place? Clearly, the company was instrumental in building a vital, if imperfect, supply line to the South. It handled capably the Confederacy's practical needs and gave tremendous assistance to some of its more obscure champions, like James Bulloch and Caleb Huse. Indeed, Fraser, Trenholm and Company did much to prolong the war, to make it a better fight. But like many other patriotic southern businessmen, Trenholm, Prioleau, and their partners were ever mindful of the fact that they were businessmen, not merely expendables to be used up and tossed aside in the grinding advance of war. Such was the legacy, in fact, of the Confederacy's merchant and planter class. Though some, most notably Trenholm, contributed much to

---

[43]Wise, *Lifeline*, pp. 223-224; *De Bow's Review*, June 1867, pp. 595-597. An excellent examination of the eight-year legal battle on both sides of the Atlantic to recover Confederate property can be found in Carvel Painter, "The Recovery of Confederate Property and Other Assets Abroad, 1865-73" (Ph.D. diss., American University, 1973). Charles Prioleau, George Alfred Trenholm, and their partners in the firms of Fraser, Trenholm and Co. and John Fraser and Co. were at the center of this struggle, as was U.S. Consul Thomas H. Dudley. The U.S. government ended up with little to show for its lawsuits, settling in 1873 for $150,000 in gold plus interest from Prioleau and the other defendants. Thus the U.S. effort to recover the reported "many millions of dollars" worth of Confederate cotton, cash, ships and other property essentially were "unsuccessful."

the war effort, economics professor Stanley Lebergott argues that on the whole they hurt the chances for nationhood by their devotion to profit — their resistance to taxes, their reluctance to send their valuable slave property to the front with their soldier sons, their running of luxury goods through the blockade, and their insistence on exporting their own cotton, denying the Confederacy the monopoly it needed to sell its cotton bonds abroad.[44] Trenholm's companies were, among southern businesses, superpatriots. But they, too, had profit in mind: survive the war, prosper from it, and then enjoy the financial windfall of victory. As it turned out, they were denied even survival by the war and its turbulent aftermath.

What became of the main players in this drama? Prioleau moved his family to Belgium, worked as a banker, and then returned to London where he died in 1887 at age sixty. Bulloch, partly because he belonged to a class not entitled to amnesty in the United States after the war, stayed in Liverpool and worked in the cotton trade. He is buried in Liverpool's Toxteth Cemetery. Dudley, until his resignation in 1872, continued to pursue and dispose of Confederate property, including naval ships that sought refuge in Liverpool. He also gathered evidence to present to an international tribunal in Geneva, resulting in an award of $15.5 million in gold to the United States from Great Britain for damages done to U.S. commerce by British-built ships, chiefly the *Alabama*. Neutral Britain had not been neutral enough. Dudley, whose struggles in Liverpool left him quite anti-British, returned to New Jersey and fought for the protective tariff until his death in 1893.[45]

George Alfred Trenholm accepted the defeat, and the liberation of the slaves, without rancor. "It pleased God to decide the contest against us," he said in a reflective letter to Prioleau while confined in Fort Pulaski. "The future is brighter to my eyes, than it is generally seen by others." For the young men, he wrote, the important thing was to forget about politics and to go to work rebuilding the South. As for the former slaves, "we must be, what we have always professed, their truest and best friends."[46] Trenholm sent three petitions to President Andrew Johnson seeking pardon. Johnson finally released Trenholm from prison on parole in October 1865, and

[44]Lebergott, "Why the South Lost," pp. 58-74.

[45]On Prioleau, see "Historical Sketch of the Prioleau Family," p. 30. On Bulloch, see *Dictionary of American Biography*, Vol. 3, p. 258. On Dudley, see Dyer, "Thomas H. Dudley," pp. 409-412; Christopher M. Henze, "The Saga of C.S.S. *Alabama*," *Alabama Heritage* 37 (Summer 1995), p. 21.

[46]Trenholm to Prioleau, Oct. 4, 1865, Fraser, Trenholm and Co. Collection, Box 1, No. 128.

pardoned him about a year later.[47] But even before Trenholm received absolution, he was at work again on big ideas. In June 1866 he led a large contingent of men from South Carolina and Tennessee to Cincinnati, Ohio, to promote construction of a railroad to Charleston via Knoxville. Trenholm signed labor contracts with his ex-slaves, helped revive Charleston's business community, invested in the new phosphate mining industry, and reviled the purportedly corrupt Reconstruction government that gripped his state. By 1874 he had rebounded from the lawsuits, sagging cotton prices, and other factors that had ruined his companies and was once again a wealthy cotton broker with a seat in the South Carolina legislature and a new summer estate called "Solitude." When Trenholm died on December 9, 1876, at age sixty-nine, the flags flew at half-mast in Charleston.[48]

As for the brick and stone building at 10 Rumford Place, the three-story, slate-roofed structure is somewhat obscured now by taller, more modern buildings. Built about 1840 it received protected historic status in 1982, and in 1991 the building was restored for use as office suites. Its "central rusticated cart entrance" was retained, and a plaque was mounted by the door beckoning, somewhat inappropriately, "Bulloch House." The renovation, regrettably, unearthed no scintillating secrets, no cache of Confederate gold, in the building that a British government document says "was in effect the Confederate Embassy in England."[49]

---

[47]Trenholm to Johnson, June 6, 1865, in Paul H. Bergeron, ed., *The Papers of Andrew Johnson* (Knoxville: University of Tennessee Press, 1967-), Vol. 8, pp. 193-194; Trenholm, from Fort Pulaski, to Johnson, Sept. 7, 1865, *Johnson Papers*, Vol. 9, pp. 41-42; "Order *re* Release of Prominent Confederate Prisoners," Oct. 11, 1865, ibid., p. 227; Trenholm to Johnson, Aug. 10, 1866, *Johnson Papers*, Vol. 11, pp. 63-64. A copy of the pardon is in Nepveux, *George Alfred Trenholm*, pp. 93-94.

[48]Robert M. Moore, from Cincinnati, to Johnson, Sept. 24, 1866, *Johnson Papers*, Vol. 11, pp. 261-263; *Dictionary of American Biography*, Vol. 21, p. 690; Nepveux, *George Alfred Trenholm*, pp. 11, 98, 104; Hanna, *Flight Into Oblivion*, p. 239; Walter J. Fraser, Jr., *Charleston! Charleston! The History of a Southern City* (Columbia: University of South Carolina Press, 1989), p. 283; *De Bow's Review*, June 1867, p. 596; *Encyclopedia of the Confederacy*, p. 1619. Trenholm's obituary was long and glowing: "It was his ambition to be a merchant in the large old sense," guided by intellect and not the speculator's arithmetic. He envisioned South Carolina as a hub for trains stabbing west and steamships sailing east. "Mr. Trenholm was wealthy when the war began. During the war his supreme purpose was to advance the Confederate cause. What advantage he gained was incidental only." "George Alfred Trenholm," *Charleston News and Courier*, Dec. 11, 1876.

[49]"Confederate Headquarters in Liverpool Sees Rebirth," *Confederate Naval Historical Society Newsletter* (October 1991), p. 1; Secretary of State for National Heritage, *Eighth List of Buildings of Special Architectural or Historic Interest, City of Liverpool (Merseyside)*, June 1985, p. 617.

TECHNOLOGY:
"AT THE EDGE OF MODERN TIMES"

CAPTAIN LANGDON CHEVES, JR., AND THE CONFEDERATE SILK DRESS BALLOON

Edited by J. H. EASTERBY

FOREWORD

The legend of the Confederate silk dress balloon appears first to have been given a wide currency through an article contributed by General James Longstreet to the *Century Magazine* in 1886. General Longstreet wrote as follows:[1]

"The Federals had been using balloons in examining our positions, and we watched with envious eyes their beautiful observations as they floated high up in the air, and well out of the range of our guns. We longed for the balloons that poverty denied us. *A genius arose for the occasion and suggested that we send out and gather together all the silk dresses in the Confederacy and make a balloon. It was done, and soon we had a great patchwork ship of many and varied hues.* The balloon was ready for use in the Seven Days' campaign. We had no gas except in Richmond, and it was the custom to inflate the balloon there, tie it securely to an engine, and run it down the York River railroad to any point at which we desired to send it up. One day it was on a steamer down the James when the tide went out and left the vessel and the balloon high and dry on a bar. The Federals gathered it in, *and with it the last silk dress in the Confederacy.* This capture was the meanest trick of the war and one I have never yet forgiven."

This account was substantially in accord with the facts regarding the operations of the famous aerostat, but in asserting that it had been made of silk dresses, presumably collected for the purpose among the ladies of the Confederacy, the writer was plucking the flowers of a plant which had probably steadily grown from a small seed cast upon the ground in the spring of 1862.

Ten years later the legend was invested with a higher authority when Captain W. A. Glassford, of the Signal Corps, in an article appearing in the *Journal of the Military Institution of the United States*, quoted General Longstreet at length without further comment than that his statement was "an interesting account of the construction, use and ultimate fate of one balloon—believed to be the only one in the Confederate army."[2] This

[1] James Longstreet, "Our March against Pope," *The Century Illustrated Monthly Magazine*, XXXI (February, 1886), pp. 601–602. The italics have been added.

[2] *Prolegomenon with Historic Sketch of the Balloon during the Civil War and the United States Aeronautical Corps*, by Captain W. A. Glassford, Signal Corps, U. S. A., Reprinted from *Journal Military Service Institution* (New York, [1896]), pp. 259–60.

endorsement by one who had made an extensive, and supposedly exhaustive, study of the use of balloons during the Confederate War was the more regrettable since the facts, as it will be seen below, were actually made available to the author a short time after his article was completed.

In his efforts to obtain information on the elusive subject of Confederate aeronautics Captain Glassford had enlisted the aid of General E. Porter Alexander, the former Chief of Ordnance to the Army of Northern Virginia, who had directed the operations of the balloon during its brief career in the Seven Days' Battle. Probably recalling that the balloon had been designed by a relative of Captain Joseph C. Haskell, his adjutant on that occasion, General Alexander in turn appealed to the latter for the desired information. Captain Haskell complied with this request, but the reports that were forthcoming from various members of his family were conflicting, and before the correct version was discovered the opportunity of preventing Glassford's repetition of the legend had been lost.

The data concerning the origin of the Confederate aerostat were first assembled by the late Mr. Langdon Cheves, a cousin of Captain Haskell. In substance they were: *first*, that the balloon had been designed and its construction supervised by Captain Langdon Cheves, Jr., an uncle of Messrs. Haskell and Cheves; *second*, that it had been built in Savannah during the spring and early summer of 1862; *third*, that it had been made of new silk; and, *fourth*, that the belief that ladies' dresses had been used for the purpose was probably to be traced to Captain Cheves's jesting remark to his daughters: "I am buying up all the silk dresses in Savannah, but not for you girls." This story was first pieced together by means of family tradition and a single written document.

With the facts in his possession General Alexander might reasonably have been expected to make effective use of them, at least, in any account that he himself would prepare. But such was not the case. When the General's *Memoirs* were published in 1907 they were found to contain the following statement:[3]

"In addition to these duties, I was placed in charge of a balloon which had been manufactured in Savannah by Dr. Edward Cheves, and sent to Gen. Lee for use in reconnoitring the enemy's lines. It was made from silk of many patterns, varnished with gutta-percha car-springs dissolved in naptha, and inflated at the Richmond Gas Works with ordinary city gas.

"I saw the battle of Gaines Mill from it, and signalled information of the movement of Slocum's division across the Chickahominy to re-enforce Porter. Ascensions were made daily, and when the enemy reached Malvern Hill, the inflated balloon would be carried down the river and ascensions made from the deck of a boat. Unfortunately, on July 4, the

[3] E. P. Alexander, *Military Memoirs of a Confederate* (New York, 1907), pp. 172–73.

boat—the *Teaser*, a small armed tug—got aground below Malvern Hill on a falling tide, and a large Federal gunboat, the *Maritanza*, came up and captured both boat and balloon, the crew escaping.

"We could never build another balloon, but my experience with this gave me a high idea of the possible efficiency of balloons in active campaigns. Especially did we find, too, that the balloons of the enemy forced upon us constant troublesome precautions in efforts to conceal our marches."

When one so well informed as General Alexander could not remember the name of the designer of the balloon and would not take the pains to correct the error regarding the materials from which it was constructed, it is not to be wondered that the legend continued to grow luxuriantly, finally attaining its highest florescence in 1921 in the following passage of William Wood's *Captains of the Civil War:*[4]

"It was the same in almost every kind of goods. The South made next to none for herself and had to import from the North or overseas. The North could buy silk for balloons. The South could not. The Southern women gave in their whole supply of silk for the big balloon that was lost during the Seven Days' Battle in the second year of the war. The Southern soldiers never forgave what they considered the ungallant trick of the Northerners who took this many-hued balloon from a steamer stranded on a bar at low tide down near the mouth of the James."

Meanwhile the true story of the silk dress balloon remained, carefully documented, in the papers of Mr. Cheves. To the materials originally used in arriving at the correct version were added even more convincing documents which had later come to light among the papers of the balloon's designer—one of them nothing less than the bill of a Charleston merchant for at least a portion of the silk used. So, in 1935, when a less credulous historian appeared in the person of Professor J. Duane Squires to ask assistance in presenting the truth, Mr. Cheves was prepared with the facts which furnished the basis of the following account, published two years later in the *American Historical Review:*[5]

"Various writers have described its construction, alleging that it was made of ladies' dresses surrendered by the loyal women of the South for the purpose. Its true origin is less romantic but not less interesting. It was built in the spring of 1862 by Langdon Cheves, jr., member of the well-

---

[4] William Wood, *Captains of the Civil War* (New Haven, 1921), p. 63.

[5] J. Duane Squires, "Aeronautics in the Civil War," *American Historical Review*, XLII (July, 1937), p. 664. Professor Squires states: "The account in this article is based on transcripts of family documents made available to the writer by Mr. Langdon Cheves, nephew of the balloon builder and a citizen of Charleston, S. C." This account has recently been repeated in Jeremiah Millbank, Jr., *The First Century of Flight in America* (Princeton, 1943), pp. 127–28.

known family of that name, captain in the C. S. A., and citizen of Savannah, Georgia. He had been stationed at Port Royal, South Carolina, earlier in 1862 and had presumably seen Lowe's balloon sent to T. W. Sherman there. It was built of new materials by Captain Cheves at his own expense in the Chatham Armory in Savannah. By the middle of June, 1862, it was complete and was at once rushed to the Richmond front. No hydrogen being available, the balloon was filled with city gas and carried to the fighting lines, affixed to a freight car. Between June 27 and July 4 daily ascensions were made and considerable useful reconnaissance work done. E. Porter Alexander, at the time Chief of Ordnance of the Army of Northern Virginia, was in charge of the balloon and 'signalled information of the movement of Slocum's division across the Chickahominy to reenforce Porter' at the battle of Gaines's Mill. After the Union forces had reached Malvern Hill the inflated balloon was put on a small armed tug, the *Teaser*, and ascensions were made from her deck from July 1 through July 4. On the latter date the *Teaser* 'got aground below Malvern Hill on a falling tide and a large Federal gunboat, the *Maritanza*, came up and captured both boat and balloon, the crew escaping.' With the loss of this balloon Confederate military aeronautics ceased. Under difficult circumstances the Southern inventors had attempted to improvise equipment to meet the new tactics developed by Lowe, but owing to the almost total lack of proper materials and trained personnel their efforts had not been a success."

When Mr. Cheves's papers came into the possession of the South Carolina Historical Society, the materials relating to the balloon were found set apart to themselves.[6] Because some of them do not appear to have been made available to Professor Squires and, more especially, because of the great interest at the present time in military aeronautics, it has been decided to publish them in full. Mr. Cheves, with his meticulous care in such matters, would probably have felt that his biographical sketch of Captain Cheves was unfinished, but this has been included as the best account that could be supplied under the circumstances. The sketch forms Part I in the following arrangement. The letters setting forth the evidence as Mr. Cheves had it in 1896, when he was corresponding with General Alexander and Captain Glassford, are included in Part II. In a later issue of the *Magazine* a third part will present the documents that were subsequently found in Captain Cheves's papers. The footnotes have been supplied by the editor.

The reader may find reasons to question some of Mr. Cheves's secondary conclusions as stated in Parts I and II, but greater significance will probably

[6] A rapid search of the Cheves Collection by Miss Helen G. McCormack has yielded three additional items. Others may be discovered in the course of time.

be attached to additions which the documents make to present knowledge of Confederate aeronautics. They will be found to reveal the fact that the balloon of the Seven Days' Battle bore the pleasing and perhaps not inappropriate name *Gazelle*. They supply the names of at least one balloonist, Charles Cevor,[6a] and two technicians, A. A. Pratt and G. D. Weigand, whose contributions to aviation may deserve attention. They show that the Confederates were experimenting with improved methods of inflation. Finally, they indicate clearly that another balloon was in process of construction and raise the question of the final result of this second attempt.

PART I

LANGDON CHEVES, JR.

A Signer of the Ordinance of Secession

Langdon Cheves was a son of the Honorable Langdon Cheves (sometime a Judge and Member of Congress from South Carolina, chairman of the Naval Committee in the War of 1812, and Speaker in 1814).[7] He was born at Charleston (I believe) on the 2d of September, 1814. His father, Judge Cheves, having been made President of the United States Bank and subsequently Commissioner under the Treaty of Ghent went to Philadelphia in 1819 and remained there and at his seat "Abbeville," near Lancaster, Penn., for ten years, and his son Langdon, the subject of this sketch, went to school at Lancaster and in Philadelphia, completing his education at the South Carolina College where he graduated in Dec., 1833. His next birthday after graduating came near to being his last. At Pendleton while practicing pistol shooting with the gentlemen of the neighbourhood he accidentally shot himself in the neck—it was supposed mortally by his companions. His mother writes: "He is a great favourite . . . a very amiable fine young man . . . the day before the accident was his Birthday, when his health and good wishes were drank in Champaign. He was twenty. His Father drank his health and said, my Son . . . I am happy to tell you you have never given me one unhappy moment."

Mr. Cheves first military experience was in the Seminole War, where he served as a volunteer, in what rank or capacity I do not know, and was actively engaged. He then read law and was called to the Bar at Colum-

---

[6a] Cevor has been mentioned in F. S. Haydon, *Aeronautics in the Union and Confederate Armies*, I (Baltimore, 1941) and will doubtless receive further attention in the volume which is to cover the later years of the war.

[7] See Susan Smythe Bennett, "The Cheves Family of South Carolina," this *Magazine*, XXXV (July and October, 1934), pp. 79–95, 130–52, where slight variations from the statements in this sketch will be found.

bia in 1836 and practiced there for several years.   He was State Reporter for the Courts of Appeal and Cheves' Law and Equity Reports (published in Columbia 1840, 41) are part of his work for this period.   He then married Charlotte, daughter of the Hon. David J. McCord, of Columbia.

After his marriage Mr. Cheves became a rice planter.   His father put him in charge of his extensive rice plantations on Savannah River in Beaufort District and later removed to his Ogeechee estate and turned over the Savannah places to himself and his younger brother Charles. He planted these places with most conspicuous skill, ability and success until the war.   He greatly assisted in the erection of the "Vernezoboe" [?] freshet bank, to protect the Savannah river plantations from its floods, and other plantation engineering works, and reclaimed and planted successfully the neglected peat or "prairie" lands, thus greatly increasing his acreage. His plantations were among the best managed and his people the best cared for in the state.   In the cholera epidemic of 185– he and his brother Charles remained with their people, removed them to camps in the pine lands, and greatly mitigated the disease and the sufferings it occasioned.

Mr. Cheves possessed a most endearing personality, winning the confidence and affection of his associates and even of his negroes, who were most loyal and devoted to him.   He was a man of unusual ability and information and was constantly called upon to assist his friends in matters of engineering and machinery so often needed on rice plantations.   Mr. Cheves was by this time known not only as a skilful and successful planter but a man of great judgment, originality, and uprightness.   He was a warm Southerner in sympathy and principle and devoted his time and resources to the cause of the Confederacy from the time of its incipiency. Mr. Cheves was chosen a delegate from St. Peter's parish to the Secession Convention and voted for the Ordinance.

On the breaking out of the war Mr. Cheves volunteered his services and devoted his time and resources to the defence of the State.   He served as an Engineer (for which his studies and his experience in plantation works, canals, banks, etc. well prepared him), and the confidence of his fellow planters of the coast in his eminent powers, justice, and integrity, their knowledge that he took personal charge of the works, and his example in sending his own negroes were of great benefit to the public defences in procuring negro labourers for them.

"In the spring of 1861 he volunteered to raise the labour for and superintended the works on Hilton Head.   After the completion of these, he became volunteer aid to General Drayton, who assigned him to engineer duty."   He was present there with Capt. F. D. Lee at the engagement with the Federal Fleet when Port Royal was taken.   He constructed the works at Red Bluff and was employed on other minor works.   In the spring of 1862 Mr. Cheves designed and superintended the construction at the Chatham Armory in Savannah, chiefly at his own expense (I believe), of the only Southern war balloon, made of ladies dress silk bought in Savannah and Charleston, in lengths of about 40 feet and of various colours. He laughingly told his daughters, "I am buying up all the handsome silk dresses in Savannah, but not for you girls." A letter of 7 June, 1862 from his brother Dr. John Cheves (then constructing, under innumerable difficulties, the system of obstructions and torpedo defences at Charleston) [says:] "Tell Lang I am using car springs dissolved in boiled oil to coat the wire (for torpedos); it is the best balloon varnish." Mr. Cheves took the balloon on to Richmond just before the Seven Days Battles and remained there to assist in using it. Several ascents were made (amongst others by the late Genl. E. P. Alexander and Capt. Jos C. Haskell, his adjutant, now chief of the Car Service Association). But the inferior coal gas and the long distance it had to be run on the railroad (attached to a flat car) from Richmond to the front and back made ascents difficult. It was finally lost at the James River, being cut off by the enemy's gun boats. Capt. Glassford, U. S. A., in his "Sketch of Ballooning in the Civil War" says: "while the use of the balloon by the Confederates is known to have been very scanty, an interesting account of the construction, use and ultimate fate of one balloon—believed to be the only one in the Confederate Army—is given by General Longstreet. He says: "The Federals had been using balloons in examining our positions and we watched with anxious eyes their beautiful observations as they floated high up in the air, well out of range of our guns. While we were longing for the balloons that poverty denied us, a genius arose for the occasion and suggested that we send out and gather all the silk dresses in the Confederacy and make a balloon. It was done; and soon we had a great patch work ship of many and varied hues which was ready for use in the Seven Days campaign. We had no gas except in Richmond, and it was the custom to inflate the balloon there, tie it securely to an engine, and move it down the York River Railroad to any point at which we desired to send it up. One day it was on a steamer down the James when the tide went out and left the vessel and the balloon high and dry on a bar. The Federals gathered it in and with it the last silk dress in the Confederacy."

Mr. Cheves brought home from Richmond the body of his nephew Lieut. Edward Cheves who had been killed in the battle. In July, 1862, he was ordered in charge of the works on Morris Island. He chose the site and built Battery Wagner, and probably suggested its name (after Mr. Theodore D. Wagner, a relative of his wife's who had contributed largely with labourers and otherwise towards its construction) and subsequently considerably improved and strengthened the work. Gen. Ripley writes (see

Charleston Year Book, 1885, p. 354) ". . . the works which had been commenced were well and solidly finished during the summer of 1862, notably Battery Bee on Sullivan's Island and Battery Wagner on Morris Island, the former under the charge of Capt. George E. Walker and the latter of Capt. Langdon Cheves." Battery Wagner and Cumins Point with some minor works on the Island were the results of his energy and skill. For more then two years he thus served his country without asking or receiving either rank or pay until about two months before his death when the War Department at Richmond conferred upon him the commission of Captain of Engineers in recognition of his services. Capt. Cheves remained in charge of the Fort until the grand attack of the Federal Fleet and land forces on the 10 July, 1863, when he was killed at the threshold of his quarters by the first shell fired from the attacking fleet.

The Charleston *Mercury* of July 13, 1863 states: "Even in the midst of our dangers and our preparations for coming trials we must pause in grief at the loss of some of our best and bravest, who fell early in the action of Friday last. Conspicuous amongst these were Captains Langdon Cheves and Charles T. Haskell. Langdon Cheves was killed by the first shell fired by the enemy at Battery Wagner . . . In the full vigor of manhood he has fallen at the Battery which he had been at so much pains to erect, leaving a record which will not unbeseem the memory of the sire whose name he bore."

Langdon Cheves

DAVID C. EBAUGH ON THE BUILDING OF "THE DAVID"

David Chenoweth Ebaugh (July 9, 1824–August 9, 1895), son of Henry and Mary Chenoweth Ebaugh of Maryland, came to South Carolina and bought timber-lands in St. John's, Berkeley, in 1855; he engaged in lumbering until that business was ruined by the Civil War. He then became superintendent of nitre works on the Cooper River near Monck's Corner, for the Confederate government. His part in the construction of "The David", a steam-driven torpedo boat, named for him, is told in the letters below. After the war, his property, appraised at $165,000, was confiscated by the Federal government. He then removed to Charleston, where he purchased as his home the LaBruce house on Columbus Street, on the site of the present cigar factory. From 1879 until 1882, he was alderman from ward 7. A pioneer in the phosphate business, he invented machinery and operated some of the earliest fertilizer factories[1] until 1891, when he organized and became general manager of a fertilizer plant in Greenville.

Through his granddaughter, Laura Smith Ebaugh, of the department of sociology, Furman University, Greenville, much of the above information was obtained from John L. Ebaugh's *John Jacob Ebaugh*, privately printed in Baltimore in 1941. The original letters were presented to the Society by Mr. and Mrs. Harold G. Guerard, Jr., of Charleston, and are reproduced here without change except the addition of punctuation when necessary for clarity.

CHEROKEE SPRINGS HOTEL

G. W. EBAUGH, PROPRIETOR

Cherokee, S. C., Oct 4th 1892

Rev. W. H. Campbell
Charleston, S. C.
Dear Sir

Enclosed please find a statement of the oragin and building of the Torpedo Boat David as requested by you when at this place.

I think it would be a good show from Charleston if they would build a Duplicate of the David and send it to Chicago for the Columbus Exposition it being the first Torpedo boat ever to run by Steam.

Very Truly Yours
DAVID C. EBAUGH

Cherokee Springs Hotel
Oct. 4th 1892

Dear Sir

According to promise I send you the history (as near as I can remember) of the building of the Torpedo Boat David, in 1864, the dates I cannot recollect, they must be obtained from other sources.

---

[1] For the Ebaugh Lime Fertilizer and Manufacturing Company, *see S. C. Stat.*, XVII, 634.

Dr St. J. Ravenel came up to Stoney landing on the Cooper river near Moncks Corner where Ravenel & Stevens had lime works. I was Supt. of Nitre works at same place for the Confederate Government.

Dr. Ravenel told me that a Torpedo had been made, that if a boat could be built to carry it and explode it under the Iron Sides we could clear Charleston harbour of Blockcadors.

He asked me if a boat could be built with a long pole in front to carry the Torpedo on and suggested to build a boat to be driven by man power. I told him it would be too slow and that two many men would be required and the danger to great. I suggested to build a Segar shaped boat and put in it a steam Engine to drive it. He remarked that a steam Engine was to big and it would make a noise. I replied saying that a steam Engine could be put in his *hat* and that I could deaden the exhaust by mechanical means.

He told me that $100,000 was offered to any person that would destroy the Iron Sides which was the terror of the Charleston Harbour. That several Gentlemen had offered $1000 each to build a boat to accomplish it.

The Gentlemen was Mr. Theodore Stoney, Cap Chevis, Theodore Wagner, Dr. Ravenel and Others.

I told Dr. R that I would build a boat on my own plans that I thought would accomplish the Object if I could get the Engine. I new there was a little double Engine that was used to drive the Machinery in the N[orth] E[astern] R[ail] Road Shop and was taken out and replaced by a larger one and if I could get it and have it changed so as to suit the boat, That Mr. John Chalk Master of Machinery at the N.E.R.R. could tell him where the Engine was, and if it could be got I would build the boat. The Engine had been removed and carried up the road, Mr. Chalk had it brought back and altered it to suit the boat that I gave him the dimentions of.

I laid out the boat full size under a Nitre shed at Stoney landing. It was 5 feet in diameter and 48½ feet long, 18 feet of the middle of the boat was same size tapering to a point at each end. The ends was made of large pine logs turned off with a grove to receive the ends of the planking, the timbers was made of 1½ inch oak doubled and riveted together, they were placed about 15 inches apart, the planking was the whole length 1½ inches thick hollowed on the inside to fit the timbers and rounded on outside, the planking was riveted to the timbers, the whole was put together at Stoney Landing, corked and launched. It was sent to Charleston to have the machinery put in. It was there hoisted out of the water by a crane on the N.E.R.R. wharf, put on a car and carried to the R. Road shop.

There it was inspected by several gentlemen among whom was Capt. Carlin, Capt Furguson, Marrion Jones (Ship builder), Theodore Wagner, Theodore Stoney, and others. Mr. Stoney wrote me that the gentlemen above mentioned condemned the boat saying it would turn over in the water and that it would not be able to carry the weight of machinery that

I was putting in it and if I would let Mr. Jones have the machinery he would build a boat in 15 days.

I replied to Mr. Stoney refusing to let Mr. Jones have the machinery and stated that it would require from 15 to 18000 lbs of iron as balast to put the boat in the water the depth I wanted it, and if Mr. Jones want to build a boat I had no objections but he could not get my machinery.

I went to Charleston the next day and employed several more hands on the boat and finished it as soon as I could. The Boiler was taken from Fort Sumter in the night brought to the R. Road shop and put in the boat. Shells was being thrown in the city while working on the boat. We moved the boat to the wharf and launched it. We put about 4000 lbs of iron in it as balast which was not enough to submerge the wheel but was all we could get in the R. Road yard. We fired up on the boiler, run the boat to Southern wharf where an Iron Clad gun boat was being built, there we got enough iron to put the boat down to where I wanted it, taking about 14000 lbs more, making about 18000 lbs of balast besides Boiler, machinery and fuel. A few days after the boat was run over to Fort Johnson and back making a speed of 10 nots per hour. After that the Confederate States navy took charge of the boat and made some alterations in the carrying of the Torpedo. They put it on the end of an iron pipe about $2\frac{1}{2}$ inches in diameter extending some 15 to 20 feet in front of the bow of the boat, it was made stationary on the end of the iron pipe the torpedo being some 6 feet under water.

I had it aranged on bars of iron extending on both sides of the boat hung on trunions so as to raise it out of the water when the boat was in motion and let it down when near the object. The Navy Dept. covered the top of the boat with plow steel about $\frac{1}{4}$ inch thick and 5 or 6 inches wide that run below the water line.

(Had they left my plan of carrying the torpedo I have no doubt but they would have blown up the Iron Sides as the Torpedo would have been much deeper in the water, the water would not have been back on the boat).

Lut. Glassell and two of the crew jumped overboard I suppose thinking the David would sink as a large body of water was thrown back on the boat, one of them swam to the boat and got aboard, the others were taken aboard the Iron Side.

The fire in the David was put out by the water thrown on it, the man fired up and brought the David safe into the harbour the Guard boats giving them a wide berth on their return.

Some time after this an attempt was made on some of the Gun Boats in Stono River without success as the Torpedo failed to go off.

Mess[rs] Ferguson & Jones built several torpedo boats after the plan of the David but I never heard of them doing any execution.

I was employed by the Torpedo Co to build two more boats of about same dimentions of the David, also a Ram, the Ram was to be 100 feet long 8 feet diameter, twenty five feet of her bow was to be of live oak, solid caped with heavy Iron, the Engines and boiler was brought from Scotland, run the blockade, these were being built at Stoney landing when Charleston was evacuated and burnt by Gen. Potter's troops or bummers.

Very Truly Yours
D. C. EBAUGH

To Rev. W. H. Campbell, Charleston, S. C.

P. S. The David was named after me.

I built two more boats at Stoney landing, one was intended to run the blockade, it was 163 feet long 12 feet in diameter, made in shape of a Segar, it was captured in Charleston after the evacuation and carried to Brookland Navy Yard, it cost $90,000. The other was a flat bottom steam boat, was confiscated and sold by a man that was afterwards sent to the Penitentiary in N. Y. or Boston for fraud.

Any further information about anything I may have knowledge of would be verry glad to write you.

Yours etc.
D.C.E.

CHEROKEE SPRINGS HOTEL

G. W. EBAUGH, PROPRIETOR

Cherokee, S. C. Dec 19th 1892

Rev. W. H. Campbell
Charleston, S. C.
Dear Sir

Your favour of 14th inst. came duly to hand and noted. The David I think was destroyed at the evacuation of Charleston a portion of her reck I think drifted on Chisolms Causeway, what became of the machinery I do not know.

The David did make an attack on the Enemys Ships in N. Edisto or Stono Rivers but the torpedo failed to explode. There was one or more Torpedo boats captured when Charleston was evacuated but not the David. The large boat I built, intended to run the blockade, was captured. She was 163 feet long 12 feet diameter. She was not complete—all the machinery was not in her She was on the Ashley river near West Point Mill at the time of evacuation was taken to Brooklin Navy Yard, N. Y.

I expect to be in Charleston in the course of next week would be glad to see you. Mrs. E. is in Summerville.

Hopeing this may find your Family and self well as it leaves me

Yours very truly
DAVID C. EBAUGH

P. S. Please do not publish anything about the David until you see me.

D.C.E.

⚹ 1213 East Preston Street
Baltimore Jan. 31st, 1893

Rev. W. H. Campbell
Charleston, S. C.

Dear Sir

Your favour of 17th reached me a few days ago I having been spending some time in Philadelphia caused the delay in writeing you.

I was in Charleston at Chrismas and intended to call on you but left hurriedly.

Since I had the conversation with you at Cherokee Springs and since writeing you a statement of the Torpedo boat David I have had an inquiry from an Attorney in Washington about a claim I had in Washington, sent there 20 years ago for property taken from me at the evacuation of Charleston, the Attorney has offered to take up the claim on a percentage. So I think it would be best for me if my name did not apear in any way at present with the Torpedo boat—at least not until there is something deffinite about the claim which is for $25,000.

I furnished the plans of the boat, built it, and spent my own money to the amount of $1500.00 not counting the lumber or my own time. Mr. Theodore Stoney I think payed some bills in Charleston. When the Confederate Navy took Charge of the boat they asked me how much the boat cost me. I told them I had spent $1500—they gave me the amount back. Dr. Ravenels suggestions about a boat was to build one to be propelled by manual labour. The engine was a suggestion of mine and the plans was originated by me and built by me with considerable opposition by several of the most influential men of Charleston.

Please do not publish anything with my name at present.

Very truly yours,
D. C. EBAUGH

CHARLESTON'S CIVIL WAR "MONSTER GUNS," THE BLAKELY RIFLES

C. R. HORRES, JR.*

FOLLOWING THE DEVASTATION OF FORT SUMTER BY LONG- range rifled artillery in the summer of 1863 and the impending loss of Morris Island, the situation appeared grim for General Pierre G.T. Beauregard and his beleaguered Confederate defenders of Charleston. A little over two years after the firing on Fort Sumter, the tides of war had changed dramatically for the Confederacy. With a fleet of twenty-three Union warships and an estimated 10,000 Union troops less than ten miles away, the possibility of Charleston falling into Union hands had become more likely. Indeed, as Beauregard affirmed to South Carolina Governor Milledge L. Bonham, preparations were underway to defend the city street by street until its complete destruction.[1]

The private citizens and military officials in besieged Charleston clung to the hopes inspired by two immense imported Blakely rifles. Many felt the guns held the promise of saving the city. Such expectations were placed on the capabilities of these technologically advanced artillery weapons that some felt the fate of the Confederacy rested on their success. The guns did not perform as the Confederates hoped; indeed, they hardly performed at all. But their story makes up a fascinating chapter of the war that took place at the edge of modern times.

Charleston's natural barriers, extensive interior lines, and strong fortifications presented significant obstacles to a force intending to conquer the city by land. Several Union advances onto James Island had established that the Confederates were prepared to defend the land accesses to Charleston. A more serious threat was posed by an invasion of the mainland or by the forced entrance of the Union's powerful naval fleet into Charleston harbor, such as had resulted in the untimely surrender of New Orleans in 1861. Adding to this possibility was the presence of large numbers of ironclad monitors. These two-gun warships had been built within a few months of the *Monitor-Merrimac* battle and were massed as a fleet against Charleston in April 1863. Encased in iron plate with guns mounted in rotating iron turrets, the monitors represented a significant

*Independent researcher, Del Mar, California. The author wishes to thank Ethel Seabrook Nepveux and Warren Ripley for their helpful comments and suggestions during the preparation of this article.

[1]Alfred Roman, *Military Operations of General Beauregard* (New York: Harper Brothers, 1884; repr., New York: Da Capo Press, 1994), Vol. II, pp. 503-504.

advance in naval warfare at a time when most warships were constructed of wood. During most of 1863-1864, six or seven remained on station off Morris Island and frequently probed the harbor defenses, slamming their fifteen-inch diameter shells into the forlorn Fort Sumter. Numerous gunboats and a formidable ironclad ship known as the *New Ironsides* were also stationed off Charleston. The *New Ironsides* carried an impressive assortment of weapons, including two Parrott rifles capable of firing 100-pound projectiles and fourteen Dahlgren smoothbores, seven each to the port and starboard, firing eleven-inch diameter shells. Its solid three-inch armor plating backed by sturdy oak planking had withstood the best that Fort Sumter and Battery Wagner could offer.[2]

The question remained how to defend the city if the feared ironclads broke through the outer harbor defenses. Beauregard had four defensive elements to protect the inner harbor — artillery, warships, mines, and obstructions. The mainstay of the harbor defenses was artillery; Charleston had accumulated a considerable number of heavy guns, predominantly eight-inch and ten-inch smooth-bore columbiads. By the end of the war Charleston District had almost 250 artillery pieces. These had been placed at White Point at the tip of the Charleston peninsula and at various locations along the waterfront and around the harbor. Castle Pinckney, in the Cooper River, was armed with two ten-inch diameter smooth bores, and sand was piled against its vulnerable brick walls. Fort Ripley, an unarmed 70-by-70-foot fort, built on pilings on a shoal area in the middle of the harbor the previous year, was ordered to be reinforced and armed. Brigadier General Roswell S. Ripley, commander of Charleston District, formulated a defense plan that involved three circles or zones of fire depending on how far the ironclads penetrated the harbor. The first was centered on a line between Fort Sumter and Fort Moultrie, the second on a line between Fort Sumter and Fort Ripley, and the third centered in a triangle between White Point, Battery Glover on James Island, and Castle Pinckney.[3]

The second element of harbor defense was to battle the ironclads on the water. Small rowboats and boarding parties were organized and equipped with ladders to attack the ironclads under the cover of darkness. In addition, much money and effort was expended by the Confederate navy and citizens of Charleston to build ironclad rams. These craft rarely ventured

[2]John Johnson, *Defense of Charleston Harbor, 1863-1865* (Charleston, S.C.: Walker, Evan & Cogswell Co., 1890; repr., Germantown, Tenn.: Guild Bindery Press, 1994), p. 212, App. B., xxi-xcix.

[3]Johnson, *Defense of Charleston Harbor*, p. 259; *War of the Rebellion: A Compilation of the Official Records of the Union and Confederate Armies* (Washington, D.C.: Government Printing Office, 1880-1901) (hereafter *Official Records-Armies*), Series I, Vol. 14, pp. 620, 733-734; Roman, *Military Operations of General Beauregard*, Vol. II, p. 507.

out of the harbor because they lacked efficient steam engines to maneuver their excessive weight in the strong currents. It was also doubtful that their armor plate would have withstood a battle against the more heavily armored monitors at close range. Beauregard was all too familiar with the fragility of the ironclad rams to depend exclusively on them. Nevertheless, the C.S.S. *Palmetto State* and *Chicora* were stationed off Fort Johnson, constantly manned and ready to engage the monitors should they enter the harbor. A much stronger ram, *Charleston*, was under construction during this critical period.[4]

Underwater mines and obstructions formed the final elements of harbor defense. As a result of its largely defensive role in the Civil War, the South developed considerable expertise in the use of explosive mines both on land and in navigable inland waters. The term used to describe these devices during the war was "torpedoes," whose meaning since has changed. Massive mines, built from powder-filled boilers equipped with electric detonators operated from shore, were planted in the Ashley River and Hog Island channels. A double row of torpedoes (mines) guarded the channel between Fort Ripley and Castle Pinckney. Beauregard reported that he had 125 torpedoes placed in Charleston waters. Shallow passages were obstructed with wood piles and the main ship channel was blocked by a difficult-to-maintain boom made of ropes and wooden floats.[5]

Of the means at their disposal, artillery was preeminent in the minds of the Confederates as a defense against the ironclads. Artillery had proven its value by defeating Admiral Samuel F. Du Pont's fleet in April 1863. The *Keokuk*, an experimental ironclad, was actually damaged so badly by Fort Sumter's artillery that it later sank. The more heavily armored monitors were a different story. Although numerous dents and gouges reminded the crews not to get too close to the Confederate guns, the monitors had proven practically invincible to the most powerful weapons of the Confederacy. Their round turrets deflected all but the most direct hits of the spherical cannon balls and led Confederate munitions designers to develop a variety of pointed or flat-faced cylindrical shot, known as bolts, to fire from the smooth-bore ten-inch diameter columbiads. Despite these improvements, Beauregard knew he needed a massive piece of artillery to fight the ironclads and petitioned Confederate Congressman William Porcher Miles to lobby the secretary of war to authorize the casting of a fifteen-inch columbiad at the Charleston arsenal. Although he received authorization

[4]Roman, *Military Operations of General Beauregard*, Vol. II, p. 507; Johnson, *Defense of Charleston Harbor*, p. 34.

[5]*Official Records-Armies*, Series I, Vol. 14, p. 620; Vol. 28, Pt. 2, p. 300; Roman, *Military Operations of General Beauregard*, Vol. II, p. 507; Gen. G.T. Beauregard, "Torpedo Service in Charleston Harbor," *The Annals of the War* (Philadelphia: The Times Publishing Co., 1879; repr., New York: Da Capo Press, 1994), p. 521.

from Secretary of War James A. Seddon to cast the gun, this task appears to have exceeded the capabilities of not only the Charleston arsenal but those of the Confederacy, for none of the 50,000-pound smoothbores was ever made in the South. After waiting nearly a year, Beauregard probably knew that the successive reports of delays from the arsenal meant he would not get his heavy gun.[6]

THE HOPES OF CHARLESTON'S DEFENDERS WERE BOLSTERED in their darkest hours by the arrival at Wilmington of two 12.75-inch rifled guns from England. On August 18, 1863, with Union shells raining upon Fort Sumter, Beauregard telegraphed Brigadier General William H.C. Whiting at Wilmington, "There are two Blakely guns, carriages, and 60 tons of shot on *Gibraltar*, belonging to John Fraser & Co., which have hastened here with utmost speed. Permit no delay." Colonel William Lamb, commandant of Fort Fisher at the entrance to Wilmington, reported on August 21 that "The Gibraltar came in this week with two of the largest cannons I know of in the World." The defenders of Wilmington were not eager to see the huge cannons go to Charleston and urgently protested to Richmond not to send both.[7]

Beauregard wasted no time requesting both for Charleston. His request to Secretary Seddon was supported on August 20 by Colonel J. F. Gilmer, chief of the Confederate Engineering Bureau. Even Congressman Miles pleaded with General Whiting on August 21: "I appeal to you not to keep from General Beauregard, in this hour of Charleston's sore trial, either of the Blakely guns." Beauregard directly telegraphed General Whiting to hurry the second Blakely on September 1, 1863. General Whiting felt that he did not have the right, under orders of President Jefferson Davis, to send the second gun. Yet given the imminent danger, Charleston prevailed in its request for both guns and on September 5 Secretary Seddon ordered the second sent to Charleston.[8]

These unique cannons were known as Blakely rifles and were said to have cost £10,000 sterling, or approximately $600,000 Confederate for the pair and one hundred rounds of ammunition. By comparison, adjusting for inflation to August 1863, a forty-two pounder, about one-sixth the weight

[6]*Official Records-Armies*, Series I, Vol. 14, p. 676; Roman, *Military Operations of General Beauregard*, Vol. II, p. 39. Warren Ripley, *Artillery and Ammunition of the Civil War* (New York: Van Nostrand Reinhold, 1970), p. 82.

[7]*Official Records-Armies*, Series I, Vol. 28, Pt. 2, p. 291; Richard D. Steuart, "The Long Arm of the Confederacy," *Confederate Veteran* 35 (1927), p. 253; J.B. Jones, *A Rebel War Clerk's Diary* (Philadelphia: J.B. Lippincott & Co., 1866), Vol. II, p. 27.

[8]*Official Records-Armies*, Series I, Vol. 28, Pt. 2, pp. 294, 329, 330, 343.

of a Blakely, would have cost about $12,600 Confederate.[9]

The Blakely rifles were purchased in conjunction with the John Fraser Company of Charleston, famous for its blockade-running activities, and delivered to the Confederacy. The correspondence of Charles Prioleau of Fraser, Trenholm and Company in Liverpool to George Alfred Trenholm of the John Fraser Company in Charleston, suggests that Captain Alexander Theophilis Blakely persuaded Major Caleb Huse, the Confederacy's minister of munitions in England, to let him build the two experimental rifles on the account of the Confederate government. They were designed by Blakely, a former Royal Artillery captain, who already had designed and fabricated a number of successful smaller-caliber rifles for the Confederacy and the Union. The Blakelys were cast by the George Forester & Co., Vauxhall Foundry, and measured 194 inches from muzzle to breech. When the guns were completed, Major Huse needed to find a steamer to transport them. Charles Prioleau offered the Confederate government the opportunity to buy back at cost the former propeller steamer *Sumter* to transport the guns. The *Sumter* recently had completed an illustrious history as a Confederate commerce raider under Captain Raphael Semmes. Fraser, Trenholm and Company had purchased the ship from the Confederacy and renamed it *Gibraltar*. Although verbally agreeing to purchase the ship, Huse had not completed the transfer before the ship sailed for America. Prioleau later was to remind Major Huse of this obligation, estimating the freight on the Blakelys at £20,000.[10]

The *Gibraltar* had to be strengthened and modified to carry the guns. Cranes were needed to load them, along with 150 solid shot weighing 650 pounds each and fifty shells weighing 450 pounds each. *Gibraltar's* holds were not designed to accommodate the sixteen-foot length of the guns in a horizontal position. This necessitated storing the guns standing upright in special slings and gave the ship the appearance of having two additional smoke stacks.[11]

The *Gibraltar* began the month-long trip from Liverpool on July 3, 1863,

[9]Josiah Gorgas, "Notes on the Ordance Department of the Confederate Government," *Southern Historical Society Papers* 12 (January-February 1884), p. 94; Richard Cecil Todd, *Confederate Finance* (Athens: University of Georgia Press, 1954), p. 198; Ripley, *Artillery and Ammunition,* p. 40.

[10]Ethel Trenholm Seabrook Nepveux, *Alfred Trenholm and the Company That Went to War* (Charleston, S.C.: Comprint, 1973), p. 65; Charles Prioleau to George Trenholm, Oct. 22, 1863, Charles Prioleau Papers (28-624-3), South Carolina Historical Society, Charleston (hereafter SCHS); Ripley, *Artillery and Ammunition*, pp. 148-155, 157, 340; Raphael Semmes, *Memoirs of Service Afloat During the War Between the States* (Secaucus, N.J.: Blue and Gray Press, 1987), p. 345; Charles Prioleau to Major C. Huse, June 5, 1863, Theodore D. Wagner Papers (11-448-2), SCHS.

[11]Stephen R. Wise, *Lifeline of the Confederacy* (Columbia: University of South Carolina Press, 1988), pp. 119-120; Nepveux, *Alfred Trenholm,* pp. 64-65.

with clearance for Nassau. The existence of the guns was known to the Union, most likely through Union spies in Liverpool, and on July 20, 1863, special orders to capture the *Gibraltar* were issued by Gideon Welles, U.S. secretary of the navy, to the commander of the North Atlantic Blockading Squadron. It was reported that Captain E.C. Reed bravely sailed the *Sumter* (*Gibraltar*) into Wilmington through the shot and shell of the blockade in broad daylight because of a breakdown of its steam propulsion system. The appearance of a ship under full sail in daylight had confused the blockaders into believing it was one of their own. Passengers arriving on the *Gibraltar* spread the rumor that the guns weighed twenty-two tons and the carriages sixty tons and that they could be fired with accuracy and immense effect seven miles.[12]

General Whiting reported to Secretary Seddon that he was ready to send the first Blakely to Charleston on August 22, four days after their arrival in Wilmington. Lifting and moving such huge objects presented his engineers a significant challenge. The gun weighed nearly 50,000 pounds and the carriages complete with all accessories weighed 58,000 pounds. Specially adapted rail cars had to be built to transport them from Wilmington. The journey across the numerous rivers between Charleston and Wilmington over wooden trestles must have caused considerable anxiety since the gun alone weighed as much as a locomotive engine of the day. The route involved transport to Florence, South Carolina, on the Wilmington and Manchester Railroad and then on the Northeastern Railroad to Charleston, a distance of almost 200 miles. On August 25, 1863, the carriage for the first Blakely was reported to have arrived at the Northeastern Railroad Terminal and occupied seven railroad cars. The gun itself arrived in Charleston on August 29.[13]

[12]*War of the Rebellion: A Compilation of the Offical Records of the Union and Confederate Navies* (Washington, D.C.: Government Printing Office, 1894-1927) (hereafter *Official Records-Navies*), Series I, Vol. 9, pp. 127-128; "Charleston's Home Defence," *Charleston Yearbook 1883* (Charleston, S.C.: News & Courier Book Presses, 1883), p. 560; Jones, *A Rebel War Clerk's Diary*, p. 21.

[13]*Official Records-Armies*, Series I, Vol. 28, pt. 2, p. 302; George W. Rains et al., *Report of Board of Officers on the Facts Connected with the Bursting of the Large Blakely Gun in the City of Charleston in September 1863*, Sept. 24, 1863, Confederate Subject File BG, p. 3, National Archives; Claude C. Sturgill and Charles L. Price, "McCabe's Impression of the Bombardment of Charleston, 1863," *South Carolina Historical Magazine* (hereafter *SCHM*) 71 (October 1970), pp. 266-268; Francis Trevelyan Miller and Robert S. Lanier, *The Photographic History of the Civil War* (New York: Review of Reviews Co., 1911; repr. Secaucus, N.J.: The Blue and the Gray Press, 1987), Vol. 3, p. 287; Francis K. Middleton to "Harry" (Harriott Middleton), Aug. 26, 1863, Cheves-Middleton Papers (12-164-17), SCHS; *Official Records-Armies*, Series I, Vol. 28, Pt. 2, p. 313. A weight of 50,500 pounds is estimated from dimensions reported by the Confederate Navy Office of Ordnance and Hydrology and from a knowledge of the density of cast iron and bronze.

Although few details are available to describe the unloading and transport to the batteries, this must have been a remarkable production. The standard equipment for lifting heavy cannons was known as a gin and consisted of a tripod arrangement of large poles at the top of which was mounted a block and tackle. It is highly likely that the Blakelys would have required two gins, one at each end, since the standard issue strained to lift an 18,000-pound columbiad. A similar two-gin arrangement has been described for lifting fifteen-inch Rodmans weighing 50,000 pounds. As the Union learned in moving the large Parrott rifles on the beach at Morris Island, cannons could be rolled by strapping wood around the diameter to create a smooth circumference larger than the protruding trunions. Because the Blakelys were much too heavy for wagons or carts of the day, a temporary railroad track was laid down King Street to assist in moving the gun from the railroad station to White Point.[14] These activities did not go unnoticed by the residents of the city. Augustine Smythe noted that on the afternoon of August 30, only one day after its arrival, the first Blakely was lying on the corner of Hasell and King streets, about half the 1.5-mile distance to its mounting site at the White Point Battery. Merchant Jacob Schirmer recorded on August 31: "Our prospects grow darker and darker every day and hour.... We are now putting up an extraordinary gun at Battery in hope of doing something there."[15]

Beauregard originally intended to put the first Blakely in the city and the other in Battery Wampler on the James Island side of the harbor. A short time later it was determined to place both at Battery Ramsey at the foot of Meeting Street from which they would have a field of fire sweeping from Fort Johnson to Mathewes' Ferry Point at Mt. Pleasant. The site of the first Blakely gun battery, on the tip of the peninsula approximately where South Battery intersects East Battery, was perilously close to nearby houses. Although the site was reported to be ready for both guns on September 4, only one would be mounted there. Eventually, the other was mounted in a battery built on the North Central Wharf at the foot of Cumberland Street known as Fraizer's (Fraser's) Wharf Battery. This battery was behind the site where the U.S. Customs House now stands and was constructed by filling in the foundation of the primary wharf used by the John Fraser Company.[16]

[14]Ripley, *Artillery and Ammunition*, p. 99, 239; *Official Records-Armies*, Series I, Vol. 28, Pt. 2, p. 248; J. Cutler Andrews, *The South Reports the War* (Princeton, N.J.: Princeton University Press, 1970), p. 328..

[15]Augustine Smythe to "Mother," Aug. 30, 1863, Smythe-Stoney-Adger Collection (24-7-9), SCHS; Jacob Schirmer, entry dated Aug. 31, 1863, in the Jacob Schirmer Diaries (11-567-10), SCHS.

[16]*Official Records-Armies*, Series I, Vol. 28, Pt. 2, p. 314, p. 337; Arthur M. Wilcox and Warren Ripley, *The Civil War at Charleston* (Charleston, S.C.: The News and Courier and Evening Post, 1991), p. 40; Nepveux, *Alfred Trenholm*, p. 7.

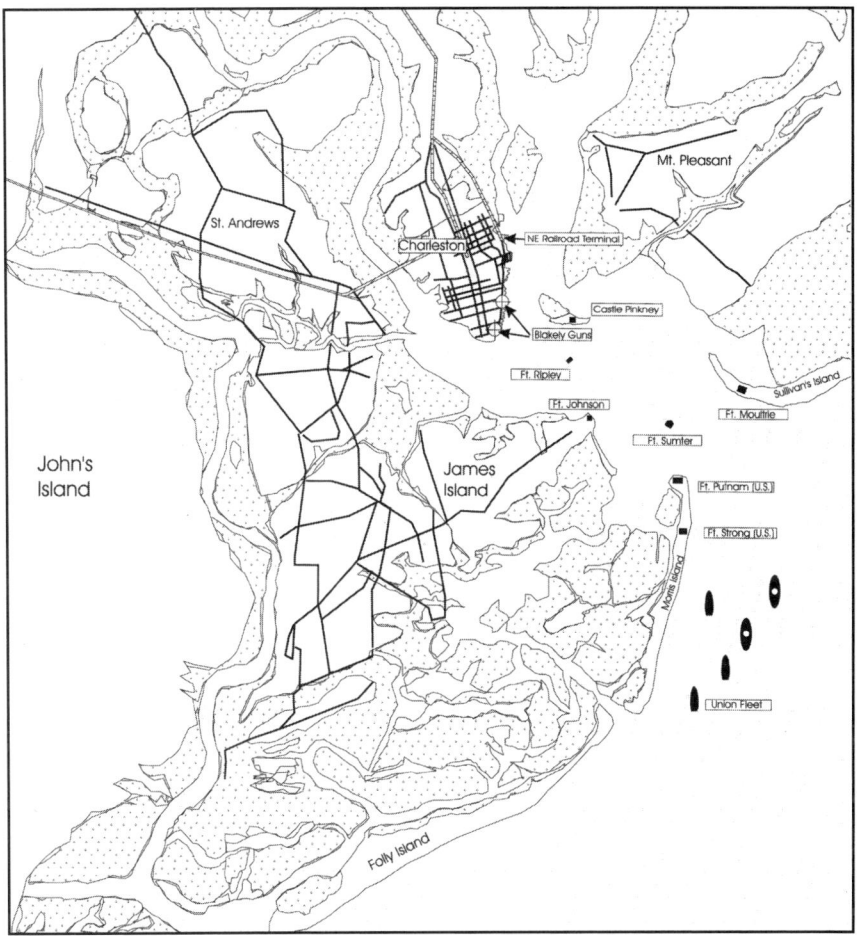

Charleston harbor in 1863 showing the locations of the Blakely batteries. Union forces occupied Morris Island and the waters of the outer harbor. Illustration courtesy of the author.

Batteries, built from mounds of earth, were three-sided affairs open to the rear. The front wall faced the expected direction of enemy fire while the side walls protected the gun and crew from nearby shell bursts. Bomb-proof magazines, constructed by covering sturdy log-cabin-like structures with more than twenty feet of earth, were located nearby to store the supplies of gunpowder. Batteries and magazines typically were covered with grass sod to prevent the wind from blowing the sand away.[17] From

[17]*Atlas to Accompany the Official Records of the Union and Confederate Armies* (Washington, D.C.: U.S. Government Printing Office, 1891, repr., New York: Random House, 1983), Plate XLIV.

their respective sites, these powerful guns could command the inner harbor.

By September 2 the first Blakely had arrived at White Point and crews were completing the foundation and carriage. News reached Richmond that one of the Blakelys was mounted in Charleston by September 7.[18]

COMPARED TO THE TYPICAL CONFEDERATE ORDNANCE, THE Blakelys were years ahead in technology. In the words of General Beauregard, "These magnificent specimens of heavy ordnance were, apart from their immense size, different in construction from anything I had ever seen." The Blakelys were designed to be mounted on sophisticated cast-iron carriages to facilitate operation. Held by its protruding trunions that allowed the barrel to tilt up and down, the gun was supported in a massive four-wheeled top carriage. The wheeled top carriage allowed the weapon to be loaded and then advanced along the bottom carriage into the firing or "in battery" position. As the weapon fired, the reaction would force the entire top carriage backwards. The sliding friction against the bottom carriage dissipated the energy and reduced the forces on the gun and carriage. By comparison, the large columbiads of the day were mounted on wooden carriages equipped with wheels on eccentric axles that were engaged to lift the top carriage just clear of the sliding surface of the bottom carriage in order to be rolled into battery. Once in battery, the eccentric axles would be turned to lower the top carriage onto the sliding surface so that the reactive force of the firing could be absorbed by sliding friction. Frequent firing loosened the wooden frame and periodic tightening of the bolts was required.[19]

The Blakely system, a more robust and easier-to-use arrangement, kept the top carriage on its wheels throughout the movement and used a band brake system on its large railroad-style rear wheels to lock them during firing. The large rear wheels of the top carriage had an outer rim that rested upon cast-iron rails of the bottom carriage and an inner rim around which a circumferential band containing protruding studs could be tightened to prevent rolling. Smaller front wheels freely rolled upon separate cast-iron rails. The bottom carriage upon which the top carriage moved front and back was of the "center pintle" variety that allowed the entire mechanism to pivot completely about a circular iron track laid in the ground. Typical of center-pintle mounts, the Blakelys were designed to fire over the surrounding protective earth parapet, as opposed to firing through embrasures (openings) in a parapet. Embrasures provided additional

---

[18] Augustine Smythe to "Mother," Sept. 2, 1863, Smythe-Stoney-Adger Collection (24-7-9), SCHS ; Jones, *Rebel War Clerk's Diary*, Vol. II, p. 36.

[19] Beauregard, "Torpedo Service," p. 524; Ripley, *Artillery and Ammunition*, pp. 207-208.

protection for the gun and crew but limited the field of fire.[20]

The Civil War was a transition period in the centuries-old artillery science. Both sides began to recognize the value of rifled artillery. Rifling was designed to impart a spinning motion to a projectile as it passes through the barrel. This motion provided several advantages over smooth-bore cannons. First, the spinning continues after the projectile leaves the barrel and stabilizes the projectile in flight, much as a spinning top can stand on its point. This stability permits projectiles to be elongated and streamlined to minimize air resistance in flight, allowing rifled projectiles to be heavier than cannon balls of equivalent diameter. For example, the Blakely 12.75-inch-diameter solid cylindrical shot was twenty inches long and weighed 210 pounds more than the 440-pound, fifteen-inch-diameter solid spherical shot of the monitors. Another advantage was that, unlike rotating cannon balls that could strike a target at any orientation, the spinning rifled projectile could be predicted to land nose first, thus allowing the use of fuses that could explode the shell on contact with a target.

The method of rifling employed in the Blakelys was unique. In American-made rifled artillery, the most common method of rifling was to equip the projectile on its base with a rim of soft material, such as lead, that would be expanded into spiraling grooves upon discharge. British-designed rifles, such as the Blakelys, Whitworths, and Armstrongs, required the projectiles to have protruding flanges, flats, or studs to engage the rifling. The Blakely used a system in which four slanting external flanges made of brass were fastened to the exterior of the projectiles with several screws or rivets. These were designed to mate with corresponding spiraling grooves in the bore of the rifle. The 12.75-inch-diameter shells and bolts were accurately turned in a lathe so that there was no discernible gap between the body of the projectile and the bore of the rifle when loaded.[21]

The Blakelys could fire powder-filled shells twenty-two inches long, weighing 470 pounds, or twenty-inch long solid cylindrical bolts weighing 650 pounds.[22] Since these weight extremes exceeded the lifting power of the gun crew to place the projectile into the muzzle, a special lifting crane with a chain reel mechanism was mounted on the barrel to lift the projectile in place. The lifting sling was designed to allow the projectile to rotate about its axis like a rolling pin while suspended at the muzzle. Rotation was necessary to permit alignment of the flanges of the projectile with the rifling grooves in the barrel.

Loading and firing these giants was a complicated process. The

---

[20]Miller and Lanier, *Photographic History of the Civil War*, "Forts and Artillery," Vol, 3, pp. 121-122.

[21]Rains, "Report of the Board," pp. 2, 4; Ripley, *Artillery and Ammunition*, pp. 158-159.

[22]Rains, "Report of the Board," p. 4.

maximum charge of black powder required for the solid bolts was fifty pounds and was encased in a cloth bag that was pushed down the muzzle with a long ramrod until the bag seated in the reinforced breech. With the powder in place, a well-greased projectile was loaded in the lifting mechanism and cranked upward. Once at the muzzle, muscle power was needed to align the shell or bolt flanges to the four spiraling grooves. Using a ramrod, several men would push the projectile against the powder cartridge. They would then release the brake mechanism on the carriage wheels and roll the gun into its forward position until the front and rear wheels rested against curved stops built into the tracks of the bottom carriage. The bottom gun carriage tilted slightly downward from back to front to allow gravity to facilitate this movement. The brake mechanism was then reset on the carriage wheels by tightening the circumferential bands. A wire tool, known as a gimlet, was inserted into the breech vent of the cannon to pierce the powder bag, the vent was filled with priming powder, and a tube-like friction primer with a long lanyard attached was placed in the vent. The loading process was then complete.[23]

The gun was aimed by elevating the barrel and pivoting the bottom carriage toward the target. Conrad Wise Chapman illustrated the Blakely with two vertical gun sights that would assist the aiming.[24] Based on the weight of the projectile and the amount of powder, a table of ranges was consulted to determine the degree of elevation required. Elevation was adjusted by means of a screw jack situated between the rear legs of the top carriage and the underside of the breech. Guns of this design could be fired from a nearly horizontal position to an elevation limit of about 30 degrees. The Blakelys incorporated a pointer on the right trunion to indicate the degrees of elevation of the barrel on a scale mounted to the carriage. The Blakely scale illustrated by Chapman indicates a maximum elevation of 30 degrees. Although maximum range for any given charge theoretically is obtained at 45 degrees, elevations above 30 degrees would place enormous stress on the gun and its carriage because the gun could not recoil effectively to absorb the reactive forces.

With the elevation set, the gun was ready to fire. Pulling the lanyard ignited the composition in the primer and forced flame down the vent which in turn ignited the powder in the chamber. Rapidly expanding gases propelled the projectile forward and the spiral grooves of the barrel developed the spinning motion that stabilized the projectile in flight. The ensuing roar and voluminous discharge of smoke would have been momentarily

[23]Miller and Lanier, *Photographic History of the Civil War*, Vol. 3, "Forts and Artillery," pp. 121-122; Ripley, *Artillery and Ammunition*, pp. 222-228.

[24]Conrad Wise Chapman, *White Point Battery, Charleston, December 24, 1863*, Museum of the Confederacy, Richmond, Va.; Philip Van Doren Stern, *The Confederate Navy: A Pictorial Review* (New York: Da Capo Press, 1992), p. 150.

deafening and blinding to the gun crew, and the action of the exploding powder upon the projectile produced an equal and opposite reaction on the 50,000-pound gun. This reaction would force the gun and its top carriage backwards along its bottom carriage two or three feet in less than one second. Before repeating the loading process, a large sponge would be dampened and used to clear the barrel of any remaining burning debris. The immense size of the guns and weight of the projectiles reduced the firing frequency considerably over the lightweight field artillery of the day. A well-served field gun could fire four rounds of canister in a minute; the fifteen-inch Dahlgrens of the monitors could fire about once every five minutes. Although not confined in a turret, the Blakelys would have taken much longer to reload and fire. During test firing it was reported that the loading went very slowly.[25]

DURING THE CIVIL WAR WEAPONS BECAME HEAVIER AND eventually the ability of the gun to resist the forces of the discharge were at the limit of the strength of available materials. Cast iron, strong but brittle, was a favorite material for the larger bore weapons and accounts of cast-iron guns bursting with disastrous results to gun crews were numerous during the Civil War. The Blakelys had several design elements to resist the enormous forces generated by a fifty-pound charge of black powder, much more violent in its exploding than modern, controlled-burning gun powders.

Captain Blakely's methods of strengthening the guns included three elements, two of which were well known to the Confederacy. The third would prove to be a source of embarrassment for the artillery officers testing the gun's performance. As was commonly practiced in the manufacture of large guns, the body of the gun was massive; almost two feet of cast iron surrounded the powder chamber. Second, for added strength, four 3.75-inch-thick bands of five-inch-wide wrought iron were heated and forced onto the outside of the breech so that they formed a nearly continuous twenty-inch wide band over the chamber of the gun. Wrought iron is about twice as strong as an equivalent cast-iron element. When it cooled, the band contracted, applying a constrictive force to the gun body to oppose the expansion forces of the powder discharge. This was described as "initial tension." Third, a 1400-pound bronze cavity, weighing more than the standard bronze twelve-pounder field piece of the Civil War, extended through the rear of the breech. This revolutionary feature was believed to have been designed to act as an air-filled shock absorber for the discharge of the black powder. The vent, a hole drilled into the powder chamber

---

[25]Ripley, *Artillery and Ammunition*, p. 228; Alvah F. Hunter, *A Year on a Monitor and the Destruction of Fort Sumter*, Craig L. Symonds, ed. (Columbia: University of South Carolina Press, 1987), p. 34; *Official Records-Armies*, Series I, Vol. 28, Pt. 2, pp. 387-388.

through which the powder charge was triggered to explode, was located just in front of the bronze chamber.[26]

In the rush to get the Blakelys to Charleston, the instruction manual had been overlooked and the function of the bronze chamber was unknown. The gun crew believed powder should be loaded into this unusual chamber, but they realized that the grooves in the barrel and corresponding flanges did not allow the end of the projectiles to reach the bronze chamber. This created a gap of thirteen inches between where the projectile stopped and the assumed location of the powder charge. The artillerists were perplexed by this gap. On September 10 they were ordered to experiment with charges beginning with twenty-five pounds. They realized that the gun could not be fired with this small amount of powder because when placed in the bronze chamber the powder bags did not reach the firing vent, and they were forced to improvise. By adding several blank cartridges in front of the charge, they were able to fire the gun without a projectile.[27]

The next day, Captain Francis H. Harleston of the First South Carolina Artillery, still not understanding the purpose of the air chamber, inserted three cartridges directly into the bronze chamber and one in the bore for a total of forty pounds. He then filled the gap between the shell and the charges with a six-inch-thick wooden plug and inserted a well-greased shell containing only one pound of bursting powder. Captain Harleston elevated the gun to two degrees to minimize strain on the gun. He knew the Blakely gun's breech, ten inches from the depth of bore to the rear of the gun, was six inches less than that of a ten-inch columbiad. Even though they chose a light charge and nearly empty shell for the trial, they cautiously attached an extra-long lanyard and fired the Blakely from the protection of a nearby bombproof. The shell, fired from a height of about eighteen feet above the harbor, flew about 800 yards, then skipped an additional 200 yards across the water. The artillerist's caution was well warranted. This very first shot was disastrous to the Blakely; the bronze chamber ruptured and was forced back about a third of an inch. The motion cracked the cast-iron breech in eleven places radiating from the outside of the bronze chamber.[28]

News of the disaster flashed to Richmond. On September 12 War Department Clerk John B. Jones noted in his diary, "We have tidings of the bursting of the Blakely gun at Charleston. I fear that this involves the fall of Charleston. Still Beauregard is there." The next day, Colonel Josiah Gorgas, the Confederacy's chief of ordnance, recorded the event in his journal in even more dire terms. "I am pained to hear of the bursting *on trial* of one of

[26]Rains, "Report of the Board," pp. 2, 3; Miller and Lanier, *Photographic History of the Civil War*, Vol. 3, "Forts and Artillery," p. 120; Ripley, *Artillery and Ammunition*, p. 366.

[27]Rains, "Report of the Board," p. 5.

[28]Ibid., accompanying sketch.

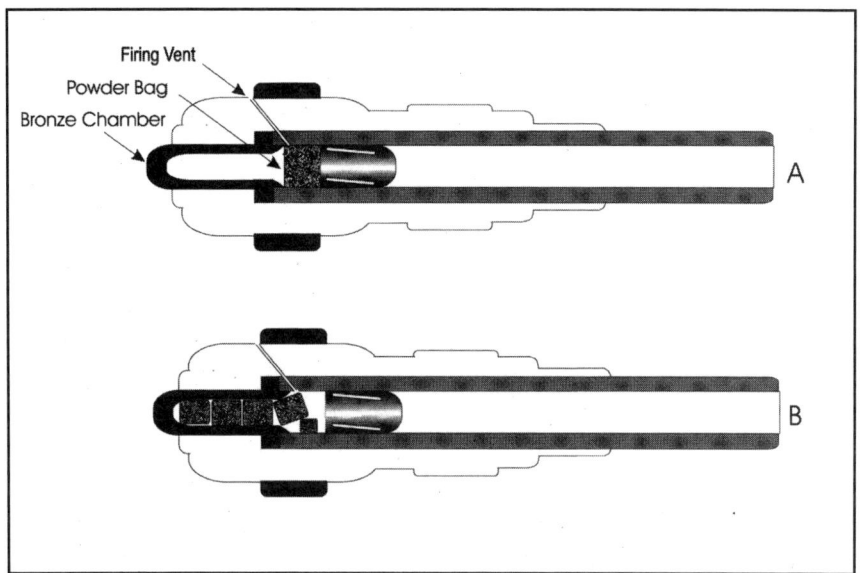

The Blakely rifles were designed (top drawing) with a bronze chamber at the rear, which apparently was to act as an air-filled shock absorber for the discharge of the black powder. When no instruction manual arrived with the first gun, the crew experimented with various means of loading it. As in the bottom drawing, three cartridges were inserted directly into the bronze chamber and one in the bore for a total of forty pounds. The gap between the shell and the charges was filled with a six-inch-thick wooden plug. When the gun was fired, the bronze chamber ruptured and was forced back about a third of an inch. The motion cracked the cast-iron breech in eleven places radiating from the outside of the bronze chamber. Illustration courtesy of the author.

the two 600 Pds. rifle Blakely guns just rec'd from abroad," he wrote. "In fact the bursting is a sort of national calamity so much was expected of these guns."[29]

Within a few months of firing the disastrous shot, Captain Harleston would earn the unfortunate distinction of being the first officer to be killed at Fort Sumter. At the time of the damage, Captain Harleston's detachment appears to have been under the command of Major Ormsby Blanding of the First South Carolina Artillery, a unit that reported to Brigadier General Roswell S. Ripley. Much embarrassment was heaped upon General Ripley by the chief of ordnance, Colonel Josiah Gorgas, among others, for allowing such an act with the precious resources of the Confederacy. In Gorgas's words to General Samuel S. Cooper, adjutant and inspector general of the

[29]Jones, *Rebel War Clerk's Diary*, Vol. II, p. 42; Sara W. Wiggins, ed., *The Journals of Josiah Gorgas, 1857-1878* (Tuscaloosa: University of Alabama Press, 1995), p. 80

Confederate army: "The destruction of this formidable gun was due to a want of forethought, unpardonable in an officer as experienced as General Ripley."[30]

Rumors of the reasons for the failure of the weapon abounded. Emma Holmes recorded in her diary that a Richmond editorial faulted the artillery men for elevating the gun too high and that the ammunition was so costly that the manufacturer never tested the guns before shipping. Charles Prioleau wrote that given the method of procurement and Captain Blakely's reputation, "their failure is no surprise to me."[31]

The damage to the Blakely led to the convening on September 18, 1863, of a special board of artillery experts to investigate the cause of the failure. The board consisted of Colonel George W. Rains of the Augusta Arsenal, Lieutenant-Colonel Joseph Yates of the First South Carolina Artillery, and Major William S. Basinger of the Eighteenth Georgia Battalion. Each officer individually inspected the damaged gun and a report was issued to Beauregard's headquarters on September 24. The board determined that the gun was made of good materials but was weak in the breech by design, that the air-chamber concept was a valuable device, and that had the gun been properly loaded it would not have ruptured with the charge used. They even recommended that a special gunpowder be manufactured for the Blakely containing one-inch-diameter grains that would burn more slowly than the conventional mixtures of large and small grain cannon powder. Considerable experimentation with all manner of guns followed until the exact function of the brass cavity was deduced. The missing instruction manual arrived on September 17, 1863.[32]

A conflict exists in the records as to whether Captain Blakely originally intended the bronze chamber to serve as an air chamber. Lieutenant J. R. Hamilton was in England during this period and saw the guns before they were shipped. He wrote that Captain Blakely never mentioned anything about the peculiarity of the chamber or its novel use as an air chamber. Rather, Captain Blakely had said something to Lieutenant Hamilton about igniting the charge from the fore end of the cartridge and allowing it to burn down into a narrow chamber. Lieutenant Hamilton added: "Even after seeing a copy of the examining board report, Captain Blakely has not

[30]*Official Records-Armies*, Series I, Vol. 28, Pt. 2, pp. 522, 388 (Gorgas quotation); John Marszalek, ed., *The Diary of Miss Emma Holmes 1861-1865* (Baton Rouge: Louisiana State University Press, 1994), p. 309; C. A. Bennett, "Roswell Sabin Ripley, Charleston's Gallant Defender," *SCHM* 95 (July 1994), pp. 225-242.

[31]Marszalek, *Emma Holmes*, p. 308; Charles Prioleau to George Trenholm, Oct. 22, 1863, Charles Prioleau Papers (28-624-3), SCHS.

[32]Rains, "Report of the Board," p. 18; Beauregard, "Torpedo Service," p. 525; Augustine Smythe to "Sister Sarah Annie," Sept. 28, 1863, Smythe-Stoney-Adger Collection (24-7-10), SCHS.

vouchsafed a single word in explanation, except to attribute the bursting to undue elevation."[33]

John Brooke, the inventor of the Confederate Brooke rifle, had strong doubts as to Captain Blakely's intentions with regard to the bronze chamber and suggested to Colonel Gorgas and General Beauregard that they use it as a "gas chamber." Lieutenant Hamilton and William N. Brooke believed that John Brooke deserved recognition for realizing the value of an air chamber. Beauregard was so impressed with the invention that he modified a number of eight-inch columbiads to employ the air-chamber effect. The columbiads were banded and rifled and were "effectively employed against the Federal iron-clads."[34]

Within a week of the damage, the first Blakely was taken down and left on the ground. It apparently lay there for some period of time while repairs were contemplated. In the meanwhile, the second Blakely had arrived in town and, although Beauregard initially ordered it returned to Wilmington, he countermanded his orders and had the Blakely temporarily placed on a wharf near the Northeastern Railroad depot. Although not specifically identified, this location may have been the Calhoun Street wharf or, more likely, the 650-foot-long wharf of the Charleston Gas Company on Charlotte Street. The Gas Company wharf had a sixty-six-foot-wide dock and was served by a railroad trestle. It would have been the closest to the railroad depot at the junction of Washington and Chapel street.[35]

On October 2 the second Blakely was fired by Colonel Joseph Yates while mounted on a skid to validate the results. Beauregard wasted no time telegraphing Richmond of its success. Some of the trials may have been observed by the U.S. Navy. Aboard the ironclad *Catskill* serving picket duty on October 12, Lieutenant-Commander Greenleaf Cilley observed a gun fired three times from near the yard where the Confederate rams were being built. The shot struck between Battery Bee and Fort Sumter, a distance of about three-and-a-half miles. From the volume of smoke following the discharge he judged the piece was a very heavy one with a large charge of powder.[36]

[33]J.R. Hamilton to William N. Brooke, Jan. 22, 1864, in William N. Brooke to Col. Wm. Garnett, February 1864, Confederate Subject File BG, National Archives.

[34]William N. Brooke to Col. Wm. Garnett, February 1864, Confederate Subject File BG, National Archives; Beauregard, "Torpedo Service," p. 525.

[35]"Cousin Anna Maria" to Augustine Smythe, Sept. 18, 1863, Smythe-Stoney-Adger Collection (24-7-10), SCHS; *Official Records-Armies*, Series I, Vol. 15, p. 110; Kimberly Grimes et al., *Between the Tracks: The Heritage of Charleston's East Side Community* (Charleston, S.C.: The Charleston Museum, 1987), pp. 18-27.

[36]Beauregard, "Torpedo Service," p. 525; *Official Records-Armies*, Series I, Vol. 28, Pt. 2, pp. 387-388, Vol. 15, p. 36.

DESPITE THEIR RELATIVE WEAKNESS, THE BLAKELYS WERE apparently capable of extreme range for a Civil War weapon. The data from the October firing reported a 470-pound shell could reach 6600 feet at an elevation of only two degrees. To reach this distance with such a flat trajectory would require a muzzle velocity of about 1700 feet per second, which is considerably higher than any other large sea-coast weapon of the day. The board of officers examining the failure estimated an initial velocity of 1300 feet per second could be reached by the shell with maximum charge. The most probable source of error between these figures would be in elevation. An increase of only three degrees in elevation would have put the calculated muzzle velocity closer to 1000 feet per second, consistent with the Armstrong and Ames rifles of the day. Confederate artillery studies had found that an initial muzzle velocity of 1600 feet per second was a maximum for the much lighter twenty-four-pounders and 1000 feet per second was a safe limit. Another possibility is that the shell skipped across the water to reach 2200 yards, a common method of insuring that an in-line target would be hit. Civil War artillery wisdom against naval targets recommended firing low over smooth water to skip a shell into a ship or target as opposed to harmlessly overshooting by aiming too high.[37]

If the Blakelys were able to develop an initial velocity of 1000 feet per second at maximum elevation, the figure of a seven-mile range rumored by the *Gibraltar's* passengers may have been correct. Serving aboard the Confederate ram *Palmetto State* in Charleston harbor, Augustine Smythe wrote that the range was six miles. Emma Holmes had also heard that the Blakelys were accurate at five miles and could shoot well to seven miles. Range figures for the largest Confederate sea-coast cannon, the ten-inch rifled and banded columbiad, indicate that at maximum elevation and a twenty-pound charge, solid shot could be fired 3.2 miles. The Confederate seven-inch Brooke rifle could fire a 100-pound shell an estimated 4.5 miles. By comparison, World War II sixteen-inch rifles could throw a 2340-pound shell 27.8 miles with muzzle velocities approaching 2700 feet per second. These sixty-eight-foot long guns weighed 146 tons and were mounted on carriages weighing thirty-nine tons. At roughly six times the mass of Charleston's Civil War Blakelys, these modern weapons had managed only about four times the range.[38]

That the presence of the Blakelys was known to the Union and their

[37]*Official Records-Armies*, Series I, Vol. 28, Pt. 2, pp. 378, 388; Rains, "Report of Board," p. 10.

[38]Augustine Smythe to "Aunt Janey," Aug. 25, 1863, Smythe-Stoney-Adger Collection (24-7-9), SCHS; Marszalek, *Emma Holmes*, p. 308; Ripley, *Artillery and Ammunition*, pp. 369, 136; Erwin N. Thompson, *The Guns of San Diego, San Diego Harbor Defenses, 1796-1947*, Howard B. Overton, ed. (San Diego, Cal.: San Diego National Park Service, 1991), p. 109.

reputation feared is a matter of record. Deserters wasted no time telling Major-General Quincy Gillmore of the new and powerful guns. A spy returning from Charleston reported to U.S Army General-in-Chief H. W. Halleck in Washington that the large gun had been repaired and planted on the battery in front of the city and that Beauregard had sent to Wilmington for another gun of the same kind. Gillmore wrote Halleck on October 20 describing the arrival of "the new 600-pounder" from Wilmington. Rear-Admiral John A.B. Dahlgren, U.S. Naval commander at Charleston, was aware of the details of the Blakelys by November. He knew where they were landed, that the first one placed at White Point had burst by blowing out its bronze breech plug and that the second had been placed on a wharf near the Northeastern Railroad and successfully fired. All this was learned from an engineer on the railroad who had deserted. Another deserter reported that he saw the White Point Blakely lying on the ground in November.[39]

From his post on Morris Island, the articulate Henry James Gooding wrote that deserters from the Confederacy were telling preposterous stories of two "monster guns" placed in Charleston to block the passage of the ironclad *Ironsides*. "It is gravely asserted that the guns mentioned will throw a projectile weighing 700 pounds!" Gooding postulated that "may be Mr. Beauregard sends the rascals over here to scare us with tales of guns and men."[40]

In April 1864 a group of ten men deserted from Battery Pringle on the Stono River and provided details of Charleston's defenses to U.S. Navy Lieutenant-Commander William Gibson. Despite a knowledge of the Fraizer's Wharf Blakely, they did not identify a Blakely among the seven guns reported at White Point, which suggests that repairs still were underway. A similar story identifying the Blakely as being at Fraizer's Wharf was told by a deserter from the ironclad *Chicora* in September 1864.[41]

The damaged gun eventually was repaired by local machine shops. Photos of the surviving breech at West Point illustrate the manner of repair. The protruding bronze chamber was leveled smooth with the breech and a flat, round plate was attached over the hole with a ring of eight large bolts, drilled and threaded into the breech. It appears that a relatively thin band was added to strengthen the damaged breech. Emma Holmes mentions the banding by the Cameron Foundry in her account of the bursting but believed that it required banding on arrival. General Beauregard noted that the injured Blakely gun was thoroughly repaired and made as efficient as

[39]*Official Records-Armies*, Series I, Vol. 28, Pt. 2, p. 103, p. 111; *Official Records-Navies*, Series I, Vol. 15, pp. 110, 232.

[40]Virginia M. Adams, ed., *On the Altar of Freedom: A Black Soldier's Civil War Letters from the Front* (Amherst: University of Massachusetts Press, 1991), p. 103.

[41]*Official Records-Navies*, Series I, Vol. 15, pp. 393, 678.

when first received.[42]

The time required for the engineers to mount the Blakelys permanently is not clear. From the deserters' reports referenced above, it would appear that the Fraizer's Wharf battery was finished before the White Point battery. It is an undamaged Blakely that is in Conrad Wise Chapman's illustration of the Charleston Battery in December 1863. Since this illustration shows a partially mounted Blakely in different location from its intended battery, the second gun may have been the model for the preliminary sketch dated October 29, 1863. Another sketch dated October 23, 1863, is virtually identical to Chapman's rendition with regard to the temporary mounting and illustrates massive cast-iron cross-bracing between the front legs of the top carriage. Both illustrations show the Blakely mounted without the bottom carriage. The complex bottom carriage would have required considerable time to assemble and permanently mount.[43]

CHARLESTON'S "MONSTER GUNS" WERE MORE OF A PSYCHO-logical value than of actual military importance. The Blakeys' performance in battle against the monitors was never tested. They certainly outclassed the 20,000-pound, banded and rifled ten-inch columbiad that previously held the honor of being Charleston's largest sea-coast piece. With the nearest enemy target at a distance of nearly five miles, the opportunity to use them during the remainder of the war was very limited. Further, from the firing results, their use in battle may have proven less than satisfactory. It was reported that the bolts had a tendency not to follow the rifling which would allow the projectile to begin an end-to-end tumbling, greatly decreasing range and accuracy. For the bolts to escape the rifling, the flanges must have been sheared off during the firing. Coupled with the disastrous bursting of the first Blakely, these factors would cast great doubt on the value of the weapons.[44]

The huge cost of the Morris Island campaign in lives and material, its relative lack of accomplishment, and the success of Union operations elsewhere kept the situation at Charleston at a stalemate through all of 1864. Charleston's Confederate defenders constantly strengthened their fortifications and prepared for invasion. The U.S. Navy forfeited the initiative gained by the army's conquest of Morris Island and reduction of

[42]Ripley, *Artillery and Ammunition*, p. 159; Marszalek, *Emma Holmes*, p. 308; Beauregard, "Torpedo Service," p. 525.

[43]Chapman, *White Point Battery*; Ripley, *Artillery and Ammunition*, p. 158; Anonymous Sketch of Blakely Gun at Charleston dated Oct. 23, 1863, in Richard H. Bacot Manuscript File, South Caroliniana Library, University of South Carolina, Columbia.

[44]Ripley, *Artillery and Ammunition*, p. 75; Johnson, *Defense of Charleston Harbor*, p. 71.

Fort Sumter by not pressing an assault on the harbor. As months passed, the ironclad fleet was in constant need of repairs and rarely gave Admiral Dahlgren the full strength he desired to challenge the harbor defenses.[45]

While Charleston was holding its own, the situation in other theaters rapidly deteriorated for the Confederacy. Sherman's success at Atlanta in September 1864 threw the entire coastal defense plan into turmoil. For Wilmington, Charleston, and Savannah, no longer was the threat from the sea but from the interior. General William T. Sherman marched unopposed to Savannah and in five days forced the surrender of a city that had stubbornly resisted three years of attack from the sea. In January 1865 Sherman feigned a move toward Augusta, then launched his seasoned legions against undermanned and weakened South Carolina defenders. No massing of troops could be made in South Carolina to give battle, and opposition to Sherman's army consisted only of delaying actions. When Sherman reached and burned Columbia, the Charleston defenders were ordered to North Carolina to join an army being formed under the newly reinstated General Joseph E. Johnston.[46]

The Confederates were determined not to leave weapons and supplies in Charleston that could be used against them. Beauregard personally had planned the details of the evacuation of Charleston and on February 15 ordered Lieutenant-General William Joseph Hardee to execute those plans. As much as could be moved by rail was brought away, but the ironclad rams and the Blakelys were impossible to remove quickly. On the evening of February 17 the rams were destroyed in spectacular explosions of their powder magazines, and the Blakelys, which had been overcharged with powder and fired, burst into hundreds of fragments. The explosion at the White Point battery left a huge block of the breech on the ground and blew a 500-pound fragment into a roof three houses away, where it remains to this day. Amazingly, the repairs to the breech survived the destruction of the gun, attesting to Beauregard's opinion of the repair work.[47]

When the Union occupiers came over from Morris Island, the Blakelys were beyond recognition. Only the bottom carriage of the gun located on White Point remained largely intact following the bursting, but the Fraizer's Wharf carriage was severely damaged. With Charleston's defenders in North Carolina, the much reviled monitors were now able to enter the inner harbor without firing a shot. In a tribute to their two-year campaign, the officers of the monitor *Catskill* were photographed in Charleston harbor with an array of Blakely and Brooke shells and bolts on the foredeck. Like the Blakely guns, the Confederacy was in the process of being demolished.

[45]*Official Records-Navies*, Series I, Vol. 15, p. 592.
[46]Burke Davis, *Sherman's March* (New York: Random House, 1980), pp. 116, 139.
[47]Roman, *Military Operations of General Beauregard*, Vol. II, p. 357, 348; Burton, *Siege of Charleston*, pp. 320-321.

SOUTH BATTERY, Charleston, S. C.
View looking West, showing the ruins of the 600-lb. Blakely Gun, exploded by the rebels on evacuating the city.

The carriage of the Blakely was left near the corner of South Battery and East Battery for many years. Photo from the collections of the South Carolina Historical Society.

Within two months, Richmond had fallen, Lee surrendered his army at Appomattox, and Johnston was entreating Sherman to stop the fighting.[48]

In the years following the Civil War, U.S. Army engineers collected many of the Confederate weapons. Most of the obsolete weapons were headed to the scrap heap and a few were to become souvenirs. The large piece of the Blakely breech from White Point was transported to the Charleston Arsenal and then to the grounds of the U.S. Military Academy at West Point. Several bolts and shells were taken to the museum at the

[48]Miller and Lanier, *Photographic History of the Civil War*, Vol. 3, pp. 120 (small insert entitled "View from the Rear" is of Fraizer's Wharf Blakely), 173; Roman, *Military Operations of General Beauregard*, Vol. II, p. 395.

Washington, D.C., Naval Yard. For eighteen years, thirty of these massive cylinders of iron were used as a border to protect a piece of the Revolutionary War fortifications preserved on Marion Square. In 1883 they were replaced by a wrought-iron fence in an attempt to beautify the square. The fencing appears on the commission's books as costing $87.70 and a receipt for $50 is noted for that year. It is possible that this receipt represented the scrap value of the bolts. Although most of the iron has been lost to the recyclers, part of the Blakely battery remains at Charleston. The foundation of the White Point gun mount was rediscovered by a crew installing a sewer line in 1976. The twelve-by-twelve-inch pine beams that supported the gun and its iron tracks were in relatively good condition after being buried beneath the roadway for more than a hundred years and they were reburied after the work was complete.[49]

The defense of Charleston was a major concern of the Confederacy and many innovative means were employed in that endeavor. It is man's nature to seek a sanctuary in a time of crisis; yet, like so many of the dreams and aspirations of the Confederacy, Charleston's "monster guns" proved but a fleeting hope to a cause that was not to be.

[49]Ripley, *Artillery and Ammunition*, p. 340; Alice R. Levkoff and Robert Whitelaw, *Charleston, Come Hell or High Water* (Columbia, S.C.: R.L. Bryan Co., 1975), p. 50; *Charleston Yearbook 1883*, pp. 466, 12, 160; Warren Ripley, "Civil War Gun Platform Found," *Charleston Evening Post*, Jan. 15, 1976, p. 1.

THE CONFEDERATE GUNBOAT "PEDEE" °

BY LEAH TOWNSEND †

According to J. R. Soley, Assistant Secretary of the Navy under Benjamin Harrison, in *The Blockade and the Cruisers*, the Confederate States went to war without naval equipment or resources of any sort except the trained officers and men who came with their states into Confederate service. As the blockade tightened and it became increasingly difficult to import guns and parts, late in 1862, S. R. Mallory, Secretary of the Navy of the Confederacy, had inspections made of possible sites for navy yards at the head of navigation of such rivers as the Pamunkey, the York, the Tombigbee, and the Pedee, where they would be unmolested while the work progressed. Flag Officer Ingraham at Charleston ordered Lt. Alphonse Barbot,[1] C.S.N., to visit and inspect inland sites in South Carolina. He reported an average depth of eight feet in the Peedee River from Society Hill landing to Georgetown, and apparently recommended the location which became the Mars Bluff or Pedee Navy Yard north of the railroad bridge on the present Marion County side of the river.

Shortly after Lieutenant Barbot's report was made, Van Rensselaer Morgan arrived with a large force—including a naval constructor, a surgeon, and a commissary, with about a hundred shipwrights and other artisans, most of whom were detailed from the army—and began the construction of the navy yard and of the vessel later named the "Pedee." Among these workers were Malcolm S. McMillan, grandfather of Congressman John L. McMillan, and Wesley W. Gregg, of Company I, 21st South Carolina Regiment.

On December 16, 1862, Secretary Mallory wrote 1st Lt. William G. Dozier, of the Confederate States Navy, in care of General W. W. Harllee, Mars Bluff:

> Sir: The department relies upon you to complete the gunboat, for the construction of which you are ordered, in the shortest possible time.

° The reader will note the variations in the spelling of "Pedee" which occur in the newspaper accounts, letters, inscriptions, and other sources herein quoted. Mills's *Atlas*, Wallace's *History*, and many other standard references adhere to the old spelling "Pedee."

† Box 266, Florence, S. C.

[1] Lieutenant Barbot was born in New Orleans in 1822. An Annapolis man, after serving in the Mexican War he resigned from the United States Navy and entered the Confederate service, returning to the United States Navy after the War, and dying an admiral.

The South Carolina Historical Magazine 60: 66-73

Mr. Murray,[2] a constructor of experience and energy, is on his way here
and will join you in a few days, and you can place him in immediate
charge of the work.

General Harllee's patriotic offer to aid in procuring timber, engaging workmen, etc., is highly appreciated, and you will avail yourself, as
far as possible, of his assistance. A paymaster with funds will join you
in a few days. I suggest that you confer freely with Gen. Harllee and
push the work on night and day. The fastening has been ordered to you.

That the boat could not have been launched in 1862, as stated on
the inscription at the base of the propellers at the Florence Public Library, is apparent from the above and from a letter written on May 27,
1862, by General W. W. Harllee, then in charge of the militia in his
district of South Carolina, to General J. C. Pemberton at Charleston.
This letter thanks him for sending four companies under Colonel
Graham to Stone's Landing to protect the railroad bridge from possible Yankee gunboat attack, but deplores his orders to Colonel Graham
to withdraw the four companies at once, it being General Harllee's
opinion that the railroad bridge could best be protected by a permanent garrison at Stone's Landing, where rafts had been arranged as
obstructions to gunboat entry, and the terrain furnished an excellent
base of operations against such boats. The letter does not mention
danger to a navy yard or boats under construction there.

Mr. James Rogers wrote in *The Florence Morning News* of December 30, 1950, that the construction of the gunboat "Pedee" was a
community project, largely financed by contributions from business men,
slave labor from plantation owners, and collections of jewelery and
silver plate by the ladies. He mentions two aunts of J. M. Napier, of
Darlington, from whom this tradition probably came. It is borne out
by an undated letter, written probably in 1925, by Mrs. Louise Harllee
Pearce to her great-granddaughter Louise Wallace (Sallenger), stating
that the money for the boat came partly from sale of their jewelry by
the ladies of this region, and that they called it "our" boat.

The workmen cut and rafted timber to the navy yard and built
what W. F. Clayton describes as the best wooden ship the Confederacy constructed. Clayton, a midshipman of the Confederate Navy,
detailed to the "Pedee" as his first assignment, later married Miss
Brown of the Claussen community and practiced law in Florence for
many years. He describes the vessel as schooner-rigged, with double
propellers, carrying two three-inch rifle guns on pivot, bow and stern,

[2] Murray is said to have come from Kentucky.

and a nine-inch Dahlgren shell gun on pivot amidships.[3] The sketch on the monument on the Florence Court House grounds shows a three-masted schooner, rigged fore and aft, with one funnel abaft the foremast; that is, the vessel was fitted for steam and sail. The *Official Records* carries a description of the "Pedee" as a wooden screw gunboat, single engine, 170 feet long, 26-foot beam, 10-foot depth.[4] James Rogers's article above states that the boat measured 110 feet from stem to stern and 40 feet at fullest width; but a Marion reporter for the *Columbia Record* of November 1, 1954, says she was 170 feet overall with a beam of 28 feet; his statement is probably a combination of the *Official Records* and personal observation. The double propellers weighed about 1,500 pounds; the engine produced some 250 horsepower; and the vessel made a speed of about 9 knots.

The inscription on the base of the propellers, now mounted on the Florence Library grounds, states that the boat was launched on the Great Pedee in 1862. This statement probably follows Scharf:

> The report of Naval Constructor John L. Porter of November 1, 1862, shows that . . . at Pedee River Bridge, a wooden gunboat had just been completed with two propellers, the engines of which were built at the naval works at Richmond, and that there was also on the stocks at the same place a small side-wheel steamer for transportation purposes on the Pedee River, as well as a torpedo-boat.[5]

The date 1862 is probably a typographical error for 1864. Mallory's letter to Dozier proves that the vessel had not been begun until the end of 1862; and the following letter of Brig. Gen. J. H. Trapier to Brig. Gen. Thomas Jordan, Chief of Staff, Charleston, dated January 26, 1864, further proves 1864 to be the proper date:

> The Confederate navy-yard at Mars Bluff, Peedee River, is assuming daily greater and greater importance. Already has there been nearly com-

---

[3] One 6.4-inch rifled Brooke gun (Serial No. S-53), weighing approximately 10,800 pounds, was begun at the Confederate Naval Foundry at Selma, Ala., April 29, 1864, and shipped to "Captain W. R. Morgan, Peedee Bridge, Marion Court House, South Carolina;" one 7-inch rifled Brooke gun (Serial No. S-46), weighing approximately 14,800 pounds, was begun at the same place April 12, 1864, and shipped to the same address July 30, 1864. The iron (Bibb No. 1 and some of Bibb No. 2) was melted in large brick reverberatory furnaces in Bibb County, near Montevallo, Ala. Records of the Confederate Naval Foundry at Selma, Ala., on file with the Navy Branch, War Records Division, National Archives and Records Service, Washington, D. C.

[4] *Official Records of the Union and Confederate Navies*, Series II, Vol. I, p. 262. Basic information used throughout this article is from this source.

[5] J. Thomas Scharf, *History of the Confederate States Navy* (Atlanta, 1887), pp. 47-48.

pleted there a vessel of war of some magnitude, which it is computed will be ready for sea in about two months. It is contemplated, as I learn, to build others, and it seems probable that important additions to our Navy will continue to be supplied from this yard as long as the war may last. The President alludes to it in his annual message, and its growing importance will naturally attract the attention of the enemy. It is my duty, therefore, to invite attention to the fact that the only defense for this navy-yard consists in the battery (White) which guards the entrance to Winyah (upper) Bay and such a defense as might be extemporized by riflemen and field batteries upon the banks of the river. I need not refer to the armament of Battery White; the commanding general of course is aware of its weakness. The position itself is a strong one, and with a proper artillery and a sufficient infantry support might be rendered almost, if not absolutely impregnable. In view of the fact that it covers a naval establishment of growing importance, and the additional fact that this may become a harbor of resort for steamers running the blockade and possibly the only one that may some day be left to the Confederacy—and that the Waccamaw, Peedee, Black, and Santee Rivers (all of which are also covered by Battery White) will if adequately protected, yield an amount of subsistence sufficient for the support of 50,-000 men, I hope I shall not be considered importunate in thus again inviting the attention of the commanding general to the subject. To me it seems one of no mean importance.

Lt. Oscar F. Johnson, an Annapolis man who had been an instructor on the Confederate Schoolship "Patrick Henry" and whose service record lists him as in command of C. S. S. "Pedee," 1864-65, came down with a complement of ninety men and officers—one of them, W. F. Clayton—some time in 1864. An article by Victor B. Stanley, Jr., in the *News and Courier*, July 10, 1938, states that the launching of the ship early in 1865 was the occasion of a public celebration:

> This was a great event and early in the morning great crowds began to arrive from Marion, Williamsburg, Darlington, Chesterfield, Marlboro and Georgetown. One witness described the day as a beautiful sunny day with the boat making a spectacle of beauty all freshly painted and sparkling in the sun. At noon the deck was filled with the crew bravely looking forward to serve the beloved Confederacy. The governor of the state, A. G. Magrath, a few Confederate officers, and hundreds of women looked on as the bell tolled twelve and Mrs. S. F. Gibson broke a bottle and said "I christen this vessel 'The Pee Dee' and may success attend her." Amid the rising cheers the boat slid slowly into the water. All those who had assembled for the launching brought lunch and a great picnic followed the christening.

Mrs. Pearce's letter describes the weather differently:

When the gun-boat was finished a great crowd went to see it pushed into the water, to be launched.

The party from my home, was my two sisters and myself, in the carriage. In a wagon, were my 3 younger brothers, 3 Whitner boys, and 2 Howards; two of our negro men servants to take care of the little boys and to wait upon us—and a large basket of lunch. By the time we reached Mars Bluff ferry, it was raining hard. When we older ones decided not to try to cross the river, in the open flat boat, all the 8 boys set up such cries of distress, that we waited.

The river was very full—"long-ferry," but when the rain stopped, all of us in the open flat—when about half way across the rain began again in torrents, and all were wet to the *skin*.

We landed on the other side, near a fisherman's log cabin. The negro servants cut fat lightwood, made a large fire where we dried the garments of the boys—but we girls could not undress there, so we kept on our wet clothing all day.

We missed the launching, but saw the boat floating on the water, and the boys enjoyed the elegant lunch.

As the "Pedee" was being completed and launched, Sherman was advancing through Georgia and South Carolina, and soon Charleston fell to the Yankee army. Only one assignment to duty was carried out by the "Pedee": She was ordered to protect Hardee's army crossing the river at Cheraw as it retreated before Sherman's advance. When she returned to the navy yard at Mars Bluff Ferry, the fall of the Confederacy was imminent. Lieutenant Johnson and his officers decided to destroy the vessel and the navy yard. Lieutenant Morgan got seven men from the commandant and sufficient horses and wagons to transport the ammunition at the navy yard to Cheraw, whence it was carried by rail to Charlotte. Before firing the vessel, the officers had a cannon ball fired into the swamp. This has been found and is now in charge of the Marion Chapter of the U. D. C. Then the vessel was blown up, sinking on the west side of the river between the old highway bridge and the railroad bridge. Stanley says that the destruction of the vessel occurred at ten o'clock Saturday night, March 15 or 18, 1865, with only the crew and a few others to witness it. Mrs. Pearce heard the boom of the explosion thirty miles away. The date given by Stanley and used in the inscription on the courthouse monument seems questionable in view of certain letters in the *Official Records.* On March 4, 1865, Major Gen. Jos. A. Mower, U. S. Volunteers, Hdq., 1st Division 17th Army Corps, at Cheraw, wrote to Capt. C. Cadle, Jr., Assistant Adjutant

General, 17th Army Corps, suggesting that a party of cavalry be sent down the river to give warning of the approach of the "rebel gunboat Pedee should it attempt to come up." Under the same date at 8 p. m., Gen. W. T. Sherman wrote to General Slocum from Cheraw: "There was a gun-boat here that had come up when the Yankees got Georgetown but it was blown up today about six miles down the river."

Whatever the date of its sinking, the "Pedee" would not stay down. Some time in September 1925, during an exceptionally dry spell, the river sank so low as to expose the vessel. According to the *Morning News-Review* of September 15, 1925, on Sunday and Monday of that week, hundreds of people went down to the river and forced their way over the three or more miles of swamp from the highway to the water's edge, where an excellent view of the vessel rewarded their effort:

> The sunken ship lies just below the Atlantic Coast Line bridge. Its propellors and boiler are plainly visible as is a large portion of the deck. The propellors are of iron, or steel. . . . The old boiler is a tremendous affair. . . . Both the boiler and the propellors are in a good state of preservation.

Souvenir hunters immediately began to destroy the hulk. The two U. D. C. chapters of Florence, taking prompt action, sent the following telegram to the governor:

> The Confederate States cruiser PeeDee, which was sunk near the A.C.L. bridge in 1865, now lies exposed owing to low water and is being mutilated by souvenir hunters. In order to preserve it for the sake of history, we, the U.D.C. of Florence, petition your excellency to give us custody of said boat so that we may preserve it as nearly as possible, for our country's sake.

Governor McLeod telegraphed Acting Secretary of War Dwight F. Davis a similar message, requesting permission to authorize recovery of the boat and disposition of it "to proper organizations for historical purposes." No reply from Davis has been found, but permission was evidently given to the two chapters to take action. The governor also telegraphed Sheriffs Barnes and Rowell of Florence and Marion Counties to prevent trespass on the gunboat and to prosecute violators. At the instance of the U.D.C. chapters, with substantial assistance from interested citizens and from the City of Florence, the propellers were moved to the grounds of the Florence Public Library and placed on granite blocks (measuring a yard long and a half-yard in width and depth) on the Pine Street side of the library, with the following inscription on the smooth fronts:

[East Block]

PROPELLERS OF THE CONFEDERATE CRUISER PEE DEE
Built at Mars Bluff Ferry and launched on the Great Pee Dee 1862
Lieut. Oscar E. Johnson, Commander
Sunk March, 1865, by its own crew to prevent capture
Salvaged 1926 by Ellison Capers and Maxcy Gregg
Chapters U. D. C. May 10, 1928.

[West Block]

Let these relics of a noble past forever testify to the patriotism of
the ninety heroic souls who manned this cruiser.

May 10, 1928, Memorial Day in South Carolina, was the occasion
of a great celebration accompanying the presentation of the propellers
to the library. The program was concluded at the Confederate Monument in Mount Hope Cemetery.

While the U.D.C. chapters salvaged the propellers, interested citizens planned to place a marker commemorating the "Pedee." The
Winnsboro Granite Company presented a rough block of granite
rounded at the top about 7 x 4 x 2 feet and weighing several tons. A
bas-relief facsimile of the vessel was cut on the smooth (south) face,
together with the following inscription:

[South face]

The Cruiser Pee Dee, C. S. N.
Built C. S. N. Navy Yard, Pee Dee, S. C. 1864
Burned to Avoid Capture March 15, 1865.
No nation rose so white and fair,
None fell so pure of crime.

[North face]

Boulder donated by Winnsboro Granite Co.
Model by P. H. Brigham.
Engraving by Dr. F. H. McLeod.
Erection by Brown Bros.

Dr. McLeod's first plan was not a granite marker, for according to
the minutes of September 22, 1927, the Florence County Governing
Board granted permission to Dr. F. H. McLeod to have erected on the
Court House Grounds "a Bronze Tablet of the Gun Boat Pee Dee."
The presentation of the granite boulder may have been the determin-
ing factor. No celebration appears to have attended the placing of this

⁶ *Florence Morning News-Review*, May 9, 11, 1928.

marker, but it is said that Dr. F. H. McLeod was in charge of a large concourse at the bridge honoring the sunken gunboat.

During the exceptionally dry fall of 1954, the hulk of the vessel again appeared above the mud of the Great Pedee. The Driftwood Company of Marion salvaged the remains and set them up on the farm of Calvin Yarborough, near U. S. Highway 301-76. The sheet-metal fence had giant-lettered advertisements of the remains, but apparently little profit came from the venture. The Historical Commission of South Carolina received several bitter protests against this treatment of the old ship. The effort was abandoned, and in midsummer of 1955 the fence had either been forced apart or had warped in many places, and the old pieced-out skeleton was there for any who wished to see. The salvage operations were rendered difficult by the depth to which the vessel had sunk in the mud of the river, by the breakup of the rotten timbers under the pull of the cable, and the wide scattering of the fragments.

The prow and stern timbers are fairly well preserved, as is the port bow; there are many half-rotted timbers from other portions of the ship, of gum, cypress, and pine, and many spikes and metal girders, grappling irons, cam shaft, and the immense single-engined boiler about 21 x 6 x 6 feet (said to weigh about 45 tons) in the center, showing the results of the explosion which wrecked the "Pedee." A full description of the vessel, still in remarkable condition for her 89 years under water, appeared in the *Columbia Record* of November 1, 1954.[7]

---

[7] In a recent renewal of interest in the "Pedee" through the negotiations of the Florence County Historical Commission with the Navy Department, an underwater crew from the Charleston base attempted to locate the guns of the Confederate vessel. A thorough search of the 200 square-foot area thought to be the location of the wreckage was begun on August 25, 1958, but failed to show any trace of the guns, and the attempt was abandoned three days later. The Commission hopes to renew the investigation at a future date.

THE HOMEFRONT:
"HOPING FOR BETTER TIMES"

EXHUMATION OF THE BODY OF JOHN C. CALHOUN 1863

The following copy of a letter from John N. Gregg, colored sexton of St. Philip's Church, Charleston, came to this Society through Mrs. Christopher G. Howe, and the Historical Activities Committee of the National Society of the Colonial Dames of America in the State of South Carolina:

230 Coming Street, Charleston, S. C.,

June 6th 1901.

Hon: T. W. Bacot.

Dear Sir:

At your request I herewith present my recollections in regard to the removal of Mr. Calhoun's remains during the War between the States. It was the Sunday after the evacuation of Morris Island by the Confederate forces, while I was attending to my duties as Sexton of dear "Old St. Philip's Church", when I noticed in the Cemetery attached to the Church Messrs: H. and R. N. Gourdin—thinking they wanted to see me, I went out and met them. Mr. R. N. Gourdin said to me: "Gregg, can you keep a secret?" I answered that I could if I said I would—then said he: "Do you know that our forces have left Morris Island?" I said that I had heard so—he continued: "Well, we want to remove Mr. Calhoun's remains for fear they may be disturbed by the 'Yankees' when they take possession of the City—we would like you to meet us here tonight about 12 O'c, and we have employed those we want to meet us at that time"—I agreed to do so, and did. When I returned that night I met the following parties: Messrs: H. and R. N. Gourdin, E. P. and A. Milliken, Mr. White the stone mason and his hands, Mr. Alley the undertaker, and my good friend R. L. Deas then Sexton of the Huguenot Church. After the slab was removed Mr. White's workmen were discharged. Mr. Alley furnished a case for the metallic coffin, and after placing the same in the box the remains were conveyed to the Vestibule of the Church and placed under the stairs leading to the South Gallery. I threw a piece of carpet over the box, and there it remained until the next night (Monday)—when at the same hour the gentlemen already named and also Captn (now Dr.) F. Miles met. During Monday I had a grave opened at the foot of the grave of Mrs. James Welsman in the Eastern Cemetery behind the Church. I told the grave-digger that I would let him know when the interment would take place—this I have yet to do. The parties present buried the remains, and my friend Deas and myself throwing in the earth—of course we made no mound, but left a smooth spot, and there Mr. Calhoun's body remained until I was about to leave St. Philip's as Sexton, having tendered to the Vestry my resignation—this was in 1870 or 1871, I am not sure as to which of those years—the late Com. Ingraham requested me to show where the body was—this I did— then I was employed to disinter the remains and replace them in the original Tomb—this was done in the Spring of the year of my resignation. I feel grateful to God that I am alive, and the only living person that was engaged in the matter. All are dead except the writer.

I submit this as a true and correct account of what took place, hoping it may be of use. I kept the secret.[1]

Respectfully

JNO. N. GREGG

[1] In the Register of Burials of St. Philip's Church appear the following entries:

26th April 1850. Calhoun, John C.—age 68 years 13 days—died March 31 (Easter day) 1850—buried April 26, 1850. Service in the Church. C. E. Gadsden. [Mr. Gadsden, then rector, later became Bishop of the Diocese.]

8th April 1871. Calhoun, John C.—died 31 Mch. 1850. From fear of spoilation by the enemy, as happened at Atlanta Ga. & other places to the dead, Mr. Calhoun's remains were removed in 1863 to the East Yard, where they rested until April 8, 1871, when in the presence of the Vestry & Clergymen of St. Philip's & others they were conveyed back to the West Yard & replaced in the vault originally intended for them. W. B. Howe, Rector St. Philip's. John Johnson, Ass't Min. [Mr. Howe, then rector, later became Bishop of the Diocese.]

THE CONFEDERATE RECEIPT BOOK:
A STUDY OF FOOD SUBSTITUTION
IN THE AMERICAN CIVIL WAR

FRANCES M. BURROUGHS*

A GREAT MANY PRIMARY SOURCES CONTAIN INFORMATION on the foodways of the Confederate military and civilians during the Civil War; information on nineteenth-century agricultural practices, military rations, supply systems, and methods of food preparation and preservation exist in diaries, letters, memoirs, newspapers, military regulations, cookbooks, manuscripts, and other sources. Yet very few books on the Civil War or on food history have in-depth information on this subject. In focusing on the civilian or homefront food situation, most references concern the bread riot in Richmond and occasionally comment on the struggles of southern women to find coffee substitutes.[1] The manuscript receipt book which inspired me to research mid-nineteenth-century southern emergency foods is located in the collection of the Eleanor S. Brockenbrough Library at the Museum of the Confederacy in Richmond, Virginia. It was donated by Mrs. Wilmot G. DeSaussure of Charleston, South Carolina, about 1895. The precise history of the volume is unknown. The full transcription of the receipt book follows as an appendix.

The receipts in this manuscript were compiled in a ledger book (six and one-half inches tall by four inches wide), covered in what the museum label describes as Confederate cloth. The dark-blue front and light-blue back covers are probably woven in wool and cotton, and the whole is hand sewn. A cracked, browned, and hardly legible paper label pasted to the front cover gives it the title of "Confederate Receipt Book." The ledger is a bank-account book from the "Bank State of So. Ca."; ledger entries were started on May 25, 1864, and ended September 21, 1864.

The manuscript receipts (the nineteenth-century word for recipes) are written in different handwritings and are copied on the back of Confederate bonds, envelopes, letters, and the pages of the ledger book itself. The envelopes are postmarked, dated, and addressed. Most names on the envelopes were carefully scratched over in ink and, in one case, the text of a letter was crossed out as well. All of the envelopes are addressed to Charleston, South Carolina, Confederate States of America. Some of the

*Graduate student in history and museum studies, Virginia Commonwealth University.

[1]Steven A. Channing and Time-Life Editors, *Confederate Ordeal, The Southern Homefront* (Alexandria, Va.: Time-LifeBooks, 1984) p. 85-86.

The South Carolina Historical Magazine 93: 31-50

receipts bear a handwritten date somewhere on the scrap of paper, perhaps indicating the date the letter was received. Only one receipt, for soap, has a date on it which could be interpreted as that of the year it was used.

This manuscript receipt book differs from others in that it contains receipts from one specific period, has no medicinal receipts in it, and though it has many differing handwritings does not seem to be necessarily the product of one family. Nothing contained in the volume indicates that there was an intent to hand it down, generation to generation.

The manuscript consists of a collection of frequently used or newly developed wartime receipts. The use of bonds as scrap paper indicates that the receipts were probably collected and bound shortly after the war ended. Several of the receipts include comments and references to "during the war." It is possible that this particular manuscript was meant to be published. If, in fact, this manuscript was intended for publication it might have been done as a fund-raising project for a charitable effort, or as a collection of southern women's receipts, highlighting regional cooking. Cookery book publications of the latter sort were quite popular in the years following Reconstruction.[2]

This manuscript volume does not duplicate any receipts found in another work also entitled *The Confederate Receipt Book*, published by West and Johnston in Richmond, Virginia, in 1863. The West and Johnston cookbook is the only one known to have been published in the South during the war.[3] The DeSaussure receipt book resembles the published volume in that it also contains a collection of receipts which were used during the war to make up for homefront shortages. A comparison of both volumes would indicate that butter, salt, leavening, meat, soap, and dyestuffs were considered the commodities in shortest supply.

The manuscript contains twenty-two non-food receipts, seven for soap and candles and the rest mainly for textile dyes. Generally, the materials that soap and candles were made of were subject to the same trade and manufacturing restrictions as foods. Dyes and other textile products were also affected, and locally grown herbs, animal and plant fibers, and other materials had to be substituted. A more in-depth discussion of this manuscript's textile and other household items, as they relate to substitution, still needs to be done. However, that is not the focus of this paper.

It seems likely that this book of receipts was compiled as a proud memento of times past and of "The Lost Cause." It serves as a record of

[2]Marion Cabell Tyree, Ed., *Housekeeping in Old Virginia, Contributions from 250 of Virginia's Noted Housewives* (Louisville, Ken.: John P. Morton & Co., 1879), title page.

[3]*The Confederate Receipt Book: A Compilation of Over One Hundred Receipts, Adapted to the Times* (Athens: University of Georgia Press, 1983), introduction by E. Merton Coulter.

hardships endured and creativity displayed by those on the southern homefront. This is also reflected in the fact that it was donated to an historical institution rather than handed down through the DeSaussure family. The Museum of the Confederacy was founded by a group of women in the 1890s who formed the Confederate Literary Memorial Society to protect artifacts used in the South during the Civil War period. They put out a call for items used by Southerners during the war and were rewarded with a rich collection of papers and objects. It is possible that Mrs. DeSaussure responded to this request with the donation of the Confederate Receipt Book manuscript.

THE DONOR OF THIS MANUSCRIPT RECEIPT BOOK was Martha Gourdin DeSaussure (Mrs. Wilmot Gibbes DeSaussure). She was born August 14, 1823, at Kingstree, South Carolina, and died at the age of ninety in Charleston, June 13, 1914. Her education was completed at Barhamville Academy, and she married Wilmot in 1845 at the age of twenty. They lived at 25 East Bay Street in Charleston. In seventeen years she bore ten children, eight of whom lived to maturity.[4] Martha is infrequently mentioned in the DeSaussure papers I have studied.[5] References concerning Martha were related to her birth, marriage, a lawsuit against her father's estate, a mention in Mary Boykin Chesnut's diary, and her obituary.

Wilmot Gibbes DeSaussure was born July 23, 1822, in Charleston and died in Ocala, Florida, following a long illness, on February 1, 1886, at the age of sixty-four. He was educated at South Carolina College and graduated in 1840 at the age of eighteen. Wilmot read law in his father's office and was admitted to the South Carolina State Bar in 1843. As a partner in the firm of DeSaussure and Son, he practiced law for the remainder of his life. He also served at least two terms in the South Carolina legislature.

In 1861, after Fort Moultrie was evacuated by the U.S. Army, Wilmot DeSaussure, newly-appointed general of the South Carolina forces, was placed in charge of the abandoned fortress. At the time of the bombardment of Fort Sumter by Confederate military forces he was in command of artillery on Cumming's Point. Later he succeeded the late General James Simons in command of the Fourth Brigade, South Carolina Militia, and held this position until the close of the war. He commanded the force of reserves which was engaged in the defense of Charleston and, after the resignation of General States Rights Gist, was appointed adjutant general of the state.[6]

---

[4]Peter G. Gourdin IX, *The Gourdin Family* (Easley, S.C.: Southern Historical Press, 1980), p. 241-247.

[5]DeSaussure Family Miscellaneous File, South Carolina Historical Society, Charleston, South Carolina.

[6]Obituary, Wilmot Gibbes DeSaussure Miscellaneous File, South Carolina Historical Society.

"Wilmot DeSaussure makes an admirable salad dressing for our tomatoes, and I am so hot, so feverish I care for nothing else," wrote Mary Boykin Chesnut. Photo from collections of the South Carolina Historical Society.

In his lifetime Wilmot was a president or member of the following organizations: the Society of the Cincinnati, St. Andrew's Society, Charleston Library Society, Huguenot Society, St. Cecilia Society, Masons, and the Odd Fellows. Being not only a lawyer but an officer, writer, and legislator, Wilmot moved in very prestigious circles in the city of Charleston. I have been unable to find any direct involvement by Martha in organized society memberships. However, as Wilmot's wife, Martha would have been expected to be as involved in her community as motherhood would allow. She was very likely active in war relief efforts in her community and in other philanthropic organizations.

The DeSaussures were friends of fellow South Carolinian and famous Civil War diarist Mary Boykin Chesnut. The DeSaussure family is mentioned often in her diaries. The published diaries contain numerous references to Wilmot's interest in foods, both domestic and military. In August 1861 Mary Chesnut writes that "Wilmot DeSaussure makes an admirable salad dressing for our tomatoes, and I am so hot, so feverish I care for nothing else."[7] She further mentions him two more times on the same subject of the tomato dressing (though she does not reveal its receipt). Mary Chesnut also notes his interest in military cookery. She describes his visit to Confederate soldiers who built stoves in the sides of hills. According to her diary he was apparently impressed with the arrangement of these ovens:

[7] C. Vann Woodward, *Mary Chesnut's Civil War* (New Haven, Conn.: Yale University Press, 1981), p. 134.

Wilmot DeSaussure in ecstasies over a cooking stove invented by the soldiers. It is cut out of the earth on hillsides. Very ingenious indeed — chimney and all perfect. Only it is a fixture. They have not faith to move mountains. So must leave the hillside with its stove cut therein when they change camp.[8]

DeSaussure's interest in food might indicate that he was one of the authors or the editor of this work. However in looking at his accomplishments and responsibilities during and after the war I think it unlikely he would have had the time to be involved in such a project. In general, manuscript cookbooks were compiled and kept by women and published works (or those intended for publication) bore the male author's name. I did not find any resemblance in Wilmot's handwriting and those of the receipts to indicate that any of them were his work, and did not have an example of Martha's to compare with the manuscript. It is conceivable that Wilmot did contribute to it, but I consider it unlikely. While there is no definitive answer to the question of who wrote the receipt book, a future analysis of the handwritings contained therein may shed some light on this mystery.

In his obituaries it was noted that Wilmot had a great "taste for historical inquiry"; perhaps this interest in history was shared by Martha and manifested itself in the compilation of these emergency food receipts. It is possible that Martha compiled this "history" of food receipts. Published cookbooks written by women in South Carolina were done so anonymously well into the twentieth century.[9]

The several styles of handwriting in the manuscript indicate that the receipts were probably collected from Martha's circle of family and friends. The manuscript contains a good representation of the most common substitute food receipts, demonstrating a variety of individual experience. The use of rice, molasses, and cornmeal, and the lack of chemical leavening agents, coffee, and meat are responsible for the greatest number of substitute food uses. This manuscript contains more receipts for emergency substitutions than any source I have found except the published *Confederate Receipt Book* and Confederate Surgeon Francis Peyre Porcher's work, *Resources of the Southern Fields and Forests*.[10]

THE ORGANIZATION AND CONTENT OF THE RECEIPT BOOK follows the form of other period manuscripts. In it there are forty-two receipts, most of them for soap, dyes, and baked goods. Very few are main

[8]Ibid., p. 164.
[9]Anna Wells Rutledge, ed., *The Carolina Housewife* (Columbia: University of South Carolina Press, 1979), p. 223.
[10]Frances Peyre Porcher, *Resources of the Southern Fields and Forests, Medical, Economical, and Agricultural* (Charleston, S.C.: Evans & Cogswell, 1863).

dishes containing meat or side dishes of vegetables. It contains little information on the preparation of fresh foods, which many published cookbooks also skim over. Considering the seeming aversion to fresh vegetables by some Southerners this is understandable.[11] For instance, Sarah Morgan noted in her diary entry of September 14, 1862, that before the war:

> Ice cream, lemonade, and sponge cake was my chief diet; it was a year last July since I tasted the two first and one since I have seen the last. Bread I believe necessary to life, vegetables senseless. The former I never see, and I have been forced into cultivating at least a toleration of the latter. Snap beans I can actually swallow, sweet potatoes I really like and one day at Dr. Nolan's I "bolted" a mouthful of tomatoes, and afterwards kept my seat with the heroism of a martyr."[12]

Like many of the manuscript and published cookbooks that predate the Civil War, the Confederate Receipt Book has a large number of baking receipts, one-fourth of the total number of receipts. This is probably due to the delicacy of bakery items and the relative difficulty in creating them. The lack of standard measurements and leavening agents made the need for explicit directions very important.[13]

Another interesting aspect of this manuscript is the use of descriptive names for several of the receipts. Three receipts have been given patriotic names: Hampton Ginger Bread (after South Carolina's General Wade Hampton), Confederate Cake, and Secession Bread. Many other receipts in later cookbooks have names which commemorate aspects of the war. The word Confederate is often used as a descriptive word for economy or the newly enforced independence from northern goods and is found in more than just receipts.[14] The following excerpt from the diary of Emma Holmes shows this use quite clearly.

> The weather was bitter cold.... The girls determined to take advantage of it and enjoy some ice cream. We had much amusement in collecting the materials, finally borrowing eggs and churn.... After many quakings and considerable excite-

---

[11]John Egerton, *Southern Food* (New York: Alfred A. Knopf, Inc., 1987), p. 27.

[12]Charles East, ed., *The Civil War Diary of Sarah Morgan* (Athens: University of Georgia Press, 1991), pp. 260-261.

[13]Evan Jones, *American Food, The Gastronomic Story* (New York: Random House, 1981), p. 23.

[14]John F. Marszalek, *The Diary of Miss Emma Holmes* (Baton Rouge: Louisiana State University Press, 1979), p. 317.

ment, at half past 10 we were regaled with an excellent Confederate article, sorghum and lemons combined, having produced chocolate cream equal to the palmy days of Mount Vernon Garden."[15]

During and after the Revolutionary War American women celebrated victory and the creation of a new nation by inventing receipts with patriotic names. It is interesting to note that a parallel development also occurred during the Confederacy's struggle for life with the ironic difference that these receipts would later serve to memorialize nationhood lost.[16]

During the war Southerners were forced to use cheaper, more commonly available local foods as substitutes for the items they had previously used. Simplified versions of fashionable receipts previously used by homemakers and cooks were adapted for use with these substitutes. Some receipts found in southern cookbooks, newspapers, and published volumes on agriculture like Porcher's work give alternatives to expensive imports and unavailable commodities. The Confederate government and some newspaper editors realized the importance of educating the public on the subject of substitute food and household items. The government assigned Surgeon Porcher to write a book on the subject, and at least one South Carolina newspaper carried a few receipts on the use of rice flour instead of wheat flour.[17]

Before the war, foods such as cornmeal, lard, molasses, sweet potatoes, and pork were considered staples of everyday life by the lower classes and slaves in the South. The upper class had the resources, access, and ability to buy the more expensive commodities such as wheat flour, butter, sugar, Irish potatoes, beef, and poultry. These preferences supplanted, or perhaps totally eliminated, some of the more inexpensive local foods from their diets. Sallie B. Putman of Richmond gave an interesting perspective to the upper class's changing situation:

> It is noticeable in connection with the scarcity of food and the high prices, that the class usually known as the poor, was not the class which experienced the most serious inconvenience, and was reduced to the most dreadful misery. They were provided for by the Common Council of the city with such staple articles of food as could be obtained, and in quantities sufficient to

[15]Ibid., p. 395.
[16]Waverly Root and Richard de Rochemont, *Eating in America* (New York: Ecco Press, 1981), p. 101.
[17]The Charleston *Mercury*, September 20, 1862, published "Directions for the Use of Rice Flour," a reprint of an 1830 handbill by S. D. Dickson.

secure them from suffering.[18]

THERE WERE MANY REASONS FOR SOUTHERN FOOD shortages food shortages which would have made it necessary to use substitutes. Among these were the lack of dependable transportation, the northern blockade of the coast, antiquated and inefficient agricultural methods, unusually adverse weather patterns (for the years 1862-1863), military supply needs, and civilian hoarding. In the wartime South food-supply problems plagued both the Confederate Army and the civilian population. Food shortages in the Confederate military are well documented through letters and diaries of soldiers and official military documents such as orders and requisitions. This is not so for the civilian population. For the most part the food was available, but the ability to transport it to consumers was often deficient — especially in the final years of the war.[19] The degree of difficulty soldiers and civilians experienced procuring food supplies varied by region, season of the year, and stage of the war. In addition there were specific areas such as northern Virginia, the Shenandoah Valley, and central Georgia which were especially ravaged by active military operations.[20]

The worst shortages occurred in the last two years of the conflict and in the first several years after it, during Reconstruction. On the eve of the war the South was ill prepared to handle its own food needs independently. In part, the South depended on European and northern sources for food, the packaging for it (sacks, barrels, boxes, etc.), medical goods (drugs and equipment), and the transportation of these commodities. Additionally, prices were inflated due to the blockade, the lack of intercontinental trade, and the monopolizing of railroads by the Confederate government and military. Because of logistical problems, food was wasted, and it often never made it to those who needed it most, the armies and the city dwellers.[21]

Other than Confederate military supplies, blockade ship cargo usually was made up of more profitable luxuries and rarely included staples in any quantity. Normally only goods which could support a large mark-up in price were shipped through the blockade. They were transported on smaller ships, which were better able to slip undetected through the blockade. Salt was the exception to the rule; it was imported through the

---

[18]Sallie B. Putnam, *Richmond During the War* (New York: G.W. Carleton & Co., 1867), p. 343.

[19]Marszalek, p. 215.

[20]Bell Irvin Wiley, *Embattled Confederates* (New York: Bonanza Books, 1964), p. 245.

[21]Putman, p. 372, and Channing, p. 30.

blockade and, unlike coffee and tea, was necessary to sustain life.[22]

Traditional southern crops like cotton and tobacco had taken their toll on the land, depleting the soil of vast amounts of nutrients. When plantation owners were asked by the government to convert their fields to food crops they tended to produce disappointing harvests.[23] The lack of modern agricultural machinery was another shortcoming. The decline in the effectiveness of slave labor due to lack of supervision, runaways, and emancipation also adversely affected food production. The North, by contrast, had surplus food to export to Europe, aligning other countries to it politically.[24]

The wholesale devastation of the southern countryside in Georgia, South Carolina, and North Carolina by General William T. Sherman's army was accomplished in an effort to starve out and psychologically crush the Confederacy. The use of armed forces on civilians had a tremendous impact on the communities, farms, and families that it touched. As one Northerner observed, the only way to break the spirit of the South was to destroy its heartland:

> Mr. Pope asked them if they (the Yankees) thought to whip the South by marching through devastating the country, unopposed except by women and children. The Yankees, replied that they did not expect to whip our armies, but meant to starve us out. "And can you do that?" he asked; the Yankee said, "Sometimes I doubt it, for everywhere we go we find such quantities of provisions. You Southerners have a rich country."[25]

The federal troops were not the only ones to ravage the countryside for military use; the Confederate Army was eventually forced to begin the frowned-upon practice of foraging.

The unavailability of food was an important factor in the outcome of the Civil War. The South, though more agriculturally oriented, lacked the industrial tradition, transportation, and the methods and techniques for

---

[22]Root, p. 183. Though food products rarely were shipped through the blockade, an ad in the Charleston *Mercury*, April 2, 1863, offered "an extensive assortment of imported mechandise," including brandy, coffee, salad oil, tea, claret, spices, and rhubarb root. The blockade runner *Ella and Annie* shipped spices, tea and coffee, and six hams. Stephen R. Wise, "Lifelife on the Confederacy: Blockade Running During the American Civil War (Ph.D. Dissertation, University of South Carolina, 1983), pp. 234-235.

[23]Channing, p. 29.

[24]Root, p. 183.

[25]Earl S. Miers, ed., *When the World Ended, The Diary of Emma Le Conte* (Lincoln: University of Nebraska Press, 1987), p. 82.

organizing a competent commissary system. The South was unable to mobilize efficiently the food resources it possessed; instead it directed most of its energy into other aspects of the war effort. Yet food problems ultimately even affected Confederate military strategy.[26]

The South lost access to tremendous meat and grain resources in portions of the upper South which were captured by Union forces early in the war. These areas were richer in those commodities than other parts of the Confederacy. In 1863 General Robert E. Lee's decision to invade Pennsylvania was influenced, to some degree, by a desire to obtain food and forage in that state's undisturbed, fertile countryside. Virginia, it seems, was already beginning to experience problems in providing supplies for the army that defended it. Southern farmers were also known to hoard food, concealing it from requisition agents and tax collectors. An editorial in the Charleston *Mercury* in 1863 pointed to another problem: high railway rates:

> Family Marketing. — Everything in the line of family supplies continues to rule at a high figure in our market. Poultry, butter, eggs, vegetables, fruits, with which the country abounds, are, for the most part, beyond the reach of families of ordinary means. What the poor do for such things, Heaven alone knows. This results from the fact that the producers in the immediate vicinity have a monopoly of the market. It should not be so, and we appeal to the only power that can remedy the evil to come to our aid in this time of general need. The railroads have the whole matter under their command, and they can well afford to relax their tariffs and do a generous act to the public.... The country people are anxious to send us their surplus produce, but the exorbitant railroad charges are an effectual barrier against them and us.[27]

BECAUSE OF THESE PROBLEMS, SOUTHERNERS were forced to turn to food substitutes. Creative planning and experimentation was required, for instance, to determine what to use in place of wheat flour, leavening agents, and butter, and how to use each. As has already been described, many of the Confederacy's wheat areas were found (relatively early in the conflict) behind enemy lines. Southerners were never able adequately to meet their own needs for wheat flour. As a result, substitutes of cornmeal

---

[26]Douglas Southall Freeman, *Lee's Lieutenants, A Study in Command*, Vol. 3 (New York: Charles Scribner's Sons, 1944), p. 28.

[27]Charleston *Mercury*, August 15, 1863.

[28]Confederate Receipt Book Manuscript, Museum of the Confederacy, Richmond, Va., App. 1, p. 3.

[29]Confederate Receipt Book, Appendix 1, p. 21.

and rice were used. These readily available (and locally produced) staples not only served as substitutes, but on occasion acted as filler. The receipt for Confederate Plum Cake offers the substitution of corn flour (or cornmeal) in place of the now-scarce wheat flour.[28] An example of the use of a substitute to stretch a small amount of wheat flour can be found in the receipt entitled Rice Bread, or "Secession Bread."[29] In this receipt cooked rice (rice being a widely produced foodstuff in South Carolina) is mixed with wheat flour to produce a bread which is not only dense and tasty but has the appearance of regular wheat bread. During the war many bakers charged very high prices for their goods and some homemakers turned back to producing breads and cakes of their own.

Shortages of hops, the major ingredient in yeast manufacture, and saleratus, a commercially available form of potash, due to their manufacture in the North, provided the South with yet another difficulty. In order to raise cake batter or bread dough, a yeast, eggs, or other leavening agent like potash (baking powder) had to be used. Potash or its more refined version, pearl ash, was a product which provided many improvements to family baking. It was a fairly stable leavening agent, unlike yeast which was more temperamental, and it allowed for the use of fewer eggs, thus lessening receipt preparation time.[30]

The substitute for saleratus was the use of lye as a leavening agent, as in the Corn Cob Yeast Powder receipt.[31] Lye is water which is drained through ashes; after the water is reduced by boiling, the powder which is left behind is referred to as potash. In this receipt the ashes are made from burned corn cobs. Though lye is mentioned as an ingredient in the Confederate Plum Cake receipt, we might assume that potash was substituted.[32] The chemical reaction of the potash, which is alkaline, mixed with the acid in the sorghum and possibly orange peel would have given off carbon dioxide which raised the batter or dough, and thus acted as a leavening agent much like saleratus.[33]

The Life Everlasting receipt was a substitute for yeast.[34] Life Everlasting (*Gnaphalium polycephalum*) is an herb which grew in the fields and kitchen gardens of the South and could have been obtained locally.[35] It was used in place of hops and according to the receipt was made the same way

---

[30]Patricia Wilson, ed., *Bellamy Mill Cookbook* (Ontario: St. Lawrence Parks Commission, n.d.), p. 6, and William Woys Weaver, *America Eats* (New York: Harper & Row, 1990), pp. 133-134.

[31]Confederate Receipt Book, App. 1, p. 13.

[32]Ibid., p. 3.

[33]Root, p. 138.

[34]Confederate Receipt Book, App. 1, p. 13.

[35]Katherine M. Jones, ed., *Heroines of Dixie, Winter of Desperation* (New York: Ballantine Books, 1975), p. 59.

hop yeast was.

Butter shortages stemmed from the difficulty in transporting available sources of dairy products from the farms to the cities and the restriction of trade with the dairying regions of the North. Often in the receipts lard (pork fat or grease) is used as the replacement for butter. The Molasses Pudding receipt gives the option of using lard in place of butter, as does Mayonaise dressing without oil, where bacon grease may be substituted for butter.[36] Although lard has a distinctive flavor, if it is well cleaned it does not impart a bad taste. The use of this product as a substitute for butter is one many people still use in the making of pastry dough.

Much has been written on the sacrifice and courage of the Confederate military effort — how ingenuity and resourcefulness could, when there was a strong will behind them, make up for lack of resources and industrial capability. What too often has gone unnoticed, however, is that an equally courageous and resourceful battle was being waged on the homefront. This battle was not being fought merely for the successful accomplishment of strategic or political objectives. This battle was for common survival. The southern generals like Lee and Jackson may have had their tactical manuals and treatises to assist them in their pursuit of victory, but to those who waited at home small and unassuming manuscript receipt books like this one meant a great deal more than just victory or defeat.

[36]Confederate Receipt Book, App. 1, p. 15-16.

APPENDIX:
THE CONFEDERATE RECEIPT BOOK

Inscription on inside leaf: The back of homespun and confederate paper
[Please note that spellings and punctuation have been left as in original]

[Page 1 of manuscript]
Confederate Cheese (meat)
Boil one shank of beef until it is tender enough to pierce with a straw, then cut up fine removing all bone, season with onion, sage, thyme, margorum, salt, red peper, mix well turning over it enough of the Stock to soften & set together. Tie the whole up in a cloth and put under a press and when cold remove the cloth and serve with pickels — "In those times considered as good as Strasburg Pie — all the stock left was treasured to make soup in combination with vegetables."
[Written on back of $100 bond dated February 20, 1863]

[Page 2]
Fricasseed Bacon
Put several pieces of bacon into a frying pan and allow them to fry

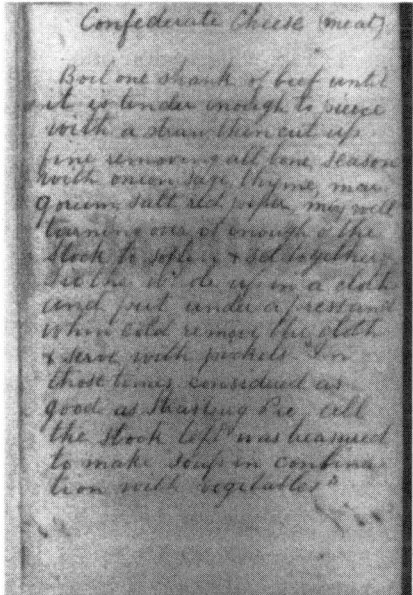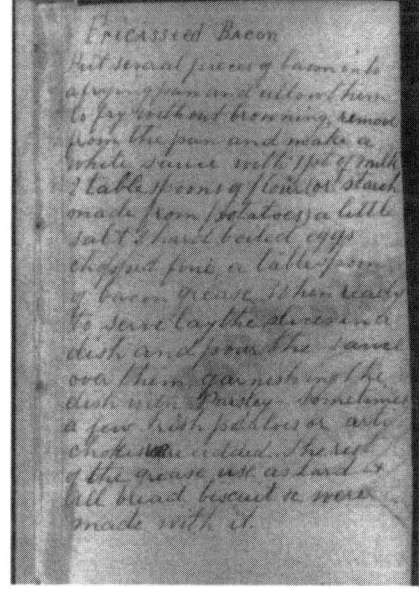

All photos of the Confederate Receipt Book courtesy of the Eleanor S. Brockenbrough Library, The Museum of the Confederacy, Richmond, Virginia. Photos by Katherine Wetzel.

without browning, remove from the pan and make a white sauce with 1
pt of milk 2 tablespoons of flour (or starch made from potatoes) a little
salt, 2 hard boiled eggs chopped fine, a tablespoon of bacon grease.
When ready to serve lay the slices in a dish and pour the sauce over
them, garnishing the dish with parsley-. Sometimes a few Irish potatoes
or artichokes were [are?] added. The rest of the grease use as Lard — &
All bread, biscuit [e]tc were made with it.
[Written on back of $100 bond dated February 20, 1863]

Confederate Plum Cake

1 lb wheat or corn flour, 1 pt Sorghum, 1 tablespoon Lard or Bacon
grease, 3 eggs, 1 pt dried apples, which must be soaked in water until a
little swelled then cut into small pieces, a little spice or dried orange peel
(obtained from native oranges) 1 tablespoon of lye. Mix and bake as
usual, adding the lye just before you bake
[Receipt written on back of envelope postmarked July 21 Newberry C.H.
(Court House) S.C. To Mr. Charles W(?), Charleston So. Ca. Penned in:
Rec in July 1862]

[Page 4]
Confederate Black Cake

1 lb. Butter or Lard, 1 1/2 pt. Sorghum, 5 Eggs, 1 1/2 lbs Flour, 1 doz.
peach nuts bleached, 1/4 lbs. dried cherries, 1/4 lbs. dried apples 1/4
lbs. dried peaches cut up the size of raisins, 1/4 lb. watermelon rine
preserves, or orange peel. Season with spices if you have them & bake in
a slow oven. The addition of a teaspoon of soda is an improvment.
[Receipt written on back of letter (ruled paper) dated: Boundary
(Baraby?) May 9, 1865]

[Page 5]
Sorghum Jelly

Beat very light 3 eggs, & add to them 1 pt. of Sorghum. Set on to boil,
stirring slowly until it thickens to the consistancy of hominy
[Receipt written on the back of an envelope to Mr. Charles (?), Charleston So. Ca. Postmark Newberry CH September 1862 SC. Penciled in: Rec
Sept 1862]

[Page 6]
Good Coffee. Sweet Potatoes

Peel sweet potatoes and slice them 3/8 or 1/2 inch thick, cut into strips
same width. The strips cut into squares so as to average the same size.
Dry in the sun three days. When dry put into bags. When for use for
coffee parch a good brown, grind and make as you would coffee berry.

Ground nuts, Okra seed (dried) cotton seed, & Rye, parched, ground and used as coffee berry were much used.
[Receipt written on back of bond: C.S. Loan February 20th 1863 The Confederate States of America will pay to the bearer Three 50/100 Dollars for Six Months Interest due July 1st 1866 on Bond No. 25-05-9 for $100 V. Johnson for Reg. of Treasy.]

[Page 7]
To make Tallow Candles
To one lb. of tallow take 5 or 6 leaves of prickley pear, split & boil with the tallow without water for 1/2 hour. Strain and mould the candles. The wicks should have been previously dipped in Turpentine & dried. By first boiling the tallow in four or five waters it will bleach it. Then harden with the prickley pear.

Myrtle wax was also used for candles. Gather the berries & boil and when cold collect the wax from the top of the water, then proceed as usual.

[Page 8]
Soap
6 lbs potash or strong lye, 4 lbs Lard, 1/4 lb Rosin beat up. Mix well together, let it remain 5 days then put it in 10 galls; warm water & for 10 days more stir twice a day. A very good soap 1862

Cotton seed soap
Put as much cotton seed in a mortar as can be mashed with a pestle. Crush it well, then boil it with strong lye and process as usual to make the soap.=
[Receipt written on back of envelope: Rec 20th May 1864 Exd 12, Charles Weissnger [?], Esq. Charleston, So Ca Confederate States. America.]

[Page 9]
Toilet Soap
1 gall: soft lye soap, 1 qt water boil 20 minutes; just before taking from the fire add a teacup of salt dissolved, stir and let it boil up once. After taking off add a teaspoon of dry salt. When perfectly cold work well with the hands all the lye out, being careful to take off all the jelly which will collect in the bottom. Refeat the whole process 4 times or until all the lye has been extracted. Color with vermillion and perfume with oil of Sassafras, or any other perfume. Make in cakes & bake in shade
[Written on green paper envelope: 1863 Mr. Charles (?) Charleston, South, Ca]

[Page 10]

Lye Soap

3/4 lb grease, 1 gall: lye strong enough to float an egg. Just before taking it off the fire pour in a little cold water to thicken it. 1 pt of Salt to every 3 galls: of lye; salt put in the last thing (after the cold water) Well stirred set away to cool — next day melt over again — then cool — Harden — cut into squares and set away — If you have cracklings instead of grease — then put one lb to 1 gall lye — The salt makes your soft soap into hard — Sept 29, 1862
[Written on envelope: Mr. Charles W(?) Charleston So Ca, Rec 16 December 1862]

[Page 11]

A nice soap can be made from myrtle berries

Gather the berries, boil them in a large quantity of water until the wax rises skim & strain this through something very thin, when cold make the soap with the wax as above directed. When cracklings are used instead of grease, a smaller quantity of lye will answer.
[Written on pink paper]

[Page 12]

Receipt for making Soap

4 lbs grease of any kind — 10 gall lye which must be strong enough to float an egg. 1/4 lb of rosin will make more soap If you wish hard soap, it must be separated from the lye with salt, one or 2 qts for this quantity will answer it must be put in when the grease is boiled away, and then put into tubs to cool. —
[Written on dark brown paper]

[Page 13]

Life Everlasting Yeast

Make a strong tea of life everlasting, adding the flour Irish potatoes [e]tc as for hop yeast & Set it to rise. When sufficiently fermented use as hop yeast — Peach leaves are an improvement.

Corn Cob yeast Powder

Reduce some corn cobs to ashes carefully to get it free from anything else. Use as yeast powder. A tea spoon ful or a little more to a quart.
[Written on $40 Bond dated Aug. 19 , 18??]

[Page 14]

Hampton Ginger Bread

Rub to a cream, 1 cup of butter or lard, 1 1/2 teacup of molasses, 3 eggs well beaten, 3 cups flour or corn flour, 1 tablespoon of ginger (or pepper if no ginger) a little salt, a teaspoon of soda dissolved in milk. Mix well, & bake in buttered tins as the soda is added.

Blacking

Boil the berry of the China tree, thicken with soot. A good drink of whiskey adds much to its efficiency.
[Written on a blue paper form, type unknown]

[All of the following receipts were written on pages of the ruled account book itself.]

[Page 15]
Confederate Cake

1 cup of Butter or Lard, 4 eggs, 4 cups flour (or corn flour)
4 cups of molasses, 1 teaspoon of Soda dissolved in milk, spice to taste & a little salt. Bake in Shallow pans.

Molasses Pudding

2 cups molasses, 1 cup butter or lard, 1 cup milk, 3 eggs, 1 tea spoon of Soda, 1 qt of flour. Add as much fruit as you like. To be eaten with sauce, which make by stirring molasses and butter to-gether, season with spice or wine. Boil the pudding in a mould or cloth put in a vessel half ful of boiling water Boil slowly 1 hour —

[Page 16]
Yellow Pudding

The weight of 12 eggs in sugar, the weight of 8 eggs in butter, cream the butter and sugar Beat the yolks well and mix with the sugar & butter, put the mixture in a puff paste and bake.

Mayonaise dressing without oil —

Mix 2 teaspoons of mustard, 1 tablespoon of butter, or bacon grease, salt to taste, pour gently on to this one pt of milk or water in which a piece of celery has boiled to give it a taste, put on the fire & when boiling thicken with 1 tablespoon of flour or starch & the yolk of 1 egg beaten with a little water. When cold beat in a wine glass of vinegar & one of <u>wine</u> if possible —

To dye with yellow paint

Take a pot of hot water, tie your paint in a piece of rag & rub it in the water until it is well coloured, boil your yarn several times, letting it dry after each boiling and the last time set your dye with a little Linseed oil.

[Page 17]

Purple Dye
Maple and Gum bark — set with copperas.

Slate Color
Maple and Hickory — set with copperas.

Green
Crab Apple & Hickory — set with copperas.

Purple Slate
Oak leaves — with copperas.

Yellow
Red clay muds — no setting

Grey
Sassafras root — with copperas.

[Page 18]

Black Dye
To 1 lb of goods take 1 oz Logwood, 1 oz blue stone, dissolve the blue stone in as much water as will cover the goods by itself, the Logwood in the same way. Put the goods in the blue stone hot and let them remain till well soaked, then empty all together with the Logwood, let them boil for at least an hour. When cold take out the goods, <u>never</u> wring them. It is advisable for cotton goods always to be put into a strong dye of Red-ash bark & Walnut with a little copperas first, after drying them, put into the above dye of Blue-stone and Logwood —

Wash out the goods in hot water and salt after dyeing them and <u>shake</u> but not <u>wring</u> them.

[Page 19]

Drab or stone color
Take the outer bark of an <u>old</u> pine tree and make a strong tea, renewing the bark until the tea is sufficiently strong, throw in a little copperas — then wet your cloth well in water and boil it in this tea for 2 or 3 hours taking care to stir it constantly so as to keep the cloth continually under water. If you desire a lighter color, a beautiful drab or stone, take the outer bark of the <u>young</u> pine — These colors obtained in this way never fade —

Yarn For various Purposes For Flannel

2 Ons cotton to six culs for chain.
4 Ons Wool to six cuts for filling. 20 Hanks of six cuts each will make chain enough for 20 yards (yd wide) and 1 Hank of six cuts filling for every yard. Woven in 600, and double sleyed.

For knitted Jackets (gents)

4 1/2 Ons to six cuts, 2 strans
4 Ons cotton to six cuts will make yarn size of No 8 factory.
2 for 12, 3 for 10.

[Page 20]

For Confederate Grey

White and blue, a little more white than blue, when these are well mixed to-gether put 1/6 black.

Blue Grey

3 lbs blue to 1 oz of white.

Black Grey

2/3 Black wool, & 1/3 cotton or white wool.

[Page 21]

Rice Bread. "Secession bread"

1 gill of rice boiled very soft, when cold mix in 3/4 lb of wheat, 1 teacup

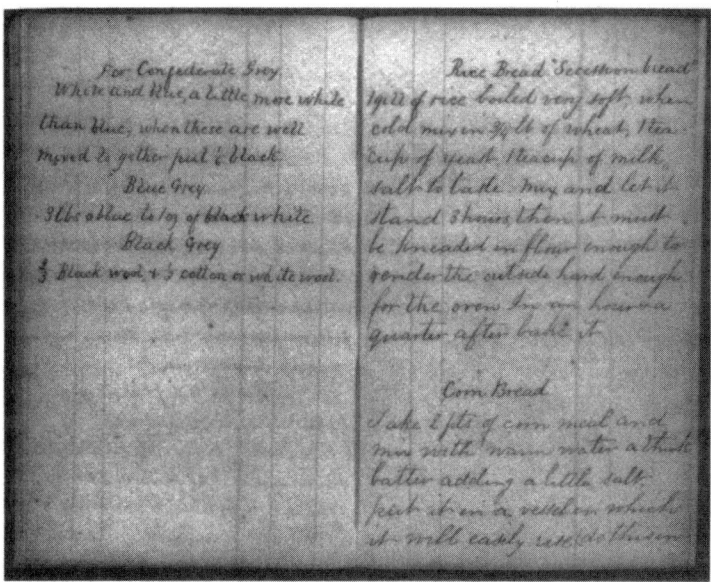

of yeast, 1 teacup of milk, salt to taste — mix and let it stand 3 hour, then it must be kneaded in flour enough to render the outside hard enough for the oven. In an hour & a quarter after bake it

Corn Bread
Take 2 pts of corn meal and mix with warm water a thick batter adding a little salt, put it in a vessel in which it will easily rise (do this in the morning when you wish it for tea) after it has risen beat well 3 eggs, add a tea cup of molasses, and a spoonful of lard & bake well.

[Page 22]
Confederate Cake
1 lb sugar or Sorghum
1 lb flour 1/2 wheat 1/2 corn
1 lb Butter
1 doz Eggs
1 qt peaches stewed with a cup of Sorghum
1/2 qt dried cherries
1 tea cup Apple brandy
1 " spoon Cream tarter
1 "   " Soda
Preserved Orange peel, spices

[Page 23]
Sorghum Pies
2 cups sorghum, 4 eggs, 1/2 cup butter, 1/2 cup brandy, spices. Bake in deep pans, crust at bottom and sides

Sorghum Pudding
4 cups Sorghum, 3 cups flour, 4 eggs, 1 cup corn flour 1 cup cream, 2 cups butter, spices — Baked in pans — 1 teaspoon Soda.

Walnut Cake
1 lb Sorghum, 1/2 lb butter, 1/2 lb Walnuts, 1 doz eggs, 1 lb flour, handful dried cherries, wine glass brandy, spices.

[Page 24]
Walnut pudding
Yolks of 8 eggs, 3 cups sugar, 1 lb Walnut, 2 cups flour, preserved Orange peel, wineglass of brandy, spices, preserved peaches or citron Bake in pans with crust at bottom —

DISLOYALTY IN THE UPPER DISTRICTS
OF SOUTH CAROLINA DURING
THE CIVIL WAR

JAMES T. OTTEN [*]

From the mass of material that has been written concerning the American Civil War, one fact has become particularly clear: the Confederacy did not go to war as one solid body and the considerable discord which existed throughout the conflict seriously impaired the war effort. An integral part of this dissension was the prevalence of much disloyalty to the cause shown through both desertion and Unionist activity. The existence of this phenomenon is not unknown to Civil War-era historians and almost every Confederate state has been the subject of a study detailing the rise and operation of this opposition to the Confederate state and national government.[1] But this list does not include a study of the state of South Carolina. Perhaps this oversight emanated from the fact that since South Carolina was the seat of secession, and that since the ordinance was unanimously approved by the secession convention, it was taken for granted that the state, *ipso facto,* was wholeheartedly aligned with the Confederacy and that its citizens were avid supporters of the cause.

This is not to say that historians of South Carolina have never acknowledged that disaffection in the form of a desertion problem existed in upper South Carolina. Charles E. Cauthen surveyed this problem and concluded that it stemmed from worsening economic conditions. It cannot be denied that the assertion is correct, but does it provide a complete explanation for the rise of dissension within the state? It is the thesis of this paper that in the upper districts of South Carolina the

---

[*] Mr. Otten is acting director of the Union Regional Campus of the University of South Carolina and an assistant professor of history.

[1] See, for example, Bessie Martin, *Desertion of Alabama Troops from the Confederate Army (New York:* Columbia University Press, 1932); Hugh G. Bailey, "Disloyalty in Early Confederate Alabama," *Journal of Southern History,* XXIII, 522-528; J. G. DeRoulhac Hamilton, "The Heroes of America", *Publications of the Southern History Association,* XI (Washington: The Association, 1907); Henry T. Shanks, "Disloyalty to the Confederacy in Southwestern Virginia", *North Carolina Historical Review,* XXI, 118-135; J. Rueben Sheeler, "The Development of Unionism in East Tennessee", *Journal of Negro History* XXIX, 166-203; Ted R. Worley, "The Arkansas Peace Society of 1861: A Study in Mountain Unionism", *Journal of Southern History,* XXIV, 445-456.

The South Carolina Historical Magazine 75: 95-110

factor which contributed most to disloyalty was the prevalence of Unionism.[2]

The mountainous area of the state, comprising the present day counties of Anderson, Oconee, Pickens, Greenville and Spartanburg (referred to as districts in the ante-bellum period, with Pickens and Oconee being joined together as one) was chosen as the focus of this study because it was here that the great majority of the state's yeoman farmers lived. It was an area of few planters or slaves and its inhabitants had little in common with the plantation aristocracy which controlled the state. If South Carolina followed the disloyalty pattern of her neighbors this area would become the center of dissension.

It should be noted that although the upper districts of the state contained the greatest amount of disloyaly it was by no means the only area in which dissension existed. Desertions occurred in most areas of the state. Negro slaves were as disloyal as they dared be and Unionist sentiments existed even among some upper district planters. These groups have received little mention in this study, however, because they were few in number and were, at best, a mere hindrance to the state government. It was, rather, the white yeoman farmers of the upper districts who were most often unresponsive to the Confederacy's call or were downright hostile to the cause. It was this group who had no sympathy with the war cause and, although merely disaffected initially, became openly disloyal as the war affected them to a greater extent. As such, the economic hardships of the war did not provide a cause but, rather, a catalyst which precipitated the transformation of these people. It cannot be argued that the resultant desertion from the front and the flagrant opposition to both the state and national governments ". . . seriously strained the fabric of the Confederate war effort." [3]

[2] Charles E. Cauthen, *South Carolina Goes to War*, 1860-1865 (Chapel Hill: University of North Carolina Press, 1950), 176. The terms disloyal and Unionist used in this study refer to those persons who not only refused to support the Confederacy but who actually worked against the government. Disaffection refers to those who were in opposition but were passive. It will be shown that few upper district deserters were passive.

[3] Quoted in Stephen E. Ambrose, "Yeoman Discontent in the Confederacy", *Civil War History*, VII, 259. For examples of S. C. disloyalty, see William Burson, *A Race for Liberty* (Wellsville, Ohio: W. G. Foster, Printer, 1867), Chapter VII; Morgan E. Dowling, *Southern Prisons* (Detroit: William Graham, 1870), 283; William B. Hesseltine, "The Underground Railroad from Confederate Prisons to East Tennessee," *East Tennessee Historical Society Publications*, No. 2 (1930), 65; John W. Deforrest, *A Union Officer in Reconstruction*, ed. by James H. Croushire and David M. Potter (New Haven: Yale University Press, 1948), 165.

As the Unionist sentiment which prevailed in the mountain areas of other Confederate States prior to 1860 was instrumental in developing opposition to the war, so too was it a factor in ante-bellum northwestern South Carolina. That area had a long history of opposition to any measures which hindered the Palmetto state's relationship to the federal union. During the nullification controversy of 1832-1833, in which the state had nullified the federal tariff law and rejected the federal system, the farmers of Greenville and Spartanburg districts remained staunchly loyal to the Union and were ready to gather enough men to march to Columbia and offer armed resistance to the nullifiers. A confrontation was averted largely through the efforts of Benjamin F. Perry, a prominent Greenville lawyer and newspaperman who urged that all legal means should first be attempted before force was used. The eventual settlement of the controversy ended the possibility of a confrontation.[4]

The citizens of the upcountry continued to remain in sympathy with the federal government until the first shots of the war were fired at Fort Sumter. During the discussion of whether or not the state's delegates should bolt the 1860 Democratic convention in Charleston if a platform not in harmony with Southern demands were adopted, upcountry newspapers, particularly the *Keowee Courier*, Spartanburg *Express* and the Greenville *Southern Patriot*, vehemently opposed such a tactic. The *Courier* noted that the entire area was opposed to such a move and to the whole secession issue. Prior to the calling of the state secession convention that same paper urged its readers not to be so hasty, and to see what the rest of the South would do after the election of Lincoln. It was the general consensus of the upper districts that ". . . the majority were far from believing that they reap only misfortune and injury in the Union and that prosperity and blessing was to be had only in South Carolina setting up for herself." [5] And while the Unionist candidates for the secession convention were defeated in these areas, their loss was due to the fire-eating statements by ardent secessionists concerning loss of yeoman

---

[4] E. R. Seabrook, "The Poor Whites of the South", *Galaxy*, IV, 689; William W. Freehling, *Prelude to Civil War: The Nullification Controversy in South Carolina* (New York: Harper & Row, 1965), 315-316. An indication of area attitude was that the "Dark Corner" section in upper Greenville District gave the nullification candidates to the December, 1832, convention only one vote out of 170 cast (see Lillian A. Kibler, *Benjamin F. Perry: South Carolina Unionist* (Durham: Duke University Press, 1946), p. 487.)

[5] Quoted in Lillian A. Kibler, "Unionist Sentiment in South Carolina in 1860", *Journal of Southern History* IV, 355; *Ibid.*, 346; *Pickens, S. C., Keowee Courier*, March 31, November 10, 1860, 2.

supremacy to the Negro. Nevertheless, even after the delegates had been chosen, a public meeting was held in Spartanburg to urge the convention to postpone its meeting for at least a month and await further developments.[6]

Much of the credit for the upcountry's eventually siding with the Confederacy must be given to Benjamin F. Perry. Although Unionist in sentiment, he elected to go along with his state and this stand by the area's most renowned figure encouraged many others to do likewise. When South Carolina issued a call for troops the upper districts, particularly Greenville's Dark Corner, were notably hesitant in their response. It was even said that approximately 600 men from the Dark Corner gathered at Greenville with the intention of marching to the capital and compelling the state to re-enter the Union. Perry was asked to quell this dissension and encourage the men to support the Confederacy. In a speech of May 20, 1861, to 200-300 Unionist sympathizers in upper Greenville District he told the men that the state had acted and they, like he, had no other choice but to obey her commands. His tactic succeeded and, as he noted, "more than two-thirds of (2) volunteer companies now in service to the state, from the upper portion of Greenville, were old Union men." [7] State officials noted Perry's influence with the citizens of this area and used this factor, along with the Negro superiority tactic, in their recruitment of soldiers. Through this strategy Pickens contributed 14 companies, Spartanburg 24 companies, and Greenville over 2,000 volunteers to Confederate service.

But many yeoman farmers had not completely forgotten their original sympathies and soon the spectre of an encroaching foe, the ignorance of the real issues at stake and the influence of the planter-oriented government would cease to instill patriotism. By September, 1861, Perry's attempts at recruitment in the Dark Corner area met with little success and upcountry volunteers declined markedly. A fugitive Yankee soldier named John Ennis also learned that Unionism was extant in the area. An officer of the 79th Highland Regiment, New York Militia, he was captured at First Manassas and imprisoned in Charleston and in Columbia, where he escaped in February, 1862. He proceeded through Unionville and Spartanburg and was directed by Negroes to the cabin of a white Unionist in upper Spartanburg District. The man told him that sympathy for the Union cause was prevalent in the area and that

---

[6] Kibler, "Unionist Sentiment", 361; *New York Tribune*, December 11, 1860, 6.

[7] Quoted in *Keowee Courier*, June 1, 1861, p. 1; Kibler "Unionist Sentiment", 351; John W. DeForrest, "Chivalrous and Semi-Chivalrous Southrons," *Harpers New Monthly Magazine*, XXVII, 341.

the citizens were passive mainly because of government coercion. He noted that his had been forced into the army and that several of the local citizens had been hanged or tarred and feathered for their Unionist sympathies. The man fed and hid Ennis and mapped a route across the mountains to other sympathizers in Tennessee.[8]

Thus, while it may be said that during the first year of the war little overt disloyalty existed in upper South Carolina, disaffection existed to a great degree and would need only a small spark to fire the spirit of open revolt. Such sparks would be provided by the Confederate government during 1862-63. The implementation of conscription acts with unfair exemption provisions, coupled with the harsh and uncertain life of a soldier in the Confederate service turned many against the government. Also, the scourges of inflation, speculation, impressment of supplies, tax-in-kind laws and the increasingly worsening economic plight of the families left behind affected not only soldiers but civilians as well.

The imposition of all these hardships upon the upcountry farmer produced a condition which the late historian, Frank L. Owsley, termed "defeatism". Any initial enthusiasm for the war had dimmed, and anger against the Yankee foe was too transient a factor to provide a basis for a protracted war. The glory of the war faded especially fast for the upper district farmers because they never endorsed the conflict. Conscription and the economic plight of the people served only as catalysts to transform disaffection into open disloyalty. By 1863 most decided they would rather die at home than be dragged forth to do battle for such a cause. The prevailing opinion among the farmers of the area was not only against the war but against the Confederacy in general. Lieutenant Alonzo Cooper, a Union escapee from Columbia, described the mood which had developed when he told of a family which gave him shelter near Walhalla:

The woman was quite bitter towards the Confederacy on account of her son having been conscripted and her being left alone, with no one to work her farm or care for her children. She was too poor to hire the work done, and was obliged to do all that was done towards supporting herself and the children as her son's pay scarcely amounted to enough to keep him in tobacco,

[8] Seabrook, *op. cit.*, 688-689; William J. Rivers, *Rivers Account of the Raising of Troops in South Carolina* (Columbia: The Bryan Printing Company, 1899), 31; Kibler, "Unionist Sentiment", 352; John W. Ennis, *Adventure in Rebeldom: Ten Months Experience of Prison Life* (New York: Business Mirror Printers, 1863), 11, 15, 25, 32; Georgia L. Tatum, *Disloyalty in the Confederacy* (Chapel Hill: University of North Carolina Press, 1934), 136.

and left nothing towards the support of his mother and a family of small children.[9]

It was in these people that dormant Unionism again came to life during the latter half of the war.

A graphic example of the effect of disloyalty-promoting factors upon the upcountry farmer-soldiers would be the trials and tribulations of Evans' Brigade. Brigadier General Nathan George "Shanks" Evans was given command of a brigade following his victory at the Battle of Balls Bluff in October, 1861. The unit consisted of: Holcombe's Legion, an infantry unit from Spartanburg District; the Seventeenth South Carolina Volunteer Regiment composed of men from throughout the upper districts; the Eighteenth S.C.V. Regiment from Spartanburg and Union Districts; the Twenty-Second S.C.V. Regiment from Spartanburg, Pickens and Greenville Districts; and the Twenty-Third S.C.V. Regiment from the Greenville District. This brigade, composed almost entirely of upper district yeoman farmers, originally numbered approximately 2,000 men. These units were pressed into Confederate service in late 1861 and it was not long before the men were tired of the war. The brigade was sent to so many different places that it became known as the "tramp brigade". In the battle of Second Manassas the Seventeenth Regiment lost 306 of its 444 men, a casualty rate of 69 per cent. Morale was further weakened because of Evans' subordinates' dislike of their commanding officer and Evans' own frequent absences and intoxication. The strain began to show early and Evans reported to Lee after the battle of Antietam in September, 1862, that only 120 men of his brigade were present for duty.[10]

The men of Evans' Brigade lost all interest in the war by the spring of 1863 because of worsening conditions at home and a like situation within the unit. The brigade was defeated at Kinston, North Carolina, in November 1862, and in the ensuing argument over who should shoulder the blame Evans court-martialed the commander of the Seventeenth Regiment. The last straw came when, after being sent to Charleston to re-

[9] Quoted in Alonzo Cooper, *In and Out of Rebel Prisons* (Oswego, New York: E. J. Oliphant, Job Printer, 1888), p. 167; Frank L. Owsley, "Defeatism in the Confederacy", *North Carolina Historical Review* III, 446-448; *The War of the Rebellion: A Compilation of the Official Records in the Union and Confederate Armies* (Washington: Government Printing Office, 1880-1901), Serial IV, II, 772. (Hereafter cited as *O.R.*)

[10] Thomas N. Spaulding, "Nathan George Evans" in Allen Johnson and Dumas Malone, *Dictionary of American Biography,* III (New York: Charles Scribner's Sons, 1929), 207, Rivers, *op. cit.,* pp. 21-23; *O.R.,* Serial I, XXVII, Part II, 587; W. H. Edwards, *A Condensed History of the Seventeenth Regiment* (Columbia, S. C.: The R. L. Bryan Company, 1908), 18; *O.R.,* Serial I, XIX, Part I, p. 143.

cuperate from the long and hard campaign outside the state's borders, the brigade was ordered on May 11, 1863, by Department Commander P.G.T. Beauregard to Jackson, Mississippi to reinforce Joseph E. Johnston's Forces. When news of the transfer was conveyed to the ranks, insubordination was rife and many left the troop train on its journey to Jackson. In fact, when Evans reached his destination he had only half the number which had embarked on the train, and he was forced to appeal for the troops' return in upper district newspapers. Two years away from home combined with other hardships had broken the morale of the farmer-soldier and "the order to go forward to the west was the signal for a general desertion".[11]

The changed attitude of the upper district farmers had a profound effect upon the fighting capability of the South Carolina troops. This is evidenced by a brigade inspection report of October, 1863. All regiments of Evans' Brigade displayed a severe lack of discipline, with the Twenty-Second (from Pickens, Greenville and Spartanburg) far behind the others. According to one roll call, the Twenty-Third (from Greenville) had only 4 of its 297 men present for duty. Beauregard noted that the brigade was in such bad shape that it should either be separated or completely reorganized. In effect, Evans' Brigade was no longer a fighting unit. The reason for this can be directly attributed to the increasing disaffection by the men who composed the unit.[12]

The fate of Evans' Brigade was not an isolated incident. The Sixteenth South Carolina Volunteer Regiment, composed of soldiers from Greenville District, was also ordered to Jackson as part of States Rights Gist's Brigade, but many of its men never completed the trip. They preferred, rather, to return to their homes. The unit was so depleted that it had to be replaced by the Fourteenth Mississippi Regiment. In February, 1864, it was reported that a large portion of the Fourth S.C.V. Regiment and three companies of the Third Regiment, composed of troops from Greenville, Pickens and Anderson Districts, had also deserted. Thus, by the middle of 1863 a great majority of the upper district farmers had decided that they wanted no part of the war and that they would resist its encroachment upon them.[13]

[11] Quoted in *O.R.*, Serial IV, II, 769; Edwards, *op. cit.*, 28-32; Douglas S. Freeman, *Lee's Lieutenants: A Study in Command*, II (New York: Charles Scribner's Sons, 1943), 478.

[12] *O.R.*, Serial I, XXVIII, Part II, 585-590.

[13] John S. Taylor, *Sixteenth South Carolina Regiment, CSA* (Greenville, S. C.: Greenville County Confederate Centennial Commission, 1964), pp. 10-12; Clement A. Evans, ed., *Confederate Military History*, V (Atlanta: Confederate Publishing Company, 1899), 208-209, 398; *O.R.*, Serial I, XXV, Part I, 560-561.

The fact that actual disloyalty, and not merely disaffection, was indeed present among the farmer-soldiers of northwestern South Carolina was vividly borne out in an August, 1863, conscription report from Major John S. Ashmore, chief Enrolling Officer for the Pickens, Spartanburg and Greenville Districts, to Colonel John S. Preston, Confederate Superintendent of Conscripts. As early as June, 1863, the Confederate government acknowledged that problems of disloyalty existed in the northwestern corner of the state as well as in other states, but this report revealed the true seriousness of the situation. Ashmore noted that deserters entering the area were daily increasing in numbers. The majority of the Twenty-Second Regiment was in the mountains above Greenville, and even deserters from Clingman's Brigade in North Carolina were coming over into the state. Local newspapers contained numerous deserter advertisements for both officers and enlisted men. "It was not at all uncommon for squads of ten to fifteen to come in from the army, having made their way across the country on foot and generally bringing their arms."[14] It was reported that many of these deserters had planned to return to their units, but when they saw the deplorable conditions at home they decided to stay. They now numbered over 1,000 and controlled an area 60 by 40 miles and 150 miles of the border with North Carolina. The deserters received active aid from their families and few people in the area were unwilling to hide deserters or counsel others to desert. No one would volunteer any information to soldiers seeking to capture the runaways. The spirit of the people was so anti-government that the deserters became quite bold. Groups of 40 to 50 would set out guards and work their farms in common, using traveling threshing machines. They would openly distill liquor, cut logs and mend fences. For their own protection, the deserters organized into armed bands and had definite meeting places. The area was prepared to resist the Confederate authorities and it was reported that at Gowensville, northeast of Greenville, a heavy log building loopholed for defense had been constructed by the deserters. This fort was evidently a serious menace, for Ashmore requested that a six-pounder be provided to destroy the blockhouse. It was noted that a band of deserters had fortified an island in the Broad River in the Spartanburg District. Ashmore concluded that "nothing but prompt and determined action can save us from ruin in the mountains of Greenville, Pickens, and Spartanburg."[15]

---

[14] Quoted in O.R., Serial IV, p. 770; Ibid., 773; Ella Lonn, Desertion During the Civil War (New York: The Century Company, 1928), p. 25; Spartanburg, S. C., Carolina Spartan, August 13, 20, 1863, 2.

[15] Quoted in O.R., Serial IV, II, p. 773; Ibid., 769-773; Lonn op. cit., 69-75.

The conscription report was a veritable bombshell and jolted Confederate and state government leaders into action. John A. Campbell, Assistant Secretary of War, stated in September, 1863, that the condition of things in the mountain districts of South Carolina ". . . menaces the existence of the Confederacy as fatally as either of the armies of the United States".[16] This same month President Davis recommended that a general officer be stationed in the mountain area of North and South Carolina to control deserters. Because of the trouble in South Carolina and other states, the Confederate Congress, in February, 1864, authorized Davis to suspend the writ of habeas corpus in order to combat the threat of disloyalty. In October, 1864, the governors of Virginia, North and South Carolina, Georgia, Alabama and Mississippi met to discuss ways of ending the menace. They recommended harsher laws, but by then it was too late for any measure to alleviate the problem.[17]

Somewhat firmer action was taken by state officials. Governor Milledge L. Bonham was horrified by the Ashmore report and immediately wrote to Governor Vance of North Carolina concerning the situation. He noted the increased resistance offered by the deserters and felt that the problem in South Carolina was only slightly less than that in her sister state. Responding to a plea of Major C. D. Melton, State Commandant of Conscripts, for a company of troops to apprehend the deserters and to the pleas of a Greenville loyal citizens committee for protection from the disloyal elements, Bonham also sent Boykin's Rangers into the Greenville area. He also asked Beauregard for a regiment of infantry to aid the state troops. These forces achieved only spotty success and it was not until a concentrated effort in May and June, 1864, that a force managed to partially suppress the violence and apprehend some deserters.

The greatest single act by South Carolina to control disloyalty in the mountain districts was the enactment of a stringent deserter law in December, 1863. The law provided that the local sheriff would now assist the enrolling officers in the apprehension of deserters. Significantly, it also stated that sheriffs who would not cooperate with the authorities were liable to a $100 dollar fine for each offense. The law further provided for a punishment of one year in prison and a $500 dollar fine for any person caught harboring, aiding, or even encouraging deserters. Al-

16 Quoted in *O.R.*, Serial II, 786.
17 John B. Jones, *A Rebel War Clerk's Diary*, II, (Philadelphia: J. B. Lippencott and Company, 1866), 46; Clement Eaton, *A History of the Southern Confederacy* (New York: The MacMillan Company, 1954), 58; Lonn, *op. cit.*, 112.

though this legislation was aimed at deserters its language indicated that it was also aimed at the numerous disloyal persons in the up-country.[18]

These measures did not succeed, however, in ending the disloyalty problem in the mountain districts. In March, 1864, the Charleston *Courier* reported that deserter bands posing as Morgan's Cavalry were stealing livestock near the Pickens District towns of Pendleton and Walhalla. Three months later that same paper, quoting a Greenville *Southern Enterprise* article, reported that deserters were very prevalent in the upper portion of Greenville District. They were stealing from everyone, but were especially bothersome because they were *burning and looting the property of rebel supporters.*[19]

From the above evidence it no longer can be said that there was only a minor deserter problem in South Carolina. Furthermore, it can definitely be linked to the Unionist position of the area's yeoman farmers who initially supported the war but eventually returned to their original positions. It is also evident that there were more than just a few recalcitrants and that they were definitely not treated with scorn by their peers.

Although the situation in the upper districts was bad in the latter part of 1863, it became even worse in 1864 and 1865. Not only did desertions continue to grow but overt disloyalty increased greatly. In January, 1864, Major Ashmore report that a Unionist meeting was to be held on January 23 in Anderson District. Conscription patrols continued to have a difficult time apprehending the mountain draftees who fled into the Blue Ridge. Those who were inducted deserted almost immediately; others resisted the Confederates bodily. John William De Forrest, a Union officer with the Freedman's Bureau in Greenville after the war, was told of several Unionists who were shot when they fought with conscription officers and heard that most of the people in the Dark Corner were in open rebellion against the authorities.[20]

The prevalent Unionist attitude of the area was further evidenced in the latter part of 1864 when the upper district farmers had an oppor-

---

[18] Letters, Bonham to Vance, August 22, 1863, and Vance to Bonham, August 26, 1863, Milledge L. Bonham Papers (South Caroliniana Library, University of South Carolina), Box 6; *O.R.*, Serial IV, II, 770; Milledge Louis Bonham, "Life and Times of M. L. Bonham" (Unpublished Biography in Bonham Papers [N. D.]), 680-681; *O.R.*, Serial I, LIII, 342; *Ibid.*, Serial I, XXXV, Part II, 478; *Acts of the General Assembly of South Carolina*, December, 1863, No. 4666, pp. 177-178; *Carolina Spartan*, October 29, 1863, 1.

[19] Charleston, S. C. *Daily Courier*, March 23, June 22, 1864, 1.

[20] *O.R.*, Serial I, XXXV, Part I, p. 536; DeForrest, *A Union Officer in Reconstruction*, VI, 37; *Idem.*, "Chivalrous Southrons", 341, 344.

tunity to aid escaping Union soldiers. The mountain people harbored many former Yankee prisoners and acted as guides to spirit the escapees through rebel lines and into North Carolina. It was well known that white "Tories" existed in these areas and De Forrest saw many of the notes of appreciation given by grateful soldiers to those who gave assistance.

The reason South Carolina prisoners did not escape prior to this time was that prior to the fall of 1864, there were no large prisoner-of-war camps in the state. But after Sherman's army reached Atlanta, the government became worried about the safety of the officer's prison at Macon and the enlisted men's prison at Andersonville, and in the summer of 1864, the prisoners were moved to Savannah and eventually to Charleston. An outbreak of yellow fever in Charleston dictated that the prisoners be moved elsewhere. Camps were established in Florence and Columbia. The stockade in Florence, for enlisted prisoners, was elaborately built and located near a swamp and only a few managed to escape. Those who did generally fled toward North Carolina, hoping to find Unionists who could guide them to the mountains and safety. The prison in Columbia was another story. Located approximately one and one-half miles from the city in what is present-day Lexington County, the camp was an uncompleted stockade in the middle of an open field, surrounded by a line of guards. As the camp had been hurriedly constructed, there were no stockade walls. The main restraining force was a "dead-line" which, if crossed, would mean death to the offender. Unfortunately, Camp Sorghum, so named by the inmates because sorghum molasses was their principal ration, lacked a sufficient guard force and was arranged so that the prisoners had to cross the dead-line to gather firewood and perform work chores. These conditions made the camp an escapee's dream and provided more opportunities for escape than any other Confederate prison.[21]

An additional and undoubtedly the most important reason for the large number of escapees from Columbia was the fact that help was nearby. Most fugitives possessed no food, clothing or money and needed assistance from the local population if they were to make good their escape. They received this aid from Negro slaves in the midlands area and from white Unionists in the upper districts. Unlike the Copperheads of the North, the slaves and Unionists of the South were not organized

[21] DeForrest, "Chivalrous Southrons", 341-342; Bonham Biography, 703; A. O. Abbott, *Prison Life in the South* (New York: Harper and Brothers, 1865), 24; Hesseltine, *op. cit.*, 60; Michael Egan, *The Flying Gray-Haired Yank: or the Adventures of a Volunteer* ([N.P.]: Hubbard Brothers, 1888), 220.

enough to plot escapes but once the prisoners were loose they were usually aided by these people.

When a prisoner escaped from Camp Sorghum he had a choice of either heading for Augusta in an attempt to make contact with units of Sherman's army or going to Knoxville, which by 1864 was in Union hands. The latter route was the longer of the two, but it was preferred because the escapees were assured of Unionist assistance once they reached the mountain area. There was no such help on the Augusta Road.[22]

That the escapees did, indeed, receive help from mountain district whites can be ascertained by consulting the narratives which the fugitives wrote concerning their exploits. One such account was that of Lieutenant Hannibal A. Johnson of the Third Maine Infantry Regiment who was captured in the Wilderness in May, 1864. He was taken to Macon and then to Columbia, where he escaped on November 21. Assisted by Negro slaves he made his way through Ninety-Six and by December 13 was near Pumpkintown in Pickens District. He became lost, but fortunately came upon the cabin of a Union woman named Prince who assisted him in every way possible when she learned that he was an escaping prisoner. She told him that her husband was a Union man but that he had been forced to enter the army and was killed in battle. After Johnson had rested, Mrs. Prince led him to a camp of Union men and deserters at the base of the Blue Ridge. These men, who had notified the area farmers to be on the lookout for escapees, then guided Johnson to other partisans in North Carolina and eventually he was taken to Tennessee. Before he crossed the border he stayed with two more Pickens District Unionist families. Interestingly enough, Johnson returned to the area after the war with the Union occupation troops and again met the Prince woman.[23]

[22] Hesseltine, op. cit., 58-59, 63, 56; Willard W. Glazer, The Capture, The Prison Pen and the Escape (Hartford, Conn.: H. E. Goodwin, 1868), 202. Although Glazer made this statement he did not follow his own advice. He attempted to reach Augusta and was captured.

[23] Johnson, op. cit., passim., 37-39. It is understandable that the reader might question the validity of these accounts as they were memoirs written after the war and in many cases were characterized by obvious hatred toward the Southern system. But in defense of their use, it should be noted most were based on diaries kept during their experiences. Also, all of these narratives have been examined by E. Merton Coulter in his Travels in the Confederate States: A Bibliography (Norman: University of Oklahoma Press, 1948), and were found to be highly factual. It can be argued that if these people were critical of the South it would stand to reason that they would not tell of Southern white Unionism were it not a fact. They even may have underestimated its extent.

The journal of Alonzo Cooper provides further evidence of upper district Unionism. A lieutenant in the Twelfth New York Cavalry captured at Plymouth, North Carolina in April, 1864, was imprisoned at Columbia and escaped in October. He traveled by way of Greenwood, through Anderson District and Walhalla in Pickens District to the mountains and was eventually captured near Franklin, North Carolina. Cooper's narrative is significant because he was befriended by two Unionists in Anderson District who told him that the entire area home guard unit sympathized with the Yankee cause and would never fight if called upon. Between Walhalla and the North Carolina border he was also befriended by an anti-Confederate farmer's wife who complained that the government took her sons and that she had very little produce.[24]

A. O. Abbott recorded an even stronger Unionist element in the Walhalla area. In a tale related to him, an unnamed major of the New York Volunteers told of his escape from Camp Sorghum in November, 1864. He followed the Saluda River, flanked Greenville and Pickens Court House and made his way to "Wallhollow". He was supplied with provisions by a Unionist white woman who had turned against the Confederacy because the government did not give her any relief committee funds since her husband was a conscript, not a volunteer. It was evidently well known that Unionists inhabited the area because the major stated that he had been given the name of a Union man to locate in Walhalla but could not find him. He concluded that there was ". . . a very strong Union element in Wallhollow".[25]

Perhaps the greatest example of Unionist sentiment was found by W. H. Shelton, an officer in the First New York Artillery. He was captured in the Wilderness and arrived at Camp Sorghum in September, 1864. He escaped in December and made his way to Cashiers, North Carolina before he was captured. He was returned to the Greenville jail and there he found a friend in the jailer, who turned out to be a Unionist who retained that position to keep from being drafted. He actually let Shelton out of jail and gave him rations, directions to North Carolina and the names of fellow Unionists in the mountains. Shelton then followed the headwaters of the north fork of the Saluda River, spent the night with a Union woman, and eventually arrived at Caesar's Head. At that location he stayed with a man named Pink Bishop whose name and political sympathies he had learned of from another escapee.

---

24 Cooper, *op. cit.*, *passim.*, 154-167.

25 Abbott, *op. cit.*, p. 235, *passim.*, 234. His story is corroborated by the tale of Lieutenant F. M. Murphy who escaped with the Major (*Ibid.*, 241-256).

He also spent a night in that area with the Case family whose two sons specialized in shooting conscription officers. Eventually he made his way to Brevard and over the mountains to Knoxville.[26]

The Confederate authorities soon discovered that Camp Sorghum was far from escape-proof, and in December, 1864, the prisoners were transferred to a stockade within the walled and well guarded grounds of the state Insane Asylum. But before these extra security measures were implemented, 373 of the 1,200 officers imprisoned at Columbia escaped.[27]

As demonstrated by the escapees' narratives, the mountain district farmers had lost sympathy for the Confederary. Here was disloyalty at its highest: aiding the enemy was out and out treason. Yet these people willingly performed this service. The term "disaffected" or "deserters" would certainly not describe this group of people by 1864.

The question naturally comes to mind, if the inhabitants of this area were, indeed, highly disloyal, were they organized like the Unionist groups in other states? Specifically, did the Heroes of America or one of the other peace societies exist in the mountain areas of South Carolina? Historians Frank L. Owsley and Georgia Lee Tatum state that the Heroes of America probably existed in the upper districts of that state, and the biographer of Governor Bonham notes that it was significant that disloyalty was strongest in those areas bordering the sections of North Carolina where the Heroes of America were most powerful. Tatum even goes so far as to say that ". . . an organization was found to exist among the disloyal in some of the countries which bordered parts of

[26] W. H. Shelton, "A Hard Road to Travel Out of Dixie", *Century Magazine*, XL, *passim.*, 942-944. The general escape routes followed the Saluda River or the Columbia to Greenville road to the latter town and thence to Walhalla or by way of Greenwood and Anderson to that town. The Walhalla route was chosen because of the vast uninhabited mountain area which began almost at the town boundary. Although Unionists could assist the escapee above Spartanburg, Greenville and Pickens, these areas were centers of troop concentrations and several miles of inhabited area had to be crossed before the mountains were reached. Once in North Carolina the escapees either followed the French Broad River or the Balsam range to the Smokies, then over the mountains to Cades Cove and Knoxville.

[27] Abbott, *op. cit.*, 150-152; *O.R.*, Serial II, VII, 1196. It should be noted that not all escapees obtained freedom. Many were caught in North Carolina and most never made their escape from the state (see the Charleston *Daily Courier*, June 22, September 30, 1964, 1). One authority, William B. Hesseltine in *Civil War Prisons: A Study in War Psychology* (Columbus: Ohio State University Press, 1930), 167, puts the apprehension figure at 75 per cent.

North Carolina in which the Heroes of America was very strong."[28] Unfortunately, little evidence is given to support such statements. Upon closer examination, however, more concrete conclusions can be reached.

Although South Carolina did not have the large organization of North Carolina, numbering 75,000 according to one observer, or many professional Union guides, such as Daniel Ellis' operation in the North Carolina-Tennessee-southwest Virginia area, the South Carolina Unionists possessed definite organization and exhibited many of the criteria attributed to the Heroes of America. They did indeed encourage desertion, as evidenced by the story of Evans' Brigade, and they did infiltrate military units with the purpose of demoralization, as in the cases of Evans' unit and the Anderson home guards. Like the Heroes in North Carolina, they did possess a semi-formal organization with signs, signals of distress and coordinated operations. Further, it was acknowledged by Governor Bonham that the Unionists in the upper districts were in communication with their neighbors across the border. And similar to other peace societies, South Carolinians were also active in assisting escaped federal prisoners and providing numerous guides to convey the escapees to other guerilla bands in North Carolina and Georgia. Thus, the South Carolina Unionists definitely possessed an organization that had all the characteristics of the peace movements of the other states except, possibly, that of size. Had the Confederate government sent agents into the mountain districts of the state as it did in southwest Virginia, Tennessee and North Carolina, the agents' reports would undoubtedly have told of the existence of a similar peace organization.[29]

From this detailed account of disloyalty in the upper districts of South Carolina it has become obvious that there was more to the yeoman farmers' break with the Confederacy than merely the dissatisfaction with prevailing economic conditions. The reason lay, rather, in the existing Unionist sentiment of a group that was never in harmony with those interests which advocated secession. It was this factor which decided whether or not the yeoman farmers would support the Confederacy and it, when combined with the other factors, determined the degree of dis-

---

[28] Quoted in Tatum, *op. cit.*, 135; *Ibid.*, 157; Owsley, *op. cit.*, 452; Bonham biography, 628. Hamilton, *op. cit.*, 10, states that the Society came into existence in South Carolina during the war but this must be a typographical error because he devotes his entire article to North Carolina.

[29] Burson, *op. cit.*, 72; Hesseltine, *op. cit.*, 65; A. Sellew Roberts, "The Peace Movement in North Carolina", *Mississippi Valley Historical Review*, XI, 196; *O.R.*, Serial IV, II, 770; Letter, Bonham to Vance, August 22, 1863, Bonham Papers, Box 6; Bonham Biography 705; Johnson, *op. cit.*, 37-39.

loyalty by these people. Since this devotion to the federal government was ingrained in these people it did not die with the cessation of hostilities. It was this same group of nonslaveholding small farmers from the mountain districts who would provide much of the white support for the South Carolina Republican Party during Reconstruction.[30]

[30] See Allen W. Trelease, "Who Were the Scalawags?" *Journal of Southern History*, XXIX, 459, for further information.

ELIZABETH JAMISON'S TALE OF THE WAR

EDITED BY DAVID J. RUTLEDGE*

When Elizabeth Jamison wrote her "Tale of the War" in the mid 1880s, she lived in Charleston, South Carolina, in a small apartment at 15 Chapel Street. At age seventy, perhaps she inscribed these words so that her children and grandchildren would have a memoir of her experiences, or perhaps she intended it for publication. When she put the manuscript away, it would remain forgotten for over one hundred years — to be discovered not in South Carolina, but in Baltimore, Maryland, in the attic of one of her descendants.[1]

Elizabeth's tale is not unusual; her experiences were mirrored in thousands of lives all over the South. Hers is a story that began with privilege and ended in poverty. She does, however, give an uncommon view of the Civil War; her voice is that of a woman on the home front who gave her sons and husband to the war, who managed large plantations in their absence, and who inherited a new world after the conflagration was over.

The world to which Elizabeth Anne Carmichael Rumph was born on February 15, 1814, was dramatically different from the world of her later years. She was the only daughter of David Rumph (1778-1835), a descendant of Swiss Germans who settled the region around Orangeburg, South Carolina, and Elizabeth Carmichael (1786 -1847). Elizabeth, along with her older brother David J. Rumph (1811-1872), grew up on a plantation near St. Matthew's, South Carolina.[2]

At the age of eighteen, Elizabeth married her first cousin, David Flavel Jamison (1810-1864), the son of prominent physician Dr. Van de Vastine Jamison (1765-1835).[3] Shortly after the marriage, D. F. Jamison built a home in Orangeburg on the corner of Russell Street and Railroad Ave.[4]

Elizabeth's husband had received his early education from Platt Springs Academy and entered the sophomore class of South Carolina College when

*David J. Rutledge is an attorney practicing in Greenville, SC.

[1] The editor wishes to thank Mrs. Thomas W. Jamison III, Westminster, Maryland, who gave him the original manuscript. It is currently at the South Caroliniana Library, University of South Carolina, Columbia, SC. It is published here in its original form except for bracketed notations.

[2] David Rumph Family Bible, Orangeburg Archives, Orangeburg, SC.

[3] "Memoir of Dr. Van de Vastine Jamison," South Caroliniana Library, University of South Carolina, Columbia, SC, hereafter cited as SCL.

[4] Plats located in the Jamison Collection, Orangeburg Archives.

Elizabeth Anne Carmichael Rumph Jamison, portrait by William H. Scarborough, ca. 1845. Illustration from a private collection.

Brig. Gen. David Flavel Jamison, portrait by William H. Scarborough, ca. 1845. Illustration from a private collection.

he˙was sixteen.[5] Unfortunately, young Jamison was expelled from the institution during his senior year for "seceding from the commons"—an act that he would repeat later in life on a much larger scale. After disgracing his family thus, he could do only one thing — study law — and he passed the South Carolina Bar in 1831.[6]

By 1835 the first of Elizabeth's thirteen children had been born, and the Jamisons had inherited her father's plantation, Turkey Hill, which was located a few miles from their home in Orangeburg. Elizabeth attended to the domestic needs of the family by preparing meals, making clothing, and overseeing a staff of house servants. Her husband spent his mornings tutoring the Jamison children. At midday he would ride out to the plantation on horseback to oversee the work and would return at night to resume his social activities.[7]

Jamison lavished attention on his children's education; he owned a library of over twelve hundred volumes on subjects ranging from literature

[5]*Charleston Mercury,* December 8, 1864; John Peyre Thomas, *The History of the South Carolina Military Academy* (Charleston: Walker, Evans and Cogswell, Co., 1893),166-175.

[6]Ibid.

[7]*Charleston Mercury,* December 8, 1864.

to history. Fluent in French and Latin, he taught these languages to his sons and daughters. His eldest daughter Caroline later would write of her father:

> You ask how my father appeared to me from a daughter's standpoint. You may not know, but my father educated me from my tenth year. I was his companion until my marriage in my eighteenth year. My girlhood was spent almost entirely in his library. I cared but little for the outside world, so content was I with my dear father's society. As I look back to those years so blessed, my father appears to my mature judgment (as he did then,) as the embodiment of all that is lovely in men, a devoted husband, a wise and tender parent, a kind master, always courteous to others, regardful ever of the feelings of inferiors. I have rarely met anyone resembling him. I have loved to recall his perfect devotion to and trust in me.[8]

D. F. Jamison's duties often carried him away from the family — leaving Elizabeth to manage in his absence. In his youth he became attached to the cavalry arm of the local militia, where he quickly rose to the rank of brigadier general, a post which he held for many years. Of his military abilities, a contemporary would later write: "He rode his horse and handled his sabre like one born to the saddle. His bearing was military, and he looked the man designed for command."[9]

Jamison also was elected to the South Carolina House of Representatives. In 1842, while chairman of the military committee, he introduced the bill that established the Citadel and served on its board of visitors from that time until his death.[10]

Of his scholarly pursuits, Jamison published several articles in the *Southern Quarterly Review*, *The Southern and Western Magazine*, and *The Magnolia* under the pseudonym "J." These articles ranged in subject from a scriptural defense of slavery to reviews on architecture and literature.[11] He

[8]Thomas, *The History of the South Carolina Military Academy*, 173.
[9]Ibid., 169.
[10]Ibid.
[11]Jamison's articles include: "The Penitentiary Question in So. Ca." *Southern Quarterly Review* N.S. Vol. II, No. IV (Nov. 1850), 357; "British and American Slavery," *Southern Quarterly Review* N.S. Vol VIII, No. XVI (Oct. 1853), 369; "'My Novel' by Bulwar," *Southern Quarterly Review* N.S. Vol. IX, No. XVII (Jan. 1854), 17; "General History of Civilization," *Southern Quarterly Review* Vol. III, No. V (Jan. 1843), 1; "General History of Civilization," *Southern Quarterly Review* Vol. III, No. VI (July 1843), 157; "Lamartin's Histoire des Girondins," *Southern Quarterly Review* Vol. XVI, No. XXXI (Oct. 1849), 53; "The National Anniversary," *Southern Quarterly*

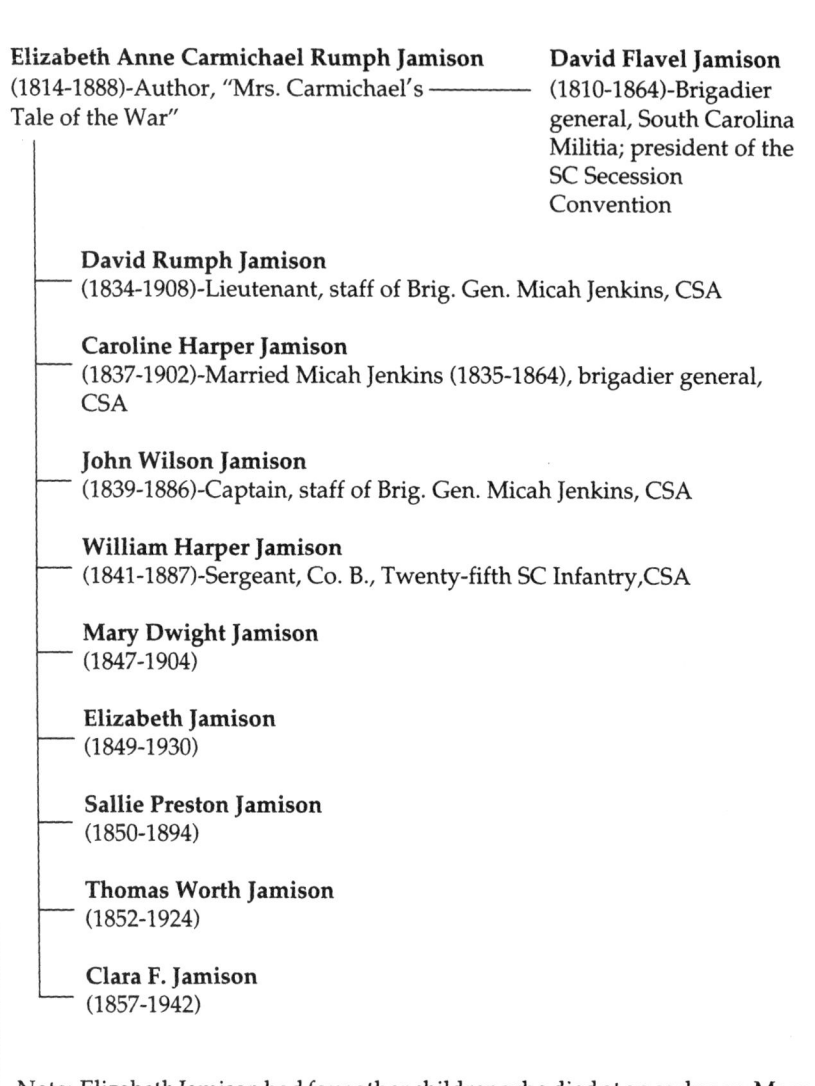

Elizabeth Anne Carmichael Rumph Jamison
(1814-1888)-Author, "Mrs. Carmichael's ————
Tale of the War"

David Flavel Jamison
(1810-1864)-Brigadier
general, South Carolina
Militia; president of the
SC Secession
Convention

David Rumph Jamison
(1834-1908)-Lieutenant, staff of Brig. Gen. Micah Jenkins, CSA

Caroline Harper Jamison
(1837-1902)-Married Micah Jenkins (1835-1864), brigadier general,
CSA

John Wilson Jamison
(1839-1886)-Captain, staff of Brig. Gen. Micah Jenkins, CSA

William Harper Jamison
(1841-1887)-Sergeant, Co. B., Twenty-fifth SC Infantry,CSA

Mary Dwight Jamison
(1847-1904)

Elizabeth Jamison
(1849-1930)

Sallie Preston Jamison
(1850-1894)

Thomas Worth Jamison
(1852-1924)

Clara F. Jamison
(1857-1942)

Note: Elizabeth Jamison had four other children who died at an early age; Mary
Elizabeth Jamison (1845), Robert Van de Vastine Jamison (1843-56), Flavel
Jamison (1851-52), and Flavel De Lessline Jamison (1855-56). E.O. Jamison,
Jamison's In America (Boston: The Rumford Press, 1901), 82-85, 526.

published a two-volume work on French history entitled *The Life and Times of Bertrand de Guesclin*. Published in Charleston and in Great Britain, it ran the blockade of Charleston harbor twice. It was beautifully printed and remains one of but a few books containing a Confederate States of America printing mark.[12]

While D.F. Jamison's star rose, Elizabeth remained at home. A devoted Christian, she was a founding member of the Orangeburg Presbyterian Church.[13] In contrast, her husband never joined that congregation and commented dryly on one worship service he attended:

> To compensate for years of puritanical affection, and eschewing of the devil and all his works, we frolicked throughout the holidays; had pleasant dancing parties every night for a week, to the great horror of Hanscombe Legare, who on the successive Sundays anathematized all fiddles, triangles, and tamarinds, ... that were ever invented and denounced all skipping, turns or dancing as inventions of the evil one. But as every man, woman, and child of his congregation or audience were implicated more or less in the offence, his logic was unheeded and his discourses were more amusing than edifying.[14]

By the 1850s the older Jamison children had entered college and had

---

Review N.S. Vol II, No. III (Sept. 1850), 170; "Raymond Lully," *The Magnolia, or the Southern Appalachian* N.S. Vol. I, No. 4 (Oct. 1842), 10; "Slavery," *Southern and Western Magazine and Review* Vol. II, No. 1 (July 1845), 2; "Annual Address before the State Agricultural Society of South Carolina," delivered in Columbia, November 12, 1856, Clemson University Library, Clemson, SC. See also, *Harper's Weekly*, February 2, 1861.

[12]David F. Jamison, *The Life and Times of Bertrand du Guesclin* (Charleston: John Russell, 1864). Jamison created his own lexicon of old French as none was available. Additionally, he traveled to France to research his work in 1859. For contemporaneous reviews of the work see *Charleston Mercury*, December 8, 1864; *Charleston Courier*, February 6, 1864; *Charleston Mercury*, February 4, 1864; June 25, 1864; *The Southern Presbyterian Review* Vol. XVI, No. 4 (March 1866), 376-384. The work was later translated into French: D. F. Jamison, *Bertrand du Guesclin et Son Epoque* (Paris: J. Rothschild, 1866). An advertisement for the book is in *Charleston Courier*, September 19, 1864.

[13]Frank B. Estes, *History of Orangeburg Presbyterian Church, 1835-1935* (Orangeburg: Privately Printed, 1935), 1. Elizabeth is listed as among those being present on May 2, 1835, when the church was organized.

[14]D. F. Jamison to George Frederick Holmes, January 28, 1847, G.F. Holmes Letter Book, Rare Book, Manuscript, and Special Collection Library, Duke University, Durham, NC, hereafter cited as RBMSCL.

begun to marry. The eldest son, David Rumph Jamison (1835-1906), was graduated from the Citadel in 1854 and, like his father, practiced law in Orangeburg.[15] Caroline Harper Jamison (1837-1902) attended a finishing school in Orangeburg and at the age of seventeen married Micah Jenkins (1835-64). Jenkins, at the age of twenty, founded the Yorkville Military Academy in the upstate. Another son, John Wilson Jamison, studied in France in 1859 and began teaching French and mathematics at Yorkville the next year.[16]

In 1859 the Jamisons sold Turkey Hill and moved from Orangeburg to the rural Barnwell District. There they settled on Burwood plantation, adjacent to Woodlands, the home of their friend William Gilmore Simms, and began construction on a large plantation house.[17]

By 1860 the clouds of secession gathered over South Carolina. When Abraham Lincoln was elected president, South Carolina was the first state to react. A convention of the people of South Carolina met in Columbia in December of that year and elected D.F. Jamison as its president. Adjourning to Charleston, the Secession Convention, with Jamison at its helm, declared South Carolina an independent nation on December 20, 1860.[18]

In the early months of 1861, D.F. Jamison served as secretary of war of the Palmetto Republic. In that capacity he prepared the fortifications of Charleston harbor and served on the Executive Committee, which ran the affairs of state. Giving a speech to the members of the convention in April 1861, Jamison proclaimed:

> This revolution, so far, has been bloodless. What a glorious consummation it would have been! What a triumph of civilization and Christianity, if the great principles involved in this movement could have been successfully achieved, without shedding a single drop of human blood! But now it seems to be otherwise. While I am yet speaking, a hostile

---

[15]Thomas, *The History of the South Carolina Military Academy*, 263.

[16]*Yorkville Enquirer*, May 3, 1860, and May 17, 1860.

[17]Deeds indicate that Jamison paid about twelve thousand dollars for his plantation. Book MM, 199-222 (November 10, 1859) and Book NN, 62 (January 20, 1861), Barnwell County Courthouse, Barnwell, South Carolina. See also, Charleston *Mercury*, January 19, 1860, which announced their move.

[18]The *Harper's Weekly*, February 2, 1861, describes the event and has a short biography and a woodcut of Gen. Jamison. See also, *Frank Leslie's Illustrated Newspaper*, February 9, 1861.

fleet is said to be approaching our shores, and before the coming night closes over us, the sands of Morris Island may be stained with the best blood of our people. May God show the right!"[19]

While D.F. Jamison reached the zenith of his military and political career, Elizabeth remained contentedly at her rural home. While D.F. Jamison and men like him sowed the winds of war, it would be Elizabeth, her children, and her children's children who would reap the whirlwind. In the end, her husband's words proved to be prophetic — the sands of a great many battlefields would indeed be stained with the best blood of a great number of people.

MRS. CARMICHAEL'S TALE OF THE WAR[20]

My "Tale of the War" is simply a plain statement of facts that came under my own observation or happened to one of my family so near me that I know all to be true.

It is with the commencement of our late war that I begin my tale of some of the anxieties and sufferings that came to myself my family and some of my friends during the four years of our unhappy struggle.

A few months after our State seceded my husband was attached to Gen. Beauregard's Staff. For some time after that I had the consolation of occasionally seeing him. My husband and my oldest son were in Charleston at the bombardment of Fort Sumter.[21] I and my daughters were not far from

[19]John A. May and Joan Reynolds Faunt, *South Carolina Secedes* (Columbia: University of South Carolina Press, 1960), 44.

[20]Mrs. Carmichael is the name that Elizabeth Jamison used in the original manuscript. Carmichael was her mother's maiden name. David Rumph Family Bible, Orangeburg Archives.

[21]David Flavel Jamison (1810-1864) was presiding judge for the Military Court of Beauregard's Corp. The term "Beauregard's Corps" in reality was applied to the Department of South Carolina, Georgia, and Florida. Charleston *Mercury*, September 16, 1864; December 8, 1864. David Rumph Jamison (1834-1908) was present at the Battle of Fort Sumter in 1861. At the outbreak of the war, he volunteered for service and entered the First South Carolina Infantry Regiment (Hagood's), as a private. Later, he was promoted to lieutenant and served on the staff of Brig. Gen. Micah Jenkins until Jenkin's death in 1864. Jamison then served on the staff of Brig. Gen. John Bratton until Lee's surrender at Appomattox Court House in 1865. D. R. Jamison, Compiled Service Records, First Infantry Regiment (Hagood's), South Carolina, and Confederate General and Staff Officers, War Department Collection

the Edisto and the waters of that river transmitted the sound of each gun as it was fired to us.[22] That was our first experience in the war. We, of course were very anxious the next day to hear the result and to know what had occurred on that eventful night. We did not know for some days that our friends had not been in danger then at all. Then followed volunteering. My son-in-law and my oldest son were amongst the first volunteers.[23] Then came forming companies, and the election of officers — then the hurrying off of the volunteer companies to Virginia. The making ready and waiting for the battles to come off was tiresome indeed, but had to be borne weary as it was.

The following summer we waited in much suspense for what we then knew must come, war in all its horrors. We who had to stay at home and wait for news from the army had many times heavy hearts. But there was much for the mothers and mistresses on our southern plantations to do. And, it was astonishing how much was accomplished too. They learned to manufacture homespun. Some of them made it nice and pretty. I had a warping bars and a loom made, and took lessons in weaving from a neighbor that I might learn one of our women to weave cloth for the use of the plantation. It took a great many yards of cloth for the domestic use of our homes as they were then. Cheerfully, the mistress attended to it all. I must say our negroes generally behaved beautifully during those years, and were true to us and to our children for a long time.[24]

But soon battles became heavier and weary waiting almost intolerable followed. My son-in-law and my two oldest sons were in Virginia. For a few months, my third son attended to his father's business at home, then he too

of Confederate Records, Record Group 109, NA, M267, roll 122, and M331, roll 139, hereafter cited as compiled service records, NA, with unit, state, or staff, and microfilm roll number. Jamison Family Collection, Orangeburg Archives. For D. F. Jamison's account of the bombardment of Fort Sumter see D. F. Jamison to Caroline Jenkins, April 14, 1861, Jenkins Papers, SCL.   D.F. Jamison's papers covering his tenure as secretary of war are located at Washington and Lee University.

[22]Burwood, the Jamison plantation, was located on the South Edisto River in the Barnwell District, South Carolina. Deed Book MM, 199-200, Barnwell County Court House.

[23]Brig. Gen. Micah Jenkins (1835-1864) was the son-in-law of Elizabeth Jamison. He married Jamison's eldest daughter, Caroline Harper Jamison (1837-1902), in 1856. John Peyre Thomas, *The Career and Character of General Micah Jenkins, C.S.A.* (Columbia: The State Company, 1903), 24.

[24]The Jamisons had thirteen "house servants" and seventy-four "field hands." Of this number three were carpenters and one was a blacksmith. D. F. Jamison Estate Records, Book J, 390, 391, 393, 394; Journal C, 473, Barnwell County Courthouse.

went off to the army, and I was left at home with my four young daughters and a younger son.[25] In '62 the fighting around Richmond was terrible, and hard was it to wait to hear the results of those battles. Many friends were struck down. Amongst the wounded was my second son who was shot in the chest as he was carrying orders across the field.[26] The shot passed across his chest touched his windpipe and one lung and lodged in his right shoulder blade from which place it was extracted the next day. An act of kindness from one who was only slightly acquainted with him I have always thought saved my son's life. When shot, he has told me, he felt a numbness and on looking down, his chest was covered with blood. Feeling weak, he thought he had best try to dismount rather than fall. He made the effort to get off but fell. [A]nother shot struck the horse he had been riding, which looked at his prostrate master a moment then galloped off. My son was then removed from the field and placed leaning against a tree. [A]t that moment the ball in his shoulder was struck and gave him intense pain for hours. The man whose act of kindness no doubt saved his life came by when the fighting ceased (my son's shoes and socks had been taken) this kindhearted man took off his own warm socks and shoes, put them on J[ohn]'s cold bare feet, placed himself back of J[ohn] and supported him during that long weary night of suffering. Had he been laid prostrate he must have suffocated from the bleeding wound so near his throat.[27] His father went on to nurse him, and for weeks he hovered between life and death, and when at length he was brought home, so changed and feeble it

[25]William Harper Jamison (1841-1887) served as a sergeant in Company B, Twenty-fifth South Carolina Infantry Regiment. He enlisted on February 24, 1862. William Harper Jamison, Compiled Service Records, NA, Twenty-fifth Infantry Regt., South Carolina, M267, roll 346. The children remaining at home were: Sallie Preston Jamison (1845-1894); Mary Dwight Jamison (1847-1904); Elizabeth Jamison (1849-1930); Thomas Worth Jamison (1852-1924); and Clara F. Jamison (1857-1942). Jamison Family Collection, Orangeburg Archives.

[26]Capt. John Wilson Jamison (1839-1886) was appointed aide-de-camp for his brother-in-law Brig. Gen. Micah Jenkins on August 11, 1862. He was wounded shortly thereafter on June 30, 1862, at the Battle of Frayser's Farm. He returned to active duty, but his position was "vacated" upon the death of Jenkins in 1864. He then was reassigned to Co. I, Third South Carolina Cavalry Regiment. Because of his war wounds, he was listed as disabled in December 1864. J. W. Jamison, Compiled Service Records, NA, Third Cavalry Regt., South Carolina, M267, roll 19, and staff, M331, roll 139.

[27]Captain Jamison related to his nephew, Robert F. Jenkins, his own account of this event as follows: "After my terrible wound and my horse killed under me, I was suffocating with blood welling out of my mouth. In charging over me one of the men seeing my condition, picked me up and lent me against a tree, and I was left with the dead and dying. A camp follower, one of the ghouls of the battlefields, was robbing

was almost hard to recognize him myself, and now, after twenty years, he is still often a great sufferer.[28]

Those were times sadly to be remembered, so full were they of anxiety for those who were going through those bloody battles. Almost daily we heard of the fall of relatives or friends. All this time, my third son had been on James Island guarding and trying to wait quietly. At length he was gratified by being in the battle of Secessionville. But his time was to come after awhile.

During these years and in the absence of masters, our colored people worked very much as usual, (a refutation in itself of the northern charges of overwork and unkindness) and made pretty fair crops.[29] We planted sugar cane and sorghum, and made syrup as most of our neighbors did. Some of them were successful in making very good sugar. The prices and scarcity of wearing apparel and groceries had become so great, that my husband sent some cotton bales through the blockading fleet to Nassau and had the cotton exchanged for groceries and dry goods. Our stockings, socks, and gloves, we knitted from homespun cotton yarn. The cotton got through safely and we received the goods in return. At length it became difficult to get salt. My husband and several of our neighbors agreed to send men with wagons mules boilers and all necessary articles for boiling salt from our salt water streams, but too far up in the country to be surprised by the enemy, and had a good quantity of the salt water boiled down into very good salt. After several weeks of fun, they returned home with each wagon laden with the salt.

During this time, the battles were more and more bloody. We heard constantly of friends who were killed, of others being wounded, and great and anxious fears filled the hearts of those at home. Many had to seek refuge in the northern parts of the State. Time passed on. The scene of war was in Tennessee. My son-in-law [Micah Jenkins]and my two oldest sons [David and John] were sent from Virginia through North and South Carolina to join in the battles that were expected to come off in Tennessee during the coming winter. They reached their destination in time for the battle of Chichamauga.[30]

---

the dead. I drew my pistol, intending to shoot him, but when he got to me I was too weak to lift my pistol up. He took the pistol out of my hand, and my watch, and robbed me." Charleston *News and Courier*, October 16, 1935.

   [28]Jamison arrived to attend to his son before July 8, 1862. Micah Jenkins to Caroline Jenkins, July 8, 1862, Micah Jenkins Papers, RBMSCL.

   [29]According to the estate records of D. F. Jamison contained in the Barnwell County Courthouse, the Jamisons had 87 slaves. D. F. Jamison Estate Records, Book J, 390, 391, 393, and 394; Journal C, 473, Barnwell County Courthouse.

   [30]Jenkin's brigade arrived at Chickamauga too late to participate in the battle. Natalie Jenkins Bond and Osmun Latrobe Coward, eds., *The South Carolinians: Colonel Asbury Coward's Memoirs* (New York: Vantage Press, 1968), 84.

From the date of their departure arose and continued the frightful anxieties of mothers wives and sisters. Desirous of news, yet fearful of its import, only a full reliance on the tender mercy of God could sustain the soul and calm the mind in times of peril such as those. It was about mid-winter that my son, who had returned to his duties too soon after his wound, was taken with a severe cough, and was sent home where he had to remain for some weeks.[31] By the time he was able to return, the army had got almost through to Virginia again. My son-in-law had been wounded again and again, though not seriously injured.[32] He was struck in his breast, the ball was turned from some cause, passed across to his arm and was extracted near his elbow.[33] Chance played some curious freaks in the manner in which he was so often struck in battle. In the first battle of Bull Run, his stirrup was struck off his foot.[34] In another fight he was struck on his knee by a spent ball, but not seriously hurt. At Chichamauga, a piece of shell cut into the bridge of his nose - an eighth of an inch more sight would have been destroyed. At the battle of the Wilderness, the ball penetrated his brain and a true hearted man, a real christian solder, a loving husband and father was taken to the "many mansions," where no doubt this warm hearted one now waits to welcome the loved ones he had to leave here to struggle through many weary years. He passed away May 6, 1864.[35]

That summer was full of anxious fears for the future. General Sherman was making his way into Georgia through Tennessee. The South had much hope in General Johnston as a Commander, but when he was removed from Atlanta, all hearts seemed to give way.

[31]Jamison was granted ninety days leave for the benefit of his health on December 19, 1862.

[32]Jenkins wrote of another incident during the Battle of Frayser's Farm: "My sword shot off with a grape, broken again by a ball, the sword knot cut by a ball, my saddle cloth cut by a ball, my horse shot under me twice, my overcoat, tied behind my saddle, cut in a dozen places with a shell, [and] I, hit upon the shoulder with a grape and upon the breast with a shell, am here to praise and bless him." Micah Jenkins to Caroline Jenkins, July 3, 1862, in Thomas, *The Career and Character of General Micah Jenkins*, 17.

[33]This occurred at the Battle of Second Manassas. See, Thomas, *The Career and Character of General Micah Jenkins*.

[34]Jenkins himself described how narrowly he escaped being wounded, saying, "Three men fell within five feet of me and a bullet knocked the stirrup from my foot." Micah Jenkins to Caroline Jenkins, July, 22, 1861, Micah Jenkins papers, SCL.

[35]For a detailed account of the life of Micah Jenkins see, James J. Baldwin III, *The Struck Eagle* (Shippensburg, Pa.: White Mane Publishing Co., 1996). *Charleston Courier*, May 17, 1864.

In August, my husband was sent to Tallahassee where he had to stay some weeks.[36] In that time a fatal fever was prevailing to a great extent. On his return he came home for one day. The day he returned to his duties in Charleston he was taken sick with a fever similar to that in Tallahassee, and in ten days he too was gone.[37] I did not know of his illness until it was all over.[38]

Previous to these sad events, my third son [William] had been in Virginia for some months. After a time he was in the trenches around Petersburg for weeks. It was a very hot summer, and he had at last to go to the hospital with a violent attack of fever, and there he lay a long time too ill to let us know where he was.[39] But at length he was found by a friend, a minister of the Presbyterian church and intimately acquainted with us all.[40]

[36]The territory for Jamison's judicial duties as presiding judge for Beauregard's Corps included Florida, Georgia, and South Carolina. *Charleston Mercury*, December 8, 1864.

[37]Jamison contracted yellow fever. Thomas, *The History of the South Carolina Military Academy*, 173; Charleston *News and Courier*, September 1, 1931, (describing his life and his death); *Charleston Mercury*, December 8, 1864. One macabre tale concerning Jamison's body relates that when Sherman invaded South Carolina, he announced that if found, the body of D. F. Jamison would be exhumed and burned upon a pyre with ex-slaves, Yankees, and the family being forced to watch. This would serve as retribution for Jamison's prominence as president of the South Carolina Secession Convention. To undermine Sherman's plans, Jamison's daughter Caroline, with the help of a servant, exhumed the body and buried it in a nearby swamp until the war ended. It was later returned to the Presbyterian Cemetery in Orangeburg where the grave remained unmarked until 1898. Statement of John Wilson Jamison, in the possession of John A. Jamison, Fredericksburg, VA.

[38]Jamison died on September 14, 1864, in Charleston. His body was transported to Orangeburg, South Carolina, by rail where it was interred in the Presbyterian Cemetery. William Gilmore Simms served as one of his pallbearers. *Charleston Mercury*, September 15, 1864; *Charleston Courier*, September 16, 1864; *Charleston Courier*, September 15, 1864; *Charleston Courier*, September 26, 1864; *Charleston Mercury*, December 8, 1864.

[39]William Jamison's compiled service records reveal that he was absent from his unit from June 29, 1863, until February 3, 1864, due to sickness. Compiled Service Records, NA, Co. B., Twenty-fifth Infantry Regt., South Carolina, M267, roll 346.

[40]This person was probably Benjamin Morgan Palmer, a noted Presbyterian minister who conducted the wedding ceremony of Micah Jenkins and Caroline Jamison. Palmer was pastor of a Presbyterian church in Columbia and counseled troops in the Army of Northern Virginia. The Reverend Benjamin M. Palmer to Caroline Jenkins, May 25, 1864, in Thomas, *The Career and Character of General Micah Jenkins*, 22; John M. Wells, *Presbyterian Worthies* (Richmond: Presbyterian Committee on Publication, 1936), 140-180.

This friend, feeling sure he could not recover where he then was, got him sent on home.[41] For some weeks he was very sick indeed, but returned to his company by the time his furlough expired.

The northern army came nearer and nearer almost weekly. I was aroused from sleep one night by many steps apparently of men coming up the steps of the front piazza. Of course I thought the Yankees had come in reality for a few moments, but soon I heard goats bleating, and knew some one had left a gate open and those animals had walked in.[42] It was a very great relief. We had these sort of frights very often about that time, but every time our men were very willing to come to our relief and always endeavored to find out the cause of our fright.

Another time as I was waiting for a girl to come in, as she usually slept in my daughters' room. I always locked the house at that time myself. I heard her talking at the well which was near the house. I leaned out of the window and said I wished her to come in as I was suffering with my head and wished to go to bed. She came in on the piazza and said "A man is under the house and won't come out." I stept [sic] on the piazza and said "Come out or go away whoever you are." There was no answer and I thought he was one of our own young negro men who was trying to frighten this girl. As I was locking the back door a large white man came from under the house and looked in the side lights at me. I walked upstairs and straight on to the piazza, and called to a woman whose house was just out of the yard, and asked her to tell the men at quarters to surround the house which they did almost as I spoke. Of course he had time to get to the woods just back of the yard. The men looked carefully but found no one. Next morning one of our men told me a Yankee soldier had come to his house in the night and told him to get our carriage horses for him. He told this man the horses were locked up, and he had nothing to do with them.

The enemy had come over the Savannah river burning houses and destroying stock. The day we were told about sunset that they were near, only a few miles off. A family who lived very near us sent a message to go with them into the fork of the Edisto [River] as they knew a gentleman living there would let us go into a large empty gin house he had there as well as other houses that he had. We packed up some valuables and clothing took horses and mules wagons and carriage and joined our friends at their gate.

---

[41] According to family correspondence, William was still quite sick in December 1863. D.F. Jamison wrote: "I regret to say that William's health improves very slowly. Since he has been with me here, he has had return of chills and fevers about every 9 to 14 days." D. F. Jamison to Caroline Jenkins, December 14, 1863, Jenkins Collection, SCL.

[42] The Jamison estate records indicate that in 1864, the family owned a herd of eight goats. D. F. Jamison Estate Records, Book J, 390, 391, 393 and 394; Journal C, 473, Barnwell County Courthouse.

We left our home near midnight. Some of our men got lightwood torches and walked before and some behind the cavalcade. We had a beautiful little colt and its mother along and they kept up a constant whinnying to each other, enlivening the way. We crossed the South Edisto a little while before day, and then waited for the morning light, preferring trying not to intrude so early on our unsuspecting neighbours. When we did make our appearance they were not a little surprised at seeing us, but would not hear of our going into any house but the one they were in, and we must wait until the two gentleman should go out and ascertain the truth of the report we had heard of. During the day we often looked in the direction of our homes, for smoke, as our houses were large. We knew we must see smoke. We saw nothing of that, though. In the course of a few hours our kind hostess had a beautiful dinner for us and all our servants. Then the gentlemen returned and told us it was a false alarm and we might safely go back to our homes, which we did, arriving there at night fall.

The autumn of '64 passed in constant anxiety. At length my son came home troubled with his wound and a cough. Very soon we knew there was truth in the report that the enemy had got as far as Pocotaligo and we felt we must leave our dear home in reality.[43] Had I known then what I knew afterwards, I would have stayed at home and let them burn, if they would. Now that the enemy were so near as Pocotaligo, the men were frequently on our place, as our servants very often told us so. We accepted an invitation from a relative of my husband to go up the country and stay with his family.[44] We took provisions of different kinds, also our mules and horses, for our friend had lost some of his by the very high freshet of that winter, known since as the Sherman freshet, as it came on as he was passing through the State.[45] After burning Columbia General Sherman seemed inclined to go on to Charlotte in North Carolina.[46] Perhaps the constant rains, that kept the roads so boggy and the rivers so high, might have induced him to cut across into the eastern portion of South Carolina. Before Columbia was given to the flames, my home and that of my oldest son too were ashes.[47] I had one

[43]Sherman left Pocotaligo on February 1, 1864.

[44]Undoubtedly, this person was Isaac Delessline Wilson of Society Hill, South Carolina. He was D. F. Jamison's second cousin.

[45]I. D. Wilson had lost the animals. In 1865 Simms wrote: "Six of my mules I propose, as the enemy demonstrates, to send over to Col. I. D. Wilson, at Society Hill who has offered to work them and feed them." William Gilmore Simms to William Gilmore Simms, Jr., January 16, 1865, in *The Letters of William Gilmore Simms*, Vol. IV (Columbia: University of South Carolina Press 1956), 481.

[46]Columbia was burned on February 17, 1865.

[47]David Rumph Jamison owned the adjoining plantation next to Burwood. Orangeburg *Southron*, March 14, 1860. Completed in 1861 shortly before D.F. Jamison's death, Burwood plantation had fourteen rooms. Innis L. Jenkins, "A Sketch of General David F. Jamison," Master's Thesis, University of South Carolina, 1927, 37.

hundred and thirty (130) bales of cotton, and a gin house packed with seed cotton — all were burned, but it matters not now that everything was gone, except a few of the servants' houses in your yard, and most of the negro quarters were left standing.[48] My son's home shared the same fate.

I was anxious to flank the enemy by going through Marion to a ferry I knew had been over the Congaree river, but was told the flat was burnt. A lady friend who was with us wished to go into Marlboro to a place of hers, and we tried to do so. We crossed the Pee Dee at Society Hill and spent a night in a house in the swamp near the river. Our men were all around too, trying to get on into North Carolina. The river was very high and still rising rapidly. The weather was very cold. We slept on blankets and comforts spread on the floor. There were fifteen of us, and some of our male friends, who hearing where we were, joined our party. The next afternoon, hearing the enemy were crossing the river, we left that house and in wagons started for the place of our friend who was with us. As night came on, it began to rain, and was very dark. I was a stranger in that part of the country.

We came to a large house a little back from the road. Our friend said "Here is Uncle S[amuel's].[49] Let's give them a call." And we did go to their door. That gentleman's daughter (whose husband had, only a short time before been killed in battle in Virginia) insisted we should get out and stay with them.[50] We did conclude to stay that night. But when morning came men wagons mules and horses all were gone, and it was some weeks before we could get back over the Pee Dee river.[51] The old gentleman and his kind

[48]The Jamison estate records indicate that in 1864 the family had 15,000 pounds of cotton worth approximately $1,500. D. F. Jamison Estate Records, Book J, 390, 391, 393 and 394; Journal C, 473, Barnwell County Courthouse.

[49]This person is Samuel Sparks (March 21, 1787-September 19, 1878). Sparks was a large planter who owned plantations in Marlboro County, South Carolina. One was located at Mineral Springs, and the other, Mandeville, was located in the Welsh Neck. Elizabeth probably was referring to Mandeville, which was the Sparks's winter residence. See, Chalmers G. Davidson, *The Last Foray —The South Carolina Planters of 1860: A Sociological Study* (Columbia: University of South Carolina Press, 1971), 213-14; See also, J. A. W. Thomas, *A History of Marlboro County: with Traditions and Sketches of Numerous Families* (Atlanta: Foote and Davies, 1897), 34.

[50]Susanna Mandeville Sparks (1834-1915) was Samuel Sparks's daughter. Ibid. Lawrence Massillon Keitt (1824-1864) was the husband of Susanna Sparks Keitt. Keitt served in the United States Congress and was a member of the South Carolina Secession Convention. He was appointed colonel of the Twentieth South Carolina Infantry Regiment in 1862, and was killed at Cold Harbor in 1864. Faunt and May, *South Carolina Secedes*, 168-69.

[51]During the early spring the Pee Dee River rises until it is almost unfordable. During these freshets, the water covers low-lying areas, cutting off Society Hill from Marlboro County.

hearted wife and daughter made all welcome that came to their house, and by dinner time they had a long table to fill.[52] All assembled around the bountifully loaded table. Several of our soldiers were there, and amongst them was my son (who had come in from his company on sick leave being still troubled from his wound) and the son of the old man at whose house we were staying.[53] Some females with their children were there too, near neighbours, who were afraid to stay alone at their homes. We were about to take up knife and fork, when in bounded a negro man calling out "The road black with the Yankee da jus coming down the hill." Everyone ran for the piazza, and sure enough the hill was covered with moving creatures that we all thought were men and horses. Our men were standing waiting for their horses. Kindhearted Mrs. L[awrence Keitt] came to where my son and I were standing together, and was just opening his overcoat pocket to drop in it a nice lunch when he turned quickly, bid me good-bye, and was gone.[54] The lunch fell on the floor. They were all gone. We then turned to look up the hill for the "Yankees." The creatures had come closer, close enough now for us to see. They were sheep and hogs being driven to a more secure place in the swamp.[55] It made us all laugh, but it was not a matter to laugh over long. We had no appetites for our dinner, for if we had just laughed we could not eat for our hearts were too anxious about our friends to feel hunger. We had heard the enemy took some little boys the size of my youngest son and carried them off and turned them loose in the swamp. Fearing they might take off my little son I had let him go into the woods with a wounded friend who had to go in a buggy, not being able to mount a horse.

We could not go to bed that night, but sat together or reclined on lounges, as we could not feel safe to take other nest. After breakfast the morning after our gentlemen friends had left us so unceremoniously, we all walked out on the piazza and were saying to each other how glad we would be to hear some news as to where the Yankees were, when two men on horseback and two others walking before them, turned in the front gate. The two on horses stopt [sic] a little at the gate. The men walked to the inner gate of the yard where we were standing. They were near neighbors.

Mrs. [Keitt] asked "What news of the Yankees?"

One man replied "Those two men are Yankees. We are prisoners."

Just then both men rode up to us.

[52]Ann Harry Sparks (June 22, 1793 -November 13, 1870) was Samuel Sparks's second wife. Thomas, *A History of Marlboro County*, 34.

[53]The son referred to is John Jamison. Captain Alexander D. Sparks (1825-1895) was Sparks's son. Thomas, *A History of Marlboro County*, 34.

[54]Elizabeth Jamison writes "L" ostensibly, so that Mrs. Keitt will not be easily identified. "Lawrence" was Mrs. Keitt's husband's Christian name.

[55]Thomas Worth Jamison, Elizabeth's youngest son was twelve in 1865. Jamison Family Collection, Orangeburg Archives.

One said "Good morning ladies. What do you think of your cause now?"

Mrs. [Keitt] answered "General Lee will tell you, when you reach North Carolina."

"General Lee has surrendered" this solder said.

There was an exclamation of disbelief.

He said again, "It is so and President Lincoln has been assassinated."

We could not believe it all. But alas, it was only too true.[56]

Just then men came pouring in from every quarter ransacking every nook and corner in house, yard, and garden. They found out from the colored people where everything was: what they did not want they destroyed. The house was crowded for hours.

In my restless anxiety I walked on the piazza. A soldier was on a large white horse at the gate. The man was very drunk. Our kind hearted old host was near the gate. That horse was a fine young animal he had raised.

The soldier called "Come here old man, and put my foot in the stirrup."

The gentleman bowed, and quietly said "I will do no such thing, sir."

His wife came out just then too.

The man said to her "Give me some whiskey."

She answered "I have no whiskey and if I had I would not give it to you."

He said "If you do not give me whiskey I will burn your house."

Again she answered "I have no whiskey ."

When he tried to get off to carry out his threat he could not so he sat still.

At this juncture a large squad rode in, several hundred, all drunk, all with bottles. They had found some old liquors that were near, from the low country, sent to that neighborhood for safe-keeping. The first set had sacked well but they were sober. The sober ones had our dinner brought in and sat down and ate it. While they were at dinner three others went down into the cellar where they found a jug containing whiskey as they thought from its looks. One came back for a tumbler directly. All three came in hurriedly walked to Mr. S[parks] and asked what was in that jug.

He said, "It is camphine.[57] We have it for burning in lamps. It is distilled from turpentine."

The man asked "Will it kill me?"

Mr. S[parks] "I don't know. As I said we burn it, never drink it."

---

[56]Sherman's foragers reached nearby Society Hill, South Carolina, as early as March 30, 1865. Mason Smith and Daniel F. Huger, eds., *Mason Smith Family Letters: 1860-1868* (Columbia: University of South Carolina Press, 1950), 84-85.

[57]"Camphine" is a purified oil of turpentine made by distilling the oil over quicklime to free it from resin.

Soldier, "Do you think if I go back to camp and take a dose of oil it will save me?"

Mr. S[parks], "I don't know, it may or it may not. That is what you get for prowling away where that you have no business to go."

We ladies glanced at each other rather amused than sympathetic. He said he drank a tumbler full without stopping, so sure was he that it was whiskey. We heard no more of him.

Before those men all left, a Capt. Guthrie rode into the yard, and handed a set of rubies to the younger lady of the house. He had taken it from one of his men. She thanked him, and asked how she should keep it. He said "Put it on." No one attempted to take it again. Two men remained until after night they said to guard the house. But we knew they were waiting to see if my son and the young Capt. S[parks]. would not come in. Just as those men were going out of the lower gate, my son rode in. One man said ["] Here is Capt. Norris now." Instantly my son determined to personate [sic] Capt. Norris. It was a clear but not a bright night. My son was riding a white horse. Capt. Norris was about my son's size and he also rode a white horse. My son demanded of them roughly, what they were doing there? They told him they were guarding the house. He then ordered them to go immediately to camp. They told him they did not know the way. They were to go to Bennettsville. My son gave directions to Bennettsville, told them where to turn off from the road and what other turns to take. But [he] had never been there himself. He then came to the house — the men rode off for camp.

I was in the hall and said, "J[ohn] those men have been waiting for you for hours. My son I fear they will come back."

He said "Yes, I met them at the gate, and they took me for their Capt. Norris. Mother, can I lie down a little? I am very tired, and suffering very much."

I said to him "[C]ome upstairs and rest on my bed."

He said "No, not upstairs." He said he had been a prisoner, to probably the same company for some hours.

The kind old gentleman came to us and directed him to an out house filled with cotton seed, but asked him to come in and eat first, but he said he was too much fatigued. He had been taken prisoner by the Capt. Guthrie who had that morning returned the set of rubies to Mrs. [Keitt]. My son and Capt. S[parks] had been together and had hid their horses in a thicket in the swamp.[58] Capt. Norris was the man who had ordered by my house burnt.

---

[58]Alexander Sparks served in Company E of the Nineteenth South Carolina Cavalry Battalion. He also served in Company L, Twentieth South Carolina Infantry Regiment. Compiled Service Records, NA, Nineteenth Batt. Cavalry, South Carolina, M267, roll 53; Twentieth Infantry Regt., South Carolina, M267, roll 316.

I asked him if it was burnt? [A]nd he said the house of a widow lady was burnt. He patted my little daughter on her head as she ran carelessly about. Before my son went to the cotton seed house, he told me he and Capt. S[parks] were walking through a newly ploughed field when they saw some of the enemy, who called ordering them to come to them. J[ohn] did not know the country around or the field. The other who did know only slipt [sic] into a ditch and was hid. J[ohn] had to walk to the fence, and over the ploughed ground and leant against the fence.

He was then questioned "Why do you walk so slow?"

["]Can't help it. [A]m just recovering from a severe wound am at home on sick leave.["]

["]Where is your Physician's Certificate?["]

He produced it. The Captain read it and told him to come over the fence. He did so. He had on horseman's boots and spurs. The men took his spurs and were about taking his boots off when he appealed to the Captain, who ordered them to let him alone.

The Captain then asked "[W]here is the man who was with him when they first saw them?"

J[ohn] said "He lives in this neighborhood and is far off in that swamp by this time. I am a stranger here or you would not have caught me."

Captain said "Well, come on to camp."

[B]ut said J[ohn] "I can't keep up with you."

Captain ordered a horse to be given him. They gave him an old mule, and offered him a drink, which he took moderately as he was tired and they had a plenty of that "old liquor" and he saw a probable chance of getting away as they became more and more under the influence of their brandy. They offered their bottles frequently to him and rode on faster, calling, "Come on Johnnie Reb." They came to a turn in the road, and "Johnnie Reb" rode off briskly far into the thick swamp tied the mule securely and got his own horse and came back to me. From all this it will be understood my son had a slim chance of getting off again should he be taken a second time. This conversation was overheard by a servant who immediately sent off and informed where he was.

Several hours later I and the wife of Capt. S[parks] were in a room near the back door. She putting her baby to sleep, I sitting on a pallet on the floor by my little daughter who was sleeping quietly. My other daughters and one cousin of theirs were sleeping on beds in the room. The night was dark but clear. We heard a rushing sound, as it came nearer, we knew more than a dozen men on horses were coming at full speed. They came right through the yard and for the cotton seed house. [where Capt. Jamison was spending the night] Mrs. S[parks] exclaimed, "Capt. J[amison], they are after him." I went out on the back piazza but could only hear horses running. At last that sound ceased. I listened for a pistol shot, feeling sure they would shoot him, but heard nothing more. How could I know they had not used something worse than a pistol shot? I went into the house at last and sat by my little child 'til day.[59] We heard no news all the next day. Is a wonder my head was almost white after that night of agony? All this time I had heard nothing of my little son. The next night Capt. S[parks] came in. He promised he would try to find my son the next day. They all did come in on the next afternoon. My son had heard them coming for him just in time to untie his horse and mount him, took a path that carried him into a corner between two fences. They saw and pursued him. As he was just about to abandon his horse, they turned off on another path and left him. But what a relief it was when they all came in, my little son and all!

The northern army had gone into North Carolina. My oldest son [David] was in Virginia with Gen. Lee's army.[60] My third son [William] was in North Carolina in those battles that were fought in that State. I heard nothing of him for a long time. I was very often walking on the road in the hope of hearing of my sons through men who were returning to their families and homes. I inquired of them for news from my two sons. At length, a man gave me a slip of paper—only a line or two from my third son, saying he was well. Then several months passed without any more news of either son. My brother too, had been taken prisoner not very far from Society Hill, although the enemy had surrendered, they carried him north and kept him prisoner until the next fall.[61] He was then released to return to his home.

In April '65 we began to make preparations to get back to our dear old home. We heard that the bridges over the Wateree at Camden, and the Congaree near Columbia were both burnt, but there were flats at those rivers. We had one wagon left. My son J[ohn] had saved his horse. [A] friend's servant rode off on one of our carriage horses when our gentleman friends had to leave us to hide in the swamp. That servant had brought the horse back to us. One mule came back to the horses she knew, and a mule

[59]Clara F. Jamison was six at the time. Jamison Family Collection, Orangeburg Archives.

[60]David Rumph Jamison surrendered with Lee at Appomattox on April 9, 1865, as a member of the same brigade that Brig. Gen. Micah Jenkins had commanded prior to his death. Bond and Coward, eds., *The South Carolinians*, 169-170.

[61]David Jamison Rumph (1811-1872) served as colonel of the Fifteenth South Carolina Militia Regiment. He changed his surname from Rumph to Rumff because he was tired of being the butt of jokes. Compiled Service Records, NA, Fifteenth Militia Regt., South Carolina, M267, roll 392. Louise Frederick Hays, *The Rumph and Frederick Families* (Atlanta: J. T. Hancock, 1942), 62.

Burwood plantation, Elizabeth Jamison's home, which Union soldiers burned in 1865. Illustration courtesy of the author.

belonging to a near neighbor who lived near our old home came to us also and we thought our friend would like to get his mule.[62] So, took the mule to his owner, as his others were all taken off, he was glad to get that one.

A relative of my husband, and a kind friend of us, as he proved himself to be, lent us a wagon and a half grown colored boy to drive, hired a white man to go with us, and return with his wagon.[63] This kind friend gave us cooked food and everything necessary for ourselves, and servants. [W]e had three with us beside the boy he sent. Also food for our animals. I can never forget the kindness and sympathy of that friend. The night after we left his house we camped at Lynches creek. My son, the white man and servants wrapped their overcoats around them, and lay by a large lightwood fire. [O]ccasionally one would get up and lay on more wood. My daughters slept well in the wagon. I alone could not get comfortable enough to sleep.

[62]In 1864, prior to this event, the Jamisons owned eight mules, two horses, one mare, and three wagons. D. F. Jamison Estate Records, Book J, 390, 391, 393 and 394; Journal C, 473, Barnwell County Courthouse.

[63]Isaac D. Wilson (1810-1889) was probably this kind friend. He was the second cousin of D. F. Jamison. His children, Isaac D. Wilson, Jr., married Sallie Preston Jamison and Elizabeth Caroline Wilson married William Harper Jamison, daughter and son of Elizabeth Jamison. May and Faunt, *South Carolina Secedes*, 227-28.

At last, I took a large blanket wrapt [sic] it around me went to the fire and lay my head on a large root of a pine tree for my pillow. My little son came to me. I covered him with the blanket, then we were all quiet until day. The blanket was as wet with dew as if it had rained heavily on us. The servants got us breakfast (they all could cook) and fed our animals, and we started for Camden. We were traveling the road the Yankees had taken from Columbia. Burnt houses, burnt fences and the skeleton of a horse were often passed. A cow or any domestic animal were scarce in truth. We reached Camden in time to cross the Wateree river before night. Such a crossing as it was! It was so near being a perpendicular bank to get up after crossing, as it was possible for it to be. There were a good many Confederate soldiers, who were returning home at the ferry, and negroes in any number. All turned and kindly helped get our wagons up. I don't see how we could have got up that river bank but for their assistance. We camped about a mile from the river. The roads were very heavy and the hills very high. One other night we were on the road, the fourth day, we dined in poor burnt up Columbia at a colored woman's house. She had been one of our house servants. Her husband's mother was a free woman, so her son was freeborn. Both mother and son were real good people and the one who had been one of our servants was a great favorite with us all. My son rode on to let her know we were coming. She got us as good a dinner as could be had there then. I asked her if she could get anything with Confederate money. She said she could get provisions and homespun. I then gave her some of that, for I had no other. One of the daughters went on with us. She, the mother went to the river to see us cross the Congaree river which was very little better than the crossing at the Wateree.

We arrived at our home on the 30th of May, 1865. That morning in passing through a town on our way, we met my oldest son. We had not heard of him before, since the surrender. He too was on his way home. It was very sad to see our beautiful home gone, only the chimneys and the underpinning left.[64] Palings and fences all burnt. We had a good orchard, and it was, well, it was well that it was a good fruit year, for at times, that summer, there was little else to eat. As everything that could be destroyed on the place was gone. Everything that I tried to save by sending it off was found and destroyed by our prying visitors whether at home or abroad, except a few articles I had intrusted [sic] to our hostess in Columbia. As soon

---

[64]Writing some fifty years later, William Gilmore Simms, Jr. described the ruins of Burwood in the following poetic manner: "General Jamison had built an elegant home upon his splendid plantation . . . and in Sherman's devastating march, house, stable, barns and hundreds of bales of cotton all perished, and where the happy household stood, the stars looked down on roofless walls." *The State*, December 18, 1910.

as the railroad was repaired she sent what she had been able to save down to me. The coloured people were no longer disposed to work. Some of ours were on the place, though many had left, and wandered about us if to show their independence, though in rags and often in want of food. One woman with eight children wanted me to take her and her family for her services. That was impossible as it was sufficiently difficult to find food for my own children. Col. Beecher and his coloured troops were stationed some six miles above and some ten miles below us. They were constantly about trying to excite those who would otherwise have been quiet, to insubordination. Murders and other outrages were committed, but no inquiries were made.

Often firearms were fired across our yard at nights. I and my daughters occupied a house in the yard, and my sons slept in another near by — two houses of some of our former house servants that had escaped the burning. My son told me never to open our door in the night for either calling or knocking, unless one of them spoke to me.

Several families not far off who were not disturbed by the northern raiders and had saved their provisions very kindly sent us food in the shape of corn, bacon and other provisions, for we were entirely destitute of all such things. One old lady friend sent some hens and other poultry to give us a start in that line. As soon as it was possible my sons commenced building a log cabin of four rooms. A neighbor told my sons he had sank some rafts in the Edisto river during the war, when he could no longer get them into Charleston. The rafts were near our landing, and he gave them to us. My sons dived for the lumber day after day, and managed to get boards in that way to floor our rooms. They even put a piazza to our cabin. My oldest son put in a log cabin also, and thus we lived and toiled on hoping for better times.

POSTSCRIPT

Better times were not to come to the Jamison family. In 1866 William Gilmore Simms wrote the following of Elizabeth and her family's plight: "She has lost every thing [sic], and with some ten children, now lives in a log house through which the winds and rains make their way."[65]

In 1869 a Charleston factor claimed that prior to the war, D. F. Jamison had owed him $800.00. Although before his death Jamison had told his wife that he owed nothing, she could not prove that she had satisfied this claim

---

[65]William Gilmore Simms to Everett Augustus Duychinck, February 20, 1866, in *The Letters of William Gilmore Simms*, Vol. IV (Columbia: University of South Carolina Press, 1956), 539.

as Sherman's men destroyed all receipts. As a result, Burwood was partitioned and sold for $1200.00.[66] Simms remarked of this event as follows: "The Jamison Estate is to be sold for debt! Eheu! It will be divided into tracts of some 3 to 500 acres and each and will be sold low, just at this juncture. Another year, it will bring five times as much."[67]

Elizabeth, evicted from her plantation, was forced to rely upon the charity of others as the following letter, which Elizabeth wrote to Simms, suggests:

> Mr. Elsey has just sent me word to haul my things as soon as possible tomorrow morning. As you so kindly said you would haul them for me, I send Mikey over at once to let you know.[68] If it is not convenient for you to get a driver, I can get one here, and send over early in the morning for your wagon and team. I do dislike to give so much trouble to you and feel much indebted to you.[69]

After the loss of Burwood, Elizabeth's younger children went to live with various members of the family. In contrast to the family's practice during the antebellum years, none received a higher education.[70] Elizabeth eventually moved to Summerville, South Carolina, to live with her son John and daughter Caroline. In 1874, she wrote her son: "John the girls have not a dollar in the wide world neither have I anything to give them to pay that tax.... If the charge must be paid, what are we to do for the girls have only their poor clothes that they work for — everything has been sold from us."[71] The amount of money, which caused Elizabeth such concern, was $17.14. Her children fared little better. David, her eldest son, lost his only child in 1871 and moved to Florida to grow oranges. After a disastrous frost, he returned to South Carolina bankrupt. When he died in 1908, he was buried in an unmarked grave near to those of his parents.[72]

[66]Jenkins, "A Sketch of General David F. Jamison," Master's Thesis, 1927, 36; Deeds showing the transfer of land in Deed Book YY, 107-116, Barnwell County Courthouse.

[67]William Gilmore Simms to William Hawkins Ferris, Nov. 16, 1869. *The Letters of William Gilmore Simms*, Vol. V, 267.

[68]Micah Jenkins, Jr., (1857-1912) who was Elizabeth's grandson.

[69]Elizabeth C. Jamison to William Gilmore Simms, December 17, 1869, William H. Ferris Collection, Columbia University Library.

[70]U.S., Bureau of the Census, *Ninth Census of the United States, 1870: Population*, 1: 272, Middle Township, South Carolina, showing that none of the Jamison children attended school the previous year.

[71]Elizabeth C. Jamison to John W. Jamison, Dec. 20, 1874, original in the possession of Albert L. Jamison, Boerne, Texas.

[72]David R. Jamison to David F. Jamison, August 4, 1899, original in the possession of Albert L. Jamison, Boerne, TX; Thomas, *Historical Sketch of the South Carolina*

Caroline Jenkins, her eldest daughter, was a twenty-seven-year-old widow when the war ended, and faced the daunting task of raising four small boys with practically no income. Utilizing the superior education her father had given her, she tutored young girls and operated boarding houses in Charleston and Summerville. Each of her four sons was educated in Yorkville at the Kings Mountain Military School; two were graduated from West Point. In early February 1902 Caroline completed a visit to her youngest son John, who was serving as an instructor at the United States Military Academy. On her way home to Charleston to visit her grandson, she was stricken with an illness and died alone in Washington, DC. Her body was taken to Magnolia Cemetery in Charleston, where she was buried in an unmarked grave next to her husband, General Micah Jenkins. She was sixty-four years old, and although considered a great beauty in her day, had never remarried.

John and William, Elizabeth's other two sons who fought during the war, also faced a world which no longer had a place for them. Both married and had several children. John taught school in Camden, while William tried farming in Society Hill, South Carolina. Both died before their mother, in their middle forties. Both left small children to be raised by their widows.[73] In Elizabeth's personal Bible is a somber reminder of John — an envelope with a withered ivy leaf. On the flap Elizabeth wrote: "This leaf came off the wreath that was on my son John's chest, his sister brought it to me."[74]

D.F. Jamison's fate was to be largely forgotten by a state to which he devoted much of his life, and he would rest in an unmarked grave for over thirty-five years. Finally, in 1897, a group of friends raised enough money to erect a small monument of South Carolina granite over his grave.[75] On this stone they wrote the following tribute:

General David Flavel Jamison
Soldier, Statesman, Scholar
Erected By His Friends
Born in Orange Parish, December 14, 1810
Died in Charleston, September 14, 1864
President of the Secession Convention

Military Academy, 263; Jamison Family Collection, Orangeburg Archives; Orangeburg *Times and Democrat,* January 31, 1908.

[73]Statements of John A. Jamison, Fredericksburg, VA, grandson of William H. Jamison, and Albert L. Jamison, Boerne, TX., grandson of John W. Jamison. *South Carolina Historical Magazine* 67 (January 1966), 42.

[74]Elizabeth Jamison's Bible is in the possession of David J. Rutledge, Spartanburg, SC.

[75]The attempt to erect a monument took many years. See, Orangeburg *Times,*

Elizabeth would survive her husband by many years. As she slipped into old age, she moved to Charleston. Aided by her daughter Bessie, she lived in poverty in a succession of progressively smaller apartments. Although Elizabeth Jamison was stripped of all that she had been born to expect (wealth, social standing, and security), she refused to become bitter or embroiled in self-pity. Her spirit is perhaps best exemplified by the following letter she wrote to her daughter Caroline near the close of her life:

My Dear Daughter:

I am very much troubled that you feel so weak and feel so badly. Dear daughter, God has taken care of us all and especially has He taken care of Bessie and me in all our trials, sickness, poverty and too much else to enumerate year after year. You know He has promised to take care of the fatherless and the widow"Leave your fatherless children I will preserve them alive, and let your widows trust in me.' Bessie bears up wonderfully - better far better in all her great pain than I do.[76] Did He not know these are the very trials we need. He would not send us so much of sorrow. He sees the end - we only the present. Try to think my own precious child that He only sends what He knows is for our eternal good. Don't you know that pride must be pretty well killed out of me? Many ladies have been very kind and thoughtful of us. I am thankful -you can imagine that I am. Often has cooked food been sent to us.... All have been very kind to us. Mrs. Jenkins is very pleasant and nice and often sends us delicacies we cannot even think of. . . . Dear daughter don't give up to troubles, try for the sake of the boys to be cheerful and pray to bear up under all that our God thinks it best to send on you. . . .[77]

Elizabeth Jamison died after a long illness on December 11, 1888, her wedding anniversary. She was buried next to her husband in the Old Presbyterian Churchyard in Orangeburg, South Carolina. On her tombstone she is remembered as the "Wife of David F. Jamison." Perhaps, her "Tale of the War" and her spirit serve as her most lasting memorials.

April 24, 1872; Charleston *News and Courier*, November 15, 1892; Orangeburg *Times and Democrat*, September 1, 1897; September 25, 1897; October 20, 1897. See also *Orangeburg Observer* July 19, 1935.

[76] "Bessie" is Elizabeth Jamison, the daughter of David and Elizabeth Jamison.

[77] Elizabeth Jamison to Caroline Jenkins, May 31, 1885, John Jenkins papers, SCL.

"ROBBING THE OWNER OR SAVING THE PROPERTY FROM DESTRUCTION?"

Paintings in the Middleton Place House

Edited by HARRIOTT CHEVES LELAND and HARLAN GREENE *

On February 22/23, 1865, Middleton Place, 15 miles up the Ashley River from Charleston, was plundered and burned. Several months later a number of boxes of paintings, books, and other items were removed from sundry caches on the plantation.

A diary of Dr. Henry Orlando Marcy of Cambridgeport, Massachusetts, and his correspondence with Williams Middleton of Middleton Place and Charleston were used to piece together this 100 year old story.

Williams Middleton (1809-1883), sixth son of Henry and Mary Hering Middleton, was born at Sullivan's Island near Charleston and was educated in England and Paris. He spent several years in Russia as an attaché with the American Legation. Middleton returned to Middleton Place about 1830. He was a member of the Secession Convention and in 1860 signed the Ordinance of Secession, helping to destroy the Union which his grandfather Arthur Middleton, signer of the Declaration of Independence, had helped create.[1]

Dr. Henry Orlando Marcy (1837-1924) became quite prominent after the Civil War, serving as president of both the American Academy of Medicine and the American Medical Association. He is credited with having introduced Joseph Lister's method of antiseptic wound treatment to America. During the Civil War, Marcy participated in the seige of Charleston and was medical director on Sherman's staff for the Carolina Campaign.[2] In the aftermath he participated in the general clean-up of Charleston.[3]

---

* Ms. Leland is Director of Research for the Middleton Place Foundation, Middleton Place, Charleston, South Carolina. Mr. Greene is a part-time staff member of the South Carolina Historical Society.

[1] All genealogical information about the Middleton family is taken from Langdon Cheves, "Middleton of South Carolina," *SCHGM,* I (1900), 228-262.

[2] *The Dictionary of American Biography (DAB),* XII, 273; *Who Was Who in America (WWW),* I, 776.

[3] Concerning this he wrote, "We detailed a force of 500 men, impressed into the service such transportation as we could procure, and, under a personal inspection of the medical staff, a house-to-house cleaning was carried on with scrupulous care, inspection of the water supply and sewage being rigidly conducted. We left the

The following article consists of excerpts from Dr. Marcy's diary and autobiography and of the original letters from Marcy to Middleton and pencil copies in Middleton's handwriting of letters evidently sent to Marcy, as well as several related letters.[4]

Middleton Place, now a Registered National Historic Landmark, was acquired by Henry Middleton (1717-1784) in 1741. Henry, a member and president of the First Continental Congress, left the plantation to his son Arthur (1742-1787), signer of the Declaration of Independence. It then passed to his grandson Henry (1770-1846), Governor of South Carolina and United States Minister at the Court of St. Petersburg. Williams Middleton inherited Middleton Place from his father Henry. The Middleton Place Foundation, established in 1975, is a non-profit, public foundation which administers the Middleton Place House and serves as a repository for Middleton family items.

Diary: February 23, 1865: We send out four or five detachments for guns left in the various forts, some of which will be absent for two days. We send out a foraging party under Capt. Armstrong. I accompany with Freeman and one of orderlies. We get strayed away on the start and lose an hour, then we are overtaken by Maj. Smith and a party of 56 th N[ew] Y[ork] V[olunteers] who orders the party to camp because they are on the road which he is ordered to explore. The Capt. submits more tamely than usual and returns. With my orderlies I push on for the Middleton place on the Ashley River.

When near the place met with an incident which came near putting a permanent end to my scouting. I was riding at a gentle gallop with my orderlies close behind—on a sharp lookout—for in this country one never knows when or where he may meet guerillas—when I heard the sharp click of gun locks and about fifty feet from me protruded two rifles from a thicket. I expected momentarily that they would fire but saw it useless to attempt to retreat and drew my revolver, when out stepped two men of the 34 th U. S. C[olored] T[roops]. The men were almost overcome with their emotions. They were just about firing when

---

city of Charleston more thoroughly sanitary, perhaps, than it has been at any time before or since." Henry Orlando Marcy, "The Surgical Service of the Civil War Then and Now—The Progress of Fifty Years," *Transactions of the Southern Surgical and Gynecological Association for 1914*, 145.

[4] Mr. Henry Orlando Marcy, IV, of St. Johnsburg, Vermont, provided transcripts of pertinant references in his great-grandfather's diary and autobiography. The letters between Middleton and Marcy are part of the Middleton Papers, owned by the Middleton Place Foundation.

they recognized me. I need not say that I felt relieved. I supposed none of our soldiers were in this direction, but it seems that a few of the 34 had received permission to visit the plantation. They were formerly slaves of Middleton.

Continued on to the mansion which I found splendidly located in the midst of extensive pleasure grounds on a slight eminence. All here was confusion. They had heard the news from their friends and they were making ready to leave. M[iddleton] had left about a week previous and moved some of his effects to Darlington. His overseer had soon followed and for some days the Col[ored] people had been alone. Everything was in confusion. The house was strewed with articles and all about the grounds things were scattered. There were many paintings yet in the house—hundreds of frames. I selected a few small ones. Met the driver and learned much of interest. The Colored people flocked around me and gave numerous demonstrations of joy. All wanted to 'shake hands.' Guess this is a custom of theirs. The Driver a very intelligent man, said he was placed in charge of a [party and teams] to go up country but he had contrived to get away with the whole party and return. He gave me a gun and [two] pistols.

Soon found my way to the library, which I think was the largest and most select private library I have ever seen. Should think 8 or 10,000 vol[ume]s. Here met Maj. Smith who had just come up. He seemed angry because I had not returned with the Capts. party. I politely settled that matter with more than usual brevity. But I sickened at the thought of such pillage as was about to occur and retired begging the Maj. whatever else he might do to spare the library.

Autobiography, page 116: I had spent perhaps an hour on the plantation when a Major with four companies of his white Soldiers arrived on their mission of destruction. I knew the Manor House was doomed, but I begged the Major to spare the Library. I had no influence over him, although his superior ranking Officer upon the Staff. I then forbad the burning of the Library, to which he replied "that he would soon make it hotter, than the place to which he would gladly consign me" and then I begged him to let me take the Slaves under my own supervision and put the books on one of the barges at the wharf and send them to Charleston.

This was all to no purpose and with a sad heart, I mounted my horse and rode away.

I could not witness the destruction of this historic place so closely interwoven with that of the State from its first Colonial settlement. I learned that Mr. Middleton had remained as long as possible upon the plantation without too great personal risk. Had loaded several teams with his more choice treasures and had escaped up the State to his famous Summer residence in the North Western part of South Carolina. . . .

On the way returning to Camp, we visited the Drayton Place, also the home for three generations of a most distinguished family. The great driveway leading to the house was through a double row of Live Oaks of two Centuries growth festooned with the gray moss common to the South. Its interlocking branches almost shut out the sun-light.

These Oaks are said to be the finest grove in the South. The many acres of gardens devoted to Azaleas in variety and beauty equal if they do not rival the Middleton gardens.

The Manor house at the Drayton plantation was not burned. It was built of bricks, of two stories with a hip roof and would have been considered very elegant if not compared with the finer Middleton House.

Diary: February 24, 1865: This morning Col. [V. W.] orders me to take a detachment of my own regiment and proceed to Middleton place and do what I can to repair the damage done by Maj. S. and 56 yesterday. He is very angry at the destruction of that library for it was burned and the col[ored] people were robbed indiscriminantly.

Took 80 men under Sgt. Batcheller and Adj. Dove. My first object was to get the col[ored] people together and advise them what to do— find there is a schooner and several flats here and as they are determined to leave I advise them to load the boats and proceed to the city. Find all the principal buildings were burned and are a mass of ruins. Tis very sad. Yesterday it was the finest place I ever saw, now all destroyed. The house was erected before the Revolution but had been well-kept and was in splendid keeping. The view here is excellent and the grounds by far the finest I ever saw. Perhaps fifty acres in the lower and pleasure gardens. The former owner was Gov. Henry Middleton and at one time Minister to Russia. There were about 700 slaves belonging to the estate. The Middleton place on the Combahee which we passed where everything had been burned in our advance was owned by him, and the property burned by *his order*.

Diary: June 5, 1865: [This entry indicates that the object] is to visit the Middleton place and obtain a quantity of books, which [I saw] last Spring hidden in the woods, for Harvard University. We were unfortunate in having a big slow boat with a sail but no wind. We found

it full 20 miles and a tiresome pull—did not arrive until 3 P. M. Find
the books much injured by dampness and mould but in other aspects
much as I left them in Feb. [In commenting on returning that night
he indicates they carried all they could of the books] "although we
left a boat load."

Charleston Sept. 16th 1866

My dear Eliza [5]

. . . I have ascertained that a certain Dr. Marcy (nephew of the
Gov. & Secretary of that name)[6] has in his possession several of my
most valuable & interesting pictures & other objects of more or less
value—having obtained them by inducing two of my negroes to row
him up to M[iddleton] P[lace] in a boat which he brought down loaded.
I enumerated many to Edward [7] so that he might if he chose to take
the trouble, recover them or some of them—many of my best books
he also brought off at the same time. . . . Believe me most affec^ately

Your's

W[illiams] M[iddleton]

23 East 37th St. New York.
18th Sept. 1866

My dear Williams

I have to thank you for your's of the 10th inst. informing me of
your discovery of the larceny of the pictures & books which you had
hitherto regarded as having been destroyed. This fate is more tolerable
to contemplate, in the opinion of the initiated, than their destruction,
even if you should never be so fortunate as to recover them, for they
may, at the least, serve to delight some enthusiast of art & knowledge
or wisdom, as the case may be, but, of course, not in the same degree
as they have always delighted us who appreciate them the more on
account of the remembered association which they conjure up in our
breasts. For this reason therefore, rather than because of their really

[5] Elizabeth Izard Middleton Fisher (1815-1890), sister of Williams, wife of
Joshua Francis Fisher of Alverthorpe and Philadelphia, Pennsylvania. *SCHGM*, I, 247.

[6] Middleton is mistaken in this reference to William Learned Marcy (1786-
1857), a three-time governor of New York and Secretary of War. According to *DAB*
and *WWW*, there is no connection between him and Henry O. Marcy.

[7] Edward Middleton (1810-1883), Rear Admiral, United States Navy, brother
of Williams. *SCHGM*, I, 251-252.

intrinsic value which may be considered as not far from great, I feel the liveliest interest in aiding you to regain possession of these heir-looms, in order that you may be enabled to transmit them to your heirs as you received them.

I have made inquiries among my acquaintances, in relation to the domicile of the alleged marauder, so far without success; but I have no doubt of ultimately succeeding in ferreting him out & in compelling him to make an admission or denial of the charge. . . . as ever, Your affect^te brother

Edward Middleton

Alverthorpe
Wed. eving. 19th Sept.

My dear Williams

I have just recd. yrs of the 16th and 17th. . . . We had just been talking about the loss of yr Pictures &c at table—& are glad to think there is any hope of yr being able to recover any of them. . . . Good night

Yr affectionate

Sister E[liza]

23 E 37th St. N.Y.
3 Oct/66

My dear Williams

. . . I have not yet succeeded in discovering the surgeon of the 35th N[ew] Y[ork] Volunteers. . . .

Edward Middleton

Cambridge Mass
Oct. 22 1867

Mr. William Middleton
Sir

I have this day received a visit from Miss Middleton [8]—a daughter of Russell M.[9]—from Newport R.I.

She supposed I had purchased of one Andrew Gray a former servant of her bro[ther] a picture which was painted by him. I had no such

[8] Either Annie Elizabeth Middleton (b. 1847), Alicia Hopton Middleton (b. 1849) or Charlotte Helen Middleton DeWolf (b. 1854). *SCHGM*, I, 255.

[9] Nathaniel Russell Middleton (1810-1890), Williams' cousin, was, among other things, president of the College of Charleston. He lived in Bristol, Rhode Island, some years after the Civil War.

painting, but have two which I obtained in Charleston. Miss M. thinks they formerly belonged to you.

They are monks & nuns at devotion perhaps 20 X 30 inches. Evidently by a good artist. They were damaged. I had them carefully repaired & reframed.

I have been informed that your collection of paintings was destroyed with the place and this would lead me to suppose they could not have belonged to you.

Middleton Place was burned by a detachment of troops belonging to the brigade of which I was Medical Director and it was reported that the destruction was complete including the Library and outbuildings—which act was greatly regretted by the Gen. in command.[10]

I remain Sir Very Respectfully

Your Obt. Servt

Henry O. Marcy

Sir

Your letter of the 22ᵈ inst has just reached me. I beg leave to state in reply that I had heard that the two pictures you write to me about viz a picture of monks under a grape arbour overlooking the bay of Naples & the pendant to it of a moonlight scene with nuns & a view of Vesuvius in the distance [11] as well as a small picture of an Italian woman in a red dress gathering grapes & sundry others & other articles— fire arms &c belonging to me were carried away from Charleston by you.

I received this information from several sources & I wrote to my brother Captⁿ M[iddleton] of the U[nited] S[tates] N[avy] to endeavour to obtain the restitution of them for me but I informed him that I believed that you were in N[ew] Y[ork]—but he told me he had striven in vain to find you there.[12]

You are mistaken in supposing that my pictures had been burnt in the destruction of my property on Ashley river. I had packed up most of my pictures in boxes which I had concealed. I have since recovered several of those which were not carried out of the country.

---

[10] According to family tradition and papers, the troops were under the command of General Van Wyck. No corroboration of this has been found except for Marcy's diary entry of February 24, 1865.

[11] The picture of "monks under a grape arbour" and that of a "moonlight scene with nuns and a view of Vesuvius" are part of the Middleton Place Foundation collection.

[12] Perhaps the search was instituted in New York because of Middleton's assumption that Marcy was nephew of Wm. L. Marcy (see footnote 6).

One box of them was burnt in my negro chapel after the Peace [13] when the Chapel, mill & buildings which had been spared by the Brigade you belonged to were consumed by special order of Genl Hatch [14] who sent a gunboat up the river to complete the devastation which he thought had not been sufficiently thorough effected by your Brigade. There were so many boxes that I cannot be positive as to the contents of each one, but I am pretty certain that the box which contained those you write about contained also two harbour views. One taken of a harbour at sunset with old fashioned ships a short distance from the quay, on which a few persons are standing in the foreground & on the right hand as you look at it some buildings with columns which stand out from them & distant view.[15] The other has a vessel at anchor . . . figures handling barrels or goods &c are on the left near a circular building near which as well as I can remember are women washing clothes at a fountain whilst across the water low grey hills form the distance.

I put in this box or the other hidden with it Sully's picture of Washington crossing the Delaware too well known to need description & a landscape with a very dark foreground on the right of which is a small pond from which some wild fowl are flying up & above this in the distance a small portion of the landscape in brighter light as a contrast— besides these there were twelve or 15 others which it would take much time to describe. I am also informed by the negroes that you carried away a good many books belonging to me. With many of these pictures & books I have associations which have formed a large portion of the pleasure of my past life.

I am Sir

Your ob[dt] Ser[t]

W[illiams] M[iddleton]

Cambridgeport
Mr. Middleton   Nov 7 1867
Sir

Your letter of the 22[d] came to hand yesterday.

I admit that the inference is a fair one that in finding two of your lost pictures, you suppose the rest are in company.

---

[13] Middleton is probably referring to either the surrender of Charleston or to Appomattox.

[14] An examination of *The War of the Rebellion: A Compilation of the Official Records of the Union and Confederate Armies* failed to locate this order.

[15] This picture is part of the Middleton Place Foundation collection.

I have in my possession two or three old oil paintings, one of which answers in some of its general characters the sea port view which you have described. It is a view of a seaport town with ships in the foreground & quite old—but as I think I mentioned in my letter they did not come from the south. The two of which I wrote are the only ones in my possession which by any possibility could have ever been yours.

These you describe as perfectly as I could have done, so that my doubts are removed as to their having belonged to your collection.

I obtained them with no feeling that I was robbing the owner, but that I was saving the property from destruction. They cost me $10. each. They were damaged. I had them carefully repaired and framed at an expence of about $30. each. They have been hung in my reception room and subject to the inspection of any one.

Now I know not of the legality of any claim which I may have to the pictures, but I shall be very willing to return them to you for the amt. which they cost me. As you know the frames are of little value except with the pictures.

I know not their value, but if you do not price them too highly, and are willing to part with them I might purchase them.

At your convenience allow me to hear from you.

Resp. H. O. Marcy

P.S. Mrs. R. Middleton called upon me a few days since in reference to the matter, but I preferred to consult you as indeed I had already written.—HM

Sir

In your letter of the 7ᵈ insᵗ your statements are so positive with respect to your not having any other of my pictures in your possession that I must beg leave to refresh your memory a little by the mention of a few circumstances which may enable you to discover the rightful owner of a good deal of the property of this nature now under your roof.

There are certain persons in this community who have a perfect recollection of having been employed by you to accompany you in a row boat about 2 months after the surrender of C[harleston] [16] to my place on A[shley] R[iver] in search of plunder which affidavits to this effect as well as to the fact of you and your companions having brought away considerable amount of property I can produce when necessary. The specification of this property is not now needed but shall be

[16] If this outing took place in April, 1865, it would have coincided with the approximate time of the clean-up operations in Charleston; *War of the Rebellion*, Vol. 100, p. 127.

furnished at the proper time. Has it escaped your memory that much of this was carried by you to the house of a gentleman on Morris Island with whom you were living and that he recognized some of these articles & expressed his surprise to Mrs. Marcy[17] that you should pack them up & send them off when he informed her where they came from & to whom they belonged?

I gave but a very general description of the pictures which I know you hold supposing that with your knowledge of the antecedent circumstances you would be satisfied that I was the rightful claimant of them & that your better nature might induce you to do justice particularly as you say in your letter to quote yr words "obtained them with no feeling that I was robbing the owner, but that I was saving the property from destruction." These laudable efforts on your part would undoubtably have elicited from me all proper expressions of gratitude had not my conviction by experience led me to know that I should have recovered it long ago, as the negroes into whose hands fortunately some of the rest fell, as soon as their evil advisors left them to themselves, were honest enough voluntarily to restore to me all that had not been mischievously destroyed. There can be no difficulty upon the score of identification as several of your most respectable fellow citizens who have seen them in my house Mr. Otis, Mr. Ritchie and others could easily satisfy any doubts on this matter, & I could myself if necessary furnish from recollection a rough sketch sufficiently accurate for any purpose of that kind.

[Copy]

Charleston Feb[y] 6th 1874.

My dear Eliza,

I have been expecting for some days to have the pleasure of a letter from you, but as I found in looking over some of my papers this morning two of the letters relating to my pictures which I so long since promised to send you I will not defer until I shall have recd yr expected letter the fulfilment of my engagement to you but write at once. I shall have both these letters copied & certified to by a Notary Public tomorrow & enclose them with this to you. You will observe at the end of the *first*, the statement as to the burning of M. Place. He does not give the details of it as furnished me by eye witnesses of the fact—viz: of the officers first taking their dinner comfortably in our old dining room and of Major Moore going down upon his hands & knees to put the fire in the closet at the head of the first landing place on the

---

[17] Marcy married Sarah E. Wendell of Great Falls, New Hampshire in 1863. *DAB*, XII, 273.

stairs &c &c; but he says quite enough to refute the vile slander which you told Hal[18] you heard during your stay in Buncombe last summer viz that the act had been perpetrated "by the infuriated Combahee negroes who had marched there in a body to revenge themselves on me." To this I had made up my mind not to condescend to make a reply. And I should not have said a word about it now but for the statement in the letter of the picture thief—of whose doings I know more than he imagines. In these letters he pretends that he has but few of my pictures, but upon my sending the sketches of others his admissions in his third letter are more full. This third letter with duplicate sketches I have not yet found, but am firmly convinced that I shall be able to do so very shortly.[19] But even if I cannot, Edward could easily identify the pictures (familiar as he must be with all except those left me by our uncle J.I.M.[20] many of which have his seal with coat of arms on the back) & without including these this man has or had, I believe, 22 or three. I need not add that I have from a most respectable source a very different account of the manner in which he (Marcy) came by them. But I will wait to expose this until the time for it comes.

For about 40 years I have made it a rule never to destroy a letter except it might be of the most trivial nature & thus you may well suppose I have a vast accumulation of them—sufficient to form a complete history of the business transactions of my life. Although my various moves from house to house have made it somewhat difficult to put my hand without some delay on any particular bundle of them. . . .

Brookline Aug. 8th '76.[21]

My dear Fisher,[22]

In answer to yours of the 3ᵈ inst. I would write that I find in a directory of Cambridge for this year the name of Henry O. Marcy Physician, 690 Main St. Cambridgeport who I hope is the person you inquire about.

Very truly Yrs

A.L. Lincoln, Jr.

[18] Henry Middleton (b. 1851), son of Williams Middleton. *SCHGM*, I 251.

[19] See final entry *infra*.

[20] John Izard Middleton (1785-1849), son of Arthur Middleton and author of *Grecian Remains of Italy*, was called by Prof. Chas. Eliot Norton, "The first American classical archaeologist." *Amer. Journ. of Arch.*, 1885, p. 3 and *SCHGM*, I, 244.

[21] The last recorded correspondence between Middleton and Marcy took place in 1867, as Marcy then studied in Europe for several years.

[22] Joshua Francis Fisher, brother-in-law of Middleton.

Charleston Aug^s. 29. 1876

Williams Middleton Esq.
Summerville SC

Dear Sir

Your letter of the 16th inst from Philadelphia came duly to hand, and the Box of pictures today. It is safely deposited in our office, where it will be quite safe against all risks except fire; and of this, there is little danger, business not having commenced, and none of the offices on the Wharf being lighted as yet in the evenings.

The box is not in our way and can remain where it is to suit your convenience. I congratulate you most sincerely on the recovery of even a portion only of your pictures, and feel pleasure that I have been able to serve you in the matter. I am very truly & respy.

I.T. Gourdin

8. a picture of Diana in centre of picture just out of a stream or pool of water surrounded by some of her nymphs whilst others are still in the water near her playing. I do not sufficiently remember the details to sketch the picture which is about 20 x 16 inches.[23]

9. Copy picture by Bruloff of an Italian girl (half-length) dressed in scarlet gathering grapes. about 12 X 12 inches.

10. Ruins of Copy of J.I.M.'s drawing in water colors. about 15 X 12 inches wide.

11. Country view with house & long waterfall in front—copy of J.I.M.'s drawing.

12. Landscape on *wood* with small cottage in centre & 1 or 2 figures approaching. *Wood cracked* across the middle, about 18 X 15 inches.

13. Monks in their grape arbour with view of the entrance to the grotto of Posilippo at the head of the road overlooking the bay of Naples. Pigeons drinking from a large earthern saucer &c. Picture about 3½ ft by 2½.

14. Nuns with view of Mt. Vesuvius in distance. Moonlight scene 2 nuns before an image on the wall. Picture 3½ by 2½. These two pictures Dr. M. has acknowledged the possession of as identified by Miss M.

[23] This picture is part of the Middleton Place Foundation collection. This list, written in pencil, may be part of the missing third letter referred to by Middleton on Feb. 6, 1874.

Errata

"'Brother against Brother': Alexander and James Campbell's Civil War": James Campbell was the older brother of Alexander Campbell. On pages 156 and 158 James is inaccurately described as the younger.

Page 165 ("An Affair of Honor at Fort Sumter"): First line, second paragraph should read "In January of 1861…."

An expanded version of "Elizabeth Jamison's Tale of the War" has been added to Ancestry.com by author David J. Rutledge.

About the Authors

Ben Bassham ("'The Bombardment of Fort Moultrie, November 16, 1863' by Conrad Wise Chapman") was a professor of art history at Kent State University. In 1998 he published a biography of Conrad Wise Chapman.

C. A. Bennett Jr. ("Roswell Sabin Ripley: 'Charleston's Gallant Defender'"), a retired physician and independent researcher, is writing a full biography of Roswell Ripley. He notes that in 2002 an Ohio Historical Society bronze marker was placed in front of the Ripley House in Worthington, Ohio.

George M. Blackburn ("A Michigan Regiment in the Palmetto State") was a professor of history at Central Michigan University. He wrote extensively on the Civil War.

Frances M. Burroughs ("The Confederate Receipt Book: A Study of Food Substitution in the American Civil War") was identified in 1992 as a graduate student in history and museum studies at Virginia Commonwealth University.

Henry Carrison ("A Businessman in Crisis: Col. Daniel Jordan and the Civil War") is an independent researcher.

Ron Chepesiuk ("Eye Witness to Fort Sumter: The Letters of Private John Thompson) was head of special collections at Winthrop University in Rock Hill, S.C. for many years. He still writes extensively on a wide range of subjects (see www.ronchepesiuk.com for titles), most recently true crime stories.

Nancy Ashmore Cooper ("When the Yankees Sacked Greenville: Stoneman's Raid, May 2, 1865") wrote *Greenville: Woven from the Past* and served as the assistant director of the Institute for Southern Studies at the University of South Carolina. Her article was edited slightly for this volume.

J. H. Easterby ("Captain Langdon Cheves, Jr., and the Confederate Silk Dress Balloon") was one of the leading South Carolina historians of his day. He taught at the College of Charleston, directed the Historical Commission of South Carolina (today the South Carolina Department of Archives and History) from 1949 to 1960, wrote on a wide variety of topics, and worked closely for many years with the South Carolina Historical Society.

W. Eric Emerson ("Lowcountry Rail Line Threatened: The Battles of Pocotaligo and Coosawhatchie, October 22, 1862") was the executive director of the South Carolina Historical Society when this article was published in *Carologue*. He now directs the South Carolina Department of Archives and History and has published two books on Civil War topics.

John E. Florance Jr. ("Morris Island: Victory or Blunder?") was identified in 1954 as an ensign with the U. S. Naval Amphibian Training Command in San Diego, California.

Viola Caston Floyd ("The Fall of Charleston") was the author of several books of genealogy and history. Her extensive collection of papers pertaining to Lancaster County has been donated to the Lancaster County Library.

Harlan Greene ("'Robbing the Owner or Saving the Property from Destruction?'—Paintings in the Middleton Place House") is senior manuscript and reference archivist at the Marlene & Nathan Addlestone Library, College of Charleston. After rising from volunteer to interim director of the South Carolina Historical Society, he has gone on to publish several novels and works of nonfiction.

John Harleston ("Battery Wagner on Morris Island, 1863"), after his service with the Virginia Rifles, worked on steamboating and railroads.

C. Russell Horres Jr. ("An Affair of Honor at Ft. Sumter" and "Charleston's Civil War 'Monster Guns,' the Blakely Rifles") is an independent researcher living in Mount Pleasant, S.C., and longtime volunteer for the Fort Sumter National Monument. In 2011 he published a children's book entitled *Jack the Cat that Went to War*.

Leonne M. Hudson ("A Confederate Victory at Grahamville: Fighting at Honey Hill") is an associate professor of history at Kent State University. Among other books that he has written or edited is a biography of Gustavus Woodson Smith.

Thomas Bland Keys ("The Federal Pillage of Anderson, South Carolina: Brown's Raid") wrote *The Uncivil War: Union Army and Navy Excesses in the Official Records* (1991) and *Tarheel Cossack, W. P. Roberts: Youngest Confederate General* (1983).

Robert Lebby, M.D. ("The First Shot on Fort Sumter") served as a physician with the Confederate Army throughout the Civil War, then held positions as alderman and registrar for the city of Charleston and surgeon-general and port physician for the state of South Carolina.

Harriott Cheves Leland ("'Robbing the Owner or Saving the Property from Destruction?'—Paintings in the Middleton Place House") is the archivist and researcher for the Huguenot Society of South Carolina and coeditor of a series of books on the proprietary records of South Carolina.

Edward G. Longacre ("'It Will Be Many a Day before Charleston Falls': Letters of a Union Sergeant on Folly Island, August 1863-April 1864") has written a number of books about the Civil War, especially biographies of generals, including Wade Hampton III and Joshua Chamberlain. He also wrote "'We Left a Black Track in South Carolina': Letters of Corporal Eli S. Ricker, 1865" in Volume 82 of the *South Carolina Historical Magazine*.

Wesley Loy ("10 Rumford Place: Doing Confederate Business in Liverpool") has been a business reporter for the *Anchorage Daily News* since May 1999.

John B. McLeod ("Skirmish on Crescent Ridge: The Last Clash of the War Between the States in South Carolina") practiced law with Haynsworth Sinkler Boyd, P.A., in Greenville, S.C.

John Hammond Moore ("The Last Officer—April 1865") is a tireless researcher who has produced many books of South Carolina history.

Larry E. Nelson ("Sherman at Cheraw") served for many years as a professor of history at Francis Marion University.

James T. Otten ("Disloyalty in the Upper Districts of South Carolina during the Civil War") taught for many years at the University of South Carolina campus at Union.

Francis LeJau Parker ("The Battle of Fort Sumter as Seen from Morris Island") spent four years on active duty with the Confederate medical service, then worked almost five decades as a surgeon. A professor of anatomy at the Medical College of the State of South Carolina, he has been described as the first surgeon to suture a nerve.

J. Tracy Power ("'Brother against Brother': Alexander and James Campbell's Civil War") is a historian at the South Carolina Department of Archives and History, where he co-coordinates the National Register of Historic Places program and the South Carolina Historical Marker Program. He is one of the state's most respected authors on the Civil War.

Elmer L. Puryear ("The Confederate Diary of William John Grayson") taught history at the College of Charleston. With Martin Abbott of Oglethorpe University he also contributed to the *Historical Magazine* a three-part series, "Beleaguered Charleston: Letters from the City, 1860-1864."

May Spencer Ringold ("William Gourdin Young and the Wigfall Mission— Fort Sumter, April 13, 1961") taught in the Department of History and Government at the Texas Woman's University in Denton and wrote *The Role of the State Legislatures in the Confederacy* (1966).

David J. Rutledge ("Elizabeth Jamison's Tale of the War") lives in Spartanburg, South Carolina, and practices law in Greenville.

Jacob Schirmer ("Extracts from the Schirmer Diary, 1860" and "Extracts from the Schirmer Diary, 1861") was a Charleston merchant whose family left to the South Carolina Historical Society the diaries he maintained from 1826 to 1880.

P. J. Staudenraus ("Occupied Beaufort, 1863: A War Correspondent's View") of the University of Kansas City also contributed to the *Historical Magazine* "Letters from South Carolina, 1821-1822" which ran in volume 58.

Karen D. Stokes ("Sherman's Army Comes to Camden: The Civil War Narrative of Sarah Dehon Trapier") has worked as an archivist for the South Carolina Historical Society since 1994. With W. Eric Emerson she coedited *Faith, Valor, and Devotion: The Civil War Letters of William Porcher DuBose* (2010).

Samuel G. Stoney ("Robert N. Gourdin to Robert Anderson, 1861") was an author, raconteur, perhaps the most iconic Charlestonian in history, and an indefatigable worker for the South Carolina Historical Society.

Leah Townsend ("The Confederate Gunboat 'Peedee'") was a longtime friend of the South Carolina Historical Society. In 1935 she published *South Carolina Baptists, 1670-1805*.

Howard C. Westwood ("Generals David Hunter and Rufus Saxton and Black Soldiers" and "Sherman Marched—and Proclaimed 'Land for the Landless'") was a lawyer with the Washington, D.C., firm of Covington and Burling specializing in airline law. He was the author of the anthology *Black Troops, White Commanders and Freedmen During the Civil War* (1992).

Kurt J. Wolf ("Laura M. Towne and the Freed People of South Carolina, 1862-1901") is a writer living on the west coast.

Ralph Wooster ("Membership of The South Carolina Secession Convention") wrote *The Secession Conventions of the South* (1962).

OTHER ARTICLES ON THE CIVIL WAR IN THE
SOUTH CAROLINA HISTORICAL MAGAZINE

"Castle Pinckney, Silent Sentinel of Charleston Harbor," by Rogers W. Young,
39: 51-59

"Captain Langdon Cheves, Jr., and the Confederate Silk Dress Balloon," edited
by J. H. Easterby, 45: 9-11, 99-110

"The Diary of Samuel Edward Burges, 1860-1862," edited by Thomas W.
Chadwick, 48: 63-75, 141-163, 206-218

"Economic Changes in St. Helena's Parish, 1860-1870," by Hermine Munz
Baumhofer, 50: 1-13

"Historic Fort Moultrie in Charleston Harbor," by Edward M. Riley, 51: 63-74,
247-248

"The Burning of Legareville," by John Jenkins, 51: 117

"The Confederate Episcopal Church in 1863," by Edgar Legare Pennington, 52:
5-16

"To Coosawhatchie in December 1861," by William D. Hoyt, Jr., 53: 6-12

"Through the Union Lines into the Confederacy," by Lucy W. Baxter, 54: 135-
140

"Some Letters of the Barnard Elliott Habersham Family, 1858-1868,"
contributed by Sarah Agnes Wallace, 54: 201-210

"Journal of Arthur Brailsford Wescoat, 1863, 1864," 55: 71-102

"Sherman Burns the Libraries," edited by William B. Hesseltine and Larry Gara,
55: 137-142

"Diary of John Berkley Grimball, 1858-1865," 56: 8-30 (1858-1860), 92-114
(1860-1861), 157-177 (1861-1862), 205-225 (1862-1863); 57: 28-50 (1863-
1864), 88-102 (1864-1865)

"Ambrosio José Gonzales, A Cuban Patriot in Carolina," by Lewis Pinckney
Jones, 56: 67-76

"State Aid for Indigent Families of South Carolina Soldiers, 1861-1865," by
William Frank Zornow, 57: 82-87

"The Confederate Archives and Felix G. DeFontaine," by James A. Hoyt, 57:
199-203

"Some Letters of William Dunlap Simpson, 1860-1863," edited by Willard E. Wight, 57: 204-222

"Diary of Captain Joseph Julius Wescoat, 1863-1865," edited by Anne King Gregorie, 59: 11-23, 84-95

"Diary of Abram W. Clement, 1865," edited by Slann L. C. Simmons, 59: 78-95

"Recollections of Harriet DuBose Kershaw Lang," edited by Rives Lang Beaty, 59: 159-170, 195-205

"Recollections of John Stafford Stoney, Confederate Surgeon," contributed by John Laurens Tison, Jr., edited by Samuel G. Stoney, 60: 60:208-220

"Beleaguered Charleston: Letters from the City, 1860-1864," edited by Martin Abbott and Elmer L. Puryear, 61: 61-74 (1860-1862), 164-175 (1863), 210-218 (1864)

"Extracts from the Schirmer Diary, 1860," 61: 163

"Excerpts from the Wartime Correspondence of Augustine T. Smythe," 62: 27-32

"Excerpts from the Schrimer Diary, 1861," 62: 182, 237

"Sue Sparks Keitt to a Northern Friend, March 4, 1861," edited by Elmer Don Herd, Jr., 62: 82-87

"Charleston Harbor, 1860-1861: A Memoir from the Union Garrison," edited by James P. Jones, 72: 148-150

"A Letter from Bleak Hall, 1861," 62: 193-194

"From Sumter to the Wilderness: Letters of Sergeant James Butler Suddath, Co. E, 7th Regiment, S.C.V.," edited by Frank B. Williams, Jr., 63: 1-11, 93-104

"Middleton Correspondence, 1861-1865," edited by Isabella Middleton Leland, 63: 33-41, 61-70, 164-174, 204-210; 64: 28-38, 95-104, 158-168, 212-219; 65: 33-44, 98-109

"The Confederate Diary of William John Grayson," edited by Elmer L. Puryear, 63: 214-226

"*The Rebel* (Columbia), January 28, 1863," 64: 13-15

"'If Fortune Should Fail'—Civil War Letters of Dr. Samuel D. Sanders," by Walter Rundell, Jr., 65: 129-144, 218-232

"A Union Soldier at Fort Sumter, 1860-1861," 67: 99-104

"The Diary of William G. Hinson During the War of Secession," edited by Joseph Ioor Waring, 75: 14-23, 111-122

"'The Correspondence of a Yankee Prisoner in Charleston, 1865," contributed by John E. Duncan, 75: 215-224

"South from Appomattox: The Diary of Abner R. Cox," edited by Royce Gordon Shingleton," 75: 238-244

"The Charleston Fire of 1861 as Described in the Emma E. Holmes Diary," edited by John F. Marszalek, Jr., 76: 60-67

"The South Atlantic Blockading Squadron: The Diary of James W. Boynton," edited by Abbott A. Brayton, 76: 112-117

"General Beauregard and the Colonel Rhett Controversy," by H. Newcomb Morse, 78: 184-190

"'We Left a Black Track in South Carolina': Letters of Corporal Eli S. Ricker, 1865," edited by Edward G. Longacre, 82: 210-224

"The Crucible of Civil War and Reconstruction in the Experience of William Porcher DuBose," by Ralph E. Luker, 83: 50-71

"An Economic Study of the Substantial Slaveholders of Orangeburg County, 1860-1880, by Jayne Morris-Crowther, 86: 296-314

"'Our Separation Is Like Years': The Civil War Letters of Deopold Daniel Louis," edited by Jason H. Silverman and Susan R. Murphy, 87: 141-147

"The Charleston Marine School," by James David Altman, 88: 76-82

"Of Mules and Men: The Night Fight at Wauhatchie Station," by John K. Stevens, 90: 282-298

"'There Goes Your Damned Gospel Shop!' The Churches and Clergy as Victims of Sherman's March through South Carolina," by David B. Chesebrough, 92: 15-33

"Maxcy Gregg and His Brigade of South Carolinians at the Battle of Fredericksburg," by Clay Ouzts, 95: 6-26

"Vox Populi and the Fall of Fort Fisher" (From the Archives), by Alexia Jones Helsley, 96: 71-73

"'Great Events Have Taken Place': The Civil War Diary of Adele Allston Vanderhorst," by Pamela J. Clements, 102: 310-334

INDEX

10 Rumford Place, 416–440
Abbott, A. O., 523
abolitionists, on sea islands, 121
    See also Gideon's Band; Towne, Laura
        M.
Adams, Charles Francis, 435
Adams, James H., 4, 15
Adams, R. N., 313
aeronautics. *See* balloon, Confederate silk
    dress
African Americans
    arming of, 74–75, 79
    charged with looting, 71
    drilling by, 88
    fading interest in taking care of, 132
    health of, 123–124
    impressment of, 146
    Michiganders' view of, 72–73
    reaction to Lincoln's death, 131
    return to South, 149–150
African Americans, refugee
    meeting regarding, 269
    numbers of, 367
    Order No. 15, 270
    Saxton on, 271–272, 274
    settlement on sea islands, 270
    and Sherman, 131, 264–267, 271, 276
    Stevens on, 361
Aiken, John, 170
Alabama, 433, 434
Alexander, E. Porter, 444–445, 446, 449
Alexandra, 430, 434
Alford, Colonel, 257
Alford, Samuel M., 240
Allison, Robert T., 15
Allston, Benjamin, 401
Allston, J. Blythe, 98, 100
Alston, Charles, 409–410, 415
Ambercrombie, John J., 291
Amnesty Proclamation, 273–274
Anaconda Strategy, 398
Anderson, Edward C., 426, 427
Anderson, Robert, 22, 24, 27–31, 43, 46,
        47, 49, 53, 113, 208, 300, 368
Anderson, S.C., 373–379
Anderson District, S.C., 512, 517

Andrews, W. H., 345
Andrews railroad raid, 94
Antietam, battle of, 214, 516
Appleby, David C., 12
Army of the James, 260
Arsenal Hill Academy, 380
art
    The Bombardment of Fort Moultrie,
        November 16, 1863
        (Chapman), 223–225, 226,
        232–233
    The Bombardment of Fort Sumter
        (Key), 233
    The Marriage of Pocahontas
        (Chapman), 225
    from Middleton Place, 557–564
Ashepoo River, 211
Ashmore, John S., 518, 520
Aspinwall, William H., 435
Atkinson, S. T., 13
Atlanta, Ga., 537
aviation. *See* balloon, Confederate silk
    dress
Ayer, Lewis M., Jr., 10
bacon, 21
baked goods, 495, 496, 501–502, 506
balloon, Confederate silk dress, 443–449,
    571
Balls Bluff, battle of, 516
banks, 406–407
Barbot, Alphonse, 478
Barnwell, *, 219
Barnwell, Edward H., 59
Barnwell, Joseph W., xiv
Barnwell, R. W., 4, 10
Barnwell District, S.C., 532
Barron, A. S., 15
Barton, D. R., 14
Barton, William B., 97, 100–101
Basinger, William S., 470
Battery Gregg, 185, 186, 191–195, 200,
    202
Battery Island, S.C., evacuation of, 143
Battery Ramsey, 462

Battery Wagner
    construction of, 449–450
    evacuation of, 193–195
    Federal assault on, xii, 161, 199–204
    Harleston's recollections of, 183–195
Battery White, 333, 339, 481
Baxter, Lucy W., 571
Beaty, Thos. W., 13
Beaufort, S.C.
    African Americans left in, 77
    arrival of Gideonites, 118–119
    Brooks's description of, 104–112
    looting of, 71
    Michiganders' views of, 70–71, 75
    whites' evacuation of, 107
Beaufort Light Artillery, 99
Beauregard, P. G. T.
    on Blakelys, 462, 464, 471
    in Charleston, 97, 456
    command of, 208
    decision to defend Morris Island, 204
    decision to evacuate Charleston, 293,
        475
    demand for Anderson's surrender, 49
    difficulties with F. L. Childs, 214
    on Federal force on Folly Island, 198
    on Fort Sumter, 53, 59, 61
    on James Island force, 197
    on Jones-Ripley dispute, 218–219
    "Journal of the Siege of Charleston,"
        228
    leadership of Department of South
        Carolina and Georgia, 171
    on Morris Island, 199, 200, 203, 218,
    need for artillery, 458
    on need to defend Charleston and
        Savannah railroad, 281–282
    popularity of, 48
    in Ransom-Calhoun affair, 168, 179
    on reduction of defenses of Charleston,
        198
    on Rhett, 181, 573
    on Ripley, 214–215, 220
    sent to Jackson, 517
Bedon, Josiah, 184
Beecher, Henry Ward, 113
Beecher, James, 287, 549
Bellinger, E. St. P., 12

Benham, Henry W., 79, 82–83, 154, 157
Bennet, William T., 289
Bennett, A. G., 298, 299
Bentonville, battle of, 220
Bermuda, 426
"Berwick" (correspondent), 295–301
Bethea, A. W., 14
Bibles, 416
Bible Society of the Confederate States,
    416
Bishop, Pink, 523
Black Island, S.C., 242–245
Blackwell, Elizabeth, 117
Blair, Frank P., 340, 341, 345
Blakely, Alexander Theophilis, 460, 467,
    470
Blakely rifles, 459–476
Blanding, Ormsby, 468
Bleak Hall, 572
Bleux, Lieutenant, 101
blockade, 21, 93, 398, 399, 400–401, 419,
    426, 432, 478, 498–499
The Blockade and the Cruisers (Soley),
    478
blockade runners, 419, 426–428
Blossom, Benjamin, 392, 396, 405
boats. *See* ships
Bobo, Simpson, 15
Bolan's Church, 282, 291
*The Bombardment of Fort Moultrie,
    November 16, 1863* (Chapman),
    223–225, 226, 232–233
The Bombardment of Fort Sumter (Key),
    233
Bonham, M. L., 219, 456, 519
Bonneau, Peter P., 10
Boonesborough, battle of, 214
Boyce, James P., 382
Boyd's Landing, 282
Boykin's Mill, S.C., 369–370
Boykin's Rangers, 519
Boynton, James W., 573
Brabham, J. J., 10
Bragg, Braxton, 354
Brannan, John M., 96–100, 103
Brigham, P. H., 484
British and Southern Finance Co., 435
Broady, George, 359

bronze, 467
Brooke, John, 471
Brooke, William N., 471
Brooks, Noah, 104
Brown, Alex H., 11
Brown, C. P., 11
Brown, Joseph E., 284
Brown, Simeon B., 374, 375, 377–378, 379
Bruns, J. D., 177
Brunswick County, N.C., 391
Bryan, Captain, 193
Bryan, George, 175
Buchanan, James, 49
Buchanan, John (S.C. Secession Convention), 13
Buchanan, John (Michigan soldier), 68, 70, 71, 73
Bulloch, James Dunwoody, 419, 424, 425, 426, 427, 432–433, 434, 437, 438, 439
Bull Run, First, battle of, 155, 514, 537
Bull Run, Second, battle of, 159, 516
Burges, Samuel Edward, 571
Burnet, A. W., 11
Burns, Samuel A., 183
Burnside, Ambrose, 65, 257
Burr, Lieutenant, 298
Burton, E. Milby, 215–216
Burwood plantation, 532
business, reaction to secession, 396
business strategy, 390–391
Butler, Benjamin F., 151, 257, 260
Butler, Matthew C., 341, 342, 345
butter, 21, 502
Cain, William, 11
Caldwell, Joseph, 14
Calhoun, John A., 10
Calhoun, John C., 165, 166, 301, 422, 489–490
Calhoun, William Ransom, 165–182
Calvary Church (Charleston, S.C.), 311
Camden, S.C., 313–331, 407, 548
Campbell, Alexander (Sandy), 155–161, 163–164
Campbell, Archibald, 285, 288
Campbell, James, 156–158, 162–164
Campbell, Jane, 160

Campbell, John A., 519
Campbell, W. H., 13
Camp Sorghum, 521–524
candles, 492, 505
Captains of the Civil War (Wood), 445
Carlisle, J. H., 15
Carmichael, Elizabeth (mother of Elizabeth Jamison), 527
Carmichael, Elizabeth (pen name), 527–552
Carn, Merrick E.. 12
Carroll, B. R., 21
Carroll, James P., 13
Cash, E. B. C., 174
Castle Pinckney, 25, 457, 571
Caughman, H. I., 14
Cauthen, Charles E., 511
Cauthen W. C., 13
Cecile, 428
Cevor, Charles, 447
Chadwick, J. R., 400
Chantilly, battle at, 159–160
Chapman, Conrad Wise, 223–233, 466
Chapman, John Gadsby, 225
Chapman, John Linton, 225
Chapman, Tom, 190–192
Charles, Edward W., 12
Charleston, 458
Charleston, S.C.
    abandonment of outlying fortifications of, 170–171
    Benham's planned attack on, 79, 82–83
    combined assault on, planned, 196–197, 234
    Confederate force in, 197
    evacuation of, 146, 293, 296–297, 320, 336, 475
    fire (1861), 573
    goal of capturing, 93, 103
    isolation of, 336
    letters from (1860-1864), 572
    reduction of defenses of, 198
Charleston, S.C., defense of
    Blakely rifles, 456–477
    coastal islands in, 211 (*See also* individual islands)
    preparations for, 456–459
    Ripley in, 206–222

Charleston, S.C., fall of
　　Berwick's description of, 295–301
　　Tew on, 304
Charleston, S.C., harbor defenses, 22, 151,
　　　　223–225, 227–231, 228, 457–475
　　*See also The Bombardment of Fort
　　　　Moultrie, November 16, 1863*
　　　　(Chapman); Fort Moultrie;
　　　　Fort Sumter; individual
　　　　batteries; individual islands
Charleston, S.C., siege of
　　public attention to, 227
　　Wightman's letters, 234–260
Charleston Battalion, 156, 200–201
Charleston Light Dragoons, 99, 102, 184
　　See also Harleston, John
Charleston Marine School, 573
Chase, Salmon P., 81, 82, 84, 87, 118
Chattanooga, Tenn., 249
Cheatham, General, 220
Cheraw, S.C.
　　description of, 336
　　destruction in, 354–355
　　explosion in, 349–350
　　Federal capture of, 345
　　Federal occupation of, 350–353
　　Hardee's march to, 336–337
　　Hardee's withdrawal from, 342
　　Sherman's attack on, 342–346
　　Sherman's march to, 332, 338–339,
　　　　341, 482
　　supplies in, 350–351
Chesnut, James R., 4, 13, 46, 169, 291,
　　　　312
Chesnut, Mary, 168, 312, 494
Chesterfield, 337, 341
Cheves, Charles, 448
Cheves, Edward, 444, 449
Cheves, John, 449
Cheves, Langdon, 4, 10, 444, 445
Cheves, Langdon, Jr., 444, 445–446,
　　　　447–450, 571
Cheves, Langdon (Judge), 447
Chevis, Captain, 452
Chickamauga, battle of, 537
Chicora, 458
Childs, F. L., 214
Chipman, Charles G., 364

Chisholm, A. R., 43
Choice, Josiah, 380
Christians, behavior of, 150–151
churches
　　in Beaufort, 106
　　Calvary Church (Charleston, S.C.), 311
　　Episcopal Church (1861-1865), 571
　　Orangeburg Presbyterian Church, 531
　　St. Andrew's Parish Church
　　　　(Charleston County, S.C.),
　　　　310
　　St. Michael's Church (Charleston,
　　　　S.C.), 147, 311, 316
　　St. Philip's Church (Charleston, S.C.),
　　　　489
Cilley, Greenleaf, 471
Citadel, The, 529
Clark, E. C., 359
Clark, Ephriam M., 11
class
　　in Beaufort, 71–72
　　and dueling, 174, 176
　　and food, 497
　　and leadership positions, 165
Clayton, W. F., 479, 481
Clemens, Jeremiah, 174
Clement, Abram W., 572
climate, 69
Clingman, Thomas L., 217
Clingman's Brigade, 518
The Club, 175
Code of Honor, 174, 176. *See also* duels
Colcock, Charles J., 98, 101, 285–286,
　　　　287, 288, 290–291
Cole's Island, S.C., 143, 145, 146, 212–
　　　　213, 252
Colhoun, Floride Bonneau, 165
Colhoun, John Ewing, 165
Columbia, S.C.
　　destruction of, xiv, 313, 321, 336, 475,
　　　　540
　　prisoner stockade, 521–524
　　vandalism in, 368
Columbia Record, 485
Confederacy, final days of, 475–476
"Confederate Receipt Book," 491–510
Conner, H. W., 11
Conner, James, 27

conscription, 515, 518, 520
convict lease program, 135
Conyngham, David P., 313
Cooper, Alonzo, 515, 523
Cooper, Samuel, 171, 217, 218, 468
Coosawhatchie, S.C., 97, 100–101, 184, 571
Corinth, Miss., 149
Cornish, Dudley, 76
Coulter, E. Merton, 423
courage, southern
    Charleston newspapers on, 157
    Michiganders' views of, 67–68
Courier (Charleston, S.C.), 157, 520
couriers, 185–195
Courtenay, W. A., 181, 184, 221
Cowan, David, 401, 404, 405, 406
Cowpens Battleground, 374
Cox, Abner R., 573
Cox, Jacob D., 290
Crawford, R. L., 13
Creighton, J. Blakeley, 339
Crescent Ridge, 385
Crocker, George H., 286
Cummings Point, 39, 40
currency, paper, 404
Curtis, Wm., 15
Cuthbert, G. B., 42
Daggett, Thomas, 395
Dahlgren, John A., 196, 201, 202, 204, 234, 334, 339, 473
Dantzler, Olin Miller, 177
Darby, A. T., 15
Dargan, Julius A., 12
Dark Corner, 383, 384, 514, 520
    See also Upcountry
David, 451–455
Davie, Ambrose, 396, 397
Davis, Dwight F., 483
Davis, Esther S., 315
Davis, Henry C., 13
Davis, Jefferson, 91, 171, 219, 374, 378, 459, 519
Davis, Jefferson C., 267–269
Davis, Martha Maria, 165
Davis, Zimmerman, 184
Dawson, F. W., 174
dead, transportation of, 151–152

Deas, R. L., 489, 490
DeFontaine, Felix G., 571
De Forrest, John William, 520, 521
Democrats, southern, 135
Department of South Carolina and
    Georgia, 171
DeSaussure, Isabel, 40
DeSaussure, Martha Gourdin (Mrs.
    Wilmot), 491, 493, 494, 495
DeSaussure, W. F., 4, 15
DeSaussure, Wilmot Gibbes, 493–495
desertion, 511, 512, 516–517, 518–520
DeTreville, Richard, 11
Devant, R. J., 4, 10
disloyalty, 511–526
doctors, female, 117
    See also Towne, Laura M.
Doubleday, Abner, 46, 48, 209
Dozier, Anthony W., 15
Dozier, William G., 478, 480
Drake, Edwin L., 392
Drayton Place, 556
Drayton, Thomas F., 151
DuBose, William Porcher, 312
Dudley, Thomas Haines, 419, 432–435, 437, 439
duels
    in American culture, 173–174
    among officers, 173
    Articles of War concerning, 172, 179
    and class, 174, 176
    opposition to, 174
    prohibition of among officers, 175
    Rhett-Calhoun, 175, 177-180
    Rhett-Vanderhorst, 176
Duncan, P. E., 13
Dunkin, B. F., 13
Dunovant, A. G., 12
Dunovant, R. G. M., 13
Du Pont, Samuel, 66, 76, 89, 93, 95, 180, 231, 300, 458
DuPre, Daniel, 11
dyes, 492, 495, 507–509
earthquake (1886), Charleston, 164
Easley, W. K., 13
Ebaugh, David Chenoweth, 451–455
Ebaugh, John L., 451
Ebaugh, Laura Smith, 451

Ebenezer Creek incident, 267–269
Edisto Island, S.C., 266
Edisto River, 211
Edwards, John J., 148
Eggleston, George C., 206
Eighth Michigan Volunteer Infantry
    Regiment, 65–75
Elford, Charles J., 385
Elliott, George, 98
Elliott, Stephen, 98, 101, 103
Elliott, Stephen Jr., 180
Elliott's Plantation, 98
Ellis, Daniel, 525
Ellis, William J., 13
Elmore, A. R., 184, 194
emancipation, debates regarding, 80–81
Emancipation Proclamation, 92
Emerson, Edward B., 365
England
    anticipated partnership with, 396
    connections to South, 417–418
    Foreign Enlistment Act, 418, 433, 434
    foreign policy, 153, 418, 434
    neutrality, 434, 439
    production of artillery in, 460
    See also Liverpool
English, Thos. R., Sr., 15
Ennis, John, 514
Epps' Bridge, 360
Emile Erlanger and Co., 424
Episcopal Church (1861-1865), 571
Eustis, Frederic A., 120
Eutaw, battle of, 142
Evans, Chesley D., 14
Evans, Nathan George, 151, 516
Evans's Brigade, 516–517, 525
Express (Spartanburg, S.C.), 513
Fair, Simeon, 14
Fairfield, Josiah, 130
Fairley, W. H., 184
Farley, Henry S., 58, 60, 61
farmers, yeoman, 512, 514, 516–517, 520,
    525
    See also disloyalty
Fay, John, 257
Feilden, Henry Wemyss, 385
Female Medical College of Pennsylvania,
    117

Fenwick's Island, S.C., 211
Fessenden, William, 83
Fifty-fifth Massachusetts Volunteers, 287,
    288
Fifty-fourth Massachusetts, xii, 110, 162,
    289, 360, 365, 369, 370
Finley, W. Perroneau, 4, 10
fire (Charleston, 1861), 573
First South Carolina Artillery Battalion,
    165, 166–167, 168, 171
First South Carolina Regiment, 109–110
Fiser, John C., 338
Flagg, Tom, 413
fleas, 69
Floating Battery, 19
Florence, S.C.
    defense of, 354
    prisoner stockade, 332, 334–335, 353,
    521
Florence (S.C.) Morning News, 479
Florida, 425, 433, 434
flour, wheat, 500–501
Floyd, Eldridge G., 240
Flud, Daniel, 12
Folly Island, S.C.
    description of, 196
    Federal fortification of, 197
    gun emplacements on, 198
    Wightman on, 238–242, 246–259
food
    baked goods, 501–502, 506
    at Battery Wagner, 187
    and blockade, 498–499
    Buchanan's comments on, 70
    butter, 21, 502
    and class, 497
    "Confederate Receipt Book," 491–510
    cost of, 142
    foraging, 367, 499
    found by Michigan troops, 68–69
    hops, 501
    Life Everlasting, 501–502, 506
    potash, 501
    prices, 21
    salt, 498–499
    shortages of, 21, 492, 498–500, 502
    substitutes for, 495, 497, 500–502,
    503–510

vegetables, 496
wheat flour, 500–501
foraging, 367, 499
Forbes, John Murray, 435
Foreign Enlistment Act, 418, 433, 434
George Forester and Co., 460
Forster, Alex M., 13, 404
Fort Beauregard, 66
Fort Donelson, 400
Forten, Charlotte, 122, 126, 127
Fort Fisher, 573
Fort Hatch, 380
Fort Henry, 400
Fort Johnson, 58
Fort McAllister, 263, 292
Fort Moultrie, 20, 228
  in assault on Fort Sumter, 209
  bombardment of, 231–232
  Chapman's drawings of, 228, 230
  evacuation of, 22–26, 24–25, 49, 51,
    208
  garrison of, 50–51
  history of, 228, 571
  modifications to, 229–231
  Ripley's command of, 209
Fort Palmetto, 171
Fort Pulaski, 77
Fort Sumter, 572
  Anderson's occupation of, 49, 51
  attack on, 209–210
  description of, 299–300
  destruction of, 202, 234, 244, 456, 457
  Du Pont's assault on, 196
  first shot on, 57–61
  loyalty of garrison in, 169–170, 179
  reconstruction of, 210
  re-raising of American flag at, 113,
    300, 368
  Rhett's command of, 180
  view of from Morris Island, 32–38
  See also Anderson, Robert
Fort Walker, 66
Forty-seventh Georgia, 287
Foster, B. B., 15
Foster, John G., 22–26, 263, 268, 281, 282,
  291
Foster, Robert S., 257
Fox, Charles B., 287

Fraizer's Wharf, 462, 473
Frampton, John E., 10
Frampton's plantation, 98, 99
Fraser, J. L., 218
Fraser, Sidney S., 398
Fraser, Trenholm and Co., 416–440, 460
John Fraser and Co., 421, 435, 437–438,
  459, 460, 462
Fredericksburg, battle of, 573
Freedmen's Bureau, 275–276
Freedmen's Bureau Act, 273, 274, 279
Fremantle, Arthur J. L., 216
French, Mansfield, 89, 90
French, Samuel G., 207
Frissell, Hollis Burke, 137
Furham, J. K., 177
furlough, 251
Furman, James C., 4, 13
Furness, William H., 116–117
Gadberry, J. M., 15
Gadsby, John, 225
Gaillard, Peter C., 156, 221
Gaines Mill, battle of, 214, 444
Garlington, H. W., 14
Garrison, William Lloyd, 116
Gazelle, 447
Georgetown, S.C., 333, 339, 358
Gibbes, W. H., 58, 59
Gibbes Art Gallery (Charleston, S.C.), 223
Gibraltar, 460–461
Gibson, Mrs. S. F., 481
Gibson, William, 473
Gideon's Band, 77, 89, 118–119
  See also Pierce, Edward; Port Royal
    Experiment; Towne, Laura M.
Gilchrist, R. C., 184
Gieger, John C., 14
John K. Gilliat and Co., 429
Gillmore, Quincy A., 112, 161, 196–198,
  200, 201, 202, 204–205, 234,
  251, 252, 259, 299, 358, 473
Gilman, Caroline Howard, 381, 382, 384
Gilmer, J. F., 459
Gist, William H., 4, 15
Gladiator, 428
Glassford, W. A., 443, 444, 449
Glover, T. W., 14
Gonzales, Ambrosio José, 571

Gooding, Henry James, 473
Goodwin, E. W., 14
Gordon, A. Burgess, 184, 185
Gordon, George H., 247
Gorgas, Josiah, 468, 471
Gourdin, H., 39, 489
Gourdin, I. T., 564
Gourdin, R. N., 27–31, 489
Gourdin, Robert Newman, 11, 39
Gourdin, T. G., 4
Gourdin, T. L., 4, 12
Gowensville, S.C., 518
Grahamville, S.C., 281, 282–284, 291–292
    See also Honey Hill, battle of
Grant, Ulysses, 249, 252, 257, 353
Gray, Andrew, 558
Gray, Captain, 97
Grayson, William John, 141–153
Green, H. D., 15
Green, Sam, 135
Greenville, S.C., 380–383, 384–386, 519
Greenville District, S.C., 512, 514, 517
Gregg, John N., 489–490
Gregg, Wesley W., 478
Gregg, William, 4, 13
Grimball, John Berkley, 571
Grisham, Wm. S., 14
Guerard, Harold G. Jr., 451
Guerard, Mrs. Harold G. Jr., 451
Habersham, Barnard Elliott, 571
Hagley plantation, 401
Hagood, Johnson, 97, 154, 221
Halleck, Henry W., 197, 266–267, 269,
    281, 282, 373, 473
Hallowell, Edward N., 357–370
Hamilton, D. H., 217
Hamilton, J. R., 470, 471
Hammond, Andrew J., 13
Hammond, Ogden, 190
Hampton, Wade, 134, 347
Hampton Institute, 137
Hanckel, Thomas M., 11
Hardee, William J., 180, 219, 264, 282,
    283, 289, 292, 296, 297, 336–337,
    341, 342, 346–347, 355, 475, 482
Harleston, Edward, 183
Harleston, Francis H., 183, 468
Harleston, John, 183–195

Harllee, W. W., 4, 14, 478, 479
Harpers Ferry, 85
Harris, D. B., 215, 217, 220, 227, 231
Harrison, Alfred C., Jr., 233
Harrison, J. J., 101
Harrison, James, 13
Harrison, James B., 374
Hartwell, A. S., 305, 368
Hartwell, Alfred, 287
Harvest Moon, 339–340
Haskell, Charles T., 450
Haskell, Joseph C., 449
Hatch, John P., 282, 283, 285, 286, 288,
    289–290, 292, 293, 296
Haughton, Nathaniel, 286
Haviland, James F., 298
Hawkins, Rush, 248
Hayes, Rutherford B., 134
Hayne, Isaac W., 11
Hayne, Theodore B., 58
Henderson, E. R., 12
Hennessy, John A., 298
Hering, Constantine, 117
Heroes of America, 524–525
Heyward, Joseph, 177
Higginson, Thomas W., 109, 110, 128
Highlanders, 154–155, 157, 159, 514
    See also Campbell, Alexander (Sandy)
Hill, A. P., 159
Hill, D. H., 206, 214, 220
Hilton Head Island, S.C., 93
Hinson, William G., 573
History of Georgetown County (Rogers),
    400
Holland, E. C., 184, 185
Holmes, Anna Helen, 421
Holmes, Emma, 178, 179, 314, 470, 472,
    473, 496, 573
Holmes, Theophilus H., 353
Honey Hill, battle of, 281, 284–294
honor, 173, 174, 176
Honour, John H., 11
Hood, John B., 219, 220
Hooper, Edward, 119, 121, 128
Hooper, Henry, 289
Hopkins, William, 15
hops, 501
Hot & Hot Fish Club, 415

Howard, Oliver Otis, 128, 273, 274, 275, 277, 278, 312, 345, 351
Howard, Stephen, 398, 399, 406, 411
Howe, Mrs. Christopher G., 489
Hubbard, Lillie, 373
Huger, Alfred, 175
Huger, Anna Isabella, 183
Huger, Arthur M., 381
Huger, B. F., 184, 186
Huger, William, 176
Huguenin, Captain, 193, 194
Huguenin, T. A., 221
H. L. Hunley, xiii
Hunter, David
    abandonment of Carolina area, 88
    assault on Fort Pulaski, 77
    attempts to enlist African Americans, 76, 78–80, 81–82
    backing of Saxton's proposal, 89
    command of Department of South, 76
    desire to take Fort Sumter, 77
    freeing of slaves, 74, 80
    report on African American regiment, 85
    resignation of, 112
    at Secessionville, 197
    and Towne, 121, 128
Hunter, Wm., 14
Huntsville, Ala., 94
Huse, Caleb, 424, 426, 431, 438, 460
Hutson, W. F., 10
Hyer, Sergeant, 184
illness, 143, 219
inflation, 142, 320, 404, 407, 498
Inglis, John A., 12
Inglis, Laura, 350
Ingram, John J., 12
Intelligencer (Anderson, S. C.), 377, 378
iron, cast, 467
iron, wrought, 467
Iverson, John F., 353
Jackson, Stephen, 12
Jackson, Thomas (Stonewall), 85, 159
James, George S., 41, 58, 60
James Island, S.C., 60, 67, 69–70, 75, 145, 147, 196, 197, 198, 204
Jamison, Bessie, 552
Jamison, Caroline, 529, 532, 551, 552

Jamison, David Flavel, 10, 527–531, 532–533, 535, 538, 549, 551
Jamison, David Rumph, 532, 536, 546, 550
Jamison, Elizabeth, 527–552
Jamison, John Wilson, 532, 535–536, 540, 542, 544–546, 551
Jamison, William, 538–539, 546, 551
Jarrott, Mrs. C. E., 352
Jeffries, James, 15
Jenkins, Caroline, 529, 532, 551, 552
Jenkins, John, 12
Jenkins, Joseph E., 12
Jenkins, Micah, 532, 536, 551
Jervey, Caroline, 381
John Jacob Ebaugh (Ebaugh), 451
Johns Island, S.C., 145, 149, 252
Johnson, Andrew, 273–274, 275, 277, 278, 439–440
Johnson, Hannibal A., 522
Johnson, J. C., 360
Johnson, John, 162
Johnson, T. H., 101
Johnson, William D., 14
Johnston, Albert, 142
Johnston, Joseph E.
    armistice with Sherman, 370
    in Jackson, 517
    reinstatement of, 475
    removal of, 320, 537
    surrender of, 331, 373, 380, 384
    Ripley's report to, 220
Johnston, Oscar F., 334, 346, 355, 481, 482
Jones, Burwell, 313
Jones, E. P., 385
Jones, John B., 468
Jones, Marion, 452–453
Jones, Samuel, 217–219, 292, 335
Jones, William, 359, 362
Jordan, Daniel W., 389–415
Jordan, Emily, 413
Jordan, Sarah Victoria, 396, 397
Jordan, Thomas, 180, 215, 227, 228, 480
"Journal of the Siege of Charleston," 228
Kate, 428
Kearny, Philip, 160
Keitt, L. M., 4, 14, 193, 195, 203, 217

Keitt, Mrs. Lawrence, 542, 543, 544
Keitt, Sue Sparks, 572
Kennedy, Robert M., 315
Kentucky, 29, 85–86
Keowee (S.C.) Courier, 513
kerosene, 392, 408
Key, Francis Scott, 233
Key, John Ross, 233
Kiawah Island, S.C., 252
Kilgore, Benj. F., 15
Kilpatrick, Judson, 263, 347
Kimball, Rodney, 249, 255
Kinard, John P., 14
King, Henry Campbell, 148
Kinsler, John H., 15
Kinston, N.C., 516
Kirk, Manning, 98
Kirke, Edmund, 359
Kirkland, Thomas K., 315
Knowles, John W., 240
labor, 22, 25–26, 409, 410, 411, 412
LaBruce, John, 405
Lamar, Gazaway Bugg, 429
Lamar, Thomas G., 154
land, 271–279
Landrum, John G., 15
Lang, Harriet DuBose Kershaw, 315, 572
Latrobe, J. H. B., 23–26
Laurel Hill plantation, 389, 406, 410, 415
Lawson, James, 380, 382
Lawton, Benj. W., 10
Lay, John F., 217, 220
Lebby, Robert, 57
Lee, F. D., 448
Lee, Robert E.
    command of coast, 211
    decision to invade Pennsylvania, 500
    defenses along coast, 93–94
    fear of mutiny at Fort Sumter, 170
    fortification along Charleston and
       Savannah railroad, 284 (*See*
       also Honey Hill, battle of)
    and Ripley's command, 169, 211
    surrender of, 331, 373, 380, 384, 543
Lee, Stephen D., 59, 60
Legareville, S.C., 571
Lehigh, 231–232
Lesesne, Henry D., 311

Lewis, Andrew F., 14
Liberty Hill (Kershaw District), 313
libraries, 555, 556, 571
library (Middleton Place), 555, 556
The Life and Times of Bertrand de
    Guesclin (Jamison), 531
Life Everlasting, 501–502, 506
Lincoln, A. L. Jr., 563
Lincoln, Abraham, 19, 27, 49, 87, 93, 104,
    131, 353, 543
Lister, Joseph, 553
Little River, 391
Liverpool, Eng., 417–440
loans, 391
Logan, John A., 312, 313, 345
Logan, R. C., 15
Long, R. D., 383
Longstreet, James, 443, 449
looting, 71, 364, 365, 376–378
    See also pillaging; plunder
Louis, Deopold Daniel, 573
Lowndes, Rawlins, 163
loyalty oath, 273–274
Lucas, J. J., 147
Luckett, Mary Elizabeth, 225
lye, 501
Lyles, William S., 13
Lynch's River, 340–341
Macbeth, Charles, 298
Mackay's Point, 96-97
Magrath, A. G., 4, 11, 169, 175, 216, 220,
    221, 481
Magrath, Edward, 175
Maguire, Matthew, 432, 433, 435
Mallory, Stephen R., 434, 478, 480
Malvern Hill, battle of, 214, 446
Manassas, First, battle of, 155, 514, 537
Manassas, Second, battle of, 159, 516
Manigault, Gabriel, 11
Manning, John Lawrence, 4, 12, 370
Manning, Richard, 46
Manning, S.C., 362
Marcy, Henry Orlando, 553–564
Marmaduke, John S., 173
The Marriage of Pocahontas (Chapman),
    225
Mars Bluff, S.C., 332, 334, 478
martial law, 143–144

Mason, John Y., 166
Masons, 385
Master, John Chalk, 452
Mauldin, Benj. F., 10
Maxwell, John, 14
Mayes, Matthew P., 15
Mazyck, A., 11
Mazyck, Lieutenant, 194
Mazyck, William, 415
Mazyck & Howard, 397, 401, 402, 405,
    411, 413
McBee, Alexander, 383
McBee, Vardy, 381
McClellan, George B., 152n, 259
McCord, Charlotte, 448
McCord, David J., 448
McCrady, Edward, 11
McCullough, James, 385
McGill, John D., 411
McIver, Henry, 12
McKee, John, 12
McKim, James Miller, 127
McLeod, Alex., 14
McLeod, F. H., 484, 485
McMillan, John L., 478
McMillan, Malcolm S., 478
McRae, Colin J., 428, 429
Meade, George G., 276
Means, John Hugh, 4, 13
Mechanicsville, battle of, 214
medicine, homeopathic, 117, 122, 123–
    124, 126
Melton, C. D., 519
Memminger, C. C., ix, 11, 404, 424, 428,
    430
Mercer, Hugh W., 97, 145, 146
Mercury (Charleston, S.C.), 157, 166, 174,
    296, 301, 450, 500
Merrimack, 144
Michigan, regiment from, 65–75
Middleton, Arthur, 403, 553, 554
Middleton, Edward, 558
Middleton, Eliza, 558
Middleton family, 572
Middleton, Frank, 102
Middleton, Harriott, xiii
Middleton, Henry A., 403, 553, 554
Middleton, John I., 4, 13, 207

Middleton, Mary, 207
Middleton, Mary Hering, 553
Middleton, Ralph, 19
Middleton, Susan, xiii
Middleton, Williams, 11, 553–564
Middleton Place, 553–564
Middleton Place Foundation, 554
Miles, F., 489
Miles, William P., 4, 11, 169, 171, 213,
    215, 458, 459
Miller, John K., 374
Miller, W. C., 419
Milliken, A., 489
Milliken, E. P., 489
mines, 205
    See also torpedoes
Mitchel, John, 175, 176, 182
Mitchel, Ormsby M., 94–95, 96, 103, 364
Moale, Edward, 23
Moale, Mary S., 23
Moale, Samuel, 23
money, Confederate, 404
money, storing, 406–407
Montgomery, James, 110, 128
Moore, J. B., 184
Moore, Thomas W., 12
Moorman, Robert, 14
Morgan, Joseph, 98
Morgan, Sarah, 496
Morgan, Van Renssalaer, 478, 482
Morgan's Calvary, 520
Morris Island, S.C.
    batteries on, 23, 52, 54 (*See also*
        individual batteries)
    Beauregard on loss of, 218
    Beauregard's decision to defend, 204
    Cheves on, 449
    Confederate force on, 32-38, 197–198
    defensive works on, 215–216
    description of, 196
    evacuation of, 193–195, 203
    Federal assault on, 198–201
    Federal capture of, 204, 474–475
    Gillmore on defense of, 204–205
    Young on, 40
    See also Battery Wagner
Mott, James, 116
Mott, Lucretia, 116

Mt. Pleasant, S.C,., occupation of, 302–308
Mountaineer (Greenville, S.C.), 383
Mower, Joseph A., 343–344, 353
Moyed, Susan, 399
Mudd, Samuel, 302
mud sills, 71–72
Murchison, Abram, 78
Murray, Ellen, 117, 121, 124, 128, 130, 134, 137
Murray, Fanny, 132
Murray, Harriet, 130
Museum of the Confederacy (Richmond, Va.), 493
Naval Brigade, 288
Nelson, ?, 102
Nesbit, Bob, 413
Newberne, S.C., 330
New Ironsides, 202
New Orleans, La., 151
News and Courier (Charleston, S.C.), 174, 221
Nichols, George W., 347
Nixon, Nicholas, 394
Noble, Edward, 10
Noe, Charles, 366
Norfolk, Va., 144
North battery, 40
Nowell, John L., 4, 12
nullification controversy, 513
Oaklands plantation, 163
Oconee District, S.C., 512
O'Hear, John S., 12
One hundred forty-fourth New York, 286, 288
One hundred second Colored unit, 290, 358, 360, 364, 369, 370
One hundred twenty-seventh New York, 287
Orangeburg County slaveholders, 573
Orangeburg Presbyterian Church, 531
Orr, James L., 4, 10, 219, 379
Otter Island, S.C., 211
outliers, 383, 384–385
Owsley, Frank L., 515, 524
paintings
 The Bombardment of Fort Moultrie, November 16, 1863

(Chapman), 223–225, 226, 232–233
The Bombardment of Fort Sumter (Key), 233
The Marriage of Pocahontas (Chapman), 225
 from Middleton Place, 557–564
Palmer, John S., 4, 12
Palmer, William J., 373, 378
Palmetto Guard, 37, 40
Palmetto State, 458
Panic of 1837, 391
Parker, Eli, 394, 408–409, 410, 411, 414
Parker, F. S., 412–413
Parker, Francis LeJau, 32–38
Parker, Francis S., 13
Parker, McKenzie, 375–376
Patton, K. N., 374
Pawnee Landing, 250
peace societies, 524–525
Peagram, Ned, 359
Pearce, Louise Harllee, 479, 482
Pedee, 332–333, 334, 346, 355, 356, 479–485
Pee Dee region, 332, 355–356
Pee Dee River
 bridge over, 336, 345, 347
 Federals' crossing of, 347–350, 354
 plan to defend bridge over, 337–338
 proposed expedition up, 334–335
 Sherman's march to, 340–341
 value of, 332
 See also Cheraw, S.C.
Pegues Ferry, S.C., 348, 349, 354
Pemberton, John C., 145, 169, 170–171, 172, 198, 211, 212, 214, 220, 479
Pembroke, Edward, 428
Pendleton, S.C., 520
Penn School, 125–126, 130, 131–133, 137
Penn School Historic District, 138
Pennsylvania, 500
Pennsylvania Freedmen's Relief Association, 130, 132
Perry, Benjamin F., 383, 513, 514
Perry, Hayne, 385
Petigru, James L., 141
Philbrick, Edward S., 111, 130
Pickens, Francis, 67, 169, 172, 182, 208, 210, 211–212

Pickens District, S.C., 512, 517, 520, 522
Pierce, Edward, 77, 81, 84, 118, 119, 121, 127–128, 138
  See also Gideon's Band
pillaging, 314
  See also looting; plunder
Pinckney, Captain, 194
Pinckney, Charles Cotesworth, 174
Pinckney, Thomas, 175
Planter, 100, 113, 143, 170
plunder, 149, 352, 359, 363, 364, 367, 368, 373–379
  See also looting; pillaging
Pocotaligo, Old, S.C., 99–100
Pocotaligo, S.C., 94, 95–100, 184, 281, 292, 540
poll tax, 135
Pope, George, 362
Pope, John, 159
Porcher, Francis J., 194
Porcher, Francis Peyre, 495
Porcher, Louisa, 381
Porter, A. Toomer, ix
Porter, John L., 480
Porter, W. D., 169
Port Royal, S.C., 66
Port Royal Experiment, 77, 265–266, 270
Port Royal Relief Committee of Philadelphia, 118, 126, 127
Port Royal Sound, 93, 211
potash, 501
Potter, Edward E., 282, 286, 287, 290, 296, 297, 314, 363, 365, 454
Potter's Raid, 314, 357-370
Pratt, A. A., 447
Pressley, John G., 15
Preston, John S., 518
Preston, Sally Buchanan, 168, 178
Price, W. P., 375
Pringle, Elizabeth Allston, 352
Prioleau, Charles E., 184, 191, 192, 194, 232–233, 423, 424, 425–426, 427, 428–429, 431, 432, 435, 437, 438, 439, 460
Prioleau, Charles K., 41
Prioleau, Mary Elizabeth, 425–426
Prioleau, W. H., 59, 61

prisoners of war
  aiding, 521–524
  in Charleston (1865), 573
  Columbia stockade, 521–524
  exchange of, 353
  Florence stockade, 332, 334–335, 353, 521
Prospect Hill plantation, 411
Pruitt, Janie, 373
Putman, Sallie B., 497
Quattlebaum, Paul, 14
racism, Towne's confrontations with, 136–137
railroads
  Andrews railroad raid, 94
  Charleston and Savannah, 184, 281–282, 284, 293 (*See also* Honey Hill, battle of)
  and food shortages, 500
  Sherman's intent to ruin junction at Florence, 353–354
  transportation monopoly, 401, 498
  use of during war, 94
  Western-Atlantic, 94
  Wilmington and Manchester, 335, 362, 363, 364, 366–367, 401
  See also Coosawhatchie, S.C.; Pocotaligo, S.C.
Rainey, Samuel, 15
Rains, George W., 470
Raleigh, Walter, 148
Ralston, Elizabeth, 155
Ralston, James, 155, 156
Ralston, Matthew, 156
Randolph, G. W., 172
Ravenel, Caroline R., 376
Ravenel, St. J., 452, 455
Ravenel, W. C., 189
The Rebel (Columbia, S.C.), 572
recipes, 491–510
Reconstruction, 113, 114, 526
Reed, E. C., 461
Reed, J. P., 10
re-enlisting, 251
Republican Party (S.C.), 526
Rhett, Alfred Moore, 165–182, 221, 573
Rhett, Edmund, 108, 168
Rhett, Robert B., Jr., 166, 216

Rhett, Robert Barnwell, Sr., 4, 11, 166, 174
    house of, 105
Rhodes, George, 10
rice, 21, 393, 395–405, 407, 411–415
Richardson, F. D., 11
Richardson, John P., 4, 12
Richmond, Va., 152, 535
Ricker, Eli S., 573
rifles, 95, 238
rifles, Blakely, 459–476
rifling, 465
Ripley, Roswell S., 44, 145, 167, 169,
        172–173, 178–179, 182, 197,
        198, 206–222, 449–450, 457, 468
Ripley Monument, 221–222
Robertson, Beverly H., 290, 354
Robinson, D. P., 13
Rogers, F. E., 360
Rogers, George, 240, 400, 403
Rogers, James, 479
Roman, Alfred, 218
Rosa, David D., 401
Rowell, W. B., 14
Ruffin, Edmund, 41, 48, 59
Ruggles, T. Edwin, 122
Rumph, David, 527
Rumph, David J., 527
Rumph, Elizabeth Anne Carmichael,
        527–552
Russell, William Howard, 421
Rutledge, Benjamin H., 11, 99
Rutledge Mounted Riflemen, 95, 102
Ryan, W. H., 145n
St. Andrew's Parish Church (Charleston
        County, S.C.), 310
St. Helena Band of Hope, 134
St. Helena's Parish, S.C., 571
St. Michael's Church (Charleston, S.C.),
        147, 311, 316
St. Philip's Church (Charleston, S.C.), 489
St. Simons Island, Ga., 88, 266
Sale, William W., 181
saleratus, 501
Salley, A. S., Jr., 57
salt, 405–406, 498–499
Savannah, 21

Savannah, Ga.
    Confederate force in, 264
    defense of, 284
    evacuation of, 264, 281, 292
    fall of, 475
    Sherman at, 263
    Sherman's approach to, 292
Sawyer, I. H., 407
Saxton, Rufus
    administration of Order No. 15, 270
    and African American soldiers, 76, 89
    coastal tour, 88
    command of, 112
    efforts for newly freed African
        Americans, 274, 275
    at Harpers Ferry, 85
    hope for African American refugees,
        271–272
    provision for African Americans left in
        Beaufort, 77
    refugees sent to, 265
    removal of, 277
    sent back to Beaufort, 83–85
    Towne's opinion of, 121, 128
Schimmelpfennig, General, 299
Schirmer, Jacob, 3, 19–21, 462, 572
Schirmer Diary, 3, 19–21, 572
schools
    funding for, 133, 135
    Penn School, 125–126, 130, 131–133,
        137
Scott, Elias B., 12
Scott, Winfield, 398
Seabrook, E. M., 10, 207, 221
Seabrook, George, 12
Seabrook, John L., 285
Seabrook Island, 252
sea islands
    capture of, 93
    plantations on, 110–112
    return of whites to, 132
    See also individual islands
secession, business reaction to, 396
Secession Convention, 3, 4–15, 532, 553
Secessionville, battle of, 83, 147–148,
        154–158, 196
Second South Carolina, 110
Seddon, James A., 215, 218, 219, 459, 461

Semmes, Raphael, 460
Session, Benj. E., 13
Seven Days' battle, 443, 445, 447
Seventy-ninth New York Infantry, 154–155, 157, 159, 514
  See also Campbell, Alexander (Sandy)
Seward, William H., 87, 435
Seymour, Thomas, 161
Shannon, William, 174
sharecropping, 412
Sharpsburg, battle of, 214
Shaw, Robert Gould, 128, 162
Shelton, W. H., 523
Sherman, Thomas W., 65, 73, 76, 77
Sherman, William T.
  armistice with Johnston, 370
  attempts to stop, 180, 283 (*See also* Honey Hill, battle of)
  devastation of southern countryside, 499
  goals of, 264
  Hardee's slowing of, 346–347
  in South Carolina, 571, 573
  isolation of Charleston, 336
  march to sea, 263, 475, 482, 537, 540
  need to break Charleston and Savannah railroad, 281–282
  Order No. 15, 270
  on provision for African American refugees, 276 (*See* African Americans, refugee)
  refugees following, 131
Shiloh, battle of, 142
Shingler, John M., 11
Shingler, W. P., 10
shipbuilders, 419
ships
  Alabama, 433, 434
  Alexandra, 430, 434
  Bermuda, 426
  Cecile, 428
  Charleston, 458
  in Charleston harbor defense, 458
  Chicora, 458
  David, 451–455
  Florida, 425, 433, 434
  Gibraltar, 460–461
  Gladiator, 428
  Harvest Moon, 339–340
  H. L. Hunley, xiii
  Kate, 428
  Lehigh, 231–232
  Merrimack, 144
  monitors, 456–457
  New Ironsides, 202
  Palmetto State, 458
  Pedee, 332–333, 334, 346, 355, 356, 479–485
  Planter, 100, 113, 143, 170
  Savannah, 21
  Star of the West, 19, 20, 22, 23, 49
  Sumter, 460
shouts, 122–123
Shumate, William T., 385
The Siege of Charleston (Burton), 215–216
Simms, William Gilmore, 532, 549–550
Simons, James W., 43, 170, 177, 493
Simons, Thomas Y., 11
Simpson, R. F., 4, 10
Simpson, William Dunlap, 572
Sims, J. S., 15
slavery, Buchanan on, 73
slaves
  Emancipation Proclamation, 92
  escape by, 402
  Hunter's freeing of, 74, 80
  Jamisons', 536
  liberation of, 407–408
  Middletons', 555, 556
  Towne's understanding of, 122–123
  See also African Americans; African Americans, refugee; soldiers, African American
slave trade, 418
Smalls, Robert, 82, 89, 90, 135, 170
Smith, B. Burgh, 385
Smith, Charles E., 374
Smith, General, 146
Smith, Gustavus W., 171, 283–284, 285, 286, 291, 292
Smith, John J. P., 11
Smith, Prince, 383
Smith, Samuel M., 97, 98
Smith, W. D., 146n, 171
Smith, William Farrar, 260
Smith plantation, 111–112
Smyly, James C., 13
Smythe, Augustine, 462, 472, 572

Sneedsborough, N.C., 348
Snowden, P. G., 11
soap, 492, 495, 505–506
soldiers, African American
    34th U.S. Colored Troops, 554–555
    102nd Colored unit, 290, 358, 360,
        364, 369, 370
    arming of, 74–75
    authorization of, 86–87, 89–92
    desertion by, 86
    disbanding of Hunter's regiment, 87
    Fifty-fourth (Colored) Massachusetts,
        110, 162, 289, 360, 365, 369,
        370
    First South Carolina Regiment,
        109–110
    Hunter's recruitment of, 76
    Hunter's regiment, 82–83
    impressment of, 146
    Lincoln's view of, 87
    Saxton's enlistment of, 76
    Saxton's proposal for, 89
    Second South Carolina, 110
    on St. Simons Island, 88
    Thirty-second United States Colored
        troops, 286–287, 288, 358,
        364, 367, 368, 369, 370
    U.S. policies regarding, 78–79
Soley, J. R., 478
Sol Legare Island, S.C., 154
South, as provincial, 152
South Atlantic Blockading Squadron, 573
South Carolina Historical Society, x
South Carolina Volunteers, Company E,
7th Regiment, 572
Southern Enterprise (Greenville, S.C.),
    520
Southerners, Michiganders' view of, 71–72
Southern Patriot (Greenville, S.C.), 513
Spain, A. C., 15
Sparks, Alicia Middleton, 181, 207
Sparks, Captain, 544, 545
Sparks, Mr., 543, 544
Sparks, Mrs., 545
Sparks, William A., 207
Spartanburg District, S.C., 512, 514, 517,
    518
Spear, Daniel G., 365

Spence, James, 419
spies, 432–433, 437
Spratt, L. W., 11
Springs, A. Baxter, 15
Springs, Professor, 183
Squires, J. Duane, 445
Stacy, Brazilliah P., 374
Stanley, Victor B. Jr., 481
Stanton, Edwin M., 82, 87, 266, 373
Star of the West, 19, 20, 22, 23, 49
States Rights Gist's Brigade, 517
Stevens, Edward L., 357–369, 370
Stevens, Isaac I., 94, 154, 157, 159, 160
Stevens Iron battery, 40
Stokes, Peter, 12
Stoneman, George, 373, 374, 377, 380–
    383
Stoneman's Raiders, 380–383, 384, 386
Stoney, John Stafford, 572
Stoney, Theodore G., 194, 195, 452–453,
    455
Stringer, Edwin Pinchback, 428
Strong, George C., 198
Stuart, Hal, 286
Suddath, James Butler, 572
Sullivan's Island, S.C., 19, 196, 197, 217,
    228–229
Sumter, 460
Sumter, S.C., 363–364, 368
Swails, Stephen A., 363
Taber, William Jr., 175
"Tale of the War" (Carmichael), 533–552
Taliaferro, William B., 161, 162, 200
Tarrh, Virginia, 351–352
Tatnall, Josiah, 144
Tatum, Georgia Lee, 524–525
Taylor, A. R., 184
Taylor, Richard, 219
Taylor, Thomas, 419
teachers, 133
    See also Murray, Ellen; Towne, Laura
    M.
telegraph, 21, 94
temperance, 134
Terry, Alfred H., 98, 103, 246
Tew, Charles Courtenay, 302
Tew, Emily Jenkins, 302
Tew, Henry Slade, 302–308

Third New York Artillery, 287, 288
Thirteenth Tennessee Volunteer Calvary, U.S.A., 385
Thirty-first North Carolina, 201
Thirty-fourth U.S. Colored Troops, 554–555
Thirty-second United States Colored troops, 286–287, 288, 358, 364, 367, 368, 369, 370
Thomas, George H., 276, 374
Thompson, James, 129
Thompson, John, 49–56
Thompson, Matilda, 120
Thompson, R. A., 14
Thompson, Robert, 50
Thompson's Creek, 338, 343–344
Thomson, Thomas, 10
Tilden, Samuel J., 134
Timmons, John M. 12
Timrod, Henry, 222
Toland, Hugh, 106
Tompkins, James, 13
Tomlinson, Reuben, 128
Toombs, Robert, 269
torpedoes, 452, 453, 458
Towne, Henry, 132
Towne, Laura M., 114–138
Towne, Rosie, 119
Towne, William, 130
Townsend, John F., 4, 11
Trapier, Edith, 322
Trapier, John H., 332, 333, 404
Trapier, Lillie, 319
Trapier, Paul, 312, 315–331
Trapier, Sarah Dehon, 315–331
Trapier, Theodore, 321–322, 328–329, 330–331
Trembly, Ralph, 105
Trenholm, Captain, 102
Trenholm, George Alfred, 416–417, 420–423, 424–429, 431, 435–436, 438, 439–440, 460
Trenholm, William, 427
Trenholm Brothers, 421
Trescot, William Henry, 213, 276, 277, 278
Tribune (New York), description of fall of Charleston in, 295–301

Trumbull, Lyman, 275
Tucker, Charles E., 360, 362, 363, 364
Tupper, Samuel Y., 183
turpentine, 390, 391–393, 405, 408–409
Twenty-fifth Ohio, 286–287, 288
U. D. C. (United Daughters of the Confederacy), 482, 483–484
Unionism, 511–526
U.S. soldiers; correspondence, 572
Upcountry
    refugees in, 536
    Unionism in, 512–526
Valentine, J., 231
vandalism, 368
Vanderhorst, Arnoldus, 175–176, 179
Vanderhorst, Adele Allston, 573
Van Dyck, Henry J., 19
vegetables, 496
Vicksburg, Miss., 151
violence, Towne's abhorrence of, 123
Virginia Bible Society, 416
Vogdes, Israel, 247, 249, 251, 254
voting rights, 133, 134
Waccamaw Neck, S.C., 389
Wagner, Effingham, 394
Wagner, Theodore, 411, 423, 435, 449, 452
Wagner, Theodore D., 11
Wagner, Thomas, 167, 169
Walhalla, S.C., 520
Walker, Henry, 156–157
Walker, Leroy P., 210
Walker, Lucius M., 173
Walker, Susan, 119, 120
Walker, William S., 95, 97–100, 102–103
Wallace, Louise, 479
Wannamaker, John J., 14
Ward, Benjamin Huger, 411, 413
Wardlaw, Francis H., 4, 13
Warwick, P. C., 218
Washington, Booker T., 137
Washington, J. McPherson, 58
Washington, T. A., 211
water, at Battery Wagner, 187–188
Watts, W. D., 14
Webster, General, 299
Webster, Moses F., 358
Weigand, G. D., 447
Welles, Gideon, 334, 461

Wells, Edward, 344
Welsman, Mrs. James, 489
Wescoat, Arthur Brailsford, 571
Wescoat, Joseph Julius, 572
Weston, Emily, 401
Weston, Francis Marion, 395
Weston, Plowden C. J., 389, 394, 398, 401, 402, 406
Wheeler, Joseph, 263, 267, 347
White, J. H., 360
Whiting, E. M., 178
Whiting, William H. C., 459, 461
Whitner, J. N., 10
Wicks, James H., 258
Wier, Thomas, 14
Wigfall, Louis T., 20, 37, 39, 43–47, 56
Wightman, Edward King, 234–260
Wilderness, battle of, 537
Wilding, Henry, 435
Williams, G. W., 19
Williams, Isaiah, 394
Williams, John D., 14
Williams, Leonard, 385
Williams, Ruben, 353, 354
William (Trapier family servant), 328–329
Wilmington, N.C., 333, 391
Wilson, Isaac D., 12

Wilson, J. H., 10
Wilson, James H., 378
Wilson, John Lyde, 174
Wilson, W. B., 15
Winsor, Nelly, 119, 130
Winthrop, Henry, 376
Winyah Bay, 333, 389, 400, 402
Wise, Henry A., 225
Withers, T. J., 13
Women's Aid Society, 117
Woods, Richard, 12
Wood, William, 445
Wragg, W. T., 177
Yarborough, Calvin, 485
Yates, Joseph, 167, 470
Year Book [of City of Charleston] 1884, 184, 187
yeast, 501
yellow fever, 219
Yemassee, S.C., 184
Yonge, Clarence, 434
Yorkville Military Academy, 532
Young, Anna Rebecca Gourdin, 39
Young, H. C., 14
Young, Pierce M. B., 341
Young, Thomas John, 39
Young, William Gourdin, 37, 39–48